MW00561155

AN AMOROUS HISTORY OF THE SILVER SCREEN

銀幕艷史

CINEMA AND MODERNITY

A series edited by Tom Gunning

AN AMOROUS HISTORY OF THE SILVER SCREEN

SHANGHAI CINEMA, 1896–1937

ZHANG ZHEN

THE UNIVERSITY OF CHICAGO PRESS • *Chicago & London*

ZHANG ZHEN is associate professor of cinema studies at New York University.

The University of Chicago Press, Chicago 60637
The University of Chicago Press, Ltd., London
© 2005 by The University of Chicago
All rights reserved. Published 2005
Printed in the United States of America

14 13 12 11 10 09 08 07 06 05 1 2 3 4 5

ISBN: 0-226-98237-8 (cloth)
ISBN: 0-226-98238-6 (paper)

Library of Congress Cataloging-in-Publication Data

Zhang, Zhen, 1962 July 8–
An amorous history of the silver screen : Shanghai cinema, 1896–1937 / Zhang Zhen.
p. cm. — (Cinema and modernity)
Includes bibliographical references and index.
ISBN 0-226-98237-8 (cloth : alk. paper) — ISBN 0-226-98238-6 (pbk. : alk. paper)
1. Motion pictures—China—Shanghai—History. 2. Motion picture industry—China—Shanghai—History. I. Title. II. Series.
PN1993.5.C4Z55 2005
791.43'09511'32—dc22

2005019256

∞ The paper used in this publication meets the minimum requirements of the American National Standard for Information Sciences—Permanence of Paper for Printed Library Materials, ANSI Z39.48-1992.

CONTENTS

ILLUSTRATIONS

ACKNOWLEDGMENTS

SOME OF THE OLDEST and finest movie theaters in central Shanghai were within a stone's throw of the neighborhood where I grew up. Behind the "iron curtains" of the cold war in the 1960s and 1970s, I enjoyed countless trips to these cinemas, especially Da Shanghai (Metropol, see fig. 7.9) on Tibet Road, where I watched the Chinese, Indian, North Korean, and Eastern European films offered in that era. Perhaps I relished more the experience of moviegoing itself, and the seemingly anachronistic modernist beauty of the theater architecture. It was at some of these venues that my generation first encountered Shanghai cinema, in particular the left-wing cinema, when it resurfaced in the early 1980s. It instantly captured my imagination, although little did I know that I would return to write this book about this cinema's place in Shanghai's history and worldly modernity. I thank those who first opened my eyes to this legacy.

The research and writing of this book has incurred many debts to numerous individuals and institutions. Miriam Hansen and Tom Gunning inspired me to enter the enchanting world of early cinema when I returned to cinema studies at the University of Chicago. Their wisdom and friendship has continuously nourished this project since I graduated and became a teacher myself. I am also grateful to the instruction and support from Harry Harootunian and Judith Zeitlin (both members of my original dissertation committee), as well as Norma Field, James Lastra, Gregory

Lee, Katie Trumptner, Yuri Tzivian, Eugene Wang, and Wu Hung during my years at the University of Chicago. Among those who contributed to my work or cheered me along a long journey, I want to particularly thank James St. André, Weihong Bao, Jennifer Bean, Tom Bender, Chris Berry, Ryan Boynton, Scott Bukatman, Yomi Braester, Xiangyang Chen, Juliette Yuecheng Cheung, John Crespi, Jonathan Hay, Lucas Hilderbrand, Anna Holian, Binghui Huangfu, Sergei Kapterev, Paize Keulemans, Eugenia Lean, Charles Leary, Judith Leeb, Cecilia Li, Sheldon Hsiao-peng Lu, Elizabeth McSweeney, Hajime Nakatani, Jackie Stewart, Jennifer Peterson, Haun Saussy, Shuang Shen, Mitsuyo Wada-Marciano, Richard Gang Wang, Paul Young, Liang Zhang, Yingjin Zhang, Xueping Zhong, Tao Zhu, Angela Zito, and, finally, my colleagues at the department of cinema studies at New York University.

My project involved extensive research in China, and I have benefited from the kind assistance of many people and institutions there. I thank above all Mr. Shu Yan, a former film critic, and Mr. Wu Weiyun, a former cinematographer, for granting me long interviews despite their health conditions. Mr. Lu Hongshi has shared with me valuable research material as well as insights on Chinese film history. Professor Li Shaobai of the Research Institute of Chinese Art, Mr. Li Suyuan and Hu Jubin of the Research Center of Chinese Film Art, and Professors Zhong Dafeng, Ma Junxiang, and Chen Shan of the Beijing Film Academy have all helped me in various ways. I thank Cui Weiping, Imma Gonzales, Tang Di, Tang Xiaodu, Wen Hui, and Wu Wenguang for their hospitality and for their friendship during my stays in Beijing. The institutions that facilitated my research include the China Film Archive, the Shanghai Municipal Archive, the Shanghai Library, the Beijing Library, the Beijing City Library, the Library at the Shanghai Theater Academy, the Library at Fu Dan University, and the Hongkou District Library in Shanghai.

A Chicago Humanities Institute Dissertation Fellowship for 1997–98 allowed me to complete the work for this book in a stimulating environment. An Andrew W. Mellon Postdoctoral Fellowship at Stanford University and a J. P. Getty Postdoctoral Fellowship made it possible for me to do further research and expand the project's scope and depth. A faculty fellowship at the International Center for Advanced Studies, and a Paulette Goddard junior grant, both from New York University, gave me additional time to think and write. As the book moved from my desktop to the University of Chicago Press, I have been very fortunate to work with Susan Bielstein and Anthony Burton, manuscript editor Mara Naselli, and series editor Tom Gunning. Their enthusiasm and professionalism made the process truly enjoyable. I gratefully acknowledge the comments and interest of the anonymous readers.

Finally, I owe my family in Shanghai a great deal for providing me a veritable home base during my research trips, and more importantly, for enabling me to reconnect with the past and the present of my native city. I thank the late "uncle" Xu Zhengming, a family friend who passed away recently, for his many gifts of books and ideas. Magnus Fiskesjö, my companion in life and intellectual adventures, has been an indispensable part of this project in countless ways. Loke's arrival during the final stage of the making of this book brought me joyful diversions. To all of them I dedicate this book, with love.

INTRODUCTION

AN AMOROUS HISTORY OF THE SILVER SCREEN

HISTORY, for Walter Benjamin, does not unfold in a "homogeneous, empty time." Likewise, historical thinking that attempts to seize in an illuminating flash the image of nonlinear time and heterogeneous experience involves "not only the flow of thoughts, but their arrest as well. . . . Where thinking suddenly stops in a configuration pregnant with tensions, it gives that configuration a shock, by which it crystallizes into a monad."[1] The year of 1931 in early Chinese film history is one of those monadic moments when history congeals and implodes, generating as much tension as energy. Everything seemed possible; all the historical actors found themselves at a masquerade ball that could last forever. Of course, it did not. Dancing, as a kinetic practice of socialization, was indeed one of the keynotes of metropolitan life, as was film culture in Shanghai in the early 1930s, a time when many events were taking place at a head-spinning speed, when past and present intertwined. While dance music entered movie theaters with the advent of sound, the fabric of urban life was lived out increasingly in cinematic terms.

At this moment the Chinese film industry, concentrated in Shanghai since the early 1910s, was suddenly seized by an urgency to reflect upon its own history on the screen, as though propelled by a desire to arrest its own image in a hall of moving mirrors. While the city grew into a veritable "Paris of the Orient" with dance halls, cabarets, cafés, and movie theaters, the film industry experienced a second boom and structural transformation. The craze of the "martial arts–magic spirit" (*wuxia shenguai*) genre was on the brink of being extinguished by multiple forces. The left-wing cinema was on the rise. The advent of sound had triggered a cacophony of public debates as well as a deluge of experiments in various formats, in particular the "dancing and singing" (*gewu pian*) genre, to incorporate sound into the silent screen. The establishment of the Lianhua Company (which quickly rivaled to the veteran Mingxing Company) and the campaign to "revive national cinema" (*fuxing guopian*) reconfigured the film industry. The Nationalist government took definitive steps to make its legitimacy felt in the film scene by instituting a full-fledged censorship program, among other restrictions. In standard Chinese film historiography, the year 1931 marked the turning point when a more progressive and patriotic cinema began to emerge following the Japanese invasion of Manchuria that same year. That shift was quickened by a new crisis: on January 28, 1932, the Japanese also bombarded Shanghai, which brought immense destruction to the film industry.

In the midst of these interconnected changes and on the eve of catastrophe, the Mingxing Company, a leading studio in the prewar Shanghai film industry, released an eighteen-reel, two-part feature, called *An Amorous History of the Silver Screen* (*Yinmu yanshi*, 1931).[2] Only an incomplete second part of the film still exists. For many decades this film has been ignored, if not purposely omitted, by Chinese film historians. Even the most recent *History of Chinese Silent Film* (1996) by Li Suyuan and Hu Jubin contains no discussion of it.[3] This film, however, is a condensed textual instance that expresses the configuration of that particular moment in history. It reveals the Shanghai film world poised on a threshold with a vividness perhaps only matched by one other contemporary film, *Two Stars in the Milky Way* (*Yinghan shuangxing*), produced by Lianhua, in the same year. One of the nine silent films made by Mingxing in 1931, *Amorous History* is unique in its direct reference to the film world on multiple levels, as suggested by the title. The film, structured as a backstage drama, showcases the Mingxing studios as a technological wonderland and a simulacrum of the everyday world. It thus also serves as a self-portrait of Mingxing and a synecdoche of the broad film world in China in the early 1930s. A docudramatic tale about the career vicissitudes of a prostitute-turned-film actress and her troubled personal life, the film presents, more significantly, an ambivalent history about Chinese women's relationship to the cinema—the promise of liberation and social mobility as well as the lure and risks of a new kind of commodification of the body by film technology.

Within this larger frame of reference, the interplay on and off the screen between fiction and documentary, between the film world and the life world, lends important insights to the understanding of this particular film as a self-referential text about filmmaking in 1931. It also directs our attention to the question of early Chinese film history as a whole. What *kind* of history could we envisage through the lens of the camera embedded in the film? Why name the narrative an "amorous history" (*yanshi* denotes an unconventional, often erotic, tale or history)? Hence, what is the relationship between such an intimate or deviant history to the master narratives of film and national culture of the prewar period as authorized by standard historiography in China? What does this self-referential gesture tell us about the embodied experience of the cinema and modernity, beyond the narrow definition of self-reflexivity often associated with the modernist cerebral obsession with language and subjectivity?

Before I proceed further into the textual space of the film, I would like to place the historiographic significance of *Amorous History* within the field of early cinema and the related question of modernity generally. What does it mean to talk about early cinema in a Chinese context? How "early"—or how "late"—was early Chinese cinema? A clarification is necessary because the term "early cinema" has a quite specific reference in film scholarship in the West. More than a period term, early cinema functions as a critical category, one that has gained increased attention and weight since the 1978 annual conference of the International Federation of Film Archives (FIAF) held at Brighton, England. It refers primarily to the cinema—that is, films as well as media intertexts, industry, and market—between 1895 and 1917. Early cinema has also been alternatively called the "primitive cinema" or the cinema "before Hollywood," that is, before the so-called classical narrative cinema—and the concomitant institutionalization of a particular patriarchal structure of looking—came to be perceived and received as a dominant mode of cinematic storytelling.[4] The FIAF conference and the annual Giornate del Cinema Muto (Festival of Silent Film) at Pordenone, Italy have provided the vital fuel for an archaeological project of rethinking early cinema's aesthetic and cultural significance, especially how it helped shape radical, new perceptions of time and space, life and death, subject and object with the onset of modernity.[5]

Scholars of early cinema have arrived at the conclusion that early cinema possessed a set of distinctive aesthetics for presenting and representing the world and lived experience, and that the classical narrative cinema, along with the seamless fictional world it created, was not the medium's necessary destiny. This new orientation in historical film scholarship highlights the importance of conjoining theory and practice, critical analysis and archival work, and has opened up many hitherto neglected areas of investigation, beyond the films themselves. As early cinema was intimately bound to the practice of exhibition, studies on early audience formation and viewing relations have relocated the experience of early cinema in a wide range of cultural practices, such as the vaudeville theater, the amusement park, shopping arcades, and so on. It became possible to envisage the film experience in the broader landscape of modern life—in the street and in the theater, in the city and in the country, and, I shall hasten to add, in the West as well as in many other parts of the world. In short, "early cinema" has not only opened new arenas for studying film, but also offered rewarding conceptual and methodological tools for placing film history in an intermedia and interdisciplinary field.

More recently, a strand of feminist film scholarship has enriched this "new film history" by highlighting the issue of gender with regard to early women pioneers, sexual coding of stardom and spectatorship, among other things.[6] This work departs from the earlier feminist preoccupation with the deconstruction of the classical Hollywood cinema as a seamlessly sutured patriarchal representational system through the opening of a new avenue for research and empowerment. By inserting the conceptual as well as historical female spectator qua modern consumer into cultural and social history of cinema, this approach reconstructs the history of women's participation in cinema as an alternative public sphere. Beyond reception and consumption, the active role women played has also been identified in the production sector, in film journalism, and especially in the area of screen performance by earlier generations of movie actresses. Gender proves to be of critical importance for understanding the vitality, if not longevity, of the direct address, intertextuality, and open-endedness of early cinema's aesthetic, as well as understanding its particular epistemology and politics.

But how shall we account for early cinema in Chinese film history? And in what ways did women contribute to the formation of the new film culture in early twentieth century China? Despite the fecundity of scholarship on early cinema, including the recent trend of feminist new history, little has been done about the subject in a cross-cultural field, let alone a consideration of its gender aspect in a non-Western culture. In the Chinese context, particularly as used by Chinese film scholars in periodization, the term *early cinema* (*zaoqi dianying*) serves loosely as a common reference to the cinema before 1949, when the Communists founded the People's Republic of China. In standard Chinese film historiography, therefore, its connotation has been mainly negative, because early cinema as a whole is not only construed as aesthetically inferior in the evolutionary chain of cultural development (which is also often the case in the Western contexts). It has also been linked to the "pre-Liberation" and hence feudal, and semicolonial political and social system. "Modern" or *modeng*, a term prevalently associated with Shanghai culture during the Republican period (1911–49), conjured up meanings of cultural decadence, sexual promiscuity, social anarchy, and Western imperialism.

Since the early 1990s, however, with the revival of Chinese cinema and renewed interest in its historical roots, scholars have been favorably reevaluating early Chinese cinema and making a finer periodization within that long "early" period. They subtly challenged prevalent ideological assumptions and tried to delineate the aesthetic and cultural significance of genres such as comedy and martial arts film, which had been largely deemed vulgar or lowbrow.[7] Underlying this diverse, albeit limited, body of scholarly work,[8] is the vexed question concerning the political and cultural status of early Chinese cinema, especially in the period before the emergence of the left-wing cinema in the early 1930s. Yet, some of these endeavors still betray a one-dimensional historical consciousness and impoverished methodology. For example, *Zhongguo wusheng dianying shi* (*History of Chinese Silent Film*), commissioned by the Chinese Film Archive to commemorate the centennial of cinema's arrival in China, was the first comprehensive account of early Chinese cinema produced by mainland scholars.[9] The book remains, however, mired in the same evolutionary conception of history, despite its sympathies for previously denounced or forgotten filmmakers, producers, actors, and their films.

The unwitting parallel of critical discourses on early cinema in the West and China, despite their divergent circumstances, motivations, and applications, offers an opportune moment to relocate early Chinese cinema within a broader cinematic modernity. The divergent origins of the term in Euro-American and Chinese contexts, and the discrepancies in periodization respectively, alert us to the heterogeneity or unevenness of the international film scene in the silent period. Rather than trying to find an equivalent—or contemporaneous—period and practice in Chinese film history that squarely fits the category of early cinema in the West, I use the term heuristically to create a critical space that negotiates its different valences, temporality, and historicity.

Two recent books in English on Chinese cinema before 1949 have made considerable contribution to the field—Hu Jubin's *Projecting a Nation: Chinese Cinema Before 1949* and Laikwan Pang's *Building a New China in Cinema: The Cinematic Left-Wing Cinema Movement 1932–1937*.[10] Hu's book, based on his dissertation completed in Australia, presents a comprehensive narrative history of Chinese cinema of the Republican period.

It includes a wealth of primary sources on both the film industry and filmmakers and their works in a manner similar to the aforementioned Chinese-language *History of Chinese Silent Film* he coauthored. Hu's book represents the revisionist historiography in Chinese scholarship on the mainland, but it is constrained by its linear narrative method and lack of attention to both cinematic texture and conceptual issues concerning modernity, urban culture, and gender. Pang's work is on the other hand more focused in terms of both periodization and thematization as she is primarily interested in a detailed study of the canonical left-wing cinema and its relation to gender politics and national culture. The particular value of Pang's work lies in her equal attention to both authorship and spectatorship, both as forms of a collective, gendered subjectivity in the making in the midst of a national crisis. Both works, though valuable as the first book-length studies on early Chinese film history, do not break significant theoretical ground. They focus narrowly on the question of national cinema and the political valence of cinema—central tropes in earlier Chinese film historiography. Nonetheless they are admirable efforts in trying to tease out the nuances and contradictions of an important part of modern Chinese cultural history.

The first Chinese film was not allegedly made until 1905, and the Chinese film industry only formed in the mid-1920s. The enjoyment of cinema, however, quickly become an integral part of urban modernity with the first public commercial showing in a teahouse in Shanghai on August 11, 1896. The lack of extant films (actualities, travelogues, educational films, and early short story films) made before 1922 has made it difficult to study that part of early cinema. Significantly, many features of the extended early cinema in China, in aspects of filmmaking as well as distribution, exhibition, and reception, resonate with similar motifs in the history of early cinema worldwide. The time lag between early Euro-American cinema and early Chinese cinema speaks certainly to the semicolonial nature of Chinese modernity, especially with regard to "belated" technological transfer and implementation. Thus, early cinema persists not so much as a rigidly defined aesthetic or period category but as an emblem of modernity, or rather competing versions of modernity, on the "non-synchronous synchronous" global horizon of film culture.[11] To disentangle ourselves from the trappings of such a time lag in periodization, a shift in focus from early cinema to early *film culture,* which includes a wide range of the film experience such as stardom, fan cults, theater architecture, fashion, as well as what happens on the screen, will allow a more productive interdisciplinary approach to the study of early film history in specific cultural locations. Such a shift will also, more crucially, enable us to expand the horizon of comparative studies of cinematic modernity. Thus for the purpose of this book I situate this multifaceted early film culture within the span of the arrival of cinema in China to the closing of the golden period of Shanghai silent and early sound film on the eve of Japanese occupation, from 1896 to 1937.

Now I return to *Amorous History,* and will use it as a case study to probe the complexity involved in the writing of early Chinese film history, particularly from a gender perspective. As I will indicate in detail below, the film opens onto the geography of film culture both through its textual inscription and material consumption. As a self-conscious gesture at "writing" film history on the silver screen, the film and its reception reveal the capacity of the cinematic medium to offer a unique historiographical register in the age of mechanic reproduction of moving images.

Let me first sketch an overview of the film. According to the synopsis written by publicists of the time,[12] the first part of the film (nonextant) begins with an establishing montage that constructs a composite, panoramic view of Shanghai's development as a modern metropolis since it was "opened" as an international trading port (*kaibu*) following China's defeat in the Opium Wars in the mid-nineteenth century. A local film industry is born in this urban landscape animated by a prosperous commercial and industrial life, dotted with skyscrapers, lined with asphalt streets, and crowded with people migrating into the city from all over China and the world. One large film company, in particular, not only boasts a studio with a host of large buildings and a contingent of "bright stars" (*mingxing*—an apparent self-reference to the Mingxing Company) but also features productions "popular all over the world" (*fengxing quanqiu*) (fig. 0.1). One of the "bright stars" in the diegesis, as well as in real life, rises from the city's pleasure quarters: Wang Fengzhen, played by Xuan Jinglin (1907–92) (fig. 0.2). Her character arrives late for a client who slaps her face. Seeing her tears flowing uncontrollably, the man (who is only given a generic name Baixiangren—playboy or hooligan) mocks her: "Since you are so good at crying, why don't you devote yourself to the silver screen to become the oriental Lillian Gish?"[13] He does not, of course, expect her to take his sarcastic remark literally, but her dedication and acting range—from the most comic to the most tragic, from that of a young girl to an old woman—quickly win her the title of "movie star" (*dianying mingxing*) (fig. 0.3). Fang Shaomei, a wealthy dandy, pursues her eagerly by coming to the studio every day and lavishly spoiling her. Wang disappoints the director who has contributed to her stardom when she begins to show signs of negligence in her work,

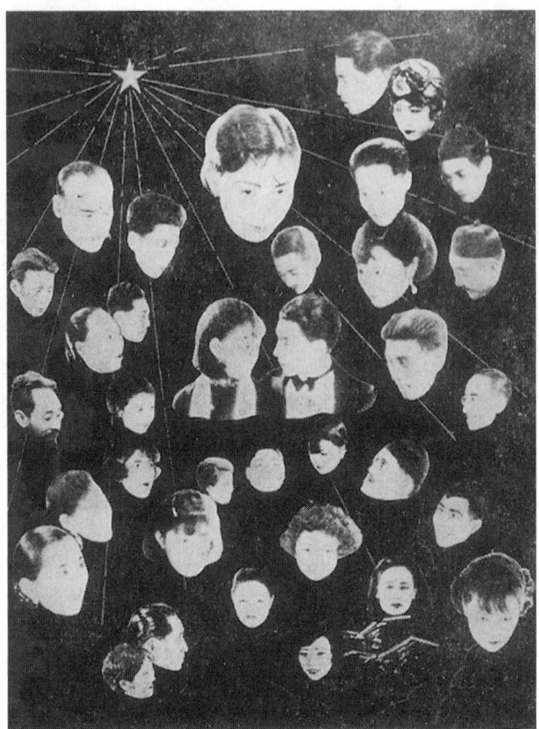

0.1 A constellation of "bright stars" of the Mingxing Company.

0.2 Mingxing actress Xuan Jinglin (*Yinxing*, no. 11, August 1927).

0.3 Xuan Jinglin in *An Amorous History of the Silver Screen*. (Courtesy of the China Film Archive)

breaching her contract with the studio by becoming Fang's concubine, or according to the fashionable term of the day, entering a relationship of "cohabitation" (*tongju*).

The extant sequel starts with the demise of Wang's domestic bliss and then moves toward her comeback to the film world. Despite her desire and effort to become a model housewife, her playboy patron-lover grows increasingly indifferent to her as he begins dallying with a dancing girl (played by Xia Peizhen [1908–?]). One day after an argument, Wang dozes off and dreams about arriving at a dance hall and finding Fang with the dancing girl. After following them to a hotel, she runs into the director who is working on a script. He reveals that she has fallen out with Fang because she is no longer a film star and encourages her to return to the studio. The next day, just as in the dream, she sets out to the hotel and confronts Fang in front of the dancing girl for the last time, only to be insulted again. She finally makes up her mind: "I will go my way. I won't die hungry for lack of a man!" Arriving at the studio, she tells the overjoyed director to quickly write a script for her so that she can resume her career on the silver screen.

Amorous History begins to take on the look of a mock documentary when the returned star is given a tour of the expanded and technologically updated studio. On that day, forty truckloads of extras arrive for several films being shot simultaneously at different studios of the same company: *The Burning of the Red Lotus Temple* (*Huoshao Hongliansi,* a martial arts serial film), *Shadow of Red Tears* (*Honglei ying,* a melodrama), *Fate in Tears and Laughter* (*Tixiao yinyuan,* a romance based on Zhang Henshui's popular novel), and *Money Demon* (*Qianmo*).[14] Wang wanders with the director through the sets for both *Money Demon* and *The Burning of the Red Lotus Temple,* impressed by the sophistication of the new equipment as well as the dedication of the production crews. The extras are organized in an assembly-line fashion, finishing make-up quickly and mechanically. Among the extras, Wang recognizes the hooligan who slapped her face back in her former life as a prostitute. Their "reunion" on the film set, following a script specially written for Wang's come-back, turns into a situation of licensed vengeance as the plot requires Wang to slap the hooligan character for a scene in a public park. Wang's resolution to return to the silver screen also magically rekindles Fang's love for her. He begins to pursue her again by driving her to and from the studio. The disenchanted dancing girl, realizing the romantic power of being a film actress, decides to try her luck in the film world herself. Along with hundreds of others, she arrives at the studio for an interview, which, without her knowing it, turns out to be a rigorous audition of her acting skill. She is provoked to cry and laugh, to be happy and angry (*xinu aile*). The film ends with her leaving the studio, hoping that she will return and become a film star.

On both thematic and stylistic levels, *Amorous History* does not merely record a significant segment of Chinese film history but also embodies the multilayered experience of the women and men who contributed to the making of that history. As a self-conscious gesture at "writing" film history on the silver screen, it reveals the capacity of the cinematic medium to offer a different kind of historiographic register, permeated with an "amorous" economy that underscores the cinematic experience both on and off the screen.

The particular attraction of *Amorous History* comes from the intertwining of a personal romance and a studio promotional showcase, feminine biography and the history of film technology. Set in the liminal space (as the daydream sequence indicates) between fictional and factual, the film indulges in cinema's potential for both realism and fantasy, or rather, the magic blending of the two, thereby creating a new perceptual experience of reality. Some Chinese film historians have pointed to the referentiality (*zhishixing*) rather than representation, romance (*chuanqi,* or fable) rather than psychological narrative, as the basic features of early Chinese cinema.[15] The elusive referentiality and hyperbolic realism of an "amorous history" (which can also be translated as "romance") inside and outside the film illustrates this observation. The contemporary fans of Mingxing productions, in particular those starring Xuan Jinglin, would readily find Xuan's life story embedded in the film. Born to a poor family (her father was a newspaper vendor) and having had only sporadic schooling, Xuan was working as a prostitute when Zhang Shichuan (1889–1953), the director and cofounder of Mingxing, discovered her acting talent. The company had her redeemed from the brothel where she worked.[16] Made one year after Xuan's return to the studio, and following the dissolution of her cohabitational relationship with a businessman, the film is in fact a biographical portrait of a cinematic Cinderella, in this case, Xuan Jinglin herself.

Xuan's rising stardom paralleled the rising fame and wealth of Mingxing.[17] The first (nonextant) part of the film chronicles her bewilderment when she first entered the film world. Mingxing, the first fully-fledged Chinese film enterprise established by Zhang Shichuan, Zheng Zhengqiu (1888–1935), and others in 1922, was just beginning to outgrow its cottage-industry mode of production and become the Mingxing Film Limited Co. when Xuan joined the company in May 1925. Mingxing's first glass studio was built while Xuan's first film, in which she played a minor role, was being shot. From 1925 to 1928, Xuan portrayed an array of characters, ranging from the country maiden to the poor widow to the dancing girl to the female gangster. By the time she joined the company for the second time in 1930, Mingxing had just begun another large-scale expansion and modernization following the commercial miracle created by the martial arts film series, *The Burning of the Red Lotus Temple.*

The new studio, which the actress in *Amorous History* tours with bewildered eyes, is presented as a magic workshop of virtual reality. When the actress marvels at the grandiose sets, high-tech lighting, and the technologically advanced production of special effects, the love story that dominates the first part of the film recedes to the background. Instead, it is taken over by an exhibitionist impulse for display characteristic of early cinema and the showmanship associated with it.[18] The romance between the actress and her unfaithful patron is now replaced by the romance between her and cinematic technology. If woman, as Andreas Huyssen remarks, has been prevalently linked to or allegorized as modern technology, as exemplified in Fritz Lang's *Metropolis* (1927),[19] the relationship between the actress and technology in *Amorous History* is organized along a different line and cannot be subsumed under the category of mechanical incorporation or alienation alone. Xuan is not overpowered by the gigantic new studio and its oversized equipment. The latter functions, rather, as a hyperbolic backdrop for her personal drama in which she redeems her independence. Unlike the dystopic vision of femininity and modern machinery in *Metropolis,* technology here emits a humorous energy—due to the comic structure of the plot—which facilitates a social transformation embodied in the figure of the actress. Xuan, playing her former self as a prostitute decked out with a huge flower on her chest, is instructed by the director to slap (back) the hooligan in front of the camera. Screen performance and reenactment of the past enable the redemption of her personal history. In front of the camera, Xuan not only literally acts out her ascendance from the lower social depth to the pantheon of movie stars, she is also able to close a painful chapter from the past. "Just as people whom nothing moves or touches any longer are taught to cry again by films," she regains the capacity to feel and emote.[20] The *act* of revenge made possible by film technology is certainly a utopian representation of women's agency. At the same time, because of the indexical rapport, or fusion, between Xuan's biographical and cinematic life, the slap is much more than a simple make-believe dramatic gesture. It serves as the point where the on-screen action unites with its social and experiential referent—a personal *histoire* with a public spectacle.

Xuan's comeback also coincided with another sea change in film technology that redefined the structure of sensory perception in early Chinese film history. Shortly after the first American talkie was shown in a Shanghai theater in 1929, several Chinese film companies began experimenting with sound despite the lack of adequate equipment. Mingxing Company once again proved to be a leader in innovation through collaborating with the Pathé recording company of Shanghai to produce the first (partial) sound film, *The Singing Girl Red Peony* (*Genü hong mudan,* 1931), using wax disks. Because the Nationalist government demanded that sound film use *guoyu,* or the standard "national language" based on the Beijing vernacular, many actors who were not of Northern origin suddenly found themselves suffering from a speech handicap. Xuan Jingling, born and raised in Shanghai, could only speak the Shanghai vernacular with a Suzhou (her maternal native town) inflection. Determined to catch up with the new technology and surpass her own image as a silent film star, Xuan took crash lessons in *guoyu* and singing. By appearing in the first Movietone film while continuing to make silent films, Xuan demonstrated that her comeback was not a mere repeat performance as an icon for the first Golden Age of Chinese silent film but a leap into a new era, embodying coexisting technologies, their ambivalent relations, as well as distinctive possibilities. It is significant that during her "tour" of the studio, the several films being produced *simultaneously* are of different genres and appeal, with one of them being a partial sound and color production, *The Fate in Tears and Laughter* (1933). She thus personifies early cinema as a critical category—that technological change does not easily translate into a shift in aesthetic modes and spectatorial address, but can expose the very contradictions of technology and its multiple appropriations.

Besides the main plot surrounding the actress's double-edged "amorous history," the film, with its numerous references to both production and reception contexts, points to the breadth and depth of a film culture far beyond the silver screen and exhibition space. In fact, *Amorous History* virtually inventories a cluster of interconnected practices that sustain and feed back into the film industry: money, stardom, fan culture, and the broader urban landscape. In this landscape film experience is interwoven with other contiguous forms of the modern experience—such as ballroom dancing and window shopping—and the constant transaction and contagion between them. The emphasis on the commercial nature of the film industry is clearly seen in a crucial scene inside the studio. The actress is led to visit the set for *Money Demon* and taken aback by the gigantic mask of the money demon descending from above and crushing onto a circle of dancing young women and men. At this moment the film is at its most self-conscious about the commodity nature of the cinema, as well as women's ambivalent place within the film world.

Throughout the film, the figure of the actress embodies not so much the glamour of stardom as the multiple and concrete social roles available to women at the time, in both the domestic and public spheres. This multiplicity manifests itself in Xuan's repertoire of characters of different ages and classes as well as in her own life experience. To be sure, women's presence in the film world remained largely confined to performing. Their visibility as public figures and the heightened social status they could enjoy were nevertheless considerable, especially at the threshold of the 1930s, when the film industry had secured its legitimate place in everyday life, if not quite yet on the altar of art. Starting in the early 1920s, the profession of film actress provided an unprecedented opportunity for many women of diverse backgrounds, such as first generation film actresses Wang Hanlun (1903–78), Yin Mingzhu (1904–?), Zhang Zhiyun (1905–?), and Yang Naimei (1904–60), just to name a few.

If these aforementioned female stars quickly faded away, Xuan Jingling proved her enduring passion for the silver screen and her ability to adjust to a fast-changing film industry, in particular with the transition to sound. Her stardom culminated in her performance as a mother—within the span of three decades—to twin daughters (both played by the erstwhile "Queen of Cinema" Hu Die) in Mingxing's sound production *Twin Sisters* (*Zimei hua*). The film was released in 1933 and played consecutively for sixty-four days, creating Mingxing's biggest box office hit.[21] After several other roles, Xuan decided to retire from the screen in 1936 due to health reasons.[22] In an uncanny way, the end of her film career coincided with the decline of the Mingxing Company, which followed the July 1935 death of Zheng Zhengqiu, a founding member of the company and screenwriter and director of many of Xuan's films. Due to the fierce competition in the sound film market, the company found itself in financial straits in 1936 and could not pay its employees. Seriously damaged by the Japanese bombing of the city on January 28, 1932, the rebuilt studio was destroyed beyond repair in August 1937, when the Japanese invaded Shanghai following another massive bombardment.

Amorous History inadvertently recorded the prime of Xuan Jinglin and the Mingxing Company, when both were crucially transforming. In weaving together personal and institutional histories in a fictionalized documentary, the film offers a compelling glimpse into prewar Chinese cinema from an insider and a woman's point of view. The historical vision presented by the film is both playful and reflexive, involved yet not without a critical distance. The self-reflexive impulse is never steeped in a psychological absorption that abstracts experience for moral edification or formal indulgence; rather, it motivates the viewer's heightened awareness of the social significance of the cinematic experience as part of the larger sensorial economy of modernity. Indeed, this self-reflexivity should be viewed as stemming from a combination of a residual aesthetic of display with a direct address to the "(in)credulous" audience, on the one hand,[23] and the impulse to "update" this early history more than three decades after the invention of the cinema, on the other.

More importantly, this self-reflexivity, unlike the often claustrophobic introspection characteristic of modernist writing, vibrated on the open horizon of audience reception, far beyond the geographic limits of Shanghai. Seeing the film, one viewer from the remote Jilin province in Manchuria wrote a long letter to the editors of *Yingxi shenghuo* (literally "shadowplay life") in Shanghai, expressing his enthusiasm for the film and gratitude to the Mingxing Company for generously sharing the "secrets" behind the scene and imparting to the audience basic knowledge about film production. He lamented the fact that, because of the remote location of his native town, it usually took months before a new film reached Jilin. The only theater there was the local YMCA auditorium, which held screenings mainly for the purpose of education. However, as an avid fan he watched everything shown there. *Amorous History,* unlike anything else he had seen, opened his eyes to what was behind the world of illusion on the screen. He was particularly impressed by the touring sequence in the film when the actress visits the sets of several films within the film, encountering famous actors, directors, and cinematographers. What astonished him most was how film technology was capable of manufacturing a different kind of reality, or a second nature:

> What a big electric fan! It makes us realize the origin of torrential rain or snow in a movie. What a big mountain and what a fast train! Now we know how a mountain is made and a train is manufactured.
>
> We know now that a skeleton is painted; a pavilion is but a miniature; a lavish living room is a backdrop; and a bustling street is artificial! Flying and leaping in the air—what impressive martial arts! But it's made possible by a hanging rope! Tears flowing—what a profusion of emotion! Do you know, though, that he is just using fake tears?!
>
> Furthermore, [we see] the way the director works, how the camera runs, and operations in the makeup room and on the sets—all the things we have never seen or heard of![24]

As Gunning underscores, the sense of bewilderment and the exhilarating enlightenment about the "true nature" of the cinema—"the magic metamorphosis rather than a seamless reproduction of reality . . . reveal not a childlike belief, but an undisguised awareness (and delight in) film's illusionistic capabilities."[25] Moreover, the revelation, or surfacing, of the cinematic magic, paradoxically, only intensified the provincial viewer's passion for the cinema. Beyond the gadgets and special effects, he was gripped by the vivid presence of the people who produced the magic—"the models draped in gauzy dress, the country women who cry and laugh hyperbolically, the directors who shout in panic through their loudspeakers, and the stars with a cocky aura." Seeing these people vicariously through Xuan Jinglin's eyes, the viewer experienced the film as a three-dimensional virtual space in which the silver screen's flatness materializes into a tangible reality. The crowded and simultaneous presence of extras, the "hidden" masters of illusion (i.e., directors and the cameramen), and the sheer size of sets and equipment endow the film with an overwhelming visibility and physicality, as well as a democratic appeal. Nothing is withheld from the viewer; every person and every object comes to the foreground, even though they are governed by a certain hierarchical organization. This experience puts the audience of a remote provincial town in direct contact with the pulse of metropolitan modernity, which the film world both fashions and symbolizes.

For the provincial spectator, *Amorous History* offered a rare occasion to "travel" to Shanghai's film scene without riding a real train and crossing mountain ranges from remote Jilin province; for me it has provided an entry point to begin making sense of a film world that existed decades ago. I encountered the film for the first time on the video screen in a shabby, cluttered room at the Beijing Film Archive in August 1995, the centennial of the cinema. My astonishment and enlightenment was comparable to the viewer's experience in a northeast China YMCA auditorium more than sixty years before, even though I had the advantage of a historical hindsight mediated through a new kind of screen practice. Just as *Amorous History* offered an introductory lesson on the ABCs of the cinema to the provincial viewer, it proved to be an eye-opening phantom ride that transported me to the early Shanghai film world. I had previously tried to envision and understand this world through arduous but inevitably intermittent library and archival research on printed sources. But in the film, that world suddenly came to life. At that moment, I was overcome by the embodying power the film transmitted. I was *moved* not so much by the rare visual encounter with an extant silent film and its story, as by the sensation aroused by the cinematic tour of the 1931 film world—by being in the company of Xuan Jinglin and her contemporary moviegoers. Here I found a precious primary source and, more significantly, a model for a film history I wanted to compose—one that traverses the lived experience on and off the screen, past and present in Shanghai and the larger world. What I try to offer in this book is a cultural history of Chinese modernity through the lens of the Shanghai cosmopolitan film culture of the prewar period. Many of the people and films I have mentioned so far will return at various points in the following chapters. Still others will also enter the scene and participate in the changing configuration of a shared amorous history.

It is, however, not my intention to write a total narrative or comprehensive inventory that exhausts—rather than illuminates—history. Instead, my trajectory will be emphatically cinematic, as in *Amorous History.* It consists of a series of long takes and close-ups on what I take to be some significant topoi in the landscape of a "vernacular" film culture—a concept I elaborate on in chapter 1 and illustrate throughout the book—and modernity in China, from the arrival of the cinema at a Shanghai teahouse in 1896 to the eve of the Japanese military invasion in 1937. Films constitute a central focus of my endeavor but not the only one; the sociological and historical landscape I delineate along the way should not be construed as the separate means or the end of the cinematic experience as the two are inexorably interwoven. On the other hand, films are not merely treated as isolated aesthetic objects that float outside sociopolitical and economical environment. I regard the films as significant works of cultural labor that invite aesthetic analysis and semiotic exegesis in relation to both larger textual or intertextual systems. At the same time, I treat them as artifacts and commodities that orbit in a broader media ecology of circulation and consumption. I delve into the contexts of their production and reception, paying equal attention to authorship, spectatorship, stylistic repertoires, the formation and transformation of genres, and the interaction or tension between art and politics. The interpretive strategies I deploy are thus not "interpretation as identification of given meaning-structures" in either a purely formalist or a deconstructive vein but rather, following Hans Ulrich Gumbrecht's proposal, the "reconstruction of those processes through which structures of articulated meaning can all emerge." The interest in textual "meaning-constitution" goes hand-in-hand with the concern for the body and other physical and material properties of signification that have been largely exiled in text- or mind-centered hermeneutic traditions until recently.[26]

There is a more practical reason why this culturally significant history of early Chinese cinema is by necessity fragmentary: Only a few dozen out of hundreds of films made before 1937 have survived the ravages of time. Most only existed on nitrate film stock and burned to ashes, especially during the two bombing raids of Shanghai by the Japanese. The films that have survived are mostly fictional narratives of varying length made after 1922. Similar to other narrative cinemas in the world, the motif of the love story in various formats and disguises runs through the history of Chinese silent and early sound film, ranging from the earliest extant comedy, *Laborer's Love* (*Laogong zhi aiqing*, Mingxing, 1922) to the horror film *Song at Midnight* (*Yeban gesheng*, Xinhua, 1937), a Chinese variation of *The Phantom of the Opera* that proved sensational in Shanghai. Crossing a number of genres and technological changes, the amorous history of this cinema is nevertheless a complicated and multifaceted one regarding the notion of narrative cinema. Indeed, as *Amorous History* attests, the permeability between cinema and other cultural forms, such as photography, serial fiction, drama, musical recording, and dancing, constantly puts the very notion of "narrative" cinema on trial. This history is then about the search for both a changing film language of storytelling and the search for an audience, and how this shared passion for the cinema shaped a modern experience in a way no other medium has achieved in China in the twentieth century.

The history—a labor of love indeed—is organized into two parts along the parallel lines of film and culture. The main theme of the book unfolds along a rough chronology, covering the late Qing period to the 1930s. The eight chapters, laid out as a series of monadic moments in the spatiotemporal constellations of modern Chinese cultural history, may be read independently of each other. The four chapters of part 1 delineate the vernacular scene as both a material and conceptual construct for the reception of the cinematic medium and the production of a domestic film industry. In chapter 1, which lays out the conceptual framework for the book, I probe the theoretical and historiographical ramifications of the vernacular and why cinema became its most important embodiment in the Chinese context, more than other parts of the world because of massive scale of a vernacularizing process. Engaging recent scholarship on vernacular modernism, as well as drawing on architectural, literary, and anthropological studies, I argue that early film culture in China, as a complex translation machine and motor for change, generated a mass-mediated social and aesthetic experience and an inclusive vernacular modernity. Modern science and technology—along with new ideas about class, gender, and the body—collided with traditional culture in some ways but were domesticated and productively absorbed in other ways. They galvanized the exploration of new aesthetic sensibilities, social positions, and epistemological orientations. As historical, cultural, and aesthetic formations, the multifaceted film culture contributed in indispensable ways to the production of a sociocorporeal sensorium and a broadly defined vernacular movement. In a nutshell, Chinese modernity cannot be adequately understood outside a modern visual culture, and cinema supplied the most synthetic and embodied form.

Any study of early Chinese cinema should not be separated from a consideration of the historical genesis of the metropolitan culture in Shanghai. The physical and cultural landscape of the city and its multifaceted film scene was nourished and supported by a broad vernacular culture involving old as well as new expressive and entertainment forms. Thus in chapter 2, I map out this rapidly evolving film culture that was deeply embedded in the urban culture throughout the silent period and the implementation of sound. I begin with an "archaeology" of the provenance of Shanghai-style modernity in the downtown Yangjingbang area and the pidgin language that incarnated this localized cosmopolitanism in the late nineteenth and early twentieth centuries. The subjects that inhabit this Yangjingbang cultural space are the so-called petty urban dwellers (*xiao shimin*), avid consumers of mass culture and moviegoers with "worldly" tastes. Among the "vernacular genres" that preceded, coexisted, and fed into the cinema as a quintessentially modern form of storytelling and socialization, I single out the illustrated newspaper and the amusement hall as the two premium examples that prepared and supplied the cinema with a new mode of visuality and spectatorship. I also argue that the visual pleasure of cinema is intimately intertwined with other modern pleasures such as reading (especially with the growth of vernacular press and film publications), eating, dancing, sporting, and dating, as the experience of film becomes deeply enmeshed in the metropolitan experience as a whole.

In chapters 3 and 4 I expand on the historical and theoretical framework mapped out in the previous chapters by delving into the rich context of the beginnings of a domestic film industry. Here I concentrate on the transformation of spectatorship during the transition to narrative cinema in the first half of the 1920s. A contextually informed close reading of the short comedy *Laborer's Love* (1922), reportedly the earliest extant narrative film, yields insights into the dynamic transaction between cinema and other cultural forms, such as the puppet shadowplay and the civilized play (a popular new spoken drama adopted from the West and Japan), which were often staged in teahouse-style theaters. The film also invites a look into the transnational composition of the audience for an incipient cinema. I then analyze the struggle to find a permanent "home" for a domestic cinema and the accompanying discourse on the ontology and social function of cinema (i.e., entertainment versus enlightenment) in the larger public sphere including the first film schools. I explore how the architectural expansion of movie theater space—from the hybrid and haptic teahouse to the exclusive, even luxury cinema—corresponded to an enlarged and uplifted film world as a whole. This included a bigger market, the increasing professionalization of film-related vocations, a more streamlined mode of production and reception, and, above all, the elevation or legitimization of the previously frowned-upon film world within the respectable segments of Chinese culture and society.

Part 1 sets the scene for the vernacular culture, which gave rise to and was in turn reshaped by the cinematic medium. Part 2 addresses competing moderns and moves from social and cultural frameworks to considerations of specifically cinematic articulations of urban modernity and vernacular experience in the golden age of Chinese silent film and early sound film. Consistently employing the method of historical intertextual analysis and engaging previously unstudied material, I focus on the competing articulations and practices that fueled cinematic expressions of modernism, commercialism, urbanism, and politics. As a whole, the films and other material analyzed in this part illustrate how the different historical moments in modern Chinese history and early film history are loaded with translated ideas, competing lifestyles, and malleable social and gender roles.

In chapter 5, I discuss the emergence of the film script in the mid-1920s as a new form of the vernacular written in "electric shadows" and its implications for cinematic storytelling, especially as manifested in two divergent forms of melodrama. Toward that end I explore early discourses about the screenwriting and trick photography of two "pearl" films—*A String of Pearls* (1926) and *Lustrous Pearls* (1927), each "translated" from different foreign sources—and show how they exemplify different aesthetic and social orientations. I argue that the narrative organizations of these films around the theme of retribution can be understood in terms of the persistence of certain traditional narrative conventions and cultural values put into service in the pursuit of new concerns. The disparities in their modes of narration reveal the unevenness in the search for a storytelling language within a heterogeneous film industry, especially as the films provide allegorical references to the intense competition in the film market at the time.

Chapter 6 canvasses the mass cultural phenomenon of the so-called martial arts–magic spirit (*wuxia shenguai pian*) film genre in the late 1920s, which was destined to have powerful repercussions in Hong Kong cinema. I first trace the genealogy of the genre in traditional folklore and contemporary martial arts fiction. The emergence of the genre is also crucially linked to an important cultural debate on the role of science in China. Aided by film technology, proliferation of the martial arts genre effected a redefinition of the body. It also created an array of awe-inspiring female knight-errant figures, reflecting the new centrality of women's bodies in the modern imagination, deploying a visual vernacular of science and magic. These films appealed to urban working classes as well as rural and diasporic populations, and drastically expanded the film market beyond the metropolitan area.

The early 1930s witnessed the transformation of a thoroughly commercialized film industry into an increasingly politicized enterprise (especially after the Japanese attack on Shanghai in early 1932). Chapter 7 locates this transformation in a number of interconnected topoi in the film landscape. This includes the prominent role of film criticism in fostering a vibrant yet contentious national cinema, the polemic battle over the so-called soft film versus hard film that erupted between modernist and leftist critics and filmmakers, and the competing aesthetics in their respective film practices. I analyze the entry of the leftist intellectuals into the film world and how this helped establish a popular version of progressive ideology in a number of productions. This is followed by a careful examination of the modernist magazine *Modern Screen* and its "soft" aesthetic. Modern girls, dandies, and revolutionaries were three most emblematic figures in Shanghai—both on and off the screen, left-wing or otherwise—who embodied the exuberance and contradictions of urban modernity in the face of national distress. The war between leftist critics and the modernists was waged over the fate of the modern girl and the meaning of urban modernity in the face of a national crisis. Despite the rising patriotic fervor, the cinema of the time remained markedly heterogeneous. Sun Yu's prolific writing and filmmaking as a whole generates a productive expression of vernacular modernism at a politically and culturally volatile time.

Chapter 8, which concludes the main body of the book, is devoted to the impact of sound on early Chinese film culture. Sound did not consolidate its status as a new "dominant" in Chinese cinema until after 1935. It in fact overlapped with the golden age of silent film. At the center of the chapter is a richly wrought intertextual analysis of Ma-Xu Weibang's *Song at Midnight* (1937). A sound film with a gothic overtone, it was made on the eve of the Japanese all-out invasion of China and occupation of Shanghai, at about the time of the demise of the silent period. I consider this film symptomatic of the unresolved tension between the silent and sound cinemas and between the persistently contending ideologies and aesthetics operating at that crucial moment of Chinese film history. Taking refuge in an abandoned theater, the disfigured hero and his disembodied voice provide the uncanny sites where unconsummated desire and repressed history resurface and are allowed to erupt. These tensions are carried over into occupied Shanghai and, later on, into Hong Kong, where segments of Shanghai cinema later migrated and where other versions of the amorous history of the silver screen would be written, and rewritten.

PART ONE

THE VERNACULAR SCENE

CHAPTER ONE

VERNACULAR MODERNISM AND CINEMATIC EMBODIMENT

THE QUESTION OF early Chinese cinema is inexorably connected to the question of vernacular modernism, a concept that has recently stirred up interests and debates in film studies and related fields. I approach vernacular modernism from a specific historical location (in this case China, particularly Shanghai) and place it within the global landscape of modernity in the early twentieth century. Here I will focus on the dynamic but also tension-ridden process of urbanization and modernization against the background of a wide-ranging vernacularizing trend in language, urbanism, mass culture, and everyday life. My theoretical investment in the vernacular joins in the emerging scholarship on the capacity of cinema for serving as both a reflection of and an antidote to the stressful and alienating conditions of modern life. More importantly, cinema as a modern global vernacular par excellence helped forge a new human sensorium and shape a synthetic and productive form of embodiment against the dehumanizing effects of industrial capitalism and colonialism.

Film culture in China between 1896 and 1937, from the arrival of cinema to the Japanese invasion, was an integral part of a profound transformation in everyday life. It changed the way the world was perceived and experienced, knowledge production and dissemination, and the formation of modern subjectivities. The creation and reception of modern imagery through the cinematic vernacular were informed by a host of old and new technologies and related cultural practices. Two interwoven dimensions are central to these concerns: First, the complex ties between cinematic modernity and the vernacular movement, and by extension, the interaction between verbal and visual culture within the broader scenario of the democratization of writing and iconography. Second is the emergence of a film culture in cosmopolitan Shanghai and the new gender relations and perceptions of the body that configured under the impact of mass media and consumerism.

Throughout the book, the vernacular is conceived as an "episteme" and a historical trope arising from a particular form of cultural experience and comprising a web of references and their signification,[1] which the cinema embodies and constantly refashions. The term *vernacular* readily invokes the linguistic mode of expression and indeed may be linked to the early conception of cinema as a new Tower of Babel. This was encapsulated in D. W. Griffith and Vachel Lindsay's vision of cinema as a modern "universal language" that would unify a world divided since the ancient fall of Babylon.[2] I subscribe to the notion that this concept is globally relevant, following Miriam Hansen's argument that "American movies of the classical period offered something like the first global vernacular" for mediating and articulating the modern experience. It impacted—but was also transformed by—different international film cultures through reception, consumption, and appropriation.[3]

My use of the concept of vernacular modernism overlaps with Hansen's, yet extends into the deeper layers of history. The cinematic vernacular in the Chinese context reveals the content of modern life and, more importantly, determines specific forms of expressibility that defy any rigid boundaries—between the verbal and the visual, the secular and the nonsecular, the material and the imaginary, the high and the low, the political and the aesthetic, and finally, China and the world. This conception has affinity with Jonathan Friedman's notion of modernity as "a field of identifications" resulting from the cyclical historical commercialization and dissemination of cultural products in the global arena and promising transcultural and intersubjective exchanges.[4] Modernism is traditionally and institutionally associated with the high-brow culture of the West (including its self-reflexive critique), which, as a symptom of globalization, also infected the Chinese intellectuals at the turn of the century. Vernacular modernism, however, is open to and dependent on a mass media–based authorship and spectatorship. The vernacular, intrinsically performative and generative, exceeds any attempt to fix its parameters. Yet it is not about a compromised middle-ground, but rather a force field that constantly produces tension as well as energy, separating or combining diverse social and material components, aesthetic traditions and trends, and sensorial and emotional flows.

Diverging from the language-centered model of film theory that has dominated the field of cinema studies, I pursue the more recent theoretical and historical moves toward a sensorial history of cinema. This history is one that parallels, intersects, and embodies the history of urban modernity in the wake of industrial capitalism in the world context. In this regard, my book presents a cultural history of the body and the affective regime created or mediated in China through the cinema in the early decades of the twentieth century. The specific films and modes—such as slapstick comedy, melodrama, martial arts film, and horror—serve as nodal points for portraying this vernacular overtly or covertly, and fit within the "body genres," which prompt visceral responses as much or more than intellectual ones.[5] This technologically and culturally mediated vernacular competed with the nativist vernacular movement that attempted to install a radically new form of modern vernacular (mixing Beijing dialect, Western grammar, and Japanese loan-words) as the standard, official language of a unified modern nation state. On the profilmic level, the cinematic vernacular includes both linguistic elements such as dialogues and texts and cinematic elements such as editing, sound, and lighting. In a broad context, it stems from the fertile ground of a vibrant vernacular culture—including the teahouses, theaters, storytelling, popular fiction, music, dance, painting, photography, and discourses of modern wonders and magic—that cuts across the arbitrary divide of the cinematic and the noncinematic, the premodern and the modern, China and the outside world. As a dialectic of home-spun formulations and "imitations" of imported movies (and lifestyles), the early Chinese silent and sound film practices manifested an energetic, if sometimes aggressive, appropriation of the global vernacular represented by Hollywood and other variants, including literary adaptations of Western and Japanese literature and drama. Thus on both domestic and international levels, in linguistic and cinematic domains, early Chinese cinema contributed to world cinema and modern visual culture with a specific brand of modernism à la Shanghai Yangjingbang—a local vernacular with unabashed cosmopolitan aspirations (this will be discussed more in chapter 2).

This cinematic vernacular came out of the tumultuous cultural sea change across the threshold of the twentieth century: Chinese people tried to come to terms with modernization spanning from the late Qing reforms, the Republican revolution of 1911, the May Fourth and New Culture movement, and the subsequent political and social upheavals until the Japanese invasion in 1937. These large-scale sociocultural transformations and waves of accelerated modernization substantially, and at times violently, altered the spiritual and physical landscape of China, especially its cities. Rather than treating this social landscape as a distant background for the cinema, I regard some of its features as significant signposts in an expansive vernacular scene—in both linguistic and theatrical senses—on which the cinematic experience is lived out and enacted, and which itself is reshaped by the cinema. Instead of tackling the specific watershed historical events head on, which has been done extensively by scholars, my focus will be on the complex interaction between cinema and history, and how the history of film culture confronts and revises the more familiar narratives of modern China.

Because the film experience is public and requires an architectural infrastructure, a history of film culture would be inadequate without considerations of the physical forms, geographical distributions, and social and aesthetic function of exhibition venues. Thus the vernacular also encompasses the urban architectural environment essential to film experience—the theaters, amusement halls, teahouses, parks, cafés, dance halls, department stores, and race courts, as well as the residential communities where these venues were often located. This environment was more than the sum of physical structures; it provided the site for a complex ecology of material conditions and sociocorporeal relations. This book does not, however, attempt to detail a social history of movie theaters and moviegoing experience. Rather, my interests in theater architecture lie more in the subtle dialectic relations between the vernacular "hardware" (locations, infrastructure, and technology) and the "software" (imaginative communities, everyday practices, social relations, and aesthetic expressions) that manifest the utility and meaning of the cinematic vernacular for the moviegoer, the quintessential modern urban subject. This subplot, which traces the changing face and place of movie theaters throughout the first three decades of cinema in China, is intimately tied with the transformation of spectatorship at different stages. For instance, in chapters 3 and 4, I connect the shift from a teahouse-style venue to the interiorized and gentrified purpose-built cinema during the first half of the 1920s. This shift in venue was simultaneous with the emergence of a morally centered narrative cinema and the discourse concerning the relationship between enlightenment and entertainment. The martial-arts film craze at the end of that decade, however, instigated a certain regression by throwing the door back open to the working class. The interactions between the linguistic, the visual, the visceral, and the architectural domains and their capacities for social change constitute the foundations of early Chinese film culture's vernacular scene.

Key to a new understanding of Chinese modernity lies in the question of women, as has been demonstrated, for example, by Rey Chow's seminal study, *Woman and Chinese Modernity,* in which she offers provocative rereadings of the urban fiction by the Mandarin Ducks and Butterflies school authors. She argues for the "modernity" of this literature—a popular literature that was systematically discredited as unworthy by the May Fourth literary discourse.[6] Early Chinese cinema was heavily indebted to this middlebrow literature. It was written in a hybrid language and disseminated widely through newspapers and magazines, and much of it was adapted to the silver screen, making it accessible for the illiterate or semiliterate audience, especially women. The cinematic translation of this literature also radically redefined the meaning of the vernacular, particularly through first generation of female actors, who embodied modernity as well as new models for Chinese women. The audiences in the theaters responded to the tears shed and laughter emitted onscreen, thereby creating a collective sensorium. This sensorium helped absorb, deflect, and overcome the shocks and stress of modern life and release the mounting tension in a society caught in between existing patriarchal codes and nascent conceptions of gender and sexuality informed by urban life style and consumer culture. The vernacular modernism formulated and expressed by the cinematic experience is therefore inseparable from the new configurations of gender relations and perceptions of the body.

In the following I will elaborate on some key theoretical and historiographical issues outlined above. I will begin with a general discussion of a body of recent scholarship that reconceives cinema as modernity incarnated. I then explore the theoretical import of vernacular modernism for cinema studies and the methodological possibilities it opens up for studying a particular film culture within the global context. Ultimately, I conceptualize early Chinese cinema in relation to the historically specific vernacular movement, and propose an embodied and gender-conscious approach to the subject as the "amorous" relationship between women and cinema significantly redefined it.

CINEMA AND MODERN LIFE

To globally contextualize the development of early Shanghai cinema, it is necessary to begin with an evaluation of the recent scholarship on the symbiotic relationship between cinema and modernity. The new critical history of early cinema has redirected attention to the epoch that provided the catalyst for cinema's birth and worldwide dissemination. What started as a tentative "archaeological" project to salvage and make sense of the legacy of early cinema has turned into a rigorous inquiry into the relationship between film and the culture of modernity—an inquiry that has hitherto only focused on the European and American experiences.

The first wave of this scholarship began in the mid-1980s with archivists and film historians—silent-film buffs who worked primarily with empirical and textual methods. A second wave of literature by film and art historians with more pronounced theoretical agendas widened the category "early cinema" beyond the narrow period of nonnarrative or preclassical narrative cinema before 1915. Borrowing ideas and methods from critical theory, these scholars have engaged the writings of Georg Simmel, Walter Benjamin, and Siegfried Kracauer, which have been more systematically translated and interpreted in the past two decades.

The second wave of scholarship on early cinema and mass culture peaked around the centenary of cinema in the mid-1990s. The endurance of cinema in the face of the explosive popularity of television and the Internet, and the cross-pollination of these old and new screen technologies and social practices further inspired critical probing into the cinema's early years. Scholars of the second wave explored mass attractions, and why this quintessential medium for storytelling and sensorial experience illuminates the phenomenon of modernity and its unfinished business in postmodernity. *Cinema and the Invention of Modern Life,* an anthology published in 1995, showcases a range of critical approaches and methodologies for linking cinema with a cluster of other cultural forms. It also declares, almost as a manifesto for the emerging field, that "cinema . . . became the fullest expression and combination of modernity's attributes" in the nineteenth and twentieth century.[7] The authors argue that the complex relationships between various precinematic or paracinematic practices, such as impressionist painting, photography, melodramatic theater, wax museums, morgues, mail catalogues, and panoramic literary genres, impacted or were derived from the cinema. As such they provide keys to the understanding of "cinema spectatorship as a historical practice."[8] Rather than a quantitative and evolutionary culmination of these preceding or concomitant modern cultural practices, the series of early or adjacent practices exerted considerable "epistemological pressure" on the emergence of cinema, which in turn "marked the unprecedented crossroads of these phenomena of modernity." Cinema congealed these "component parts" of modern life into "active synthesis with each other. . . . In providing a crucible for elements already evident in other aspects of modern culture, cinema accidentally outpaced these other forms, ending up as far more than just another novel gadget."[9] Thus, it is not only fruitful but also imperative to ground early cinema in the matrix of everyday life in modernity—abundant forms of mass and commodity culture that intertwined with the flourishing of the cinema, as well as the political, social, economical, and cultural transformations.

Cinema and the Invention of Modern Life is a collective effort to map out the terrain of an emerging field in which cinema studies rejoins the study of visual culture and sociocultural history. A number of monographs have also treated the subject. The underlying theoretical interests of Lynne Kirby's *Parallel Tracks,* an exhaustive study of the early American and British railroad films, stem from the fascination with the manufactured kinetic sensations of both cinema and trains. These emblematic modern machines engender and transform the human sensorium and social behaviors. Drawing on Wolfgang Schivelbusch's influential study of the railway's impact on landscape and human perception,[10] Kirby applies the rail passenger's "panoramic perception" of the moving landscape to the experience of cinema. Because both kinds of "journeys" are predicated on spatiotemporal discontinuity and the "shock of surprise" (accidents, shifts in point of views), the spectator-passenger embodies a modern urban subject "jostled by forces that destabilized and unnerved the individual." This unstable collective subject is thus "hysterical or, in the nineteenth century terms, 'neurasthenic' subject."[11] Its formation is also intertwined with nation-building, colonial expansion, and American cinema's claim to universality. Because a large number of railroad films stage scenarios of romance and transactions of libidinal economy, multiple gender performances and transformations unfolded along the parallel tracks of the railroad and cinema.

Critical investment in the question of gender and historical forms of female spectatorship has yielded some significant studies, conjoining early cinema, feminism, and critical theory in productive ways. Anne Friedberg's book on the correlative mode of cinematic gaze and "window shopping" found in the viewing practices in both early and postmodern cinema is one of the early attempts to apply Benjamin's writings on *flânerie* to a feminist inquiry on film spectatorship of the "past, present and the virtual." Central to Friedberg's argument is that cinema and its ancillary forms of viewing, such as panorama, diorama, urban strolling, and window shopping at department stores in *fin de siècle* Paris, created a "mobilized virtual gaze" that distinguishes itself from traditional sedentary forms of spectatorship (opera, for example). This "imaginary flânerie" of cinema spectatorship, argues Friedberg, "offers a spatially mobilized visuality but also, importantly, a temporal mobility."[12] More importantly, this mobilized gaze is attributed to not simply the aloof male intellectual *flâneur* profiled by Benjamin by way of Baudelaire,[13] but indeed to the urban crowd as a whole, particularly women, or *flâneuses,* who made rapid inroads into the public arena in that period.

Lauren Rabinovitz's *For the Love of Pleasure,* on the other hand, canvasses Chicago's turn-of-the-century film and mass culture and identifies women as active yet ambivalent consumers of this culture.[14] From the world expositions to the department stores, from the amusement parks to the neighborhood nickelodeons, women enjoyed unprecedented, albeit circumscribed, visibility and freedom in the public space. We also find this in Shanghai to varying degrees. While Friedberg concentrated on the theoretical and historiographical significance of early female spectatorship, Rabinovitz is concerned with locating the historical female spectator in a particular time (the turn of the twentieth century) and place (Chicago). Unearthing and engaging a wide range of historical and filmic sources, Rabinovitz's reconceptualization of *flânerie* and the *flâneuses* revises Friedberg's (and Susan Buck-Morss's)[15] "exaggerated" celebration of the uninhibited *flâneuses.* The supervised appearance and movement of women (prostitutes, shoppers, and pleasure-seekers) suggests that gender hierarchies, while being challenged, were not overturned. By characterizing women's "urban travels" as vacillating between motion and stillness (for example, waiting and standing), between seeing and being seen, Rabinovitz offers a more differentiated account of women's presence in public space. Quite different from the self-reflexive, radical image of *flânerie,* "female urban consciousness" has more to do with the collective "rituals of urban commodity consumption."[16] Such patterns of behavior and ambivalence—"the double-edged process of subjectivity and objectification"[17]—were carried into the film experience.

The aforementioned studies focused on the *flâneuse* or female spectator as an anonymous collective body, afloat in the wonderland of modern pleasures (and potential dangers). Giuliana Bruno's work on early Italian film culture bridges spectatorship with female authorship by excavating the (fragments of) films by Elvira Notari, Italy's first and most popular female filmmaker. Taking the contemporary reader on a series of "inferential walks" on the "ruined map" of the turn-of-the-century Neapolitan urban landscape and vernacular traditions—reminiscent of the port city Shanghai on the other side of the vast Eurasian continent—Bruno weaves an intermedial tapestry of cinema, architecture, photography, medical discourse, and literature. Employing what she calls a "typoanalysis" of spectacle and spectatorship, Bruno grounds her exploration of Notari's cinema and writings in the physical and mental geography of her milieu. Ultimately, from intertextual restorations of cinematic fragments and other transdisciplinary operations that cut across high culture and popular culture, Notari's panoramic visions chart an urban culture, along with women's lives and desires inscribed within it. In this instance, the figure of the *flâneuse* is at once an individual and a collective body, both spectatorial and authorial, an agent of both cultural reception and production.

These explorations of the kinship between cinema and modernity have prompted David Bordwell to rather dismissively characterize this emerging field and its attendant methodologies as "the modernity thesis."[18] The core of this criticism resides in the suspicion of Benjamin's view that urban industrial modernity profoundly altered modes of human perception, and that cinema represents the synthetic embodiment of this sea change. A related criticism has to do with the allegedly fuzzy demarcation between modernity and modernism—or between sociocultural, economic factors and formal transformations in literature, cinema, and other arts.

Ben Singer in *Melodrama and Modernity* attempted a sustained engagement with Bordwell's criticism by way of a substantiation of the "modernity thesis."[19] While the book's primary historical materials are the American theatrical and cinematic sensational melodramas from 1800 to 1920, Singer devotes nearly half of the book to investigating the nature of a historical era marked by the advent of modernity and capitalism. He theorizes melodrama as both a product of modernity and a training ground for the modern subjects to adjust to the "hyperstimulis" of the metropolis.[20] Singer's book is rich with insights into the issue of spectatorship, even though it is not at the forefront of his project. Through an investigation of the social demographics of the American city and the audiences of melodrama, Singer shows that the "massive" urban working class and the white-collar, "burgeoning lower middle class"—both products of modern capitalism's great bureaucratic expansion—were the main participatory spectators and consumers of the "manufactured stimulus" offered by sensational amusements such as melodrama on stage and screen.[21] Sensational melodrama attracted both female and male spectators through its representation of "a new kind of independent, energetic woman—the New Woman," who was an object of fascination and a novelty. Beyond being a cultural symbol of urban modernity, the New Woman was also a "real flesh-and-bones social entity," and sensational melodramas centered on such figures provided an "iconology of popular feminism" for a vast number of women entering the work force and public spaces such as the theater and cinema.[22]

As an illuminating interpreter of Benjamin's, Kracauer's, and Adorno's writings, Miriam Hansen has brought a crucial dose of theoretical rigor to the argument for the discursive corollary between cinema and modernity. Her more recent work has steered the discussion on cinema as an alternative public sphere, especially in *Babel and Babylon: The Emergence of Spectatorship in American Silent Film,* toward a series of polemics on cinema's role in the "mass production of senses." Hansen makes a systematic attempt to open up the question of aesthetics precisely to address yet again the ontological status of cinema, which had so long been confined to the abstract apparatus theory of a different paradigm. In Hansen's essays, the return to aesthetics is intertwined with the return to history because the two trajectories constitute a common inquiry into the history of modern senses as witnessed and shaped by the cinema. The writing of film history thus necessarily entails histories of embodied and lived experiences of cinema as a constitutive part of modern life. Highlighting Benjamin's etymological parse of the word *aesthetics*, or the "theory [*Lehre*] of perception that the Greeks called aesthetics," which he employed to critique its narrow definition associated with the bourgeois institution of art, Hansen underscores the historical significance of Benjamin's investment in the term. Writing at the moment of danger—the rise of fascism and its appropriation of technology (war machines as well as mimetic machines such as cinema) for destructive purposes—Benjamin called for a revised and expanded notion of the aesthetic in an effort to rescue technology from reification or abuse by both the bourgeoisie and fascism.

Hansen observes a crucial link between this revived notion of the aesthetic and the concept of innervation in Benjamin's thinking on the social, productive reception of technology. This emphasis on aesthetics as perception and sensation (rather techniques or tastes accessible only to a few), and on technology as a medium for overcoming alienation and anaesthetization in the industrial age, shifts the focus of philosophical debate on modernity from mind to body, from messianism to actuality, from superstructure to infrastructure, from the sublime to the profane, from that of the individual to the collective. The political implications of the notion and practice of innervation are profound, as Hansen explicates:

> The crucial issue is therefore whether there can be an imbrication of technology and the human senses that is not swallowed into the vortex of decline; whether Benjamin's egalitarian, techno-utopian politics could be conjoined with his emphatic notion of experience / memory; whether and how the "profane illumination" he discerned in the project of the surrealists could be generalized into a "bodily collective innervation," the universal and public integration of body- and image-space (*Leib- und Bildraum*) that had become structurally possible with technology.[23]

Hansen reasons that Benjamin's conception of innervation is tied to his broader visions of humanity's future. It was produced through an eclectic mixing and retooling of Freud's psychoanalysis (particularly his neurological and anthropological accents), contemporary perceptual psychology, developmental psychology, reception aesthetics, and acting theory (Eisenstein's theory of the "expressive movement" derived from Meyerhold's biomechanic theory). To accomplish the imbrication of second technology (mechanically mediated) in capitalism and the human senses, it requires cultivation of "discarded powers of the first, with mimetic practices that involve the body, as the 'preeminent instrument' of sensory perception and (moral and political) differentiation."[24] However, the reactivation of the abilities of the body and the reignition of the instinctual power of the senses must not be construed as a nostalgic return to the pastoral era before technology and modernity. For technology has irrevocably altered the vectors of the historical process and the conditions for experiencing and transforming the world. As technology has so deeply penetrated or "cut" into the modern landscape—(the railway, for example, manufactured the experience of "panoramic travel"),[25] any attempt to achieve "bodily collective innervation" goes hand-in-hand with a collective innervation of technology. For the restoration of human senses could only be done by "passing through" technology that permeates the air of modern life.

Three major lines of theoretical and historiographic concerns are shared by the examination of the relationship between cinema and the experience of modernity: (1) the grounding of cinema in the phenomenology of the metropolis and the kaleidoscopic cultural space of modernity; (2) the decentering of the cinematic object for writing a new intermedial and transdisciplinary cultural history of the screen experience. This history is horizontally distributed and open-ended instead of reproducing a linear, text-centered, teleological film history; and (3) the foregrounding and rigorous historicization and affirmation of gendered and embodied moviegoing experience. These endeavors have not only reenergized cinema studies but together they have applied concepts about the cinema of attractions to related issues in the 1920s and beyond, well after the purported hegemony of Hollywood narrative cinema worldwide. In this regard, "the concept of cinema of attractions allow us to look at classical Hollywood cinema as a dynamic process," and to uncover the "interaction between spectacle and narrative so frequently found in Hollywood genres."[26] This expanded notion of the cinema of attractions, as I will show in later chapters, is particularly productive when studying other national cinemas where there is no "early cinema" comparable to the Euro-American periodization.

The expansion of cinema as a distinctive industry (or dream factory) and its penetration into everyday life paralleled the intensifying modernization and capitalist production. Aggravated sensory overload in the Taylor labor system and urban environment inflicted both deeper trauma and numbed the modern urban subjects' sensorium. This deprived them of the initial sense of thrill and astonishment as typically seen in the cinema of attractions or sensational melodrama that often featured the country rube encountering the city. Cinema (especially American cinema) responded to such routine forms of shock or "hyperstimulus" in work and leisure with streamlined narrative formulas and a vertically integrated studio system modeled after the Taylor's labor system. At the same time, however, this further loss of "aura" or decline of experience—(the diagnosis of modern culture made by Benjamin in his artwork essay)[27]—in both life and the mimetic arts created ever greater needs for "ever more powerful aesthetic techniques, ever more spectacular thrills and sensations, to pierce the protective shield of consciousness."[28] The spiral-effect and subsequent exponential increase of the desire for pleasurable compensation or distraction feeds into the symbiotic relationship between modern life and the culture industry. By the same token, the film and media culture that transformed and thrived beyond early cinema continued to manifest the attributes and symptoms of modernity in an ever more complex combinations of containment and excess, anaesthetization and stimulation, conformism and anarchism.

PLAYFUL VERNACULAR MODERNISM

A proliferation of *youxi,* or play and playfulness, appeared in a plethora of media and discourses—vernacular press, amusement halls, mechanical theaters, and electric shadow plays—in urban China around the turn of the twentieth century. At these locations of collective play and performance, people experimented with modern mimetic gadgets to reflect and represent an increasingly technologized everyday life. If "'Lunarparks' are a prefiguration of sanatoria" where numbed senses and alienated body parts convalesce, then places like the Great World and New World in Shanghai where the urbanites play, gamble, eat, drink, and flirt not only recreate the metropolis, but also serve as a playground for old and new mimetic technologies. It is hardly surprising that such playgrounds were the first homes to cinema. Not only were many early films made in and about amusement parks, they were also among the first projection venues for the toy-like cameras and childlike performances on the screen. Modern *youxi* is not only a concentrated form of urban socialization and entertainment, it also quickly lent inspiration to early filmmakers. Zhang Shichuan, Zheng Zhengqiu, and their colleagues who started China's first film enterprises, readily looked for material and frames of reference in the "profane" world of *youxi,* in particular vernacular theaters and amusement halls that resembled the new medium.

As a unique technology that integrates the apparatus and the human body (the actors as well as the spectators), Benjamin saw in cinema a unique medium for such a redemptive process, a medium for the interplay between nature and humanity. This idea was made famous by his artwork essay but had been in ferment in *One Way Street,* a collection of sketches and essays written in 1928. Hansen elaborates:

> Film assumes this task not simply by way of a behaviorist adaptation of human perceptions and reactions to the regime of the apparatus (which seems to be the tenor of parts of the artwork essay) but because film has the potential to reverse, in the form of *play,* the catastrophic consequences of an *already failed* reception of technology. . . . Because of the medium's technicity, as well as its collective mode of reception, film offers a chance—a second chance, a last chance—to bring the apparatus to social consciousness, to make it public.[29]

The notion of play as a concrete form of bodily and collective innervation is critically important. On the one hand, it captures Benjamin's fascination with the figure of the child and the implications of children's playful and performative "mimetic faculty" with which they explore new objects in the world and boundaries of their bodies. Play destabilizes the dichotomy between subject and object and creates an interactive and repeatable mode of contact and communication, a "mode of cognition involving sensuous, somatic, and tactile forms of perception; a noncoercive engagement with the other that opens the self to experience."[30]

For Benjamin, one of the most representative or allegorical sites for the radical playfulness of bodily innervation is found in the gestalt of Chaplin, the childlike clown whose body and sentimentality literally passes through and survives technology repeatedly, as seen in the assembly-line scenes in *Modern Times* (1936). The worldwide popularity of Chaplin, a figure whom André Bazin characterizes as "a man beyond the realm of the sacred,"[31] is a testimony to the appeal of a childlike, bodily cinema that is border-defying, curiosity-rousing, and universally intelligible and translatable. Among the first series of shorts made by the Asia Company, a small Sino-American joint venture, are two Chaplin-in-China films. In the first, (the imposter) Chaplin, played by Richard Bell, a British resident of Shanghai who worked as a clown at the New World, arrives at the docks of Shanghai on an ocean liner and then proceeds to visit the city, making a fool of himself along the way (figs. 1.1 and 1.2). In the other film, Chaplin and Harold Lloyd (this time played by two Chinese actors) make a big scene in a theater.[32] The films are in fact pidgin

1.1
The King of Comedy Tours Shanghai: at the harbor. (Courtesy of the China Film Archive)

1.2
The King of Comedy Tours Shanghai: in a sedan chair. (Courtesy of the China Film Archive)

versions of a global cinematic vernacular à la Shanghaiese, with the copycat Chaplin "going native" as its embodiment.

Yet the child or the childlike person as the vernacular hybrid who grapples with the joys and pains of technology is a complex player on the cinematic playground; it is a figure rather than a specific demographic. Traditional discourses on early cinema are riddled with the use of the child figure to denote a "mythic childhood of the medium" in a patronizing and evolutionist vein. According to Tom Gunning, however, the first film audiences of astonishing sights such as the *Black Diamond Express* or the electrocution of an elephant were anything but credulous children. Instead, early film spectators, like spectators of other attractions such as freak shows and wax museums, were sophisticated connoisseurs of modern sights and sounds and understood the aesthetic of astonishment—the swing between shock and distraction. The combination of wonderment and (profane) education, directly bound to the "lust of the eye" (rather than the mind) creates an (in)credulous spectator who is a child-adult hybrid, a "freaky" performer who is part of the show rather than a distanced contemplative subject. Gunning reminds us that this childlike spectator is also a well-tempered modern subject who constantly has to navigate in the agitated urban milieu.

> The panic before the image on the screen exceeds a simple physical reflex, similar to those one experiences in a daily encounter with urban traffic or industrial production. In its double nature, its transformation of still image into moving illusion, it expresses an attitude in which astonishment and knowledge perform a vertiginous dance, and pleasure derives from the energy released by the play between the shock caused by this illusion of danger and delight in its pure illusion. The jolt experienced becomes a shock of recognition.[33]

Gunning's conceptualization of the aesthetic of astonishment and identification of the (in)credulous spectator's "vertiginous dance" with new forms of urban attractions is germane to the notions of innervation and play, two sides of the same coin minted by Benjamin. The anchoring of this collective body in the concrete architectural space of the cinema (from Grand Café in Paris to the picture palaces in Berlin to the Art Deco-inspired cinemas in Shanghai) calls for a history of cinema in relation to a history of moviegoing and exhibition practices. This resonates with Hansen's reading of *One Way Street* in terms of the urban metaphor of the street and traffic. By replenishing the neuropsychological term with a productive meaning and applying it to film and mass culture, Benjamin envisioned cinema to be a two-way process that cuts through both the nerve-pathway and the avenues traveled by the urban dweller. This would have likely included a stop at a movie theater. If film presented itself to be a "prism" that could expose the "optical unconscious"[34] and transform our worldviews, the "moviegoing experience would therefore seem to be the logical site for thinking through the possibility of a bodily collective innervation, as the condition of an alternative interaction with technology and the commodity world."[35]

The attempt to locate the spectator in the urban environment and the movie theater brings us closer to identifying the historical spectator, who is not so much a quantifiable empirical statistics as a condensed figure, indeed a collective body. This body of the crowd is embedded in the metropolitan life. If the figure of the *flâneur* represents the (male) writer in the capitalist marketplace who "botanize[s] on the asphalt" and feels at home in the arcades ("a city, even a world, in miniature"),[36] then the collective body of the urban crowd that frequents the amusement parks, variety shows, and cinemas via the "two-way street" of innervation constitutes a mass *flânerie*—a vast array of "physiologies" or "metropolitan types" in the urban scene.[37]

One of these metropolitan physiologies that Gunning discerns to be the embodiment of the cinematic mass *flânerie* as opposed to the solitary dandy-*feuilltoniste* is the gawker, a street-level spectator qua performer.[38] For Gunning, this plebian figure is the quintessential representative of the early moviegoing experience that is woven into in the urban fabric. Through this figure, "attractions do more than reflect modernity; they provide one of its methods." The gawker's desire to stop, stare, and marvel reflects not only the ebb and flow of the distracted urban crowd but also a new culture of consumption and pleasure through an aggressive visuality. The gawker, who paces the sidewalks, is a spectator of the urban scene and its participant. Many early film showmen are, in fact, gawkers who literally peddled shows on the sidewalks while watching the surrounding street scenes. Such was the case in China as well. The Electric Shadowplay on Fourth Avenue, which featured a band promoting teahouse movie shows, furnishes a telling example (fig. 1.3). "The Whole Town Is Gawking" is a vivid portrayal of the omnipresence of the gawker with both childlike curiosity and a petty urbanite's consumer desire. The sidewalks and cinema houses allowed the mutual recognition of disparate urban subjects and the formation of a public as well as a collective urban subjectivity. At the same time, in ascribing to the city itself the attributes of the gawker, especially its mass and mobile character, Gunning grasps the phenomenology of the metropolis as well as cinema as an embodied vernacular experience.

If the turn of the century mass attractions offered the *flâneuse* and the gawker a democratic, even playful appeal, their effects are usually considered to be trampled by the emerging hegemonic force of classical Hollywood cinema. However, Hansen ventures into the realm of classical cinema, so often seen as the bastion of conservative and patriarchal ideas, in an attempt to place the "bad object" in a new light by teasing out its imbrication in the "mass production of the senses." This development is consistent with her earlier elucidation of Benjamin and Kracauer's fascination with American cinema as the emblematic form of bodily innervation, especially from the perspective of a Europe overshadowed by war and fascism.[39] This vernacularization of an institutionalized type of narrative cinema based on universal mental structures and transhistorical aesthetic norms seeks to relocate classical cinema in the historical context of modernity and the practice of modernism in other contemporary arts.

1.3 "A Social Phenomenon in Shanghai: The Noisy Shadowplay on Fourth Avenue" (*Tuhua ribao*, no. 36).

The move from "modernity" to "modernism" is a deliberate one. It is made possible in part by the retooled, wider notion of the aesthetic—"one that situates artistic practices within a larger history and economy of sensory perception that Benjamin, for one, saw as the decisive battleground for the meaning and fate of modernity."[40] At the same time, it attempts to escape from the trappings of the social-scientific frameworks that hold little regard for aesthetic questions. Rather than replace modernity as an all-encompassing social theory with modernism as a narrowly formal regime, the modifying term *vernacular*—as opposed to *classical*—accounts for their intertwining. By proclaiming that Hollywood cinema presented something like the first "global vernacular," Hansen brings cinematic modernism back into the arenas of history and international film culture. Manufacturing and promoting itself as the embodiment of youth, energy, gender equality, and above all, contemporaneity, American cinema streamlined an intelligible, translatable mass-based cinematic idiom that appealed to the widest possible range of audiences worldwide, often accompanied by aggressive marketing strategies. Through a complex chain effect of circulation and transformation in different cultural locations, this vernacular is in turn modified and localized. Thus in a dialectical way, precisely through its contact with other cultural contexts, Hollywood at once offered a reflexive horizon for mediating the global experience of modernity and became provincialized as other film cultures tried to challenge its dominance.

The transformation of Russian cinema, in particular the emergence of montage theory (a modernist / avant-garde canon), during the revolution illustrates Hansen's argument on the mediating role of American cinema. The rather quick shift from the Old cinema characterized by slow-paced melodrama yet multilayered mise-en-scène to the New cinema accentuated by close framing and rapid decoupage seems to have taken place through a "process of Americanization." Yet this American accent is acquired through a complex process of sifting and recombining disparate elements. Yuri Tsivian suggests that two kinds of Americanism were at work in this cinematic transition. Many directors, for narrative efficiency and coherence, borrowed from stylistic elements such as "American montage" or "American foreground" (standard idioms of classical cinema). The Russian films of the period, however, carried deep imprints of the "lower genres" in American cinema, particularly the body-centered and kinetically charged adventure serials and slapstick comedies.[41] The coexistence of the two influential currents in the transformation of Russian cinema and the appropriation of American "cinematic pulp fiction" by the Russian avant-garde demonstrate both the malleability of the American cinematic vernacular and the reciprocal relationship between classical cinema and modernism.

Reception gives vernacular modernism concrete, situated meaning. By outlining the double trajectory of American cinema's universal ambitions and provincialized realities in the international context, Hansen was able to extend the theoretical discussion of Benjamin's "bodily collective innervation" as a utopian idea into the domain of comparative cultural histories of the film experience. In a subsequent article, Hansen takes up Shanghai silent film as an instance of vernacular modernism that paralleled yet distinguished itself from the "global vernacular" represented by Hollywood.[42] Discussing a body of silent films screened at the Pordenone Silent Film Festival in 1995 and 1997, Hansen finds that the hybrid visual style and star performances in some of the Chinese classical works from the 1930s illustrate the mechanism of vernacular modernism "as a sensory-reflexive discourse of the experience of modernity and modernization, a matrix for the articulation of fantasies, uncertainties, and anxieties."[43] The figure of woman—the on-screen heroines as well as stars Ruan Lingyu and Li Lili—articulates the polyvalent meanings and contradictory promises of modernity. Li's masquerading *performance* of her character in *Daybreak* (*Tianming*, directed by Sun Yu, 1933), especially in the execution scene, resonates with Marlene Dietrich's in Josef von Sternberg's *Dishonored* (1931). The American-educated Sun Yu in this and other films liberally borrowed from American and European cinemas and used Chinese aesthetic motifs and artistic repertoires. His visual style and social concerns indeed mark him as perhaps the most important master of vernacular modernism in Chinese film history (discussed more in chapter 7).

In her essay on Shanghai silent film, Hansen tested her general theory of cinema, American cinema in particular, as an exemplary instance of vernacular modernism. But her foray into Chinese silent film also stressed the importance of local *conditions* of the reception or rather, translation, of foreign cinema and the production of a domestic cinema. She alludes to the "wealth of intertextual and intermedial relations both within individual films and in Shanghai film culture," which informs our project here. The extensive, though by no means exhaustive, historical work required to excavate and reimagine the multiple, crisscrossing "intertextual and intermedial relations" that Hansen's brief essay called for is one of the foundations of this book. In the process of explaining the production of the vibrant cinema within Shanghai urban culture in early twentieth century, I develop and recast the concept of vernacular modernism through specification and amplification, approaching it from a set of intersecting angles. These approaches are intertwined with discussion of embodiment, yet anchored in the historical context of the vernacular movement in China.

Vernacular in this manner is a less ideologically loaded term than *popular*, yet rich with social, political, and aesthetic implications. It departs from its clichéd definition of a static (and largely agrarian) tradition and a lack of stylistic sophistication, as often deployed in the field of architecture.[44] Yet the emphasis on craftsmanship, democratic appeal, and on the use of local materials, techniques, and forms in vernacular architecture is to some degree relevant to the way a local film culture is shaped and disseminated. In architecture studies the vernacular has traditionally been posited against the monumental and the modern and ascribed to the prosaic and preindustrial landscape and way of life.[45] However, as Amos Rapoport argues, the vernacular is situated in a fluctuating and relational "continuum" of the primitive, vernacular, popular, and high styles, such that a movie palace may be regarded as an emblem of high class in comparison to a nickelodeon, but it is still vernacular next to an opera house.[46] My reworking of architectural discourse, which was borrowed from nineteenth-century linguistics, emphasizes the interpenetrating of the old and new temporalities and attendant spatial practices. As both "language" and physical structures the cinema manifests the dynamic transactions between the cosmopolitan and the local, the high and the low, the decline of aura and the retooling of the archaic.

In its original homestead of language and literature, the vernacular, invoking both heterogeneous experience and the polymorphous forms of language, has always attracted the avant-garde in search of a radical language bound to the materiality of the signifier. Among the modernist artists who experimented with typography Guillaume Apollinaire's calligrammatic poems stand out for their striking figural dimension that is enmeshed in the realm of experience. As Johanna Drucker stresses in her study of the futurist and Dada experiments with typography, Apollinaire's rejection of ossified classical poetic structures was "accompanied by coming to terms with the richness of spoken language and an infusion of vernacular, daily speech patterns into his poetry."[47] Quite different from his contemporaries' (including Eisenstein's and Pound's) whimsical intellectual deployment of the Chinese ideograph, Apollinaire's interest in the ideograph as "a contemporary hieroglyphic, a dense bearer of visual / verbal values" was informed less by esotericism than by a vernacular sensibility focused on the "simple, evident, even banal forms." His overall method is characterized by a "sensual leap to the work" or a "presentational mode" rather than "intellectual processing."[48] The typographic attempt to create the visible word is fueled by an impulse to render the world legible and tangible. As such it comes close to some of the aesthetic manifestations of early cinema: the direct address, the presentational mode, and the teeming presence of everyday life and vernacular expressions. Apollinaire's and other avant-garde artists' affinity with the "mystery" of the everyday may have resulted in a certain form and idiom of the modernist vernacular. The sensuous, "experimental" language of the cinema of attractions, which, as Gunning has underscored, has a direct bearing on the historical avant-garde and hatches a vernacular modernism that would subsequently diversify and transform in different historical contexts.

Because the vernacular is "discovered" by both linguists and architects alike as a pervasive background against which modern towers of Babel may be erected,[49] the modern is inevitably and simultaneously shot through with the vernacular as a source of inspiration or nostalgia, alternately an object for derision and colonization. Rather than two antitheses, the vernacular / modern is indeed a pair of Siamese twins—inextricably connected yet existing in permanent codependence and competition. In this ambivalent symbiosis the hand joins the machine, primitive technology penetrates the second nature. Hardly a timeless tradition, the vernacular "landscape" is made up of material culture (including architectural forms such as the amusement hall and the movie theater), as well as social and affective experience in modernity. It is inherently porous, dynamic, and generative. It evolves from a homegrown culture while drawing and even thriving on global forms of communication and representation spurred by modern technology and cosmopolitan culture. The constant transformation of the vernacular, as persuasively argued by Sheldon Pollock, is simultaneously propelled by the attractions of "cosmopolitan universals" (communicative media such as literature and cinema) and "affective attachment to old structures of belonging." Both the attractions of the new and attachment to the old can be profoundly intertwined and ambivalent. As Pollock reasons, any vernacular movement inevitably "consists of a response to a specific history of domination and enforced change, along with a critique of the oppression of tradition itself, tempered by a strategic desire to locate resources for a cosmopolitan future in vernacular ways of being themselves."[50]

In sum, my theoretical investment in the vernacular is not simply motivated by a desire to get away from the much-contested and delimiting categories of the "popular" or "mass culture" deployed in discourses on marginality vis-à-vis hegemony, or subversion vis à vis domination. Rather, it is fueled by an urge to reestablish the historical connection or dialogue between film culture and modernity, and between the cinema and other media. At the same time, early Chinese cinema does manifest the ambivalence toward Euro-American culture, in particular the global vernacular embodied by Hollywood cinema. The emergence and survival of the Chinese film industry is thus a tension-ridden process of negotiation between cosmopolitanism and nationalism, between film as a utopian "universal language" on the one hand and local vernacular(s) on the other. In that sense, the vernacular experience from which the early Chinese film culture emerged and in turn refashioned is inherently polyvalent and resilient. It was constantly being experimented with, lived out, and redefined.

Stemming from but ramifying beyond the domain of language, the vernacular thus encompasses the realm of the everyday, including architectural and urban space, and the impact of cinema as a commingled media on the experience of modernity. As such it functions as a conceptual and experiential scaffolding that, in locally specific yet globally significant ways, reconstructs the twentieth century Tower of Babel. The vernacular, retooled and conjoined with the phenomenology and representation of modern life, has the potential to account for competing forms of modernism, the relationship between high and low cultural repertoires, and globalizing formulas and localizing permutations—including subversive mimetic play and appropriation.

THE PAINFUL EXPERIENCE OF ENLIGHTENMENT

As articulated in early Shanghai cinema, vernacular modernism had distinctive historical and cultural markers. The international culture of modernity, largely a product of industrial capitalism and colonialism, resulted in the uneasy coexistence of cosmopolitan yearnings and nationalist aspirations. As noted earlier, one of the most consequential changes effected by the movement took place in the domain of language and literature, that is, the promotion and institution of the vernacular language (or Mandarin, based on the Beijing dialect) as the standard modern Chinese. The "discovery" of the vernacular by the late Qing reformers and then the early republican intellectuals coincided with the emergence of a modern urban culture and the introduction of cinema in China. When we move from the vernacular movement as a "literary revolution" (*wenxue geming*), conceived and practiced by the intellectuals, toward the embodiment of the vernacular experience in Shanghai cinema, the perspective of film and cultural history reveals fruitful insights on the very question of Chinese modernity.

Print culture and popular literature flourished in the late Qing period. New print technologies made texts more accessible to an expanding reading population with varying level of literacy, and reshaped a new vernacular culture. The pressure to modernize and open up to the world impelled the reformers to explore a more democratic form of writing that would not only represent the proliferating forms of modern life but also cohere the motley of local vernaculars into a recognizable, standardized script shared by the elite and the populace. In 1905, as part of the reform program, the institution of imperial examinations was abolished. With it, the supremacy or official status of classical Chinese (*wenyanwen*), a sophisticated written language largely isolated from the different spoken vernaculars, was dismantled (although its usage continued in less rarefied forms). *Baihuawen,* the new vernacular, was a written language based on colloquial speech. Easy to understand and unencumbered by arcane allusions, it was quickly adopted by the new print industry, especially in newspapers catering to the expanding urban population and in textbooks for new-style schools. *Minbao,* the earliest newspaper using the vernacular, appeared in Shanghai in 1876 as a supplement of the middle- to highbrow *Shenbao.* Between then and the end of the Qing dynasty in 1911, there were more than 140 vernacular newspapers all over China, with 27 based in Shanghai alone (some of which catered to communities of provincial sojourners in the city).[51] They functioned largely as portable instructions for enlightenment (*qimeng*), appealing to women, children as well as other semiliterate "petty urbanites" (*xiaoshimin*) such as shop clerks and workers. Even the newspapers using classical language frequently published texts in the vernacular to widen its readership. To increase comprehensibility, vernacular newspapers adopted punctuation and sentence breaks, onomatopoeia and dialect terms—features largely absent in canonical classical texts. Responding to a flourishing mass culture, a number of newspapers specialized in entertainment and leisure, such as *Youxibao* founded at the end of the 1890s by Li Boyuan, a famous middlebrow fiction writer.[52] The proliferation of the illustrated newspapers, on which I will have more to say in chapter 2, was also part and parcel of this surge of vernacular press. This trend, which aimed to achieve mass literacy in both language and modern consciousness, created a fusion of communicative and expressive forms that emphasized intelligibility and performativity. The new vernacular liberally drew on storytelling (*shuoshu*), public speech (*yanshuo*), and the popular theater. Qiu Jing, the legendary female revolutionary and poet who also started a vernacular paper in 1904 in Japan, emphasized that the new writing form must not overshadow its oral origins. Rather, she insisted that printed texts supply the ready source for public speech and storytelling that appealed to the illiterate.[53] Within this broad vernacular movement, the boundaries between the written and the spoken, the image and the text, and the presentational and the representational were often blurred. This in turn stimulated the growth of the new-drama (*xinju*), a modern form of theater that used vernacular speech and was modeled after the naturalist spoken drama of the West. (In chapters 3 and 8, I will discuss how this vernacular drama supplied the impetus and ready material for Shanghai cinema.)

Standard Chinese film historiography produced in the mainland has consistently regarded the film practice of early Chinese cinema, in particular that of the 1920s, as part of the nonprogressive popular culture, outside of the May Fourth movement that was intimately bound to the vernacular movement.[54] In an influential but rather biased essay, the veteran screenwriter and film critic Ke Ling asks rhetorically, "Why didn't the strong shock waves of the May Fourth movement reach the film circle?"[55] According to Ke Ling, it was only after the Japanese bombing of Shanghai in January 28, 1932 that left-wing writers began to enter the film world, and that Chinese cinema belatedly connected with the New Culture movement. Briefly, the movement stemmed from a particular political movement, namely, the surge of Chinese nationalism triggered by the students' demonstration in Beijing on May 4, 1919. The students, mostly from Beijing University, and Beijing citizens protested the imminent signing of the post–World War I Versailles treaty, which would allow the Japanese to take control of Shandong province from Germany. The incident was a pivotal point within a decade-long (1915–25) radically antitraditional and iconoclastic cultural movement, alternatively labeled the "Chinese Enlightenment."[56] The two banners of the movement upheld by the May Fourth intellectuals are Mr. Democracy (*Demokelaxi xiansheng*) and Mr. Science (*Saiyinsi xiansheng*), first articulated by Chen Duxiu in an article published in the radical journal *New Youth* (*Xin qingnian*), in January 1919.[57] As part of its modernization program, the movement sought to carry out the unfinished enlightenment launched by late Qing reformers and intellectuals: to eradicate superstitious beliefs, popularize mass education, and replace the classical language and literary canon with a new vernacular literature.

Countless studies in English on the origin and impact of the vernacular movement have centered on the literary revolution in the May Fourth movement and the literary corpus it generated. Little effort has, however, been made to locate the question of vernacular writing and modern print culture beyond the confines of literary history, in a broader inquiry on the "technologizing of the word" and its interaction with the cinema.[58]

Early Chinese cinema was related to the vernacular movement and May Fourth culture in a complex way. The adoption of the vernacular language and its wide-ranging impact on culture paved the way for the emergence of a film culture in China. By the late 1910s, the vernacular press had extended beyond popular education to highbrow literature as well as political, intellectual, and scientific discourse. Attempts were made to standardize the pronunciation of the vernacular language and homogenize the vast dialectal differences across China. In 1918 the ministry of education promulgated a standard table of phonetic signs. The standards were met with a lukewarm reception because they were difficult to master, especially in the South where the Mandarin, the new Northern-based national language, was rarely spoken. In the subsequent years several revised proposals were presented but none proved satisfactory.[59] Yet the standard vernacular became increasingly formal and sophisticated—so much so that it began to lose touch with its sources. Thus, within the vernacular culture itself, new hierarchies were formed along levels of education as well as social and political proclivities. The language the May Fourth writers devised and promoted, heavily indebted to Japanese loan words and Western grammars, eluded the masses they intended to engage and enlighten. In fact, it became detached from traditional popular Chinese literature and drama as well as spoken languages, and this modern language effectively became the elite cosmopolitan parlance of those well-versed in Western and Japanese literary and philosophical canons.

The strand that had closer connections with traditional popular and modern mass cultures evolved into a more syncretic vernacular form that mixed the classical, the vernacular, and the foreign, as well as different media. This vernacular language and its sensibility were carried into the film culture. In a sense, this polyphonic, vibrant trend in language constituted an unofficial vernacular movement that refused to be institutionalized and turned into an edifice of the nation state. The inclusiveness of this vernacular allowed it to be a lively cultural form rather than simply a strictly codified artificial language to deliver, process, and digest the top-down vernacular movement. The film culture in urban China that emerged in the first three decades of the twentieth century exemplifies such inclusiveness and synthesis. Many modern ideas about social reform, mass education, and scientific knowledge were absorbed by filmmakers of various ideological and aesthetic inclinations. The actual presentation of these ideas in their films were, however, often mediated through a combination of techniques derived from a wide range of sources, compounding modern and traditional beliefs, values, and notions of embodiment and representation. Because early filmmaking in China was a conspicuous commercial venture, the high-flung May Fourth movement's progressive ideas were confronted with the capitalist tendencies of the film industry, and the supposedly low- or middlebrow tastes of the petty urbanites.

To further connect the discussions on vernacular modernism in the field of cinema studies to the specific context of the Chinese vernacular movement, it is useful to flesh out the term *experience*. This will help trace its global circulation and local articulation in the age of mechanical reproduction, particularly because it was a cornerstone of the vernacular movement. My theoretical and practical interests are grounded in the two interlocking categories of experience and embodiment and their potential for conceiving the cinema as a unique catalyst for the production of a global vernacular and a modern sociophysiological sensorium. Benjamin memorably spelled out the double-layered meaning of experience in his corpus. It is essential to note that there are two German terms for experience. The first term, *Erlebnis*, denotes a singular event and adventure—often a fragmented piece of information and or sensation in the modern city—and is perhaps closer to the English word *experience*, which also contains the root of experiment.[60] *Erfahrung*, on the other hand, underscores the vector of bodily movement and its temporal duration. It is associated with the holistic way of life and the storytelling tradition that the modern life threatens with atomization and sensationalism.[61] In his famous essay on Baudelaire, Benjamin traces the bifurcated term to the tradition of "philosophy of life," from Wilhelm Dilthey's *Das Erlebnis und die Dichtung* (*Experience and Poetry*) to Henri Bergson's *Matière et mémoire* (*Matter and Memory*). Arguing that this philosophical tradition tends to isolate experience in the realm of nature, rather than locating it in "man's life in society," Benjamin proceeds to excavate, via Proust's "discovery" of *mémoire involontaire,* the transmutation or restructuring of experience in the age of industrial production. For him, the singularity of Baudelaire's poetry lies in its recognition of and confrontation with the fracturing of experience—or the "disintegration of aura"—in the age of shock and sensation and in its desire to give expression to an innervated experience regaining the sense of wholeness and liveness for the collective sensorium.[62] Rather than a complete replacement, this new *Erfahrung* would always contain the traumatic kernel of shock when individuated *Erlebnis* is jolted into a collective—and reflective—modern experience. However, the reflexivity imbued in the aftershock experience is hardly the property of the intellect but rather stems from the new "physiology" of the modern urban life, to which the virtual sensation of "seasickness on dry land" belongs.[63]

We encounter yet another linguistic and cultural problem of translation when we try to allocate the Chinese equivalent for *experience.* Although the term *jingyan* had existed in the Chinese lexicon denoting a more embodied cultural practice before the introduction of Western empiricism,[64] its modern usage has, over time, acquired the reified positivist meaning connected with *jingyan zhuyi.* The latter is a sinicized translation for empiricism as an epistemological and methodological practice based on observation and quantified accumulation of knowledge, as well as the abstraction or objectification of lived experience.

The concept of experience came to play an important role in Chinese intellectual and cultural history at the turn of the century, particularly through the vernacular movement and related transformation in literary and artistic expression. Hu Shi (1891–1962), one of the Western educated intellectuals who spearheaded the Chinese enlightenment, was an avid advocate of experience as an antidote to orthodox traditional rituals and doctrines, such as those perpetuated by Confucianism and the imperial court. He had derived the term *jingyan* largely from the pragmatic philosophy of John Dewey with whom he had studied at Columbia University.[65] Hu Shi's status as the "father" of the vernacular movement was established instantly when he published "Some Modest Proposals for the Reform of Literature" in *New Youth* in 1917.[66] Hu Shi put forth a literary and linguistic program for a "living literature" (*huo wenxue*) written in the vernacular (*baihua*), so that the latter could take over the canonical status traditionally accorded literature and historiography written in the classical language (*wenyan*). The proposals contain eight remarks, summarized as the "eight do-not-ism" (*babu zhuyi*), which quickly became a mantra for the vernacular movement:

1. Writing should have substance
2. Do not imitate the ancients
3. Emphasize the technique of writing
4. Do not moan without an illness
5. Eliminate hackneyed and formal language
6. Do not use allusions
7. Do not use parallelism
8. Do not avoid vulgar diction[67]

The first and last remedies Hu prescribed are particularly suggestive for his aesthetic of experience as a social intervention. Interestingly, Hu Shi's program for a modern vernacular reform draws heavily upon a particular traditional canon derived from folklore and oral literature. The first "remark" emphasizes "substance" (*wu*), or "matter," which Hu Shi associates with "feeling." He substantiates his point by citing the famous "Great Preface" of *Book of Poetry,* a foundational collection of ancient poems: "Feelings come from within and are shaped through language. If language is insufficient, then one may chant or sing; if chanting or singing is insufficient, then one may dance with one's hands and feet." The equation Hu Shi tries to draw between vernacularity and embodiment of emotions, which was to remain an unrealized dream of the actual May Fourth literature, would have unintended implications for the cinema. Hu Shi envisaged a literature that stemmed from the lived, sensory world in which a "living language" was borne out of "the creation of new phrases to describe and portray what people see and hear with their own eyes and ears or personally live through."[68]

In the last remark, Hu Shi actually performs an archaeological excavation of the vernacular tradition. He traces the origin of vernacular canon formation to the translation of Buddhist scriptures into Chinese and their subsequent dissemination in Buddhist lectures and catechism, which resulted in the "dialogue" (*yulu*) form. According to Hu Shi, the tradition of a living language ran through the Song Neo-Confucians and, to some extent, the Tang-Song poetry, the Yuan dynasty drama (960–1368), culminating in the formation of "an incipient popular literature, out of which emerged the novels *On The Water Margins, The Journey to the West,* and *The Romance of the Three Kingdoms* and innumerable dramas."[69] "At that time [Yuan dynasty], Chinese literature came closest to a union of spoken and written languages, and the vernacular itself had nearly become a literary language."[70] Hu Shi lamented that if that tradition had not been "arrested" in the Ming period by the ascendance of a literary "archaism" (*fugu*) and the imperial institutionalization of the "eight-legged essay" (*baguwen*), China would have had a "living literature" comparable to those in Europe, which emerged from "vulgar" replacements for Latin. It is interesting to note that Hu Shi deploys, in a positive way, the Chinese word *su* for *vulgar,* which was later often used by May Fourth ideologues to attack popular literature and cinema. It is, however, within the overlapping semantic space of the "vulgar" and "vernacular" (*su*) that Hu Shi's vernacular poetics may be productively wrested out of the orthodox May Fourth ideology.

While studying at Columbia University, Hu Shi also began the radical experiment of writing poetry in vernacular Chinese to prove the empiricist theory of "experience." Even more than prose and drama, poetry as an art of the educated elite had been composed primarily in the classical language. His book of poetry, *Collections of Experiments,* became a model text for the vernacular movement, and the poem "Dream and Poetry" is its centerpiece.

All are but ordinary experiences
All are but ordinary images
When they rush into dreams by chance
They are transformed into so many new and strange patterns!

All are but ordinary feelings
All are but ordinary words
When they encounter a poet by chance
They are transformed into so many new and strange poetic lines!
Having been drunk, one knows the strength of wine
Having been in love, one knows the heaviness of feeling:
You cannot compose my poem
Just as I cannot dream your dream.[71]

In the postscript for the poem, Hu Shi describes the poem as a manifesto for his "poetic empiricism" (*shide jingyan zhuyi; jingyan zhuyi* literally means "experientialism"). It is hard to miss the recurrent quotidian imagery in the poem carried by the word "ordinary" (*pingchang*). In his attempt to do poetic justice to everyday material, Hu Shi was not, however, simply envisioning a democratic literary space crowded with tangible objects. His emphasis on the "transformation" of experience points to the tension or interpenetration between concreteness and abstraction, content and form that is crucial to his "poetic empiricism." Reality as such is not static but is rather malleable and even magic (*bianhuan*). The last stanza goes one step further in foregrounding the body not only as a sponge absorbing the "influence" of life but, more crucially, as a medium for processing worldly experience and subject formation.

The visceral experience of writing in the vernacular is nowhere more pronounced than in the preface he wrote for the fourth edition of the collection.[72] More strikingly, here he compares the vernacular experiment to the physical pain of unbinding feet (*fangjiao*) that many Chinese women were experiencing at the time:

> Now when I look back on the poems I wrote in the past five years, it feels as though *a woman who has unbound her feet* looks back on the changing size of her shoe pattern. Although they have enlarged year after year, each shoe pattern is tinged with the *bloody smell* of the foot binding era. . . .
>
> But women with bound feet can never regain their natural feet. I have once again sorted through my "shoe patterns" over the last five or six years, selected some while omitting those that are totally shapeless and even potentially harmful [to readers]. There remain some "small patterns"; by retaining them, however, I hope people can learn something about the *pain* of foot binding. If that would serve some *historical purpose*, then I would not worry as much.[73]

The use of foot binding (and unbinding) as a metaphor for cultural renaissance resonates with Rey Chow's claim for Chinese male intellectuals' masochist identification with (oppressed) women. She argues that, by assuming the position of the premodern female subject, the male intellectual came to terms with the traumatic encounter with the West and the process of modernization.[74] Chow's psychoanalytical and feminist approach has heralded a body of scholarship concerning gender and national culture in the study of modern Chinese literature. What concerns me here is the sliding interchangeability between writing and body in the production of the vernacular as a cultural practice beyond the limits of language and literature. In other words, the bodily metaphor carries a quite referential weight. The grafting of a linguistic experiment onto the social body of modernity as a lived, gendered experience—pain as well as liberation—suggests that the cultural ambition of the vernacular movement extends into a larger cultural domain, including the transforming perception of the body and its epistemological status. Rather than the exclusive property of language, the vernacular is grasped as an affective experience enmeshed in the larger referent of everyday life and social reality (e.g., the unbound feet), as well as a discursive formation that demands the creation of a flexible sign system (e.g., the shoe pattern).

The production of the vernacular entails the production of a historical trope (or "purpose") and its attendant forms of expressibility. Language is an integral but by no means the only way this historical trope gets articulated. Hu Shi's effort to anchor the process of vernacularization in the flesh and blood of the female experience of becoming modern remained a literary masquerade (by borrowing the identity of the suffering women with bound feet). But the historical impulse behind recognizing the vernacular as an embodied experience has a heuristic implication for my conception of early Shanghai cinema as the quintessential medium of the vernacular. Thus instead of a semiotic approach championed by Christian Metz and his followers, who treat the cinema, or rather, its narrative coding, as a form of language that has a self-contained sign system and narrative structure,[75] I proceed along a different route, one that does not seek to conceptualize cinematic language in terms of verbal language only. Rather, it places cinema in a historical context as a larger signifying field, in which body and affectivity are crucial conduits of collective and individual expression.

ORNAMENT, EMBODIMENT, EMPOWERMENT

In grafting cinema studies onto the social and experiential body of a modernizing vernacular culture in China, my primary concerns lie with the parallel and intertwining vernacular movement and Shanghai cinema. The latter manifests itself as a complex ramification of, contribution to, and intervention into the former. The vernacular here is configured as a cultural (linguistic, visual, sensory, and material) "processor" that blends foreign and local, premodern and modern, high and low, cinematic and other cultural ingredients to create a domestic product with cosmopolitan appeal. This processor—a worldly technology, a translation machine, and a cultural sensorium—allowed for different levels of mediation and forms of synthesis. It continually catered to and changed the local audiences' tastes, shaping and reshaping their worldviews. The cinema substantially fashioned China into something of a modern democratic society, and as such it imagined and configured new perceptions of the body, gender, and sexuality. These changes were exemplified by the first generation of screen actresses and cinematic renderings of the martial heroine, the dandy, the revolutionary, and the Modern Girl.

Hu Shi's psychosomatic poetics of the vernacular experience, informed by a scientific impulse, emerged largely outside of the early Chinese film culture. However, the desire to incorporate modern science into a poetic sensibility was not entirely divorced from a prevalent cultural sentiment shared by the emerging Shanghai cinema, which began to sprout around the same time as the vernacular movement. Rather than hastily denouncing the applicability of experience because of its origins in modern Western science and subject formation, I choose to reenergize the term by locating it in the realm of embodiment.

Writing in the vernacular took on great importance for the Chinese intellectuals and their project of modernization. Even more importantly, expressing oneself and living in the vernacular, especially in the emerging urban centers, went beyond the linguistic and literary domain of the term, bringing it into a heterogeneous field of cultural production and consumption. For these reasons, I find *jingli* and *tiyan* (either functioning as verbs or nouns), in place of *jingyan,* to be better terms for encompassing a shifting and lived experiential horizon because these compounds incorporate the words for history (*lishi*) and embodiment (*tixian*). Embodiment as such includes sociocultural practices that are directly expressed through the body and a form of "sensuous" knowledge and memory production that extends beyond textual inscription or hermeneutics.[76] To reintroduce the notion of experience at this point historicizes its multilayered nature and its embodied articulation.

The shifted emphasis from intellectual discourse to lived experience, from representation to embodiment, has methodological implications for writing a materialist cultural history. Taking the body as a being-in-the-world, an experiential agent rather than an object or sign, and placing it at the center of a historical analysis of cultural change and subjectivity formation allows for a "radical empiricism" as advocated by an emerging strand of ethnography.[77] In his critique of the dominance of semiotics over phenomenology in anthropology in the wake of poststructuralism (a situation shared by cinema and literary studies as well), Thomas Csordas proposes a new synthesis of the methodologies that would place body and text in a dynamic, complementary relationship. Not to jettison text and textuality altogether as useful analytical categories, he rather juxtaposes to them the "parallel figures of the 'body' as a biological, material entity and 'embodiment' as an indeterminate methodological field defined by perceptual experience and mode of presence and engagement in the world." The paradigm of embodiment is thus offered as a "dialectical partner" to texuality, and a fruitful combination of both opens up possibilities for explorations of intertextuality (semiotics) and intersubjectivity (phenomenology).[78]

The cultural etiology of the bound feet, deployed by Hu Shi to convey the pain as well as the liberation that characterizes the vernacularizing process, allows me to take the word *movement* in the expression "vernacular movement" even more seriously and quite literally. The vernacular movement was not a static or pedantic enterprise concerning only a few modernist intellectuals. It involved the production of a pervasive, if often contradictory, historical force and the emergence of a new collective social body and, as a consequence, individual, gendered bodies. This theoretical move resonates with Vivian Sobchack's invocation of Merleau-Ponty's view of language as an embodied and enworlded experience for restoring the sensuous power of the motion picture to signify. As a new vernacular "language" for perception and expression, the cinematic experience is always already situated (hence the term "*address* of the eye") in the "flesh of the world" and grounded in the embodied existence and material world.[79]

The embodied experience, with both local inflection and global resonance, enables the understanding of modernity as a fusion of disparate yet connected cultural sensibilities and worldviews. These worldviews then acquire unprecedented palpability and global appeal when the "world itself has taken on a 'photographic face.'"[80] It conditions us toward a new perception of the phenomenal world, one in which physicality is revealed and recreated by the "optical unconscious" of the camera described by Benjamin. If photography inaugurated a mechanically reproducible means to arrest reality and congeal life in a split second, the cinema was able to reassemble the "still" images and put them into motion, or rather, as Kracauer saw it, back into the "flow of life."[81] The cinema is a "new mode of embodiment" in modernity, not simply because of its photographic indexicality and visual immediacy,[82] but also because it stimulates and reorganizes a whole range of sensory experiences, such as tactility, smell, taste, and sound through mass mediated technology. Susan Buck-Morss has argued, extending Benjamin's view on the tactile quality of the "optical unconscious" of photography and cinema, that the film screen is a prosthesis of sense perception.[83] It is through the (re)enactment of physiological movement and everyday life that the cinema emerges as the exemplary "mimetic machine" for embodying the fractured and constantly metamorphosing experience of modernity. Within the virtual space between the original and the copy, fidelity and fantasy, the mimed and the mime, an embodied sense of alterity and the revived faculty to experience springs, even just momentarily, out of the prison world of alienation and fragmentation.[84]

Kracauer's work is particularly helpful as we attempt to conceptualize cinema as an embodiment and constituting force of vernacular modernism. His conviction that cinema presented both the historical opportunity and the means for the "redemption of physical reality," is systematically laid out in his *Theory of Film,* first published in 1960. But his interest in the subject stems from his early writings in Weimar Berlin and from his exile in France during the war. Indeed, as Miriam Hansen points out in her introduction to the most recent edition, the "material aesthetic" inherent in film can be traced back to photography. The "photographic nature" of film endows the medium with an indexical relationship to reality in a particular temporal and spatial composition, mimetically reproducing and also revealing the lived world it represents.[85] Kracauer's "photographic approach" to film is encapsulated in the opening of his essay, "Photography," published in *Frankfurter Zeitung* in 1927, in which he describes a photograph of the female star of a cinematic *tour de force* similar to Chinese incarnations examined later:

> This is what the film diva looks like. She is twenty-four years old, featured on the cover of an illustrated magazine, standing in front of the Hotel Excelsior on the Lido. The date is September. If one were to look through a magnifying glass one could make out the grain, the millions of little dots that constitute the diva, the waves and the hotel. The picture, however, does not refer to the dot matrix but to the *living* diva on the Lido. Time: the present. The caption calls her demonic: our demonic diva. Still, she does not lack a certain look. The bangs, the seductive position of the head, and the twelve lashes right and left—all these details, diligently recorded by the camera, are in their proper place, a flawless appearance. Everyone recognizes her with delight since everyone has already seen the original on the screen. It is such a good *likeness* that she cannot be confused with anyone else, even if she is perhaps only one twelfth of a dozen Tiller girls. Dreamily she stands in front of the Hotel Excelsior, which basks in her fame, *a being of flesh and blood,* our demonic diva, twenty-four years old, on the Lido. The date is September.[86]

The photographic image of the diva on the cover of an illustrated magazine has a great deal to say about the changed meaning of memory and history when the appearance of the whole world undergoes a photochemical process. If photography has created a new kind of depository for historical truth in place of memory-images that "outlast" time, this depository is no deeper than the surface of a glossy magazine cover that flattens time into a spatial continuum. However, this flattening process does not necessarily lead to petrifaction. The photograph registers not only a flawless appearance but also a moment of origin and an exterior of a concrete location—"a means of expression as generally intelligible as language." What has animated the life of the film diva out of the stockpiled dots is the "demonic" power embedded in the "life of the original," to which the image provides access for the contemporary beholder. For the knowing reader who has seen the film diva on the silver screen, her photographic pose relates to a context, a situation he or she has lived through in the movie theater. The film diva cannot be reduced to a fashion photo because the reader / viewer is constantly reminded of her corporeal reality, as herself as well as the characters she portrays. The surface of the magazine is thus shot through with a "being of flesh and blood." The readability of the image—"intelligible as a language"—relies on this sense of immanence and palpability in spite of the fact that its meaning, unlike a traditional artwork, is stockpiled in and produced by the photochemical process rather than accumulated over time. The contingency and materiality of the photographed "history" can hardly authorize a total history with a deep-seated truth; rather, "this history is like a monogram that condenses the name into a single graphic figure that is meaningful as an ornament."[87]

The idea of this "[photo]graphic figure" as new "writing" (*graphe*) and as a condensed "ornament" invokes Kracauer's fascination with the collective figure of the Tiller girls, referred to in the passage cited above. The singularity and corporeality of the film diva are subsumed under the mass image of the Tiller girls, the revue dancers popular in the Berlin scene from 1924 to 1931.[88] In "The Mass Ornament," an essay published shortly before "Photography," Kracauer spells out his ambivalence toward the aesthetic of "surface," as manifested in the "body culture" of the Tiller Girls. The mass ornament, inherently photogenic, can be alternatively read as "mass embodiment." The exteriority or spatial quality of the mass ornament is compared to "aerial photographs of landscapes and cities in that it does not emerge out of the interior of the given conditions, but rather appears above them."[89] Kracauer finds in the production of the "mass ornament" a potential analogy of social reification and dehumanization effected by the Taylorist system—the "hands in the factory corresponded to the legs of the Tiller Girls." Body parts are interchangeable with machine parts; thus, "[t]he mass ornament is the aesthetic reflex of the rationality to which the prevailing economic system aspires." The individual bodies of the Tiller Girls are emptied out in the process—or on the assembly line in the factory of distraction. But it would be beside the point to try to redeem the individual body and return it to a pristine natural order. The Tiller Girls could attain their expression and vitality only through the "assemblage" of a second nature or the "body without organs."[90]

Rather than leading to total rationalization and social abstraction, the production of the "mass ornament" paradoxically triggers the *formation* of a new physicality and organicism that create a self-legitimating *"aesthetic pleasure."*[91] With this Kracauer was able to defend the "mass ornament" and its capacity to "bestow form" upon life material in an epoch that was increasingly losing touch with itself. This "aesthetic" goes beyond the realm of conventional representational art, such as painting or sculpture, and is charged instead with the kinetic power aroused by the undulation and movement of the Tiller Girls. The "mass ornament" represents both the means and the end in bringing the aesthetic back to reality. With this realization, Kracauer concludes, "No matter how low one gauges the value of the mass ornament, its degree of reality is still higher than that of artistic productions which cultivate outdated noble sentiments in obsolete forms—even if it means nothing more than that."[92]

Toward the end of his essay on photography, Kracauer envisions the contribution that the cinema might offer to a new, however "provisional," configuration of nature and its meaning amidst the ruins of alienation or fragmentation. Photography created the confrontation between human consciousness and lived reality by stripping the latter of its "natural shell" and disintegrating the "original order" of things. The loss of context and the danger of the reification of experience constitute what Kracauer calls the "go-for-broke game of history" in the turn to photography. The image of the film diva may be recuperated only through the production of a new sense of context, aided by the cinema and the movie-going experience. The revolutionary potential of the cinema lies not simply in its "capacity to stir up the elements of nature" but also in the way it "combines parts and segments to create *strange constructs.*"[93] The new cinematic reconstitution of the relationship between the human world and natural order that Kracauer envisions differs radically from any return to an organic origin within a linear history. Instead, closer to the logic or formula of dream, the "strange constructs" of the cinema will yield newfound connections between images and experiences.[94] In this light, the daydream episode in *Amorous History* takes on a critical significance. The actress sees herself wandering in a disjointed urban landscape, a place where she soon finds herself. In the story that follows, especially as she slaps the hoodlum, the actress succeeds not so much in taking revenge as in making connection between past and present experience—and between different registers of reality.

Kracauer's critical insights on the relationship between technology, mass media, and social (self-)representation supply useful conceptual tools for the understanding of early Chinese film culture. But more significantly, his sociophenomenological observations on urban modernity in Berlin in the 1920s and early 1930s delineate a cultural landscape similar to Shanghai during the same period. The Tiller Girls did in fact come to Shanghai as well, in the form of both revue shows and film musicals. A scene in *Money Demon*, one of the films shown in production during the studio tour in *Amorous History*, features a group of Chinese girls and boys dancing under the spell of the "money demon." The scene of the extras' synchronized act of putting on make-up offers yet another instance of the cinematic mass ornament in a Chinese dream factory. *Queen of Sports* (*Tiyu huanghou*, 1934), Sun Yu's ambiguous contribution to the Nationalist New Life movement, also features mechanic choreography of female athletes' robust legs. The film vacillates between the body cultures of dancing and sport, embodying the dual nature of the "mass ornament"—its utopian potential for the liberation of the senses as well as the danger of ideological exploitation of bodily energy, as happened *in extremis* in Germany under fascism.

The "mass ornament" has a global appeal, though its configuration is contingent upon the local conditions of any mass-mediated cosmopolitan culture. "Simultaneity" (*Gleichzeitigkeit*), which Kracauer found to be the underlying structure organizing work and leisure under the industrial mode of production,[95] can certainly be expanded to envisage the mass ornament as a global experience of modernity. On this coeval horizon, the early Shanghai film culture—(the same argument could be made about other metropolitan centers such as Tokyo, Bombay, and Rio de Janeiro)—participates in the local production and transformation of the global mass ornament. How the "mass ornament" became "Shanghai-ed" is part of the main story of this book. The link between the readily intelligible language embodied by the Tiller Girls' legs in Kracauer's diagnosis of mass culture and the unbound feet in Hu Shi's cultural pathology of the vernacular language may at first seem arbitrary. What is so strikingly similar in their visions, however, is the investment in the energy and anxiety unleashed by the physical entrance of women into the public arena and the cultural statements they make, consciously or unconsciously. These women represented a utopian potential of a new "language" for reconnecting aesthetic expression and lived experience, or representation and its referent.

Hu Shi did not realize that, when he was writing about the pain of unbinding the feet of vernacular literature and trying to resuscitate true experience in its endangered form of poetry, the first Chinese female film star Wang Hanlun (1903–78) entered the cultural scene with her unbound feet. Wang became an instant celebrity in 1922 after portraying a widow convinced of the virtue of education in *Orphan Rescues Grandfather* (*Gu'er jiuzu ji*, 1923), produced by the Mingxing Company. If the silver screen made her unbound feet, referred to at the time as "civilized feet" (*wenmingjiao*), visible to the public (fig. 1.4), it was the life story of her unbinding herself from the fetters of an old society that made her an urban legend of her day.[96] Born into a gentry family, Wang Hanlun was forced to marry a stranger in her late teens. After a hard-won divorce, she moved to Shanghai. Emboldened by the "swelling [movement] of women's rights," she entered the work force and acquired marketable skills.[97] At first supporting herself by teaching in an elementary school, she then worked as office clerk at a foreign company and later as a typist for an international sports association (*Wanguo tiyuhui*).[98] Unsatisfied with mere economic independence, she felt that she "wanted to find a different path, to do something on a grand and spectacular scale." Though Chinese cinema was emerging and still met with disdain (including by her family), she decided to "sacrifice" herself to the new medium.[99] Wang Hanlun abandoned her original family name Peng and took Wang as her new name: the Chinese character for Wang (which also means king) is part of the complex Chinese character for tiger—a fearless creature.[100] Hanlun, on the other hand, was derived from her English name "Helen." Director Zhang Shichuan recalled years later that Wang was one of the few "modern girls" (*modeng nülang*) of the time; her fashionable dress and makeup deeply impressed him and his colleagues.[101] Her linguistic gifts—being able to speak Mandarin and English in addition to the Shanghai dialect—added to her modern flair. Not only did Wang boldly show her unbound feet on the screen during the shooting of a film in 1926, she also had her long hair cut in front of the camera. Though required by the plot, this "cut" (from her past) added another bodily token to her image as a modern girl.

The cinema created new vocations for women as well as significant social positions and public images. Because many women contributed substantially to early film ventures in capacities that went beyond acting, it is not too far fetched to consider them pioneers of Chinese cinema and film culture as well. Traditionally Chinese women had been largely excluded from the public arena. Only the few very chaste or filial women who sacrificed themselves for patriarchy could be regarded as public models for emulation. Before the coming of the cinema only women from poor or marginal social groups worked as actors, mainly in all-women traveling opera troupes catering to the rural population or lower-class town residents. Women and men neither were to appear on the same stage, nor allowed to sit together in the audience, if women were admitted at all. While the cinema as a mass attraction drastically changed the gender makeup of audience and women quickly became avid spectators, the earliest Chinese films only featured male actors, mainly with theatrical backgrounds. In 1913, Yan Shanshan became the first Chinese woman to appear on the silver screen, in the short story film *Zhuang Zi*

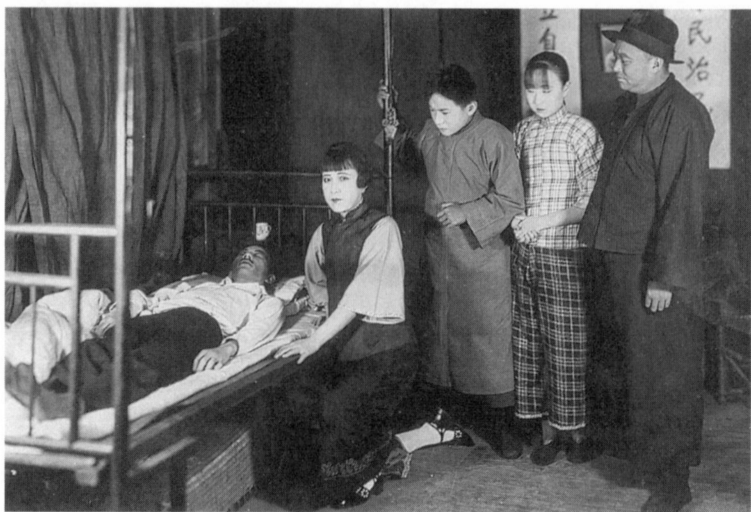

1.4 Wang Hanlun (center) with her "civilized feet" on screen. (Courtesy of the China Film Archive)

Tests His Wife (*Zhuang Zi shiqi*), directed by her husband Li Minwei. Ironically, Yan played the minor role of the maid while Li played Zhuang Zi's wife.[102] At the time, it was still inconceivable for women to appear in film, much less playing leading roles. Before becoming a film actress, Yan was known as a member of the female bomb squad during the Republican Revolution in 1911. Even after her breakthrough there were hardly any women playing female roles until 1921, when Wang Caiyun, a theater actress-turned singsong girl, played the leading role as a prostitute in *Yan Ruisheng*.

The cinema boom in the early 1920s—especially the proliferation of long narrative films and a growing popular "taste for reality" and melodrama—created a demand for actresses not just to fill the scenes but also to play leading roles.[103] The profession of screen acting thus provided an unprecedented opportunity for many women of diverse backgrounds, including the new-style female students who defied family and societal prejudice to embrace the cinema as well as courtesans or singsong girls who saw in the medium a chance for improving their social standing. With the help of the print media, including early trade journals and fan magazines, the beginnings of a star system were already in place. Actresses including Wang Hanlun, Yin Mingzhu, Yang Naimei (1904–60), Zhang Zhiyun (1905–?), Zhang Meilie, Fu Wenhao, Li Minghui, Xu Su'er (?–1931), Zhao Jinxia, Wang Huixian, and Cao Jianqiu displayed their courage in embracing a modern mass medium, which was still shunned by the elite society.[104] Their stardom partly derived from their image as champions of the modern lifestyle in many aspects—in fashion, hairstyle, car-driving, and unconventional sexual life (such as having boyfriends or choosing cohabitation over marriage).[105] They were in fact the first generation of Chinese "modern girls."

Among them, Yin Mingzhu and Yang Naimei were probably the most prominent. Yin, born to a gentry family, studied at a Western-style women's college in Shanghai. She was known for her skills in dancing, singing, horse-riding, biking, and car-driving. Because she always dressed as foreign movie stars, she came to be called Miss F. F. for Foreign Fashion.[106] Together with Dan Duyu, an artist-turned- director, Yin founded the Shanghai Shadowplay Company (Shanghai yingxi gongsi), one of the early cottage-industry ventures. Beside her involvement in the operation of the company, Yin was the leading star of their popular productions. Yang Naimei, on the other hand, was famous for her "romantic" life style and her penchant for "strange clothes" (fig. 1.5). The only daughter of a successful Cantonese businessman, Yang went to a girls' school and indulged in performances. After a small role in a Mingxing box-office hit, *Jade Pear Spirit* (*Yu Li hun,* 1923), she quickly became a major star and character actress, specializing in playing wayward, amorous women. Her off-screen hobbies, like high-speed driving through the main thoroughfare in central Shanghai, also brought her notoriety. Yang's fame outraged her father who saw acting as nothing less than prostitution and consequently disowned her. In 1926, Yang wowed the film world by appearing in tableaux vivant fashion during the screening of *The Resurrection of Conscience* (*Liangxinde fuhuo,* 1926), dubbing live the Kunqu tune "Song of the Wet Nurse," which she sang in the film. Unsatisfied with being dictated by male directors, she founded her own company, the Naimei Film Co. and produced a film about a legendary modern woman in 1928. None other than she played the protagonist.[107]

Wang Hanlun's film career also culminated in the opening of a film company under her own name, and producing and starring in the feature *Revenge of the Actress* (*Nüling fuchou ji*) in 1929.[108] It was practically a one-woman enterprise. She hired a director but had to take care of all other aspects of production herself, including editing. Because of the negligence of her partners, she eventually bought the shooting script from the director and finished the postproduction by herself. With the aid of a manual projector, she completed editing the film at home. Afterwards, she traveled with the film all over China, going as far as Ha'erbin in Northeast China and performing live during intermissions.[109] The profit generated by the film enabled her to retire from the screen and

1.5 Actress Yang Naimei was famous for her "romantic" life style and her penchant for "strange clothes." (*Silverland*, no. 33, 1931).

establish the Hanlun Beauty Salon, which became an eye-catching spot in Shanghai.

The ascendance of Wang Hanlun and Xuan Jingling as screen stars and icons, despite their different social origins, exemplifies the transformative power of the cinema. It presented both women with a chance for a second life on and off the screen. At the same time, their disparate backgrounds and ways of living out their potential demonstrate the heterogeneous origins of early Chinese cinema and Shanghai's urban culture. Whereas Wang came from a wealthy family and received her education at a missionary school, Xuan belonged to the lower strata of society and was hardly literate when she entered the film world. One escaped from an arranged marriage and cut her ties with a traditional family, the other left the pleasure quarters and later the confines of modern concubinage. The film world became their new home as well as their university of life. Although the sense of liberation and empowerment felt by Wang and Xuan was incomplete and often ambivalent, the silver screen nevertheless allowed them to experience their changing self-perception through performance and role-playing. Through this act of play, which functions as a "mirror, a doubling split between action and actor,"[110] they could attain a sense of alterity and enjoy the experience of transgression. Through the blending of these early film actresses' personal histories with the lives of the characters they played on the screen, the collective experience of Chinese women, poised on the threshold of different worlds and destinies, began to receive meaningful articulation. If the movement toward embodiment in Hu Shi's vernacular poetics remained symbolic, the reenactment and transformation of the lived experience of the first generation of film actresses on the silver screen carried the weight of a particular historical indexicality and concreteness.

CHAPTER TWO

WORLDLY SHANGHAI, METROPOLITAN SPECTATORS

ALL ABOUT SHANGHAI, a well-known guidebook compiled and published by English and American expatriates in Shanghai in the mid-1930s, opens with a hyperbolic hymn to the city and its spectacular manifestations of modernity:

> Shanghai, sixth city of the World![1]
> Shanghai, the Paris of the East!
> Shanghai, the New York of the West!
>
> Shanghai, the most cosmopolitan city on the world, the fishing village on a mudflat which almost literally overnight became a great metropolis.
>
> Inevitable meeting place of world travelers, the habitat of people of forty-eight different nationalities. Of the Orient yet Occidental, the city of glamorous night life and throbbing with activity, Shanghai offers the full composite allurement of the Far East.
>
> Not a wilderness of temples and chop-sticks, of jade and pyjamas, Shanghai in reality is an immense and modern city of well-paved streets, skyscrapers, luxurious hotels and clubs, trams, buses and motors, and much electricity.[2]

The rather blatant Orientalism notwithstanding, this introduction to Shanghai underscores the world-class nature of its modernity, its cosmopolitan character with its "composite allurement." Instead of the usual exoticization of the "wilderness of temples and chop-sticks" often found in foreign sojourners' travelogues, the authors of this "standard guide" to the Chinese metropolis placed the city on the same level as, if not higher than, the most prominent cities in the Western hemisphere. With its wide streets, bright lights, soaring skyscrapers, and exuberant urban life, Shanghai is deemed ultramodern mainly because the facades of this modernity seem on par, or perhaps even superior to, those found in Paris or New York.

During the late nineteenth century and the early decades of the twentieth century, Shanghai was a hotbed for the production and consumption of mass culture, including the cinema. Baptized "Paris of the Orient," the city was seen as a major metropolitan center in the modern global geography. Its urban infrastructure and cultural trends indeed had much in common with the Paris immortalized in Benjamin's *Arcades Project,* Berlin under the observing eyes of Kracauer, and even more with New York, a coastal multicultural metropolis in the new age of global capitalism. Shanghai was hardly slow in consuming and recycling all sorts of mass culture and brands of modernism imported from America, Europe, and Japan. On the contrary, the growth of the city into a major metropolis also involved the emergence of a vibrant Chinese culture industry that included cinema.

In the above-quoted eulogy to Shanghai's honorary status as a haven for global capitalism, the city's multifaceted vernacular culture and social unevenness is made invisible. These aspects are precisely what I desire to reveal, through the looking glass of film history as an emblematic cultural history of modernity. It is hardly my goal here to uncover an "authentic" oriental jungle of "chopsticks, jade and pyjamas," which only existed in the fantasy of the exotica hunters roaming about in a vast Chinatown. Nor is my aim to reclaim Shanghai for various brands of Chinese nationalism that have always harbored a deep suspicion toward the city's cosmopolitan legacy, particularly its manifold manifestations of material culture and entertainment industry. Rather, this book tells how its vibrant film culture, which has almost become synonymous with the world city of the Republican period, contributed crucially to a culturally anchored and mass-mediated cosmopolitan experience.

Beyond the bulk of guidebooks and travelogues authored by old and new Western and Eastern Shanghai aficionados, a large body of Shanghai scholarship has overwhelmingly focused on perspectives of its political and social life to explain or describe the city's role as the harbinger of Chinese modernity.[3] Recently, more attention has been directed to the flourishing forms of material culture and everyday life that characterized what Leo Ou-fan Lee terms "Shanghai Modern" in the Republican era.[4] For instance, in his book Lee engages the popular print culture, including newspapers, magazines, advertisements, and calendar posters, to write a broadly contextualized literary history as part of a modern experience. Cinema, however, remains largely a backdrop or playground for scholars of modernism.[5] This approach, in part inspired by the effort to both reinstate the historical role of literary modernism in modern Chinese literary and cultural history and compare it with its Western counterparts, nevertheless perpetuates the tradition of author-centered literary criticism. Its explanation of urban modernity and cosmopolitanism remains text-bound and elite-oriented rather than attending to its embodied mass participation.

The cinematic legacy is an indispensable link in the history and conceptualization of modernity in China. It is an integral part of Shanghai's metropolitan identity through the late Qing, the Republican period, and beyond. Early Chinese film enterprises and audiences were overwhelmingly concentrated in this rapidly expanding trading port and urban center, which attracted large numbers of people from other parts of China and the world. While the golden age of Chinese film familiar to Shanghai fans is often equated with the Shanghai modern of the 1930s and 1940s, the early years of Chinese film history have rarely been considered as an integral part of the story of Chinese modernity. Alongside towering skyscrapers and luxurious clubs and exclusive hotels teemed a world of vernacular culture and mass entertainment. It was a part of the city that was more readily accessible and affordable for the Shanghai population at large—a broad and fluctuating social strata of the so-called *xiaoshimin,* or petty urbanites. "Electric shadows," as the cinema was called, belonged in the world of electric power that fueled the city's industry and illuminated the phantasmagoria of commodities. In order for us to understand the significance of this film culture as the embodiment of the Shanghai modern, we must revisit the origins and transformation of the metropolis, and reconsider the reasons for its peculiar mode of modernity and for being the cradle of Chinese cinema.

SHANGHAI MODERN, YANGJINGBANG STYLE

By no means was Shanghai a "fishing village" prior to its opening as a treaty port in the aftermath of the Opium Wars and the signing of the Nanjing Treaty in 1843.[6] In fact, Shanghai had been a thriving commercial port for hundreds of years. Nevertheless, the pace of Shanghai's transformation into a world city in the second half of the nineteenth century and in the early twentieth century was breathtaking. During this period, the complex social fabric and the corresponding urban geography gave the city a particular modern character that was at once vernacular and cosmopolitan. I choose to make sense of this character through the term *Yangjingbang* (or pidgin) style rather than the more entrenched and glamorous term, *haipai,* or the Shanghai style.[7] The Shanghai style—the "visual equivalent of an attitude"—has acquired inflated and ahistorical valences, but the sense of "big-city edginess" identified by art historian Jonathan Hay in the late Qing Shanghai school of painting remains the kernel of its various expressions.[8] It was also during this period that Shanghai truly became, literally and figuratively, *Da Shanghai* or Big Shanghai (not unlike the Big Apple), as it is still referred to by the rest of China. When the port opened, Shanghai was a county seat of 540,000 people. By the dawn of the twentieth century, it had emerged as the largest city in China, boasting a population of 1.08 million. By 1915 this number was nearly doubled to 2 million, and by the end of the 1920s, the population had risen to 3 million.[9] A significant portion of the Shanghai population at any given time during those decades was comprised of "floating" subjects, including foreign travelers and refugees (notably Russians) and Chinese migrants (who often arrived in waves in times of war and natural disasters). As a result, there were probably as many nationalities and languages as there were Chinese regional identities and dialects that filled the city streets.

The population growth paralleled the rapid, often chaotic, and hardly adequate expansion and transformation of the urban space. The city map was frequently redrawn by both the Chinese and foreigners, in order to reflect and define the constant physical and demographic changes (fig. 2.1).[10] After the Republican revolution of 1911, Shanghai's designation was changed from *cheng* (town) to *shi* (city). While the former connotes etymologically a walled city, the latter suggests more the notion of the market place, a modern city as a municipal entity.[11] This makes particular sense as the wall enclosing the small and crowded Chinese area (Nanshi) was torn down in 1912, shortly after the Republican revolution that ended China's dynastic history. Where the wall once stood, there now runs a wide, paved street with ceramic sewer ducts underneath. The street was given a quaint composite name, Fahua Minguo Road (French-Chinese Republican Road, now Renmin lu or People's Road). Many of the dried-up, stinky canals were filled, more roads were paved, and bridges were built (most importantly over the Suzhou River, which runs through the northern part of the city and into the Huangpu River). A mass transportation system was installed,[12] thus making the boundaries more permeable between *zujie* or the foreign concessions in the North (international settlement) and the West (French concession) of the old city, and

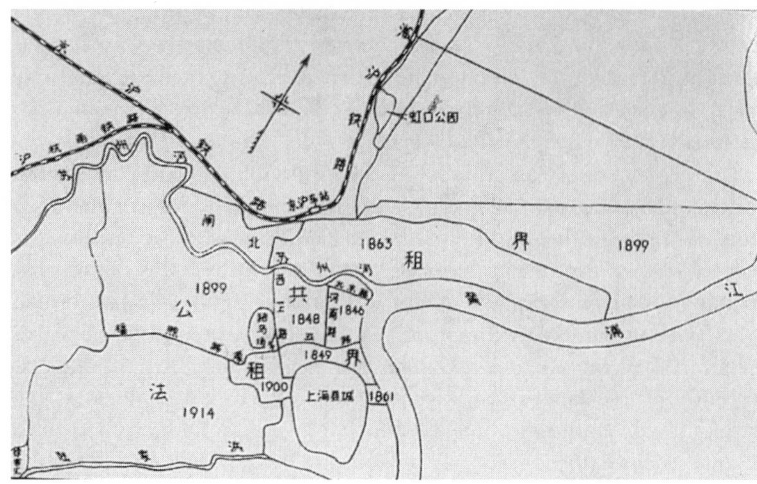

2.1 Shanghai at around the turn of the twentieth century.

the Chinese areas (including Zhabei on the north side of the Suzhou River). These new urban infrastructures enabled people, money, and commodities, as well as languages, ideas, and lifestyles to circulate widely and quickly through the city. In the process, the basis of a syncretic yet uneven metropolitan identity emerged, mapped out on an equally uneven urban geography.

Prior to the tearing down of the wall, large numbers of Chinese residents had already entered to live or work in *zujie,* especially in the wake of the Taiping Rebellion that seriously affected the Chinese old city. They contributed to the building of the wealth and glamour of the so-called *shili yangchang* or "ten miles of foreign land" (one *li* is about half a kilometer); many of them also became the first Shanghainese to speak a pidgin English or Chinglish, inflected with Shanghai and other dialects. In the early years following the opening of the Shanghai port, foreign settlers (mainly British subjects) had constructed and lived in a relatively segregated area alongside the embankment of the Huangpu River northeast of the walled city. The Chinese first regarded this area as a *yichang* (barbarian's land). With the illegal expansion of the concessions and the increasing coexistence of foreign and Chinese residents and businesses, the term *yichang* gradually gave way to the less pejorative *yangchang.*[13] It refers primarily to the Bund area and the Nanking Road (then Huayuan Long) lined with shops, offices, and banks. The commercial prosperity and thriving entertainment establishments in *yichang,* with flashy advertising banners, billboards, and electric lights, became a modern spectacle and earthly wonder in the eyes of both the Shanghai residents and visitors. The more neutral term *yang* denotes foreign and exotic things (*yang* also means "ocean" or "beyond the horizon") as well as connotes things and manners that are stylish in an uninhibitedly modern, even cosmopolitan way. Over time, *yangpai* (foreign style), became interchangeable with *haipai* (Shanghai style), especially as both *yang* and *hai* means ocean.[14] The name of Shanghai itself is almost synonymous with "going to sea" (*shanghai*) or "on the sea" (*haishang*) due to its proximity to the China Sea and the Pacific Ocean.[15]

This change of terminology and perception is significant in that *zujie*, a product of unequal treaties, acquires new meanings as the concessions became increasingly domesticated and diversified. Over time, shocking foreignness gave way, though unevenly and never entirely. The Chinese taking residence in the concessions rapidly outnumbered the foreigners; many Chinese found it legitimate (this was China after all) and sometimes even profitable (one could evade the taxes and other laws leveled by the Chinese authorities) to live and do business there.

Yangjingbang, a peculiar Shanghai vernacular expression, is perhaps the single emblematic token of this grassroots metropolitan consciousness and ambivalent semicolonial experience. Popularly known as a form of pidgin language spoken by Shanghai residents, Yangjingbang was originally the name of a canal dividing the British and French concessions, not too far from the old Chinese City just to the south (fig. 2.2). It was the area where the foreign and Chinese interaction was most intense, due to its proximity to the docks along the Huangpu River. The embankments of the shallow canal were popular sites for migrants' shelters, shops, and brothels. Many tour guides, porters, translators, middlemen, flower girls, and prostitutes made a living there doing business with foreigners. As the well-known late Qing reformist thinker Wang Tao observes in his *Nuying Miscellaneous,* perhaps one of the first books to record the emergence of modern Shanghai, "The Yangjingbang area is a floating world, . . . whenever one enters the Yangjingbang area, the sights and sounds there are extraordinary."[16] The canal was filled in 1915 and became Edward Road—(or Aiduoyalu in pidgin via French, renamed as Yan'an Donglu after 1949)—in a move to facilitate the connection between the two concessions, and to "clean up" the area (fig. 2.3).[17]

Yangjingbang marks the site of the correspondence of spatial and linguistic practices. Perhaps because of the ambiguous character of the social geography of the canal-turned road, over time the name became a Chinese reference to *zujie* as a whole. More significantly, the geographical term coalesced with the linguistic term for pidgin (or "business") English developed by the Shanghai residents of lower classes in daily trans-

2.2 The Yangjingbang Canal.

2.3 The canal was filled in 1915 and became Edward Road.

actions with foreigners.[18] Irreverent of grammatical rules and full of chance (and sometimes creative) combinations, the Yangjingbang speech mixed English, Chinese (including local dialects), and elements of other languages that permeated the city. Bernard Shaw allegedly spoke highly of the Yangjingbang language after his visit to Shanghai in 1931 and commented that one day it might become a world language.[19] In an early urban study of Shanghai, Yao Gonghe, author of *Shanghai xianhua* (Idle Talk of Shanghai), attributed the birth of the Yangjingbang language to the self-employed "outdoor translators" (*lutian tongshi*) congregating in the area. These translators were partially responsible for inventing a new phonetic system for transcribing English sounds with radicals taken out of Chinese characters.[20] Several English dictionaries and glossaries marked with Chinese transliterations were published to popularize and "standardize" this hybrid vernacular.[21] The oft-cited pidgin terms are *delüfeng* for telephone, *kangbadu* for comprador, *namowen* for Number One. Other terms show the wit of the transcribers such as *heiqi bandeng* (black-lacquered bench) for husband and *leidesi* (tired to death) for ladies.[22]

With the rise of mass print enabled by new technologies (lithography and photography) and the rising demand for cheap cultural products and entertainment by the migrant Shanghai citizens, Yangjingbang also found its way into newspapers, magazines, and popular fiction (including translations).[23] Prior to the official adoption of the standard vernacular language in 1905, most publications from Shanghai catered to the moderately educated readership. The publications were liberally illustrated and employed a vernacular that mixed classical (written) and spoken Chinese, Shanghai dialect sprinkled with Yangjingbang words.

The popular dissemination of the Yangjingbang speech and sensibility also contributed to the quick reception of cinema in Shanghai following the first screenings by traveling foreign showmen. Although early silent "moving photographs" (*huodong xiezhen*) did not require reading skills in any language whatsoever, the increased use of intertitles, especially with the advent of story films between 1900 and 1920, did not create a significant barrier for Shanghai audiences who had been accustomed to Yangjingbang pidgin. Running commentaries by the showmen or "explainers" (*jieshuo*), who functioned as a cinematic *tongshi* (translator), also helped Shanghai audiences. The Mandarin Ducks and Butterfly writers quickly took up the task of penning film stories, intertitle cards, and programs for foreign and domestic films using a peculiar trademark Butterfly-style Chinese. This style produces a mosaic text that interweaves the vernacular or colloquial (*bai*) language and the classical or literary (*wen*) language, and is often interspersed with Yangjingbang words.

Yangjingbang, a direct product of the so-called *huayang zaju* (Chinese-foreign mixed residences), became more of a norm than an exception in late nineteenth-century Shanghai. Beyond a mere linguistic phenomenon, Yangjingbang constituted and gave expression to both a spatial practice and a form of everyday life that placed Shanghai in the world and the world in Shanghai. The emergence and proliferation of this "spatial vernacular" has less to do with the tearing down of *zujie* boundaries than the interpenetration and collision of diverse forms of life and consciousness.[24] Naming both *zujie* and the pidgin with the residual name of an erased locality, the Chinese residents were able to reclaim the concessions for themselves and for their everyday use. In the process, a unique urban experience crystallized, which in turn forged a particular metropolitan identity. This juxtaposition and mixing of the Chinese and foreign mores and ideas made an impression on the physical look of the urban space and city's architectural style.

Cultural historians interested in the Shanghai modern have shown a fascination with the eclectic Western architecture in Shanghai, especially the landmark structures built in the high modern period of 1930s. The pervasive vernacular establishments and housing, however, have been relegated to the background. The recent Shanghai nostalgia is essentially a postcard collection of these colonial remains. The Bund in particular has been widely acknowledged as the emblem of the World's Fair (*Wanguo bolanhui*) style architecture.[25] The vast collection of neoclassical and art deco buildings and design in Shanghai are singled out as proof that Shanghai was a world-class city. This cosmopolitan splendor, in the eyes of the ordinary inhabitants and migrants, was by and large a "mirage," "a world of fantasy which cast a mixed spell of wonder and oppression."[26] The Chinese-foreign coresidence was by no means harmonious and equal. With the flourishing of material emblems of urban modernity, Shanghai became radically divided. The well-to-do foreign taipans and Chinese compradors resided in luxurious mansions or apartment hotels. The majority of lower-middle and working class Chinese lived in modest and ill-equipped quarters, in particular the so-called *longtang*—housing particular to Shanghai that mixes the Western row house and the Chinese courtyard model. The first row houses were wooden Chinese-style structures built by the British settlers to rent to the refugees from the nearby provinces. After a big fire in 1870, a safer material used for rebuilding more liberally combined Western and Chinese style of vernacular housing.[27] The even less fortunate migrants and coolies concentrated, however, in the shantytowns of Zhabei and other Chinese areas where the living costs were far lower.

Making up the broad, fluctuating middle strata of Shanghai are the so-called petty urbanites or the *longtang* residents. They constituted the backbone of the consumers of popular culture and were avid theater- and moviegoers. The skyscrapers on the Bund and Nanjing Road, the villas with private gardens, and luxury art deco apartment buildings in the French concession stood for the Western face and the "upper" end of Shanghai Modern. The vast *longtang* neighborhoods and communities of

2.4 *Longtang:* Shanghai style vernacular housing (photo by the author).

commerce and culture in surrounding areas, on the other hand, are spatial and social manifestations of the Yangjingbang vernacular (fig. 2.4). Yet these two sides of the cosmopolitan city presuppose each other, existing and evolving in a symbiotic relationship. On a representational level, early Chinese films, the majority of which were set in Shanghai, *longtang* was a ubiquitous and often essential element of the mise-en-scène for tales of urban life, as can be glimpsed in such classics as *New Woman* (*Xin nüxing,* 1935) and *Street Angel* (*Malu tianshi,* 1937). Although there are gradations between old style (more crowded and less modern) and new style *longtang,* an average *longtang* compound is an alley (usually off-limits to cars) with a main entrance on the street and lined with two-story rowhouses and an inner courtyard. While the more affluent took up an entire unit, more often it was shared by more than two families, with each family only occupying a single room. Occasionally non-Chinese residents also lived in *longtang,* sharing not only space but also lifestyles and languages with their Chinese neighbors. The easy access from *longtang* to major commercial thoroughfares and entertainment and cultural establishments such as teahouses, theaters, and bookstores, however, allowed the *longtang* residents to readily participate in the broader arena of urban life. In that sense, if Yangjingbang is an erased geographical entity (the canal and its environs) whose spirit lived on in the Shanghai pidgin, the sprawling *longtang* housing stands as the physical, and more domesticated, incarnation of Yangjingbang. Through this built environment, the diversity and unevenness of the Shanghai modern finds salient vernacular expression.

Yangjingbang as a mixture of geographical, linguistic, and social practices occupying the same temporal plane endows the treaty port with a composite worldly character, which is at once cosmopolitan and local, ambitious yet pragmatic. This double-edged worldliness was reflected in the world of mass entertainment. In this playground and laboratory a particular form of cosmopolitanism emerged. Inseparable from the conditions of modern colonialism and industrial capitalism, the Yangjingbang style of Shanghai modern illustrates what Ackbar Abbas aptly calls a "cosmopolitanism of extraterritoriality." Shanghai's architectural legacy and other forms of cultural production, including cinema, embody "a shallow kind of cosmopolitanism, a dream image of Europe more glamorous than Europe itself at the time."[28] This shallowness casts into relief the promises as well as contradictions of the modern experiment away from the metropole(s) in the West. At the same time the delight in "shallowness"—rather than elitist indulgence in high-minded cosmopolitanism—opens up the physical and social space of mass culture.[29] While *longtang* represented the more domestic and subdued side of modern life, the teahouses and amusement halls that gave rise to an early film culture stood for the spectacular and playful aspects of that life in public domains. Shanghai modern, an arbitrary convergence of modernity, spurred an "unintended" city with a host of different social groups and urban identities that laid their own claims to the city and its cosmopolitanism.[30] As manifested in the Yangjingbang phenomenon and vernacular architecture of *longtang,* this form of urban modernity expresses a complex cultural experience and historical process.

ATTRACTIONS OF THE CITY, CINEMA OF ATTRACTIONS

With the influx of large number of immigrants and migrants to the city came an explosive demand for leisure. With the expansion of the city, countless entertainment joints, gambling parlors, teahouses, brothels, and eventually movie theaters crowded and transformed the urban landscape. Many of these establishments clustered, as they had in the past, in the old Yangjingbang area.

For those newly arrived from the countryside, the city itself was an attraction that inspired shock as well as wonderment. From tall buildings to bridges made of concrete and steel, from escalators to revolving doors, from trams and trolleys to shop windows, from women's fashion to the strange countenance of the foreigners, Shanghai was an earthly mirage overflowing with novel objects, vehicles, and all kinds of people. For

2.5 *Xiyangjing:* a peep show of the kaleidoscopic world.

many, coming to Shanghai meant "opening [one's] field of vision" (*kai yanjie*) or broadening one's horizon, to gaze into a giant kaleidoscope of a magic world (*kan xiyangjing*) (fig. 2.5). To these migrants and visitors, the very name Shanghai was tantamount to modern spectacle. In fact, many men of the country gentry became so infatuated with the sights and sounds of Shanghai that they decided to take up residence in *long-*

tang and devote themselves to the enjoyment of the city. These *yugong* (apartment misters) formed a prototype of an urban-based "man of leisure" (*baixiangren*) that emerged in the late Qing period. Many more petty urbanites also sought diversion and pleasure to relieve the fatigue or stress from work and from daily routines. Street scenes alone could not satisfy the craving for novelty, spectacle, and escape. The hustling and bustling urban space was stressful and even dangerous, as attested by the deluge of press reports on traffic accidents and other urban perils of the time. Two major forms of affordable, accessible recreation and relaxation allowed people to experience metropolitan attractions without the anxiety caused by the "real" city or the drudgery of the everyday: the illustrated newspapers and amusement halls.

Illustrated Newspapers

In the late nineteenth century the attractions of the city were instantly reproduced as attractive features in newspapers and magazines. The illustrated newspapers (*huabao*) occupied a central place in the display and representation of the pleasures and dangers of the modernizing city. The dynamic combination of texts and images, which created a vividness, immediacy, and docudramatic effect, may be seen as one of the precinematic forms that fostered what Benjamin discerned as the "optical unconscious" in the age of mechanical reproduction. For the less-educated or illiterate people, and particularly women and children, the illustrated newspapers were cheap and easy to understand. It was no coincidence that the first illustrated newspaper founded by Western missionaries in 1875 was called *Xiaohai yuebao* (Little Children's Monthly).[31] In the late Qing period, there were ninety-eight illustrated papers published all over China, the majority of which were based in Shanghai, the capital of mass print industry. Among them, the most famous and long lasting *Dianshizhai huabao* was founded in 1884. Its team of illustrators consisted of leading painters of *fengsuhua* paintings (such as Wu Youru, Jin Zhanxiang, and Ma Ziming), which depicted contemporary and vernacular scenes with a combination of Chinese and Western techniques. Due to popular demand, about twenty distribution agencies for *Dianshizhai huabao* (Dianshizhai Illustrated) were set up in other cities. An additional paper, *Feiyingge huabao* edited by Wu Youru, was created in 1890 and sold at the same price: a mere five cents.[32] Many text-based papers also added illustrated supplements to satisfy the craving of mass readership for visualization and novelty.

Through its innovative synthesis of image and text portraying a large inventory of incongruous subjects *huabao* appealed to a readership across different ages, genders, and classes; in effect it created a modern visual vernacular that was part and parcel of the Yangjingbang culture. Through *huabao,* the petty urbanites could access or open their "field of vision" to a wide array of metropolitan attractions and world phenomena in a printed simulacrum, free of danger and anxiety. In the inaugural issue the editors announced that their paper "would choose the more unique and interesting news from regular newspapers, such as the invention of a gadget or the spotting of a new thing, and explicate them through illustrations and words in order to make the readers believe."[33] The illustrated papers remained popular until about 1912, when copperplate photography became less costly for mass print and widely adopted. The glossy *Tuhua zhoukan* (Pictorial Weekly), *Liangyou huabao* (The Young Companion), *Rensheng huabao* (Life Magazine), and the early 1920s movie magazines are representative of this new kind of *huabao,* replete with black and white or even color photo plates.

In addition to serving as a portable public school for the masses, *huabao* also functioned as a printed newsreel that showcased happenings in the city and in the world, as well as intrinsically modern spectacles, such as skyscrapers and trains. The breadth of its coverage is often suffused with vivid details: from observations of urban daily life (the neighborhood market, new trolley lines) to reports of the extraordinary (murders, ghosts, fire, war). The best-selling attractions were tales of strange urban phenomena that blended the Chinese and Western mores as well as old and new values, such as Shanghai women playing golf,[34] or descriptions of novel, magic (*shenqi*) gadgets such as the x-ray and elevators.

The high point of *huabao*'s popularity coincided with the appearance of cinema in urban China at the turn of the twentieth century. *Tuhua ribao* (Illustrated Daily), published by Around the Globe Press (Huanqiushe) in 1908 (fig. 2.6), was a major *huabao* that consistently showcased new modern attractions and people's reactions to them, including the cinema, then called "Occidental shadowplay" (*xiyang yingxi*). The seventh issue from August 1908 reported and illustrated "Noisy Shadowplays on Fourth Avenue" as a particular social phenomenon in Shanghai. The writer of the story appears amazed at the use of trumpets and even Chinese gongs and drums in front of the teahouse to promote the foreign shadowplay. Not only are the films being shown inside the venue advertised, the boisterous on-location publicity, in Yangjingbang style, presents an urban attraction in its own right. Throngs of people (mostly men) filled the streets to watch the live advertisement while a few women passing through in the sedan chairs also showed their curiosity (see fig. 1.3).

Tuhua ribao also devotes much space to popular entertainment or performance of all kinds that coexisted with the foreign shadowplay, such as

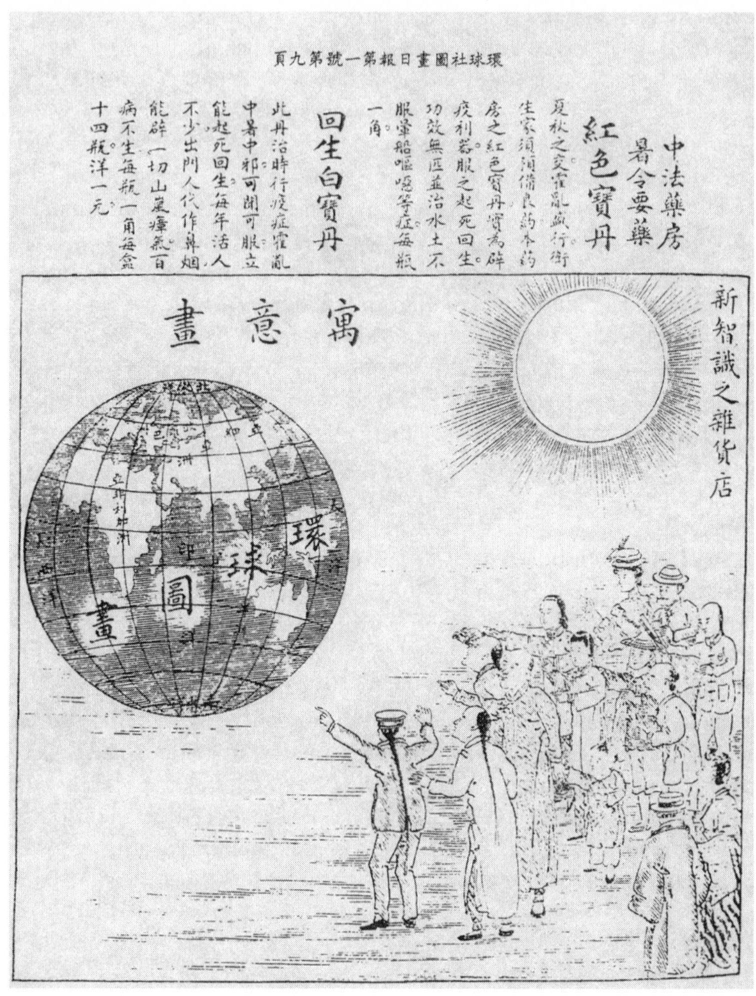

2.6 *Tuhua ribao* (*Illustrated Daily*): "A grocery store of new knowledge."

new-style Peking opera, the civilized play (*wenmingxi,* spoken drama using the vernacular), puppetry, storytelling, and magic shows. The clientele of this teahouse culture consisted mostly of urban commoners of varying means who patronized venues appropriate to the depth of their pockets. Both men and women attended shows, though the seating was sometimes segregated. The audience usually was seated around tables; waiters with big trays carried teapots, cups, and snacks to them. Fanning themselves, women chatted and gossiped. Such a space was often depicted as a hotbed of women's freedom and sexual desire and hence a constant source of public anxiety. For instance, the phenomenon of summer night gardens (*ye huayuan*) allegedly provided a haven for romantic rendezvous, and the illicit liaisons in certain theater houses between female spectators and actors scandalized the public.[35]

Not only is *huabao* linked to the new phenomenon of cinema through its coverage of contemporary mass culture, its thematic repertoire and presentation format are structurally similar to the cinema of attractions that characterized the early cinema before the institutionalization of narrative cinema and its corresponding spectatorship.[36] The term "cinema of attractions," coined by Tom Gunning, made a vital contribution to the new historical turn in cinema studies in the mid-1980s and provided a key to the reperiodization of film history before (and to some extent after) narrative integration and the solidification of classical Hollywood cinema. Gunning's concept challenges the previous text-based psychoanalytical theories of spectatorship. The latter posited the spectator as a homogeneous disembodied male (or hysterical female) voyeur inscribed in classical Hollywood cinema. Unlike the commercial narrative cinema produced within the parameters of the studio system and attendant narrative or genre formulas, the content and presentation of early cinema possessed qualities that created a more heterogeneous experience. While frontal tableaux and minimal camera movement or editing are often associated with the "primitive" form of early cinema, the true aesthetic and historical visage of early cinema is best understood not in terms of its evolutionary ("low") value with respect to later film forms but rather to be appreciated with regard to its unique mode of address and its social and cultural implications. The cinema of attractions, argues Gunning, consists "less of a way of presenting stories than as a way of presenting a series of views to an audience, fascinating because of their illusory power . . . and exoticism."[37] Rather than voyeurist, the appeal or form of this cinema is inherently "exhibitionist" and as such it offers a more diffused and alternative form of visual pleasure—a kinetically oriented experience of the cinema. Its mode of address hinges on display, immediacy, and participation, thereby mobilizing rather than repressing the viewer, as typified by the Hale's Tours shows of simulated train rides, which placed the audience at the center of the *motion* picture.

By virtue of its portability, affordability, novelty, and its nature as a commingled media, the illustrated newspaper prepared for the cinema and served as its companion; at the same time, cinema effectively functioned as a sort of *live* newspaper. The kaleidoscopic range of thematic content carried over to the silver screen in various forms and combinations. The twelve news categories covered by *Tuhua ribao* resemble the "genres" of early cinema: (1) scenic sites, (2) architecture in Shanghai, (3) portraits of famous historical figures around the world, (4) biographies of Chinese or foreign heroines, (5) fiction with social themes, (6) detective fiction, (7) world news, (8) social phenomena in Shanghai, (9) sketches of the marketplace, (10) the "grocery store" [column] of modern knowledge, (11) illustrated news of other cities, (12) miscellaneous.[38] The world covered by the illustrated newspapers was both microscopic and macroscopic; the multifarious knowledge and pleasures they disseminated explicitly catered to the petty urbanites at large. Readers around the country found themselves virtually in the same temporal and spatial realms, gaining practical know-how to navigate daily life in the metropolitan environment as well as basic knowledge in world politics and national culture. The vast number of readers who consumed illustrated newspapers to make sense of their rapidly changing world became modern subjects and citizens in the viewing process, forming a ready film audience.

Amusement Halls

While *huabao* presented an approximate or protocinematic experience through its visual immediacy, thematic variety, and low price, *youlechang* (amusement halls) that mushroomed in the 1910s and continued to thrive well into subsequent decades offered similar yet even more competitive pleasures, also at an affordable price. Not only could the urban attractions be experienced in three-dimensionality, the visitors were also encouraged to regard a trip to these funhouses as an attraction and diversion in itself. One Chinese scholar called the craze for amusement halls in the 1910s a "world fever" (*shijiere*), an apt description because many of these entertainment complexes included the word *shijie* (world) in their names.[39] But why "world"? What does that pervasive name tell us about the "worldliness" of this sort of secular Mecca of leisure and fun for the masses? And in what ways were the amusement halls related to early film experience?

A sociological survey of Shanghai public culture in 1933 defines these *worlds* as "*amusement resorts that cater to patrons with moderate means*" (emphasis in original).[40] They came in different sizes and capacities, but cheap admission and a variety of shows and services were standard. Louwailou (The Tower beyond Towers), founded by Jing Runsan in 1912, was essentially a big glassed-in teahouse on top of the Xinxin Wutai Theater on Zhejiang Road. The attractions featured there, in addition to the regular acrobatic and drum-singing numbers, included distortion mirrors imported from Holland near the entrance and, for an extra dime, an el-

2.7
The New World entertainment center.

2.8
The Great World entertainment center, ca. 1917.

evator that would take the visitor directly to the top floor.[41] The place was always crowded; many came for the fun while others simply wanted to be at the center of happenings in the city. Cheap admission, social conviviality, and diversity of programs and popular regional performances were particularly appealing to the working class and migrants.

The success of Louwailou inspired many more to follow suit. Xin Shijie (New World) and Da Shijie (the Great World) appeared in 1915 and 1917 respectively, each with imposing multistory structures and even more diverse attractions (figs. 2.7 and 2.8). Many more "worlds" of pleasure sprung up all over the city, in Chinese areas as well as in the concessions: Shenxian Shijie (The World of Fairies) on Simalu (now Fuzhou Road), facing the famous Qingliange Teahouse; Daqian Shijie (The World of Myriad Spectacles) on Shimeng Road in the French concession; and Xiao Shijie (Little World) near the north gate of the old city. The Great

World, which was the largest of all and remained open (despite several transmutations) until recently, was erected in 1917 at the crossroads of Edward Road and Tibet Road, a densely populated triangle zone that linked the different concessions. The simulacrum of urban attractions (and conveniences) within the Great World was made more complete with a daily newspaper and a twenty-four-hour bank of its own (to encourage visitors to stay longer and spend more money, of course). This artificial cosmos even boasted a mini zoo housing lions, tigers, and peacocks.[42]

The amusement halls were a kind of urban Coney Island and World's Fair à la Shanghainese, a "phantasmagoria which a person enters in order to be distracted."[43] They possessed the full-blown form of what Jonathan Hay calls the "architecture of spectacle" that emerged in late nineteenth-century Shanghai, "frankly embodying the excitement of big-city life as spectacle."[44] This type of architecture is crucial to the understanding of the emergence of the metropolitan crowd and mass spectatorship in urban centers in China. Most of these earthly wonderlands were located in the center of the city, in particular around the former Yangjingbang area. These entertainment venues catered mainly to ordinary city dwellers and functioned as a "virtual emporium of cultural motifs"[45] where diversity and hybridity—from local operas to skating rinks and mini golf courses—embodied and amplified the Yangjingbang legacy.

Unlike the more respectable and genre-specific public entertainment venues such as the theater house, where largely fixed and segregated seating limited movement and social intercourse, the amusement halls allowed women to delight in their accessibility, diversity, and freedom. With a few cents, they could spend a whole day inside the world of phantasmagoria until closing time at midnight, moving from booth to booth and stage to stage. The amusement halls were also dubbed "Love Exchange" (*Aiqing jiaoyisuo*), for lovers as well as those who sought romantic encounters with the courtesans from the nearby brothels clustered around Simalu.[46] The social marginality yet public visibility of the courtesans ironically gave them early exposure to new forms of urban attractions such as the "foreign shadowplay" and the "flying ship," which hovered in the open space above the large indoor arena. In these floating "worlds" the Butterfly writers would find material for their stories and scenarios, as well as their heroines. In his memoir, Bao Tianxiao, one of the foremost Butterfly writers, recalls his experiences in the amusement halls.

> I recall that it was at the Great World founded by Huang Chujiu where I first saw films. Inside there was also a small Peking opera

> theater called "Little Peking Troupe." It had a male-female mixed cast. Although it was inside the Great World, the theater charged a separate entrance fee. It was merely 30–40 cents. The show would start at 8 p.m. and end at midnight. It was then followed by movies, lasting till around 1:30 a.m. The movies were even cheaper, at just about 10–20 cents. Business was especially good at these hours. The "sisters of flowers" [courtesans] would come together, because they would have some free time by then. . . . There was no silver screen to speak of, only a piece of white cloth. The people in the movies jumped around even when walking, while the houses were also on the move. There were lots of exterior scenes, but the stories were confusing. . . . I often asked those "sisters of flowers": "Do you have any idea what kind of characters are in these movies?" They would reply, "We know there are three types of characters: women, good people, and bad people." Really succinct and clear, smart words spoken by smart girls.[47]

It was while working at this New World that Zhang Shichuan first spotted a lively Xuan Jinglin with pigtails inside the donkey riding court. Years later, working as director at Mingxing, Zhang rediscovered Xuan, who starred in *Amorous History of the Silver Screen*.[48] Besides being spectators or consumers, women also worked as performers in the amusement halls, presenting shows that sometimes played with or revised established cultural repertoire and crossed gender boundaries. In addition to the male-female mixed troupe stationed inside the Great World, as mentioned by Bao, the World of Fairies featured an all-women Peking opera troupe (*mao'er xi*).[49]

The popularity of amusement halls was contagious. Several major department stores on the Nanjing Road, including Xianshi (Sincere), Yong'an (Wing'an), and Xinxin (Sun Sun), also opened rooftop amusement gardens.[50] Sincere Company, founded in 1900 on the site of a teahouse, was among the first retail establishments to install a roof garden, which featured, among other things, an all-female Cantonese opera stage (fig. 2.9). The twenty-fifth anniversary album of the company is filled with poetic proclamations by the Butterfly school writers, eulogizing the "fairy" world of the garden and the elevators (*shengjiangji*) that lifted one's body as well as spirits. A poem penned by Li Liying captures the thrill of entering this otherworldly urban jungle:

> Going straight up to the "Tower that Touches the Stars"
> Enjoying the panorama by the railings
> Precariously, the building stands on the boulevard
> Trees far away hint at a cool autumn

2.9 Roof Garden on top of Sincere Department Store.

> The city feels near with the sound of the crowd
> The theaters opens with flickering electric shadows
> This paradise is unique and hardly vulgar
> Men and women flaunt their fashionable and unconventional style.[51]

The architecture of amusement halls and rooftop gardens is particularly conducive to physical interactivity and the production of a "mobilized gaze" through a kind of "window shopping," which, as Anne Friedberg argues, was characteristic of the perception and experience of early cinema.[52] A foreign visitor's observation connects this mobilized gaze with a mobilized "taste":

> [The crowd] shuffles slowly from one hall into another, here watching a juggler or magician, there listening to the high-pitched squeaking singsong of a girl, sipping tea on a rock roof-garden, taking a donkey-ride in a miniature menagerie, laughing at their distorted images in concave mirrors, dictating a family letter or taking a bite of some delicacy from a far away province of China.[53]

These structures—amusement complex or rooftop recreational gardens—were derived from late imperial Chinese gardens (as a miniature world) and teahouses; they were also inspired by the world's fairs. Vestiges of traditional landscaping were juxtaposed with modern building materials and equipment, particularly the elevator and electric lighting. Due to the high land price in central Shanghai, the exquisite, elite hermitism associated with gardens or pavilions found in the architecture of elegant leisure in the Jiangnan region gave way to multistory establishments replete with sights and sounds.[54] The combination of horizontal panoramas (or series of views) with the thrill of vertical movements (enhanced by elevators) puts the patrons onto a constant roller coaster of visual and kinesthetic sensations as well as virtual tours of the world. The diversity of attractions, popular genres, and modes of presentation and address traversed the boundaries between the old and new, Chinese and foreign, high and low. These constant border crossings helped to turn the urban crowd into a worldly—that is, both cosmopolitan and vernacular—body of spectators and, to some extent, public actors.

The structures of the Great World and the New World were most representative of this integrated architecture. Both were located at major intersections and had a circular facade; their size and capacity gave them the imposing air of a department store. The former was an extended two-story building resembling a sports arena when viewed from above. It was decorated with several Chinese-style pavilions symmetrically arranged on top of the second floor, and large commercial advertisements were painted on the outer walls. In 1925, after a major fire, the structure was rebuilt with four stories and an eight-floor tower, which looked like a pagoda yet included definitive baroque features, and was placed on top of the main entrance. Inside, in addition to the assortment of entertainment booths, there were various "scenic" spots modeled after the Chinese garden. On the meandering elevated passageway (*tianqiao*) linking various booths, stages, and pavilions, visitors of different ages, genders, and classes brushed shoulders, made associations, and even brokered deals (fig. 2.10). The New World, on the other hand, was a compact three-story building with identically shaped arched windows and balconies on both the inside and outside, so it was easy to see and be seen. Before later renovations, it also featured a central tower and Chinese-style eaves. The complex boasted Shanghai's first skating rink and billiard room, in addition to a completely tiled and well-lit underground passageway, which was decorated with an aquarium and linked its North and South buildings across Jing'ansi Road (Bubbling Well Road, now Nanjing Xilu).[55]

Because amusement halls were among the first venues of film exhibition in China, they occupy a significant place in early Chinese film history. Their importance is underscored by their contemporaneity with the

2.10 The Tianqiao (Heavenly Bridge) inside the Great World.

beginnings of domestic film production by people closely associated with the culture of amusement halls, such as the Butterfly writers and members of the civilized play troupes. Both played a crucial part in the formation of a domestic cinema. The amusement hall, more than the illustrated press, fostered an embodied metropolitan mode of spectatorship with a mobilized gaze trained by the variety of live performances and attractions. Inclined toward a "taste for reality," this viewing habit prepared them for a new medium that would synthesize and transform the experience of being metropolitan subjects.

THE PETTY URBANITES AS COSMOPOLITAN AUDIENCE

Because these media and experiences intertwined in the public space, readers of the illustrated papers and visitors to the amusement halls and rooftop gardens actually constituted the early film audiences. The "optical unconscious" embedded in these earlier or contiguous forms of participatory reading and viewing gave rise to a mobilized virtual gaze that absorbed urban shocks and sugarcoated the attractions. It also participated in the formation of a mass mediated vernacular culture, of which cinema was an integral component. These overlapping bodies of audiences belonged to the broad social base of petty urbanites—street vendors, clerks, students, actors, migrants, courtesans, and middle-lower-class men and women in general.[56] As a broadly and vaguely defined social class, the petty urbanites were a composite urban formation of the traditional and modern nonagrarian workers, small merchants, and the petty bourgeoisie. They included an emerging white-collar class (of both genders) that staffed banks, law and accounting offices, hotels, and department stores.[57] The majority of them occupying lower or lower-middle class positions are *xiao* or "petty" because of their nonelite socioeconomical status (not, however, at the bottom of society), young age (often because of their immigrant origins), and limited education and outlook (yet endowed with a measure of cosmopolitan spirit). For the most part they were residents of the *longtang* and modest apartment buildings. Their cultural tastes and commercial acumen, a conspicuous marker of the Shanghai social character, were eclectic, curious, and worldly (*shisu*) in both senses of the word. The petty urbanites approached the middlebrow. Their participation in the production and consumption of a burgeoning mass culture gave rise to a distinctive metropolitan culture, which voraciously mixed popular entertainment with cultural aspirations, cosmopolitan yearnings with everyday concerns. Though conceived as petty in its relative social position, the petty urbanites were large in number and enormously significant in their social and political potential. As their population and demographic expanded in Chinese domains as well as the European concessions (in residential areas, entertainment establishments, and industrial and professional sectors), they became the very flesh and blood of the city.

The elasticity of the social and cultural orientation of the petty urbanites, both fostered and exploited by consumerism, frustrated the elite May Fourth intellectuals devoted to modernity as a teleological project for national strengthening. In fact, some of them are responsible for coining the term *xiao shimin,* a pejorative word that persists today as a stereotype. They regarded the petty urbanites as an anarchic social body corrupted by both "feudal" values (because of the rural origin of many migrants) and modern evils of the city (due to their economical aspirations and urbane tastes). In his essay on "The Feudal Arts of the Petty Urbanites," Shen Yanbing (pen name Mao Dun), a writer known for his realist novels on Shanghai, reacted unfavorably to the popularity of the Butterfly fiction and popular film genres such as the martial arts film and family melodrama that attracted a wide following across China.[58] Zhou Zuoren, a representative of the *Jingpai* (the Beijing school, as opposed to *Haipai,* the Shanghai school) writer, attributed the emergence of the petty urbanite class in any modernizing Chinese city to a certain "Shanghai air" (*Shanghai qi*) that infected and corrupted their mind and body.[59]

The formation of this massive urban crowd paralleled the emergence of an incipient film culture in Shanghai and beyond. To be sure, when the "Occidental shadowplay" or electric motion pictures entered the teahouses and theater houses around the turn of the century, it was by no means a commanding medium. Films first appeared in teahouses in Shanghai in 1896 and in Beijing in 1902, but the early film exhibitions by traveling foreign and Chinese showmen quickly spread to other trading ports and cities. At that stage, cinema was but one novel attraction among many and was seen as a variation on—or extension of—the existing puppet shadowplay. Before long, the power of cinema increased dramatically as the movie-only venues were built to house the growing number of films and audiences. Several Chinese entrepreneurs also began to produce films set in China and about Chinese lives. It is widely believed that attempts were made to record and exhibit Peking opera episodes by the Fengtai Photo Studio in Beijing, beginning in 1905, but a studio fire abruptly ended the project. Beijing ceased to be the main site of Chinese film production for other reasons as well. Some scholars have attributed the abortive start to the conservative attitude of the more homogenous Beijing citizenry, as well as that of the imperial family, toward what was seen as a new and dangerous medium. In Shanghai, however, the worldly population, including the petty urbanites, supplied both enthusiastic audiences and amateur filmmakers. The unique Yangjingbang style of modernity also contributed to the ready acceptance of this novel technology and the ferment of a less ideologically charged alternative vernacular culture. Thus, some argue that it was historically "accidental" for Beijing to be the first site for Chinese productions, whereas it was "inevitable" for Shanghai to become the cradle of Chinese cinema.[60]

Unlike the Peking opera recordings produced in Beijing, the early cinema of attractions made in Shanghai were distinctively concerned with contemporary subjects, ranging from current affairs, slapstick comedies, and scenic panoramas to educational materials. From around 1900, a handful of foreign sojourners in Shanghai shot footage of local street scenes for exhibition at local venues, as well as for export. In the 1910s, many Chinese picked up secondhand cameras and began experimenting with the medium. The number of films made domestically and exhibited in Shanghai during this period was still limited, yet the range of subject matter and production modes was remarkable. Foreign-Chinese collaboration was sporadic yet still the prevalent mode in the early 1910s; in the later half of the decade all-Chinese productions emerged and eventually led to the establishment of a domestic film industry. The Asia Company, cofounded in 1913 by Zhang Shichuan, Zheng Zhengqiu, and a couple of Americans, shot its first films in an outdoor "studio" on Hong Kong Road near the Bund. The dozen short comedies (mostly one- or two-reelers, except for the four-reeler, *The Difficult Couple*) depict everyday scenarios of the petty urbanites—country bumpkins having fun or running into trouble in the city, bicycle accidents, gambling brawls, and satires on arranged marriage. The titles alone offer a taxonomy of the *xiao shimin* taste:

> *Thieves on Trial* (*Da Chenghuang,* literally, "hitting the god at the city temple")
> *A Gambler Plays Possum* (*Dutu zhuansi*)
> *The Silly in Town God's Temple* (*Erbaiwu baixiang Chenghuangmiao*)
> *A Funny Love Affair* (*Huaji aiqing*)
> *Bride Meets Ghost* (*Xinniang huajiao yu Bai Wuchang,* a.k.a. *Huo Wuchang*)
> *Bicycle Accident* (*Jiaotache chuanghuo,* a.k.a. *Hengchong zhizhuang*)
> *A Deal* (*Laoshao yiqi,* literally, "the old and the young swaps wife")
> *Die for Marriage* (a.k.a. *The Difficult Couple; Nanfu nanqi*)
> *Family's Blood* (*Sha zi bao,* a.k.a. *Jiating xue*)
> *A Corrupt Official Returned* (*Tanguan ronggui*)
> *Mascot Is Coming Here* (*Wufu lingmeng,* a.k.a. *The Playboy Monk, Fengliu heshang*)
> *New Camellia* (*Xin Chahua*)
> *An Overnight Fidget* (*Yiye bu'an*)[61]

The subjects of these shorts are not entirely unique to China; themes such as the country rube's encounter with the city were staple ingredients in early cinema as a whole.[62] They echoed the thematic repertoire of, among others, Max Linder and Charlie Chaplin, who were popular among the Chinese audiences and embodied a global image of the petty urbanites and immigrants, complete with their upwardly mobile but precarious social positions. Yet these films, which are set (mostly on location) both in the Old City and in the concessions, carry geographical indices of Shanghai and specific cultural inflections. For example, the setting of the *City God Temple,* the contested cultural practice of arranged marriage, and popular beliefs in retribution and ghosts are featured in this group of comedic sketches that portray the ambivalence of modern life. They recorded the everyday experience, the pleasure, and the anxiety that petty urbanites faced through a mixture of old and new situations and choices in the metropolis. Several films address the issue of money and moral corruption in an intensely commercialized society. One of the films, *The Shop Apprentice Who Lost His Lottery Ticket,* offers a satire of the capitalist lottery system and its problematic promise of social mobility. The apprentice is so worried that he may lose his ticket that he glues it on a door. As it turns out, he has the winning number, but unable to peel the ticket off, he has to carry the whole door to claim his prize.[63] The comedic mode (*huaji*) that solicits both laughter and reflection, much like the distortion mirrors at the amusement halls, accentuates the incongruity and absurdity of the "composite allurement" of a Chinese metropolis driven by an inflated money economy and commodity culture. Deploying a film "language" of imported and local vernaculars, these early Chinese films made in Shanghai articulate a cinematic Yangjingbang that is derived from the encounter between the city and the world, the petty urbanites and a new mass medium.

The production of story films of varying length coincided with the mushrooming of film exhibition venues in the city. The intertwining of cinema and the city thus receives more salient expression in the physical forms and social function of this novel kind of architecture. It includes the teahouses, theater houses (which often featured the interlocking film-dramatic play, or *lianhuanxi*), and increasingly the exclusive cinemas, which sprung up around the *longtang* residential areas in central Shanghai and some outlying areas. While the theater houses were built and owned by mostly Chinese concerns, the first movie houses were predominantly foreign establishments, such as the chain run by the famous Spanish showman Antonio Ramos who started his career in the Qingliange Teahouse. Within a few years following Ramos's Hongkew Theater, which was built on a skating rink at the intersection of Zhapu Road and Haining Road in 1908, a number of cinemas quickly became new urban attractions. They included Victoria (Weiduoliya) at Sichuan Road and Haining Road, Apollo (Aipuluo) on North Sichuan Road, Helen (Ailun) at Haining Road and Bei Jiangxi Road, Olympic (Xialingpike, later called Embassy) on Jing'ansi Road (Bubbling Well Road), Republic (Gonghe) on Minguo Road, Isis (Shanghai) on Bei Sichuang Road, and Willies at the intersection of Haining Road and Zhapu Road (fig. 2.11).[64]

While these foreign-owned establishments showed mostly imported films, the large theater houses Gongwutai (Hubei Road and Hankou Road) and Xinxin Wutai (Hubei Road and Jiujiang Road) provided provisional screening space for Chinese films.[65] Incidentally, the early shorts were mostly made by people involved in the theater circles (notably Zheng Zhengqiu and his troupe) in their spare time. *The Difficult Couple,* which is adapted from one of Zheng's plays, screened at Xinxin Wutai Theater in September 1913 along with a documentary about the uprising in Shanghai in the revolution, *The War in Shanghai* (*Shanghai zhanzheng*).[66] This venue also premiered a few Chinese productions in the ensuing years, including *Victims of Opium* (*Heji yuanhun,* 1916), based on a phenomenally successful play about the destruction of a family by opium addiction, which had been staged in the same theater.[67]

2.11 A cinema built in the 1920s: Willies Theatre.

The well-appointed purpose-built cinemas and the cinematic use of large theater houses, as opposed to the more hybrid, cheaper teahouses and amusement halls, significantly altered the landscape of the local film culture; the venue changes signaled the emergence of narrative film and also a certain gentrification of cinema. This trend was in part a reaction to the encroachment of long foreign and serial films (such as Italian epic costume dramas and Diva films, French film d'art, and the newly established Hollywood narrative cinema). At the same time, this change resulted from a domestic discourse and public debate centered on the ontology of cinema and the relationship between enlightenment and entertainment, which will be discussed further in chapter 4.

VISUAL AND OTHER MODERN PLEASURES

After the cinema became a legitimate cultural institution, widely accepted as a young "seventh sister" of the other established arts, the film experience in Chinese cities, especially Shanghai, continued to be embedded in and actively produced the polymorphous space of urban modernity. Such an expanded experience involved a cluster of cultural practices and venues beyond the confines of the theater. As elsewhere in the world, the history of early Chinese film culture is emphatically also a history of the moviegoing experience, imbricated with the larger sensorial and libidinal economy of a modernizing society. It is also a history of film-related publications including fan magazines, which, due to the lack of a substantial number of extant films, provide the richest sources for the understanding of early film culture. The illustrated newspapers had inculcated in the reader an "optical unconscious" that prepared them for the moving images and texts on the silver screen. The print culture surrounding the booming film industry underwent a significant expansion in the 1920s. New voluminous film magazines and other film-related publications offered indispensable assistance to help viewers make sense of the moving images and participate in an expansive film culture.

In the first half of the 1920s, the print industry was also shifting en masse to standardized modern vernacular Chinese. The increase of the vernacular press during the period was not simply an after-effect of the vernacular movement initiated by May Fourth intellectuals in the late 1910s. The vernacular press contributed to the movement in its own right by providing concrete forums and tools for mass literacy, yet the effect disturbed radical May Fourth writers when the vernacular movement inadvertently energized Butterfly-style literature and the film industry. The popular urban fiction provided not only raw material for screen adaptations but also produced China's first generation of screenwriters, which I will discuss more in chapter 5.

The rise of the Mandarin Ducks and Butterflies literature was intimately related to the rise of Shanghai as a commercial and cultural center in the late Qing and early Republican periods. The rather florid nickname accorded to the literature allegedly comes from a poetic couplet in the late Qing courtesan novel *Traces of Flower and Moon* (*Hua yue hen*), which recycles the poetic trope of paired Mandarin ducks and butterflies as an allegory for sentimental relationships between scholars and courtesans.[68] Until the 1910s, Butterfly literature was written primarily in a semiclassical language and included a large bulk of modified translations of international urban fiction, including the Sherlock Holmes's detective stories. It appealed to a reasonably well-educated urban middle-class (consisting largely of the disenfranchised former rural gentry families that moved to the city), partly because of the relatively expensive cost of books, as modern print technology was still a novelty and implied luxury.

This picture was dramatically altered in the 1920s. The paradigmatic shift in the literary market concurred with a radical reconfiguration of readership, as Butterfly writers adopted and updated the old vernacular style and produced more original stories instead of producing extrapolated translations. The literature as a whole became commercially accessible to a wider audience as the prices of books and magazines lowered. Serialization in daily newspapers also increased affordability and access. The new readership included a large segment of lower social groups—readers who had acquired basic literacy through various institutions, such as the new-style schools and evening classes. The visible consequences brought by this surge in the vernacular trend to the urban scene are not, however, merely limited to the expanded readership per se. Rather, the restructured reading space and mode of reception carved out a significant space for privacy and fantasy. In a fast-growing metropolis like Shanghai, the constant stimuli and distractions coming from the street, work, and marketplaces induced the desire in the urban dwellers to retreat to the quietude at home and seek relief and comfort in books and magazines. Perry Link reasons that this popularized need for privacy was part of the "general inward-turning tendency," though he stops short of elaborating further. It is not surprising that this inward-turning took place concomitantly with the gradual dissolution of a traditional vernacular "reading" space, in which fiction, or *xiaoshuo,* was often performed by storytellers and listened to by an illiterate or semiliterate audience in teahouses and marketplaces.[69]

The new interiorized reading space, however, was not a totally homogenized cocoon of isolation. In fact, a large number of "readers" also found themselves enjoying Butterfly literature through forms of storytelling such as films, comic books, stage plays, and drum-singing storytelling.[70] Popular fiction thus offered writers and readers a host of opportunities to take part in an increasingly commercialized vernacular space, which in turn redefined privacy and interiority. In the 1910s, a publisher was content with a circulation of 3,000 copies for a book or magazine in order to cover production cost; in the 1920s, the multimedia dissemination of most popular Butterfly stories reached at least into the hundreds of thousands, if not more than a million.[71] The purpose-built cinema emerged in this period was at once a visible public venue enacting Butterfly literary sensibilities and an interiorized comfort zone for the more isolated viewer. This spatial and cognitive reorientation in both the reading and viewing experience effectively bridged private and public domains. In short, Butterfly fiction metamorphosed from a late Qing literary genre written for the amusement of the leisured and educated classes into a lucrative multimedia business. It became a protean component and catalyst of a modern vernacular culture, out of which early Chinese cinema was born and in turn reshaped the literature substantially.

Verbal discourses on film previously only appeared sporadically in the form of spontaneous reviews and translated articles in newspapers or news magazines, and in the form of the so-called shadowplay story (*yingxi xiaoshuo*) or film story (*dianying xiaoshuo*—summary plots of foreign films) in literary magazines or booklets.[72] By the mid-1920s discussions of film had become an established mode of vernacular expression. Readers of Butterfly fiction, many of whom would presumably also attend films based on the literature as well, overlapped with those readers of film publications, especially fan magazines and film programs. The two comprehensive encyclopedia of the film world in China published in 1927, Cheng Shuren's *China Film Yearbook* and Xu Chiheng's *Filmdom in China,* featured bibliographies of periodicals, popular books, early textbooks, and a "film beauty calendar." Cheng's book boasts a complete list of special issues (*tekan*) on specific productions from twenty-one film companies based in Shanghai, complete with mailing addresses.[73] Xu's book, on the other hand, gives an annotated introduction to a dozen film publications including magazines, pictorials and Cheng's book as well.[74]

In short, the expanded vernacular press provided a fertile ground for the emergent film culture. At the same time, through the adaptation of Butterfly literature onto the screen, early filmmakers were able to incorporate a vast portion of the reading public into the moviegoing enterprise. Although China's first film magazine had been published in 1921,[75] it was not until some years later that a boom of film magazines and daily newspaper columns on film appeared; at this point, a specifically film-related discourse began to play an influential role in shaping the film industry and the moviegoing experience. These film publications include *Yingxi congbao* (Shadowplay Gazetteer, February 1921, Beijing), *Dianying zhoubao / Tiaowu shijie* (Movie Weekly / The Dancing World, November 1921, Beijing), *Yingxi zazhi* (Film Magazine, December 1921, Shanghai), and *Chenxing* (Morning Stars, 1922, Shanghai). *Yingxi zazhi* was the first full-fledged fan magazine devoted mostly to foreign films and *Chenxing* committed itself to promoting Chinese films. The mid-1920s saw the publication of more film magazines, such as *Dianying zazhi* (Movie Monthly), *Yingxi chunqiu* (Movie Weekly), *Yingxi shijie* (Motion Picture World), and so on (figs. 2.12 and 2.13).[76] Between 1921 and 1926, there were nearly thirty film magazines in print at one point or another.[77] During the 1930s, with cinema becoming a more widespread national pas-

2.12–13 Film magazines of the 1920s: *Dianying zazhi* and *Yingxi shijie.*

time, far more film magazines appeared. Early in the decade, the left-wing playwrights and critics launched a concerted takeover of the film and arts supplements of almost all the major newspapers in Shanghai, including the widely circulated *Shenbao.* The colorful world of film publications catered to a diverse group of fan, and readers had varying knowledge of and involvement in the film medium. Leading studios such as Mingxing and Lianhua ran their own trade journals, while film buffs with a literary or theater background would also occasionally spring onto the scene with their individually colored magazines. Some magazines catered to laymen fans, others were designed mainly as publicity outlets, and still others featured more sophisticated reviews and criticism.

Film publications were also a form of entertainment as well as a verbal and visual extension of the moviegoing experience. Beside the regular magazines and topical books, studios produced special issues (*tekan*) to promote specific releases, often sold in the theater lobby as a more authoritative guide than regular theater program pamphlets (*shuomingshu*). Film magazines or trade journals, though often just as short-lived as the many film companies that came and went, provided moviegoers with an amplified film experience. The readers were grateful for a reading space to linger in before or after seeing films. They could learn about plots, institutional organization of the industry, film technologies, biographies of Chinese or foreign stars, directors, and even cinematographers, as well as forecasts of what films were in production. Through their active participation in the magazines, the readers also engaged in the shaping of the broad film culture.

Dianying zhoubao (Saturday Screen News), published by the Morning Society (Chenshe) in Shanghai, started a new edition in April 1925. The editor-in-chief proudly justified the renumbering of the magazine:

> The previous edition was only a one-page newspaper that hardly satisfied the expectations of our readers. They sent in numerous letters asking us to expand its volume and publish it as a magazine. Now we are fulfilling their wishes. As regards the content and editing method, we have also made some changes. So we should not be held accountable for being inconsistent. We are "setting up a separate kitchen" [with the new edition], so why not have the changes?[78]

One of the eye-catching changes suggested by the editor was the adoption of copperplate printing, which gave the magazine a colored cover and other photo illustrations, making the publication more visually appealing. The large size and attractive appearance of the magazine, however, was not meant to contradict the avowed seriousness of the editors. The opening address of the new edition announced that the function of the magazine was to promote the development of the domestic film industry, an important force in revitalizing the Chinese economy. For this lofty mission, the magazine would limit the scope of the public discussion to that of "film scholarship, history, and news," and exclude any sensational news about stars or groundless attacks on any specific persons. With the third issue of the new edition, the magazine was already able to demonstrate the successful implementation of its policy. A student sent in a letter expressing his excitement at the appearance of the new edition:

> I am a student who is very fond of going to the movies, and especially like to watch Chinese films. As soon as there is a Chinese film showing somewhere, I will hurry to see it like a magnet attracted to iron. Yet, I often found myself disappointed afterwards because there were no adequate film publications to guide viewers like me.

He continued to say that, although there had been other publications, they were either shabbily printed or often erroneous in content. He found the new edition very "exquisite and beautiful" and hoped it would adhere to its principles. As a responsive and responsible reader he even made some specific suggestions, such as limiting the number of illustrations of foreign films, opening a reader's debate corner, and avoiding inserting advertisements in the middle of an article because it obstructed the reader's sight.[79] Instead of an American star, the cover girl of the next issue featured the Chinese actress Zhang Meilie. She starred in several hits in the mid-1920s, including the knight-errant romance *Love After Robbery* (*Jiehou yuan,* Lianhe, 1925), lavishly advertised in the same issue.

Not only did film magazines function as a public sphere for disseminating the films being shown in town, they were also the most strategic sites for advertising commodities. Reading a film magazine simulated both the moviegoing and window-shopping experience. The April 1925 issue of *Yingxi chunqiu* (Movie Weekly) carried a set of peculiar advertisements. Under the half-page advertisement for *True Love* (*Zhen'ai,* Xin Dalu, 1925)—the "first ever grand tragedy in China," based on a story by the Butterfly writer Zhou Shoujuan—there is also an advertisement for Dayou walnut snacks (fig. 2.14). The titillating caption reads: "Watching a shadowplay and eating Dayou's new walnuts product: isn't that heaven!" The description is written in the format of a film program, detailing its attractions and benefits for health. A similar advertisement for the famous Guanshengyuan (located on Nanjing Road) candies appeared

2.14 Ads for the film *True Love* (1925) (top) and for walnut snacks (lower right) in *Yingxi Chunqiu.*

76 |

2.15 "Window shopping" Lux soap (featuring the late Ruan Lingyu). The Chinese characters on the top read *Memorial Portrait* (from *Lianhua huabao,* vol. 5, no. 2).

everywhere in *Yingxi shenghuo* in the early 1930s: "Watching a shadow-play and eating Guanshengyuan's candies. The taste as well as the fun are beyond words." Through such juxtaposition, visual pleasure is collated with the pleasure of the palate and the well-being of the body, and snack concessions were already an integral part of the moviegoing experience. In fact, the connection between moviegoing and eating as a combined aesthetic pleasure surfaced most palpably in the Yangjingbang transliteration of the word *movie* (*muwei*) which literally means the "taste of the screen."

Film magazines also contributed directly to the formation of a star system and its attendant mythology. The stars perceived themselves to be, and were in turn also used as, icons for a modern lifestyle, especially fashion. Certain advertisements skillfully exploit stars' fame by putting them on the screen of the print advertisement to speak for manufactured products. *Lianhua huabao,* published in the early 1930s, ran a prominent advertisement for Lux fragrant soap (*Lishi xiangzhao*) in almost every issue. Potential consumers are pictured as spectators sitting in a movie theater and engaged in conversations about how beautiful a certain star on the screen looks (for example, Chen Yanyan or Ruan Lingyu) and how smooth her skin appears (fig. 2.15). The implied reason is, of course, that she uses Lux soap. More intriguingly, the advertisement in each issue has a slightly different graphic format, and the star occupying the screen is never the same. These serial ads also provide a glimpse of the actual auditorium atmosphere, which—judging from the images of these talking heads—was really not so quiet. Theaters were clearly spaces that interlaced with the urban lifestyle as a whole and allowed for polymorphous identifications.

SILVERLAND AND SPORTS WORLD

While there was a heightened interest in narrative for the exclusive film theater in the 1920s and 1930s, this picture of cinematic containment is complicated by an intricate network of urban spaces that proliferated during this time—sports venues, department stores, cafés, jazz bars, and dance halls. The cross-fertilization of the cinematic and other urban experiences, especially dancing and sports, is manifested in film magazines as well. The amphibious *Xin yinxing yu tiyu shijie* (Silverland Sports World) gives equal coverage to film and sports (fig. 2.16).[80] Another magazine has an ingenious dual set-up, with one cover entitled *Dianying zazhi* (Film Magazine) and the other *Tiaowu shijie* (The World of Dancing), assuming an overlapping readership consisted of moviegoers and dance-hall patrons. One of the most famous movie-dance crossover stars is Liang

Saizhen, whose fans followed her from movie theaters to the dance floor inside the Dahu Dance Hall. In 1935, she and her three sisters, two of whom also worked as dance hostesses, played themselves in Lianhua's *Four Sisters* (*Si zimei*), a film about four dancing girls in fashionable Shanghai.[81] As Gong Jianong wrote in his memoir, the favorite destination of night outings for actors and actresses was the Carlton Dance Hall near the Park Hotel, which also had a theater under the same name.[82] More than mere leisure space for the movie stars, the dance hall and sports venues also became ubiquitous spatial tropes in the films produced in the 1930s.

Queen of Sports (1934) was a silent classic written and directed by Sun Yu. As in many other contemporary films about a country girl going to—and sometimes losing her way in—the urban jungle in Shanghai, it is filled with typical tropes of metropolitan life. The rise and fall of the queen of sports Lin Yin, played by Li Lili, parallels her zigzagging trajectory between the stadium and the dance hall. While (good) sports were represented as a means to discipline the body and nurture the mind, social dancing stood for excessive pleasure and decadence. The film opens with a steamship arriving at a harbor on the Huangpu River. Using her tree-climbing skills, the excited Lin gets to the top of the chimney to gain a bird's eye view of the city. After disembarking, she rides in an open car with her relatives and admires the skyscrapers in downtown Shanghai. Lin starts her new life as an aspiring athlete enrolled at a boarding sports school for women. The school is cinematically rendered through a series of scenes in which the girls go through rigorous training. From morning exercises in bed to brushing teeth to taking showers to training in the field to studying anatomy or the international history of sports in the classroom, everything is executed in an efficient fashion. Lin Yin's skills and diligence lead her to break several records at the National Sports Games (*Quanguo yundonghui*). However, intoxicated by the success that has made her a "Queen of Sports" in the press, Lin's lifestyle begins to show signs of change (fig. 2.17).[83] She reads fan letters in the classroom and wears high heels and sexy dresses; she also allows herself to be courted by college playboys and attends dance parties. Lin learns a big lesson at the National Trials for the Far East Games (*Yuandong yuxuan dahui*): that the true spirit of sports lies in collective effort, not individual glamour. The didactic message about the need to harness the individual body—in particular, the female body—for nation building is not to be missed. But the many hyperbolic scenes in which the girls flaunt their youthful legs, either in the dormitory, on the running track or the dance floor, forestall any facile moralist containment of the energy and modernity embodied by the female athletes.

2.16 *Xin yinxing yu tiyu* (*Silverland Sports World*)

2.17 *Queen of Sports* (1934) with Li Lili (1915–2005). (Courtesy of the China Film Archive)

The mass appeal of *Queen of Sports* is attributable to its fictional reworking of a real sports event. The director Sun Yu wrote the script right before the opening of the Fifth National Games held in Nanjing in October 1933. On the first day of the Games, shooting crews from three major Shanghai studios—Mingxing, Tianyi, and Lianhua—were present at the stadium. Sun and his crew members, representing Lianhua, tried to shoot the film "on location," but had to abandon the plan after a few days because the authorities only allowed the shooting of documentaries.[84] Some footage the crew shot, however, was instantly shown in local theaters, and partially incorporated into the completed feature. Cheng Ying, now an elderly Shanghai woman whom I interviewed, told me that she was an avid moviegoer and dance aficionado, and for that reason she was chosen as an extra in the film. According to Cheng a large part of the on-location shooting took place in the newly finished Jiangwan Stadium, built to host the Sixth National Games in 1935. The stadium was part of the Great Shanghai Project (*Da Shanghai jihua*), an effort by the Nationalist government to create a separate Chinese-ruled Shanghai in the northern suburbs of the semicolonial metropolis. Lin's roommates, who displayed their muscular legs and white teeth in the dormitory, were played by students (including my informant) from an actual women's sports college located near the studio. True to the conception of the film as an intertext between fiction and documentary, or for that matter, the "silverland" and "sports world," Li Lili's fans entered the film to play her partners. The girls were treated to an exclusive screening after the film was finished.[85] Although *Queen of Sports* might be a rather particular case, it shows that a film cannot be simply treated as a closed representational entity. As a cultural object, it is produced and circulates in a complex network of cultural practices and reception. Between different but frequently overlapping audiences or patrons—of film, sports, dancing—who are part of the "games," the boundaries were never clearly demarcated.

METROPOLITAN SOUND AND CINEMATIC WRITING

The advent of sound in the late 1920s and early 1930s not only aroused intense public anxiety toward modern technology and the intrusion of American talkies, it also drastically reordered the hierarchy of the senses. To be sure, the movie theater in the silent period was never quiet. In fact there always existed a plethora of sound practices in the form of either musical accompaniment (phonograph or orchestra) or the live speech of an interpreter (like the *benshi* in Japan), for the benefit of the illiterate and to generate a communal atmosphere of storytelling. The arrival of sound, partly due to the high cost required for changing or upgrading production and exhibition equipment, initially had very mixed effect on the moviegoing experience in China. The undubbed American talkies were only embraced by a certain stratum of spectators who went to watch and listen to them out of sheer curiosity or simply for the pleasure, and in some instances under the pretense, of "understanding" a foreign tongue.[86]

It has almost become a cliché that Chinese silent narrative film (especially the left-wing cinema) reached its golden age in the 1930s despite the advent of sound. Reasons behind this are so complex that it would require a separate investigation beyond the space allowed here. As I will discuss in considerable detail in chapter 8, the film scene of the golden age was far from being homogeneously "silent"; nor was it aesthetically or ideologically uniform. The slow transition to sound in China, roughly between 1930 and 1936, was characterized by the cohabitation of different temporalities as well as cultural imaginaries and practices. All-silent, semisilent, partial-sound and total-sound films, which were produced and projected with an array of technologies, coexisted. *Metropolitan Scenes* (*Dushi fengguang,* 1935), *Lianhua Symphony* (*Lianhua jiaoxiangqu,* 1937, an omnibus production with eight films of varying length and technologies), and *Street Angel* (*Malu tianshi,* 1937) were all Lianhua productions incorporating sound in various ways. These are only a few examples for the kaleidoscopic multiplicity of this transition period. The advent of sound, in conjunction with other audiovisual entertainment forms such as the radio and revue theater, definitely foregrounded aural enjoyment. The dynamic but troubled coexistence of the visual register and sound track in this protracted transition constantly reorganized the sensorial economy as well as the cultural and ideological hierarchy of technological resources.

These polyphonic and multisensory events took place both inside and outside the movie theaters. They were also prepared by or carried over into film magazines. Increasingly we find song-sheets inserted in the magazines, counterbalancing the verbal and visual sections. The early 1930s was a time when film critics and writers of conflicting aesthetic and ideological interests camped out in various film magazines or supplements, generating a veritable polemical symphony on the social function and meaning of the cinema. In 1934, the left critics began to stage an attack on the so-called soft cinema (*ruanxing dianying*) represented by Liu Na'ou, Huang Jiamo, and others of the Yihua Company, with regard to the relationship between technology (including the use of sound) and ideology, aesthetics, and politics. The verbal battle culminated in 1936, when the national distress reached a new point of crisis. The roots of the "soft" aesthetic, often condensed in the humorous sentence, "cinema is ice-cream for the eyes, and a sofa for the heart," must be traced back to a slightly earlier moment. When *Xiandai dianying* (Modern Screen), a film magazine edited by Huang and Liu, began to publish a series of articles advocating the soft film aesthetic in 1933, the "New Sensationalist" (*xin ganjue pai*) literature was reaching its full bloom.[87] The Chinese term for New Sensationalism was directly borrowed from the Japanese *shinkankaku ha,* which flourished as a literary school in 1924–27. Liu Na'ou, who grew up in Japan, first translated *shinkankaku ha* writings into Chinese.[88] This modernist group of writers clustered around a series of journals: *Wugui lieche* (*Trackless Train*), *Xin wenyi* (*La nouvelle littérature*) and *Xiandai* (*Les contemporains*).[89] A great deal of Chinese literary criticism has been unleashed against the New Sensationalist petty-bourgeois sensibility and decadence since the 1930s and onwards. It is noteworthy that in the recosmopolitanized Shanghai at the end of the twentieth century, New Sensationalist writing had not only received its due place in literary history but has also been ghettoized in new urban genres, in particular, the snapshot like *dushi sanwen* (urban jottings) and sensational autobiographical fiction by "beauty" writers such as Wei Hui (*Shanghai Babe*) and Mianmian (*Candy*). However, critics remain reluctant to reevaluate the soft cinema, because it would entail rewriting of Chinese film history as a whole.

What I find most striking about the New Sensationalist writing is its palpable texture, which seems to have largely derived from the cinema, with its montage technique, mobile points of view, screenplay-like form, and rhythmic "editing" style. Mu Shiyin's "Street Scenes" (*Jiejing*) and "Shanghai Fox-trot" (*Shanghai wubu*), Shi Zhecun's "At the Paris Theatre" (*Zai Bali daxiyuan*), and Liu Na'ou's "Flux" (*Liu*) and "Formula" (*Fangchengshi*)—in fact, the entire collection of his *Scène,* or *Dushi fengjingxian*[90]—are just a few titles from a body of texts that I call "cinematic writings." Their work as a whole manifests a sustained fascination with the relationship between vision and body, as well as with a wide spectrum of urban experiences suffused with sight and sound: speed, stimuli, shock, trauma, heightened or frustrated material and sexual desire. This body of writings also richly depicts the moviegoing experience in Shanghai in the 1930s. In fact the city is often perceived as an enormous movie theater, or a simulacrum, in which moviegoers also act out their own social and gender roles in cinematic terms.

Shi Zhecun's short story, "At the Paris Theatre," invites us to vicariously participate in the moviegoing experience at a real theater space as the complex gender economy unfolds inside. The Paris Theatre (*Bali daxiyuan*) is located on Xiafei Road (now Huaihai zhonglu) in the then-French concession in Shanghai (fig. 2.18). The original theater (Donghua) was built in 1926 during the cinema boom and was given the com-

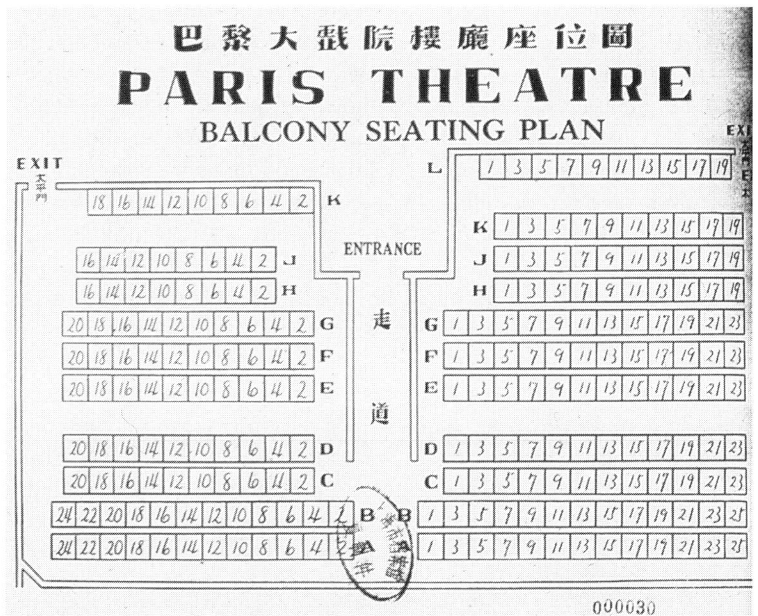

2.18 Interior of the Paris Theater, balcony seating plan. (Courtesy of Shanghai Municipal Archive)

paratively exotic name appropriate for its setting in 1930.[91] The form of the story is a prolonged neurotic monologue of a Shanghai *flâneur* in the course of his movie date with his mistress, a young city girl. Set in a time when sound film had only recently entered the urban scene in Shanghai, the jarring stream-of-consciousness narration has the effect of a sound track that is still searching for a way of articulating psychological interiority and narrative cohesion. The reader has to negotiate constantly between the dissonant or even contrapuntal relationship between the acoustic and the visual trajectories in the story, which unfolds like a film. Temporally, the story takes place over the whole duration of a film.[92] Spatially, it covers the trajectory of two lovers going to a movie theater on a typical urban date: queuing up to buy the tickets, picking up a program in the foyer, being ushered to the seats, watching the set of films offered (we learn that the program contains a cartoon before a foreign feature), experiencing body smells and intimacy inside the auditorium, commenting on the plot and the actors, buying and eating snacks (chocolate ice-cream) during the intermission. After more subtle interactions between the couple, the lights come on, and finally the couple leaves the Paris Theater.

This narrative itinerary, which provides a rare glimpse into the physical layout of the theater interior, the program and its services, the multisensory experience (with fragrance, ice cream, sexual arousal, and so on) may seem routine. It reveals, though, that moviegoing as a social practice is enacted within a concrete urban geography and physical theater space, in which men and women interact rather than being completely passively interpellated by some invisible ideology emitted from the projection room. The liminal atmosphere of the space, the unstable and dilated sensations (pleasure as well as displeasure) felt and lived out in and between the bodies of the spectators are portrayed as more central than the film plot. The texture of the story as a whole acquires a multidimensional quality. What is written down by Shi Zhecun, or for that matter, what happens in the male character's head, is reflected by what's shown on the screen (a European romance starring the Euro-Russian actor Morodin) on one hand,[93] and the couple's interaction, or lack thereof, in the theater on the other. The limited first-person narration (or mumbling) does not detail to us what the film is about, as the male spectator-narrator "hardly glanced at it." All the while he has been trying to penetrate the mind of his inscrutable girlfriend, an elusive Modern Girl. But the film on the screen and the drama in the auditorium seem to intertwine, when the man eventually experiences a moment of identification—which he has been resisting (it was deemed unsophisticated for an educated man like him to "sit glued to the screen all the way through")—he "talks" to himself in a monologue:

> Now what's happening on the screen? He's taken his former wife's ring off and thrown it away in front of that woman, hasn't he? Morodin's got a fine expression on his face. Look how anguished he looks! . . . Isn't this my wedding ring? If I should throw away the ring my wife gave me right now, what would be her [the mistress'] reaction? . . . Right, I'll give it a try. It's coming off now. And now I'm holding it between my finger and thumb.[94]

Then he hears a loud sigh coming from the audience, which seems to react both to the heroine's act on the screen and to his awkward gesture. Moreover, he suddenly finds his girlfriend gazing at him nervously grabbing the wedding ring in his hand. Up till that point, the man has been watching her every move and expression, as if she embodied a film herself, in order to figure out whether or not she loves him. After all, he is a married man with a wife—the "gentle and rather pitiable creature"—left in the countryside. He has secretly scorned the girl for her lack of knowledge about the UFA company, been baffled by her fascination with the "stern and cold" male star ("If [he was] someone like Valentino, then perhaps!"), and annoyed by her fickle attitudes toward him (including her body language). His sustained attempt to understand this Modern Girl, who seems even more enigmatic than the flickering images, remains unsuccessful. He could not understand why she refused to go for a snack with him as couples usually did after a movie, "but instead flagged down a taxi and went off by herself," thwarting his desire to "take her all the way home." Yet she gives him a mixed signal before taking off: she offers him a new date to go to a park the next day. What's the message? "I don't understand," the man mumbles to himself. Thus ends the story and a brief psychological confrontation that took place in a movie theater between a *flâneur* who thought he knew it all but suffers from neurasthenia, and a *flâneuse* who resisted the self-absorbed male fantasy and staked out her own terms for desire and pleasure.

The story illustrates what Shu-mei Shih calls a "textually mediated cosmopolitanism" characteristic of the new sensationalist writers and an emasculated or impoverished male subjectivity, which could not reconcile the difference between his imagined glamorous cosmopolitan identity and the uneven social and economical reality of a semicolonial city.[95] But for my purposes the story demonstrates that a film is more than just a printed (foreign) text that only the educated urbane male could appreciate. Its power of embodiment and its popular appeal allowed a larger audience to access these cosmopolitan products; the Modern Girl was not required to know German or Russian to "meet" and fall for Morodin, after all. The movie theater proved to be a unique public space of social intercourse—a stage for rehearsing emerging yet real metropolitan identities. Its darkness and the sensorial stimuli transformed the medium into a fertile ground for fostering "illegitimate" social and sexual dynamics outside the more regimented and moralizing public world. It was a space of shared, but never uniform, pleasures, where people of different genders, ages, classes, and races (especially in a cosmopolitan city like Shanghai) congregated and confronted each other's tastes and values. The language of this story in particular and the New Sensationalist writing in general not only informs us about the everyday content of an intense urban life, complete with its often evasive and inchoate details, but is itself also actively constituted by the moviegoing experience. In other words, it renders the representation as well as the actual form of urban life increasingly cinematic, which, in turn, refashions the lived experience. In this sense, the fragmented montage surface of the New Sensationalist literature is a salient manifestation of a modern life mediated and embodied by the cinema.

METROPOLE AND PERIPHERY

From the end of the nineteenth century to the high-modern 1930s, the historical conditions present in Shanghai secured the city's role as the natural habitat for a local film industry and a cosmopolitan film culture. It is important to bear in mind, however, that Shanghai was neither the starting nor the end point of the film experience in China in this period. The entry of the "Occidental shadowplay" to China took place first in the port city of Hong Kong in early 1896.[96] In fact, the traffic between Shanghai and Hong Kong, and between the film cultures in these two most Westernized Chinese cities, remained consistent and strong throughout the Republican period.[97] Hong Kong served as an indispensable relay point for the Shanghai film industry to reach the vast Southeast Asian diaspora market. Early exhibitions by traveling foreign showmen also quickly spread to a number of Chinese cities, including Beijing, Tianjin, and Wuhan, and gradually, albeit with great difficulty, to the interior provinces.[98] As noted earlier, the first film productions by Chinese allegedly began in Beijing, an ancient city but also the center of late Qing reform, which was poised for modernity. It was, however, the combination of social, political, economic, and cultural circumstances that ultimately allowed the new medium to find its home in the new city of Shanghai.

This modern Chinese metropolis was less constrained by, though by no means free from, the long history of traditional culture (as in Beijing) or the complete colonial domination (as in Hong Kong). Unmistakably a product of modern capitalism, Shanghai belongs to the international family of those "great cities, Grosstadt, metropolis, even Weltstadt, [that] were larger in population and in spatial coverage than any previous cities." The cradle of modern life, the metropolis, through its exuberant life of consumption, also differs fundamentally from a mere industrial city (the seat of production).[99] Shanghai certainly befits this description. It was and remains the most important center of industrial production in China, but it was really its energetic and sometimes unruly commercial and cultural life that made it a metropolis. The city's ambiguous and ambivalent relationship to both the world and China, enhanced by its opportune geographic location and demographic syncretism, endowed this former outlying county seat on the Eastern seaboard with a historical opportunity to play a major role in the shaping of a modern vernacular culture, including the cinema.

As a center for film production, exhibition, and distribution, the city functioned as a nexus in the larger matrix of a national, regional and international film culture. By virtue of its Janus-faced identity as a world-class city on a par with other metropolitan centers in the world and an entry port to a vastly underdeveloped country, Shanghai's position in the geography of global modernity carries the characteristics of both the metropole and the periphery. Shanghai was an ideal laboratory of global modernity as well as an emblem of its glaring uneveness and contradictions. The external and internal configurations of geopolitical and cultural relations render the city in general and its mass culture in particular an exemplary "heterotopia" or "site of alternate social ordering." As "places of otherness" the heterotopia, according to Foucault's deployment of the medical term, is composed of juxtaposed sites of radical contrasts or incongruity within a social body or a text, always carrying with it something excessive and unsettling.[100] The complex layering of Yangjingbang as a spatial, linguistic, and cultural repository and embodiment of Shanghai's metropolitan identity, which gave rise to a worldly citizenship of petty urbanites with complex stratification, amply testifies to the multifarious, excessive, and even grotesque character of its cosmopolitanism.

Shanghai film culture and its urban modernity did not exist within the bounds of the city per se. Shanghai cosmopolitanism makes sense only in relation to both foreign influences and Chinese interests (inside the country as well as the diaspora). On the level of representation Shanghai was, as Laikwan Pang aptly put it with specific reference to the left-wing cinema of the 1930s, "a cultural space as well as a symbol."[101] In terms of production and marketing practices, the scarcity of Chinese-owned theaters in Shanghai impelled major studios to systematically expand toward both the inland and Nanyang. Many cities in China emulated Shanghai and participated in the dissemination of the metropolitan film culture on a national scale. While big Shanghai studios had their sales offices in major cities, many local cinephile businessmen built their own theaters, distribution networks, and sometimes even production companies. By the mid-1920s, the craze for film was so contagious that small film companies also appeared in Beijing, Tianjin, Guangzhou, Shantou, and Hangzhou, although most of them had only brief lives.[102] While most productions from Shanghai studios are about and made in Shanghai, a significant number also dealt with the city-country connections and contrasts and were even shot on location in sites outside of Shanghai, as the self-referential *Two Stars* shows in vivid detail. Film magazines published in Shanghai also constantly carried reports on local film enterprises and the reception of Shanghai-produced films throughout China.

The Jilin reader's letter to *Yingxi shenghuo* (Movie Life) about his viewing of *Amorous History* quoted in the introduction documents this double-edged center-periphery interaction mediated through both film and print. The dissemination of moving images from and about the metropolis to the less-modernized interior was aided by lightweight film magazines that traveled faster and cheaper than the movies in those days. The provincial spectators in remote areas of China thus became petty urbanites at large and took part in the construction of a domestic film industry and a cosmopolitan film culture that was never simply about Shanghai.

CHAPTER THREE

TEAHOUSE, SHADOWPLAY, AND *LABORER'S LOVE*

MOVIEGOING EMERGED as an important part of modern everyday life, and also quickly became imbricated in a larger film culture that remapped urban geography, both physically and discursively. In this chapter, I trace how a film experience embedded in a haptic teahouse space gradually gave way to an interiorized experience with the spread of the exclusive movie theater in the first half of the 1920s. At first film was seen as a form of play (*youxi*) and part of variety shows offered to a mixed and participatory audience at teahouses. This transformation coincided with the founding and consolidation of Mingxing in 1922, the first full-fledged Chinese film enterprise. It also overlapped with the emergence of a broad film world (*yingxi shijie,* or *yingjie*) consisting of a great number of studios of varying size, distribution agencies, movie theaters, film schools, film publications, and other related institutions.

This multifaceted film culture paralleled, intersected, and diverged considerably from the May Fourth cultural movement. Early Chinese filmmakers, exhibitors, and especially critics, who aspired to use the cinema as a means of vernacular education by way of entertainment, embraced a modern mass medium. The intellectuals, however, despised and dismissed it as the "vulgar" dregs of the petty urbanites. Even Lu Xun, the revered writer, joined the crusade against popular Chinese cinema.[1] The May Fourth writers busily engaged themselves with the print medium to "rewrite Chinese" from the classical language to a modern vernacular and to promote a loftier literary and ideological episteme for the more educated.[2] The nascent film industry on the other hand sought a more heterogeneous audience among the teahouse and theater visitors, as well as students and other new urban subjects. The early filmmakers and exhibitors—many with experience in the theater—aspired to use the movie theater as a pedagogical space for transmitting modern knowledge and values to the public at large. However, market pressure and changing tastes of the audience constantly placed demands on the production sector, complicating its effort to create a cinema of "business plus conscience" (*yingye jia liangxin*), a slogan coined by Zheng Zhengqiu, Mingxing Company's cofounder, and widely considered the "father" of Chinese cinema. In the process, the filmmakers were compelled to reconcile the tension between enlightenment and entertainment by seeking a film language for storytelling largely centered on family melodrama. Meanwhile, the filmmakers and critics also set out to define the ontological as well as cultural implications of the Occidental shadowplay, an effort that in effect constituted an incipient film theory and film criticism in China. Instead of the antitraditional radicalism and iconoclasm advocated by the May Fourth ideology, the popular storytelling cinema, and the porous vernacular culture that surrounded it, then tried to create a more malleable and inclusive public sphere. The latter allowed not only the negotiation of conflicting values and ideas but also the processing of fractured experiences of modernity, not to mention projections of the good life for both the society and the individual. The tension between entertainment and enlightenment was to persist during the silent and early sound period and certainly continued as a *leitmotif* in the Chinese film history as a whole.

LABORER'S LOVE IN CONTEXT

Laborer's Love (*Laogong zhi aiqing*, a.k.a. *Zhiguo yuan*, 1922) is allegedly the earliest complete extant Chinese film. A silent film with bilingual intertitles (Chinese and English), this thirty-minute short comedy is one of more than a hundred films made by two pioneers of Chinese cinema: director Zhang Shichuan and screenwriter Zheng Zhengqiu.[3] The film is a plebeian story about how a carpenter-turned-fruit vendor wins the hand of an old doctor's daughter, and was among the few short comedies made by Mingxing in 1922. These shorts reportedly failed to become box office hits, which subsequently impelled the company to manufacture more "long films and serious dramas" (*changpian zhengju*) in order to make up financial loss.[4] It is surprising that such a noncanonical work, deemed "frivolous or vulgar,"[5] should have survived the ravages of history to stand now as the "beginning" of Chinese cinema. It has toured around the world as the "earliest extant Chinese narrative film."[6] To what extent can this accidental residue or leftover from Chinese film history help critics today reimagine the cultural "chronotope" of early Chinese cinema?[7] And how can we situate the genesis of this particular cinema—or at least this particular film—in the field of early cinema as a cultural as well as critical category? I do not intend to use *Laborer's Love* here as an all-purpose text to answer these large historical and theoretical questions, which are inevitably interrelated; the film serves rather as an intersection where a number of contextual meanings traffic through and collide. This singular film acts upon film history even though it was long relegated to oblivion. Precisely because the film was not seen as exceptional in mainstream Chinese film history, its vivid details and rich cultural context may actually offer us a compelling glimpse of early Shanghai cinema and its complexity.

Laborer's Love is a romantic comedy that provides an explicit caricature of traditional arranged marriage. The film thus suggests that early Chinese cinema was not entirely divorced from the May Fourth cultural movement for which free love was a central theme in its narrative of emancipating the individual from the shackles of feudalism. For the first time the film created a screen image of a "laborer" (*laogong* was a modern term for the emerging urban working class) in Chinese film history.[8] This film was in fact a prelude to a profusion of films released in the first half of the 1920s, mostly derived from the popular Mandarin Ducks and Butterfly urban fiction that centered on questions of love, family, and ethics in a rapidly modernizing society. Overlapping some May Fourth ideas on similar issues, this early narrative cinema, with its melodramatic excess and sensational appeal, searched for an effective and affective mode of storytelling to account for the impact of urban modernity.

Until recently, many film scholars of the West with an eye on non-Western cinemas had been particularly enamored with Japanese cinema. A central concern fueling this passion seems to be the possibility that a non-Western cinema, in this case, the Japanese one, could offer a counter-Hollywood or alternative cinematic discourse. Noël Burch's *To the Distant Observer* is typical of how Japan became the vehicle for this academic radicalism. Burch aims to identify prewar Japanese cinema as the "only national cinema to derive fundamentally from a non-European culture," hence distinctly and radically differing from the "standard 'Hollywood style' of shooting and editing adopted by the industries of Europe and the U.S., as well as by colonized nations."[9] In other words, Japan simply became a convenient metaphor in a political project challenging the hegemony of Hollywood cinema. The second related reason, according to Burch, for the originality or purity of the Japanese case is located in Japan's avoidance of the "colonial stage" in the late nineteenth century. The former great civilizations, such as India, China, and Egypt, Burch laments, were colonized or infiltrated by Western powers and have failed to fully develop indigenous original modes of filmic representation. Consequently, he argues, they have failed to produce "masterpieces" as Japan has. For Burch, the muddiness of inauthenticity of film that is not radically different from Hollywood cinema, complicates his clean-cut program of buttressing Western theory by means of non-Hollywood practice. Quoting some figures from Jay Leyda's *Before Hollywood: Turn of the Century Films from American Archives,* Burch finds early Chinese cinema to be a hybrid existence enslaved by American cinema, from film stock and cameramen to visual style.[10] In other words, the formative period of Chinese cinema was characterized as infantile dependence and mimicry.

Burch all too hastily draws pessimistic conclusions about early Chinese cinema based upon Leyda's statistical figures. Early Chinese cinema was largely produced and consumed in Shanghai in the early decades of the twentieth century. If American films comprised 90 percent of the films shown in China in 1929, that does not mean that China did not have a film industry of its own. Nor can one conclude that before and after this low ebb in the late 1920s, due to the onslaught of American sound cinema, Chinese film production failed to attract a Chinese audience. In fact, the 1920s were an enormously lively and complex time in Chinese film history. It was a period marked by the consolidation of the Chinese film industry as well as the transformation from a "cinema of attractions" to longer narrative features early in the decade and the difficult transition to sound at the threshold of the 1930s. Although only a handful of films from the 1920s are extant today, more than 500 films were produced. The number of registered film companies around 1925 was 179, of which 142 were in Shanghai.[11] Though many quickly went out of business, some 40 companies actually produced films, and many others were presumably involved in film distribution and exhibition in some way.[12] The wide variety of films produced in this period includes box-office successes: Ren Pengnian's gory crime story *Yan Ruisheng* (Zhongguo yingxi, 1921), Zhang and Zheng's moral tale *Orphan Rescues Grandfather* (*Gu'er jiu zu ji;* Mingxing, 1923), Hou Yao's women's rights advocacy film *The Abandoned Wife* (*Qifu;* Changcheng, 1924), and Wen Yimin's martial arts adventure *Red Heroine* (*Hong xia;* Youlian, 1929) featuring a female protagonist. These films' successes reveal interesting aspects of early Chinese cinema: (1) the thematic and stylistic obsession with traditional arts; (2) the propensity for theatrical adaptations; (3) the tendency to address modern issues. The film stock and cameras used to produce these films were imported from Europe or America, and the majority of film production was concentrated in the westernized concessions of Shanghai. Nevertheless, these films were Chinese productions preoccupied with attracting urban, and to some extent, rural audiences still largely immersed in the traditional and theatrical performing arts. Far from being thoroughly westernized or colonized, early Chinese cinema long lingered in a different mode of perception and presentation while strenuously trying to accommodate an entirely new visual apparatus imported from the West.

It would, however, be erroneous to draw the conclusion that Chinese cinema—deeply indebted to indigenous forms of presentation and representation—was also essentially or radically different from the Hollywood style. Given the particular quasi-colonial context of the city, the uneven industrial development in China, the international circulation of the film medium, and the diverse styles of individual filmmakers, there was certainly no such thing as a purely "original" Chinese cinema. At the same time, to conceive of early Chinese cinema in terms of total dependence and mimicry—(as opposed to the "autonomy" of the Japanese case in about the same period)—is even more removed from the complex cultural context to which *Laborer's Love* now stands as a compelling, albeit silent witness.

A return to the beginning of Chinese cinema can provide some insights into a highly syncretic Chinese film culture. However, generalizations are a risk when revising a chaotic historical period, which began with a brief, accidental slapstick comedy. My challenge here concerns the status of the individual text in any theoretical and historical analysis of cultural production. In his article, "Film History and Film Analysis: The Individual Film in the Course of Time," Tom Gunning attempts to rescue film history from the tyranny of theory, in particular, the brand rooted in linguistic structuralism and Lacanian-Althusserian theory of subject positioning that has dominated film studies until recently. Yet he also cautions against any confusion of a historical approach with naive misconception of history as a "chaos of facts drawn out in an endless chain and the endless round of predictable recycling."[13] Analysis of the individual film, argues Gunning, "provides a sort of laboratory for testing the relation between history and theory," as the individual text often reveals the "stress points in each as they attempt to deal with the scandal of the actuality of a single work as opposed to the rationality of a system." Certain "transitional texts" that "contain a conflict between older and more recent modes of address" are instances that manifest the interplay and interpenetration between the "synchronic slice" and the "diachronic axis" in a given situation.[14]

My analysis of *Laborer's Love* as such a "transitional text" will be an exercise in historical textual analysis that aims to reveal the "complex transaction that takes place between text and context, so that one never simply functions as an allegory of the other."[15] In the following I will demonstrate how some historical data may be mobilized as part of a larger textual field, rather than being relegated to "historical background" or simply providing prehistory of the narrative cinema that followed in various versions of Chinese film history. In such a field, a confluence of cinematic experiences of production, exhibition, and spectatorship is woven into the individual film, which is seen treading the tightrope between different aesthetic and cultural norms, thereby transforming spectatorial expectations. Situating the film in this broad historical scenario, I argue that this short comedy made in 1922 has a long story to tell us about the transition from a "cinema of attractions" to a "cinema of narrative integration," and the changing configuration of production, exhibition, and consumption modes as well as the emergence of a mass audience. My reading of the film is thus anchored in a particular vernacular scene, the teahouse. Embodying the Yangjingbang-style architecture situated in an urban culture, its transformation is crucial to our understanding of early Chinese cinema as a product of a vibrant, tension-ridden modernizing urban culture and vernacular experience.

SHADOWPLAY AT TEAHOUSES

Cinema arrived in China only months after the Lumière brothers' show in the basement of the Grand Café in Paris on December 28, 1895. On August 11, 1896, the allegedly first projection by some French showmen took place in the Xu Yuan teahouse in Shanghai which usually featured traditional operas, magicians, firecrackers, and acrobats. The film program was integrated into the live shows and attracted a large audience. In the next few years, a number of European and American showmen entered the trading port to exhibit films at teahouses such as Tianhua, Tongqing, and Shengping.[16] American showman James Ricalton's showings of Edison films received an enthusiastic review, entitled "Watching American Shadowplay," in the *Youxibao* (Leisure and Entertainment) in Shanghai on September 5, 1897. This first printed piece of Chinese writing on film beams with excitement and wonder at the arrival of cinema:

> Recently, there are [shows of] American electric shadowplay, which seems to be made in the form of shadow lantern yet can make wondrous changes totally unexpectedly. Last night, in the cool of the evening following a shower of rain, I went to the Qi

[teahouse] garden with my friends to see a show. After the audience gathered, the lights were put out and the performance began. On the screen before us we saw a picture—two occidental girls dancing, with puffed-up yellow hair, looking rather lovely. Then another scene, two occidental men boxing. Then a woman bathing in a tub. . . . In another scene a man puts out the light and goes to bed, but he is disturbed by a bug. To catch it he throws off all the bedding, and when he finally puts it in the chamber pot, he looks very funny. . . .

One wonderful scene, which was repeated, is a bicycle race. One man rides in from the east, another from the west. They collide, one man falls down and when the other tries to help, he falls down, too. Suddenly many bicycles come in and all fall down, making the audience clap their hands and laugh out loud. . . .

Another scene is an American street [Fifth Avenue] with tall street lamps, carriages going to and fro, and pedestrians in great numbers walking along. The spectators feel as though they are actually present, and this is exhilarating. Suddenly the lights come on again and all the images vanish. It was indeed a miraculous spectacle.[17]

This peculiar mode of exhibition, that is, the coexistence of the foreign shadowplay (*xiyang yingxi*) and indigenous popular performances in a variety show venue, continued well beyond 1908 when Antonio Ramos built Hongkew Theatre, a simple sheet iron structure boasting 250 seats and the first movie house in Shanghai.[18]

The teahouse was a significant spatial trope in Chinese urban culture around the turn of the twentieth-century and figured strongly in the history of early Chinese cinema. It was not, as typically representing in the exotic imagination, as a place where Chinese scholars in long gowns discussed intellectual matters over cups of green tea. In many cases teahouse (*chayuan*) and playhouse (*xiyuan*) were interchangeable terms for entertainment establishments where traditional opera pieces and other popular variety shows were offered, along with tea, snacks, and cold towels for refreshment. The typical traditional teahouse / playhouse, with a maximum seating capacity of 1000, is a square or rectangular enclosed space with an ornately decorated stage (usually flanked by wooden pillars and railings) that takes up one entire wall and protrudes onto the main floor. The walls on either side and opposite the stage are lined with two-story seating compartments or balconies, usually reserved for aristocrats, officials, and rich merchants.[19] The old playhouse inside restaurants and later teahouses was popular in Beijing since the early eighteenth century, but it took on pronounced modern features when it spread to the South. Concentrated in the concessions, in particular near the Yangjingbang area, the teahouses / playhouses in Shanghai installed electric lights (replacing paper lanterns) and mechanical devices (such as the rotating stage) years before Beijing. Instead of the vertical placement of tables and chairs, Shanghai theaters opted for horizontal placement allowing viewers to face the stage directly. The crowded main floor, traditionally reserved for poorer patrons who could not afford (or were not allowed to book) the high-rated seats on the sides and balconies, was made into the most desirable seating area. Another visible social change was that these venues began to allow women, although in many instances separate entrances and seating arrangement were made to ensure gender hierarchy and propriety.[20] In the 1910s the more traditional hybrid teahouse / playhouse began to give way to, or compete with, modern theaters with "mirror-frame style" (*jingkuangshi*) stage and numbered seating after the New Stage (*Xin wutai*) was built in Shanghai in 1908.[21] The teahouse / playhouse tradition and its modern manifestations created cultural and material conditions for reception of the Occidental shadowplay.

At the same time, multifunctional gardens (such as Zhang Yuan, Xi Yuan, Yu Yuan), roof-top gardens on top of department stores, and amusement halls, were also venues for a wide selection of both traditional and modern forms of mass entertainment. For instance, fireworks, magic shows and electric shadowplay were reportedly the main attractions of Xi Yuan, which was lit with hundreds of electric bulbs at night. Some larger establishments were also notorious sites for gambling, prostitution, and gangster activities, such as the Qingliange on Simalu (now Fuzhou Road), where Antonio Ramos made his projection debut in a rented booth (fig. 3.1).[22] Even the more refined teahouse Wenming yaji (literally, "the civilized and elegant gathering place") on Second Avenue (now Jiujiang Road), where calligraphers and painters used to gather, once featured a wax figure show and a simulated train ride show accompanied by landscape films similar to the popular "Hale's Tours" in American amusement parks.[23]

Before cinema's arrival other screen practices existed, including the modern slide show (fig. 3.2). Qian Huafo, a theater actor at the time, reminisced that leather puppet shadowplay and slide shows were "preludes of the films." He saw a slide show by Wu Zhihui, who was to become a prominent educator and had just returned from France with slides of Chinese students there. Qian also describes the primitive condition of the Huanxian Theater, which had only a makeshift ceiling, a muddy floor, and some wooden benches. The films shown there included

3.1 The Qingliange Teahouse.

3.2 Slide-show as shadowplay (as written on the hanging lanterns) in a teahouse (*Dianshizhai huabao*).

a newsreel about the Empress Dowager Cixi's funeral. Following the films variety shows were often staged.[24] Zheng Junli, a famous 1930s actor and director who wrote the first theoretically informed account of early Chinese cinema, considered Huanxian the first nickelodeon in China.[25]

Significantly, before and even after Western cinema's arrival in China, the teahouse served as a venue for many kinds of shadowplays. The leather puppet show in particular, staged behind a screen illuminated by gaslight, has generally been considered by Chinese film historians to be the bedrock of the Chinese cinematic (un)conscious. The age of this shadowplay has been the subject of controversy,[26] though most claim the earliest record came from a Song dynasty source that describes Emperor Wu of Han Dynasty's (reigned 141–87 BC) experience of a staged shadowplay to meet the soul of his deceased wife (fig. 3.3). Other forms of shadowplay such as the "horse-riding lantern" (*zoumadeng*) and "hand shadowplay" (*shouying*) have been considered part of the genealogy of this indigenous art form.[27] One should, of course, be mindful of the risk involved in any such attempt to fix an original moment or a self-contained trajectory of a cultural category. The overlap of the puppet shadowplay and Occidental shadowplay in the late Qing and the early Republican period nevertheless deserves critical attention, if one considers cinema both an international and culturally specific practice.

Most existing accounts describe the flat shadowplay puppets as made from donkey skin painted with vivid colors. The performances consisted of a white cloth screen dividing the spectators from the puppeteers, who narrated and sang while manipulating the puppets behind the screen and in front of the light source. Usually Chinese orchestras accompanied the shows.[28] Although themes and styles differed according to troupes' genealogical and geographical particularities, the common repertoire consisted of popularized versions of classical tales, vernacular stories, religious legends, and adaptations from various local operas. The shows also varied from collections of unrelated vignettes to serialized long dramas. While some puppeteers read from scripts, others relied on memory and improvisation. Beijing alone had two major schools. One dominated the eastern part of the city (*Dongcheng*) and used scripts; the other, which did not use scripts, flourished in the western part (*Xicheng*) of the city.[29] Leather puppet shadowplay also flourished in Shanghai,[30] and as late as the mid-1930s, some venues featured nonelectric shadowplay as a staple program.

Until the early 1930s, cinema in Chinese was predominantly called *yingxi* (shadowplay), especially in the South, before the term *electric shadows* (*dianying*) gradually became more standardized. The term *yingxi* in-

3.3 Han Wu Di meets his deceased wife through a shadowplay (drawing by Zhang Zhengyu, ca. 1927, from Xu Chiheng's *Filmdom in China*).

dicates its umbilical tie to the puppet show and other old and new theatrical arts, in particular the modern stage drama, the civilized play (*wenmingxi*). *Wenming,* a loan word from Japanese (*bummei,* a key banner of Meiji Restoration), was a popular term referring to anything modern or new, including modern-style wedding (*wenming jiehun*) and women's unbound feet (*wenmingjiao*). It is noteworthy that many pioneers of modern spoken drama, like Ouyang Yuqian, had a background in Peking opera. While studying in Japan, they were inspired by the Japanese version of Western drama (*shimpai geki*) and began to perform it in Chinese. *Wenmingxi* is a folk term for this new type of drama (*xinju*).[31] Advocates and practitioners of a truly "modern" and progressive spoken drama (*huaju*) distanced themselves from *wenmingxi,* as the latter retained many vestiges of traditional theater and catered to an urban audience who sought pleasure and entertainment more than didacticism or refined art. Though it departed significantly from the traditional opera in that it is mainly "spoken" in the vernacular, it retained many features of old Chinese drama.[32]

The emphasis on *play* rather than *shadow*—in other words, the play (*xi*) as the end and shadow (*ying*) as means—has, according to the film historian Zhong Dafeng, been the kernel of Chinese cinematic experience.[33] As the pioneers of Chinese cinema were deeply immersed in traditional Chinese theater while also enthusiastically espousing the transplanted modern spoken drama, the notion of *xi* became, if unconsciously, the guiding principle in their film practice. Some of the earliest Chinese films are recordings of Peking opera performance (featuring opera stars such as Tan Xinpei and Mei Lanfang) and adaptations from *wenmingxi* plays. This illustrates not only a thematic predilection for *xi* but also attests to the shooting style that foregrounds the frontal, tableau effect of stage performance. Such a visual style is certainly congenial to the stagy aesthetic of early cinema before Hollywood—that is, before the onset of a diegetically absorbed cinema. The persistence of the "cinema of theater people" (*xiren dianying*) in China and its attendant stylistic strategies (including the prevalence of medium-long shot, nonperspectival spatial relations) requires, however, a consideration of its specific cultural texture.[34] This theatrical proclivity by no means signifies "tradition" in a rigid sense; in other words, early Chinese cinema cannot be simply seen as a process of Westernization of Chinese culture or Sinicization of Western technology. The modern spoken drama played a significant part in negotiating "play" and "shadow" in Shanghai's syncretic urban culture. The first successful commercial films, such as *Victims of Opium* (1916) and *Yan Ruisheng* (1921), were adapted from sensational *wenmingxi* plays. Yet the awareness of the film camera as a visual apparatus and of the cinema as a far more complex modern commercial practice than the theater, also impelled the early filmmakers to explore the "shadowy" side of film's potential.

Laborer's Love is very much a product of this nascent aspect of the urban culture and of a confluence of discourses and practices of shadowplay in Shanghai. Before they established Mingxing Company in 1921, the creators of the film, Zhang Shichuan and Zheng Zhengqiu, had collaborated eight years earlier to make some Chinese films for the Asia Company, a small joint venture with two American businessmen. Zhang and Zheng had been directly involved with other forms of mass culture before their accidental encounter with cinema in 1913, shortly after the revolution that abolished the ancient imperial rule. As mentioned earlier, Zhang had been a manager at the entertainment complex the New World located at the heart of the city.[35] Zheng, on the other hand, was already making a name in news supplements as a Peking opera critic, and was well connected in theater circles. The two embraced the new medium simply "out of curiosity," Zhang later recalled. "Because it is about shooting shadow-'play,' I naturally thought of old Chinese theatrical 'plays.'"[36] "Xinmin New Theater Research Society" and "Asia Shadowplay Co.," two signs in front of their makeshift "studio" located near the Bund in the international settlement, signify a marriage of the modern Chinese play and Occidental shadow (fig. 3.4).[37] Their first film, *The Difficult Couple* was a parody of feudal arranged marriage "scripted" by Zheng and "directed" by Zhang with all the enthusiasm of innovation. With stage actors of their acquaintance and a static camera running until the end of the reel, the

3.4 The Asia Shadowplay Co.: Zhang Shichuan and Zheng Zhengqiu on the set

four-reel film had a discernible narrative (but hardly a narrative structure) and has been hailed as the beginning of China's "narrative" cinema.[38] This early attempt at using the cinematic medium to expose the absurdity of arranged marriage predated the publication of the play *A Lifetime Affair* (*Zhongshen dashi*) about the same issue by Hu Shi, the "father" of the new vernacular literature, in *New Youth* (*Xin qingnian*) six years later in 1919. Far from lagging behind or being divorced from the New Culture movement, the early cinema proved to be a unique medium in disseminating ideas about social reform and modern life while entertaining its audience.

After this film Zheng left the company to form his own civilized play troupe; Zhang continued to film a number of short subjects, mostly comedies without sustained narrative and didactic concerns that catered to the "petty urbanites." Standard Chinese film historiography tends to dismiss these films as frivolous, vulgar, and in bad taste; they are often considered merely shoddy and nonprogressive interludes at drama performances. Zhang had to cease filming when World War I cut off the supply of film stock from Germany, but after a new American film stock source was secured, Zhang's new film company, Huanxian (Dream Fairy), along with other companies turned out a wide array of short and long films. Their range encompassed actualities, travelogues, comedies, educational films, adaptations of Peking opera, and true crime detective films. Most were all-Chinese productions, and with them Chinese cinema as a domestic culture industry seemed to have come of age.

The early 1920s saw an unprecedented cinema craze in China. After a stock market crash, many speculators turned to investing in the nascent film industry. As mentioned in chapter 2, this was also a booming era for Chinese journalism and popular literature, which had great impact on film production. In particular, the popular romance genre of Butterfly literature, which was mostly serialized in literary supplements and magazines, provided ready-made stories for the screen. Butterfly literature originally derived from traditional vernacular fiction sentimentalizing the romances of, usually, a poor young scholar and a beauty willing to sacrifice her wealth or family name for love. In the early twentieth century, however, the genre diversified and included detective stories, muck-racking reportage, martial arts romance, and some ghost fiction. This literary phenomenon's popularity reached its heyday in the 1920s and had a definitive impact on the emergence of a narrative cinema in the same period. Many popular fiction writers, seeing the new medium's potential, also began to write "shadowplay" scripts. But the link between popular fiction and cinema, as scholars have noted, was largely filtered through civilized clay, which first adapted successful Butterfly literature for the stage, often with major editorial changes.[39] Such mediation enhanced theatrical effect in the cinema at the expense of narrative coherence and closure.

It was in this sizzling ambiance that Zhang and Zheng began their second collaborative venture, this time with a larger budget and greater ambition. Instead of the open-air, mud-floored tiny studio where they filmed *The Difficult Couple* in 1913 with rudimentary filmic control, the new company, now named Mingxing, was housed in Zhang's former stock market company building and had a sizable staff. From the very start, they also established the Mingxing Shadowplay School to train professional actors and actresses. The company was no longer just an amateur artisan workshop experimenting with rendering stage drama into electric shadowplay; it was a business serious about its ability to produce popular and profitable films.

What was happening to Mingxing in particular and the Chinese film industry in general at that time may be conceived in terms of a gradual and tension-ridden transformation from what Tom Gunning termed the cinema of attractions to narrative integration, characterized by changing dynamics of spectatorial pleasure. Gunning argues that early cinema, in "its ability to *show* something," is an "exhibitionist" cinema, contrasted to the voyeuristic tendency in later narrative cinema.[40] The institutional ambition of Mingxing and its growing narrative impulse stemmed from a similar epistemological shift in cinematic perception. An increasing awareness of the electric apparatus behind the shadowplay and its commercial power, coupled with the consolidation of a drastically different mode of exhibition and spectatorship, forced Chinese film production to be conscious of a more varied audience and a less predictable market. No longer confined to the customers of Shanghai teahouses or theater houses, the film industry had to consider far larger potential audiences patronizing the more sophisticated but also less noisy and spontaneous film theaters—audiences in the interior cities, rural areas, and diasporic Chinese communities. Together they constituted a veritable cosmopolitan audience for Chinese cinema.

This transformation, however, was less apparent and more gradual than any retroactive conceptualization tends to suggest. As discussed in chapter 2, the demographic and social makeup of Shanghai citizenship formed the backbone of a film spectatorship heavily informed by the petty urbanites' worldviews and viewing habits. Their changing cultural tastes in turn impressed upon the aesthetic and social orientation of early Chinese cinema. The emergence of this spectatorship paralleled the expansion of this social body in number as well as in its commercial and social power. These viewers not only contributed to the construction of the city as a "kaleidoscopic world" (*huahua shijie*) but also became avid consumers of this world's offerings. Cinema—as moving images as well as public spaces—came to occupy a significant place in this cultural and commercial enterprise. The technology of cinema not only allowed the petty urbanites and other urban constituents to experience the world and modern life in a dramatic new way but also created a sensory-reflexive horizon through which their metropolitan identity was articulated. Similar to but more effective than the illustrated press or amusement halls, cinema facilitated the formation of a distinctive public sphere through the constitution of a metropolitan audience, an uneven yet composite *public* body. Moreover, this public sphere was engaged in dialogue with but not necessarily conforming to the ideas and programs of the New Culture movement. The film circles—the producers as well as the audiences—began to exhibit a growing awareness of cinema as a powerful medium for raising social consciousness and for possible personal and collective transformation (*jiaohua*) in the age of mechanical reproduction.

SCREENING SENSATIONAL REALISM

Several early Chinese "feature-length" productions from mid-1910s to the cusp of the 1920s tested such changing spectatorial expectations, at-

3.5 *Victims of Opium,* a popular civilized play staged in 1910.

tempting to reconcile and transcend the seemingly contradictory commercial and cultural (and even political) concerns. Based on sensational stage productions on contemporary urban issues (opium addiction, prostitution, and murder), these films addressed the persistence of a worldly or sensational taste of the petty urbanites as well as a sense of social immediacy and participation. This preoccupation with shocking "reality" carried over the petty urbanite's taste for reality and live attractions as a detached viewer (or *kanke,* a paying audience member) in the amusement halls and teahouses. Yet it also underscored the importance of imminence and novelty as the loci of urban modernity in forming (or recruiting) the mass spectator as a unified collective subject. In the process, the taste for sensational melodrama gave way to an acquired ability to appreciate melodramatic realism and accept it as a chief mode of cinematic representation.

The significance of *Victims of Opium,* an adaptation of a popular civilized play of great social impact, had less to do with its length (nearly two hours) than with the contemporary nature of the subject matter (fig. 3.5).[41] It also intimated the drive toward the so-called long and serious drama, a socially concerned melodramatic form advocated by Zheng Zhengqiu in the 1920s. After the loss of the Opium Wars, addiction wrecked havoc on millions of Chinese families, which explains the great success of the play. The screen adaptation revolves around the attempt of a wealthy man Zeng Huodu (in Shanghaiese, true fool) to prevent his son Zeng Baijia (true family destroyer) from becoming a philanthropist (hence family wealth destroyer) by turning him into an opium addict. He figures his son will stay home that way, away from the corruption of the city. Of course, misery ensues. Zeng Huodu dies of regret and anger, followed by his grandson's accidental death from swallowing some raw opium. Baijia's wife drowns herself, unable to change her husband's habit or tolerate his abuse, and their daughter Zhenzhen (true and true) is sold by unfaithful servants Bu Yaolian (the shamless one) and Mei Zhishi (the ill-educated one) to a brothel. Eventually the father and daughter reunite by chance when Zhenzhen goes out on call-out service finds her decrepit rickshaw puller is none other than her father. The brothel owner takes Zhenzhen away while Baijia dies at the city gate.[42]

The film was made mostly out of commercial interest: the popularity of the play ensured profit because a film print could do away with the expense and contingencies of multiple live performances. Inadvertently, the film laid the ground for a kind of family ethic melodrama that would become the staple repertoire of Chinese cinema (and TV soap opera) in years to come. More importantly, in its mass appeal to the petty urbanites as a broad social base, the film signaled the emergence of a cinema that would create and gratify a set of particular spectatorial expectations. Entertaining (through familiar theatricality and comic antics), educational (through overt or covert didacticism and moralizing), and cathartic (through the motif of retribution and solicitation of identification and sympathy), this play-film processed some emblematic and painful sociopolitical experiences caused by the contradictions of modernity since the Opium Wars.

The move from sensationalism toward realism was punctuated with trials and tribulations. After a hiatus during World War I, local productions of long films were resumed. The biggest box-office hit among them was *Yan Ruisheng*, a ten-reel docudrama that aspired to "reflect" reality[43] (fig. 3.6). This film was also based on a hit civilized play, which in turn was inspired by a real crime that shocked the city. In June 1920, Yan Ruisheng, a playboy working at a foreign company, devised a plan to rob a famous prostitute in order to pay his gambling debts. He lured the prostitute for a drive to the country with the help of his friends. They drugged and strangled her before fleeing Shanghai with the stolen jewelry. Yan was caught at the train station of a provincial city and taken back to Shanghai where he was promptly executed. After Xinxin Theater's success, numerous copycats appeared in teahouses, theater houses, amusement halls, and storytelling courts, forming a citywide craze.[44]

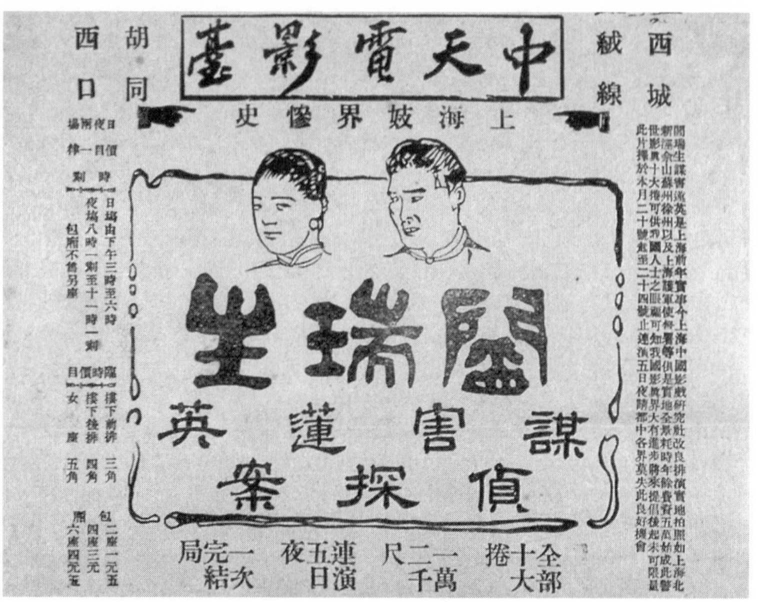

3.6 Ad for *Yan Ruisheng* (1921). (Courtesy of the China Film Archive)

Again, a provisional association called Shanghai Shadowplay Research Society set up shop in a lane off Nanjing Road before embarking on the project of developing a cinematic mise-en-scène. The main cast consisted of members of the Society who turned out to be closely related to the actual people involved in the case. Wang Caiyun, a reformed prostitute who happened to have the same surname as the murdered prostitute, Wang Lianyin, became the first Shanghai woman to appear on the silver screen. According to the advertisement published in *Shenbao,* the film was a product superior to the theatrical version because of its "realness," respectability, and narrative "economy." Literally going where the theater production could not, the film canvassed and inventoried the entire metropolitan landscape—from the center to the suburbs and beyond—and recreated an urban geography on the screen:

> The play *Yan Ruisheng* as staged in many theaters is very loose and extended; it requires two to three evenings to see the whole play. The theater patron [*kanke*] has to sit for long hours; when his or her back and legs begin to hurt the play is only halfway through. We have deployed the most economical "methods" [or tricks—*fazi*] to make this shadowplay. It takes only one time to watch the whole

> thing. Besides, the seats are more comfortable. The audiences will surely feel satisfied.
>
> The main actors are young men with high education. Moreover, the actors who play Yan Ruisheng and Wang Lianyin bear striking resemblance to the characters. This makes the film all the more unusual.
>
> The various locations include: Baihuali, Fuyuli, Wang Dechang Teahouse, Horse Racing Court, Yipingxiang [Restaurant], Wheat Fields, Sheshan Hill [Church], Xuzhou Train Station, Longhua Military Police Station and so on. They are all real locations, very different from painted backdrops.[45]

This advertisement also indicates that ticket prices ranged from 1 yuan for main floor of the auditorium and 1.5 yuan for balcony seats. These rates were considerably more expensive than admissions to the amusement halls and low-ranking theater houses. Nonetheless, the film premiered at the Olympic Theater on July 1, 1921 to a packed house. The daily box-office receipts amounted to more than 1300 silver yuan, and the week's profit reached more than 4000 yuan, an unprecedented record for a domestic production. "Afterwards, the fact that Chinese production could also generate profit began to be impressed on the minds of Chinese audience."[46]

The film's appeal can largely be attributed to the sensational nature of the story in particular and the penchant for modern fads and stimuli among the Shanghai petty urbanites in general. As an exposé film (*baolupian*) set in the "ten miles of foreign field," the authenticity (*zhenshixing*) of *Yan Ruisheng* hinges more on the capitalization on social news (*shehui xinwen*) and its reality effect than on critical or social realism. The ideological efficacy of the latter, which gained increasing influence in the 1930s, thrived on fictional representation and psychological interiorization of the characters as well as the spectators. Yet precisely as the optical unconscious exposed the life world, the film re-created a lived experience shared by the city as a whole. *Yan Ruisheng* revealed the embodied nature of photographic "true realism" through the exposure of the corrupt metropolis as a public and private space, a playground and a crime scene.[47] Such a photographic realism, according to André Bazin, constitutes the ontology of cinema in "its power to lay bare the realities."[48] If Bazin had in mind the surrealist intervention in deploying photography for revolutionizing the perception of the objective world, *Yan Ruisheng* unwittingly became the first hyperrealist work in Chinese film history. What distinguished *Yan Ruisheng* from most Chinese films is its glaring modernity, which both delights and disgusts just like the "sin city" of

Shanghai itself. Through a concoction of realist and hyperbolic objects and gestures, sincere yet ironic perspectives this compelling film witnessed, recorded and offered a "reverse" (*fanmian*) lesson in the manner of the distortion mirrors so ubiquitous in amusement halls. The images refracted from such mirrors are at once real and monstrous, indexical and representational. Unlike the mirrors, however, the film demonstrated its uncanny capacity to "embalm" bodies and time, reproducing a perpetual present through "an impassive mechanic process."[49]

What made this kind of early venture in filmmaking more remarkable was its amateur nature. The Research Society was modeled on the theater fan club (*piaoyouhui*) often associated with the stage performance world, as were many other short-lived companies that came before and after it. Such practice carried over the interactive spirit of the amusement halls and put on hold, however briefly, the professionalization of the cinema as a cultural institution and organized capitalist production. Even after the formation of a fully functioning domestic film industry in the mid-1920s, the mushrooming of small family or fan-made companies often disrupted the monopoly of big companies like Mingxing and Tianyi (which later became the Shaw Empire).

THE BRICOLEUR FROM NANYANG

The rise of Mingxing Company is inseparable from this tortuous prehistory of the Shanghai studio era. The newly established Mingxing retained many vestiges of the earlier cottage industry. In fact, it took nearly a decade to establish a full-fledged studio (comparable to those in Hollywood, Europe, or Japan); Mingxing produced the first Chinese sound film in 1931. Its first four productions, *Laborer's Love* among them, continued the spirit of earlier attractions, short or long. Two comedies featured a local incarnation of Chaplin, and another longer film, *Zhang Xinsheng* (1923), was based on an actual crime story first adapted as a civilized play and similar to *Yan Ruisheng* in its exploitation of journalistic sources and hyperrealist gory details.[50] In addition, Mingxing also produced five newsreels on sports events and public ceremonies, including a funeral. These films are largely products of Zhang's production philosophy, which centered on experiment (*changshi*), entertainment, and instant mass appeal: "Always pursue the current attractions and tastes, in order to bring out merry laughter from the people" (*chuchu wei xingqu shishang, yiji boren yican*).[51] But these short films of "attractions and tastes" failed to produce large returns for the company. Mingxing soon found itself following Zheng's line of thought to make more long films and serious dramas. This strategy not only answered the market demand in a timely fashion but also seemed better suited to a politically turbulent and culturally fragmenting China in the early 1920s.[52]

Laborer's Love, the only extant film of these early Mingxing productions, is a peculiar film in that it combines presentational and representational impulses—in other words, theatrical and cinematic practices. Its stylistic features tend to oscillate between those of a cinema of attractions and a cinema of narrative integration. If the latter is often marked by a certain representational closure, or, in Thomas Elsaesser's term, *interiorization,* the film *Laborer's Love* still shows its stubborn exaltation of theatrical and performative exteriority while flirting with narrative interiority. For Elsaesser, *interiorization* refers to the shift from the diverse practices of early cinema to streamlined Western narrative cinema in the late 1910s, coterminous with the emergence of an increasingly institutionalized (and isolated) spectatorship in the wake of the establishment of picture palaces and other fixed exhibition outlets. He writes, "For the very pressure towards longer narratives coming from the exhibition sector meant that the struggle for control once more shifted away from the mode of presentation to the mode of representation, though defined by the new commodity-form embodied in the multi-reel film, which required self-sufficient fictional narratives."[53] In other words, the stress on interiority and the segregation of audiences the picture palaces are linked to new forms of closure and the "interiorization of the narrative instance" in film production.

The narrative trajectory of *Laborer's Love* is clear, but the film is less concerned with the internal psychology of the characters than with their actions, which often amounts to a *show* that disrupts any incipient diegetic absorption. While the film skillfully uses cross-cutting and temporal continuity for the sake of narrative cohesion, the emphasis on *mechanical* movement and optical experiment often foreground the cinematic apparatus, betraying a sustained fascination with the medium that had first brought Zhang and Zheng to cinema nearly a decade before. This obsession with movement and optical play is inscribed in the seemingly harmless story of a romance between a fruit vendor and a doctor's daughter. The story is in fact a frivolous commentary on the question of social mobility, implicitly mocking the feudal and patriarchal codes regulating marriage and family. The film also serves as a commentary on the early 1920s film culture, and on a cinematic perception and spectatorship in transformation.

Laborer's Love is staged between two kinds of spaces: the exterior and the interior, the theatrical and the cinematic. Moreover, its setting evokes an unmistakable but changing teahouse milieu. The three-reel film can be divided into three parts. The first establishes the basic pattern for a narrative "exchange": the vendor desires the doctor's daughter and proposes marriage. The second part describes how the vendor arrives at the idea of turning a nightclub's clients into the doctor's patients to win his approval. The last part simply executes the vendor's idea, which leads to the predictable happy ending.

The first part, with exclusively exterior, frontal tableau shots, weaves the dynamics of desire between the fruit shop, the doctor's shop, and the hot-water shop (*laohuzao*).[54] The first shot of the film, an introductory intertitle, tells the audience that carpenter Zheng returned from overseas (Nanyang, or the South Seas—referring to Southeast Asia) and changed his profession, becoming a fruit vendor. The following tableau shot shows the fruit vendor cutting melons and peeling sugarcanes with his carpentry tools. Next to his stand is the teashop where some local hooligans hang out. The old doctor (played by Zheng Zhengqiu), nearsighted and clad in his long robe, practices traditional Chinese medicine in his shop located opposite the fruit shop and the teashop. The mise-en-scène of the doctor's open shop, which consists of a Chinese calligraphic couplet and antique furniture, is clearly established as a stage of spectacle, framing his young daughter as object of desire for the vendor and the hooligans at the teashop alike. We are told the doctor is in dire financial straits, with no patients visiting his shop. His daughter mends his gown in public, betraying the deteriorating situation of a traditionally elite class.

The vendor's business, however, is booming. He looks longingly at the girl doing embroidery in the left corner of the shop, and uses a rope to swing his ink marker box filled with fruit over to her—a mechanical maneuver attributable to his carpentry skill. This "sending over" (through alternating shots) links the two opposite shop spaces, injecting a pleasurable movement (of desire) into an otherwise static frontal framing. By using a string, the movement also invokes a traditional Chinese motif for love and marriage, hence the other name of the film, *Zhiguoyuan*, literally, "fruit-throwing love connection," which is derived from a folktale. One of the hooligans at the teashop gets jealous and walks across the street to tease the daughter. She quickly sends back the box, alerting the vendor to her situation. The vendor throws an apple at the hooligan. He moans and the doctor mistakes the hooligan for a patient, as all the exchanges have escaped his nearsighted notice.

The same movement of desire in relation to vision is repeated when the doctor tries to find an auspicious date in the fortune-telling calendar to pray for his dwindling business. He takes off his spectacles and unwittingly puts them in the box, sent by the vendor for the second time. Unaware of this, the daughter sends back the box, along with a handkerchief (again, a classical motif for "pledging love through an object," or *yiwu chuanqing*) and the spectacles. The vendor delightedly smells the kerchief but is confounded by the spectacles. As he puts them on, a point of view shot shows an unfocused world. The vendor's altered vision ceases to relay any voyeuristic desire, and the smoothness of the narrative is suddenly halted: there is nothing to see but the *frame* of the spectacle(s). The doctor, standing on the other side of the street deprived of his glasses, also becomes confused and disoriented. Thus, in her unwittingly mischievous gesture, the daughter momentarily disrupts both men's visual pleasure.

In the remaining half of the first part of the film, the pattern of desire moves from staging to acting. After the "denial" of male vision, the daughter takes the initiative. She crosses the street to buy hot water from the teashop. The hooligan once again tries to make advances, but she walks instead to the fruit shop to chat with the vendor. By intruding upon both sites of male desire and showing her preference for the vendor, she asserts her role as a subject of desire rather than simply remaining a desirable living prop in her father's shop. The vendor shyly proposes to her and she advises him to go talk to the doctor—she still has to observe the "time-honored" patriarchal codes regarding matrimony. The vendor brings melons and sugarcane over to her father to make a proposal. Here the mockery of traditional arranged marriage could not be more obvious. The Chinese educated elite has always harbored a deep contempt for the mercantile class. In a previous time, when social hierarchy was more rigorously observed, it would have been unthinkable for a petty vendor to propose to a doctor's daughter with only fresh fruit as gifts. But the poor doctor is desperate as his vision is failing him and traditional medicine seems increasingly out of fashion. He will allow the marriage only if the vendor will make his business prosper. Feeling dejected the vendor closes his shop and goes inside to rest.

The second part of the film shifts into a primarily interior space with more sophisticated filmic control. As we have seen, the treatment of space in the first segment remains largely theatrical, characterized by frontal framing and presentational performance. This part, shot mostly in the vendor's bedroom and the nightclub upstairs, experiments with such cinematic techniques as superimposition, cross-cutting, and editing (for instance, between close-ups and long shots) to articulate narrative logic, movement, and development. First we find the vendor in his room again in a frontal shot, drinking water and smelling the girl's handkerchief. But quickly the film surprises the viewer with two dream-balloon shots showing the vendor's daydreams of the girl and the doctor's stern face. The vendor's interiority, or subjectivity, is thus "contained" within the

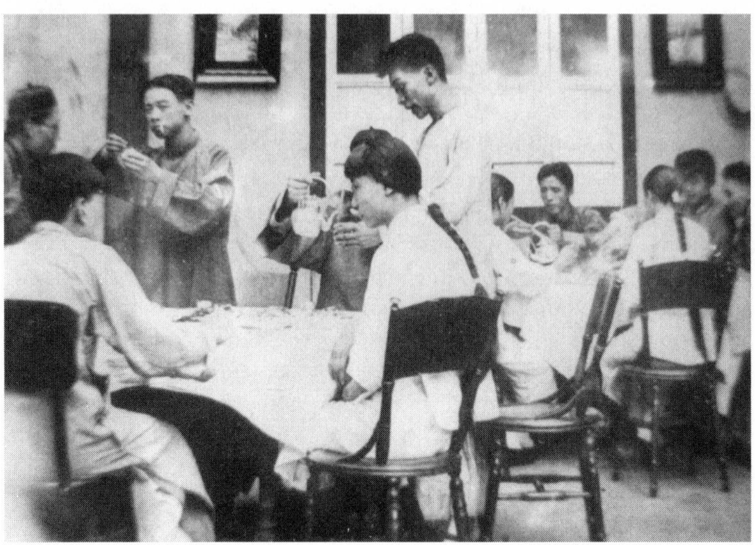

3.7 *Laborer's Love:* Interior of the Teahouse All-Night Club. (Courtesy of the China Film Archive)

narrative frame. In the next shot, the vendor looks at the table clock, and a following point of view shot shows the clock at 9:47. The vendor yawns and goes to bed. This sequence is intercut with the staircase outside leading to the club. The cross-cutting thus links temporal and spatial movement, the interior and exterior space.

The nightclub is the interior extension and elaboration of the open teashop (fig. 3.7). Unlike its "primitive" form, which serves merely hot water, tea, and a view of the street, the All Night Club (*Quanye julebu*) signifies an interiorized spatial figure of modern urban entertainment, particularly in the more sophisticated large film theaters that thrived on exclusivity and closure. The transition from the vendor's bedroom to the interior of the club is accomplished through a mini sequence of mahjong playing. A close-up of the mahjong table with hands mixing the tiles signals the emergence of a different space, and the following long shot brings the club into full view. Two subsequent medium and close-up shots refocus the attention of both the diegetic and filmic viewer onto the mahjong game: someone wins, everyone in the room stretches to see. Two hooligans fight over a seat next to a girl, and the slapstick wakes the vendor downstairs. Another point of view shot of the clock: 2:56 a.m. The elliptical editing here is smooth and convincing. As he hears some clients descend the staircase, the annoyed vendor gets an idea. But he puts a finger on his lips, gesturing to the camera—that is, the spectator—to keep the secret for him. As a whole this segment demonstrates a clean and cinematic handling of narrative progression. The interiorized narrative and subjective space becomes subtly analogous with a cinematic space. Yet, as my analysis has noted, a number of theatrical elements persisted: the slapstick fight resonates with the earlier fight at the teashop, and the final shot of the vendor gesturing at the spectator breaks the fairly tight diegetic space cultivated up until that point.

The two kinds of spaces are juxtaposed and integrated in the last part of the film. The morning after his sleepless night, the vendor visits the doctor's shop and strikes a deal with him: the doctor will have many patients, and the vendor will marry the daughter. While customers keep ascending the staircase to the club, the vendor makes a trick staircase to replace the original one. In the next exterior shot, he fixes every step in the staircase onto his device and tests it. By pulling the device, he can turn the stairs into a slide. By pushing, the slide will reconfigure as stairs. Meanwhile, a reconciliatory banquet goes on upstairs, presided over by an old man who admonishes the young playboys and hooligans against infighting. He exits, only to become the first victim of the trick stairs. As the banquet reaches its end, more people exit the club and make their repetitive "fall," an unequivocal reference to the comic "slide effect."[55] In this sequence, the editing alternates between the interior of the club and long shots of the entire slide scenario and medium shots of the moaning victims at the bottom of the staircase. The long shots of the scene clearly retain the virtuosity of a theatrical space: with the magic staircase diagonally dividing the screen, the vendor on the left side and under the stair is kept "invisible" to the victims on the right side of the frame. As some Chinese critics point out, such a "hypothetical plane space" renders the causality of action visible to the viewer by placing both cause and effect within a single frame.[56] This treatment of a haptic space effects a kind of internal cutting within the same frame; the exposure of cause and effect renders *at once* linear progression redundant. The vendor's secret is truly an open one, since the audience is in on his trick.

This scene is also crucial to my view of the film as a celebration of social mobility as well as a commentary on a transitional cinema. On the one hand, the film satirizes through the literal sliding of the leisure class the thriving but also often chaotic teahouse culture in modern urban space.[57] The fall of his victims in turn becomes the stepping stone leading to the vendor's climbing the social ladder. The old man who first slides down the staircase can be seen as a double of the doctor whose social and physical decline places him at the same level as that of the vendor; what the viewer witnesses here is thus also a *dramatic* transformation of the ex-

3.8 *Laborer's Love:* The fruit-vendor cum carpenter makes a trick sliding staircase. (Courtesy of the China Film Archive)

isting social hierarchy. After being mobilized by the carpenter-vendor's mechanical intervention, the magic stair turns squared-off, static steps into a smooth slide. This play with movement, based on the erasure of the fixed repetition of steps, paradoxically precipitates the multiplication of bodies. The vendor repeats the act of pulling the steps into a slide many times, so that finally the entire crowd from the nightclub is turned into a mass of injured bodies on the street (fig. 3.8).

The excess of the vendor's (and our) perverse pleasure becomes as overwhelming as the excess movement caused by the loss of equilibrium; the downward sliding proves far more dizzying than the theatrical horizontal crossing in the first part of the film, hence the intensification of movement at the end of the film. The partying crowd, now the potential clientele of the doctor, swarms to the doctor's shop for treatment. Silver coins are piled into the money tray one after another in close-up shots as the patients fill the shop only to receive cursory mechanical treatment for their wounds. The doctor handles the bodies in a fashion similar to the way the vendor handles the fruit and the stairs. Seeing the doctor overloaded with work, the vendor comes over and volunteers to help, thus literally joining the social rank of the doctor. In a frenzied acceleration of screen action the two "doctors" twist heads and limbs, knock chests and spines as if on an assembly line. The identities of the patients are blurred and the whole scene spins out of control. This optical confusion recalls the previous gag featuring the loss of sight triggered by the displacement of the spectacles, only now the blurry vision is saturated with an overinvestment of *head-spinning* movement and a polymorphously perverse pleasure rather than the male scopophilic pleasure centered on the body of the daughter.

Both instances exemplify, hyperbolically, the kind of fascination and ambivalence with which the earliest generation of Chinese filmmakers regarded cinema as a modern perceptual and communicative medium. The carpenter-vendor character may be viewed as an on-screen representative figure of this emerging "cinematic *bricoleur,*" a term Thomas Elsaesser employs to describe the makers of the Weimar cinema of the 1920s.[58] The latter are said to be preoccupied with the "Edisonian imaginary," or a realization of the technological and epistemological potential and risk the cinema brings. Elsaesser locates the "Edisonian imaginary" in the "'defective' narratives of the Weimar cinema, their undecidability, their peculiar articulation of time and space, and their resulting problematic relation to visual pleasure and the look, all [of which] point to a form of perception that is neither altogether voyeuristic-fetishist nor an imitation of 'normal vision.'"[59] His overvaluation of the status of the "auteur" (though more a composite form than a single director) over the "spectator" in discussing the historical and perceptual genesis of Weimar cinema is certainly problematic. The concept of the "cinematic *bricoleur*" is, however, useful to the understanding of *Laborer's Love* and other films produced in the early 1920s by Zhang Shichuan and Zheng Zhengqiu. They still treated cinema as a curious, if not "Edisonian," imaginary before launching longer narrative moral dramas.

The problematization, albeit with a jocular overtone, of narrative and visual pleasure in *Laborer's Love* is anchored in the specific cultural milieu of early Chinese cinema. The oscillation between and the imbrication of the theatrical and cinematic spaces in the film—that is, its hesitancy to inscribe voyeuristic-fetishist pleasure or to embrace "an imitation of 'normal vision'"—have to be understood in relation to the "undecidable" position of the first generation of Chinese filmmakers. In a sense, the carpenter-vendor in *Laborer's Love* is a bricoleur par excellence. The magic staircase is his quintessential mise-en-scène, linking the theatrical and the cinematic, exterior and interior spaces. The professional and the social status of this bricoleur remains ambiguous throughout the film, although he is consistently referred to as "Carpenter Zheng." (As Zheng is the last name of both male actors, and one of them is the "screenwriter," this self-referentiality underscores the identification between the carpenter-vendor and the cinematic bricoleur.)[60] Yet he is no longer practicing traditional artisanship, especially after his return from Nanyang, one of the most popular destinations of Chinese emigration since the nineteenth century.[61]

The allusion to Nanyang or Southeast Asia is significant, as it obliquely underscores the importance of what was the biggest market for Chinese films from this period.[62] Historically and stereotypically, overseas Chinese of Nanyang have always been associated with commercial skills in the colonial or semicolonial Southeast Asian countries. Carpenter Zheng is presented as a worldly-wise man who returns to his hometown to become a businessman, engaging in exchange rather than production. But instead of abandoning his past altogether, he adapts his carpentry skills to vending fruit (an allusion to the tropical Nanyang, of course). And when his desire is at stake, this skill is also utilized in courting and bridging a social gap between his fruit shop and the doctor's place. In other words, he transcends the old mechanical role of carpenter and masters both production and exchange at once. And while the vendor sells flawed bodies to the doctor in exchange for the daughter, the cinematic bricoleur manufactures and mobilizes an incipient narrative of desire.

This narrative economy, however, remains defective or complicated in two respects. The first has to do with the bricoleur's ambivalence toward interiority. He never enters the interior of the club where we have observed the most cinematic moment (in the classical sense) of the film, in the mahjong playing. Although he is granted a couple point-of-view shots of the clock and two dream-balloons, the film is at pains to perform his secret desire and his carpentry magic in the theatrical open space. *Laborer's Love* is thus very much a "last echo of an early cinema," at once embodying and challenging Zhang Shichuan's faith in "attractions and tastes."[63] The second "defectiveness" is related to the displacement or blurring of visual pleasure discussed above. The configurations of vision and desire in the film are resonant with Miriam Hansen's remark on the spectatorship of early cinema in relation to a gendered public sphere: "The polymorphously perverse energies that animated the cinema of attractions were not yet channeled into the regime of the keyhole, the one-way street of classical voyeurism which has led feminist theorists to describe the place of the female spectator as a 'locus of impossibility.'"[64]

In the film, before the doctor's daughter denies the male vision in the scene of the spectacles, she had already glanced directly into the camera in her first appearance. Facing the street working on her embroidery, she is a spectator of, as well as a participant in, public life. The desire that motivates the narrative as well as gender *performance* is hardly a "one-way street" as she crosses the street to express her equal infatuation with the vendor, and tacitly agrees to be the future proprietress of the fruit shop. This exchange underscores not so much the theme of social mobility as a simple reversal of social hierarchy to a more democratized distribution of labor. The more fluid social mobility and gender relations thus includes demographic and spatial changes in trade, migration, and immigration.

The insistence on the double identity of the carpenter-vendor is very much an insistence on bricolage. While the film delights in an incipient form of filmic narration, it also passionately adheres to the formal conventions and themes derived from traditional and modern theater, popular literature, and folklore. Momentarily flirting with the "Edisonian imaginary," *Laborer's Love* nevertheless refuses to be absorbed completely by the magic power of the apparatus. The final words are given to the human heart and hand, as indicated in the calligraphic couplet hung in the doctor's shop: "A benevolent heart saves the world / A magic hand can bring back spring" (*Renxin zai jishi, miaoshou ke huichun*). The cliché is given new meaning at the end of the film.

The film as a whole frankly acknowledges the presence of film technology and the impact that mechanical reproduction had on traditional cultural practices (e.g., Chinese medicine and calligraphy). The humorous image of the bricoleur as a versatile filmmaker, who uses his hands as much as his entrepreneurial skills, represents the struggle of the first generation of Chinese filmmakers to balance between art and profit, craftsmanship and modern technology, tactile and haptic cinema and psychological narration. The cinematic bricoleur who rebuilt the staircase and rearranged both the cinematic and social space, as we shall see in the next chapter, would be compelled to build a larger and more clearly defined "film world" beyond that of the New World or Great World amusement complexes. The bricoleur strove to entertain and educate on a far larger scale, searching for readers, students, consumers, and spectators to inhabit that brave new world.

CHAPTER FOUR

BUILDING A FILM WORLD

DISTRACTION VERSUS EDUCATION

I HAVE SUGGESTED that the institutional and aesthetic transformation from a cinema of attractions to a cinema of narrative integration in the early 1920s largely corresponded to and, to some extent, was constituted by a spatial and architectural reconfiguration. The teahouse milieu, though never completely uprooted, was dramatically superseded by the onset of large and ostensible cinematic venues. By the mid-1920s, the electric shadowplay had taken root not only in Shanghai—which was being inundated by a tide of luxury movie theaters—but in the hinterlands, too, where a network of distribution agencies and exhibition outlets were bringing film to the rural population. Based on information from U.S. trade commissioners stationed in major cities all over China, including Shanghai, Canton, Peking, Hankou, Harbin, Yunnanfu [Kunming], Changsha, Dalian, Tianjin, Jinan, and Xiamen [Amoy], an American diplomat compiled a report on the wide distribution of film. The report opens with a description of how cinema finally reached a small town in Shanxi province, "about 900 miles distant from Shanghai," in 1922.[1]

This inward turn, both in terms of a more interiorized film-viewing experience and the opening of an interior market (paralleling the expansion of the Nanyang diaspora market), demanded the supply of long features. The narrative features were believed to be able to sustain profitable exhibition programs and offset the costs of shipping and the construction and maintenance of purpose-built cinemas. To understand this situation we have to take into account that American narrative cinema, especially the serial wild west and detective films, had begun to assert a pronounced presence in China after World War I cut off film stock supplies essential for domestic production. European countries, in particular France and Germany, exerted cultural influence as well. The report cited above indicates that "whereas in 1913 only about 190,000 feet of American films were sent to China, this amount has increased to about 3,000,000 feet in 1926."[2] Also significantly, the shrinking delay before new American releases reached the Chinese market signaled that the Chinese urban film market was becoming nearly synchronous with and implicated in the international scene at large. The local film industry was compelled to produce feature-length films in order to compete with foreign imports and gain access to foreign-owned first-run theaters. Chinese producers and distributors realized the importance of exhibition venues and began to take over foreign-owned establishments and build new ones. This effort, a cultural war indeed, went hand in hand with other projects to create building blocks for a legitimate and viable domestic film industry, including the establishment of film schools and discourses to train both film professionals and spectators.

A CINEMA IN SEARCH OF A HOME

Within only a few years in the early 1920s, the cinema craze mirrored the stock exchange craze. In both instances, the anxiety of surplus generated intense instability. The initial stock exchange craze was largely conditioned by urban development in Shanghai. After World War I, domestic industries were overpowered by the dumping of Western goods and foreign manufacturers' return to Shanghai; Chinese investors then turned to more fluid sectors that could generate fast returns without long commitment. Real estate, bonds, and currency trading were among the lucrative options in a city under rapid spatial and demographic expansion. Yet, the unstable economical situation (including the poor regulation of stock exchange) was exacerbated by social fragmentation as a result of the incessant feuding between the warlords, ultimately causing the stock market to crash. The large-scale transfer of Chinese capital to cinema was a peculiar phenomenon. While the nascent Chinese industries were thirsty for capital, a large surplus of cash wandered around desperately searching for a material body to manifest its magic power. The sensational success of the three long story films, each made by a one-film company (*yipian gongsi*) in 1921–22—the murder case-inspired *Yan Ruisheng,* the ultra modern romance *The Sea Oath,* and the detective thriller *Red Beauty and Skeleton*—offered a timely solution for the imbalance between growing capital and lean output. Despite the growing investment and popular interest in Chinese cinema, however, there were still a shortage of the exhibition venues. The former stock speculators, who had reinvented themselves as film producers, suddenly realized that film was a peculiar brand of "stock." It would not generate returns without the endorsement of spectators; the shimmering moving images' value had to be converted into a fully embodied commodity before box offices could yield meaningful profits. Without this mediation, reels of film were superfluous, which explains why numerous small companies, unable to find exhibition venues, quickly vanished from the scene.

Up until the early 1920s, film distribution and exhibition in China was predominantly controlled by Western companies and their Chinese agents. During World War I, Hollywood cinema, along with American film stock and equipment, made rapid inroads in Asian markets. It was reported that "an average of about 75 per cent of the motion pictures shown in China are of American origin." In Kunming and Fuzhou where French influence was stronger, American film showings accounted for only half of the total, but in cities like Hong Kong, Shanghai, Beijing, and Dalian nearly 90 percent of all films shown were American.[3]

This statistic, however, cannot be taken at face value. Michael Walsh's meticulous study of the troubled mission of United Artist's Far East Department between 1922 and 1929 reveals some deep-seated tensions in the American presence in East Asia. United Artists (UA) had originally chosen Shanghai as the center for its Asian operations: in the free trading port the company could be protected by U.S. law in the International Settlement. Instead, the company settled in Tokyo. Japan had a comparatively higher standard of living, and there American films "enjoyed a popularity that was not restricted primarily to colonialist foreigners, as was the case in other Asian markets such as the Chinese treaty ports and the Dutch East Indies." The attempt to attract a wider audience in those regions was also complicated by the problem of subtitling and the high degree of illiteracy.[4] Indeed, as most imported films were not translated or subtitled into Chinese, the language issue was a key obstacle for foreign films seeking to gain a local audience.[5] The Chinese war and revolution in the 1920s, the boycott of Japanese goods, and the Japanese financial crash in 1927, in addition to the high rental price for American film and outrageous expense of maintaining American personnel abroad, steadily undermined UA's commercial ambition. Until the advent of sound, the enterprise proved "too brittle"[6]—a losing game resulting in mounting deficits.

One important effect of this volatile American presence is the room it created "for local productions which could operate on a smaller margin exploiting smaller and subsequent second- or third run houses, the larger indigenous base, and longer release patterns employing rural centers as well."[7] The Chinese producers in the 1910s and early 1920s mainly resorted to the guerrilla strategies described by Walsh. Most films made in this period still adhered to the principles of attractions; some were direct stage adaptations. As such they were very much at home in the teahouse milieu, although Chinese studios occasionally rented foreign-owned cinemas for major releases, such as *Yan Ruisheng* and *Red Beauty and Skeleton.* By the mid-1920s, however, the rising number of film companies and long features created intense competition. Not only did Chinese producers need increased access to the upscale and better-equipped foreign owned first-run theaters, but they also sought to form their own distribution networks and acquire exhibition venues.

An imminent sense of danger descended on the booming film industry in 1925. That year, the April issue of *Movie Weekly,* printed three bold-faced warnings (*jinggao*) in oversized characters to alert the Chinese film world:

> **Warning 1:** All Chinese film producers unite! Resist a certain country's sabotage and monopoly!
> **Warning 2:** With only studios and no distributors, even if we shoot thousands of yards of film every day, there will not be a single inch of space for exhibition. Alas, this is no way to survive! The greatest crisis!
> **Warning 3:** Friends! Wake up! Don't think only of shooting films! Open your eyes and see: Where can you show your film when it's finished?[8]

The "certain" country referred to in warning 1 was undoubtedly the United States. But a closer scrutiny of that issue of the magazine reveals that the main trigger for this outrage was the purported buyout of small or second-run movie theaters by the British-American Tobacco Company, which also had a film department. The opening page of the issue carried an editorial explicitly exposing the Tobacco Company's plot to engage small theaters by showing "foreign serialized detective films" to the "middle-lower society so as to promote the sale of their tobacco." The editor claimed that if this strategy succeeded then Chinese films would lose their only venues and their "investment money earned with blood and sweat [*xueben*] would not be salvaged." The only "way of survival," he declared, was to "form a Chinese film producers' association and collect funds to build a theater of its own."[9] Another column in the same issue, entitled "Painful Words on Shadowplay," also lamented the fact that Chinese films were already at the mercy of foreign-owned theaters. With small Chinese-owned theaters being co-opted by the Tobacco Company, Chinese films were running into an obvious impasse.[10] Metaphors of claustrophobia, bodily pain, and blood loss permeated the discourse at a moment of excessive production and fierce competition, but there would soon be a major turn-around.

In 1926 Shanghai Cinemas Company (*Zhongyang yingxi gongsi*) took over a number of theaters owned by Ramos—the most pivotal event in the city's film scene at the time. Shanghai Cinemas Company was owned by none other than Mingxing manager Zhang Shichuan and Pathé Shanghai manager Zhang Changfu.[11] We recall that Ramos set up the first cinema in a roller-skating rink in 1908 and subsequently made himself the city's foremost film exhibition mogul. In 1925 Zhang Shichuan and Zhang Changfu bought Shenjiangyi Theater (*Shenjiangyi dawutai*) and turned it into Central Theater (*Zhongyang daxiyuan*) to exhibit Mingxing's and other domestic productions. This was a concrete and speedy answer—barely twenty days later—to the outcry in *Movie Weekly.* The theater that had been an important forum for the civilized play and modern-style Peking opera performances was now converted to and crowned the Palace of Chinese Cinema (*guopian zhi gong*). A witness describes the "gorgeous and pleasing-to-the-eye" look of the renovated theater and the extravagant inauguration ceremony attended by more than a thousand people. The ceremony consisted of speeches by Zhou Jianyun (chair of Shanghai Cinemas Company and financial manager of Mingxing), among others, a vaudeville program, and a film screening (incidentally, not a Chinese film).[12] *Orchid in the Empty Valley* (*Konggu lan;* Mingxing, 1925), a film adapted by Bao Tianxiao from his translation of a Japanese novel, broke the box-office record for a Chinese silent film in February 1926, drastically elevating the status of Chinese-made films in a market dominated by foreign films.[13] Ramos's retirement back to Spain presented a golden opportunity for Chinese producers to form their own distribution and exhibition network. Through this buyout, the Shanghai Cinemas Company secured seven major theaters as a stronghold for the "exclusive engagement" of Chinese productions.[14] The event marked the end of foreign monopoly over exhibition.

Although there were a number of other Chinese-owned cinemas—many of them also serving as distribution agents—participating in the promotion of Chinese films, the market in the city alone proved to be limited. At an extraordinary pace, modern theaters were erected one after another in Beijing, Tianjin, Hankou, Quanzhou, Chongqing, and Kunming. "With this market expansion, film was finally popularized all over China."[15] At the same time, the Nanyang market also grew and consolidated, with many Nanyang distributors setting up offices in Shanghai to keep pace with, and sometimes to influence, the production sector. In turn, film producers and distributors were stimulated by news from the Philippines, Singapore, and the Dutch East Indies where Chinese films received enthusiastic reception by local Chinese communities.[16]

The pressure to exhibit and produce a cinema of narrative integration goes hand in hand with the demand for a new kind of exhibition space that would provide more bodily comfort and allow more psychological absorption. The first half of the 1920s witnessed the opening of more than fifty large luxury theaters in Shanghai alone, such as Empire (*Songshan,* opened in 1921), Carlton (*Changjiang,* opened in 1923), Odeon (*Audi'an,* opened in 1924), and Peking (opened in 1926).[17] Among them, Odeon was perhaps the "most pretentious," "a new half-million dollar theater located on the North Szechuen [Sichuan] Road extension."

> It took approximately fourteen months to build this theater, and now that it is finished it makes an imposing addition to Shanghai's amusement places, and indeed, is probably the best picture house in all China. No expense has been spared to make it modern in every respect, and the result embodies the latest in theater architecture. . . . The theater has a seating capacity of 1,420. The seats on the lower floor are of modern design, and those in the balcony heavily upholstered. . . .
>
> The inside of the theater is finished in light blue and cream and prettily decorated. . . . A smoking room has been provided for ladies as well as for men. Both the ladies' and the men's smoking rooms and the bar are commodious and well furnished.[18]

Unlike the more casual and open teahouse venues where film attractions were shown in a variety program (which continued to exist in a lesser degree), these standardized movie theaters were promoted as self-contained art sanctuaries and architectural wonderlands. The facades and interior designs of the teahouses, despite their hybrid functions, were largely traditionally Chinese and furnished with carved furniture and Chinese porcelain tea service. The new breed of movie theaters took pride in international design and modern equipment, in addition, of course, to a large seating capacity. Interestingly, these new theaters were, following the existing theater houses, mostly called "Grand Theater" (*da xiyuan*). The emphasis on large size is obvious. However, the retention of the element *xi* (play/drama) in these names suggests the persistent influence of theatrical art (including shadowplay).

Beyond the sheer scale and luxury, theaters also highlighted other

北京大戲院

最新建築規模宏大中國唯一之影戲院

上海北京路貴州路口　電話中央七四一〇

本院之十大特色

（一）交通　（二）建築　（三）裝璜　（四）座位　（五）路燈　（六）光線　（七）影片　（八）衛生　（九）價格　（十）招待

4.1 Ad for the Peking Theater (from Xu Chiheng's *Filmdom in China*)

features that contributed to the viewing experience. China's first comprehensive film encyclopedia, *Filmdom in China,* published in Shanghai in 1927, carries an enticing advertisement for the Peking Theater located at the corner of Peking Road and Guizhou Road in central Shanghai (fig. 4.1). Under the pompous rubric "Newest Architecture, Grand Scale, Unique Shadowplay Theater in China," the advertisement lists ten lucrative features categorized according to transportation, architecture, interior design, seating, lighting, projection, film selection, hygiene, price, and service. Beside the boastful remarks on its accessibility and magnificent facade, it is noteworthy that most other selling points are exclusive to opulent modern interior and the quality of the viewing experience. The well-being of the spectator's (motionless) body and his or her unobstructed sight were the theater owner and designer's chief concerns. Some of the features in the ad deserve full translation here, as they vividly illustrate what Kracauer called the "optical fairyland," the picture palaces "aimed at the masses":[19]

> *Architecture:* Magnificent, solid, and modern. Moreover, *there is no single pillar inside the theater obstructing the spectator's view.* The vast size of the lobby also eliminates the queuing crowd at the box office.

Decoration: All done uniquely by specially commissioned art designers, as lavish and luxurious as they can execute. From the combination of colors to lighting fixtures, *everything is artistically conceived* and may be regarded as the best in the Far East.
Seating: Carefully arranged, felicitous in size and height. Regardless of distance, *all lines of vision are directed* [*to the screen*]. Yet the space is large and comfortable.
Aisle lighting: The newest kind of lamp is installed to provide convenience to the spectators, yet *it in no way obstructs the viewers' sight.*
Projection brightness: Equipped with two American projectors of the latest model whose lenses are very clear. Empowered by a large-size generator to produce sufficient electricity, *the effect of projection is extra bright and clear.*
Hygiene: The air in the theater is well ventilated. There is adequate equipment to provide *appropriate temperature comfortable to the body either in harsh winter or steaming summer.* (emphasis mine)

The ad also professes to select films that are of "special value" with "noble-minded" plots. Finally, as if to reconcile its commercial interest with noble features of the cinema palace, the price category promises that, "as film is for the service of social education, in order to popularize it, the theater has set the ticket price especially low."[20] The "cult of distraction" embodied in the "surface splendor" and physical externality is also paradoxically "raised to the level of culture."[21] The theater owners aim to attract and create a specific audience that expects to be conditioned by sensorial indulgence and exposure to the larger, utopian world on screen.

The Peking Theater, owned by a Chinese show businessman He Tingran, opened on November 29, 1926. It was but one of a dozen or so grand and ambitious theaters inaugurated in Shanghai in the mid-1920s to outshine the preexisting theaters and teahouses.[22] The city was suddenly turning into a big cinema wonderland, not only by the sheer number of the theaters densely dotting the urban geography but also by their "magnificent" and "artistic" design that prioritized visual "attention."[23] These theaters further enhanced their lofty prominence with promises to serve as pedagogical spaces for mass spectators. He Tingran, a former schoolteacher, was considered a vanguard in carrying out this mission.

Another full-page, illustrated advertisement in *Filmdom in China*, graphically framed in a theater facade, features for the World Theater (*Shijie daxiyuan*) located in the mostly working class district of Zhabei, north of the Suzhou River (fig. 4.2). Not only is the address of the theater printed on the theater's two columns but a couplet also spells out the

4.2 Ad for the Shijie (World) Theater (from Xu Chiheng's *Filmdom in China*)

management's goals: "Revitalizing Business in Zhabei, Popularizing Social Education." A lengthy caption states that the theater was constructed with reinforced concrete and had two stories with 600 seats. Modeled after the "new-style" theaters in the United States and Europe, the World Theater was equipped with electric fans, radiators, and ventilators. The silver screen, purchased from a foreign company, could display film images with maximum clarity. However, as the pictures in the advertisement show, this auditorium still had a few pillars that might have obstructed the viewer's line of vision. The theater also boasted that, despite a considerable loss at the box office, it abided by the principle of showing "top-notch" domestic and foreign films for the purpose of promoting local business and universal education. The advertisement showcases a mixture of aspirations for high quality films (and their projection quality) presented in a modern theater with classy interior design, and for attracting and educating ordinary people by selling affordable tickets. The aesthetic and social function of this new breed of theaters is emblematic of the cinematic experience in China during this period of major expansion and transformation. Elements of the previous teahouse mode of perception, and along with it, the attractions, were absorbed into an institutionally well-designed and expanded film world.

The success of several early feature-length Mingxing films exemplifies the tension in the conception of cinema as both a commodity form and a pedagogical tool for social betterment. After the less-than-satisfactory performance of *Laborer's Love* and other films, Mingxing's seventh production, *Orphan Rescues Grandfather* (1923), was a "serious long moral drama" that has been described as the "first narrative feature" in standard Chinese film history. What distinguished this film, according to Zhou Jianyun (manager of Mingxing) was its reliance on emotions rather than laugher—fictional realism rather than hyperbolic comedy—for soliciting audience sympathy. Notably, it was also the first film made without foreign involvement.[24] In the film, a pregnant widow (played by Wang Hanlun) is driven out of her father-in-law's (played by Zheng Zhegu) house due to an evil relative's plotting. Impoverished, she gives birth to a son (played by the director's own son Zheng Xiaoqiu) who later attends a charity school founded by the grandfather he has never met (fig. 4.3). In an unexpected turn of events, the orphan rescues the old man from danger. At the end, the estranged family is reunited.[25] The film, which premiered at the Apollo Theater (Aipuluo), was a big hit. Its success was overwhelmingly measured in commercial terms: "The day after [the opening], distributors ordered film copies at high prices. (A Nanyang dealer even paid eight to nine thousand yuan for projection rights.) The turnover was several times more than expected."[26] The fascination with

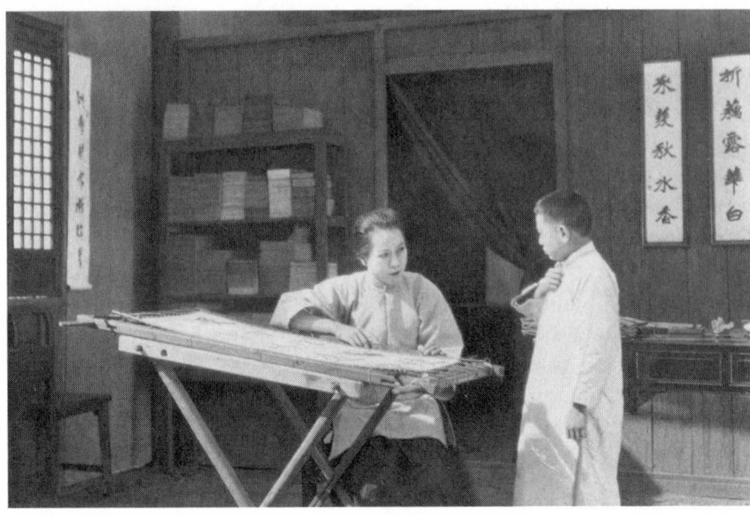

4.3 *Orphan Rescues Grandfather* (1923) (Courtesy of the China Film Archive)

4.4 *Orchid in the Empty Valley* (1925) (Courtesy of the China Film Archive)

numbers was emblematic of a post–stock craze era of an inflated number of companies and fierce competition. Between 1924–26, Mingxing released twenty-four films in all. As with *Orphan Rescues Grandfather,* most of them were long films and serious dramas. Among them, *Jade Pear Spirit* and *Orchid in the Empty Valley* continued the saga of success with similar melodramatic tales about public education for the poor (*pingmin jiaoyu*) and moral retribution that appealed to the mass audience (fig. 4.4).

The enlarged market and theaters simultaneously reshaped the mechanism of production and reception of cinema, both as an institutional practice and as a perceptual experience. A growing obsession with gigantism and ornamentation pervades this structural reorientation. Anxieties about the "loss of blood" were soothed by an aggrandized sense of triumph in taking over foreign-owned theaters and building new, resplendent modern ones. The most successful studios began drawing up blueprints for technical upgrades and institutional sophistication on par with Western studios. The Great Wall Company (*Changcheng*), transplanted to Shanghai from Brooklyn, New York by a group of American-educated students, boasted a 3000-square-yard glass studio where three films could be shot simultaneously (fig. 4.5–6). The company planned to relocate again to the suburbs in order to build a large steel-structure studio, "which would contain at least five film sets at once," and its own office building and dormitories for its employees. Among Great Wall's more sophisticated projects was establishing a film school to train directors, actors, and skilled technicians. Emulating vertical integration in the United States, the studio also planned to build its own theater, "especially because of the large population and hence large number of movie-goers in Shanghai."[27]

An adequate explanation of these fascinations with large-scale, solid metal structures, and with ownership and professionalism requires forays into territories beyond the industrial history delineated thus far. The

4.5 The Great Wall Company, founded in Brooklyn, New York. (Courtesy of the China Film Archive)

4.6 The Great Wall Company's staff and equipment. (Courtesy of the China Film Archive)

architectural space of the film world, transformed by the modern look of the "magnificent" theater facade, ornamental art deco motifs, and colorful light displays promised spectators something more than glittering, distracting surfaces. As the advertisements for Peking Theater and World Theater illustrate, the dimly lit, hygienic interiors and the films being shown were what counted. Simultaneously indulging the viewer's body and creating a psychologically attentive spectator proved a task too complex to be tackled at the theater alone. In this sense the expanded theater is writ large in a broader vernacular scene of cinema, which constantly vacillated between education and distraction, social reform and commercial interest.

DISCIPLINING ELECTRIC SHADOWPLAY

The cinema, an intermedial cultural form and forum, increasingly came to be viewed and used as a vernacular school for modern life and social transformation. Early film schools, though often short-lived, supplied the first group of professionals for the film industry and, more importantly, developed the cinema as an avenue for social mobility and an emblem of modernity.

As early as 1919, the late Qing reformist and industrialist Zhang Jizhi, who was a top graduate (*zhuangyuan*) of the imperial examination system before the collapse of the Qing dynasty, established an actor's school (*lingong xuexiao*) in Nantong, a small city north of Shanghai. This was done in collaboration with the China Film Production Company, Ltd. (*Zhongguo yingpian zhizao gufeng youxian gongsi*). The acting school, in conjunction with the Gengsu Theater owned by Zhang functioned mainly to train young Peking opera actors, typically coming from poor backgrounds. Instructors included Ouyang Yuqian, a prominent playwright, actor, and director, who later also became involved with cinema. Under Ouyang's direction, several students acted in the filming of *Village of Four Heroes* (*Si jie cun*, 1919), a Peking opera episode full of eye-catching martial arts action.[28] In his memoir Ouyang recalls that a key part of the curriculum of the acting school was teaching students reading, writing, and "basic social knowledge." This included giving them May Fourth journals such as *New Youth* and *New Tide*. His reform agenda also involved setting up strict regulations on the morale inside Gengsu Theater. Not only did the theater have acoustics that surpassed those of major Shanghai theaters, the management also took pains to insure that seating was numbered, that noise, spitting, and garbage were outlawed, that ushers were uniformed, and that actors were not allowed to sit in the auditorium. His ambition to transform the old-style acting training (*keban*) into a modern professional school was met with much resistance, although his program for changing the teahouse environment into a disciplined performance space centered on dramatic representation had considerable success.[29]

Several other attempts were made to establish acting schools in the early 1920s. When Mingxing was founded in 1922, it briefly also ran an acting school. The more rigorous China Film School (*Zhonghua yingye xuexiao*) run by Shanghai Theater (*Shanghai da xiyuan*) manager Zeng Huantang and taught by several noted artists attracted two thousand applicants in 1924. Among them was the future "Queen of the Cinema" Hu Die, who saw a newspaper advertisement for admissions by chance. The program would last half a year and the tuition was minimal. Although it was mainly an acting school, the students had to study several subjects on administration, drama history, cinematography, screenwriting, and studio shooting and directing. Twice a week, there were also free screenings of foreign films for "emulation." As the teachers were volunteers and most students had day jobs, the classes met from seven to ten in the evening. The school ended operation after only one term due to a lack of funds and other administrative problems.[30] Such a short-term experiment was typical of a nascent film world in which many projects had ample aspirations and talents but not enough institutional and financial backing. Public enthusiasm for film education, however, persisted in multiple forms. The film magazine quickly became a unique medium for education. One reader even wrote to the editors of *Movie Weekly* asking the magazine to open a film school.[31] Another reader (an art student) who claimed to have acted parts in films but felt disenchanted by the corruption in the studios wrote to the editor asking for advice about film schools in France. The editor replied by directing the reader to a relevant answer in an earlier issue and asking him to wait for a response from Xu Hu, a cinematographer trained in Paris.[32]

The public desire for the dissemination of technical film knowledge went hand in hand with the intellectual attempt to probe the ontological status of cinema in Chinese culture. This necessarily involved an inquiry into the medium's relationship to other arts, especially drama and literature. In linking the mass-mediated experience of cinema to the larger arena of vernacular culture—especially with regard to its social efficacy—this incipient film theory gave cinema a heightened social and cultural profile for the first time in public.

The first comprehensive correspondence film school, complete with published textbooks and a core faculty (including former students of the China Film School), appeared in 1924. Wang Xuchang was head of the school, and faculty members included Hong Shen, Zhou Jianyun, and Cheng Bugao. Located in a lane on Xinzha Road in the International Settlement, the school promised to mail reading materials to students on a weekly basis.[33] Its formality and commitment were manifested in the publication of a set of textbooks, *The Teaching Materials of the Changming Correspondence School for Film* (*Changming hanshou yingxi xuexiao jiangyi*). According to an advertisement in the August 10 issue of Shanghai's biggest newspaper, *Shenbao,* the school opened on July 10. The ad also included an outline of its first course in *An Introduction to Shadowplay:*

1. The definition of shadowplay
2. The origin of shadowplay
3. The history of shadowplay
4. The ontology of shadowplay
5. The purpose of shadow
6. The function of shadowplay
7. The classification of shadowplay
8. The two grave shortcomings of shadowplay
9. The national character of shadowplay
10. The future of Chinese shadowplay

The course was to be taught in eight sessions, and its content was described as "erudite and detailed, explaining many previously unknown things." The student body was very large, and even included students from Japan, the Philippines, and other Nanyang islands.[34] Three subsequent courses, projected to be more specific, focused on directing, script writing, and cinematography. The whole program had ambitions to systematize and popularize film knowledge, as well as to endow the Chinese practice of electric shadowplay with a theoretical aura that would legitimize its international standing and its modern professional status. As the *Introduction* was the first comprehensive Chinese text that tried to systematically define the aesthetic and pedagogy of cinema, a close examination of it will illuminate the intellectual reception of the medium undergoing a structural change.

Introduction was written by Zhou Jianyun and Wang Xuchang, illustrating the extent to which the production sector eagerly engaged in the public discourse on cinema. Zhou cofounded Mingxing and its management miracle; he was also an active editor and writer for early film magazines, especially Mingxing's own trade journals. Wang studied at École du Cinema in France. After returning to China, he was hired as director of cinematography at Mingxing. In 1924 he established Changming Correspondence Film School with Xu Hu, who had also studied film in Paris. The same year, they and several others founded the Shenzhou Film Company, which produced a number of "social films" (*shehui pian*) aimed at using artistically executed films to "exert a subtle influence on people's thinking (*qianyi mohua*)."[35]

In *Introduction* Zhou and Wang trace the genealogy of shadowplay in both Chinese and international contexts. Although *cinema*, or *motion picture*, had regionally disparate equivalents in Chinese (*yingxi, dianying, huodong yinghua*, etc.), the authors argued in favor of the term *shadowplay* (*yingxi*):

> [S]hadowplay is made of drama performances, and not painted pictures . . . *Huodong yinghua* [literally, motion pictures] is both too long and beyond the point . . . , to be concise, we should adhere either to *shadowplay* or *electric shadow*. However, considering the fact that action and expression in shadowplay are even more delicate and natural than in stage drama, how can we ignore the crucial function of *Drama* [English in original]? For the purpose of consistency in naming, and for the ease of recalling the meaning when we look at the name [*guming siyi*], let us use *shadowplay*.[36]

Having set the name straight, the authors justify, in broad strokes, their insistence on the "dramatic" quality of cinema. The family tree they sketch covers several thousand years of arts, culminating in shadowplay. Opera was traced back to poetry and folk song, and modern expressive drama was connected to dance drama and puppet shows, which in turn were supposedly evolved from spontaneous and later choreographed dance. Similarly, the roots of shadowplay could be found in slide shows, photography, various hand-shadows, lantern-shadows, and other similar shadow-based screen practices. They emphatically state that shadowplay is linked to all these arts except for song, as (silent) film is soundless.[37] This theoretical effort to give cinema a historical depth and ontological complexity is laid out in an elaborate chart that places shadowplay as the synthesis of historical confluences:[38]

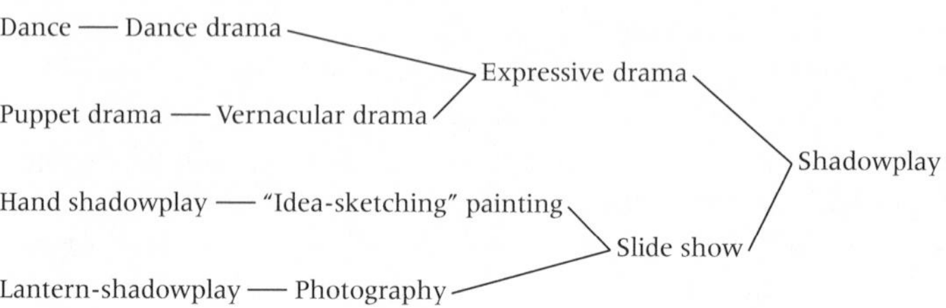

For all its evolutionist overtones, the chart demonstrates a dialectical understanding of the history of aesthetics, as it rests the complexity of shadowplay on a simultaneously diachronic and synchronic axis. Rather than simply restricting the Chinese practice of shadowplay to a self-contained cultural repertoire, the cinema as conceived here is an intermedial and culturally cross-fertilized product, a mosaic of the multiple crossings between play and shadow, embodiment and representation.

This genealogy, however, is insufficient to account for the more protean form that the actual electric shadowplay would take in the modern theater. When it comes to the original matter (*yuanzhi*) of shadowplay, the writers enumerate literature, science, psychology, sociology, technique, and fine arts as its basic components. This systematic exposition contains some obvious debts to Gu Kengfu's famous opening address in the first issue of China's earliest film magazine, *Yingxi zazhi,* published in 1921. But it is striking that Zhou and Wang not only added psychology, sociology, and the fine arts to Gu's essay but also reversed the order of the categories.

Let us examine Gu Kengfu's essay briefly. His inaugural editorial for the magazine is commonly regarded as the first "theoretical" treatise on the definition and function of electric shadowplay. It is much less formal and programmatic, yet outlines some issues that have proven to be foundational in early film discourse in China.[39] Gu regards shadowplay as a kind of drama that best achieves verisimilitude (*bizhen*) yet remains quite modest about the prospect of this "genre," suggesting "whether or not [it] will play an important role in the future is hard to know." He considers technique (that is, the art of acting), literature, and science the three basic components of shadowplay. Using Peking opera as a reference point, he stresses that "shadowplay has only *zuo* [stylized bodily movement or action] and no singing or speech, therefore its technique lays weight mostly on facial expression and movement."[40] For him the performance in shadowplay is "life-sketching" (*xiesheng shi*) whereas Peking opera is "patterned" or stylized (*tu'an shi*). So shadowplay must serve as a model for reforming Chinese drama. Gu contends that, although drama was a "sharp instrument for exalting cultural tradition and extending education [to the masses]," shadowplay is superior in carrying out these missions.

As for literature, Gu sees the script as a subgenre of literary fiction that originated in the "hands and pens of famous writers." The crucial analogy between the script and filmed shadowplay is their shared economy (*jingji*) in words and images, which creates lively movement instead of the "dead" stage's static effect and artificial set designs. Shadowplay, unlike drama or literature, can be staged "everywhere" in "natural" settings. Clearly, in drawing analogies to existing cultural forms, Gu was adamant about the uniqueness of the cinematic medium and its capacity to reproduce living situations.[41]

The section on science in his essay further highlights the phenomenological specificity of shadowplay and its efficacy as a mass medium. Gu first briefly focuses on the optical nature of shadowplay and its embeddedness in modern science; he then comments on its efficiency in propagating scientific knowledge and eradicating superstition, thereby baring the influence of enlightenment ideology. He emphasizes the vividness and simultaneity of the cinematic perception: "When the spectators watch science films, it is as though they are watching teachers carry out experiments in the laboratory." In the same way, commercials for factory products could function as special "educational" films. Shadowplay, according to this logic, could replace slides for the doctors and hygiene specialists to demonstrate the causes of diseases more captivatingly. The "scientific" quality of shadowplay ultimately boils down to economics again. Compared to ordinary drama performance, shadowplay is advantageous in the following respects:

1. In terms of *expense* (without the costs of transportation and food for a whole traveling troupe);
2. In *time* (with rapid train transportation and multiple prints of the same film shown simultaneously in different cities);
3. In *price* (saving big salaries for theater stars like Mei Lanfang, "for a couple of silver dimes, we can see an American star who earns tens of thousands of dollars a month");
4. In *reprise* (as films are never "dead," whereas big theater stars are irreplaceable);
5. In the [increased] *number of spectators.*

The last point anticipated the race toward the expanded movie theater. The author underscored the crucial difference between sensorial economies involved in drama and film reception respectively:

> The shadowplay theater building can be constructed larger than the normal theater. Because light-waves are transmitted farther and faster than soundwaves, even viewers seated far [from the screen] can still see clearly. In a normal theater, if you sit too far away [from the stage], then you can hear nothing. And if you can't hear anything, what's the point of seeing a play?"[42]

Despite his utopian enthusiasm for the medium, Gu's overall observation on the significance of shadowplay for "education" remains largely on the level of scientific and medical experimentation as attraction, if not simply for the purpose of disseminating information or providing consumer guides. This is hardly surprising given that the essay was written almost two years before Mingxing decided to formally adopt Zheng Zhengqiu's "long film and serious drama" principle both as a commercial strategy and pedagogical intervention. Gu's essay in particular and his film magazine in general nevertheless inaugurated the beginning of a public discourse on film in China. His ideas on the appeal of democracy and science were clearly in dialogue with the May Fourth ideology, albeit presenting them from a perspective specific to the cinematic experience. While aspiring to raise the social and aesthetic bar of the new medium, Gu remained committed to its mass appeal and entertainment value.

The Changming school textbook greatly amplified Gu's vernacular film theory but prioritized literature first, science second, (acting) technique next to last. The literary section literally copies Gu's essay, stressing mimesis and the "economy" of words and images as the common ground for literature and shadowplay. The science section was written, however, like an exuberant futurist manifesto on the power of material civilization (*wuzhi wenming*), especially with respect to optics, chemistry, and electric engineering. It even cites the recent invention and exhibition of sound cinema in Germany as evidence of technology's mighty impact on cinema. The book cites a Shanghai YMCA screening of a film on Einstein's theory of relativity to demonstrate that "profound axioms that are hard to explain in language can be easily grasped through film showings." The interesting twist at the end of this otherwise material determinist manifesto arrives in a dialectical reversal: "Although shadowplay is a product of science, the latter also relies on the former for development." This technophilic impulse and the attempt to inscribe film within it were no doubt in tune with the May Fourth exaltation of enlightenment and modern science. But unlike the latter's lofty intellectual program, which was primarily confined to verbal discourses, the film school teachers grasped that the moving image was the best vehicle for not only transmitting but also transforming popular science. While the modern aura of science considerably divested shadowplay of the low status traditionally accorded theater people in China, the more *cinematic* appeal (associated with optics and chemistry) of the profession also granted the new trade the potential to confer respectable modern subjectivities. The film school, if nothing else, at least taught its students how to make and view films more intelligently as initiated "insiders."

PSYCHOLOGICAL ORGANS AND SOCIOLOGICAL PERFORMANCE

The parts on psychology and sociology in the introduction manifests an investment in the subjective interiority of both the spectator and the cinematic representation. The particular section starts with some Chinese proverbial wisdom on the interconnection between physiognomy and personality, surface and interior. But the vocabulary soon slips into one of modern neurological psychology, emphasizing the effect of age and sex differences and the importance of the circulatory structure of the human body in relation to sense perception, memory, and imagination.[43] The nervous system is most susceptible to sensorial impressions and stimuli. Connecting the brain cortex, eyes, ears, nose, tongue, skin, and muscle while mediating contact between the organic body and external forces, its "perceptual" nerves transmit external perceptions to the inside, and are dependent on any slight change in the sensorium. However, the "motor" nerves, mainly manipulating the muscles upon receiving commands from the brain, will relay internal feeling to the body's surface.

This description resonates strikingly with Georg Simmel's portrayal of the "mental life" in the modern urban milieu. For Simmel, "the psychological foundation, upon which the metropolitan individuality is erected, is the intensification of emotional life due to the swift and continuous shift of external and internal stimuli." The individual molds a "protective organ" as a shield against the constant assault of these stimuli.[44] If Simmel is concerned with the general profile of the "metropolitan type" in the wake of urban modernization, the Chinese shadowplay pedagogues directly conceived of this urban subject through the figure of the film spectator. The "enlarged individual horizon" set against the expanding backdrop of physical urban space and population that Simmel described can also be grasped synechdochically. It could be linked to the enlarged movie theaters rising in major urban centers in China and elsewhere in the world, not least Weimar Berlin, on which Simmel carried out his sociological anatomy in the same period.

Carefully working through the mass spectator's body, from its outer shell to inner psychology, the authors of the Changming textbook were able to differentiate emotion from perception, reordering the relation between the two. Moreover, they introduced a third category, mood (*qingxu*), to negotiate the dualism between interiority and externality. While emotion is seen as subjective and volatile, and perception is seen as originating in exteriority, mood is a "complex mechanism due to a combination of several kinds of emotions." It is also intimately linked to perception and memory, which in turn facilitate the mental faculties of expectation and imagination prone to speedy change. In other words, "mood" is a manifestation of the chimerical link between exterior stimuli and interior reactions. This formulation is akin to the "protective organ" diagnosed by Simmel, which is a psychosomatic bodily extension or a sensory product of reaction-formation. The Chinese writers assert: "If someone has a dull perception, his/her mood must be very underdeveloped." As an "intermediate" activity, "mood" is essential in establishing communication between the actor and the spectator. They further single out vision as the privileged site of this identification, or "correspondence":

> Shadowplay is after all a kind of drama that depicts human moods. Recent shadowplay works, due to the improved [skills] of actors, have come to focus on "interior acting" [*neixin biaoyan*], which works basically, through facial expressions, by bringing out the mood hidden inside the heart which moves the spectator deeply. Therefore the highest artistic acting is not only concentrated on the face, but ultimately in the *eyes*. If the actor does not completely understand the human individual character and personality, and if the actor does not know something about psychology, how can he/she act out those expressions?[45]

These cinematically reproduced and enhanced eyes could be seen as the organs of "mood," linking the external stimuli and interior emotion, surface and depth, the body and the psyche. In this sense, the eye stands out as the "organ of tactility," an exegesis the anthropologist Michael Taussig has offered of Benjamin's famous notion of the "optical unconscious."[46] The expressiveness of film actors' eyes was certainly enhanced by cinematographic techniques such as close-up and editing that came to be widely used in narratively integrated cinema by this time. Director Chen Shouying complained that, although the actors had learned not to "look at the camera," most of them had yet to learn how to "act to the camera."

If they failed to act to or "register" (English original) their performances on the camera, they subsequently failed to "act for the spectator."[47] This clearly indicates the recognition of the power imbued in cinema's "optical organ" and of its relation to the spectator's interiority. But this tendency toward interiorization does not necessarily have to be understood as internalization. It is rather a process of giving a palpable materiality to the psychological experience of both the actor and the spectator. Mood thus functions as a sensitive glue between the "feeling" on screen and in the auditorium, which is subject to the rapid change of both shadowplay and the urban life it captures.

As if conscious of the potential pitfalls of exclusive individuality implied by psychology, "sociology" is then deployed to situate the interiorized spectator and the "nerve system" of shadowplay in a large social system. Within the larger social realm countless modern "problems" (such as the "labor problem," the "women's problem," the "divorce problem," the "family problem," and the "child problem") await solutions. A tinge of elitism is detectable in Zhou and Wang's sociological concerns when they pictured the "masses" as essentially "blind" and lacking "discerning power." It would be a few intellectuals' task to intervene and lead in this crucial "transitional period" and shadowplay, the epitome of modern society, would be most befitting for "performing" (*biaoyan*) social reality. Among all kinds of shadowplay, the "social drama" was considered the most viable as it "contains suggestions as how to solve the problems, and leaves impressions on spectators that are deep enough to compensate for what cannot be achieved by writing books or making speeches."[48]

The sociological mission accorded shadowplay also places a higher demand on technique—an aspect alluded to in the psychology section. The writers here denounce the civilized play's prevalent tendency to uncritically borrow from various existing performances, such as the "playthings in the amusement hall," instead of cultivating "facial expression" and "movement." They criticize such playthings as "off the point" and as merely "low (or obscene) circus tricks" to win the "mere laughter of the spectator." The object of this self-righteous critique is obviously Zhang Shichuan's earlier production that was philosophically centered on attractions rather than psychology. However, the cultivation of the psychologized performance is not to be understood as passivity and immobility. By highlighting the distinction between stage performance and screen acting, the writers emphasize the inherently fragmented, yet mobile, nature of cinema:

> While on the stage performances are consistent and continuous, the expression and movement on the screen is fragmented and divided into parts. On the stage there is speech as a tool to assist [per-

> formance] whereas on the screen it is pure performance that delivers meaning. Seen from this perspective, the acting techniques of stage actors and shadowplay actors, though similar on the surface, are actually different in nature. When the two are compared, of course, a more complicated shadowplay is also more meticulous and refined.[49]

Such complexity and refinement also include modern skills of dancing, driving a car, flying an airplane, or even steering a hot-air balloon. And the authors caution aspiring actors that "commonsensical" bodily techniques are acquired through careful observation and practice in real life, not taught in any film school or studio.[50] Resorting to the university of everyday life and modern trends, the pedagogy adopted here is radically different from traditional ways of learning to read or act, be it a school practice dominated by book copying and memorization or an apprenticeship in a theater troupe governed by disciplined repetition.

As though these ways to perfect the performance and reception of shadowplay were not complex enough, the last item in the list for the "original matter" of shadowplay uses "art" as a culminating category for setting the standards of shadowplay. This is a programmatic aesthetic statement of which "beauty" is the buzzword with "truth" (or authenticity) and "goodness" as foils. Here "art" is an amalgamate category that includes the "beauty" of script, sets, acting, costume, lighting, intertitles, and camera work. It is an art of comprehensiveness and structure "because shadowplay is an art of division and cooperation, not something that can be independently done by a few people."[51] In other words, in order to attain the respectable status of art, shadowplay has to be divested of its reputation as a mere trick or plaything in the teahouse or amusement hall. Film production is recognized as large-scale collaboration, rather than the cottage-industry that characterized earlier film making. It has to be perfectly coordinated without erasing the professional distinctions of each filmic component.

There are some apparent contradictions in these theoretical attempts to define the multifarious ontology of shadowplay. One chief paradox lies in the effort to endow shadowplay with a more distinctly cinematic, artistic aura, and perhaps also an institutional grandeur. At the same time the authors continue to cling to some aesthetic aspects of drama, seeking in it an organic "spirit" that would bring "electric shadows" to life—or to give life-content to the "empty," almost ghostly, form of film. In this regard, the "spirit" also stands in for flesh and blood, as a displaced form of embodiment. This phantom body, at once metaphysical and materialized, serves not only as a metaphor for the cinematic body but also as a concrete site for contending external and internal forces, perception and emotion, the psychic and the social, the diachronic and the synchronic, the individual and the collective. This paradox is related to the tension between the lofty "artistic" ideal about the kinds of film that ought to be made and a populist impulse to replace the traditionally privileged writing system with this visual Esperanto.

Before moving on to elucidate the more practical "function of shadowplay," the writers find it necessary to remind their students of the "national character" of shadowplay. Until the "world has become truly universalized" (*shijie datong*), they contend, shadowplay is necessarily a national project charged with the mission to "propagate and represent" national history, culture, character, customs, industry, and crafts. They advise the spectator not to blindly worship foreign films and see through their racial discrimination. This brief patriotic discourse stops short of being schematic and rhetorical.[52] A lengthier meditation on the popular, yet hardly "low," quality of the medium, steers the discursive flow back to the pedagogical track tinged with a utopian universalism.

ATTRACTIVE NARRATION

In the section on the "function of shadowplay," the authors deal more explicitly with cinematic modernity. The first and foremost function of shadowplay is its "entertainment spirit." Harking back to the arguments on psychology, the authors prescribe shadowplay as a panacea for modern subjects who labor long hours and suffer from nervous exhaustion. If people do not have access to "appropriate" (*zhengdang*) entertainment, they may go morally astray or become dejected and suicidal. Although there are many kinds of "low-class" folk entertainment forms available, those are regarded as poisonous to the body and the heart. Music, art, and drama are "adequate" forms of entertainment but are too "pure" or one-dimensional. Only shadowplay, with its rich assortment of genres, is the most appropriate and comprehensive form of entertainment that satisfies all kinds of needs and pleasures. For a low price, it can "mold a person's temperament and benefit the body and the heart."[53]

"Appropriate" entertainment is necessarily "popular education." It should guide society and become people's friend and teacher. The writers compare shadowplay to other existing forms of entertainment, arguing that only shadowplay is capable of both entertaining and edifying. Various traditional opera forms are either too highbrow (e.g., the *kunqu* opera) or too restricted by regional and dialectical specificity. They also tend to be overly stylized in their use of elaborate lyrics, music, masks, and props, not to mention the "magic-ghost plot, deafening gongs and drums, and supernatural martial-art episodes." The vernacular spoken drama may be seen as a form of popular education, "but some of the actors, instead of standing in front of the people, only follow behind them; they cater to the society rather than try to correct it. Some have become Peking operalike while others turned to low amusing games—neither donkey nor horse. As a whole they keep declining."[54] In stark contrast to this degrading mishmash, shadowplay is absolutely "close to truth" and "complete with a beginning and an end." Not only is it capable of reflecting the human condition and shifting the audience's mood, it can also have an impact on social progress. For these reasons, shadowplay appeals to all social groups regardless of age, gender, or level of education—exerting imperceptible influence and ultimately transforming their minds.

This experience of enlightenment does not, however, have to be pedantic and passive. A powerful aspect of educational moviegoing is its ability to induce vicarious kinesthetic sensations of traveling all over the world. The spectator can "go" anywhere and see anything via the silver screen: from the ancient ruins of Egypt and Rome to the modern scenes of New York and Paris, from African wild animals to the Great Wall—all the sites and things that "our ears have heard so much about but our eyes haven't seen." Confined as we are by our jobs and our small income, shadowplay take us "on the scene in person" (*shenlin qi jing*), far beyond what newspapers could offer. The writers cannot help citing, and transplanting, some proverbial sayings here:

> People say reading a travelogue makes one "travel while lying down (*woyou*)"; seated in the movie theater watching newsreels and landscape films then amounts to "traveling while sitting down (*zuoyou*)." There is an ancient saying: "A scholar knows the affairs of the world without leaving his study." I would change it to: "Everybody can know the affairs of the world without going out of the door."[55]

The analogy of "traveling while sitting down" reminds us of simulated landscape travel films or the "phantom ride" shows at teahouse venues. The remarkable thing is that the authors, having privileged social drama and artistic aura in the section on shadowplay's ontology, are indulging here in travelogue films that generate bodily sensation and vernacular knowledge rather than moral edification and purgation. As in the earlier illustration of cinema's comprehensive quality, travelogue, newsreel, comedy, detective stories, and social drama are enumerated equally for their distinctive entertainment and educational values.

It is possible to speculate that, in making the transition to a more narratively integrated cinema and its attendant viewing protocols, early Chinese film theorists and producers were not necessarily advocating an exclusive narrative cinema targeted at a homogenous audience. Their critique of early Chinese shadowplay's parasitic relationship to traditional performance, vernacular spoken drama, and other forms of entertainment was at times belligerent but usually reserved and ambiguous. Rather than turning the theater into a thoroughly psychologized space of narrative absorption, they wanted the cinematic interiority to be anchored in, if not superimposed onto, the public world at large. The preference for photographic "verisimilitude," or realism, as manifested in *Yan Ruisheng* and *Zhang Xinsheng,* suggests a persistent interest in the cinema of attractions, instead of a closed fictional world. There is little indication that film viewing should be entirely intradiegetic, either. Therefore, forms such as the educational lecture (*yanshuo*), aided by film projection, are deemed highly commendable as an integrated film experience. The educational purpose can be accomplished by repetitively showing or "demonstrating" the same film, replacing clumsy and costly laboratory equipment. The powerful camera lens can also expose microscopic views of plants and bacteria that the naked eye cannot see.

To the extent that the cinematic attractions are mobilized to aid a wide-reaching public education of modern science, this utopian project is nothing short of a search for what I will call a cinema of "attractive narration." While continuously regarded as immanently appealing to the senses, the cinema of attractive narration presents film as an object of knowledge and presupposes a viewing subject conscious of but not completely surrendering to its didactic function. This desire to use the inherently sensuous medium as a visual vernacular for disseminating scientific knowledge underscores the conception of the medium as an eminent vehicle for affective knowledge. Thus using the movie theater as a public school for this *informed pleasure* is not so much about discipline and representation as about staging a "living tableau" of the everyday experience.[56]

Toward the end of *Introduction,* the authors express their affirmative view of film as the best museum of history—or rather, reservoir of memory—in a world full of transient happenings and novel curiosities. To invoke Bazin again, because the body "embalmed" in shadowplay outlasts any mortal body, film can preserve ancestral images and the unparalleled art of famous actors for future generations. The authors mention the art of Yu Jusheng and Tan Xinpei, two leading Peking opera actors, as best candidates for "eternal preservation" through film.[57] Had photography been invented long ago, the authors claim, it would have been much more effective to study history by viewing films than by reading a history book that is easily forgotten. The exaltation of a filmed body's indestructibility is thus not reserved for great names and their "everlasting" art only; it is extended to the plebian universe as well. "Even an ordinary person's life may be filmed in order to be remembered by that person himself and provide a model for his offspring." Due to its liveliness, durability, reproducibility, and, above all, democratic appeal, the filmic image is regarded as the optimal medium for the embodiment and representation of history of all ages.

Ultimately, the shadowplay's reproducibility and affordability could aid in reaching a wider audience than literature and drama—forms privileged by classical aesthetics. The authors seem to have plagiarized Gu Kengfu wholesale on this point. But a notable addition is the term *minzhong hua* (popular orientation, or popularization) juxtaposed to *pubian xing* (universal nature). Thus the emphasis is not simply on the numerical size of the audience per se but rather on the broad social base of spectators and their potential mobilization for social change. The Shenzhou Company, which Wang Xuchang helped establish, sought to make films about "common knowledge" and take them to rural areas to show "ordinary women and children" (*yiban furen ruzi*) for free.[58] In this way, they might open their eyes a bit to the outside world.[59] More crucially, shadowplay could also, without resorting to conventional education, impart basic knowledge that the "citizens of a twentieth-century republic" ought to possess. If this plan were to succeed, it would immensely benefit the "ignorant mob" (*yumang*). This utopian and largely elitist intellectual vision did not immediately materialize, as the company had to compete with both domestic and foreign rivals in a market that craved narrative features with commercial value. Modeled after Mingxing's practice, Shengzhou made several long and serious films. Their elaborate technique in storytelling and attention to "artistic appeal" (such as embellished intertitles) became known as Shenzhou style (*Shenzhou pai*)."[60] The pursuit of stylistic sophistication and psychological complexity, however, limited the appeal of its films primarily to students and intellectuals in the cities, a result far from its initial intention to use shadowplay to enlighten the massive population in China's vast rural interior.

CENTERING THE SPECTATOR

The Changming Correspondence Film School's pedagogical ambitions to employ shadowplay as a paraeducational medium of mass communication, knowledge dissemination, and moral guidance were shared by many filmmakers and critics at the time.[61] Such a mass-oriented ontology of the cinema increasingly placed the spectator at the center of the exclusive theater space as well as the larger social space of the film experience. The mid-1920s was a high time for Zheng Zhengqiu, comaker of *Laborer's Love* and the foremost ideologue of the long film and serious drama. His homespun production philosophy—"business plus conscience, 'ism' combined with popular taste"—was being materialized in numerous Mingxing productions and was widely adopted by other studios after the success of *Orphan Rescues Grandfather* in 1923.

It is significant that the chief mise-en-scène in *Orphan Rescues Grandfather* is a public school funded by the rich grandfather to provide free education to poor children. The disinherited grandson is a studious pupil there who aspires to become a "refined and courteous, smart and witty" educated person despite his "humble" origins. The old man does not know the model student is his own grandson until after its revelation. After the happy reunion, the widowed mother is convinced that the school was the key to the solution of the "gross injustice" inflicted upon her family. She decides to invest her retrieved wealth in opening more charity schools so that "poor children who could not afford normal schools might get the education necessary for life."[62]

The education of the "orphan" saved his grandfather's life and averted a financial disaster for the family, while the sensational commercial success of the film steered Mingxing out of difficult financial straits. More importantly, the film attracted a mass audience, both domestically and in the Nanyang diaspora, that was to last for a long time to come. Although the traditional family was still the centerpiece in this first long film and serious drama, its redemption hinged upon the modern-style public school that materialized the reformist vision for a more egalitarian society. The widow is not only welcomed back to the family but is given the ownership and management of its entire property, which effectively makes her a matriarch. The grandfather, embodying the disintegrating traditional order, has to abandon the old house and make the charity school his home as a premise for the reunion of the family, which in the end becomes an expanded educational community. An analogy can be drawn between this expansion of the school in the film as the fruition of private yet ethically motivated investment and the expansion of the film world as a potential vernacular school at large. The film indeed exemplifies Zheng's conviction of the theater as the most effective school: "Theater is the laboratory for social education while actors are good teachers imparting this education."[63] If Mingxing's early nondidactic ventures failed to create a stable pedagogical situation in the teahouse milieu, *Orphan Rescues Grandfather*'s success and the consolidation of long film and serious drama marked the emergence of a broad but more unified spectatorship in the enlarged theater, both physically and socially.

Amid a profusion of film discourses in the mid-1920s, Zheng once again proved to be a provocative voice in the spectator's central position. Unlike many Western-educated critics and filmmakers, Zheng has had a direct and intimate relationship with his audience, the petty urbanites, beginning when he wrote theater reviews and initiated the revival of the civilized play. Although he was instrumental in pushing Chinese cinema toward a more narratively integrated cinema, he refused to be carried away by the crazes for the full-fledged film script (and hence diminished importance of improvisation) and for turning shadowplay into "art" alone. In his seminal essay, "My Expectations of the Audience," Zheng urges filmmakers and critics to focus on the audience and their needs. He opens his argument in a polemic tone:

> As regards whether or not the future of drama will be good, and whether or not a theater house or a film company will be prosperous, many readers seem to agree that the real power rests in the hands of the screenwriter. In my opinion, however, most of the power rests with the spectators, because even the screenwriter often has to change his mind due to the inclinations of the audience. Old theater houses were like that; new drama is like that. Today film companies, I am afraid, have to follow suit as well.[64]

He nevertheless agrees with the Changming textbook writers that any piece of drama (or shadowplay) has to convey some message of social critique in order to make the audience aware of the problems surrounding them. Responding to provocations to make "pure" art films, he proudly states that he is not ashamed of what he has been doing. Zheng confesses that he has made countless experiments to achieve prevalent artistic standards. The results, however, have been that "either the financial sponsors find the films too 'high' [to accept] or women viewers and people in the world of commerce are totally baffled." What he has found more rewarding for both filmmakers and audiences is adding one or two artistic elements at a time in a film, which as a whole should still cater to the audience's general tastes. This is because shadowplay producers are not subsidized by the state, and for the purpose of staying in business, it is natural for them to cater to the psychology of the spectators (*guanzhong xinli*). In other words, it is through the enactment of interactive communication or a symbiotic relationship between the sender and the receiver that the medium will "imperceptibly embark on the path of art." "Art" here represents more an intersubjective process of establishing formal conventions than an abstract aesthetic ideal. Only then "will my taste and that of the audience improve," writes Zheng. "Taste" is clearly regarded as product of a cultural habitat and historical process.

Zheng was a firm believer in individual and collective transformation through cathartic storytelling. For Zheng, who abandoned the traditional path of social ascendance (i.e., the imperial examinations) as a youth to willingly sink into the theater world's lower depths, the theater space was the most effective school of life. In this public space meaningful social and ethical lessons can be delivered through the time-honored pedagogical method of "good systematic guidance with skill and patience" (*xunxun shanyou*), which will eventually lead to enlightenment and transformation in an ethical project rather than an ideological one. The model of Zheng's ideal cinematic school is thus a bricolage of traditional drama and teahouse practice, Confucian ethics and modern style education, which *Orphan Rescues Grandfather* helped to visualize.

Published after the media uproar over the planned buy-out of the British-American Tobacco Company's small theaters and the May Thirtieth incident in 1925,[65] Zheng's essay was not oblivious to the political potential of the film audience. Although Zheng is reserved about the "artistic" vogue or bourgeois trend among film critics and well-educated urban spectators responding to the rise of art cinema (or "pure cinema") in Europe and Japan, he is adamant about the need for Chinese-made films to survive and succeed in a competitive market. In closing, he asks that the spectators give something in return: to tell relatives and friends not to attend the showing of foreign films that do not benefit the country, and to bear with Chinese films, even though each film may have only one commendable aspect or may seem less stimulating technically. Audiences can promote good films by word of mouth, which is more effective than writing. When they find films that are inappropriate to the "national condition," they should write letters to caution the filmmakers, and if that proves ineffective, they should compose essays to attack them until filmmakers make amends. In short, Zheng expected the Chinese moviegoers to be involved in the public sphere at large. Public opinion, according to Zheng, had the power to improve the Chinese film enterprise at a time when quantity overshadowed quality but when it also had a golden opportunity to grow in the market. Zheng Zhengqiu's motto "business plus conscience" crystallizes a balanced integration of his long-term partner Zhang Shichuan's inclination for attractions and commercial profit on the one hand and his own penchant for socioethical education through dramaturgy and storytelling on the other.

To recapitulate, the film world in the first part of the 1920s was an expanded architectural and social space created by different participants of an emerging public sphere—architects, theater owners, distributors, producers, directors, writers, technicians, critics, actors, and, most importantly, spectators. It functioned as a forum for a host of perspectives. Within it, many critics and filmmakers attempted, if often with deep ambivalence, to reconcile business and art, high-brow and low-brow taste, enlightenment and entertainment, modernist impulses and traditional ethos. The Central Theater and its exhibition chain was a synecdoche of a vibrant and rapidly expanding film culture in Shanghai and other urban centers. This massive reorientation not only required the recruitment of a far larger audience than that of the previous teahouse environment, but also placed substantial pressure on the filmmakers and theater owners to take into account a changing mode of visual perception and consumption. The corollary between the theater's spatial interiority and the socialized spectatorial psychology reflects some tension in the social engineering of the isolated individual spectator within a communal cinematic experience. This tension was articulated in the incipient discourse on the ontology and social efficacy of the cinema. The mass production of long films and serious dramas, or popular melodramas about families, social ethics, and mass education proved to be commercially viable in this period of rapid urbanization. More significantly, the commercial interest was intertwined with a conscious moral investment—hence Zheng Zhengqiu's slogan "business plus conscience." The cinema was as a democratic medium imbued with the potential for social transformation. Inasmuch as this moral and artistic conscience was often conveyed through sensational plots and melodramatic excess endowed with social purpose, the narrative integration of this cinema remained unsettled, or rather, open to more possibilities in a constantly evolving film world.

PART TWO

COMPETING MODERNS

CHAPTER FIVE

SCREENWRITING, TRICK PHOTOGRAPHY, AND MELODRAMATIC RETRIBUTION

THE FILM WORLD in Shanghai of the 1920s was crowded with a great number of companies, films, and a profusion of cinematic discourses. In this period long narrative films bloomed and diversified. *Orphan Rescues Grandfather* not only saved Mingxing from a financial crisis but also provided the film industry as a whole with the impetus to move toward institutionalization and industrialization. One critic praised the film for departing significantly from formulaic stage art: "The whole film is redolent of a shadowplay ambiance. The New Drama–like acting is diminished."[1] This remark anticipated a broad discussion that tried to systematically define cinema vis-à-vis drama—especially the civilized play. The textbooks of the Changming Correspondence Film School discussed in chapter 4 were but part of this impulse to endow the film profession with social and artistic legitimacy. At the same time, the notion and practice of the film script as a new form of modern, vernacular writing began to occupy a prominent place in both cinematic discourse and practice.

In this chapter I chart the complex genealogy and cultural geography of a melodramatic mode of cinematic storytelling and its variations in the mid-1920s. Rather than offering an exhaustive account of that dynamic period, I will instead focus on the rise of, and resistance to, the film script and the related question of cultural translation. The increasing importance of the script, while effectively bridging the verbal conception of a film and its visible manifestation on the screen, generated anxieties over the ontological status of the cinematic medium and its social and ethical implications. I begin with a discussion of the art of screenwriting as conceived by Hou Yao (1903–42) and Xu Zhuodai (1881–1958), who were at once filmmakers, screenwriters, and critics. Xu's fascination with trick cinematography also calls for an inquiry into the contemporary discourse on and practice of photography with regard to the "composition" of the modern subject in China. This places the film experience within a larger field of experimental cultural vision as still images were *mobilized* to embody the playful and mobile yet anxiety-ridden modernizing process.

Then I turn to two rather distinct films about pearls: *A String of Pearls* (*Yichuan zhenzhu,* Changcheng, 1926), the earliest extant narrative film written by Hou, and *Lustrous Pearls* (*Ye mingzhu;* Huaju, 1927). Both liberally draw upon foreign and indigenous sources and point to the heterogeneous aesthetic and social orientations characteristic of the period Zheng Junli called the "booming era" of Chinese cinema. The two pearl-centered films related differently to the ascendance of the script (or, screenwriting, in a quite graphic sense), and to a particular storytelling mode heavily reliant upon the notion of retribution (*baoying*). In vernacular usage, retribution suggests repetition and balancing of moral or economical debts across time and space, including the boundary between life and the afterlife. The cinematic adoptions of the Buddhism-influenced concept and other traditional notions permeating Chinese everyday life are complicated because the medium, as a mechanical mimetic machine, gives new shapes and meanings to the human soul and body. The circulation of pearls and, indeed, the circular narrative trajectory bound to them can be viewed as materialization of retribution undergoing stressful transformation—at times quite literally.

Both films contain explicit elements related to retribution. *A String of Pearls,* meticulously scripted by Hou Yao for the patriotic Changcheng Company and based on Guy de Maupassant's short story "The Diamond Necklace," seamlessly harnesses those elements to create a cautionary tale about female vainglory and a moral allegory of urban modernity's corruptibility. The cycle of exchange in the film, while continuing to bring back the specter of the commodity fetish embodied by the necklace, is also suggestive of a gender relation in a state of upheaval. By contrast, *Lustrous Pearls,* scripted by and starring Zhang Huimin, a self-styled film entrepreneur and a Shanghai local hero (as a famous fire-brigade chief), freely mixes elements of folktale and the American "serial-queen drama" series which were quite popular in China. *Lustrous Pearls* may not seem to originate in any elaborate dramaturgy or film theory, as did *A String of Pearls.* I am inclined, however, to view the film as an extension of a film aesthetic and practice rooted in the earlier teahouse mode of production and presentation, which emphasized spontaneity and physical action over artful realism and psychological absorption. In Zhang's action-packed film, a group of athletic male and female characters stage adventurous acts in a wild landscape—a far cry from Hou's interiorized urban theater and family drama.

The films' different narratives can also be understood allegorically in relation to the intense competition in the Shanghai film scene at the time. The disparities reveal the plural approaches in the search for a language of storytelling, particularly the melodramatic form (or forms), within a fast-developing film industry and market. Together they represent a historical moment laden with translated ideas, competing lifestyles, and polymorphous gender roles—a cultural landscape permeated with new possibilities and residues of a lingering past. My analysis of the two films thus serves in part to contrast the different narrative models available to Shanghai filmmakers at the time, especially with regard to their uses of existing storytelling conventions and modes of address.

SCREENWRITING AS "COMPOSITION"

As examined in chapter 3, no systematic distinctions were made between the "director" and the "screenwriter" in the teahouse mode of film production. Up until the early 1920s, the bulk of the Chinese cinema of attractions consisted of actualities, travelogues, short physical comedies, and filmed sensational civilized plays. The early short story films such as *Laborer's Love* had a lean outline but a shooting script was unheard of. The sketchy scenario outline, derived from the *mubiao* practice of the civilized play,[2] served as a production's haphazard reference point rather than a rigorous blueprint. With the onset of the long story film, however, a synopsis was no longer adequate for a cinema that relied on a sustained plot and dramatic conflict. The increased number of characters also required sophisticated dialogue and other intertitles to convincingly help the narrative unfold. For the silent cinema, this increased verbality created a heightened importance for the written word.

This new trend attracted a number of fiction writers, particularly the Mandarin Ducks and Butterflies school, including Bao Tianxiao, Shen Zhengya, Zhu Shouju, and Zhou Shoujuan. Many of these writers began to get directly involved in cinema in a period when Butterfly literature itself adopted the vernacular and gained an unprecedented mass appeal. The May Fourth writers such as Lu Xun, however, relentlessly attacked this literature on the grounds that it catered to the "feudal" taste of the petty urbanites and indulged a leisure-seeking readership.[3]

In Bao Tianxiao's memoir, he vividly recalled the first time he ventured into film as a screenwriter. In 1924, the booming Mingxing Company was suddenly beset by a serious shortage of scripts (*juben huang*), as it was no longer possible or desirable to rapidly churn out skeletal *mubiao* for long films. One day, Zheng Zhengqiu called upon his friend Bao, then an editor at the newspaper *Shibao,* with a request: Mingxing wanted to engage him to write a script based on his widely popular novel *Orchid in the Empty Valley.* The novel had been successfully adapted into a civilized play by Bao and Zheng ten years earlier. Bao, knowing nothing about the film business, humbly replied, "You are really asking a blind man for directions. I don't know anything about screenwriting, and have never seen a script. How can I start writing one?" Zheng replied that it would be simple enough—Bao only needed to concoct a plot with complicated twists and turns plus some tragicomic elements, and the company would then expand and divide it into scenes and acts (*fenchang fenmu*). Bao had always considered himself a believer in Hu Shi's pragmatic "experimentalism," willing to try any new literary form or medium. Beside immense curiosity, another factor that motivated him was the lucrative payment: a hundred yuan for the script. Compared to the meager rate of two yuan per thousand characters for his serialized fiction, the screenwriter's job would give every written word much more value, not to mention glamour. When the film turned out to be a big hit, the veteran writer, seeing his name on the screen as the screenwriter (*bianju*), was a bit ashamed as he knew the finished film was rather far from his "script."[4]

What made this earlier screenwriting practice peculiar was the indispensable role played by the writer of intertitles, the *shuoming* (explicator)—a title may have derived from the oral announcer or interpreter in early exhibition practice. Generally in the credits, the name of the explicator was juxtaposed with the screenwriter. In the strictest sense of the word, screenwriting was a composite act performed in production and during exhibition.[5] The prominence offered to Bao Tianxiao was likely a ploy to capitalize on his popularity and turn his vast number of readers into film audience members. Although the intertitles bear some visible traces of the original story, the script had little to do with the film. For *Orchid in the Empty Valley,* Zheng Zhengqiu assumed the role of the explicator, masterfully rendering the soul of Bao's script into a visible body. The cinematic vocabulary (such as framing and editing), however, was largely left to the director.

This doubled-up screenwriting process was further complicated by the diversity of writing forms that separated the verbal and the visual. The synopsis and intertitles for the third-person narration were mostly written in a semiclassical language quite similar to the early Butterflies literature, whereas the dialogue titles were in the contemporary vernacular prose. In *The Science of Screenwriting,"* [6] a Changming textbook, the authors offered some explanations for this hierarchy of writings:

> In Chinese shadowplay, the main intertitles (*zong shuoming*) should be written in the simplified classical language while the minor intertitles (*fen shuoming*) should be in the vernacular. This is a very good division. The intertitles in a shadowplay should avoid the use of abstruse words, especially unfamiliar allusions, because *within a short time, the glances of the spectator pass quickly and there is no time for elaborate thinking.* Some people suggest that the intertitles should use only unrefined language, and that it is not necessary to pay attention to the literary value. This is really a shallow man's superficial view and the crazy talk of the uneducated! If a very valued literary work will be used as the material for adaptation, how can you use a vulgar language in intertitles to trample on the men of letters and spoil the canon? [7]

Authors took pains to balance the distance between the loftier status of major literary works and the vernacular taste of the mass audience, because the popular nature of the film experience leaves little room or time for recondite learning in the classical language. It also reveals some of the fundamental contradictions of the vernacular movement. The teaching resonates with Hu Shi's "eight do not-ism" manifesto, in which he called for a literary language that would, among other things, be free of classical allusions. By upholding the canons' "literary value" yet acknowledging cinema's vernacular appeal the writers exposed the ambivalent relationship between popular cinema and the vernacular movement. In spite of its democratic intentions, the movement quickly evolved from a mass-oriented project into a "neoclassical language" as criticized by the Marxist critic Qu Qiubai.

However, the situation with cinema was arguably different because the written word was only part of its experience. In a pragmatic sense, the task of the filmmakers and critics was to negotiate between the diverse cultural resources and interests that gave rise to this new cinematic trend. The cohabitation of classical and vernacular, written and spoken languages created a shared space for disparate cultural sensibilities and temporalities.[8] This composite method provided an innovative means for inventing screenwriting at a time when the cinema was deeply enmeshed in a multitude of cultural practices and representational forms. More importantly, it resonated with the host of languages, including their inflections and accents, heard or seen in the streets, the newspapers, and the theaters in Shanghai and elsewhere.

While Chinese silent cinema was heavily indebted to the rich repertoire of old and new vernacular literature, a number of attempts were made to adapt world literature to the Chinese screen for both local and diasporic audiences. In part these adaptations derived from the highly institutionalized practice of translating world literature into Chinese, which had flourished since the late Qing period. Existing filmographies indicate a few dozen or so foreign adaptations, which comprised a persistent strand of Chinese silent cinema from the early 1910s through the early 1930s.

In her study of the "composition" of the New Woman in late Qing China, Hu Ying finds that this highly gendered image appeared in translation as a collective production of the modern imaginary. The Chinese New Woman was an imported cosmopolitan product bearing resemblance to *La dame aux camellias,* Sophia Perovskaia, and Madame Roland de la Platiere. Yet, as she was being composed in(to) Chinese, she took on features and behaviors of her would-be literary ancestors and sisters in the Chinese literary tradition. Thus it was not surprising to find a revolutionary who was also a filial daughter, or a chaste widow who recited a poem from *Romeo and Juliet*—in short, a composite figure that was neither "original" nor "coherent."[9] Hu's study demonstrates that translation, just as with the creation of the Chinese New Woman, "bristles with implications about the difficulties in presuming either 'fidelity' of translation or adequacy in representing cross-cultural experience." Translation as such, beyond the literal and literary domains, is thus "a tension ridden 'contact zone.'"[10]

I have identified approximately thirty films that are apparent adaptations, including *A String of Pearls,* although some original sources remain obscure. I say "apparent" because, as Hu Ying's example of *Jade Pear Spirit* (a popular novel second-handedly based on *La Dame aux camellias*) shows, there are often opaque translations and derivatives that do not correspond directly to their sources. Not surprisingly, the screen adaptation of Shen Zhengya's novel, a text in classical prose derived from the Camellia story, was a box-office hit in 1924. Shen's serialized story was a far cry from the French original, which had been first translated into classical Chinese by Lin Shu in 1898. Shen transfigured the famous Parisian courtesan into a Chinese widow who, painstakingly trying to obey the Confucian codes of chastity, renounces her desire for her own child's teacher, a young handsome scholar, only to die of depression and melancholy.

As a comprehensive aesthetic and cultural form, the cinematic experience was deeply implicated in the translation and domestication of Western technology and ideas. Early film exhibition more often than not involved the instrumental presence of a simultaneous "interpreter" or explicator. Their commentaries could be very far from what the images "intended" to say and often served as means of mediation between foreign sights and local tastes. In the process, the exotic images were infused with a set of new meanings and became, to use Hu's wording in a cinematic sense, a "composition." Their "translingual practice"[11] not only crossed the linguistic barriers but medial and cultural thresholds as well.

SOULS TO THOSE SHADOWS

Xu Zhuodai,[12] author of *The Science of Shadow-play* (1924), and Hou Yao, author of *Techniques of Writing Shadowplay Scripts* (1925, hereafter *Techniques*),[13] were two prominent film personalities who uniquely represented the energetic small companies in the colorful film world of the 1920s. At the outset, Xu and Hou seem to have embraced two opposite positions on cinema's relationship to drama. Xu explicitly argued for the singularity of shadow (*ying*) in the cinematic experience, whereas Hou persistently adhered to play (*xi*) as the foundation of cinema. Yet Xu said elsewhere that "shadowplay is really about play."[14] Obviously, *xi* has two meanings here. It represents serious "drama" for Hou Yao, whereas for Xu *xi* is derived from *youxi,* or play (and playfulness) that is not necessarily confined to the theater space. Both shared an obsession with the soul (*linghun*) of shadowplay. For Hou, this soul has recourse to a new form of verbal art, the film script. For Xu, who was known for his versatility as both a comedian and a popular writer, however, the shadowy "soul" was found in the unstable identity of the photographed body.

Despite their different and even contrary ideological and aesthetic persuasions, each harbored a dramatist and, to some extent, pedagogical zest for ethical education, now mediated through the magic of cinema. While Hou was serious about creating a film language for dramatizing tragedy and his disenchantment with the May Fourth enlightenment, Xu was committed to carrying over the spirit of comic relief and quotidian entertainment into the cinematic venture. Hou's ambivalence toward cinema stemmed from his adherence to a naturalist dramaturgy that emphasized mimetic representation and its social function. By contrast, Xu embraced cinema as a new form of mass entertainment and found in cinematography the potential for a playful embodiment of modern subjectivity.

During this period, the space of the movie theater was structurally transforming to condition spectators physically and psychologically for a cinema of narrative integration and moral edification. Thus the attempt to inscribe the "soul" of shadowplay underscores a desire to establish an organic and more stable connection between the spectator and cinema. The script could endow the electric shadows with traces of tangible substance, pacifying the anxiety over the ontological status of the medium. The institutionalization of the script not only incorporated popular Butterfly literature writers into the film world but also attracted progressive spoken drama playwrights including Hou Yao, Hong Shen, and Tian Han (1898–1968) to write for the silver screen. With cinema becoming popular and commercially viable in a booming urban culture, the question whether or not cinema had a distinguished, authorial soul behind or transcending the flat screen suddenly acquired urgency.

In the preface to his *Techniques,* Hou states that the "script is the soul of a film." In the book, however, he consistently views the cinema as a new form of drama. To be sure, soul was hardly a novel category in Chinese dramaturgy. For centuries, the Chinese theater, deeply embedded in folk religions, has been, among other things, the familiar habitat of wandering souls. The theater has functioned as a liminal space for the living to appease, exorcise, and encounter the souls of the diseased and religious deities in order to come to terms with them.[15] The actors were often liminal figures, too, since they themselves often came from among "ignoble," marginal social groups.[16] Frequently staged in town squares or village temples during festivities or funerary rituals, the collective experience of the theater, so vividly depicted in Lu Xun's Temple Theater (*Shexi*), also provided the point for social conviviality and cultural initiation of the young.[17]

As many actors of the traditional theater were often illiterate or semiliterate, the scripts were often passed on orally and through rigorous hands-on teaching by the masters. Actors often started as young children, joining the troupe, which was organized as family, in lieu of attending school. Even in the early twentieth century, as Ouyang Yuqian recalls, the many Peking opera plays he authored were not intended for publication. He taught other actors orally and used scrap paper with lines and directions, but there were hardly complete scripts. Some were simply recorded by other theater teachers during performances. Published plays attributed to him were sometimes quite different from the versions performed.[18] The spirit of a stage play seemed largely consigned to the contingency of performance and lodged in the bodies of the actors, much different than Hou's attempt to relocate it within the screenwriter's mind.

As mentioned in chapter 3, the story of the Emperor Wu of Han Dynasty meeting his deceased concubine's soul was reconstructed as the earliest instance of the proto-shadowplay by film commentators in the 1920s. A performing artist had a square cloth screen lined up, behind which a woman resembling the concubine danced in dim candlelight. In the evening, watching the moving shadow of the actress on the screen, the emperor was convinced that he saw his deceased concubine.

The association of a projected image with an embodied soul was still current but acquired new meanings when photography and cinema were introduced to China in the mid- to late nineteenth century. Growing up in that period, Lu Xun observed how the Chinese believed that the camera would steal the subject's soul; some even imagined Westerners' eyes as minicameras ready to suck out the Chinese hearts to make pickles. Even those who dared to be photographed avoided a bust portrait, because it would look as though one had been chopped in half—a traditional execution method.[19] Many late Qing illustrated newspapers and magazines (e.g., *Dianshizhai huabao* and *Tuhua ribao*) carried numerous drawings of the horror and wonder evoked by photography, telegraphy, and X-ray. It was widely believed that electricity was a form of the soul, or that it could be embodied through transmission.[20] One of the gifts that the Dowager Empress Cixi received for her seventieth birthday celebration in 1904 was a projector and some film reels from the British Minister at the embassy in Beijing. Shortly after the show started, however, the power generator exploded. Cixi was frightened and decided that the cinema was inauspicious. The deadly lore of the cinema was augmented by another incident involving members of the imperial family showing films in the palace when several attendant officials were killed by yet another explosion. Henceforth, film was not allowed inside the imperial palace.[21]

By the mid-1920s the power of the electric shadowplay, associated with life and death, was transformed into a commercial miracle that rivaled the theater and the print media. Even after the May Fourth enlightenment, which relentlessly attacked the so-called feudal superstitions, the vocabulary of the immaterial soul in relation to the spectral moving shadows persisted in the discourse on film.

Hou Yao was one of the few early cinema personalities who actually had a direct tie to the May Fourth movement proper. In the early 1920s, before Hou joined the Great Wall Company as a screenwriter-in-chief, he had been involved in the Literary Association (*Wenxue yanjiuhui*), a major May Fourth intellectual organ founded by Zheng Zhenduo, Shen Yanbing (Mao Dun), and Zhou Zuoren in Beijing in 1921. The association consecutively clustered around the two foremost progressive vernacular literary journals, the *New Tide* (*Xinchao*) and *Fiction Monthly* (*Xiaoshuo yuebao*). The latter was owned and operated by the Commercial Press, the Shanghai media giant. Hou embraced the humanist principle of art for life's sake (*wei rensheng de yishu*) of the Literary Association and believed art should "represent life, criticize life, harmonize life, and beautify life." His passion for the theater, however, also stemmed from a pedagogical principle. Because he had studied education at Nanjing University and was active in the New Drama, Hou's conception of the theater was not far from Zheng Zhengqiu's: "Theater is the laboratory for social education. Actors are the best teachers to impart this education." In his preface to *Techniques* he described himself as a gardener (*yuanding*) charged with the responsibility of cultivating the sprouting Chinese cinema. The horticultural metaphor, often used to describe a devoted educator in China, also subtly invokes the term *pear garden* (*liyuan*), which traditionally stands for the theater world, or rather, the "school" where young pupils are disciplined by their mentors. Hou's insistence on equating life with theater—a rather old view, in fact—was most clearly spelled out in the opening of his book: "Life is really an endless drama. Human beings have to continue to act out those sad partings and happy reunions, living and aging, becoming sick and dying, declines and growths, gains and losses. . . . The theater is really the epitome of human life."[22] The modern shadowplay constituted for him a privileged subcategory of drama far more capable of achieving collective catharsis through its mass appeal and vividness.

For Hou, the life-world, like the theater world, is comprised of problems that make it possible to transform notions from the traditional theater of suffering and redemption in the afterlife into a set of burning modern concerns. Two modern Western writers in particular influenced him: Ibsen and Maupassant, whose plays and stories were enthusiastically translated by the May Fourth writers, especially members of the Literary Association. Hou's first script for Great Wall, *The Abandoned Wife* (*Qifu*, 1924; starring Wang Hanlun) (fig. 5.1), was based on his eponymous stage play. In essence an exposé of the "problem of women's employment," it ponders the after effects of Chinese Nora leaving home. The script, written entirely in the May Fourth-style vernacular, complete with scene numbers and camera setups, was appended to *Techniques*.[23]

According to the screenplay, the female protagonist Wu Zhifang has left her unfaithful husband, seeking independence and respect from society. But the modern city, seemingly a haven for educated and professional women, proves to be another prison. She works as a secretary at a press where the boss demands sexual favors from her and her male colleagues harass her. Her maid goes to school, only to be looked down upon by the school principal and her classmates. Wu then devotes herself to the suffrage movement but has to flee the city when her estranged husband and the police begin to persecute her for being a radical. She eventually dies of illness, hunger, robbery, and shock when the police come to arrest her in a mountain nunnery where she has sought refuge. Crying over the dead body of this women's liberation martyr, the maid condemns society for devouring women and vows to fight on. Here, Wu's

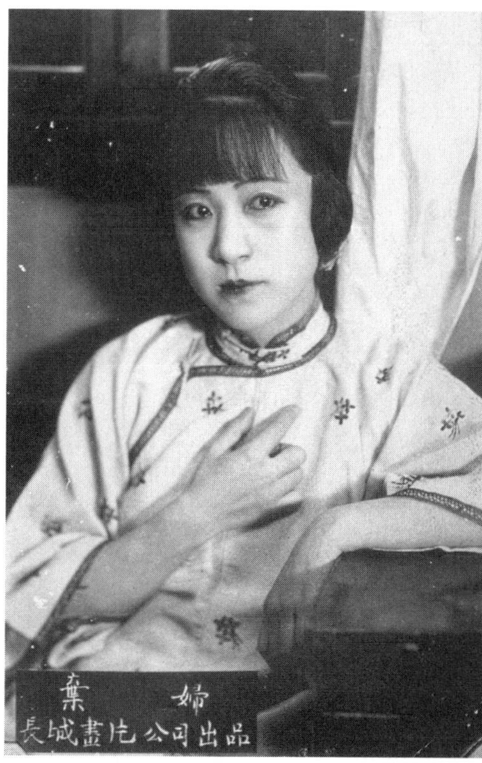

5.1 *The Abandoned Wife* (1924) starring Wang Hanlun. (Courtesy of the China Film Archive)

corpse becomes an effective "living" mise-en-scène statement against a corrupt, male-dominated society. There is no need to revive Wu's soul since her maid, who has practically become her sister after they left the oppressive home, stands as her incarnation. The film, however, has not survived the ravages of time; only its script was retained in Hou's text.

THE SORCERY OF TRICK PHOTOGRAPHY

One year before Hou Yao wrote his *Techniques,* Xu Zhuodai had already published *The Science of Shadowplay.* Xu did not explicitly assert the centrality of the script as Hou did; instead, he seemed obsessed with the notion of the photographic shadow and its peculiar, playful relation to the soul. While Hou was a keen admirer of Ibsen and Maupassant, Xu reveals himself to be a fan of German expressionism and its progenitor, romanticism, and the technique of *tuolike* (trick) using double-exposure. In the very first chapter, he sets out to distinguish film drama (*yingpianju*) from theater drama (*wutaiju*), using the early German film *Student of Prague*

(1913) as an independent art consisting of moving shadow pictures.[24] It is appropriate that the short sample script (only a synopsis and the first scene were included) in the book is called *Shadow* (*A Thought Drama*) (*Ying* [*sixiang ju*]). This story is obviously modeled after Paul Wegener's film, about a student's Faustian bargain. The hero is a young medical student who is "well versed in philosophy and science" but deeply tormented by his dread of death. An evil demon encourages him to go on living as a misanthrope. A good (redeemed) demon tries, however, to cure him by advising him to look toward light instead of his own shadow. He tells the student that light stands for eternity and shadow stands for the present. The fear of death originates in the student's obsession with his shadow, that is, his own mental shallowness and lack of substance. The good demon gives the student a drug that can keep his shadow exposed near the radiant light. Day in and day out, the student diligently works without complaining. As a consequence, his shadow becomes less and less ugly; more surprisingly, it begins to overlap with his body. The student is thus able to sleep without the fear of death. At the end, the good demon revisits the student, telling him from now on there will be neither life nor death, except for the eternal light. Finally redeemed, the soul of the student walks alongside the good demon toward boundless transcendence.

While *Shadow* bears striking resemblance to *Student of Prague*, it also diverges from the latter in some crucial aspects. The duality embodied by the two demons clearly rehearses the romantic motif of the doppelgänger in *Student of Prague*. But in the latter, the double is played out between the student himself and his own reflection, which is sold to the devil for the money needed in his pursuit of an aristocratic woman. The Prague student loses his mirror image but cannot get rid of his own haunted soul, and ends up killing the other "self." The loss of the symmetrical vision (the bodily self and the reflection) is the cause of spiritual destruction in his pursuit of social ascendance. Once severed, the wandering shadowy self is no longer the friend in the mirror, but a deadly repetition beyond salvation. In *Shadow* the student confronts his own double along a different trajectory. The redemption of the student here proceeds from the opposite: his shadow (rather than reflection) has to be reunited (rather than killed) with his body in order for him to attain existential harmony, or take form in the "projected" (not present) life-world. The soul at peace is an asymptotically embodied being rather than a vacuous ghost image. The shadow here is not a replica (or reflection) of the self, but rather a chimerical demonic force associated with darkness, which ultimately, through "exposure" by the chemical effect of the medicine, is submerged and awash in light, thus completing the "development" or metamorphosis of the negative into positive.[25]

In both instances, the allusion to photography is unmistakable, yet with certain variances. While *Student of Prague* accentuates the perceptual confusion between the body and the soul, *Shadow* is more concerned with the moral conflict highlighted by the allegorical play between shadow and light, evil and goodness. In the German film, the drama revolves around the tragic effect of the mimetic infidelity between the student's body and his mirror image. The image retaining traces of his past as a poor student, which he left behind, haunts him like a living corpse, or "wanders ghostlike through the present."[26] Once the image is sold as a commodity, it takes on a separate life of its own. Without the familiar reflection framed in the mirror, it is no longer clear which version of the student is the authentic one; and the two cannot converge except in the event of (second) death, which erases both the original and the copy.

In Xu's sample script, we are confronted with a shadow that is not an exact mirror image. The whole episode resembles a nightmare in which the spectral sensation arises in the liminal space between sleep and awakening. The moment when the student dissolves his shadow into eternal light approximates when a dreamer feels the "action of light upon the eye or other sensitive medium" (such as film).[27] If the emergence of the spectral shadow into embodied light in this story suggests the process of film projection, it carries all the social and ethical implications as well. When the good demon waves his hand (in a manner typical of the early photographer addressing the sitter) and calls forth the young man's shadow, the latter rather resembles the evil demon that the student believed to be his own image. The instruction for shooting indicates that a trick shot is needed here to have the same actor appearing twice simultaneously in the frame (*erchong zhiyi*) through double-exposure. The writer cautions the actor to be particularly careful, not to confuse his two distinct positions.[28] A close-up displays the grotesque, greedy expression of the shadow. The emphasis on the incongruity, not only in substance but also in physiognomic form, of the split sides of the self, leaves space for transformation rather than confusion, thereby foregrounding the potential of moral redemption.

The fascination with *tuolike* (trick) technique—(Xu devoted a whole chapter to the techniques of reproducing transparent ghost images or daydreams [fig. 5.2])—resonates with a peculiar cultural perception of the body and objective reality, beyond simple toying with the camera. Xu's own film productions (as director and actor) in the mid-1920s included subjects that required extensive use of trick cinematography: *The Invisible Coat* (*Yinshen yi*, 1925), *The Magic Club* (*Shenxian bang*, 1926), *The Mobile Safe* (*Huodong yinxiang*, 1926), to name a few. But in addition to playing with trick techniques, Xu seems more interested in its implication for the role of the actor. In *The Science of Shadowplay* the fictional names of many actors contain the character *ying* (shadow), as though a whole breed of Chinese actors is camera-ready for double-exposure.[29] The penchant for "double-roles" may be traced to the civilized play actors who indulged in playing different, or even antithetical, parts both on- and offstage. Many early popular magazines often carried photographs of actors in various disguises and, more tellingly, their split or multiple personalities within the same trick image [figs. 5.3–4]. This theatrical trend, however, has to be placed in a larger cultural framework.

In his satirical essay on the practice of photography in China, written in the same year as Xu's text, Lu Xun summarizes the form of photography as "essentially . . . sorcery." He recalls that although a photography studio opened in his hometown S (Shaoxing) in the late nineteenth century, only those who either had "bad luck" or were "radicals" were eager to have their souls taken by the camera. The "famous/Bohemian personages and fashionable dandies" (*mingshi fengliu*) of the time experimented with a prevalent genre or composition called the "two-self picture" (*er wo tu*) (fig. 5.5), in which the sitter would pose twice in different attire and expression, and then the two exposures would be made into a single photograph. This format was also called "separate body photographs" (*fen shen xiang*) (fig. 5.6). "But if one self sits in an arrogant posture while the other self obsequiously and pitifully kneels down in front the former, the name is then different and is called 'the self begging the self picture' (*qiu ji tu*)." As though the irony were not obvious enough, the photographed subject would later caption the picture with some poetic lines. This, according to Lu Xun, is akin to the traditional practice in which men of letters would inscribe their own art and the artwork they possessed, before they hung them on the wall in their study.[30] For him, these photographic forms vividly illustrate the master-slave dialectic. Despite his patently satirical tone, Lu Xun recorded a critical moment in the history of photography in China. It called attention to an at once fragmented and recomposed subject caught between separate yet superimposed worlds, or, in Homi Bhabha's phraseology, on the "split screen of the self and its doubling" in a colonial setting.[31]

This tension-ridden double-life, when processed by the photographic double-exposure or sorcery effect, takes on the spectral forms of the "two-self picture" and "self-begging picture." These staged split images are kindred spirits of the double professional roles in trick shots, as visualized by Xu. They all seem to acknowledge the epistemological, ethical, and social dimensions imprinted on the photographed image. Appearing in China at a time of tremendous cultural change and unsure identities, the uncanny power of photography generated a double-edged knowledge that linked a modern medium with certain superstitious beliefs

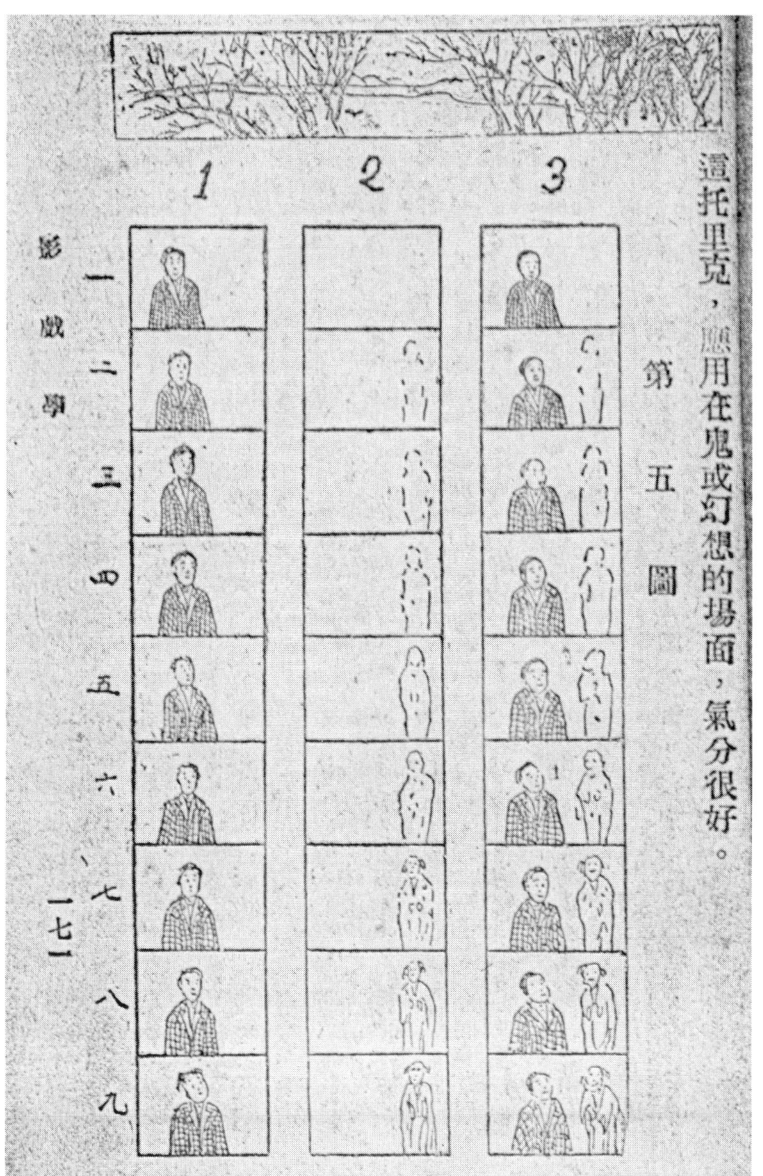
還托里克，應用在鬼或幻想的場面，氣分很好。

第五圖

1　2　3

一　二　三　四　五　六、七　八　九

影戲學　一七一

5.2 Illustrations for trick cinematography in *The Science of Shadowplay.*

5.3 Xu Zhuodai (Xu Banmei), the author of *The Science of Shadowplay*, in a female role.

about appearance and soul, body and selfhood, physiognomy and character. Even the daredevil fashionable dandies, as modern incarnations of the traditional literati, embraced photography as a sort of spiritual medium. It enabled the bodily manifestation of one's ambivalent phantom other(s), and the mobilization of multiple perspectives on selfhood

5.4 Actors playing with trick photography.

5.5
The two-self picture
(*er wo tu*).

5.6 Separate body photograph (*fenshen xiang*).

and the external world through the manipulation of juxtaposed exposures of the same actor. In this sense, the self-begging picture and the double professional roles of the actor resemble the spiritualist images in early photography and film found in other cultures. Tom Gunning sees the phantasmagoric quasi-religious images used by the spiritualists as "modern manifestations." They are modern because, although some served as "evidence of a supernatural metaphysical existence, the spirit photographs also present a uniquely modern conception of the spirit world as caught up in the endless play of image making and reproduction and the creation of simulacra."[32]

To be sure, there are not only vast regions of historical time but also paradigmatic cultural and technological differences separating the worlds of the Han emperor's simulacrum and trick photography studio at the dawn of the twentieth century. While the emperor contented himself with a live performance and remained an external spectator of the female image in a private "screening room," the becoming-modern dandy was aided by the magic power of photography to publicly exhibit an ambivalent narcissism. The latter fabricated not only a multiplied selfhood but also a self-conscious, three-tiered viewing subject: the dressed-up "master" watched the "slave" and vice versa, and the third, the "original" or predisguised author-sitter who posed for and signed the photograph with epigrammatic poetry for daily introspection.

The self-begging picture is also suggestive of a cinematic impulse, as it is essentially a heterogeneous product made of two (or several) different frames, moving from stasis toward mobility or transformation.[33] The final composition, ornamented with poetic lines (like title cards in a silent film), presents a trick shot laden with narrative tensions between a series of originals and copies, distributed unevenly across different social and ethical planes. The impulse to use backdrops and mise-en-scène props inside the studio—a practice carried over from portraiture tradition and stage performance—also anticipated the use of painted backdrops and real objects in early film practice.

In Xu's sample script *Shadow,* the student finally attains his soul by renouncing the dark forces within him. This renunciation or, rather, exposure, tends to erase traces of a heterogeneous subject. In his interpretation of Benjamin's historico-philosophical conception of the medium, Eduardo Cadava writes: "The conquest of darkness by the increased light of photography conjures a link of fidelity between the photograph and the photographed. Yet it is precisely the conviction in the coincidence, in the photographic possibility of faithful reproduction, that marks the decline of photography." What spurred Benjamin's reaction to this decline was the "forgetting of the photography's ghostly or spectral character" as a result of the rise of a "mimetic ideology of realism" fueled by the technical perfection of the apparatus.[34] Xu's brief sample script, subtitled a "thought drama," remained an unrealized idea. Despite the eventual forgetting of death and exorcism of the uncanny dark force, the story as a whole shows its author's lingering attachment to "photography's ghostly or spectral character." While Hou tried to find the soul of narrative film in the legitimate theater and literature, Xu pursued it in cinema's debt to photography, acknowledging its transformative power, especially its capacity for composing modern subjectivities.

A STRING OF PEARLS: RETRIBUTION OF COMMODITY DESIRE

Having explored the inchoate relationship between the ascendance of the script and competing perceptions of soul and body operative in early twentieth-century Chinese media culture, I now return to Hou's *A String of Pearls* to examine how he applied and projected his theory on screenwriting onto the silver screen (fig. 5.7). It was one of the many films he scripted for Great Wall, a studio founded in 1924 by film enthusiasts who had studied in America. Hou Yao, who had not studied abroad, joined the company that year. In an attempt to differentiate itself from other commercial companies that relied heavily on the Butterfly fiction, Great Wall emphasized the importance of the independent script: "Without good scripts, we'd rather not hastily make any films in three or five months that might . . . corrupt the society, humiliate the country."[35]

5.7 Ad for *A String of Pearls* (1926). (Courtesy of the China Film Archive)

Despite his insistence on imposing the naturalist drama's mimetic function on cinema, Hou was conscious of cinematography's power to embody a film's moral soul, or to rekindle the magic of the written word. In the film, this soul is writ large in the animated word-image-thing of the fateful pearl necklace, making concrete the ambivalence toward the cinema's double identity—a potential vehicle for mass literacy and education as well as a mass-mediated commodity. Hou's critique of commodity fetishism and urban modernity, and elevation of writing over image, paradoxically resorted to cinema's capacity for retooling the primitive power of mimesis or closing the distance between words and things.

Hou's script transplants Maupassant's story to a Chinese setting, turning it into a "family problem drama" set in Shanghai's emergent urban culture. The original short story is about a young couple that borrows a diamond necklace from a rich friend so that the wife can wear it to a ball. But the necklace is lost on their way home, and the couple has to work very hard for ten years before they can repay the debt. Only then, after all the hard work and social degradation they have endured is the truth revealed. The lost necklace is in fact a fake. They have paid 35,000 francs to purchase a new necklace: the fake one only cost 350 francs.[36]

In Hou's version, all the characters assume ordinary Chinese names and the setting of the story has been changed to a private party in Shanghai during the Lantern Festival, celebrating the full moon on the fifteenth day of the first lunar month (fig. 5.8). Several other key elements were replaced to enhance the narrative function of the necklace and its commodity nature, as well as its cultural and cinematic appeal to the Chinese audience. Instead of diamonds, the necklace is now a string of pearls, a familiar motif in traditional Chinese folklore and literature. The

5.8 *A String of Pearls:* "Lantern Festival" in electric writing.

wife's name contains the character *zhen* (precious), which is a prefix for the word *pearl* in Chinese (*zhenzhu*, literally, "precious beads"). The residual hieroglyphic elements in Chinese characters make it easier to reveal such connections (or connotations and puns) between things and people's character, especially as Chinese names can be made out of almost any character in the dictionary.

The round shape of pearls (and the string, or *chuan*) and their literary association with tears combine to make the necklace a pertinent narrative vehicle for a melodrama about the commodity circulation and desire in an emerging Chinese metropolis. *A String of Pearls* underscores the danger to the nuclear family in a modern city by adding a child to the picture and foregrounds the moral conflict encountered by the urban woman, who is poised between the private and public spheres. Feeling obliged to provide for his wife, Wang borrows a string of pearls from a friend who runs a jewelry store. The husband works at an insurance company (rather than a government bureau, as in Maupassant's story), which allows the narrative to unfold in a different direction. The necklace belonged to a female customer who had brought it to a jewelery store for repair. Wang tries to borrow money from relatives and friends, but without much success. In the end, he steals money from his company's safe to buy a new necklace, gets caught, and is promptly sent to prison. Xiuzhen moves to a slum, barely surviving by mending clothes (fig. 5.9, 5.10).

Hou also made bold alterations to the second half of the story, spinning a subplot into a circular tale of moral retribution. With that resolution, the sexual imbalance caused by the (woman's) desire for material display is readjusted and the family and social order recaptured. After his release, Wang does menial labor at a factory where a certain Mr. Ma works as an accountant. As it turns out, Ma had hired a hooligan to steal the necklace after he saw at the party how much the party hostess Fu Meixian admired it. He won Fu's heart with the stolen beads and married her. The hooligan, however, has been blackmailing Ma, who in turn has been taking more money from the office safe to keep the secret. Finally, Wang "coincidentally" finds himself rescuing Ma from a violent attack by the hooligan. At the hospital, Ma repents, revealing the truth. Fu buys back the Wang family's house, and things return to normal—except that the inauspicious pearl necklace has been excised from the picture.

A String of Pearls makes visible the cultural and economic presence of the West in Shanghai. Hou's script, however, results from "borrowing" as much as from cultural translation, enabled by a global sphere of mass culture, exchange, and consumption.[37] By placing the centerpiece of mise-en-scène—a string of pearls—in a prolonged economic trajectory,

5.9 *A String of Pearls:* At the party. (Courtesy of the China Film Archive)

5.10 *A String of Pearls:* Reunion after the husband is released from jail. (Courtesy of the China Film Archive)

Hou's revision of the original story produces a highly dramatic effect of reversal and accentuates the uncanny logic of repetition, reciprocity, and social reproduction in a modernizing city. The exchangeability of the social positions of the husband, who borrows the necklace to satisfy his wife's vanity, and the friend, who steals the necklace to buy his fiancée's affection, constitutes a double that is redolent of the doppelgänger motif in trick photography discussed earlier, only here no double exposures are needed. Throughout the film, the necklace, once appearing, then vanishing, functions as a red thread linking different narrative elements and characters, and thereby connecting an interior family drama to a larger public scene and urban marketplace. This enigmatic object of desire and an ornamental artifice wreaks havoc on a nuclear family of the new urban white-collar class. Through the narrative cycle, the necklace lives out its full life as a quintessential commodity form, taking on a hieroglyphic significance and haunting those who come into contact with it.

Even before the plot unfolds, several elements place the film in an ambivalent space of cinematic consumption. The first appearance of the company icon is formed by pearl-like dancing dots and then transfigured into bricks of the Great Wall, a stylized but clichéd emblem of Chinese civilization. In the print I saw, a statement in both Chinese and English announces: "The Chinese Moving Picture Company's Manila distributor has exclusive distribution rights in the Philippine islands." This indicates that the film entered the lucrative Nanyang market, which was vital to the Shanghai film industry at the time. The following credit displays the film title encircled by a giant pearl necklace, which again forms a visual reincarnation of the ancient Great Wall (fig. 5.11a–b).

The collusion of the iconic Great Wall and the pearl necklace illustrates the production of a cinematic hieroglyph with a Chinese inflection.

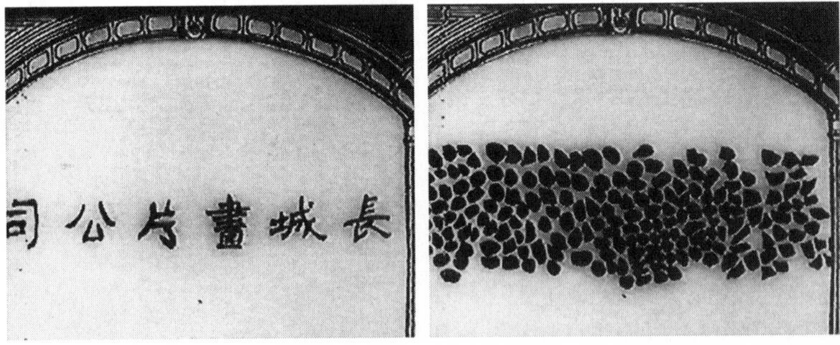

5.11a–b The company name is transformed into dancing dots (and then into the "Great Wall").

Marx's classical definition of the commodity form as a hieroglyphic rests on a reconceptualization of the fetish as both a magic object and a "perverse" image that lies at the heart of the "fantastic relations" between things. He describes commodities as "social hieroglyphics" that ask to be deciphered like a language or code.[38] Prefiguring Benjamin's remarks on the "forgetting" of photography's historical genesis in its "decline," Marx points to the mechanism of collective amnesia as a crucial condition for the production of a fetish, as "the intermediate steps of the process vanish in the result and leave no trace behind." The modern day commodity fetish is doubly desacralized because it appears as though it is a natural daily object free of any magic touch and has no historical grounding.[39] In a proposition that links Marx's commodity theory to a broader conception of a mediatized mass culture, Theodor Adorno reasons: "As image, the hieroglyphics [of mass culture] are the medium of regression in which producer and consumer collude, as writing, they supply archaic images to modernity."[40] Miriam Hansen goes further and argues that the "regression" that Adorno describes parallels the "reversion of Enlightenment into myth and the resurfacing of the archaic in modern forms of domination." In industrialized society, while language becomes increasingly instrumentalized, mass culture has acquired the "archaic" appearance as a "language of images." However, it is precisely through the unwitting return to the mimetic faculty of language based on hieroglyphic writing that modern mass culture resuscitates the ancient desire for aesthetic signification without the distance between the sign and the image, the "producer" and the "consumer."[41]

In *A String of Pearls*, the chimerical necklace—commodity, adornment, graphic design, and writing—exerts its capacity of imaging mass culture "in which producer and consumer collude." Here the hieroglyphic apparition is even more emphatic and literal because of the cultural history of ideogrammatic symbolism through Chinese characters. The impulse to return to the archaic system of writing via the means of electric shadows is ensconced, rather ambivalently, in a desire to showcase the lure as well as the calamity of modern commodity culture. In a key moment, the image of the necklace and the two Chinese ideographs meaning "misfortune" collapse into legible animated hieroglyphic writing—or the "language of images." This takes place in the sequence after Wang has gone to jail and Xiuzhen must mend laborers' clothes. Xiuxhen's nightly sewing is intercut with a masked shot of her husband's forlorn posture inside the cell. She is still at work at dawn, when the lyrical intertitle reads: "My tears must stop, for every drop / Hinders needles and thread." As though evoked by the classical poetic allusion that links tears and pearls, Xiuzhen, in a flashback, revisualizes the earlier scene when women at the party admired her necklace. As visual tokens of the "tear drops" and "needles and thread" in the preceding monologue, the threads and buttons on the table suddenly come to life, animated into formation of two gigantic ideographs, *Huo Hai* (misfortune or catastrophe), thereby closing off the flashback (fig. 5.12a–b). The pearl necklace eventually "dances" back into the shape of the threads and buttons, the humdrum daily objects and tokens of a life in the urban lower depth. This stop-animation brings back the necklace as a haunting specter, a hieroglyphic literally inscribing the moral soul of the film on the screen. Its significance within both the daydream sequence and the plot as a whole vividly illustrates the other meaning of specter, namely—according to the Epicureans—"an image or semblance supposed to emanate from corporeal things, those that assail the soul when she ought to be at rest."[42] By deploying trick cinematography as a modern form of magic—one that effectively links the commodity fetish to Xiuzhen's social degradation and spiritual regression to archaic animism—in the service of a carefully constructed narrative, the filmmakers demonstrated "film to be the ritual cure for modern misfortune."[43]

The circular movement of both the necklace and the plot, however, is

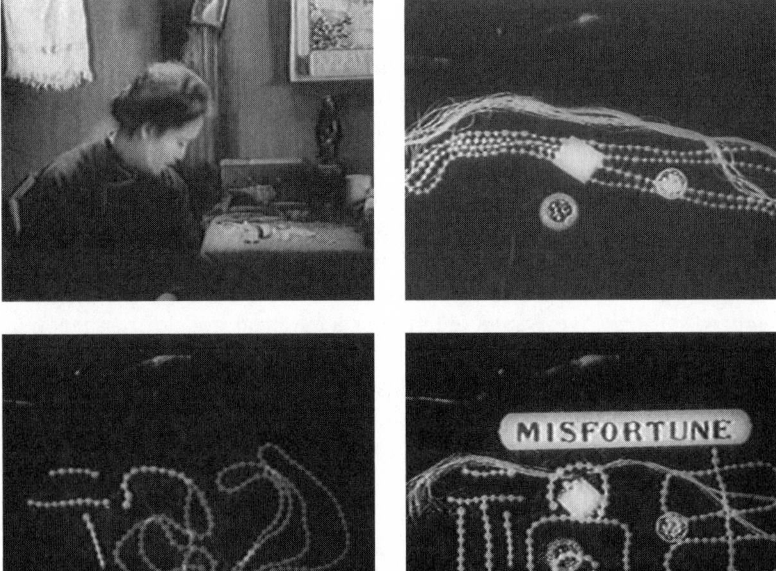

5.12a–d *A String of Pearls:* The animated reenactment of "Misfortune."

fraught with pressure points. The narrative upheaval, as captured in the animation, exposes commodity fetishism and the hieroglyphic, anachronistic character of mass culture. The artistic and pedagogical intent of the film is complicated by its very visual indulgence in displaying and circulating the valuable yet superfluous object. The film's (or for that matter, Great Wall's) dependence on the market, especially on the consumption power of the overseas Chinese in Nanyang, who may or may not read Chinese, presents *A String of Pearls* itself as a hieroglyphic commodity. As universal "image," it is highly readable; as Chinese "writing," it relies on translation for deciphering. Yet the very presence, or, indeed, the primacy of the Chinese language on the screen reminds and reassures the uprooted Chinese communities living in the doubly foreign (non-Chinese and colonial) setting that they are kindred spirits of the civilization within the bounds of the cinematic Great Wall.

On the thematic level, *A String of Pearls* also delivers mixed messages regarding gender and modern consumer culture in urban China while invoking traditional notions about woman's desire and social order. The first title card right after the credit is a didactic ballad directed at the viewer:

> Don't you know? Don't you know?
> A string of pearls is equal to a million rings of sorrow.
> If a woman drags herself down the road of vanity,
> Her husband will be her victim surely.

This ballad's direct address, commonly used by a narrator or storyteller of traditional vernacular tales, spells out the central narrative trope. A string of pearls is multiplied quantitatively and qualitatively into a million rings of sorrow prefiguring the narrative trajectory as an allegory for moral lapse and the threat of retribution. The transaction of desire, the female body, and jewelry recalls the famous vernacular story "The Pearl-Sewn Shirt" by Feng Menglong. The late Ming writer adapted the story from a classical tale and also took a keen interest in folklore. Many of his stories, including this one, were made into films in the 1920s in the craze for "classical costume drama." Hou's modern fable on modernity and materiality unabashedly rehearses a deeply entrenched misogynist notion in Chinese cultural tradition—that a woman of vanity is the source of destruction to the family and state. Thus, in its first verbal interpellation of the spectator, the film bares its uneasiness with woman's desire for adornment and consumption.

A String of Pearls is structured in a particular way in order to induce a solution to a larger social issue. If woman's vanity is an age-old "problem," the opening of the film updates it by bringing it right into the heart of the quintessential modern setting in China: a tracking shot of the mesmerizing night-scene of Nanjing Road in Shanghai. The flashing neon signs of the department stores are unequivocal signposts for modern consumption. The film then cuts to the Wang family's living room. The interior is crowded with furniture; the ornate pattern of the wallpaper and the fabric of the sofas are so perfectly matched as to render the space claustrophobic. Xiuzhen holds the baby and her husband reads while smoking his pipe, seated quietly as if they have nothing to say to each other. This tableau forms an archetypal still of the middle-class nuclear family transfixed in boredom. Yet the intertitle reads: "There is nothing in the world more precious than a sweet home." This beginning, which contrasts the urban space brimming with motion, stimuli, and desire with the static tableau of a self-contained nuclear family, establishes a basic pattern of parallel yet contrasting narration that oscillates between the public and the private spaces.

The rest of the film navigates the viewer through the urban maze, linking locations marked with social disparities along the trails of the necklace. From the street full of moving vehicles and lined with shops, to the insurance company where Wang works, to the jewelry store, and to the lavish Fu family garden where the Lantern Festival party takes place. The top of the pavilion in the garden is decorated with light bulbs forming two gigantic characters, *Yuan Xiao,* meaning the "Lantern Festival." This electric writing formed by pearl-like bulbs ominously spells out the setting for the imminent "misfortune." Later we are led to the teahouse where Ma finds a hooligan to steal the necklace, the prison, the working-class neighborhood, the factory, and finally the hospital where the mystery surrounding the necklace is revealed. The numerous tracking shots of locations where characters will pursue the necklace form a dizzying itinerary. After the necklace is stolen, the jewelry becomes a wandering phantom evading its pursuers in the labyrinthine city, yet contaminating everything and everybody. The urban space, wrought with mobility and possibilities, is also unpredictable, violent, and socially segregated. Crucially ironic, Wang, an accountant for an insurance company, is not only incapable of insuring the astronomical value of the necklace but is socially degraded by the object as well. Similarly, the man who arranged to have the necklace stolen is also plagued by the object, eventually winding up wounded and hospitalized. As an accountant, he must repeat what Wang has done: removing the money in the company's safe to pay off the moral debt.

The jewelry store, which literally supplied the necklace, serves as a pertinent location for revealing that the commodity bears far more exchange value than use value. The string of pearls is in fact, in the context of the film, a transitional fetish that embodies both traditional craftsmanship and a modern fashion of exchange. The setting, with its outrageously priced jewelry on display, functions almost like a stock exchange where big sums are dealt precariously. The store owner may be observing a traditional code of trust when he loans the necklace to Wang, but the modern metropolis proves to be too risky a place to base social relations on trust and mutual aid. By the same token, when Wang embezzles money to buy an expensive replacement necklace to protect his honor, he too misses the point.

While the men, despite their respectable professions, seem so ill-prepared to function in a modern city, the women in the film are portrayed as reckless consumers. The crisis of masculinity is thus linked to the excess of women's desire to consume, and male honor is seen as undermined by female vanity. Before Wang enters the store to ask his friend for help, a group of shots is smoothly edited to place an anonymous female customer in the center of the store for no apparent narrative purpose. She walks into the store and examines the jewelry in the glass cases. A shop assistant pulls over a chair for her to rest one of her legs. Another assistant enters the frame in a low-angle medium shot and begins to mop the floor. The mop leads his gaze to the woman's leg, and he stops mopping and sizes up her body. The mop suddenly falls on the woman's leg, but she is too preoccupied with the jewelry to heed what is happening behind her. An onlooker catches the assistant's lurid expression and pushes him down to the floor. Only then does the woman discover his presence and laughs at him with the crowd. The miscreant man is pulled out of the frame but the mop once more touches the woman. Another assistant tries to clean her skirt with a handkerchief, but the annoyed woman rejects his advances.

This sequence is typical of the comical interlude (*chuancha*) prevalent in early Chinese cinema, yet in this context it bears more narrative weight than a mere light moment. It carries over both the spontaneous elements of the cinema of attractions and theatrical interludes (made up of martial arts or clown performance) in the Chinese theater. In spite of the impulse to master a tighter narrative control in *Techniques,* Hou himself lists "interludes" (moments of comic relief or spectacle) as useful ingredients to make a script more "vivid and interesting."[44] However, this particular interlude, reminiscent of Porter's *The Gay Shoe Clerk* (1903), is not a piece of mere comic relief. Seemingly irrelevant to the development of the plot, it nevertheless foreshadows the hardly comical fate to befall the Wang family. The vain female customer is so enthralled by the jewelry that her body is "defiled" by both the male gaze and the dirty mop.

The stain left on her skirt becomes an insignia of her vanity and loss of moral chastity. We also get the sense that as soon as a woman enters the public space overwhelmingly associated with commerce and consumption in Shanghai, she throws herself into a perilous world. This woman also prefigures the anonymous greedy female customer whose necklace was loaned to Wang and who angrily goes all the way to Wang's office to demand her necklace back, humiliating him in front of his sadistic boss. Wang tells her that he has bought a necklace worth $15,000 in return because he does not want his friend "to share [his] dishonor." The woman relents by saying: "Since it is worth $5,000 more than my original one, I may as well accept your kindness now." The surplus value pacifies the vain woman, whose "loan" has accrued interest over time.

The interlude or, rather, prelude smoothly incorporates elements of the cinema of attractions at the service of a long moral drama. It also stands out as a pivotal point where a sexual economy is thrown out of balance. Not only are the necklaces exchangeable but the female characters, whose vanity is their common "epithet," also become interchangeable in the circulation. The missing necklace puts Wang's family on the path of rapid social decline as it also threatens to bankrupt the jewelry store by destroying the business's foundation: trust. The male shop assistants, now rollicking at a sexual joke, would all endure the dire consequences of unemployment faced by Wang and Ma. On a broader social register, the two accountants' embezzlement exposes the dirty tricks that undermine the larger financial structure of the commercial culture.

Something other than the necklace is soon revealed to be what really triggers the gender imbalance. Sitting in front of a large dressing mirror in the bedroom, Xiuzhen puts on the necklace while the husband is rocking the cradle. The following intertitle, with a drawing graphically reproducing the previous scene, displays two lines in the mode of traditional boudoir poetry:

> After finishing her makeup [she] whispers to her husband,
> [*zhuangba disheng wen fuxu*]
> "Am I not dressed up fashionably?"
> [*"huamei shenqian rushi wu?"*]

Wang carefully examines her with a circling gaze and shows his satisfaction. This scene is metonymic of the gender structure within the emerging urban middle class family, even though Hou tries to conceal its modern significance with classical diction. In his seminal treatise on the rise of the modern day "leisure class" in industrialized society in general and on "dress as an expression of the pecuniary culture" in the United States in particular, Thorstein Veblen observed that a woman's elaborate dress and "necessary" paraphernalia were markers of being able to "consume vicariously for the [male] head of the household; and her apparel is contrived with this object in view." He points out that this conspicuous display of the female body as an icon for "leisure" originates in the fact that women are still "in the full sense, the property of men," "the performance of conspicuous leisure and consumption came to be part of the services required of them." She is the "chief ornament" of the household, whereas her master gets the credit of social respectability.[45] The misogynist remarks in the opening title card only mask a displaced desire. As the head of the modern nuclear household, Wang is driven to borrow the expensive necklace not simply out of Xiuzhen's vanity but of his own compulsion to display her in a public setting and be a part of the leisure class.

Having created a Chinese Nora in *The Abandoned Wife,* Hou could not help but give a measure of agency to Xiuzhen to reveal the troubled gender relations. On her way out to the party, leaving Wang to attend the baby, she says to him, "Please try to be a mother to-night." While she is enjoying the sight, sound, and the crowd at the festival, Wang struggles impatiently to impersonate the mother role. The parallel editing here works effectively to play out the ironic contrast between the private sphere now devoid of the crucial mother figure and the public space where Xiuzhen can flaunt her femininity. The baby's incessant cry is "echoed" (through editing) by the spectacular fireworks. The women clapping hands and cheering the burning paper lantern with a male figure in it seem to mock the inept surrogate "mother" back at home, trying in vain to use a bottle of milk to calm the baby. He falls asleep, unaware that the baby has slipped out of his arm and dropped onto the floor.

The nuclear family is in disarray because the gender roles are (momentarily) reversed with dire consequences. Henceforth, the balance sheets of both the family economy and the insurance company face disorder. Xiuzhen is a successful "pecuniary" display at the party; after the necklace is stolen, however, her presence has to be concealed in the deep recesses of the private home. When the storeowner comes to ask for the necklace back, Wang lies to him by saying that his wife has not returned home yet, although she is just coming downstairs. Wang quickly walks over to the stair, obstructing the view of the storeowner. First surprised, but then realizing the situation, she quietly returns upstairs before the owner sees her. The disappearance of the ornamental fetish object thus necessitates her body to become absent. She has to remain invisible until her husband finds a substitute for the missing object to redeem his masculine honor.

Once the truth behind the necklace is exposed, the family is also socially, and spatially, removed from the leisure class. Xiuzhen's new lifestyle is shot in soft, almost idyllic light, but at night Xiuzhen feels the visceral pain of poverty, again encapsulated in Hou's poetic diction—now in a vernacular vein "fitting" her current low social station:

With fingers weary and worn
With eyelids heavy and red
Stitch, stitch, stitch
In poverty, hunger, and dirt.

After Wang is finally released from jail and returns home, Xiuzhen proudly shows him the twenty dollars that she has saved over the year, an unbearable duration that has elapsed through elliptical editing. Between the astronomical price of the necklace and her tiny savings earned, the Wangs have lost their home and social status but regained their conscience. This redemptive process aptly exemplifies Hou's preference for (internal) repentance to the (external) legal and moral punishment as a solution for the "family problem" in particular and social problems in general.[46]

The Wangs' social decline, however, turns out to be but a larger interlude in the circular narrative. Applying the principle of "winding and interesting, not too fast nor too slow" to the ending, as outlined in his *Techniques,* Hou has the story return to the characters involved in the loss of the string of pearls and paves the way for a major reversal of fortune. Wang not only gets the opportunity to witness Ma (who stole the necklace) mirroring his own past but also the chance to play the hero, reestablishing his social and physical prowess. In the last flashback in the film, Ma recounts how he masterminded the theft and subsequently proposed to Fu with the jewelry as an engagement gift. Everyone shows relief at hearing the truth about the mighty necklace that brought catastrophes to their marriages, and no one wants to touch the inauspicious object again. Wang replaces Ma as the accountant, and the rich Fu family buys the house back for the Wang family. Things have come a full circle after all the tribulations, and people return to their proper stations.

Chinese film historian Li Suyuan has argued that, similar to the Butterfly literature from which the cinema partly derived, one of the basic characteristics of early Chinese narrative cinema is the propensity for a big reunion (*datuanyuan*). *Datuanyuan* refers to a conclusion that rests upon the completion of a circular formula rather than closure of a Hollywood-style linear narrative.[47] The cliché happy ending cannot fully account for the cultural meaning precipitated in the term *datuanyuan.* The key element here is the round shape that over time has become a culturally conditioned cognitive construct in tandem with cosmological symbols, such as the full moon (and moon-cake), and daily objects like the round dining table (around which the family shares food or settles domestic matters. The round table is an especially central mise-en-scène element in early Chinese cinema (fig. 5.13). Around it many dramatic conflicts and resolutions take place, as for example in *Jade Pear Spirit* and *The Last Conscience,* both of which are Mingxing productions from 1925. The "roundness" of the plot lies primarily in the configuration of a set of causal relationships that, however, do not necessarily entail any recourse to a rational procedure. More often than not, predestination and coincidence act as rules of a moral order heavily influenced by basic Buddhist notions of retribution and karma and override any linear resolution that presupposes the separation of cause and effect.

Retribution (*baoying*) plays the chief role in the melodramatic loops of *datuanyuan.* In everyday practice and popular understanding, retribution entails balancing out moral (sometimes in the form of economic) debt incurred, whether purposefully or by unwitting transgression. The balancing can take place within one's own lifetime or in the afterlife (i.e., in the chain of lives) and may take various manifestations: family reunions, felicitous marriages, the return of favors or gifts, revenge killings, financial ruin, and so on. The underlying moral principle goes: "goodness reaps

5.13 The mise-en-scène of narrative "roundness" in *Last Conscience* (1925). (Courtesy of the China Film Archive)

benefits, evil deeds lead to evil payback." Another popular metaphor renders it even more vernacular: "Those who plant melon seeds get melons, those who plant bean seeds get beans." The edible plants in this proverb both suggest roundness and fruition, and the causal relation is conceived as organic and "natural." We recall that Hou imagined himself as a gardener of good deeds. For him the drama (the theatrical and the cinematic) is capable of cultivating both the good and the evil in people. True to his May Fourth convictions, Hou aspired to use cinema to demonstrate the possibility of change. But he did so in part—and in ways similar to a number of Western and Japanese modernist writers and artists—by having recourse to "primitivism,"[48] the "unscientific" logic of retribution, rather than to rational social intervention.

In his study on *pao* (that is, *bao*) as a multifaceted historical construct in Chinese culture, Yang Liansheng emphasizes that its meaning carries semantic dimensions of report, reciprocation, retribution, revenge, and response. The most crucial aspect where this construct comes into play is in interpersonal relations (and to some degree between humans and nature) that constantly require a balance of emotional or material obligations. However, the interpersonal relations also fall within larger networks of kinship and social transactions, which demand an individual's constant awareness of reciprocal responsibility and the observance of existing ethical and cosmological orders.[49] Quoting an ingenious philological discovery made by Wang Guowei (1877–1927), Yang states that in the ancient oracle bone inscriptions, the earliest known Chinese writing system, the protoform of the *bao* pictogram is associated with a particular sacrifice at the ancestral burial ground.[50] In this sense, retribution is rooted in a belief in the existence of the deceased's soul, and the sacrificial ritual is meant to complete a cycle of reciprocity. Buddhist influences both reinforced and transformed the Chinese beliefs and practices of retribution by extending the hierarchy of familial and social obligation to a larger moral universe that included even animals and plants, and introducing ideas of individual karma and reincarnation. Over time, *bao* has become an everyday category that comes into play in both religious and seemingly secular practices of retribution. Its varied and changing forms are ubiquitous in popular literature, drama, and other performance arts.[51]

The May Fourth ideology attacked what was seen as superstitious beliefs, including ethical fundamentals such as the concept of retribution. That attack was also aimed at the popular Butterfly literature, which, as in traditional vernacular and oral literature, largely relied on *datuanyuan* and *bao* as central storytelling devices. Especially for those who migrated into the cities, the traumatic *déclassement* of traditional sociomoral orders (such as the extended family and an agrarian lifestyle based on a cyclical temporality) created the need for comfort and the assurance of a better life to come. They were concerned that certain old values and virtues could still retain a place, even a fictive one, in a rapidly modernizing society fraught with problems associated with the "new style" life.[52] *Datuanyuan* provides a digestible narrative form for organizing the often chaotic, unpredictable experience of modern life and for the reembedding of communities in the metropolitan setting. Its structure allows superimposition of the old and the new as well as staging of the reconciliation of conflicting values and lifestyles; this integration accounts for its popularity.

However, the very juxtaposition of incongruous ideologies and narrative strategies also render *datuanyuan* a protean ground for formal experiments and social critique. It contributed to the development of a highly sophisticated form of melodrama or *qingjieju* with heavy Chinese inflections. Newspaper serialization was the common form for most Butterfly literature. This form was inclined toward multiple episodes that loosely fit within a large narrative, leaving ample room for play and improvisation. Its "broken-up forms," argues Rey Chow, constitutes a "very different kind of subversion at work—a subversion by repetition, exaggeration, and improbability; a subversion that is parodic, rather than tragic, in nature."[53]

Notwithstanding his early connection with the Literary Association in the May Fourth movement, Hou's rather liberal revision and extension of Maupassant's story with retribution revealed his mixed feelings about the May Fourth ideology. More akin to naturalism than to realism, Hou saw life as structured like theater, constantly staging "sad departures and happy reunions, life and aging, sickness and death, the diminishing of plenitude and compensation of lack, gain or loss, rise or decline." Such an endless, episodic life-drama renders any teleologically oriented narrative resolution superfluous. Within this repetitive or cyclic construct, the final message of the film is writ figuratively in the beaded and rounded shape of the fateful necklace.

At the same time, however, this adaptation of a foreign story at a time of fierce commercial competition and large-scale transformation of theatrical space demanded a mode of narration to absorb the audiences' attention and money. In this regard, the several flashbacks efficiently create suspense and a sophisticated psychological interiority, both of which would have been much more difficult to seamlessly produce onstage. The overt clockwise circular structure, which is otherwise appropriate for the relatively formulaic (linear but not teleological) logic of early story film, is significantly complicated by the counterclockwise movement (i.e., flashbacks and hallucination), allowing in-depth explanations for the characters' seemingly driven actions. These flashbacks provide the plot with some rational explanations, even though the overall retributional structure of the film keeps suggesting that a precarious modern world is hardly immune to a fatalistic value system. At the same time, social anonymity and increased exposure to danger has rendered modern urban life more prone to the overdetermination of chance, which becomes a modern variant of fate. At those moments, *A String of Pearls* crystallizes the multiple, competing narrative strategies adopted by pioneering Chinese writers and filmmakers to present a collage of historical landscapes and subjectivities.[54] In this sense, the use of retribution becomes an effective gesture to expose the doubling logic of adaptation. Embodying the tension between imported values and traditional moral codes, retribution also proffers a rhetorical possibility for articulating a collective ambivalence toward modernity.

Hou's retooling of an archaic cultural trope interweaves the modern trajectory of commodities' global circulation and their attendant lifestyles—of which cinema is the premium medium. The logic of retribution, in which a cyclical temporality breaks down the binary of tradition versus modernity, could also work the other way around with adaptations of classical Chinese tales or drama. It is thus not surprising that in the late 1920s craze for costume drama, Hou adapted the celebrated classical play *Romance of the Western Chamber* (1927)—this time as both screenwriter and director—for the Minxing Company.[55] This film is studded with spectacular pyrotechnic displays and special effects made possible by trick photography and postproduction devices. For example, during a scholar's dream, his brush magically enlarges into a phallic weapon to rescue his maiden. The fulfillment of the scholar's desire is finally encapsulated in a typical *datuanyuan* but with a twist—the formulaic reunion of the beauty and the scholar appears in silhouette shot through a paper window screen. With this denouement Hou is obviously bowing to the shadowplay aesthetic; at the same time, this playful conclusion reminds the audience that the "scholar-meets-beauty" romance has become emphatically a modern day cinematic rendition.

A String of Pearls and *Romance of the Western Chamber* represent two opposite poles on the spectrum of Hou's adaptations, as well as for much of early Chinese narrative film. His use of *datuanyuan,* however, directly contributes to the patterning of circulation and redistribution of desire in each film. In both films, male social impotence is finally canceled out by bringing women back to their proper place: home and matrimony. Only when the external threat—the temptation of modern commodity consumption or the untamed masculine banditry—is cleared, can the fractured moral universe and social order be repaired. Yet, the recovery (of the necklace or virility) remains highly improbable due to the scandalously irrational nature of retribution. The consummation of erotic desire at the end of *Romance* is abstracted by the two-dimensional shadowplay. The hieroglyphic value of the necklace in *A String of Pearls,* on the other hand, can hardly be domesticated. As an inauspicious fetish it was literally exorcised from the house before the Wang family could safely return. But there was no guarantee that it would not come back to haunt them.

LUSTROUS PEARLS: MELODRAMA IN THE WILDERNESS

A String of Pearls internalized the archaic trope of retribution in adapting a Parisian tale as a Chinese urban fable, and skillfully dovetailed it with explicit cinematic techniques, such as stop-animation, flashbacks, and parallel editing to create a convincing moral allegory. *Lustrous Pearls,* however, presents an altogether different picture of the circulation and redistribution of wealth and desire. The film is neither adapted nor is it a serious drama promoting social or moralistic interventions.

The plot of *Lustrous Pearls* also has many twists and turns but they are not narratively motivated. Unlike *A String of Pearls,* the bilingual intertitle cards in *Lustrous Pearls* are kept to a minimum, as if words were redundant, and the characters busily engage in playing hide-and-seek games rather than being enveloped in a psychologically absorbed drama. The film does not have an urban setting (though the characters all have a certain urban flair), nor does it revolve around family problems as in *A String of Pearls.* Yet the look of the film is unmistakably modern. Notably, the Huaju Company, founded by Zhang Qingpu and Zhang Huimin,[56] distinguished itself in producing "modern-costume romance" (*shizhuang yanqing pian*), at a time when most other companies turned to "classical-costume drama." The title cards display the film's modern look. Though sparse, they are decorated with Art Nouveau style drawings of seminudes adorned with roses. The characters themselves parade in European style (*Ouhua*) clothes (such as riding breeches and boots), even though they are supposed to be living in a fishing village, and strangely shaped concrete buildings dot the seaside landscape.

Four young fishermen have harvested two large-size lustrous pearls from the sea, but once they come ashore, their brotherhood is put in jeopardy by the impossibility of evenly distributing the treasure. Xin Xiong, played by screenwriter Zhang Huimin himself (also a company co-owner), appears to be the big brother among them. He decides to give the pearls to his cohabitant (*tongju*) girlfriend Yu Zhiyin and his sister for safe keeping.[57] But the three other young men, unable to get a share of either the pearls or the girls, vow to seek revenge. The three brothers-turned villains come to Xin's place to demand the pearls, but Xin insists that he harvested them. A series of physical ordeals ensues. In the first trap, the villains tie Xin up with a rope and leave him on a rock offshore. Spotting his helpless figure, his girlfriend swims over and rescues him. In the second trap, his sister is kidnapped and one of the three men forces her to marry him. Master Yang, "a crafty and ambitious bandit in retirement," gets his hands on the pearls when he steals them from the jewelry box next to the sleeping girls.[58] Xin Xiong seeks help from a friend who betrays him and abandons him in a desolate valley.

Seemingly docile objects of male desire in the beginning, the women unexpectedly prove themselves to be the real heroes of the film. The girlfriend and the sister set out as disguised knights-errant to find Xin. In a suspenseful sequence full of vertiginous vertical pans and horizontal tracking shots, the heroines rescue the trapped hero, and the three of them run from the villains through the rugged landscape. Meanwhile, the villains finally get hold of the treasure, only to be caught in the same predicament of uneven distribution. The two female knights-errant in male disguise proceed to rescue Master Yang's daughter, who was captured by the villains. To show his gratitude and repay his moral debt, Master Yang tracks down the bad guys and recovers the pearls. Xin is so impressed by the women's capability that he gives them one pearl each. The lovers are reunited as the sister happily watches over them, in a manner similar to the "big reunion" of the *Western Chamber.* Yet no indication is given that this resolution necessarily leads to matrimony and social harmony.

On both thematic and stylistic levels, *Lustrous Pearls* echoes many features in the American serial-queen melodramas between 1912 and 1920. The significance of this "other melodrama" for female fantasy and empowerment is revelatory. The serial-queen drama films, which were shown in China (numerous mentions of the American "adventure/detective" series appear in Chinese film magazines), typically featured the tribulations of an androgynous heroine (most famously the actress Pearl White), and were "essentially antithetical to Hollywood's domestic melodrama."[59] The insistence on unabashed "externalization," that is, the idea that "everything happens on the outside," and the "total banishment of the figure of the mother," yield particular interests for a reading of the genre as an important intertext for the modern mythology of the New Woman.[60] Ben Singer argues that the female inclination for novel and risky experiences in this genre expresses female fantasies of mastery at a time when women were rapidly entering the public world outside the home. But at the same time, the recurrent imagery of imperilment, trapping, and violence sends cautionary messages about the risks involved in this liberation. Similar oscillations between empowerment and containment in *Lustrous Pearls* is clearly seen in the figure of Master Yang's daughter, who steals the pearls and tries to elope with one of the villains only to be cheated and abandoned on the seashore and driven to a suicide attempt. The two heroines also eventually resume the roles of the (unwed) wife and the sister in relation to the hero, when they receive one pearl each from him as reward.

The promiscuous textual and sexual economy of *Lustrous Pearls* suggests that many features of an early heterogeneous cinema outlasted the institutionalization of a narratively integrated cinema with loftier social and pedagogical ambitions. Although the trope of retribution is also central to this loosely linked film, the films' diffuse and erratic temporality does not allow any seamless crystallization of a self-contained narrative. The film is replete with sequences of suspenseful chases in spectacular and discontinuous landscape—oceans, hills, woods—which constantly disrupt any sense of spatial realism. What actually seems to link the disparate segments together is the prominent role played by the numerous traps (*jiguan*) and ropes—devices common in the serial-queen dramas—that bring about surprises and coincidences in a constantly displaced cinematic space. The spatial jolts and leaps created by these devices constitute a temporality that is, in Tom Gunning's words, "explosive, surprising, and even disorienting."[61] The first use of ropes in the film leads to the explosion of the house. From that moment on, the film embarks on a journey in the wilderness dotted with show-stopping and breathtaking actions that are not oriented toward creating a diegetic totality yet filled with a spontaneous storytelling energy.

Gunning's conceptualization of the temporality of attractions as "that of the alternation of presence/absence . . . embodied in the act of display" is also germane to the role the two pearls play in the film. From the first moment the pearls land in our view, the spectator is engaged less in the unraveling of the plot than in a game that is played out in both visible and invisible spaces—spaces of exposure and disappearance. The spectator gets entangled in the permutation of numbers: two pearls, three maidens, one master/father, four brothers, and several other friends. The hieroglyphic function of the pearls here conveys a strong picaresque air, especially as they are being shuffled between different hands and landscapes without a clearly justified narrative motivation. The pearls are treated more like the folkloristic motif of mythic treasure, evoking stories in which the recovery of riches incites the hero's many trials and final return and restoration.

CINEMA AS MODERN FOLKTALE

To better account for the significance of this forgotten early narrative film, I will now turn to an allegorical approach inspired by but not confined to Propp's seminal study of the folktale form.[62] The latent folktale structure of both *Lustrous Pearls* and *A String of Pearls* is given new and palpable expression by the cinematic technology. Propp's syntagmatic (rather than paradigmatic) schemata in dissecting formal elements (or "motifs") of the Russian fairy tale centered primarily on the linear trajectory of dramatis personae. His morphological study has revolutionized folklore study and challenged a Lévi-Straussian structuralist binarism. His formalist approach, however, has been criticized as too confined to the action and internal composition of the folktale, failing to account for the larger cultural contexts and local variations.[63] Although Propp's schemata are useful in understanding the picaresque pattern of action in *Lustrous Pearls,* which I see as a modern folktale, my analysis of the film as a fable of that period's commercial film industry will attend to motifs that fall outside of the tale proper. Yet, these external motifs constantly point back to various components of the film. The transaction between internal and external meanings invites an interpretation of the context of its production and reception, whereas a mechanical use of Propp's categories in analyzing a Chinese film would be quite misleading. The applicability of Propp's morphology to this cinematic tale produced in the age of mass-mediated modernity is at best rhetorical or ironic.

There are numerous signposts in the film other than the ostensible Art Nouveau–styled intertitles that urge a reading outside the internal morphology of the tale per se. The film and the Huaju Company itself are deeply implicated in a vibrant commercial cinema in which even "conscience" has to be reconciled with profit. The preoccupation with wealth and the attendant problem of distribution (among the brothers or partners) in *Lustrous Pearls* reveals its self-conscious link to the competitive distributive system of the film world at large. The arrival of the ship and the unloading of cargo in the beginning of the film paves the way for the first mythic appearance of the lustrous pearls and locates the film in a port market that trades overseas, especially in Southeast Asia. Throughout the film, the four brothers, who look identical in their white Western shirts and hairstyles, are caught in a war of pursuing and sharing the invaluable and indivisible treasure. Among the sparse intertitles, two keep recurring:

"How [are we/you] to divide it?"
"How [are we/you] to repay [the debt]?"

This anxiety over payment and distribution (of dividends, in a literal sense) seems less strange considering the organizational plurality, confusion, and fierce competition that beset the Chinese film industry in the late 1920s. The competition among dozens of small and medium-sized companies over access to the means of production and the distribution system was intense and even ruthless among the unequal players. These companies had no choice but to fight to win the attention of distributors, exhibitors, and, ultimately, audiences.

Indeed, many film companies still retained the early cottage industry mode of production, essentially operating as family businesses. The legendary earliest family company (*jiating gongsi*) was Dan Duyu's (1897–1972) Shanghai Shadowplay Company founded in 1920. His wife, the famous "Miss F. F." (Foreign Fashion), Yin Mingzhu (a.k.a. Pearl Yin), and his nephew Dan Erchun constituted the main cast of Dan's productions. Dan Duyu's *A Family Treasure* (*Chuanjiabao*) was made a year earlier than *Lustrous Pearls* and portrays several cousins' search for and vain attempt to divide a magic antique coin, a legacy from their deceased grandfather. When the two parts of the halved coin are pieced together, it reveals an inscribed epistle admonishing the young generation not to feud over material gains but to instead form harmonious bonds within the extended family.

In 1924, two years prior to the two elder Zhang brothers' establishment of Huaju, their younger brother Zhang Huichong (1898–1962) had already set up Lianhe, which produced several short and medium-length films, including *Seizing a National Treasure* (*Duo guobao,* 1926).[64] In 1927, the same year *Lustrous Pearls* was made, he founded a new company with his own name, Huichong, and made several of China's first martial-arts films, heralding the commercial craze for the genre in late 1920s. Beside the Zhang brothers, the Shao brothers (Shao Zuiwen, Shao Cunren, Shao Renmei, and Shao Yifu) established Tianyi in 1925.[65] One of Tianyi's early productions was called *A Lustrous Pearl* (*Ye guangzhu,* 1928).[66] The Tianyi version (which may have stolen the idea from the Huaju film), however, has the stolen magic pearl go to the urban jungle in Shanghai where the kidnapped maiden is then taken to the wilderness.

In all these variations on (or, in Propp's terminology, "species" of) family members feuding over a precious treasure, the object of desire constantly plays hide and seek with the characters as well as the spectators. The different players in the games, who often happen to be brothers, friends or lovers, keep shifting their allegiances. There is, furthermore, unfailingly the character of a servant who, in his blind (but not totally unjustified) ambition to rise above his station, betrays the master/mistress. Such "treasure-hunting" folktales, with a visible modern makeup, constitute a particular cinematic landscape in the 1920s. The pressures of competition for the film market unwittingly stimulated the desire to experiment with various forms, old and new, indigenous and translated, while also unleashing a near neurotic drive to run ahead of others to find the secret of success.

The vocation of cinema no doubt presented an unprecedented opportunity for great fortunes in the mid-1920s Shanghai. At the same time, it also created real anxiety over the chance of survival and the likelihood of financial success. Many small companies proved to be disposable instances of modern life in which "all that is solid melts into air."[67] The oversized rare pearl as a hieroglyphic index for this anxiety is most pertinent because the pearl, although considered a piece of precious jewelry, lacks the permanence of metals or minerals that allow the accumulation of antique value. Once taken out of the protective shells, it will literally melt away over time if not carefully processed and preserved. At a telling moment in *Lustrous Pearls,* the hero teaches his girlfriend that "the gems are calcareous concretions deposited for centuries in layers around a central nucleus in the shells of a pearl oyster. They are known as carbuncles or lustrous pearls." This emphatically modern, "scientific" discourse underscores the long durée of the creation process from the "raw material" to "art."[68] It also conveys a tension between the film as a hastily churned-out marketable modern folktale in the age of mechanical reproduction and the desire on the part of the filmmaker to create an artwork that transcends monetary motives. The use of Art Nouveau motifs that frame the title cards and the rough trajectory of the pearls seem to provide contrapuntal traces of this dilemma. The "artistic" makeup is, however, precisely the selling point of the film: it revolves around the circulation and transaction of something (i.e., the pearls) that is both a natural aesthetic object and a valuable commodity.

The collage of old and new values—scientific ideas and folkloric motifs—demands a consideration of the historical conditioning of retribution storytelling. Walter Benjamin's diagnosis of the aesthetic paradox in storytelling at the dawning of modernity in his essay, "The Storyteller," sheds light on the issue at stake here. While the demise of traditional society unleashed destructive forces on community-based modes of storytelling and social networks, the rise of modern communication does not necessarily entail an apocalyptic ending to the past as much as a radical new beginning. He cautions us not to dismiss outright the transitional mode of narration as a "symptom of decay" but to treat it rather as a historical "concomitant":

> The art of storytelling is reaching its end because the epic side of truth, wisdom, is dying out. This, however, is a process that has been going on for a long time. And nothing would be more fatuous than to want to see in it merely a "symptom of decay," let alone a "modern" symptom. It is, rather, only a concomitant symptom of the secular forces of history, a concomitant that has quite gradually removed narrative from the realm of living speech and at the same time is making it possible to see a new beauty in what is vanishing.[69]

The "new beauty" brought by the "secular forces" of the ruins of a dying history is singular in its own right, because it manifests the dynamic production of new modes of address. This productive process links the dying and nascent forms of storytelling and reception. The penchant for the compounded (traditional, though not necessarily native) "folktale" plus (modern) "adventure/detective" genre in films discussed above may thus be seen as stemming from a desire to search for narrative solutions at a particular juncture of film history. The increasingly institutionalized systems of distribution and exhibition called for long features that would at once cultivate and cater to spectators' tastes. The various manifestations of this storytelling mode—at once frivolous and balanced, exotic yet familiar—are testimonies to the "concomitant" storytelling effect outlined by Benjamin. The success of Great Wall's and Huaju's modern-style fables can be largely attributed to their awareness of both the commodity nature of the cinema and its attractions as a novel aesthetic form. Demographically speaking, this cinema, irreverent of any single tradition, also directly addressed a highly diversified audience ranging from the educated to the illiterate—those who preferred "European style" as well as those who still relished the teahouse mode of storytelling and the power of retribution.

This sets up a stark contrast to the failures of Tian Han's (1898–1968) early cinematic efforts to visually represent the folklore movement as a purely artistic project. A prominent May Fourth playwright and poet, Tian spent his formative years (1916–22) studying education in Japan, where he was also drawn to folklore studies and cinema, particularly the film aesthetics of the Japanese modernist writer Tanizaki Jun'ichirô. In 1921 Tian, along with Guo Morou, Yu Dafu, and several others studying in Tokyo, founded the Creation Society, a small literary coterie known for its "art for art's sake" banner. Returning to Shanghai, its members were engaged in polemics with the May Fourth cultural movement flagship organ the Literary Association. The latter adopted the slogan "art for life's sake" as its institutional motto. The famous literary magazine, *Fiction Monthly* (*Xiaoshuo yuebao*), edited by Mao Dun and published by the Commercial Press in Shanghai, was the chief forum for discussion of the large amount of the "fiction of problems." The magazine was promoted as the counternarrative to the "playful" Butterfly fiction but with limited success. Both the Creation Society and the Literary Association, in spite of their antagonistic slogans, played a major role in the vernacular literary movement. At the time when Tian Han began to experiment with the cinematic medium, the Creation Society was also steering toward more progressive pursuits.

After returning to Shanghai from Tokyo, Tian scripted and directed *Going to the People* (*Dao minjian qu,* Nanguo Film and Drama Society, 1926) and *Lingering Sound of a Broken Flute* (*Duandi yuyin,* Shanghai College of Arts, 1927) for the Nanguo Film and Drama Society. Nanguo was a fraternal and collegiate association rather than a commercial film enterprise. Both films were left unfinished due to lack of funds and entrepreneurial skills. In his memoir Tian called the aborted *Going to the People* "an unfinished silver dream." He recalled that the chief source of inspiration for the film was a poem by Ishikawa Suzuki, a Japanese poet of the late Meiji period. Suzuki expressed his impassioned desire to mobilize his contemporaries to follow the example of the Russian *Narodnik* (Go to the People) movement of the 1890s.[70] The film, however, transplants this poetic spirit into a romantic tale set in China about some young urban intelligentsia's ambivalent relationships to rural reconstruction. Interestingly, the film has an alternative title: *Dance in Front of the Tomb* (*Fengtou zhi wu*).[71] The story centers on a newlywed couple who settles among the peasants and choreographs new "folk dance" to show respect and pay their moral debt to their dead friend, who killed himself out of regret over his failed love and life. The New Village becomes an exotic setting for a highly improbable *ménage-à-trois* story of the petty bourgeoisie. Their attitude towards folk culture, particularly the so-called "folk dance" as opposed to the Western ballroom dance in the city, is both naive and patronizing. The film, like the Go to the People pioneers it portrays, died prematurely.

In part *Going to the People* satirizes the frenzy of the stock market, one of the main causes of the young man's suicide. The failure of the Nanguo production itself nevertheless suggests that "going to the people" was not as simple as gathering a little money for a charitable cause. At a moment when the film world was dramatically transforming itself into a complex network of industrial and commercial enterprises, Tian's sentimental artisan attempt at the silver screen was ill-fated because he did not take the market or the audience into account. The folklore movement as a high-flung idea imposed from above by the self-styled avant-garde became a thwarted "silver dream," unable to find a legitimate place in popular cinema. Its dead spirit could only be encased in the film's alternative title, waiting to be revived at a later point in Chinese film history.[72]

The modernity of *Lustrous Pearls* as a folktale incarnate owes a great deal to its portrayal of women. Instead of the trite folktale trope of the "hero rescues the beauty," the film sets the stage for the two female "pearls" to transform themselves from passive or victimized maidens to able-bodied heroines (or helpers, to use a folkloristic term) in androgynous masquerade. They rescue the endangered hero and recover the treasure.[73] The erratic itinerary of the two bright pearls through the film, ostensibly a narrative device like that of the necklace in *A String of Pearls,* is associated with the imbalance in sexual economy but departs significantly from the more rigorously regulated gender configuration in Hou Yao's film adaptation. Unlike *A String of Pearls* in which the drama about moral debt and male honor takes place in an interiorized family drama of the rising urban white collar class, the erosion of gender roles in *Lustrous Pearls* is inscribed in the physical landscape and measured by bodies in motion and transformation. The latter film is emphatically about the the mobile, indestructible heroine bodies that dare challenge any natural or artificial obstacles. The film is permeated with too many long shots of feet and legs on the move and of bodies wrestling to tell the difference between the female and male characters.

A String of Pearls makes a serious attempt to penetrate the psychology of the new urban subjects, who constantly moved from one interior setting to another. The whole story is in fact "framed" from beginning to end within the domestic space of the nuclear family except for a few disastrous digressions into the public space. In contrast, *Lustrous Pearls* is emphatically about the freewheeling spirit of the often indestructible bodies that dare to challenge all obstacles. Unlike the docile and sacrificial maternal figure in Hou's melodramatization of Maupassant's story, the unwed (but not necessarily "pure") maidens in Zhang Huimin's modern folktale wander recklessly in the wilderness with chimerical identities and bizarre outfits. They defy any prescribed femininity by showing off their swimming and cliff-climbing skills. Their intelligence as well as prowess seems probable precisely because the film is not structured along a logical story line; instead it relies heavily on chance and the mutability of the social, physical, and economic environment.

If Hou Yao harnessed the traditional conception of retribution to accommodate a subdued social commentary, he does so at the expense of rendering women culpable of male disgrace and the disintegration of the proper social order. By contrast, the tribulations of retribution in *Lustrous Pearls* are hardly "strung" together to produce a closure. The weight of the concept is relocated from the claustrophobic psychosocial and moral interiority to the more externalized material and social world.

Above I have tried to delineate the emergence of a particular mode of narration and its variations in the mid-1920s. The historical trajectory of this change, albeit often contradictory and multidirectional, is marked by a sustained interest in reworking the traditional socioethical concept of retribution and its protean presence in folklore into a cinematic vernacular of storytelling. The ingrained cultural obsession with moral recyclability releases new "secular productive forces of history" (as for Benjamin) into social reproduction and representation against a modern background. This deeply entrenched concept of retribution as a narrative device was ubiquitous in popular fiction and folklore before and after the 1911 demise of dynastic history, which organized itself according to the cyclical lunar calendar and the "repetition" of dynastic temporality. However, its manifestations were effected by the radical transformation of modern modes of production and reproduction. New notions of the copy versus the original developed in response to new technological—and consequently epistemological and historical—changes, in particular with the onset of mass print technology, photography, and the cinema. Photography and cinematography not only made the soul and body, the original and the copy, or a series of selves simultaneously visible on single planes, but also they set in motion new modes of identity formation. As a result, the culturally conditioned cognitive susceptibility to notions such as retribution, soul, and afterlife took on a renewed but qualitatively different valence and, quite literally, visibility.

The ontological preoccupations with the cinematic soul in early Chinese film and the afterlife of the written word in the moving image, particularly as evidenced in Hou Yao's and Xu Zhuodai's writings, are symptomatic of a widespread anxiety. As a process of translation, the cinematic adoption of retribution and other cultural elements involved a series of successive or concomitant practices, such as photography, the New Drama, popular Butterfly fiction, and the May Fourth intellectual discourse. Their overlap changed, but never overhauled, traditional structures of experience and perception. The return of retribution—often under various modern disguises and in competing melodramatic forms—became in this sense a historical "revenge" against the enlightenment narrative critique of superstition and other feudal residues. Yet, these stories also actively engage with modern concerns and desires provoked by rapid urbanization, industrialization, modern technology, and commodification of social relations. The collusion of these competing discourses and practices is visually embodied in the form of the pearls, so graphically illustrated in two of the few extant films from that period. The mysterious pearls function as mobilized, visible words that signal the constant sliding and superimposition of the commodity, the verbal sign, and the visual register. Such a dynamic interaction, while threatening the distinction between the sign and the referent, also magically revives the mimetic faculty of human imagination as shown in the dance of the animated string of pearls in Xiuzhen's daytime reverie.

At the level of gender representation, the folklore formula is also significantly rewritten. The tales of pearls, traditionally laden with meanings associated with sentimentality and femininity, are "translated" by Hou and Zhang from diverse origins into different cinematic visions of modernity. Although both films use the trope of retribution as an organizing device of storytelling, their social and aesthetic interests embarked on disparate itineraries. The May Fourth-influenced Hou Yao's version primarily examined the nuclear family as the mirror of larger social problems. The necklace tale's circular structure serves to redeem the urban white-collar nuclear family as a modern institution at the expense of curtailing women's desire to break out of the bounds of domesticity. Hou's pedagogical impulse is most obvious at the end of the film, in his reworking of the "big reunion" vernacular idiom into a scene of moralizing edification. Its message is reinforced by the formal emphasis on the necklace's circular shape, which exploits the culturally overdetermined sensibility of retribution. Similarly, Hou's skillful vernacularization of classical poetry using parallelism in several key intertitles dramatizes and purges the evils of modernity. The numerous misogynist ballads elaborately reinscribed as folk wisdom in semiclassical diction function as a verbal straightjacket for urban women instead of creating a new language for gender relations. As it tries to incorporate the oral tradition as a critique of modernity, the very process of appropriating the oral tradition into writing via the cinematic medium turns that critique on its head. Moreover, such a critique, true to the film's circular hermeneutic structure, mobilizes the conservative components within folklore—especially when it comes to gender and sexuality—in order to affirm the male subject's masculinity in the modern urban setting.

The unabashedly exhibitionist *Lustrous Pearls,* by contrast, can hardly be called a self-contained narrative predicated on spatial realism and psychological interiority. Its interest is emphatically *elsewhere* in the disjointed exterior space or, rather, the concomitant spaces of nature and culture, the urban and the countryside, the cosmopolitan and the parochial; such heterotopic spaces provide playgrounds for both male and female, old and new subjectivities. The film presents a new kind of "extended family" in the making: ambivalent business partners and ambiguous sexual relationships that refuse to be contained by either the traditional kinship structure or the modern nuclear family. The film does not aim to manipulate emotional responses from the spectator as *A String of Pearls* does through its carefully wrought and, quite literally, inscribed story. The narrative logic of *Lustrous Pearls* contains far fewer verbal traces. The film has very few intertitles, nearly all of which are in the vernacular or Pidgin English. In other words, although the film does not tell or pose as a folktale, its externalized folktale structure, loosely stitched together by ample leaps, bounds, and repetitions, embodies an experimental impulse of storytelling through a more accessible visual vernacular.

Because *Lustrous Pearls* is not aimed at creating full-fledged fictional individuals, its women's new physicality, prowess, and performativity can be interpreted as a formulaic revision of old and new mythic gender types,[74] whether the martial-arts heroine or the New Woman. And because the film works within an evolving genre (the adventure/detective/treasure hunting film), the actresses who played similar roles and who embodied the ambivalent figure of the New Woman in urban China in the 1920s also enter the picture. Leaving the theater, the audience would expect to see Wu Suxin, who played the heroine in all Huaju productions from 1927 to 1931, return in a new film as a reckless spirit, playing tough games with men in various settings. Her action-oriented heroines in Huaju productions, her gender performances within the wild sociophysical landscape, and her penchant for masquerade prefigured the "knight-errant" heroine (*nüxia*) that was about to dominate the film scene by the end of the decade. *The Valient Girl White Rose* (*Nüxia Baimeigui,* 1929), also starring Wu Suxin, will constitute part of my discussion on the martial-arts film fever in chapter 6.

The films and the discourses on film informed by differing ideologies and aesthetics discussed in this chapter should by no means be construed as consciously polarized representations or critiques of modernity. Rather, the different attempts made by Hou Yao, Xu Zhuodai, Zhang Huimin, Tian Han, and their contemporaries to meet the challenges posed by the cinematic medium—and to envision new possibilities for personal and cultural expression—were translated from a vast wealth of sources and experiences. Thus no simple lines can be drawn between China and the World, the East and the West, the old and the new, the city and countryside, and the oral and written traditions. Their serious or playful experiments constitute a spectrum of practices that paralleled or engaged the iconoclastic May Fourth movement and cinematic modernity as competing global phenomena.

CHAPTER SIX

THE ANARCHIC BODY LANGUAGE OF THE MARTIAL ARTS FILM

LUSTROUS PEARLS, with its emphasis on the body, the landscape, and the spirit of chivalry and play, prefigured the martial arts films that flourished and declined in Shanghai between 1928 and 1932. Some fifty studios produced about 240 martial arts films and hybrid "martial arts–magic spirit" films (*wuxia shenguai pian*) during those four years[1]—comprising about 60 percent of the total film output. Eighty-five films were released in 1929, the peak year of the craze.[2] The widely popular genre proved to be a commercial miracle, and Nanyang distributors rushed in to order copies, sometimes producing films themselves.[3]

In essence, most martial arts films made in this period were fast and cheaply produced commodities that fed the seemingly insatiable appetite of the market. The impact of the genre's reception was equally astounding. Some spectators were so enthralled by the superhuman power and freedom embodied in the image of the knight-errant (*xiake*) that they went to the mountains to become disciples of martial arts or Daoist masters.[4] One frequently cited story in film magazines at the time was about how spectators started burning incense inside a theater to worship the almighty spirits appearing on the screen.[5] The whole film world seemed to be swept into frenzy; producers, distributors, critics, and spectators alike became mesmerized and confused by the commercial power and social energy generated by the genre.

The phenomenon spurred strong reactions from film critics and cultural bureaucrats of the Nationalist government, established in 1927, who considered themselves the custodians of the growing Chinese film industry. After a brief period of excitement over its political and aesthetic emancipatory potential, the liberal critics lashed out at the genre for its overt commercial interests, shoddy quality, superstitious indulgence, and vulgarity. The official censors were more concerned with the anarchic tendency manifested by the genre and the film industry as a whole. From 1931, the authorities sought to regulate and streamline the production of the genre, closing down many small studios that prospered from making low-budget martial arts films and banning many films from release or reshowing. Several companies continued to work sporadically with the genre, but as experimentation with sound film began and left-wing filmmakers came to occupy a substantial place in the film scene, this mass cultural phenomenon quickly receded into the background.

My return to this early martial arts genre will be a "flight" in a double sense. First, on a quite literal level, it was a major step to take in the early experiments to cinematically create the kinesthetic experience of flying, which in turn became a staple ingredient for the martial arts film. Second, flight as a dialectic trope is employed here in a way that invokes Walter Benjamin: it attempts to reconnect the past with the present on a simultaneous plane. A flight to the past, as in Benjamin's "tiger's leap" to nineteenth-century Paris, is thus by no means an escape to a phantom but a laborious archaeology of the modern experience enmeshed in the here and now, which in effect "blasts open the continuum of history."[6] My fascination with flight as both a cinematic and historical experience embodied in the martial arts film has led me to encounter a cluster of issues that are deeply implicated in the question of modernity, in particular the question of science and its bearing on the magical new art of cinema in the Chinese context. Far from being formulaic and homogeneous, the martial arts film stems from a promiscuous family tree that complicates any facile definition of the genre as such. Particularly of note, a prominent subgenre situates the female knight-errant at the center of dramatic tension and visual spectacle.

A perusal of film titles from the period reveals an array of the term *nüxia* (female knight-errant). This subgenre gave rise to a group of actresses whose physical dexterity and prowess drastically changed the image of an earlier generation of actresses who, despite their modern looks, had the residual features and constrained body language of the traditional woman. The names of actresses such as Wu Suxin (starred in *Lustrous Pearls*), Wu Lizhu (1910–78, nicknamed the "Oriental Female Fairbanks") (fig. 6.1–2), Fan Xuepeng (1908–74), Xia Peizhen (1908–?), Xu Qinfang (fig. 6.3), and Hu Die became synonymous with the swordswomen they

6.1 Actress Wu Lizhu. (Courtesy of the China Film Archive)

6.2 Wu Lizhu (right), the "Oriental female Fairbanks" (from *Dianying yuebao*).

6.3 Actress Xu Qinfang. (Courtesy of the China Film Archive)

portrayed.[7] Appearing in anachronistically dramatic attire and sporting superhuman or supernatural skills (rendered by special effects), their performance or disguise in various chivalrous roles created a constellation of empowering, though often ambivalent, female images. As I will show in more detail later, this iconographic ambiguity, which often involves blurred gender identity, is coextensive with a larger cultural ambiguity operating in the contemporary discourse on the role of science, technology, and human agency. Thus the subgenre, besides generating female power for some and a threat for others, also alerts us to the tension-ridden relationship between nature and culture (including their redefinitions) in a modernizing society.

What is the historical and cultural significance of the invention and reception of the martial arts–magic spirit film, a genre that has left lasting echoes in Hong Kong cinema to this day? What is the relationship between its aesthetic of excess and the political anarchism pervading social, cultural and cinematic discourses in a larger historical framework? To what extent is the proliferation of the *nüxia* or martial heroine suggestive of the anxiety toward women's exponentially growing public presence and the social power they embodied? Ultimately, these questions are bound up with issues concerning the role of science, the tension between elite and popular culture, the relation of this cinema to the vernacular space of folk culture, and the gendered meaning of the body as it was articulated through this hybrid genre.

The scarcity of extant films makes researching the brief yet explosive popularity of the genre difficult. Only one fragment of eighteen still exists of the most celebrated film(s), *The Burning of the Red Lotus Temple* (*Huoshao Hongliansi,* Mingxing, 1928–31) (fig. 6.4), which allegedly ignited the craze with its phenomenal box-office success. As it is impossible to survey the genre as a whole, I will concentrate on the few films I have had access to, excavating and imagining lost connections and contexts. Indeed, the fragmented nature of this body of films is indicative of the volatile fate of the genre in particular and early Chinese cinema in general. Our incomplete records inevitably bear upon our present inquiry and challenge any facile narration of history. Among the few extant films, there are three of the *nüxia* subgenre: *The Red Heroine* (*Hong xia,* Youlian, 1929), *The Valiant Girl White Rose* (*Nüxia Baimeigui,* Huaju, 1929), and the sixth episode from *The Swordswoman from the Huangjiang River* series (1930–31). This accidental "abundance" provides us with a precious entry point into both this subgenre and the martial arts–magic spirit film.

A careful tracing of the genre's genealogy and close examination of several films show that the genre's cultural significance extends beyond the commercial miracle it created. By concentrating on the motif of flying—the genre's trademark—this chapter addresses technology and social transgression, and their implications for new perceptions of the body. The genre also generated, or made visible, a particular vernacular social space—a utopian folk culture that blurs the boundary between premodern ethos and modern aspirations, popular taste and the avant-garde. In a sense, the martial arts–magic spirit film carried over the spirit of the

6.4 *Burning of the Red Lotus Temple* (Hu Die, second from left; Xia Peizhen, second from right). (Courtesy of the China Film Archive)

cinema of attractions and the attendant exhibitionist mode. The dynamic interplay between production and reception, formula and variation, special effects and storytelling mark the genre as an exemplary form of cinematic folktale.

THE FAMILY OF A PROMISCUOUS GENRE

To study the formation of a genre, according to Rick Altman, is like asking the question, "How did the whale become a mammal?" It is about establishing a corpus in light of a particular historical paradigm. The inquiry is in fact comprised of a cluster of interrelated questions:

> What genre is, what it does, why it exists (and who makes it exist), what diverse roles industry, critic, and public play in genre functioning, how (and how not) to define a genre, . . . how to identify and delimit subgenres, and, in a broader sense, how to recognize and theorize the relationship between generic functioning and the strategies of the society that spawns a genre.[8]

If genre can be defined essentially as the order of things,[9] the martial arts–magic spirit film that evolved into a mass phenomenon in Shanghai in the late 1920s is emphatically a hypergenre characterized by disorder, chaos, and cross-fertilization. Since its inception, the genre has received mixed reactions. On the one hand, the audience and critics marveled at the spectacular pyrotechnic display and the entertaining suspense produced by dramatic or supernatural elements. It was hailed as a "new art" that could bring "new knowledge, new technique, new ideal and new courage," and was considered democratic in its address.[10] Its immediate origin can be found in the teahouse milieu, where the storytelling of traditional tales and folklore catered to the taste of the layman.[11] The valiant fortitude and physical prowess in martial arts–magic spirit films were regarded as particularly empowering by a people who had internalized the image of the "sick man of the orient" (*dongya bingfu*) since China's defeat in the Opium Wars and the subsequent suppression of the Boxer rebellion by Western powers. On the other hand, when the genre quickly expanded in quantity and variation, attacks were launched at its outlandish use of "superstitious" motifs, cinematic tricks, sexual promiscuity, and gender ambiguity. Major studios such as Mingxing and Tianyi were especially challenged by the fact that dozens of small companies swarmed the market with their low-budget productions, causing frantic competition and confusion.

Ma Junxiang finds the coexistence and the mutual sustenance of the avant-garde cinema and genre-oriented entertainment cinema in the West virtually absent in early Chinese film history. If the farcical and slapstick comedy (e.g. *Laborer's Love*) may be regarded as an oblique substitution for the avant-garde cinema in China, reasons Ma, then the invention of the martial arts–magic spirit film was the second wave to create a genre cinema, assimilating or repackaging experimental elements of the early comedy, particularly the focus on optical play.[12] In this sense, the early stage of the martial arts–magic spirit film served the dual function of both experimental cinema and commercial entertainment in a form that may be called "avant-pop." This aesthetic fuzziness largely determined the slippery nature of the genre, further complicated by the fact that a multitude of studios of varying size and resources had diverse approaches to style and production value.

Insofar as this emerging genre experimented with trick photography, special effects, camera movement, and editing, it proved to be a vanguard in modernizing the Chinese cinematic language. Its attraction and popularity overshadowed the slow-paced socioethical film, love film, and a large part of the classical costume drama burdened with theatrical fabrication and stasis. Many film advertisements of the time boasted "magnificent sets" and "strange special effects."[13] While some films were adapted from traditional tales and folklore, most were either derived from contemporary martial arts fiction or simply filmmakers' spontaneous inventions. The latter were more concerned with creating spectacular and profitable motion pictures than being faithful to any received notions or practice of the martial or other esoteric arts.

The genre was by no means an *ex nihilio* self-generated cinematic event; rather, it filtered through diachronic and synchronic cultural layers. China, of course, has a long tradition of martial arts practice and literature. The root ethos of the martial arts (*wuxia*) is the idea of *xia,* for which the inadequate English equivalent is "knight-errantry." James Liu, in an early treatment on the subject in English, lists eight basic tenets of *xia:* altruism, justice, individual freedom, personal loyalty, courage, truthfulness and mutual faith, honor and fame, and generosity and contempt for wealth.[14] Ancient records or descriptions of *xiake* (the person with a chivalric aura) can be found in the early historiography *Shiji* (*Records of the Historian*) by Sima Qian (145–86 BC), which contains chapters called "Biographies of Assassins" (*Cike liezhuan*) and "Biographies of the Wandering Knights-Errant" (*Youxia liezhuan*).[15] As a social and moral trope, the origin of *xia* is commonly traced to the Warring States (ca. 403–221 BC), when political chaos and feudal divisions gave rise to a distinct group of independent warriors who dispensed justice and offered protection to the weak and the dispossessed. These social agents were regarded as the embodiment of moral superiority and physical strength; their mastery of military arts, especially the sword, was indispensable to their heroic aura. The genealogy of *xiake* runs through a subsequent long, turbulent dynastic history until the late Qing period, as profusely demonstrated by literature (in both classical and vernacular languages), drama, and storytelling. Usually of commoner origins, they were essentially self-made men (and sometimes women) who, in times of disorder and disaster, embarked on self-imposed missions to restore a moral conscience to the social body, which often involved redistributing wealth and power by force. The chief characteristic of a *xiake*'s chivalry or righteousness was his faith in a transcendental moral order and the ultimate equality or mutual respect in human relations (as manifested in friendship or fraternity) outside the mainstream, corrupt social order, even though its achievement would often entail a measure of violence and sacrifice.[16]

Over time, the historical authenticity associated with the early figures of *xiake* gave way to more mythic representations, branching into popular literature, iconography, and folklore. The Ming novel *On the Water Margins* (*Shuihu zhuan*) is an exemplary text amalgamating historical accounts and the popular imagination, weaving the two into a sustained narrative of both political and magic power, and spelling out the lure and trappings of marginality.[17] The novel's creation of a "family" of 108 knights (including a few women), most of whom came from humble origins, was its most celebrated aspect. Many knights are endowed with some form of supernatural power, such as flying or swallowing flames. This expanded tribal family, consisting mostly of sworn brothers and empowered by its proximity to nature (woods, swamps, mountains), stands as a symbolic counterpart to culture (i.e., the court) and the flourishing urban civilization under its dominion. As a self-contained power, this unique family in the wilderness posed a serious threat to the imperial court and its purported heavenly mandate. Ultimately, however, the family on the "water margins" is dissolved by forces from within and without. When the head of the family, Song Jiang, a disgraced former official of literati origin, fails to resist the temptation of a prominent post in the court, the stronghold on the Liangshan Mountain is quickly reduced to historical ruins.

On the Water Margins is but one exemplary instance in the large corpus of traditional knight-errantry lore ambivalent to civilization and its corrosive forces throughout Chinese history. The ancient ideal of *xia* did not pass through literary and oral tradition down to modern times in a continuous flow. To be sure, the historical imagination surrounding *xia* was resurrected in the twentieth century by the cinematic medium, benefiting from the unprecedented visual spectacle of moving images. The most crucial catalyst for this resurrection, however, was the proliferation of popular martial arts literature in the early Republican period, largely made possible by the spread of vernacular literacy, modern print technology, and other mass media. In fact, the term *wuxia* (with emphasis on *wu* or martial arts), as it has been known in modern times, was allegedly only coined and began to be widely used in this period by the translator and novelist Lin Qinnan (Lin Shu) as well as other writers and literary historians.[18] This modern martial arts literature coincided with both the emergence of narrative cinema and the vernacular movement. It is more polymorphous and sophisticated in both form and content with multiple subgenres, daring expression of amorous chivalry (*qingxia*), and amplified description of martial arts techniques.[19] The boom and diversification of the Butterfly literature created space for this new breed of martial arts fiction. Significantly, the new martial arts fiction widely adopted colloquial Chinese as opposed to the classical language in which much of early martial arts literature was written. Many newspapers and magazines serialized popular martial arts works. Pingjiang Buxiaosheng's (pseudonym for Xiang Kairan, 1890–1957) *Tales of Strange Knights-Errant in the Wilderness* (*Jianghu qixia zhuan*), began its serialization in 1920 in *Red Magazine* (*Hong zazhi*) and was published in book form in 1928, totaling 150 chapters. It is often seen as the pioneering text that "raised the curtain" of the surge of modern martial arts fiction.[20] This daily or weekly form of storytelling through arbitrary suspense is no doubt a modern form of literary production contingent upon the cycle of periodical production and circulation. But it is also reminiscent of the *zhanghui* structure of the traditional novel with interlocked chapters, which was in turn modeled after the serial forms employed by professional storytellers to hook the audience in teahouses and theaters.

Indeed, as elsewhere in the world, mass-produced serialization was one of the hallmarks of the culture industry in the Shanghai of the 1920s when modern mass media began to pervade the fabric of everyday life. Popular fiction, comic strips, various forms of drama, and cinema, all, in one way or another, adopted the serial format. The cultural market of the time was inundated with products recycled from one popular genre to another, creating a chain effect that blurred the boundaries between different venues of cultural consumption. Part of *Tales of Strange Knights-Errant in the Wilderness* was adapted for the screen by Mingxing in 1928.[21] *The Burning of the Red Lotus Temple* became an instant hit, which led to three sequels in the same year and another fourteen over the following three years. Serial illustrated books (*lianhuan tuhua*) based on the film(s) quickly appeared on street corners, satisfying the cravings of children and the poor who could not afford to see the movie. The whole city was aflame with a passion for the saga of the Red Lotus Temple. In the film industry alone, the fire quickly spread to other studios, which tried to repeat Mingxing's success. A host of films that had titles containing the word *burning* (*huoshao*) filled the silver screen. Though no other studio was as ambitious and affluent as Mingxing, which produced eighteen series, many attempted several series or at least one sequel. Just as Bao Tianxiao and other Butterfly writers had been recruited by the expanding film industry to serve as screenplay writers, so too, the martial arts fiction writers also became natural candidates for adapting prose fiction to the screen. Gu Mingdao, author of *The Swordswoman from the Huangjiang River,* wrote the screenplay for Youlian Company's eponymous film. Between 1929 and 1932, thirteen series of the film were released. The circular nature of the cultural context that gave rise to the genre interestingly paralleled the open-ended narrative structure of the film series. Prone to prompt more installments, episodes were never complete narratives but existed in a loose but suspenseful relation to what came before and after, in a manner similar to the use of "cliff-hangers" in the American serial queen drama.

The birth of a genre is more about the production of form—or "formula"—than content,[22] which nevertheless cannot be divorced from its origins. Form as such is thus never complete and self-sufficient. Given the syncretic nature of the intertextual and intermediatized seriality, the commonly accepted view that *Burning* is the first martial arts–magic spirit film in Chinese film history requires some qualification. Although the film was the first big-budget attempt at institutionalizing the compounded genre and turning it into a mass phenomenon, it derived from a series of experiments in the preceding years. These experiments may not have directly contributed to the formation of the genre proper, but they nevertheless created a vital contextual field in which the genre evolved. Jia Leilei traces the "prototype" of the "martial arts" film to *Robbery on a Train* (*Che zhong dao*) produced by the motion picture department of the Commercial Press in 1919.[23] Adapted from a story by Lin Qinnan based on an American film (most likely *The Great Train Robbery*), the Chinese version boasts a series of chase scenes and martial arts fighting sequences. It also features a hero, who, with the help of a flower-vending girl, catches the villains. The director Ren Pengnian (1894–1968) later made a couple of films set against the background of the 1911 revolution that contained a more pronounced theme of "knight-errantry" and were inflected with patriotic sentiments.[24]

Red Beauty and Skeleton (*Hongfen kulou*), modeled on a translated detective novel, was released by Xinya Company (using the facilities and equipment of the Commercial Press) in 1922. One of the earliest Chinese feature-length films, it features a disguised heroine who rescues her lover from the villains' den with the help of his detective brother. Screenwriter and director Guan Haifeng, who was involved in the adaptation of the sensationalist play *Victims of Opium* in 1916, chose the topic because the Shanghai audience was very attracted to films with a martial arts plot (*wuxia qingjie*) at that time.[25] The film, containing plenty of on-location shooting, is replete with elements of "the detective, adventure, martial arts, romance, and comedy."[26] Before entering the film industry, Guan had been active in Peking Opera and New Drama. He even adapted an American detective film *The Phantom Bandit* for the stage. Guan introduced several mechanical tricks or devices (*jiguan*) into *Red Beauty and Skeleton* to produce a thrilling sensation of horror and mystery. In this sense, the film may be a progenitor in combining elements of both the "martial arts" and "magic spirit;" it also prefigured the emergence of the horror film, which I will discuss in chapter 8.

In these early experiments the spirit of *xia* is deployed in varying degrees to articulate a number of modern character types, such as the urban hero or heroine (often refigured as a detective) or the revolutionary assassin. Interestingly, these modern incarnates of the classical *xiake* are akin to those heroic characters on the New Drama and civilized play stage around the Republican revolution a decade earlier. The blending of entertainment with patriotism, adventure with revolution, attraction with narration, popular tastes with artistic play, and theatricality with cinematic experimentation endows these nongenre-oriented films with an exploratory and synthetic style and appeal.

With the rise of Mingxing and the long film and serious drama in the first half of the 1920s, the impulse to make martial arts films, however, did not vanish entirely. The two directors qua actors who contributed most significantly to the perfecting of the modern (i.e., in modern clothing and setting) martial arts film are Zhang Huichong and Zhang Huimin, the two brothers mentioned in chapter 5. The former started his acting career at the motion picture department of the Commercial Press in 1922 and played the knight-errant hero in many films. He is regarded as the first major actor of martial arts films in China, long before Mingxing made *Burning*.[27] Zhang Huimin and Wu Suxin, who formed a strong partnership both on screen and in their private life, demonstrated their unique modern orientation in the midst of the "burning" craze when most martial arts–magic spirit films had either a salient or a vaguely archaic look.

While the Zhang brothers represented the modern style martial arts film, the boom of the so-called unofficial history film (*bishi pian*) and the classical costume drama (*guzhuang ju*) between 1925 and 1927 installed a traditional look on the Shanghai commercial cinema—at least on the surface. The first experiments with historical subjects made by the liberal-minded Commercial Press in the early 1920s were directly influenced by the intellectual movement of "reordering national heritage" (*zhengli guogu*) advocated by, among others, Hu Shi, the "father" of the vernacular movement. Tianyi set the trend in 1925. Its founders were the famous Shao (Shaw) brothers. It launched a campaign to "propagate Chinese civilization" (*fayang Zhonghua wenming*) through cinema as a means of countering Western modernity. However, the kind of "civilization" unearthed and remolded for the petty urbanites and diasporic audiences was mainly the vast reservoir of folklore, traditional literature, and unofficial history. The materials that most attracted producers were tales with strong supernatural and amorous elements. They included the famous legend White Snake (about a love affair between a scholar and a snake spirit appearing as a beautiful woman) and episodes from classical novels and their extrapolated popular versions (e.g., *Investiture of Gods* and *Journey to the West*).[28]

The aesthetic emphasis of these cinematic adaptations was on the narrative devices of "strange machination" or "wondrous coincidence" (*xuanji*). In spite of Tianyi's original aim of "focusing on old morals and ethics" (*zhuzhong jiu daode, jiu lunli*), many costume dramas often appear ultramodern, replete with contemporary fashion, expressionist sets, and even seminude scenes. *The Cave of the Spider Spirit* (*Pansi dong,* Shanghai Film Company, 1927), adapted from an episode in *Journey to the West,* is a spectacular example (fig. 6.5). Originally a beauty-calendar painter, the

6.5 *The Cave of the Spider Spirit* (1927). (Courtesy of the China Film Archive)

director Dan Duyu was known for his obsession with the look of his films. The cave in which the spider queen reigns is designed in both "realistic and magnificent" ways to evoke an animate yet ghostly ambiance. The boundaries between the human and the nonhuman, the dead and the living, are blurred as the main characters—the spider queen, the monkey king Sun Wukong, and the pig Zhu Bajie—keep taking on different disguises. The biggest attraction of the film seems to have been the scene of swimming spider-beauties shot through an underwater camera, the first of its kind in China.[29] A 1927 adaptation by the Fudan Company from the classical romantic novel *Dream of the Red Chamber* simply had the cast appear in modern fashion, with the female protagonist Lin Daiyu in a flowing long robe and high heels, her hair adorned with white ribbons. The color cover of the special issue for the film published by the company is rendered in art nouveau style, featuring a scantily clad romantic couple ascending into the sky amid clouds. The famous *Burning* also owes its sensational success to its presentation of titillating scenarios of seminude beauties shown in the midst of violence and esoteric rituals (fig. 6.6).

The provocative, and often erotic, appeal of costume drama created a phantasmagoria of overlapping temporality; the alternative versions of "history," when rendered cinematic, became the place where magic and

6.6 *Burning of the Red Lotus Temple:* temple as harem. (Courtesy of the China Film Archive)

technology, archaic fantasy and modern desire fused into a feast of visual display. The genre was immensely popular in Nanyang, which created a competitive edge for Chinese cinema over American cinema.[30] These experiments with the magic spirit of the cinema in rendering the past palpable also paved the way for the emergence of the commingled genre, the martial arts–magic spirit film. The latter became a new formula for tossing together both visual attraction and narrative suspense, physical action and psychic power, natural wonder and supernatural forces. The supple and cunning female figures in *The Cave of the Spider Spirit,* though portrayed as negative forces in the film, may be seen as the prototype of *nüxia* (martial heroines) who were to crowd the screen in less than a year.

As a whole, the cultural labor involved in the making of the martial arts–magic spirit film was transmedia in form and heterogeneous in nature. The genre as such was a meeting place for a variety of experimental cultural and filmic practices, creating an alchemy of traditional obsessions with the fantastic and the strange, and modern fascinations with the new and the changeable. Engaging and translating the vast wealth of folklore and oral histories with the aid of modern mass media, the costume drama as a diffused genre practice provided an important springboard for the martial arts–magic spirit film—an implosion of the vernacular culture of both past and present.

BODIES IN THE AIR: SCIENCE OR MAGIC?

The critical vector of martial arts–magic spirit film discourse shifted dramatically over the period from 1927 to 1931, including the perception of the body and its relationship to cultural representation. When the first full-fledged martial arts films appeared in 1927, critics enthusiastically welcomed the foregrounding of bodies, specifically, the cinematic display of various bodily techniques. In contrast to the emphasis on sentimental close-ups of facial expression prevalent in the interior-bound melodramatic film, the actor's physical dexterity and martial skills acquired paramount importance. By 1931, however, the authorities officially banned the production of films with explicit "superstitious" elements. The body, now seen as the vehicle of dangerous desires and spirits, was a source of degeneration of Chinese cinema and national spirit. Measures for containment and restructuring of the industry were implemented.

The emergence of the martial arts–magic spirit film marked a turning point in the presentation and perception of the body in early Chinese cinema. Until this time the narrative and performing style of the dominant genres such as the socioethical film, romance film, and a bulk of costume drama was generally characterized by *wen*—which has a polysemous meaning of literary, restrained, and elegant. As I have shown in my analysis of *A String of Pearls* in chapter 5, close-ups on subtle facial expressions, continuity editing, and the focus on the interior space were crucial to the construction of narrative cohesion and moral persuasiveness. The martial arts film, on the other hand, embodied the spirit of *wu* (which means the state of being virile and military).[31] The spectacle of *wu* consists of martial arts and related instruments, the physical landscape, and even driving a car in instances of the modern-dress martial arts film. In other words, the body in motion, in direct contact with the physical world and basic elements, is a distinct trademark of the genre. The body's kinetic experience and its transformative power become the emphasis. However, the body does not roam about in a totally externalized physical landscape; in fact, it constantly moves in the unstable zone between nature and culture, the society and its margins. The physiological character of the body is thus inscribed in the social landscape at large. The abundance of visual delight and magical effects so crucial to the martial arts–magic spirit film serves another purpose as well; it contributes to the cultivation of *xia* as a kind of embodied aura in a modernizing and alienating society. For this reason, the genre was seen by a critic as a "stimulant," which could "lift [one's] aspiration for the martial spirit [*shangwu jingshen*]":

> The martial spirit is something everyone ought to possess. Yet, if there is nothing to awaken it, it will always be shrouded and will never attain exciting expressions. As a result, one will look like a weakling. Wouldn't that let down one's aspiration for the martial spirit? Those stirring and extraordinary martial arts films, however, demonstrate all kinds of shocking yet gratifying action [*dongzuo*], as well as depicting events that solicit everyone's sympathy. . . . These are really the special merits of the martial arts film.[32]

Physicality is thus preeminently fraught with moral and cultural significance. Most of the *wuxia* films unfailingly convey the message of "eradicating villains and wiping out despots, redeeming the good and aiding the poor" (*chujian chubao, jiuliang jiping*). This heroic aura is typically masculine because *wu* is traditionally associated with male warriors and swordsmen with superhuman powers. This critic however, suggested that the martial spirit could awaken a collective spirit in the audience when embodied through cinema. He believed the martial arts film, more than any other genre, could "direct the world," filling the void where education or propaganda could not penetrate.

This ambiguity of the genre lies in the sense of wonder evoked by the "shocking and gratifying action" and its sense of purpose as a social remedy—contradictory conceptions of its aesthetics and politics, magic and science. In a broader cultural context, such contradictions speak to the valorization of modern science, which had acquired heightened currency in the May Fourth movement and especially the 1923 extensive controversy over "science and metaphysics" (*kexue yu xuanxue*) in 1923. The critical focus was centered on both the sensual physicality *and* the socioethical power it embodied; this conflict was further complicated and amplified by the discourse on technology—the flying machine in particular.

"NEITHER HORSE NOR DONKEY," OR THE LORE OF THE FLYING MACHINE

One of the modern martial arts films produced by Zhang Huimin's Huaju Company, *The Great Knight-Errant of Aviation* (*Hangkong daxia,* 1928) (fig. 6.7), was based on a real-life story of Zhang Huizhang, the first pilot to successfully complete a long distance flight in China.[33] Zhang Huimin

6.7 *The Great Knight-Errant of Aviation* (1928), a modern martial arts film (from *Dianying yuebao*, 1928, no. 7).

himself played the pilot-knight-errant, described as one who "practiced knight-errantry and observed loyalty" (*renxia haoyi*) (fig. 6.8). The modern knight-errant is always ready to rectify injustice, tempted neither by money nor treasure. One day, riding the train after completing a "knightly mission" (*xingxia*), the pilot catches sight of a bandit, nicknamed the Flying Tiger, threatening a young woman (played by Wu Suxin). He rescues the beauty and rides away with her on horseback. The bandit and his underlings have to give up the chase when they see the couple vanish into the sky, where an airplane is dancing like a dragonfly. As it turns out, he has rescued his future wife, betrothed to him by their parents when they were children. Then, against a beautiful sky, the reunited lovers spend their honeymoon cruising the open space, the traditional practice of arranged marriage thus reconciled with free love, emblematized by the flying machine.

Ostensibly parading as a martial arts film, *The Great Knight-Errant of Aviation*, contains, however, no swordplay or classical costumes.[34] Rather, the virtuoso displays the wonder of the flying machine and the fantasy of modern science. Yet a sensational effect is produced by blending chivalric knight-errant routines and the shop-worn motif of extending the martial hero's prowess and speed with a horse as well as modern transportation. As in Gaston Bachelard's conception of productive ruptures in scientific knowledge, transforming martial arts stock elements through

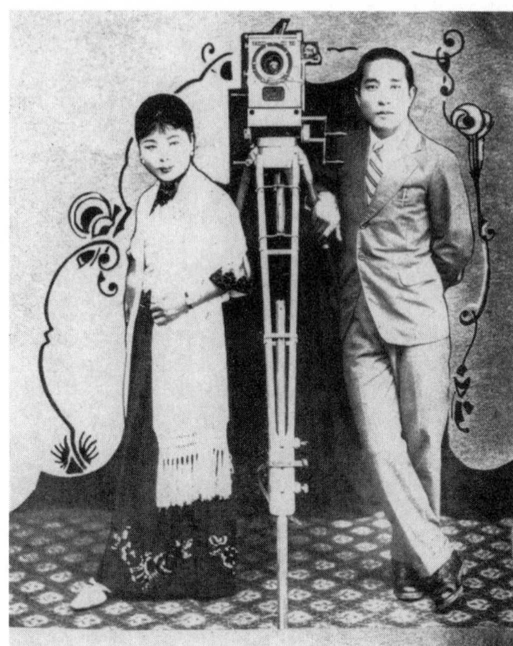

6.8 Zhang Huimin and Wu Suxin, with the company's camera (*Silverland*, no. 10, July 1928).

cinema's spectacle may be seen as recasting (*refonte*).[35] These breakages and leaps are realized by techniques such as editing, trick shots, superimposition, and sometimes animation that materialize the transfers between different forms of knowledge, representation, and genre. In the case of *The Great Knight-Errant of Aviation,* the instant spatiotemporal transition from the scene where the hero rides away with the woman on a horse in the wilderness is literally sprung into the next shot of the airplane in the sky. The attraction here rests not so much in any logical narrative progression, but in the spectacle of speed and compressed metamorphosis from organic martial arts to mechanical virility.

The "flight" in *The Great Knight-Errant of Aviation* is not portrayed as a painful transition from nature to culture or the premodern to the modern but rather as a delightful crossing of contiguous realms of experience. Just as the hero effortlessly inhabits the double identity of the archetypal knight-errant and the pilot in his modern armor, the airplane and the horse are not necessarily antithetical symbols of different temporalities and consciousness. The airplane may be seen as a winged horse, a mechanized creature that gives the martial arts plot a touch of the magic spirit. Given that airplanes were still rare in China at the time, its traceless appearance and disappearance were perceived as "natural" precisely because of its mythical aura. According to a contemporary description of the film, "when weak and oppressed people hear the engine of the plane from afar, their faces are lit up as though in a shadowplay; their sad distressful expressions are replaced by happiness and relief."[36]

The reception of cinematic recasting was not uniform. During the years immediately preceding the martial arts film boom, one commentator on the "craze for classical drama" regarded certain ways of "revising old drama" (*guju xinbian*) with shock and disdain. Citing the examples of Zhuge Liang (a historically-based character in the classical novel *Romance of the Three Kingdoms*) fighting Sun Chuanfang (a warlord of the 1920s), and of Tang Sanzang (the monk in *Journey to the West*) riding a motorbike instead of a white horse on his pilgrimage to fetch the scriptures in India, the critic accused the studios of blindly catering to audience curiosity (*xinqi*) in order to make quick cash.[37] The question to be asked, however, is why the audience was so enthralled by "curiosities" that were considered "neither horse nor donkey" (*feilü feima*).[38] What really disconcerted this critic was perhaps the cross-fertilization of the past and the present, the body and the machine, and literary canon and cinematic technology that effected a temporal collapse and disintegrated a certain order of things. The cartoonlike image of the legendary monk riding a motorbike is outrageous because it redefines the sacrosanct body of the pious monk by aligning it with the machine age. While the classical figure is associated with a rugged natural landscape, the motorbike takes him directly into the urban jungle.[39] In his twentieth-century incarnation, Tang Sanzang is no longer a passive victim of worldly desire; he instead becomes the icon of commodity desire itself. In that sense, the cinema updates archaic texts as part of modern urban folklore.

The opposition between the organic folk world and the mechanical world or for that matter, the premodern and the modern, popular in traditional folklore studies encounters a challenge here. Just as the plane was to the pilot, the motorcycle to the monk became an "extension of his bodily scheme"; the apparatus at their disposal is not presented as something ontologically transcending, but rather intimately related to the operating agents and their awareness of its [practical] function.[40] It is thus hard to distinguish the objectification of the body from the anthropomorphism of the machine. As Hermann Bausinger points out, inventors and technicians often treat their work in technology as something beyond the realm of science. When a new gadget or machine is first tested, the experimental impulse and anxiety are evoked more as an "experience," often tinged with "demonic power."[41] In this experiential dimension the boundary between the rational and irrational becomes quite irrelevant as the body and the machine constitute a new kinesthetic fusion.

NAVIGATING THE LANDSCAPE OF MODERN SCIENCE

The voracious mixing of traditional tropes and modern technology, canonical literature and commodity culture, is part and parcel of a larger cultural discourse about technology and modernity in China in the early twentieth century. The connection and interpenetration between the human body and machines had already captured the Chinese imagination in the late Qing fin-de-siècle period. The popular illustrated newspaper *Dianshizhai huabao* (1884–96) carried numerous reports and illustrations of how various new apparatus and instruments dramatically altered people's perceptions of the body in time and space. X-rays, cameras, trains, and airplanes appear most frequently. Airplanes were seen as mythic flying ships cruising over exotic landscapes (fig. 6.9).

If these illustrations displayed the vernacular scientific imagination in a visually palpable way, the literary and intellectual discourse, though still couched in the classical language, was hardly slow to respond. Huang Zunxian (1848–1905), the innovative late Qing poet, reformist, and diplomat, wrote a set of poems in his late years about the modern expe-

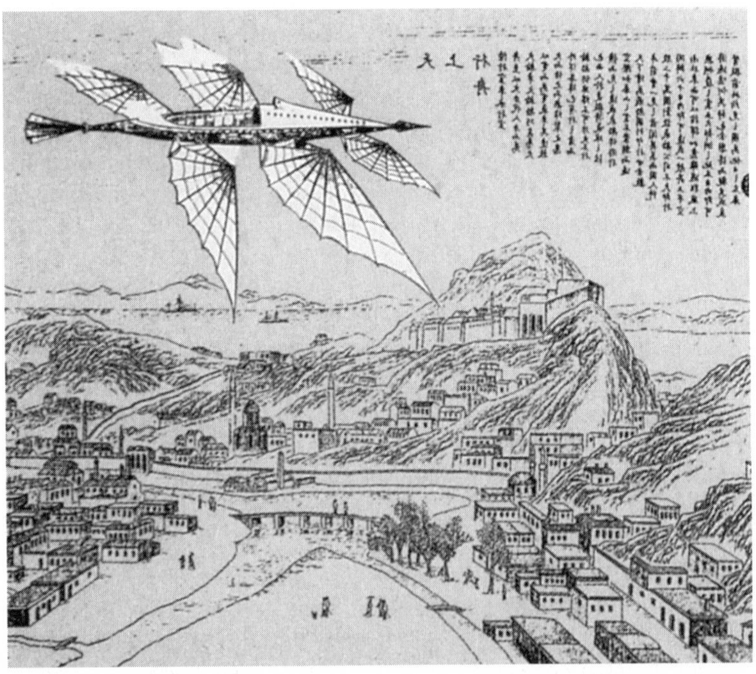

6.9 The winged flying machine (*Dianshizhai huabao*).

rience of parting and nostalgia affected by photography, the telegraph, the steamship, and the train. Fast and efficient as these instruments and vehicles are, they "conspire to increase the sorrow of people parting" because tight schedules, punctual timetables, and high speed allow no indulgence in bidding farewells. Sentimentality is redundant as a steamship vanishing over the horizon long before the people who send off the passenger get home. The self, when "transported" by these mechanical vehicles over time and space, becomes shot through with technology's unsettling power.

Of the telegraph Huang wrote about an entirely new mode of mediatized personal communication. In these lines he considers these messages from his lover,

> But this letter I am reading is not from your hand
> And it seems to be lacking your personal touch
> I did read my sweetheart's name just at the end,
> But I suspect the signature was forged by someone else!"

Huang searches for an answer outside his window:

> In front of my gate two rows of straight poles
> March in perfect order to a place over the horizon.
> Metallic strings run along each row,
> Strings that connect one pole to the other.
> I really don't understand how you mail all these letters,
> And how they arrive so quickly, one after another.
> There are hundreds of minutes in each single day,
> But how do you find time to send so many notes?
> If I don't have your news for just one moment, darling,
> My face turns ashen with anxiety and worry.
> I wish I could travel at the speed of lightning,
> And flash in one moment to my lover's side![42]

The poem questions the nature of the disembodied written word without the personal touch of a calligrapher. The classical poetic sensibility associated with Chinese calligraphy (and hence ideogrammic characters) gave way to the transnational digital coding of the telegraphed message. Yet, the compound sense of wonder and anxiety over telegraphy's "speed of lightning" incites his will to "flash" his body to the faraway lover's side like those wired characters. The poems on "modern parting" are accounts of disjunctive bodily and spiritual movement on the "confused horizons" in the late Qing moment.[43] Huang's observation of (and on) the

Eiffel Tower in 1893 elucidates the vertiginous experience of a vertical movement that radically transforms one's worldview.

> An elevator car suddenly shoots up its cable,
> And I leap when I hear the whine of its engine.
> I really am flying, without any wings on my back,
> Soaring on a journey to the heavens above![44]

This dizzying experience of rapidly ascending an artificial peak and the new perspective it offers was rendered visible by a contemporary illustration of the world's "Tallest Building" in *Dianshizhai huabao*. The twenty-eight-story building, supposedly located in Boston, has inflections of Chinese architecture, such as the flying eave and arched windows, yet features external basket-like machines that transport people up and down.[45] The human body in these poems and visual representations was no longer the solitary subject of classical poetry who contemplates the wonder of nature and travels in real time (as on a horseback or in a wooden boat). Rather, the body was quite literally "carried away" by machines that generated speed and kinesthetic sensation. Despite the anxiety and lamentation over a passing world, these poems and pictures about the transformed experiences deliver a humorous recognition of a paradigmatic change in human perception. They explored the possibilities in the broadening of the cultural horizon and facilitating communication in a world context that was at once shrinking (due to technology) and enlarged (by an expanded consciousness). Though still written in the classical language, Huang's poetry was regarded by Liang Qichao (1873–1929) as a pioneering voice in the "revolution in the poetic realm" (*shijie geming*). For Liang, Huang's poetry exemplified the reformist vision of "casting new ideals in old styles" (*rongzhu xin lixiang yi ru jiu fengge*).[46] Well before Hu Shi's *Experiments*, Huang Zunxian was certainly among the vanguard that brought a vernacular impulse and a global outlook to the classical Chinese poetic tradition.

Huang's modern poetic views were echoed by his contemporaries. For instance, reformist intellectual Tan Sitong pioneered the concept of sexual relations as a physiological mechanism and wrote of the human body as "an intricate machinery which could be adjusted and regulated."[47] The leading liberal magazine *Eastern Miscellany* (*Dongfang zazhi*), first published by the Commercial Press in 1904, was a forum where much up-to-date information and knowledge on modern science (including cinema) was disseminated. Its August 1911 issue carried a photograph of a "machine-man" (*jixie ren*), or a robot. The "man" in the picture, a machine body with a human head and even a beard, is named Oceutus (meaning the "incredible"). He can "mimic all human behaviors, such as speech, laughter, screaming and singing." Although Oceutus would obey any human instruction to perform like a clown, he is not a "monster, nor fantasy play." In short, he is not human but like a human.[48]

These incipient discourses were related to the political discourse on "enriching the nation and strengthening the military" (*fuguo qiangbin*) and subsequent intellectual discussions on the roles of science and technology in a modernizing China.[49] As modern technology was also associated with Western imperialism, many late Qing debates focused on the advantages or disadvantages of introducing new technology, including weaponry and warships. In the second half of the nineteenth century, under internal and external pressure, court reformers were able to carry out the "self-strengthening" (*ziqiang*) program that allowed modern military schools, factories, and shipyards. But reformists rationalized that Western science only ought to be regarded as a useful tool, whereas the "body" of Chinese learning to remain intact.

After the fall of the Qing dynasty in 1911, the clamor for more radical changes in social infrastructure and cultural consciousness culminated in the May Fourth movement, the two chief banners of which were "democracy" and "science." The humiliating events at the Versailles conference in 1919 convinced the intellectuals that the reasons for China's inferiority was its slowness in embracing the project of Enlightenment and modernity. For the same reason, any residual feudal beliefs and Confucian values should be cast into the historical trash bin. The cult of science went hand in hand with the iconoclastic antireligious movement and an extensive effort to reevaluate and reorder the traditional heritage. Antiquity was studied through scientific methods that had been introduced to China in the late nineteenth century and further developed in the early 1920s in the wake of the visits by John Dewey, Bertrand Russell, and other Western thinkers. Even folklore became an object of scientific study, which attempted to record and categorize folk traditions of the past while removing "superstitious" elements.[50]

The supreme status accorded modern science was seriously challenged in 1923–24 in a debate on "science and metaphysics"—also known as the polemic on "science and the view of life" (*kexue yu renshengguan zhizheng*)—that intensified the rift among the intellectuals. Liang Qichao's book, *Impressions of a European Journey,* written after his visit with a group of Chinese delegates to the Paris Peace Conference and to war-torn Europe in 1918–19, provided a prelude to the debate. The book contains an essay called "The Dream of the Omnipotence of Science," a pessimistic reflection on the destructive power of modern technology, and the decline of Western material civilization:

> Those who praised the omnipotence of science had hoped that, as soon as science succeeded, the golden age would appear forthwith. Now science is successful indeed; material progress in the West in the last one hundred years has greatly surpassed the achievements of the three thousand years prior to this period. Yet we human beings have not secured happiness; on the contrary, science gives us catastrophes. We are like travelers losing their way in a desert. They see a big black shadow ahead and desperately run to it, thinking that it may lead them somewhere. But after running a long way, they no longer see the shadow and fall into the slough of despondency. What is that shadow? It is this "Mr. Science." The Europeans have dreamed a vast dream of the omnipotence of science; now they decry its bankruptcy. This is a major turning point in current world thought.[51]

A promoter of the "poetic revolution" more than a decade earlier, Liang saw modern science as an instrument of mass annihilation instead of democratic emancipation on a global scale after his own journeys to the West. He directly took "Mr. Science" to task, comparing him to a shadowy illusion—a provocative metaphor as it negates the substantive character associated with modern innovation. His "impressions" were confirmed by his meetings with Henri Bergson, Rudolf Eucken, and Bertrand Russell during the trip, as these philosophers had already begun to critique the material obsession and the supremacy of Western civilization following the World War I.

Liang's view was shared and propagated by Zhang Junmai (Carson Chang), a Beijing University professor in the delegation to France. In his lecture "View of Life" at Qinghua University on February 14, 1923,[52] Zhang argued that one's general relation to the world could not be resolved by a pragmatic scientific perspective alone. Rather than privileging logic, causality, objectivity, and uniformity, he proposed that complex life phenomena, including psychological experience, might be better perceived—if not explained—in terms of an intuitive, nonquantitative, and inclusive approach. Such an approach could account for problems in ethics, religion, literature, and philosophy, which science tended to leave out or circumscribe.[53]

Zhang's views were quickly refuted by the geologist Ding Wenjiang (1887–1936), also a member of the delegation, on the grounds that they extolled a combination of Western and Chinese metaphysics.[54] Despite their friendship, he called Zhang "possessed by the ghost of metaphysics" (*xuanxue gui*) in his article "Metaphysics and Science."[55] He insisted that politics, metaphysics, and education, rather than science, should be held responsible for the war. The "God of Science" (*kexue shen*) was more than ever needed in China in order for it to modernize.[56] The dualism between Western materialism and Eastern spiritualism, as underscored by Zhang in his lecture, appeared arbitrary. In spite of his hard-line empiricism, Ding's polemic is ironically "scientific" in its use of categories such as "ghost" and "God." In his desire to expel the specter of metaphysics—be it imported Western agnostic philosophy or the much-heeded Wang Yangming intuitionist school of Confucianism—he advocated the "new religion" of science, which paradoxically ran counter to the iconoclastic May Fourth rhetoric.[57]

The impact of the debate was far reaching. Extending over a year and a half, it involved leading intellectuals of diverse persuasions and ideologies who published more than forty polemical essays in influential magazines. Similar discussions carried into later decades, including the 1980s, when the modernization agenda was once again highlighted. If the debate would seem divorced from the realm of the popular, its visibility in mass print media wove it into the larger social fabric. Some of the basic issues resonated in the conflicting discourses on the martial arts–magic spirit film a few years later. After the establishment of the Nationalist government in Nanjing in 1927, in the midst of the martial arts–magic spirit film boom, a number of publications on the subject appeared in an effort to evaluate and conclude the earlier debate.[58] The prevalent film criticism rhetoric of science vis-à-vis superstition in and the eventual censorship of the popular genre cannot be disassociated from this extensive debate on modern science and the fate of the modernity project in China.

Popular cinema, largely operating on the margins of the May Fourth movement yet occupying a substantial space in the vernacular culture, engaged with the contemporary controversy and its aftershocks in indirect but complex ways. The plots of most films were largely derived from traditional sources; however, the adaptations often privileged strange, magical, and improbable elements in order to enhance narrative suspense and visual effect. The bold use of film technology for these effects turned adaptation into a distinctively modern experience. The cinematic realization of the fantastic and mythical world, made possible with editing techniques, multiple camera set-ups, superimposition and so forth, rendered the impossible not just possible, but even believable. The sword-fighting scene in *Romance of the Western Chamber* was reportedly shot from several camera angles at once and edited afterwards. The result is a complexly patterned pyrotechnic display of light and shadow at high speed, redolent of the avant-garde film aesthetic. *Burning* was the first large-scale production that combined "martial arts" with "magic-spirit" and experimented with film technology to create special effects and a

6.10 The special effect of the "light of swords competing in magic arts." (Courtesy of the China Film Archive)

mystical ambiance. The cinematographer Dong Keyi (1906–78) found an ingenious way to solve the problem of spatial contiguity by aligning the temple roof painted on glass with the roofless life-size backdrop, creating a "magnificent" piece of virtual architecture.[59] By putting together the performance of actors and cartoon "stunts," the effect of the "light of swords competing in magic arts" (*jianguang doufa*) is achieved (fig. 6.10). His most important invention, partly taken from an idea in an American magazine, is the flying knight-errant (*feixia*), which quickly became a trademark of the genre.[60] The headdress of the heroine was dyed red, highlighting the prominence and androgynous look of the female knight-errant.[61] The film magazines of the day also copiously published articles on modern, state-of-the-art techniques used behind the scenes, revealing the secrets of cinema's magic spirit.[62] Through the innovative play between science and magic, film technology and folklore, avant-garde aesthetics and popular tastes, the cinema came to embody the multiple "faces" of modernity.[63]

These interwoven faces create new perceptions of the body at once corporeal and metaphysical, visible and invisible, material and magical, human and mechanical. Here the boundaries between nature and culture, the irrational and the rational, the traditional and the modern, were much less fixed than perceived by those of Enlightenment-minded intellectuals. If the "body is man's first and most natural instrument," as Marcel Mauss put it, the "techniques of the body" in the martial arts–magic spirit film constitute a particular habitus in which the body is both the medium (instrument) and the message (aim) of a cultural practice.[64] In early twentieth-century China, this habitus could be located in the composite space of traditional folklore and an emergent urban mass culture. The term *jianghu* traditionally signifies both the geographical and imaginary habitat for the "world of martial arts" and the liminal social space inhabited by the outcasts and outlaws in a predominantly rural landscape. Sam Ho put it succinctly, "the domain of the marital arts is therefore a subculture, at once a part of the real world but also apart from it."[65] The urban teahouses and amusement halls, where so much martial arts and magic spirit storytelling took place and where cinema first appeared and remained, are concrete examples of this renewed folk space. In other words, the world of *jianghu* had extended into the metropolis of Shanghai (and later Hong Kong), both as cinematic imagery and social organization. The martial arts–magic spirit film, stemming from a promiscuous body of cultural forms, sensibilities, and social experiences, articulated the ambiguity of the space of modern folk culture.

The flying body of the knight-errant may be seen as the quintessential embodiment of this mosaic and contentious space. The cinematic technology transforms the magic power—to borrow Robert Stam's formulation in another context—into an "aesthetic resource, a means for breaking away from the linear, cause-and-effect conventions of Aristotelian narrative poetics, a way of flying beyond the gravitational pull of verism, of defying the 'gravity' of chronological time and literal space."[66] Suspended in the air by invisible devices or various stunts (*tisheng* or "replacement body"), the body's movement and speed generated visual and kinesthetic experiences that effectively materialized the previously imaginary tricks of oral tales, literature, theater, and pictorial art. The hero's body and spiritual aura were fused together in this technologized liminal space. Such an extraordinary skill was certainly practiced and realized to varying degrees in the past (*On the Water Margins* abounds with such descriptions). However, the technique was mostly considered a superhuman skill possessed only by a few masters. In the late Qing period, flying and walking on air came to be perceived as acts that ordinary people could perform as well (fig. 6.11). When the film actors were able to perform these skills "effortlessly" and repeatedly on the silver screen, the flying body became the site of mass attraction and identification. This prompted many teenagers to go into the mountains in pursuit of such magical skills, a frenzy that, in part, led the cultural elite and the authorities to denounce the genre for corrupting the innocent and to take mea-

6.11 The art of walking on air: "female thief leaps onto the roof" (*Dianshizhai huabao*).

sures to curb its feverish production and consumption. Before going into more detail on the eventual censorship of the genre, I will deepen my discussion on its social implication and cultural effect through a close look at several *nüxia* films, bringing the gender subtext to the forefront. This may in turn help to explain the popularity and paranoia about the genre as a whole.

MARTIAL HEROINES: MASQUERADE AND AMBIVALENCE

As a mass-produced cultural product marketed beyond major urban centers, the martial arts–magic spirit film's appeal to rural Chinese audience and overseas Chinese communities was overwhelming. A revival of the martial spirit was much desired in a time of political instability and social fragmentation to compensate for the image of the "sick man of the Orient." The martial hero, such as the pilot in *The Great Knight-Errant of Aviation,* became an icon for modern masculinity. His superman-like image and pilot gear created an aura charged with mobility and velocity that epitomized the new epoch.

However, the martial aura and magic spirit were not reserved for men alone. Although the male martial hero is a more familiar archetype, the genre was distinguished and became increasingly popular through the proliferation of the female knight-errant.[67] This no doubt corresponded to the proliferation of swordswomen characters in contemporary martial arts fiction,[68] which provided raw material for screen adaptations. Although very few films of this subgenre have survived, the list of select film titles below, with the character *nü* (female) and *xia* (knight-errant) appearing in each one, testifies to the popularity of the subgenre with martial heroines:[69]

- *Nüxia Li Feifei* (*The Female Knight-Errant Li Feifei,* Tianyi, 1925)
- *Mulan congjun* (*Mulan Joins the Army,* Tianyi, 1927)
- *Ernü yinxiong* (*Hero and Heroine,* Youlian, four series, 1927–30)
- *Xianü jiu furen* (*The Female Knight-Errant Rescues the Lady,* Mingxing, 1928)
- *Wunü fuchou* (*Five Vengeful Girls,* Minxing, 1928)
- *Jianghu qingxia* (*He and She,* Youlian, 1928)
- *Feixia Lü Sanniang* (*The Flying Knight-Errant Lü Sanniang;* Da zhonghua beihe, 1928)
- *Nü dalishi* (*The Great Woman,* Da zhonghua beihe, 1929)
- *Nüxia bai meigui* (*The Valiant Girl White Rose,* Huaju, 1929)
- *Hong xia* (*Red Heroine,* Youlian, 1929)
- *Langman nü yinxiong* (*A Romantic Heroine,* Xintian, 1929)
- *Nü haidao* (*The Female Pirate,* Da zhonghua baihe, 1929)
- *Huangjiang nüxia* (*Swordswoman from the Huangjiang River,* Youlian, thirteen series, 1929–32)
- *Lan guniang* (*A Girl Bandit,* Huaju, 1930)
- *Nü biaoshi* (a.k.a. *Guandong nüxia, A Woman Bodyguard,* Yueming, four series, 1931)
- *Nüxia Hei mudan* (*The Female Knight-Errant Black Peony,* Yueming, 1931)

Unfortunately, only a few of these films still exist. Huaju specialized in the modern style martial arts and action film, but Youlian was most prolific in producing *nüxia* films.[70] *The Red Heroine,* the most complete extant film from Youlian, exemplifies the diverse yet overlapping aspects of the genre (fig. 6.12). Its most striking feature is the alliance between the

6.12 *The Red Heroine* (1929): shooting on location. (Courtesy of the China Film Archive)

desexualized heroine Yungu and an old Daoist master called (and resembling) the White Ape (*Baiyuan Laoren*), who not only rescues her but also teaches her martial arts and the magic of flying.[71] Surrounded by a bevy of half-nude girls and his minions (including one with protruding wolf teeth), a decadent bandit represents the force of evil. All of them reside in a secret, sumptuous palace in the wilderness. The orphaned heroine, abducted by the bandit, avenges her grandmother's death and also rescues another maiden from the claws of the bandit. Her abilities include such feats as instantly transporting her body in a puff of smoke, evoking similar dazzling feasts in Méliès's and Pathé's films of magic transformations.

Another extant film, *Uproar at the Lujiao Valley* (*Danao Lujiaogou*), is the sixth episode of the thirteen-series *Swordswoman from the Huangjiang River* and features a heroine (played by Xu Qinfang, 1909–85)[72] who roams Northern China's rugged landscape and saves villagers from monstrous birds. Another mission in the episode involves a visit, masquerading as an old woman, to a martial heroine in a neighboring village. After a sisterly swordplay competition, the two join hands to raid a bandit's den to avenge the young heroine's father's death.

The Valiant Girl White Rose from Huaju, again starring Wu Suxin, is a shorter feature (extant in incomplete from) that carries over many of the chase and rescue elements of *Lustrous Pearls* discussed in chapter 5. The difference here, however, lies in the foregrounding of the heroine. In the film Wu acts as a double for her feeble brother in order to assist their sick father in fending off intruding bandits. The theme of masquerade is consciously deployed to render the plot more dramatic and the gender relations more ambiguous. The mistaken identity also provides ample material for comic relief, an element clearly carried over from the civilized play and early physical comedy.

In all three instances, and in the *nüxia* subgenre as a whole, the heroine is usually pushed onto the stage by default, due to either the absence or enfeebled condition of a male heir in the family—suggesting variations of the Hua Mulan legend. Having assumed the role of avenger for an unjust death in the family and guardian of a community under external threat, the heroine embraces the challenge and renounces or postpones her sexual desire. Her transformation is usually signaled by visible changes in her iconography (costume and facial make up) and body language, in addition to her newly acquired martial skills. Her obligatory departure from her home community for a specific quest in a far away place also propels the narrative to enter, quite literally, an otherworldly dimension.

These films typically open with the "telling" of an emergency situation befallen an ordinary community. *The Red Heroine,* for example, literally opens in the mouth of a villager who announces the imminent arrival of the bandits. This expression effectively acknowledges martial arts film's roots in oral storytelling. At the same time the formally provocative framing, while betraying an experimental impulse, attracts the audience through a sensory organ and demonstrates the embodied nature of cinematic storytelling. Against the background of emergency, the narration gradually gravitates toward a more fantastic representation of reality with the heroine's transformation from a country lass into a woman warrior. From that point on, the unfolding of the film tends to operate on two parallel lines—often through crosscutting. One continues with the realist presentation of the distressing situation at home involving the people who are related to the heroine; the other follows the heroine's trajectory of transformation, mediated by magical powers that complicate or intervene in the logical unfolding of the plot proper. These films' resolutions typically fall within the happy reunion (*datuanyuan*) paradigm, often culminating in marriage or a family gathering. However, such an ending does not always return the heroine to her original maiden form, at times surprising the audience with disconcerting developments.

Unfailingly, the heroines are endowed with extraordinary bodily techniques that mark them as supernatural creatures. One such technique is the effortless ability to move horizontally or vertically, such as flying or leaping over walls or across chasms. In other words, overcoming gravity or temporality makes the instant bodily transportation from one location to another possible. It is thus only natural that the name of the female knight-errant in *The Red Heroine* is Yungu, the "maiden of clouds."[73] After three years of training in the holy Emei mountain, Yungu's name is figuratively spelled out in the sky when she returns home walking on the clouds in a classic *nüxia* outfit. It includes the flowing turban that covers her hair and her maiden identity, and the unisex "martial arts" dress completed by a pair of boots. Diagonally flying down from the upper right corner of the frame toward the audience, her appearance is a shocking contrast to her image in the sequence of three years ago. Back then she was a virgin captured as the bandit's sexual slave and appeared with her long disheveled hair over her bare shoulders, stripped to her black slip.

A mysterious old master, the White Ape, comes to her rescue. In a revealing moment, the bandit pulls the curtain open to find the ape-man leisurely smoking a pipe in her place. Here the mise-en-scène, resembling a magician's theater, establishes a prelude for a dramatic transformation. As though the ape-man was her papier-mâché facade, Yungu emerges from behind him. The powerless Yungu suddenly turns into an avenging goddess when she lifts a huge vase and crashes it on the head of a bandit. Yungu never appears with her long hair and feminine dress again. At the end of the film, after she fulfills her role as the matchmaker for the maiden and her cousin the scholar, she disappears in a cloud of smoke rising from the ground. In the next shot, from the young couple's point of view, she is shown in the sky brandishing her sword and moving rapidly. Her forward approach ultimately overtakes the screen, which can no longer contain the velocity and energy of her body in the air (fig. 6.13).

Similarly, the heroine Fang Yuquin in *Uproar at the Lujiao Valley* is also capable of overcoming gravity, if not precisely flying across vast distances. After entering a cave to rescue a boy kidnapped by the monstrous golden-eyed bird, she holds the boy in her arms and jumps over a precipitous chasm. This spectacle in silhouette is accomplished in a long shot with the aid of animation technique and the shadowplay aesthetic. In a later sequence, at a temple where Fang meets her nemesis (who killed her father), she performs an effortless jump over a tall wall into the courtyard. Likewise, with a strong and supple body, Nian, a girl from another village, invites Fang to assist in avenging her father's death. In one remarkable sequence, Nian jumps onto a wall carrying a huge pair of round grinding stones (passing for weights). The back-lit lighting makes Nian's image atop the wall extremely imposing, amplifying the earlier im-

6.13 *The Red Heroine* (1929): Yungu fighting against the bandits. (Courtesy of the China Film Archive)

age of Fang jumping over the chasm. This performance is presented as a public spectacle in front of the villagers. These sudden insertions of shadowplay-like images, accentuated by backlighting, foreground the martial women as larger than life figures. Nian's performance is also presented as a spectacle, enacted in the midst of a crowd. Fang, disguised as an old beggar with her sword hidden in her luggage, happens to witness the show. Through this repetition and identification, the two forge their sisterhood in the world of *jianghu*.

Bai Suyin, the heroine in *The Valiant Girl White Rose*, performs her flying technique on a swinging rope. The theme of *xia* here playfully unfolds through masquerade and a series of chase scenes, recalling similar treatment in *Lustrous Pearls*, also starring Wu Suxin.[74] Unlike the other two *nüxia* films, which are set in mythical time and rural space, *White Rose*, as with Huaju's other films influenced by the serial queen dramas and Westerns, opens in a conspicuous modern setting: the stadium for girl's school sports tournament. In an almost documentary fashion (and prefiguring Sun Yu's *Queen of Sports*), the camera tracks the women in T-shirts and shorts parading into the stadium and performing Western-style gymnastics. Bai Suyin, the student leader who excels in all sports including target-shooting, wins a bow and a martial arts costume that includes a cowboy hat. Soon after, she assumes her brother's masculine-sounding name Bai Tiemin (Tiemin means "iron people"), puts on the martial costume, attaches a mustache, and embarks on a journey toward the North to save her father from a local tyrant.[75] During her adventures she repeatedly has to prove her martial skill and (male) virility. The rope, a common device used in early comedy film to generate motion and scene connection,[76] is deployed time and again to escape from danger or to demonstrate dexterity, as when she confronts and defeats the villains by swinging on a rope back and forth across the screen. Skillfully flying in the air by using the rope almost as a prosthetic extension of her body, White Rose even takes a moment to salute the camera! She also uses the rope to bind the captives while jumping onto her horse and leading her game back to her father's ranch. All the while, her real identity remains concealed. Only when she is ordered to have a bath with her father does she confess the truth.

The device of masquerade and identity change is important for the latent theme of female bonding or even love in these films. In *The Red Heroine,* Yungu, after her return as an androgynous knight-errant, rescues another girl who is trapped. Unlike the heroines in other films who enter the world of martial arts to avenge or aid their fathers, Yungu's mission is to avenge her grandmother's death and to rescue the neighbor's daughter. Her role as a surrogate parent to the girl becomes apparent at the end of the film when she presides over the engagement between the girl and her scholar cousin (who had been keen on Yungu before her transformation). She then vanishes into the sky. Similarly, Fang Yuquin, disguised as an elderly woman, encounters the younger heroine who has solicited her help to avenge her father's death. Their duel in the courtyard, with each gazing into the other's eyes, is not so much a competition as a ritual of bonding—a practice common in the world of *Jianghu,* especially among men. After the competition, in which the more experienced Fang wins, the two heroines drink wine to cement their bonding as sworn sisters.

In *White Rose,* Bai Suyin, acting as a man, becomes the love object of two sisters who study martial arts with the man whom Bai secretly adores. In one sensuous scene, Bai enters two sisters' bedchamber by mistake. The romantic, feminine ambiance of the set is accentuated by a door shaped like a huge crescent moon.[77] For a brief moment, this martial arts story enters the inner chamber of the intimate female space. The mistaken sexual identity here provides the occasion for the staging of an ambiguous rendezvous between the three women. Inadvertently, this "mixed-up" relationship also cancels out the subplot of the heterosexual relationship in the film. In addition to his fear of offending his friend the bandit, the male protagonist refuses to help Bai Suyin upon discovering the romantic interlude. These fleeting scenarios of female bonding and mistaken love are perhaps signposts of a fledgling longing for a feminist utopia, where women help and love each other and form connections outside of kinship and the reproduction-oriented extended family.

The image of the martial heroine, in its diverse narrative and iconographic expressions, conveys a mixed message. On the one hand, the heroine, embodying technologized freedom, social mobility, and even transcendence, offers the viewer an empowering image of a modern woman. Her androgynous look and body language make her appealing to all kinds of spectators—men and women, old and young—thereby representing multiple potential identifications. The fact that the martial heroine has to conceal her gender or even to assume a male identity, however, continues to subordinate female power to a patriarchal order. This ambivalence is further played out regarding the issue of female virginity and the association of women with nature or primitive forces.

The overwhelming presence of nonhuman or semihuman figures—apes, birds, and other forms of uncanny embodiment—and their affinity to women in these films complicates the ambiguous social and sexual identity of the female knight-errant as a cultural icon. As in the case of contemporary martial-arts fiction, the proliferation of the image of the female knight-errant on the screen was almost invariably accompanied by the collective image of sexually victimized women, which sometimes borders on misogynist violence. Instances include the decorative seminude girls in the bandit's palatial den and the reference to rape in *The Red Heroine;* similar motifs occur in *Burning,* where lecherous monks keep young women in secret cells.

The martial arts–magic spirit film has to a certain extent developed from science fiction and other forms of popular culture in the late Qing and the early Republican periods. The thrill of fantasy, previously accessible through storytelling, print media, and theatrical performance, was visually materialized and enhanced by cinematic technology. The screen incarnation of the female knight, as typified by Yungu, may be considered a protocyborg figure that combines attributes of the woman, the primate, and the machine. This multifarious female subject defies anthropocentric reproductive laws and social hierarchies. In making the phantom leap into the sky, Yungu literally approximates the Unification of the Heaven and [Wo]man, the traditional ideal the literati had sought. The leap into a new dimension, or a cinematic space, accentuated by the martial-arts outfit that endows her with the sartorial attributes of an androgynous angel, also considerably alters her social and gender identity. She is no longer bound by social norms regulating marriage and family.

This change, however, does not necessarily entail an escapist transcendence. Instead, Yungu's expanded physical capacity and supernatural power enable her, if at a remove, to serve her native community in the most effective way. It is this combination of being at once a supernatural creature, a social subject, and a technological hybrid that makes her "a condensed image of both imagination and material reality."[78] Through this distillation, fantasy becomes a lived experience, magic an embodied reality.

As the only complete extant *nüxia* film, *The Red Heroine* is also more complete in its portrayal of a female knight-errant who evades conventional matrimony, unlike *The Swordswoman* and *White Rose.* Faithful to the original novel, the heroine in *The Swordswoman* ties the knot with her male comrade at the end. Similarly, in *White Rose,* after all the mishaps of her masquerade, Bai Suyin marries the man who refused to aid her revenge plot after her rendezvous with his sisters. Fang Yuquin and Bai Suyin are both bound by their passion for, if not devotion, to the other sex. Their knight-errantry is chiefly conditioned by their private missions to avenge their fathers and is therefore caught in the trappings of safeguarding or restoring a patrilineal order. Yungu's heroism, on the other hand, is mainly motivated by her allegiance to women. Her blind grandmother's death by a stampeding crowd, her own captivity, and the rape of the neighbor's daughter exemplify how women are the most downtrodden subjects in a society dominated by men. Thus, Yungu's transformation into a "maiden of the clouds" constitutes a vertical movement that not only dissolves the boundary between the social and the supernatural sphere, but also breaks up the patriarchal hierarchy that places women at the bottom of society. Yet, despite her role as a superhuman savior, she does not entirely evolve into a celestial creature bereft of social bindings. Her double identity as an insider, who is loyal to her fellow villagers and victimized women, as well as a semidivine agent dispensing justice through *deus ex machina* spectacles, positions her at the threshold of the personal and the communal, spiritual transcendence and social immanence.

The final scene of the film encapsulates this multifaceted character through a double narration of the familiar and the strange, the earthly and the magical, all wrapped in an unconventional happy ending. After Yungu descends from the sky, she conducts an engagement ceremony between her cousin and the neighbor's daughter—an act that would have been reserved for an elderly male member of the family. Yungu's transformation into a semidivine subject not only endows her with the power to perform this ritual but, more significantly, gives the ritual a magical touch. When she vanishes in a cloud of smoke from the scene, the engagement—already simplified in that no relatives are present and it is set in the wilderness rather than a conventional social space—is further bereft of its normative meaning. The role Yungu plays here is by no means an authority imposing an arranged marriage but a witness and catalyst of a liberal romantic relationship. The issue of virginity is here once more brought up when the maiden apologetically tells the scholar about the "loss of her body" (*shishen,* to the bandit presumably). If her apology confirms the tenacious conservativism regarding female sexuality even in the post-May Fourth late 1920s, the fantastic happy ending effectively removes the weight of that guilt. The maiden, now also donning a martial arts outfit, stands out more as a duplicate of the transformed Yungu than a victimized village girl. The film thus achieves a happy ending that is both conventional and refreshing. Its narrative closure of romantic fulfillment (Yungu's earthly desire will be vicariously lived out by the girl) is charged with a supernatural power that renders the ending more phantasmagoric than logical, more ambiguous than normalizing. If this ending is reminiscent of similar closures in *Romance of the Western Chamber* and *Lustrous Pearls,* in which a woman also witnesses a romantic union, it departs from them through magic female power.

THE TAMING OF THE MONSTROUS

The proliferating and profitable martial arts–magic spirit film came to an abrupt halt in 1931 when the newly established National Film Censorship Committee (NFCC) of the Nationalist government officially banned the showing of many films. After its establishment in November 1930, the FCC (a forerunner of NFCC) had already begun to issue licenses to films. The extremely successful *Burning* received a license on June 27, but it was soon revoked on July 21. *The Flying Female Knight-Errant Lü Siniang* (Lianhua), *The Knight-Errant with Double Swords* (Youlian), and *The Ghostly Shadow on a Strange Island* (Dadong) were among other censored films in this first wave of legal containment.[79] Within three years, more than sixty films in the genre were exiled from the silver screen, some of which simply never made it there.

This massive onslaught against the genre was part of the Nationalists' antisuperstition campaign,[80] as well as a response to the outcry of the cultural elite in and outside the film world. The genre was considered a dangerous vehicle for feudal ideology and a threat to the health of a modernizing society and the film industry alike. In other words, the Nationalists were concerned with disciplining the film culture as part of its program to create order and inculcate citizens with its party ideology and modern values.[81] The Nationalist regime had come to explicitly acknowledge the political and pedagogical instrumentality of the cinema and consequently even set up an official film studio, the Central Studio, in Nanjing for producing propaganda and educational films. The censorship of the martial arts–magic spirit film thus inadvertently paved the way for the 1934 New Life movement with its similar but more rigorously defined goals.

To be sure, film censorship was neither a novel invention nor only directed at the martial arts–magic spirit films in the early 1930s. Censorship had existed prior to the Nationalist era and could be traced to the early 1910s when cinema began to assert an increased presence in public space. Theater morality (such as the segregation of the sexes in seating) and tax collection (as film became recognized as a new commodity) were among the chief concerns of the early censors. Film censorship was a topic of concern in public discourse after the social impact of cinema became rather visible.[82] Cheng Shuren's 1927 *China Film Yearbook* also contains a section on censorship, which includes several official pronouncements and police ordinances regarding production and exhibition.[83] Domestic and foreign productions censored during the early 1930s were either banned or ordered to be cut because of nudity and eroticism, torture and murder, anti-Chinese and racist elements, or religious and superstitious subjects.[84] However, the martial arts–magic spirit genre comprised 70 percent of all banned Chinese films. Censorship quickly extended to printed martial arts fiction as well. *Tales of the Strange Knights-Errant in the Wilderness,* the serialized novel that inspired Zhang Shichuan to make *Burning,* was deemed "absurd in content" and ideologically "counter to the Party doctrines" by the NFCC. The Ministry of Education and the Ministry of Internal Affairs joined the NFCC in issuing orders prohibiting the publication and adaptation of such fiction.[85] The mass appeal of the genre's anarchism, both on and off the screen, obviously caused the paranoid reaction of the fledgling regime.

Official censorship notwithstanding, the May Fourth writers and ideologues had also been waging a war against Butterfly literature from which fertile ground the films had launched their commercial successes. Their attack against this literature had begun in the late 1910s and the early 1920s when the May Fourth movement was in full swing. The writers who spearheaded the attack include Lu Xun, Mao Dun (Shen Yanbing), Qu Qiubai, and Zheng Zhenduo. In 1919, Lu Xun had already voiced his distaste for fiction about knight-errantry and scholar-beauty romance as a whole in *New Youth,* the leading journal of the New Culture movement.[86] In a newspaper article called "Names" published in 1921, Lu Xun listed pen names of popular writers whose writings he would not bother to read, including A Knightly Soul (*Xiahun*) and A Strange

Knight-Errant (*Guaixia*). Despite his overall sensitivity to popular culture, Lu Xun's view of the martial arts fiction and the films remained negative and dismissive.

In the early 1930s, the May Fourth intellectuals' resentment and envy toward Butterfly literature intensified, especially as the martial arts–magic spirit film brought unprecedented popularity to the genre. In a seminal article on the failure of the May Fourth "literary revolution," Qu Qiubai lamented that the literary scene, twelve years after the revolution, was still dominated by a wide range of popular literature and arts that fell outside the May Fourth ideological orbit. Martial arts fiction and other popular genres enjoyed wide readership among the moderately educated commoners, who could indulge their favorite readings at street-corner libraries, which were essentially neighborhood rental joints. Those who were illiterate or semiliterate could resort to serial cartoons and teahouse storytelling. According to Qu, popular (or old-style) vernacular literature was so influential among laymen because its readership was organized in a "mobile" fashion. Through a rental club, a book could be circulated among many readers very cheaply. One old-style novel was worth eight or nine new-style novels.[87] As a staunch May Fourth critic, Qu's point was hardly to affirm the cultural significance of such popular literature; on the contrary, he perceived that body of vernacular literature as inherently reactionary because it skillfully repackaged "feudal virtues" and "bourgeois" values to satisfy the tastes of a mass readership.[88]

Shen Yanbing (Mao Dun), another prominent May Fourth writer, directly attacked the martial arts–magic spirit film and welcomed the Nationalists' censorship on the genre. For him, both the film genre and its fictional progenitor were nothing but the "feudal arts of the petty urbanites," which Shen also alternatively defined as "petty bourgeoisie" (*xiao zichan jieji*). Shen thought that after seeing *Burning,* audiences would be so obsessed with Jin Luohan and Hong Gu (the male and female leads) that the knights-errant would later appear in their dreams. His condescension notwithstanding, Shen offers an ambivalent eyewitness sketch of the genre's reception in a Shanghai movie theater:

> As soon as you arrived at a movie house, you could witness the great appeal of *The Burning of the Red Lotus Temple* for the petty urbanites. As cheering and applauding are not prohibited in those theaters, you are from the beginning to the end surrounded by the [noise of the] fanatic crowd. Whenever the swordsmen in the film begin to fight with their flying swords, the mad shouting of the spectators [*kanke*] is almost warlike. They cheer at the appearance of the flying Hong Gu, not so much because she is played by the

> female star Hu Die, as because she is a swordswoman and the protagonist in the film. . . . For them, a shadowplay [*yingxi*] is really not "play," but reality![89]

The eruption of the crowd, which Shen describes with a mixture of sarcasm and paranoia, in fact dramatizes a spectatorship that is constituted by a dynamic interaction between the magical power of the films (and the actors) on the screen and participatory auditorium practice. What Shen failed to see was that this genre, at once absorbing and distracting, like Dada for Benjamin, "hit the spectator like a bullet . . . thus acquiring a tactile quality."[90] The excessive identification of the fans with on-screen knights-errant, especially through the kinesthetic stunts that defied physical and social laws alike, illustrates how a particular kind of cinema could rekindle or reinforce the mimetic faculty of alienated metropolitan and dislocated diasporic subjects. This form of mimesis, as Jennifer Bean has persuasively argued with regard to the "hypnotic" spectatorship of the serial-queen dramas, "stresses the reflexive, rather than reflection; it brings the subject into intimate contact with the object, or other, in a tactile, performative, and sensuous form of perception." In the contagious and tranformative realm of embodied mimesis, "it is the body of the fan that becomes extraordinary—the material on which the cinematic 'real' acquires its most palpable, historical register."[91]

Such a mass-mediated mimetic desire or "burning" passion for the martial arts–magic spirit film, as Shen observed, also spread outside the theater, taking a truly "mobile" character. The junior petty urbanites would continue their daydreams about the martial heroes through "those crudely illustrated serial fiction" (cartoon books) adopted from the screen version. In the countryside and towns inland where there were no movie theaters, the cartoon books of *Burning,* though much shabbier and less tangible compared to the screen version, simply assumed the place of the film, providing a vicarious cinematic experience. The martial arts–magic spirit film, incarnated in polymorphous forms and reaching a greater public than the petty urbanites in Shanghai thus became a wandering monster, capturing utopian dreams of millions. What this mass-scale escapism through cheap entertainment and magic embodiment really suggested was in fact a collective desire and effort to recuperate a popular imagination and utopia as an antidote to the disappointing social and political reality in which they lived.[92]

In Shen's theory, the "knight-errantry craze" (*wuxia kuang*) was simply a "bowl of magic potion" concocted by "feudal forces" to distract the people by channeling their frustration and anger toward corrupt society and the ruling class into a fantasy world. Shen's rhetoric smacks of an elitist sarcasm, and his theory about the invisible "feudal forces" persisting in modern entertainment is characteristic of the May Fourth discourse; yet, his reaction toward the official censorship betrays a strain of ambivalence toward the popular craze. He attributes the genre's appeal to the "petty" people, in particular, the youth, to its providing a "way out" for their disillusionment with reality. He speculates that Nationalists initially tolerated the genre because of its direct or indirect critique of the feudal past, especially the Qing dynasty and the warlord period that preceded it, which could help to legitimize the new Nationalist regime. However, the anarchic energy generated by the cinema began to have a widespread social impact. It posed a real threat to the official program of modernization and its nationalist ideology, inadvertently foregrounding the political impotence of the status quo, which could hardly top the heroic image of the knight-errant. Realizing the social significance of the petty urbanites, the Nationalist regime, which Shen equated with other contemporary "fascist regimes" in Italy, Germany, and Japan, was nevertheless eager to stabilize or appease this expanding social power. Shen concludes that it was under such sociopolitical exigencies that the Nationalists decided to take measures to outlaw "monstrous" and "feudal" films such as *Burning*, which propagated the cult of the "superman."[93]

In spite of their opposing political and ideological interests, the official censors and the May Fourth intellectuals were united in their denunciation of the genre (from fiction to film to comic books) as essentially "unscientific" and "feudal." As a fiction writer devoted to promoting social realism, Shen also found fault with the retributional narrative pattern (*shan you shanbao, e you ebao*) in the genre, which he linked to fatalism (*dingming lun*).[94] These charges defined the genre as nothing but feudal residues and thus politically regressive. The left-wing writers were eager to exorcise the demon of the martial arts fiction in particular and Butterfly literature in general to make room for May Fourth realist fiction, which was deemed capable of inspiring social change. The Nationalist government, on the other hand, was primarily concerned with establishing a culture industry at its service rather than one that caused unrest. For both the Left and the Right, the impact of the genre generated a surplus "misdirected" social energy counter to the project of Enlightenment and modernization.

Ironically, both parties choose to overlook the vernacular modernism manifested in the genre, especially its cinematic form and popular appeal. As Shen's rather paranoid account of the spectatorial sensation in the theater suggests, it was not the film *Burning* itself that upset the status quo or the leftist critic. At stake was the emergence of a sociophysiological sensorium inside and outside the auditorium that seemed to have exceeded the political imagination of both the Right and the Left. The eruption of the magical power on the screen was echoed by the audiences' kinesthetic energy, creating a near anarchic experience that was predicated on mobility, sensation, intensity of enjoyment, and identification rather than passivity, stability, and conformism. The physical and political freedom of the knight-errant, articulated through his or her capacity to transcend the confines of time and space and realized through the technology of cinema, created a modern phantasmagoria where the images of the feudal knight-errant and the romantic modern superman (or superwoman) amalgamated. Out of this superimposition came a modern folk hero who did not quite fit the ideological projections of either the Nationalist regime or the May Fourth intellectual camp. Seen in this light, it is not surprising that a didactic section about the nationalist anti-Qing movement in *Burning* failed to interest the audience because it appeared to be rigidly imposed from outside the story proper.[95]

The immense size of the audience, which ceaselessly grew beyond the bounds of the urban setting and even the nation, was matched by its demographic complexity. In fact, the biggest market for the martial arts–magic spirit film was in the diaspora Chinese communities in Nanyang. The rentals for these films were cheaper than other kinds of features (e.g., the socioethic film). The genre embodied a certain version of the Chinese heritage through its evocation of the traditional lore of knight-errantry, yet it required only a minimal knowledge of the written language (for reading intertitles) to understand the plot. The overseas Chinese audiences, despite their geographical distance from China and its contemporary social situation, could identify the cultural icons in the traditional folklore. The simultaneous recognition and geographical distance created a degree of self-exoticism in the reception of the genre, which has the hybrid look of both the familiar and the strange, the archaic and the modern. *The Cave of the Spider Spirit, The Swordswoman of Huangjiang, Journey to the West,* and *Burning* were allegedly among the best-selling films among the Nanyang distributors and theater owners.[96] In fact, because their representatives stationed in Shanghai were always inclined to pay more for prints than local distributors, the Nanyang distributors had a direct influence on what kind of films were to be made. The martial arts–magic spirit film thus became a staple product in the lucrative Nanyang market for a long time to come.

The overseas saga of the genre's reception demonstrates how its attraction literally crossed national boundaries and marketed an image of China at odds with the blueprint of the modernizers at home. This multifaceted genre shows a stubborn resistance to any single prescribed ideology, but rather stems from the social fabric of quotidian life, further intensified by transnational migration as well as the expansion of mass media and technology. While the mainstream project of modernity laid a heavy emphasis on rationality and standardization, the martial arts–magic spirit film exemplified an alternative yet powerful cultural dimension that celebrated the mobility and heterogeneity of modern experience.

A crucial component of the Nationalist ideology and the May Fourth Enlightenment program was the cultural iconoclasm that sought to topple the real and imagined idols of the feudal past. In the wake of the two waves of antireligious campaigns—the first during the Republican revolution (1900–15) and the second after the inauguration of the Nanjing government (1927–30)—"images of popular gods were desecrated or forcibly removed from rural temples and the temples themselves were refashioned into elementary schools and offices for local government."[97] The violence against iconographical representations of folk religions and beliefs went hand in hand with the drive to enlighten the people who had largely been excluded from the elite literary culture. The erection of schools on the ground of temples was symbolic of the self-righteous Enlightenment ideology that sought to replace idolatry with literacy, folk belief with scientific knowledge.

This structural and architectural reform, imposed from above, unwittingly recycled the entrenched supremacy accorded to the written word in the traditional political and literary culture. The May Fourth intellectuals, despite their radical vision, were surprisingly insensitive to the significance of a technologized visual literacy that had already begun to reshape everyday life in China since the late nineteenth century. Even Lu Xun, a giant of modern Chinese literature and an astute cultural critic, voiced his deep suspicion of the cinema early on. The now classic story about his visceral, and patriotic, reaction to a slide show about the decapitation of a Chinese while he was studying medicine in Japan between 1904–6, has been redeployed by Rey Chow in her anatomy of the May Fourth writers' denigration of image.[98] Chow argues that the impressionable young Lu Xun, who upon seeing the show abruptly left the auditorium and switched his vocation from medicine to literature, crystallizes the "circumvention of visuality" in the "(re)introduction of literature and writing" as the primary instruments of modernization.[99] Such cultural iconoclasm, progressive in its intention yet regressive in its effect, helps explain why the May Fourth writers "simply refused to take the film medium seriously" and "expressed nothing but contempt for the cinema."[100] The democratization of culture remained on superstructural level where literature was assigned a paramount role. Vernacular iconography and mass entertainment were regarded as incapable of accomplishing the lofty goals of nation building. Throughout the 1920s and until the outbreak of the "national salvation" movement in the 1930s, the May Fourth intellectuals, many of them active in the Shanghai literary scene, kept conspicuous distances from the film world even if they were avid moviegoers in their leisure time.[101]

The attempt to turn temples into schools in the second antireligious campaign paralleled the censorship of the martial arts–magic spirit film. It is no coincidence that *Burning* was the chief casualty in this purge. Indeed, the temple (*simiao*) was ubiquitous in this body of films both as a central mise-en-scène and as a cultural reference crucial to the martial arts culture. Typically situated in or near wilderness, beyond the reach of ruling powers, the temple (of a particular kind) is a spatial trope in classical tales and folklore closely associated with esoteric arts and magical powers. Its geographic marginality and political neutrality (or, rather, ambiguity) has also made it a popular place of retreat for either political or personal reasons.[102] In this sense, this kind of temple is really a nodal point of the anarchic social landscape of *Jianghu*, the world of martial arts. The cinematic multiplication of the temple image associated with martial arts could hardly be the direct cause for paranoia on the part of the state; yet, the power of the cinematic mise-en-scène produced a virtual *Jianghu* space, transplanting remote temples right into the heart of the urban space. Such relocation elides the boundary between the geographical and the cinematic, the rural and the urban, recreating a landscape both familiar and strange to urban dwellers who came from the countryside. The uprooted experience of migration to the cities, further exacerbated by the crowded urban space, is vicariously compensated for by a virtual trip to faraway landscapes where freedom can be attained and justice rectified. When spectators began to burn incense inside the theater and kowtow to knightly and mythical spirits onscreen, the space was literally transformed into a temple. Martial arts–magic spirit films not only created much-needed palpable heroes and heroines but more importantly, transformed the theater into a modern shrine of anarchic energy and utopian yearnings.

The censorship of the genre, however, was soon complicated by the political turmoil following the Japanese invasion of Northern China and subsequently the bombardment of Shanghai on January 28, 1932. This national crisis not only directly affected the official policy toward the film world but also brought about a structural reconfiguration in the film industry and exhibition. Prior, the establishment of the more progressive Lianhua Company and the gradual entry of the May Fourth writers (as a new breed of screenwriters) into companies such as Mingxing had already begun to steer commercial genres toward more socially concerned themes. In July 1932, NFCC gathered representatives from major domestic film companies at a conference, demanding the producers to refrain from making films with explicit reference to "class consciousness." "Tragic materials" that might depress the audience should also be avoided.[103] The year 1933 marked a crucial transition point. With the release of *Wild Torrent* (*Kuang liu*, Mingxing, 1933) and other films scripted by left-wing writers, an incipient *puluo-jino* (proletarian kino) movement began to come to the foreground.

Alarmed by the quantity and influence of the progressive films being made within a few years' time, the Nationalist government's propaganda organ promptly put more pressure on the NFCC to target this new cinema. As the Nationalist army was busy dealing with the "red bandits" (*chifei*, i.e., the Communist army) in the mountains, the left-inflected cinema also came to be labeled as "bandit-making" (*zaofei*).[104] The martial arts–magic spirit film was now taken over by the left-wing cinema. This time, however, the censors were faced with a far more complicated case. The onscreen world of martial arts and the knights-errant who inhabited it were perceived as supernatural, a reality in a mythical past. In contrast, the mountains in Southern China, where the communist Red Army was waging guerrilla warfare for an ambitious political agenda for the future of China, was a real place at the present time. The taming of the red monster was to prove to be very arduous and with unpredictable consequences.

CHAPTER SEVEN

FIGHTING OVER THE MODERN GIRL

"HARD" AND "SOFT" FILMS

LIKE OTHER METROPOLISES of the world, Shanghai during the first half of the 1930s was the site of high modernism and attendant forms of social and cultural upheavals. No other period in Chinese cinema history matches the intensity and complexity of this period of high idealism as well as everyday strife. It was an age that left a rich yet troubled legacy. A new generation of filmmakers (such as Sun Yu, Cai Chusheng, Shen Xiling, and Yuan Muzhi) and actors (such as Jin Yan, Li Lili, Wang Renmei, Gao Zhanfei, and Zheng Junli) entered the center stage; the Shanghai film industry as a whole restructured. More importantly, their entrances were accompanied by numerous film critics who held considerable power in defining contemporary or epochal (*shidai*) cinema. Film criticism—and with it the writing of the literary script—became a highly professionalized and politicized cultural institution. The raised status of a modern writing style associated with the New Culture movement pressured for changes in cinematic expression and spectatorship, and hence the meaning of the vernacular. Against this contentious background, further complicated by censorship, the directors, screenwriters, actors, critics, and the studios often espoused differing or overlapping aesthetic and political tendencies simultaneously and shifted their allegiances constantly.

In the midst of this major transformation, a debate on the so-called soft film (*ruanxing dianying*) and hard film (*yingxing dianying*) was staged in the modernist film magazine *Modern Screen* (*Xiandai dianying*) and other film-related publications in 1933–35. This debate started in the realm of aesthetics but quickly escalated into an ideological battle in the shadow of war and the Nationalists' modernization project, in particular the so-called New Life Campaign. It had profound implications not only for film production and reception but also for the fate of cosmopolitanism represented by Shanghai's film and urban culture.

Not so surprisingly, the battle over what constituted the cinematic in relation to the political was waged over the body of the modern girl and her destiny in the metropolis. The modern girl and the vicissitudes of her transformation emblematized a flourishing urban modernity and intensified social division and political turmoil. Gone were the 1920s students or widows torn between self and family. The amorous maidens in classical costume and androgynous martial heroines with otherworldly auras had been replaced by a new breed of Chinese Noras, trapped in what had liberated them, primarily the modern urban lifestyle. The cinema produced in this period bears a starkly contemporary look accented by a vibrant cityscape and the 1930s design and fashion—as well as by the patriotic and revolutionary fever galvanized by a national crisis. The true meaning of this epoch emerged, however, in the contestation about its forms, material registers, cultural representations, and gender inscriptions (or prescriptions).

Historicizing a highly mythologized era, this chapter proffers a remapping of the heterotopic landscape of 1930s film culture. I focus on two interrelated facets: the emergence of the left-wing film discourse and the debate on "soft film" featured in *Modern Screen,* and the respective literary and film production of its key members. My goal is to carefully differentiate and periodize this debate by outlining the many crisscrosses and exchanges within this pivotal moment in Chinese film history. The material I use to facilitate this investigation is embedded in the multifaceted spaces of production and reception and the metropolitan space of Shanghai, which the Nationalist government tried to refashion (as can be glimpsed in Sun Yu's *Queen of Sports,* discussed in chapter 2). These texts and the debates surrounding them engaged the tension between aesthetics and politics, elitist discourse and vernacular experience, cosmopolitan yearnings and nationalist sentiments in the first half of the 1930s. It is neither possible nor productive here to conduct a comprehensive survey of the most contentious and perhaps richest period of Chinese film history.[1] I hope my focus on the imbrication of the changing shape of the modern girl will shed light on the nature of a cinema caught between competing modernist claims and vernacular praxis. Despite their avowed oppositions in a polemic war, these competing moderns shared an obsession with the question of urban modernity and national identity in the shadow of war.

THE LEFT TURN: RADICALIZING THE CINEMATIC VERNACULAR

The early 1930s witnessed the transformation of a thoroughly commercialized film industry into an increasingly politicized enterprise, especially in the aftermath of the Japanese occupation of Manchuria in 1931 and the bombing of Shanghai on January 28, 1932. In the existing Chinese and Western historiographies of Chinese cinema in the 1930s, the period from the 1932 bombing up till the overall Japanese invasion of China in 1937 has been labeled the first "golden age."[2] Its inauguration has habitually been linked to the ascendance of the left-wing cinema that emerged early in the decade, culminating in the so-called National defense cinema (*guofang dianying*) launched in 1936. Aptly couched in an urban terminology, this paradigmatic shift was called the "left turn" (*xiangzuozhuan*).[3] The political and aesthetic implications of the rise of this socially engaged and patriotic hard cinema by its critics have received much scholarly attention. Both to its advantage and disadvantage, patriotic cinema has been apotheosized into a myth ever since the Communists' Yan'an years. In the late 1970s, this myth was further consolidated after the rehabilitation of many 1930s filmmakers and actors who were persecuted under the directives of Jiang Qing (an actress in the 1930s Shanghai and Mao's wife) during the Cultural Revolution. The erstwhile "poisonous weeds," as Chris Berry has noted, were reinstated as "national treasures" through this revisionist enterprise.[4]

The political rehabilitation was accompanied by a series of public activities in exhibition (both national and international), research, and publications in the early to mid-1980s.[5] The most extensive exhibition took place at the China Film Archive in Beijing in September 1983 where some 20, 000 people saw forty-three films, many deemed left-wing. Veteran critics and writers such as Xia Yan, Yang Hansheng (1902–93), and others inaugurated the exhibition; a scholarly conference was held concurrently.[6] It was nothing less than a rescue operation, especially as many filmmakers and critics active in the 1930s were rapidly aging or dying. Numerous memoirs were hastily written; copious compilations of the left-wing film criticism were published; and symposia on representative left-wing directors were held one after another. This extensive effort has no doubt helped salvage and organize a significant amount of historical material. The sifting and interpretation of the archival material by and in the interest of a few surviving members of the left-wing group, however, have yielded a fairly one-sided story that is not so much a history as an updated myth.[7]

The version reinforced repeatedly is that the left-wing cinema movement was created and guided by the Communist Party (the headquarters of which was then far away in the mountainous region of Jiangxi). It saved the Chinese cinema by defeating the feudal and imperialist forces in the Shanghai film scene, in particular the advocates of the so-called soft cinema. The heterogeneity of the film world in the period has been reduced to a binary opposition between the "hard" and "soft" stances, or between the patriotic or revolutionary and the escapist or reactionary. Within the left-wing itself, the differences between its core coterie—mainly the critics and script writers who were party members (Xia Yan, Ah Ying, Wang Chenwu, Shi Linghe, and Situ Huimin)—and the often shifting outer circles of progressively minded but hardly dogmatic creators have been smoothed over, creating an image of the left-wing as a more pervasive and centralized movement. The rescue operation in the 1980s succeeded largely because their major opponents died long ago and thus were not able to participate in this retrial, in which the latter were judged to be "historical sinners" or "national traitors" in absentia once and for all.

More recent studies have challenged this myth and have come up with some new insights into this rich yet complicated period. This revisionist approach tries to demystify the existing historiography by situating the left-wing cinema in the broad landscape of the syncretic Shanghai film culture of the 1930s. Far from being an isolated radical movement within the predominantly commercial Shanghai film industry, the left-wing cinema emerged and thrived in a moment in Chinese and international film history when multiple ideological and aesthetic inclinations coexisted and commingled as much as they collided. This complex web of allegiances and conflicts together created a film culture torn between competing brands of modernism. Demythologizing does not discredit the historical importance of this progressive cinema, but rather traces its history, in particular its interaction with urban modernity and a mass culture of consumption and entertainment.

The veteran film historian Li Shaobai leads this reevaluation of the 1930s progressive film movement. While acknowledging its origin in the left-wing drama movement, Li argues that the term *left-wing cinema* is a latter-day construction. Li notes that the term only appeared once in the "outlines of present action" of the left-wing association of dramatists, which was founded in September of 1931. The outlines did, however, stress the film medium's importance and urged members to actively seek opportunities to launch a Chinese *puluo-jinuo* (proletarian kino).[8] However, for about two years this orientation only existed as a loosely connected patriotic and progressive tendency in the film circle, after the establishment of the Lianhua Company in 1930 and the Japanese invasion of Manchuria in 1931. This tendency took on the more salient form of a cultural front with the formation of the Association of Chinese Film Culture (*Zhongguo dianying wenhua xiehui*) on February 9, 1933. Its membership was hardly exclusive, open to almost anyone who worked within the film industry in Shanghai.

Rather than an insular political group with a uniform doctrine, the association was a broad democratic forum of patriotic filmmakers and other cultural workers who shared the desire to join forces and create a socially concerned and economically viable domestic cinema. They responded not only to the national crisis that directly affected the Shanghai film industry but also to the encroachment of Hollywood.[9] Its manifesto proclaims, in a somewhat utopian spirit, that the association's primary goal is to "expand our powerful avant-garde movement in film culture and build a new silvery world [*yinse shijie*]."[10] Under the banner of patriotism, economic survival, and cultural resistance, members of different studios and the critics' circle from different generations and with different ideological outlooks united to begin a new chapter of Chinese cinema. Collectively they responded to the urgent situation, although their methods of achieving this common goal varied. The left-wing cinema was, strictly speaking, a subsegment of a multifaceted cultural movement, while the political exigencies pushed many to adopt a receptive attitude toward a progressive social and aesthetic orientation.

Above all, the left-wing cinema was a screenwriting and film criticism movement, with its origins in the New Culture movement and its strong print media. The effort to channel the May Fourth ideology of the modern vernacular fiction into the domain of entertainment, especially cinema, coincided with the film industry's crisis after the quelling of the martial arts film, and the Japanese attacks. Zhou Jianyun, the cofounding manager of Mingxing, made the first contact when he approached Ah Ying (Qian Xingcun), also a native of the province of Anhui, and asked him to help introduce famous writers to "consult" on Mingxing script production.[11] Mingxing was hit hard in the Japanese bombing and had been losing its competitive edge after the establishment of Lianhua, which thrived on its contemporary subjects starring new, youthful, athletic stars. In 1932, Mingxing only managed to turn out three silent features whereas the up-and-coming Lianhua produced eighteen (including works by the three energetic and prolific young writer-directors, Cai Chusheng, Bu Wangcang, and Sun Yu).[12] In the next two years, Mingxing released a number of films scripted by left-wing writers, in particular Xia Yan and Ah Ying, to considerable critical and popular acclaim.

They include Xian Yan's *Wild Torrent* (*Kuang liu*, directed by Cheng Bugao, 1933), *Spring Silkworms* (*Chuncan*, 1933, based on Mao Dun's fiction), *Rouge Market* (*Zhifeng shichang*, directed by Zhang Shichuan, 1933), Ah Ying's *Year of Plenty* (*Fengnian*, directed by Li Pingqian, 1933) and *Three Sisters* (*San zimei*, directed by Li Pingqian, 1934). The left-wing writers also adopted the tactic of working closely with directors who had built careers making commercial films in the 1920s but were now seeking change. This method was described as "trailing on the playing field." While Xia Yan worked with Cheng Bugao at Mingxing, Tian Han wrote scripts for Bu Wangcang at Lianhua.[13] To avoid the suspicion of both the Nationalist and foreign censors, the writers would sometimes assume pseudonyms or have the directors take the credit as screenwriters.

These script-centered films, though to some extent each carrying their individual director's style, are markedly different from films of the civilized play or Butterfly literature tradition, both of which relied heavily on formulaic theatrical or traditional storytelling conventions. These new films were elaborately written, using the idioms of critical realism, which May Fourth writers applied in their antifeudal and anti-imperialist literary enterprises. As a whole they inaugurated a new genre in cinematic writing by infusing the May Fourth literature and drama into the "silver world." This effectively redefined the meaning of the vernacular on the screen, which up to that point had been dominated by mass entertainment, traditional theater arts, and popular urban fiction. The obvious changes can be seen in the increased number and length of intertitles, their political didacticism, and in the replacement of the (classical) vertical format with a horizontal format. For instance, *Spring Silkworms*, hailed as the "first sound of adapting the New Culture to the screen" by director Cheng Bugao himself, literally put Mao Dun's words on the screen. Cheng related how he painstakingly tried to "visualize every word and sentence in the story and not to stray from [the story]." The result: a faithful "sketch" of the original.[14]

Soviet cinema and film theory and Japanese radical film writing catalyzed the flourishing of the May Fourth-style script.[15] The diplomatic relationship between the Soviet Union and China established in December 1932 made public dissemination of Soviet film culture less risky, though the nationalist authorities and the colonial administrations kept a constant eye on such practices. On February 16, 1932, *The Road of Life* (*Shenglu*, directed by Nikolai Ekk, 1931) premiered in Shanghai. In 1933 and 1934, nine Soviet films were shown in Shanghai, including *Golden Mountains* (*Jinshan*, directed by Sergei Iutkevich, 1931), *Storm over Asia* (*Yaxiya fengbao;* a.k.a. *The Heir to Genghis Khan*, directed by Vsevolod Pudovkin, 1928; released in 1929), and *Marionettes* (*Kuilei*, directed by Iakov Protazanov, 1934).[16] The progressive filmmakers were elated to discover a new film language and quickly incorporated the so-called Soviet shots (*Sulian jingtou*), referring to the montage technique as well as the social and political form these shots constructed. The Soviet fever among the radical intellectuals resulted in a series of translations and publications in 1932–33. Xia Yan and Ah Ying translated Pudovkin's *On Film Direction* and *On Screenwriting*, respectively. Most film-related publications, including popular fanzines, increased their coverage of Soviet cinema and culture. Suddenly, *puluo* (proletariat) and *jino* (kino) became fashionable cinematic vocabulary within the educated strata; the exuberant utopian spirit and aesthetic in Soviet cinema captured the imagination of both the left and modernist filmmaker and critics. The Soviet connection provided Chinese cinema its first forays into the global arena in a grand style. A delegation, including Hu Die, the "Queen of Cinema," was dispatched to Russia to attend the Moscow International Film Festival in 1935. The famous Peking Opera actor Mei Lanfang also appeared on stage there, where he enthralled Sergei Eisenstein. Among the Chinese submissions, Cai Chusheng's *Fishermen's Ballad* (1934) became the first Chinese film to win an international award.

The crop of films with heavy May Fourth literature inflections primarily appealed to the intelligentsia that fervently responded to the national distress. Hardly surprising, then, this May Fourth-styled cinema was embodied in the recurrent male writer, poet, or actor, who undergoes transformation from a dandy to an awakened, even radicalized social agent. As such, the progressive and high-minded turn in cinema created a new orientation in film spectatorship. If the entrance of Butterfly writers into the film world in the mid-1920s marked the first fusion of vernacular literature and screenwriting, this new wave of literary and cinematic convergence was motivated by entirely different reasons and had different consequences. The flourishing Shanghai cinema in the 1920s capitalized upon the social anarchism and political polycentrism of the time. The Nationalist regime in Nanjing, established in 1927, however, tried to eradicate the martial arts–magic spirit film that was deemed "superstitious" and socially threatening. It also took measures to contain the Communist influence in the arts and mass media. Censorship and confiscation of radical literature and drama were diligently practiced. However, barely literate working class people and other petty urbanites with a taste for popular culture had limited interest in the lofty May Fourth style literature, which adopted Western grammar and syntax and complex intellectual ideas. This further impelled progressive writers and dramatists to use cinema accessibly to proselytize their political ideals. Yang Hansheng, a May Fourth writer-turned screenwriter, recalls: "At that time, the number of copies for a novel was limited. Those that sold well had a print of five thousand to ten thousand copies whereas those that did not sell had but only two to three thousand. Moreover, they were subject to the censorship of the Nationalists and often confiscated at the postal office. Cinema was, however, entirely different. Each film could have millions of audiences. For that reason, we encouraged many people working on stage to strengthen cinema."[17] The radical political momentum created by the 1932 confrontation with Japan and American plans to build Shanghai studios abated as the city and the film industry quickly recovered, although the New Film Culture movement had became a broader yet polymorphous cultural phenomenon. In order to pass the censors and appeal to studio producers, left-wing screenwriters often resorted to tactics that compromised divergent demands or concealed radical messages behind popular formulas, such as selectively adapting, and subtly altering, Butterfly-style film titles or romantic plots. One interesting example, again related by Yang Hansheng, is the title of *Tieban honglei lu,* which literally means "A record of iron boards and red tears," couching the hard message in soft romance. When Yang confessed that he did not know how to write a film script, Hong Shen, a Mingxing veteran screenwriter and director, told him to "just write it like a novel" and Hong would modify it for the screen. He assured Yang that such an ambiguous title would easily pass censorship.[18]

Left-wing writers successfully infiltrated the film studios while other business-savvy producers and directors continued to make films catering to audiences that craved sentimental melodrama and other genres. Mingxing and Lianhua, where the left influence was most palpable between 1932 and 1935, also churned out conventional genre pictures, often by the same directors. Sound films were carving out a distinct space where the new technology focused the filmmakers' and viewers' attention on singing and speech, a topic to be tackled in chapter 8. While also participating in the New Film Culture movement and producing several patriotic films, Tianyi, the stronghold for costume drama and Butterfly romances, never ceased to make its signature commercial films. Directors sympathetic to the progressive cause who also continued to indulge their popular taste were regarded by the hard-line left critics as "fellow travelers" at best. Their works were subject to relentless ideological dissections, a practice carried into the People's Republic era. Ideological critique reached its devastating climax during the Cultural Revolution, when film criticism became mass campaigns that forced filmmakers and actors to denounce themselves and others or commit suicide.

Indeed, through film criticism the left-wing cinema emerged as an ideological discourse and institution. Its explicit goal was to transform an urban mass culture represented by the cinema. With this movement, serious film critic's (*yingpingren*) social status became visible in the film scene, overtaking other film journalists working in a popular idiom with much less theoretical rigor or political passion. In the early 1930s, the film press boasted a big expansion. Popular fanzines and trade journals included *Movie Monthly* (*Dianying zazhi*), *Screen Weekly* (*Yinmu zhoubao*) (fig. 7.1), *Movie Fans' Weekly* (literal translation of *Yinmi zhoubao*), *Mingxing Bimonthly* (literal translation of *Mingxing banyuekan*), the *Film Magazine* (*Yingxin zazhi*, Lianhua's trade journal, later changed to *Lianhua huabao*), and *Qingqing Film* (*Qingqing dianying*). A new breed of film publications took the form of newspaper supplements, which quickly became the chief battleground for the left critics, including *Morning Daily*'s "Daily Film," *Shibao*'s "Shibao Film," *Minbao*'s "Film Forum," and *Dawanbao*'s "Silhouette [*Jianying*]." Xia Yan and Ah Ying's translations of Pudovkin's works were first serialized in "Daily Film" before they were published in book form. Xia Yan's script, *Wild Torrent*, was published, as an appendix (or illustration) of the monograph *On Film Direction*.[19] Some supplements, such as "Daily Film," resulted from complicated negotiations between political objectives and commercial interests. "Film Forum," edited by Lu Si and supported by a team of critics from the league of left-wing dramatists, occupied the far left position in the spectrum. It also systematically introduced Soviet film theory and cinema, particularly films screened at Shanghai theaters. The critics often attended the films together, held discussions, and even collectively signed the reviews.[20]

This organized film criticism practice, joined by about three dozen well-educated intellectuals and film professionals, quickly launched polemic debates on cinema and national culture in the news supplements, magazines, and a cluster of urban public settings. They made moviegoing a serious profession and roamed about the city armed with their notebooks and ideological lenses. These modern men of letters and ambivalent cinephiles spent hours watching imports and domestic products and took them apart at "film tea party" (*dianchahui*) gatherings at restaurants or teahouses, before going home to write up reviews for print overnight.[21]

This self-styled group of avant-garde critics, however, was not uniform in its ideological stance and personal attitude toward urban culture. At the film tea parties they often argued vehemently about specific films and issues concerning Chinese film industry, as well as over personal differences. Such contentions were reported in great detail in film magazines.[22] A few hard-line Leninist critics (such as Yu Ling) rejected nearly all modern forms of Shanghai entertainment and leisure and, as a social statement, wrote their reviews at street food vendors' eateries. But many took advantage of the numerous coffee shops in the concessions where they sat in anonymity and wrote their articles over beef tea (*niucha*) or

7.1 The modern look of *Yinmu zhoubao* (*Screen Weekly*).

club sandwiches. The payment for film reviews was very low, typically two yuan for a thousand characters (which could only pay for two sandwiches).[23] Some of them, despite their radical polemics, nevertheless enjoyed other urban pleasures in addition to cinema that the city provided, especially dancing with dance hostesses.[24]

While helping to construct a film theory and, to some extent, a Chinese national cinema, radical film criticism tended to hold a patronizing and judgmental attitude toward Shanghai filmmakers and their films. The critics were eager to turn the vast number of urban masses into *pu-luo* (proletarians) after the Soviet model and make cinema an instrument for the ideological and cultural war against feudal remnants and imperialist forces. They thus regarded any film practice not entirely and explicitly in service of these ends as either politically backward or outright reactionary. The films deemed problematic were often those that either indulged in "exposing" the glamour (and sins) of metropolitan pleasures or the ones that adhered to previous melodramatic formulas, stressing the "ethical" or "fateful" dimensions of social relations and conflicts. Leftist film criticism left behind a formidable but also ambiguous legacy. Its rigor and political vision radicalized the cinematic vernacular and enabled a paradigm shift in Chinese cinema from a popular entertainment to a political instrument. At the same time, its exclusionary dogmatism, though practiced within a public sphere that allowed considerable dissention, planted seeds for more totalitarian forms of discursive (and sometimes physical) violence. It was directed even toward some of their own or "fellow travelers" in Yan'an and after 1949, the year the Communists took power.

By and large, this culture of high-minded film criticism was part of a print-centered masculine public sphere and a form of male intellectual flânerie. Hardly any women were involved in the circle other than as quiet companions to their male friends.[25] Yet interestingly, one of the key points of contention among different factions of the critics was the question of woman's relation to urban modernity. Her changing iconography and the social and epistemological status of her body were of critical importance to the transformation of Chinese cinema and its spectatorship during this anxious "left turn."

REMAKING THE "SILVER DREAM" AND THE MODERN GIRL

The left-influenced film circle, formed in early 1933, seized a great political opportunity when Shanghai became more closely tied to the country's fate and took on more salient nationalist overtones. For many outside of the core group, embracing left-wing cinema was part of a conversion experience. Some old-style figures, such as Zheng Zhengqiu, attempted to update their social aspirations by "embarking on a progressive road."[26] More romantic ones saw the national crisis as a chance to channel their petty bourgeois, narcissistic sentimentality toward sympathy for the underdogs of capitalism and imperialism. The movement's frontline was hardly uniform as conversion and allegiances within the left-wing varied as the political tides shifted.

This conversion was often described as waking up from a daydream world, which signaled a fundamental change in cinema's perceived ontology and function. For some, the conversion had actually begun before the national distress became an emergency and before the New Film Culture movement was officially formed. Tian Han, a central figure of the movement's left-wing component, is a case in point. His essay "Out of the 'Silver Dream'" has often been cited as the signpost of both the personal and collective conversion for Western and especially Japanese-educated intellectuals (Lu Xun among them). As mentioned in chapter 5, since his return from Japan in 1924 the poet and playwright Tian Han tried to make films with the Nanguo Film and Drama Society, but financial constraints hindered the completion and distribution of *Going to the People* and *Lingering Sound of a Broken Flute*. Both productions, lasting intermittently for two to three years, were undertaken with very few resources, though he did obtain some support from the Shanghai Art College where Tian Han taught and briefly served as its president.[27] Just like the amateur drama (*aimeiju*) that Nanguo advocated and practiced, the two films were low-budget ventures and possibly the first fruits of independent art cinema in Chinese film history.

For Tian Han the poet, cinema presented the unique medium for "manufacturing dream" (*zaomeng*) in the twentieth century.[28] His passion for and ideas about cinema stemmed from his student years in Japan. In his earlier writings on cinema published in the film magazine *Silver Star* (*Yingxing*) during 1927 and later collected in a book, *Yinsede meng* (Silver Dreams), Tian recalled his experience as an avid "cinemafan" in Japan, where he watched more than a hundred foreign films in seven years. Moved by the image of a girl too poor to buy a pair of shoes she desired, Tian wanted to send her his own savings but later realized his own naiveté after he saw her appearing again as a queen in another film.[29] His belief in cinema's "manufacturing dream" was largely inspired by Tanizaki Jun'ichirô, a famous New Sensationalist writer and an active member of the pure cinema (*jun'eiga*) movement.[30] As I will show later, the influence of Tanizaki and the New Sensationalist aesthetic was also instrumental for the "soft film" advocates.

Tian's idea of imparting a "silver dream" art cinema to the then predominantly commercial Shanghai film scene was directly borrowed from Tanizaki. In his English-titled first installment of *Silver Dream*, "Day Dream," Tian Han defined cinema by way of translating Tanizaki's film theory and practice:

> In some sense, film is perhaps a clearer dream than ordinary ones. People have simple dreams when they sleep; they like to dream

> even whey they are awake. We go to the movie theaters precisely to have "day dreams" [in English]. It is perhaps for this reason that I enjoy going to the movies in daytime, and in the spring and summer seasons. Especially in between the two seasons when one feels a bit sweaty, [cinema] can best induce all kinds of fantasy. Returning home, these fantasies still linger in one's mind while in bed, communicating with dreams in sleep. In the end, it becomes hard to know whether it is dream or film, but only leaving a lingering beautiful illusion in the mind. Film can indeed be called the dream made by men with machines! [31]

Besides inspiring Tian Han through his writing and films, Tanizaki even had a real role to play in Tian Han's realization of his "silver dreams." [32] During production of *Going to the People,* Nanguo Film and Drama Society hosted a tea party for Russian writer Boris Pilnyak, and two Japanese writers, Tanizaki and Sato Haruo, who were visiting Shanghai. Footage of the meeting was allegedly included in the film.[33] This encounter between the Chinese, Japanese, and Russian modernists is but one of many occasions when Shanghai served as a hub for cosmopolitan networks in the 1920s and 1930s. The Russian intellectuals saw Shanghai as a laboratory of revolution, whereas the Japanese modernists found Shanghai to be an Eastern metropolitan center rivaling the West after much of Tokyo was destroyed overnight in the 1923 Kanto earthquake.[34]

Tian's only fully realized silver dream prior to his "left turn" was his script for *Spring Dream on the Lakeside* (*Hubian chunmeng,* Mingxing, 1927) (fig. 7.2). The film, though nonextant, seems to have fulfilled his modernist reverie and bears striking affinity to Tanizaki's *The Lust of the White Serpent* (*Jasei no yin,* 1921). Its use of psychoanalytical motifs and a corresponding aesthetic style made this silver dream unique in the late 1920s. When most Chinese films were either ethical melodramas or historical subjects, this poetically rendered psychological drama stood out as modernist and Western.[35] Directed by Bu Wangcang, known for his "European style," and starring Yang Naimei, the famous modern girl and trendsetter in Shanghai, the film presents a sadomasochist love triangle between writer Sun Pijiang and two women. The male writer (played by rising matinee idol Gong Jianong) is frustrated by his love for a stage actress (played by the famous female impersonator Mao Jianpei) and goes to the dreamy lakeside of Hangzhou. There he finds solace in the icy beauty Li Yibo (Yang Naimei), whom he first encountered on the train and who reappeared in his dream. Li turns out to be a woman with a penchant for beating her love objects. She whips him until he bleeds and then licks his blood off with her tongue like a vampire. He indulges in the

7.2 *Spring Dream on the Lakeside* (1927). (Courtesy of the China Film Archive)

painful pleasure. The "silver dream" motif is foregrounded in a scene when he is shot in the arms in his dream.[36] When he wakes up in the morning, he returns to Li Yibo's house, seen in the dream, only to find a silver-haired old woman there. "How mesmerizing this is! Just within a blink of the eye, rouge is turned into gray hair," an enthralled critic comments.[37]

According to the synopsis and reviews of the film, mirrors were frequently used to enhance the haunting atmosphere and psychological intensity. Mirrors reflect the unstable relationship between reality and dream, functioning as devices of metamorphosis between different states of mind and temporality. Tian's modernist daydream is realized as a cinematic fairy tale about the painful transformation of modern male and female identity. Sun Pijiang's character stands for a confused masculinity caught between desire for both conventional love and anomalous pleasure, between city life and the genteel pastoral landscape. The two modern girls, one consumed by her worldly ambitions and the other an ethereal phantom, are both presented as femmes fatale and hence Sun's impossible objects.

The cult of the unobtainable modern girl seems to have traveled to urban China from Japan in the late 1920s. Xu Xiacun's short story, "Modern Girl" (titled in English), offers an unsentimental sketch of a Japanese

Mo-ga, Xinzi, a café waitress who has resurfaced in Shanghai's foreign concessions.[38] The story places the modern girl squarely in midst of the urban scene and film experience. The narrator Mr. S encounters Xinzi while strolling on the bustling Sichuan Road before a movie showing. Descending from the bridge over Suzhou River and entering the jungle of restaurants and department stores, he feels suffocated by a "crudely manufactured urban air." He observes that while cars and trams are screeching ahead on the paved street, the "crowd let themselves get sucked into brightly decorated movie houses and Japanese dance halls that send out strands of Jass [*sic*] music." "Mr. S!" Xinzi calls him in Japanese. Taking her to a tearoom, Mr. S (alias Eureka) recalls his meeting with her years ago in Tokyo.

A "true modern girl" and a Francophile, Xinzi also writes poetry, and is an avid fan of Rudolph Valentino. Mr. S describes her features as devoid of the usual Japanese feminine beauty; rather, the creator of "this sculpture" seems to have mistakenly used angular male lines on her, with flat chest and buttocks. Although her "Bebe Daniel" hairstyle looks impeccable, her generic round face can be found on any advertisement and her big hook nose makes her look like an old woman. The reader learns that she is promiscuous, often dating several men at once. Abandoning her student boyfriend, she hangs out with older men. In the end, Xinzi becomes an enigmatic figure; her gender identity is as ambiguous as her cultural identity. The cosmopolitan modern girl gets lost in Shanghai's urban jungle just as the Chinese male flâneur once did in Tokyo. Because the brief encounter occurs before the movie Mr. S has planned to see, the reader is left with an uncertain feeling that this could well be a "silver dream" that he has conjured up.

PINK DREAM

The leitmotif of the modern girl, or temptress, and male fantasy takes on a more domestic visage in Cai Chusheng's film *Pink Dream* (*Fenghongse de meng,* Lianhua, 1932). The film has been historically seen as Cai's last petty-bourgeois indulgence before he converted to the progressive camp. Cai was reinstated as a master of the left-wing cinema in the early 1980s, particularly due to his award-winning *Fisherman's Ballad* and his phenomenally successful postwar melodrama, *A River Flows East* (*Yijiang chunshui xiangdongliu,* 1947). His films before his "left turn," however, manifest a mixture of Zheng Zhengqiu's slow-paced ethical melodrama and Tian Han's aesthetic romanticism.[39] Decidedly anchored in the urban space of Shanghai, *Pink Dream*'s narrative was also structured around a male writer and his two women. The film opens with these introductory intertitles:

> Intertitle 1: In a corner of Shanghai, our literary artist Luo Wen is working hard.
> Intertitle 2: The beautiful pink dream has finally disappeared in the deep night. What remains is but a faint trace of smile in Luo Wen's lingering dream.

After a series of superimposed flashbacks of their romantic youth, the film quickly cuts to a scene showing the routines and oppression of everyday life in the city (for instance, the lack of money to pay rent). Like many other melodramatic films made in this period, the male protagonist is torn between family obligations and erotic temptation, work and pleasure. Luo Wen and his family live in an ordinary Shanghai *longtang* apartment. While he tries to conjure up a romantic novel, his wife teaches classes in the room next door to support the family.

When the writer's desire for romantic and sexual fulfillment seems frustrated by the sterility of domestic life, he directs his gaze to the flickering city outside the window, as though the city's nightlife would supply the erotic stimulants he sorely needs. To get inspired, he opens a trendy magazine and finds a picture of the "social flower" (*jiaojihua*) Li Huilan. The next shot cuts to the real-life modern girl, as though Luo's desiring gaze has brought her to life. As the camera tracks backward, they are already in a dance hall, soon to meet. Lou quickly falls in love with Li, who is presented as a figuration of the city's temptations. She lives in a luxurious art deco apartment where she entertains her suitors, dressed in semitransparent flowing gowns, although how she affords this lifestyle remains a mystery. Luo's newfound "pink dream" takes him into the world of pleasure and fantasy, in the form of nightclubs and the modern apartment of the "worldly and seductive" modern girl.[40] In a revealing scene, sitting on a couch in the apartment, Luo flips through a copy of *London Life* while Li flaunts her legs, striking a pose similar to the foreign model in the magazine. By conquering the foreign-flavored Shanghai "flower," Luo has tasted a European dandy's erotic pursuits (fig. 7.3). After a series twists and turns, Luo Wen wakes up from his prolonged "pink dream" and reunites with his chaste wife, who has written the novel *The Tears of an Abandoned Wife* under his name during her self-imposed exile in a country school.[41] Meanwhile, the modern girl, married to Luo briefly, has eloped with her new beau with his advance for a novel about their romance, called *Paradise*. Of course, the real paradise turns out to be domestic bliss, not the ephemeral "pink dream." By and large the film is a typical Mingxing production, rooted in the melodramatic tradition cultivated and perfected by Cai's mentor Zheng Zhengqiu.

The film was made in the midst of the Japanese attack of Shanghai. Cai, shocked by the bombing, postponed the film while engaged in the

7.3 *Pink Dream* (1932). (Courtesy of the China Film Archive)

collective production of an explicitly patriotic film, *Share the Burden of the National Crisis* (*Gongfu guonan*, 1932), which he codirected with Sun Yu, Shi Dongshan, and Wang Cilong.[42] Afterwards Cai completed *Pink Dream*. Despite its implicit social critique, the film was met with harsh criticism from left critics. Together with several other films that centered on the question of moral degeneracy in the city, the film was accused of smacking of "imports" (*polaiping*)—that is, Western lifestyle and Hollywood film—and of cultivating a *modeng* (modern) look, while also intending to criticize it. The "happy end" (English original) and the large number of dance hall scenes—a clichéd trope in most urban films of the period, or a cipher for both Shanghai's spectacular metropolitan culture and its danger—were singled out as instances of American influence.[43] Another critic also found Cai's indulgence in things that are "good to look only" troublesome (English in original), referring to the "beautiful" shots of women's legs, semitransparent dresses, and a new car in which the modern girl rides.[44] Lu Si, a hard-line critic, pointed out that while the chaste wife was a "feudal" figure, the modern girl represented the "metropolitan leisure class that was underdeveloped but already morally bankrupt." In short, she was a "social parasite, a plaything." Lu Si admonished the screenwriter to say goodbye to these subjects about "flowers, the moon and my lover," and to speak instead for the "oppressed and weak nation," turning entertainment into a movement to help realize a "bright and great new epoch."[45]

In the eyes of the left critics, Tian's "silver dream" and Cai's "pink dream" were waning symbols of the feudal or bourgeois demons that ought be exorcized from Chinese cinema, along with the modern girl and the chaste domestic woman. They demanded that the filmmakers dispense sentimental humanism and the attendant expressive form of melodrama, characterized by hyperbolic plots, contrast of good and evil, reliance on coincidence, retribution, and happy ends. After the 1932 bombing, which pushed filmmakers of different generations and backgrounds to embark on the "progressive path," the trope of "waking up" became common in their films. Tian Han, the famous "cinemafan" and "daydreamer," became a forerunner of the left turn.

Tian Han's conversion took place as early as 1930. Lu Mengshu, the former editor of *Silver Star,* asked him to contribute a follow-up essay on cinema to the new film magazine, *Dianying,* as part of an effort to launch a new cinema movement. The result was "Waking up from the Silver Dream," in which he rejected Tanizaki's "Day Dream" theory and embraced the ideological (*yishi*) nature of cinema.[46] He also renounced the rise of Japanese jingoism and celebrated the Soviet Republic, the only "proletarian" homeland in the world. He cited several incidents that helped cause his change of heart.[47] During a twenty-fifth anniversary celebration of their victory in the Russo-Japanese war, more than one hundred Japanese school children were killed or injured in a film projector fire in a dance hall. "They had planned to send them to die fighting in the battlefield but accidentally killed them in the cinema," wrote Tian Han. He concluded that the war films that the children saw and the ideas to be inculcated in them were by no means "beautiful dreams" but "evil propaganda" controlled by the imperialists. Tian's realization of the sheer political use of cinema as a means of war mobilization in Japan provided a major trigger for his conversion. His earlier interest in the ontology and aesthetics of cinema now gave way to a certain instrumental use of the medium for sociopolitical purposes. In the next few years, he put his new conviction to practice, churning out film scripts one after another and becoming one of the most prolific left-wing screenwriters.

THREE MODERN WOMEN

Three Modern Women (*Sange modeng nüxing*), directed by Bu Wangcang, was Tian's quintessential contribution to the remade silver dream.[48] Significantly, in his new cinematic vision, the two types of women reconfigured as three models. They were all single, urban professionals with varying degrees of "moderness," while the "happy ending" in marriage and family was replaced by a combination of tragic outcomes and somber sociopolitical awakenings. The complexity of the modern girl was fleshed out by the triple constellation, while their sexuality was ultimately banished from the scene.

Tian's renewed love affair with cinema aptly takes place within the film circle. The male protagonist Zhang Yu (played by Jin Yan) is a movie star torn between three modern women (rather than a wife and a lover), between personal pain and collective consciousness, between the lure of the metropolis (in particular, the world of cinema) and the calling of the nation. Here the multifaceted image of the modern woman makes Tian Han's tale different from previous commercial and Butterfly-inflected metacinematic films, such as *Amorous History* and *Two Stars* (1931). The modern girl, either a phantom femme fatale as in *Spring Dream* or a caricatured worldly "social flower" in *Pink Dream,* took on multiple faces: a "sentimental girl" (Chen Ruoyin) who commits suicide out of her unrequited love for the movie star, the "femme fatale" Yu Yu who has all the paraphernalia (fashion dress, car, mansion) and sexual appetite of a modern girl, and finally the virtuous *and* progressive telephone operator (Zhou Shuzhen, played by Ruan Linyu) whom the movie star jilted in their hometown.[49] The screenwriter took pains to anchor this quadrangle love story in the political exigencies of the nation.[50] As in his other scripts, the September 18 incident in Manchuria in 1931 and the January 28 attack in Shanghai in 1932 constitute the metanarrative motivation through their structural presence. Shuzhen moves to Shanghai after the Japanese invasion of Manchuria and finds work as a telephone operator. By chance she encounters Zhang Yu, who fled their arranged marriage earlier and became a movie star in the city. Zhang Yu's awakening from his silver dream and playboy lifestyle is attributed to Zhou's guiding him into the "real" world. The narrative shifts from the interiority of male fantasy to the expansive urban milieu that includes the battleground, the slums, a worker's evening school, factories, and docks—in other words, a larger social and political world beyond "flowers, the moon, and romance" (fig. 7.4).

The ambition of the film lies in its redefinition of the term *modeng* by divesting its connotations of urban leisure, consumerism, glamour, and decadence. As with his scripts for *Maternal Light* (*Muxing zhi guang*), *Color* [*Se*], and *Children of Troubled Times* (*Fengyun ernü*) written in this period, Tian Han strove to demonstrate his new "social consciousness," pursuing the possibility of using art for political ends.[51] During a crucial scene in *Three Modern Women,* Zhou Shuzhen spoils Yu Yu's fashionable party by

7.4 *Three Modern Women* (1933). (Courtesy of the China Film Archive)

delivering a speech about the plight of people in the Northeast under Japanese occupation. Moved, the movie star pronounces (as the writer's mouthpiece) that the true modern woman should be one who is "most independent, most rational, most courageous, and most concerned about the public welfare." Chen Ruoyin's subsequent suicide during the shooting of a film with Zhang and Yu Yu's moral bankruptcy pave the way for the emergence of Zhou as the embodiment of a new type of modern woman, desexualized while politicized. In the end, even though Zhang and Zhou reach a mutual understanding, they become more like comrades rather than lovers.

Despite the references to national salvation, the use of militant rhetoric, and the fashioning of a progressive modern woman, ultra-left critics still found fault with *Three Modern Women.* Tian Han was praised for creating a transparent political vision of collective mobilization in several of his scripts devoid of a romantic plot, for example *National Survival* (*Minzu shengcun*), *Golden Age* (*Huangjin shidai*), and *Song of Victory* (*Kaige*).[52] Those structured around urban youth and the fate of their love lives in a turbulent epoch, however, retained vestiges of the *modeng* look, especially in characterizing different types of modern women. In order to expose the vacuity of the material modern girl and the emergence of the utopic New Woman, the screenwriter seemed to find it imperative to set the "waking up from the silver dream" story in the metropolis and its dream factory. While acknowledging the film as a progressive "social problem drama" and applauding the new modern woman articulated through Zhang Yu, the critics found the "negative" exposure outweighed "positive" description. The negative aspects are multiple, including the emphasis on the luxurious lifestyles of the fashionable urbanites and their romantic entanglements; the large amount of overly literary and ornately displayed intertitles; and above all, the flawed characterization of the "most modern woman" Zhou Shuyin. They would have liked her to be a true blue-collar proletariat (rather than an educated telephone operator, an embodiment of modern technology), who lived in miserable conditions and, of course, did not wear a perm (which the star Ruan Lingyu did). They would have also been more satisfied if the decadent Yu Yu had been scripted a bad ending (perhaps also a suicide) and if the movie star fell all the way down with her.[53]

NEW WOMAN

These demands were answered by *New Woman,* directed by Cai Chusheng (and written by Sun Shiyi) two years later. With this film, Cai completed his "left turn," leaving behind his pink dream for good. While the triple women configuration remains,[54] the quadrangle romance is disposed of. The change of the imported term *modeng* to *xin* (new) marks a paradigmatic shift in the representation of modern urban women. The latter term explicitly reconnects with the May Fourth discourse of women's liberation as part of the Enlightenment project and has less to do with urban modernity. The clichéd "social flower" disappeared altogether and

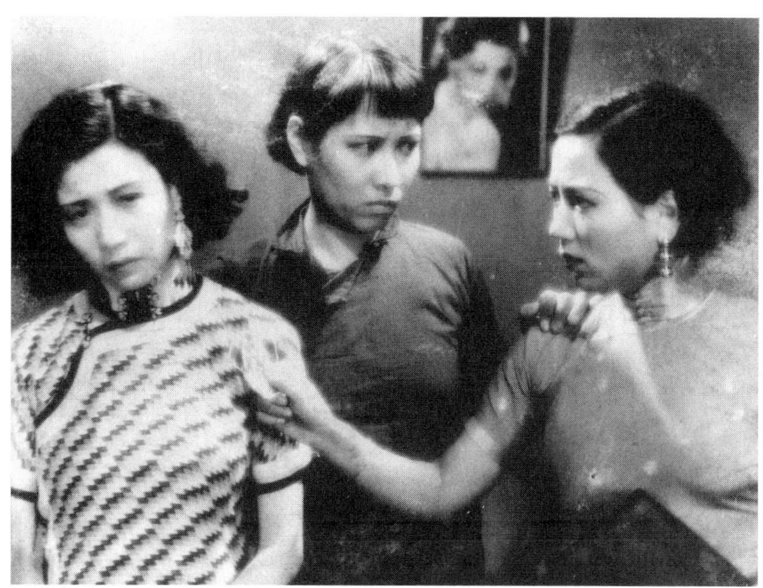

7.5 *New Woman* (1935). (Courtesy of the China Film Archive)

was replaced by a repressed married middle-class housewife—an old classmate of the protagonist. And the sentimental girl has been changed to the struggling professional woman Wei Ming (again played by Ruan Lingyu), who teaches music in a school. She also writes a novel (pointedly titled *The Tomb of Love*) but ultimately commits suicide out of despair (but not for love). The telephone operator from *Three Modern Women* is refashioned here as a true working class woman with a proletarian name Li Ahying, who teaches at evening school rather than studying. Li, as the paragon of New Woman, does not have a perm and is portrayed as a masculinized strong woman who physically overwhelms a man who tries to take advantage of Wei. Whereas the angular physique and boyish charm of the Modern Girl in Xu Xiacun's story were traits of an androgynous yet sensuous female sexuality in the modern age, Li is a cardboard figure devoid of any sexuality (fig. 7.5). This is literally reflected in her giant shadow, powerful yet immaterial, on the *longtang* wall near their residence in one of the key scenes. Even some leftists thought the screenwriter and the director had gone too far to create such an "abstract" "ideal" character without "real flesh and blood."[55]

The film has been treated in considerable detail by several recent studies, especially with regard to the startling reverse mimesis of Ruan Lingyu's star text (and her suicide shortly after production) with regard to the ambiguous feminist stance of the left-wing filmmakers.[56] As we have seen in *Pink Dream*, the male writer is clearly at the center of the film and naturally the "owner" of many subjective shots (or erotic fantasies). In *New Woman*, Ruan Lingyu's character stands at the center stage (though only to die there), highlighting several different women's lives; she is also granted numerous subjective shots.

In a key sequence, Wei's awakening is cinematically projected first on a live performance inside the Seaside International Dance Club. Performed by two Caucasian (likely Russian) dancers, the show has the man whipping the woman in a stylistic fashion. Wei, half drunk, sees herself in the Caucasian dancer in prison clothes and chained feet. The pain inflicted on the dancer's skin is so visceral that a tactile, bodily identification takes place here. Her embodied vision is carried into next sequence, when the street view on the car window fades into flashback of her life. Though deploying cinematic techniques similar to *Pink Dream*'s, these hallucinatory projections serve entirely different functions. The petty bourgeois sensibility and illusion of this quasi-modern girl is shaken off completely in the process, as if cinema afforded her an extraordinary sensory capacity to see through reality and reexperience the past. If *New Woman* achieved a more thorough reshaping of the modern girl than *Three Modern Women*, it does so by turning dancehall culture into a theater of cruelty and a transcultural allegory of women's fate. Yet, ironically, the gender play of a modern girl erotically whipping an effeminate dandy in *Spring Dream* is turned upside down here. Wei Ming is not only physically and psychologically abused but also ultimately forced to commit suicide, just as the actress Ai Xia (on whose life the film was based) did. And Ruan Lingyu was soon to follow on March 8, 1935, shortly after the film's release.[57]

The conversion experience of these writers and directors, Tian Han and Cai Chusheng in particular, appears inexorably bound to the transfiguration (and death) of the modern girl on the one hand, and the "awakening" of the male writer or artist figure on the other. The exorcizing of the modern girl, as if she is a demon in a nightmare (often through her association with nightlife), guarantees the metamorphosis of the literary dandy into a progressive, if not quite revolutionary, subject. The seductive forces of Shanghai nightlife and its mythological embodiment in the modern girl retreated as male screenwriters, directors, actors, and critics rose to the social and political challenges of the day. The experience of awakening is brought into optical and class *consciousness* and made literal by a newly encoded cinematic vernacular centered on the trope of the "dawn" or "morning," which harked back to the ethos of the Enlightenment movement.

Indeed, many films made in 1933–34 are explicitly structured around the new temporality of an energetic "morning" that belonged to work, not leisure, and hope, not despair. In early 1933 Cai Shusheng published an essay entitled "Morning Light" (*Zhaoguang*), in which he pronounced his disentanglement from the "nightmare" of the past. He wrote: "When I rush out to the staircase still shrouded in the dim air caused by the night fog coming from outside of the window, my vision begins to perceive the first ray of morning light of 1933."[58] In the same year, he completed *Morning in the Metropolis* (*Dushi de zaocheng*), which used the melodramatic plot of a capitalist's two sons' diametrically opposed fates in the service of a class allegory. The kind of petty bourgeois sentimentalism evident in his early works is entirely disposed. The remaining partying scenes are depicted as the denizen of the metropolis designed to trap innocent women; the evil figure now is the depraved playboy, the capitalist's legitimate son. The film had a successful run of eighteen continuous days after its release.[59] With *Fisherman's Ballad, New Woman,* and *Lost Lambs* (*Mitu de gaoyang,* 1936), Cai's pink dream forever faded. He descended down the night-fog shrouded "staircase," marched into the street, and trained his camera on the victims of, and potential rebels against, an unjust society.

THE MANY FACES OF *MODERN SCREEN*

Film-related journalism became a battleground in the early 1930s as numerous intellectuals of different political and social orientations tried to influence this important aspect of mass culture. Cai Shusheng's above-cited essay "Morning Light," in which he declared his "left turn," was published in the inaugural issue of *Modern Screen* in March 1933. Unlike the motley of trade journals and fanzines, this modernist magazine stood out as a well-designed and sophisticated publication that took cinema seriously. This seriousness, however, was more concerned with aesthetic modernism than with political mobilization and hence became the target of polemical critique from left critics.

While left film critics had dominated the art and film supplements of major periodicals—and in some instances created their own film magazines (for example, *Film Art* in 1932),[60] trade journals and popular fan magazines continued to flourish. Compared to the 1920s, the fan magazines of the 1930s had a conspicuously modern look in graphic design and a heightened consciousness about the imbrication of the cinema in urban modernity. An art deco–inspired international style, began to replace the previous straight-forward "cover-girl" or "cover-boy" style, as the December 1932 issue of *Screen Weekly* (*Yinmu zhoubao,* published by the respectable liberal Eastern Publishing House) shows. Fashionably dressed modern girls and dandies stroll leisurely on the street of a futuristic metropolis crowed with skyscrapers and expressways (see fig. 7.1).

Many such magazines were as ephemeral as the urban life and the

7.6 Inaugural issue of *Modern Screen*, featuring Ruan Lingyu.

celluloid dreams they celebrated. *Modern Screen* was first published on March 1, 1933 (fig. 7.6), and only ran (intermittently) until June 1934. This magazine was particularly noteworthy for its apparent "highbrow" approach to cinema, its flagrant modernist name and design, and, most crucially, its debate over the so-called soft film. Despite its cosmopolitan style, its editors (Chen Binghong [Benjamin Chan], Liu Na'ou, Huang Jiamo and others) prided themselves on the fact that their high quality magazine, featuring sixteen pages of exquisitely reproduced photos, cost only twenty cents—a one of a kind phenomenon in the business of film journalism. The eight thousand copies of its first issue sold out in less than ten days, so the editors decided to add two thousand more for the second issue.[61]

The magazine assembled an impressive team of contributors—in fact, a mixed company of liberal critics and leftist filmmakers and actors, in addition to its own contributing editors. Shu Yan, a critic active in the left-circle, for instance, contributed articles. Leading directors who were instrumental in the New Film Culture movement, such as Cheng Bugao, Sun Yu, and Shen Xiling also regularly published in the magazine. Sun Yu even held a small column called "Cinematic Chop-Suey Shop" (*dianying zasuiguan*), in which he offered his reflections on the current state of Chinese cinema in the form of a miscellaneous essay (*zawen*). Rising stars including Ai Xia, Li Lili, and Gao Zhanfei (who played the dandy writer in *Pink Dream*) also penned essays or poems as modern women and men of letters off-screen.[62] On the whole, the magazine cultivated a cosmopolitan look and refined taste, catering to the educated urbane movie fans.

The modern cinephiles were also given a primer for all the necessary accessories of modern life through the magazine's carefully designed and worded advertisements. The commodities and lifestyles advertised were often tied to cinema. For instance, Hujiang Photo Studio, located on the Bubbling Well Road, called itself the Artistic Palace of Photos for the Modern Girls, the Treasure House of Photographic Images of Modern Stars, and claimed to provide numerous images for the magazine. Sports products and venues are patronized by Li Lili and Wang Renmei, two new Lianhua starlets standing for the "healthy beautiful" body culture of the New Life movement (fig. 7.7). Li Lili also lent her bright white teeth and handwriting to ads for toothpaste. Other stars graced makeup products, such as nail polishes, with cinematic close-ups of their hands and fingers. The Rolls Self-Winding Watch and the Buick car recurrently associated themselves with the modern girl. Female stars and moviegoers, more than their male counterparts, were presented as both embodiments and consumers of the machine age characterized by speed and the commodity desire it fueled. The overwhelming presence of feminine faces and body parts, seen in ads and graphic embellishments for articles, gave the magazine an especially soft look and feel.

The ostensible appeal of cosmopolitan consumption cultivated by the magazine (which was not atypical for popular press at the time) was

7.7 Li Lili: the "great jade pillar," or the embodiment of athletic beauty. (*Modern Screen*)

oddly juxtaposed with a lofty mission. According to Huang Jiamo's inaugural editorial, the magazine's major objective was to elevate Chinese cinema's cultural status. Despite their ultimate differences that caused the soft film debate, the modernists and left critics agreed upon the importance of building a viable national cinema to resist Hollywood's imperial cultural dominance. They also agreed on the necessity of rescuing Chinese cinema from the "low-level taste" of previous film trends, in particular martial arts and costume dramas. In other words, both sides wanted to focus on the contemporary condition of the city and its inhabitants. Huang opens his essay in an optimistic spirit: "In China, cinema has become widespread. There are movie theaters in every large city as well as small towns. It has obviously taken over drama, attracting a youthful China. . . . After a decade or so of pioneering work, Chinese cinema has entered the stage of maturation." He underscores that the unpopularity of foreign sound cinema provided a great opportunity for Chinese cinema. With it, China could produce films that would compete with imports. Not only would they help Chinese viewers to promote national products (*tichang guohuo*), Chinese products could also be exported, thus "spreading the light of the nation" (*fayang guoguang*). Yet such products should be of high artistic quality and thoroughly modern. Huang reasons:

> Today, the general public—the general modernized (*modenghua*) young men and women all regard cinema as the greatest solace and highest degree of enjoyment of in their life. In addition to attending the movies, they also need a good film magazine to serve as a regular movie guide, companion of study, and reference for judgment in order to raise their consciousness about modern film art. This is because cinema is not simply a product for leisure. It is the synthesis of art—including literature, drama, fine art, music, and science (such as electronics and optics). Thus forms the most advanced kind of modern entertainment. At the same time, it also serves as the sharpest weapon of education and propaganda. The arts are her soul, whereas science is her bone structure; thus she is the crystallization of the new arts of the twentieth century.[63]

From the second issue on, however, *Modern Screen* began to make its agenda more explicit. A series of articles by Huang and Liu Na'ou, the magazine's two leading voices, launched an aesthetic theory of film and spectatorship while criticizing the ideological critique in vogue. In a nutshell, their views of cinema were informed by convictions in the primacy of film form and sense, and in cinema's capacity to alleviate modern people's pain and ennui through laughter, sentimentality, and vicarious fulfillment of erotic desire.

In June and July 1934, left-wing critics of several news supplements staged an attack on the soft film advocated by *Modern Screen*. The polemics largely concerned relationships between technology and ideology, aesthetics and politics, and the notion of the "masses" (*dazhong*). The modernists saw the latter as increasingly valorized by the left as a uniform spectatorship for a national cinema. Several authors in *Modern Screen* complained about the "misuse" or "abuse" of the term and iconography of the "masses" in *Three Modern Women* and *Daybreak*. The "workers" in such films, in their view, were wholesale imports from Soviet films—and as such offered unrealistic depictions of the Chinese life.[64] For the modernists, the "masses" were a broad social spectrum embodied in the moviegoers. They defined the metropolitan audience (*dushi guanzhong*) as patients suffering from neurasthenia and modern malaise who sought remedy in the movies. These remedies, neither ancient nor imported, could "dissolve phlegm and clean up the [bad] energy" or cleanse the intestines and nourish the stomach."[65]

The modernist's contention that the Soviet-styled *puluojino* with revolutionary figures was fashionably opportunistic was not altogether groundless. Their advocacy of an apolitical, "pure" art cinema for the sake of sensuous indulgence, however, ultimately betrays their "glaucoma-infected vision,"[66] fixated on the aestheticization of everyday life. Leading left critics Xia Yan, Tang Na, and Chen Wu indicted soft film for its indulgence in bourgeois sensibilities, decadence, and escapism in the face of a national crisis. The attack from the left was motivated in part by a sustained reaction against "soft" romantic melodramas and martial arts films.[67] In fact, the modernists also detested these popular genres as "feudal" and "low-taste."

The advocates of the "soft film" commonly claimed, "cinema is ice-cream for the eyes and sofa for the heart and the mind" (*dianying shi yanjing de bingqilin, xinling de shafayi*). The sentence appeared in Huang Jiamo's essay, "Hard Film versus Soft Film," published in the December 1933 issue of *Modern Screen* (fig. 7.8).[68] As the focal point of the controversy, it deserves a close look. Only one page long, the article consists of five short sections. The much-debated quote is found in the opening section. Huang's basic justification for the slogan is readily given in the section title: "Film is made of soft celluloid" (film negative in Chinese is called "soft film," or *ruanpian*). Owing to the medium's specificity, Huang asserts, film as representation of the human drama ought to sustain its "power of entertaining attractions." In the second section, "Chinese [soft] film has turned hard film," Huang laments the fact that contemporary Chinese cinema has become "starched" or "hardened" by overt ideological interests and left-wing "isms," turning cinema into a propagandist instrument while depriving it of its entertainment appeal. Huang argues that, although this "hardened" cinema is supposed to educate and even mobilize the people, it has in fact alienated both the popular and the more educated audiences because of its unabashed political preaching and romanticizing of the "masses." The argument goes thus: "Modern viewers are rather straightforward people. They are practical and have little patience for pretentious preaching. After they are just liberated

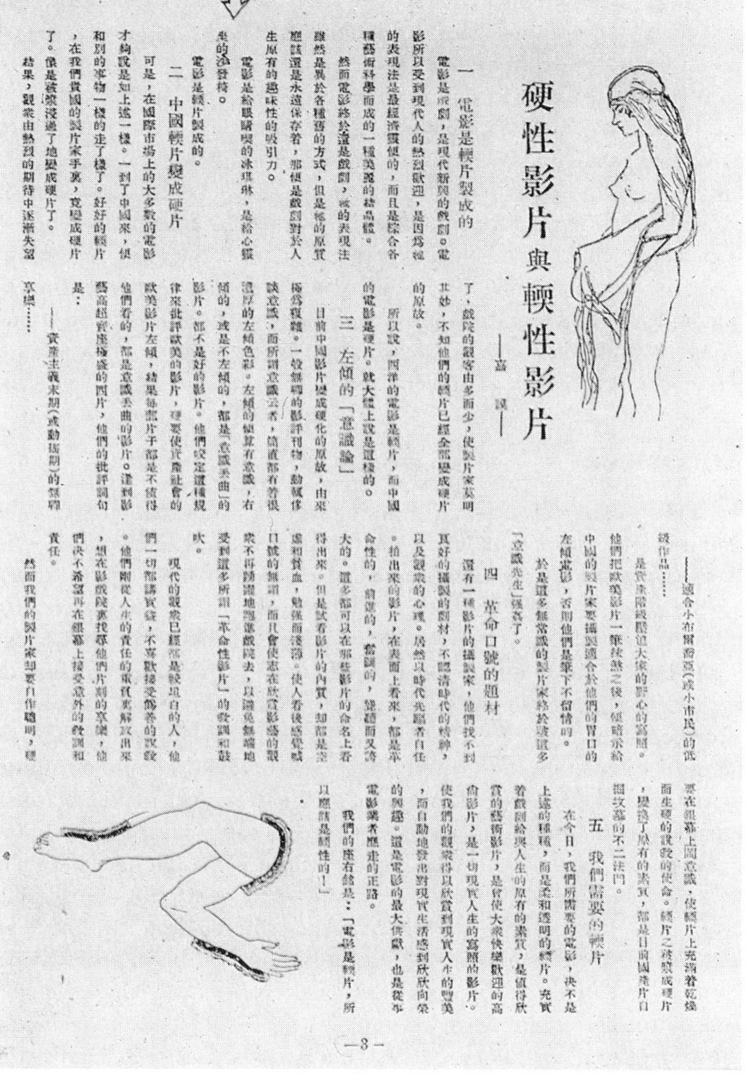

硬性影片與輭性影片

——嘉謨——

一　電影是輭片製成的

電影是戲劇，是現代新興的戲劇。電影所以受到現代人的熱烈歡迎，是因爲牠的表現法是最經濟靈便的，而且是綜合各種藝術科學而成的一種美麗的結晶體。

然而電影終於還是戲劇，牠的表現法雖然是異於各種舊的方式，但是牠的原質應該還是永遠保存着，那便是戲劇對於人生原有的趣味性的吸引力。

電影是給眼睛喫的冰琪琳，是給心靈坐的沙發椅。

電影是輭片製成的。

二　中國輭片變成硬片

可是，在國際市場上的大多數的電影才夠說是如上述一樣。一到了中國來，便和別的事物一樣的走了樣了。好好的輭片，在我們貴國的製片家手裏，竟變成硬片了。像是被漿浸過了地變成硬片了。

結果，觀衆由熱烈的期待中逐漸失望了，戲院的觀客由多而少，使製片家莫明其妙，不知他們的輭片已經全部變成硬片的原故。

所以說，西洋的電影是輭片，而中國的電影是硬片。就大體上說是這樣的。

三　左傾的「意識論」

目前中國影片變成硬化的原故，由來極爲複雜。一般無聊的影評刊物，動輒侈談意識，而所謂意識云者，簡直都有着很濃厚的左傾色彩。左傾的便算有意識，右傾的，或是不左傾的，都是「意識歪曲」的影片。都不是好的影片。他們咬定這種規律來批評歐美的影片，硬要使資產社會的歐美影片左傾，結果每部片子都是不值得他們看的，都是意識歪曲的影片。這種影藝高超資產極盛的西片，他們的批評調句是：

——資產主義末期(或動搖期)的頹廢享樂……

——適合小布爾喬亞(或小市民)的低級作品……

是資產階級麻醉大衆的野心的寫照。

他們把歐美影片一筆抹煞之後，便暗示給中國的製片家要攝製適合於他們的胃口的左傾電影，否則他們是筆下不留情的。

於是這多無常識的製片家終於被這多「意識先生」強姦了。

四　革命口號的題材

還有一種影片的攝製家，他們找不到真好的攝製的劇材，不認清時代的精神，以及觀衆的心理。居然以時代先驅者自任。拍出來的影片，在表面上看來，都是革命性的，前進的，奮鬥的，標題而又誇大的。這多都可以在那些影片的命名上看得出來。但是試看影片的內質，卻都是空虛和貧血，勉強而淺薄。使人看後感覺喊口號的無謂，而且會使志在欣賞影戲的觀衆不得躊躇地踏進戲院去，以避免無端地受到這多所謂「革命性影片」的教訓和鼓吹。

現代的觀衆已經都是較坦白的人，他們一切都講實益，不喜歡接受偽善的說教。他們剛從人生的責任的重負裏解放出來，想在影戲院裏找尋他們片刻的享樂，他們決不希望再在銀幕上接受意外的教訓和責任。

然而我們的製片家卻要自作聰明，硬要在銀幕上圖意識，使輭片上充滿着乾燥而生硬的說教的使命。輭片之被變成硬片，變換了原有的素質，都是目前國產片自掘墳墓的不二法門。

五　我們需要的輭片

在今日，我們所需要的電影，決不是上述的種種，而是柔和透明的輭片。充實着戲劇給與人生的原有的素質，是值得欣賞的藝術影片，是會使大衆快樂歡迎的高尚影片，是一切現實人生的寫照的影片。使我們的觀衆得以欣賞到現實人生的雙美，而自動地發出對現實生活感到欣欣向榮的興趣。這是電影的最大供獻，也是從事電影業者應走的正路。

我們的座右銘是：「電影是輭片，所以應該是輭性的！」

—3—

7.8 Huang Jiamo's essay, "Hard Film versus Soft Film." (December 1933 issue of *Modern Screen*)

from the burden of daily responsibilities, they go to movie theaters to seek momentary enjoyment. They never expect to receive uncalled-for lessons and responsibilities." What these modern viewers need are "soft" and "transparent" films that show the "beauty" of real life and infuse in people a sense of joy. Huang's views are blatantly self-righteous about the need to make "feel good" movies, such as comedies, for urban dwellers who have to endure mental and physical assault outside the movie theater. Some "hard" films full of "revolutionary slogans," in his eyes, lacked substance and suffered from "emptiness and anemia."

What exactly was the nature of the "soft film" advocated by editors of the *Modern Screen*? If hard film was never uniformly hard (in the form of emotional excess and decorous sets and costumes), then it seems doubtful the soft film was as soft as both its advocates and detractors claimed. Instead of this opposition, other historically specific terms of reference—such as film style, reception, star text, and indeed, cinematic modernity—suggest a more complex controversy. A closer examination of the essays and graphic design, as well as the films they refer to, reveal an abundance of contradictions that suggests much more was at stake than a mere polemical exchange of metaphors.

THE SPEED OF FLESH: ANATOMIZING THE SOFT FILM

A famous Shanghai dandy with an ambiguous racial background, Liu Na'ou was the more prolific and sophisticated architect of *Modern Screen.* Well-versed in several languages, his contributions in the magazine cover a wide range of aesthetic topics in film theory and criticism, including "The Problem of Depth Description in Chinese Film" (1:3), "On Choosing [Film] Subjects" (1:4), "On Film Rhythm" (1:6), "The Structure of the Camera: A Treatise on the Mechanics of Camera Position" (1:7), and "Interpretations of European Classical Films" (1:3). In one article, Liu points out that the verbose intertitles of some hard films (especially those with a rural theme or setting) contradict their mass orientation because the majority of Chinese, in particular peasants, could hardly read. Liu advocated a visual language, telling stories through the interplay between light and shadow, mise-en-scène, editing, and other cinematographic properties. He goes as far as to suggest that, with the decline of the "star system" in Hollywood and the "director system" in Europe, one should anticipate a cinema centered on the "camera system," which would emphasize the materiality of the medium.[69] This celebration of cinema as the aesthetic and cultural synthesis of the machine age—its soft desires and hard gears—renders the label "soft film" somewhat ambiguous. Similarly, the hard film was not always a direct reflection of hard-line leftist dogma. These aspects of ambiguity and layers of mediation call for an alternative argument that places the two camps in ambivalent relation rather than in diametrical opposition to each other.

Liu's most entrenched criticism of hard film rests on formal ground. Indeed, the discursive split between the soft and hard films was largely drawn along the line between form and content, the question of technology and the meaning of urban modernity. Because most left critics were not directly involved in film production and came mainly from literary backgrounds, their writings were by and large centered on thematic representations and dramatic characterizations of the social world. They were primarily concerned with utilizing narrative to mobilize the masses (often conflating the movie audience with the abstract notion of the "revolutionary masses") toward national salvation; the medium itself only served this objective. In Lu Si's view, "form and content" could not be separated.[70]

Liu regarded cinematic form as foundational to the medium and is unique. In another article, under the original French title, "Ecranesque," Liu Na'ou argues that speed and motion constitute the quintessential form of the cinema. He writes, "the cinema is the art of motion arising from the combination of artistic sensibilities and scientific rationality. Just as [modern] architecture embodies the purest form of the rationality of mechanical civilization, that which can most uniquely represent the social environment of mechanical civilization is the cinema." This passage is instructive for understanding the soft aesthetic beyond its glossy appearance in the magazine. Rather than isolating the cinema as a pure aesthetic object, Liu was convinced that cinema's synthetic power to represent and recreate reality was embedded in its material base and concrete social infrastructure. The architectural metaphor and passion resonated with a wave of new Shanghai theaters, such as the Grand (*Da Guangming*) on Jinansi Road, the Metropol (*Da Shanghai*) on Yu Qiaqing Road (Xizang zhonglu), and Cathy (*Guotai*) on Joffrey Road (Huaihai zhonglu). These new entertainment venues redefined the Shanghai skyline (fig. 7.9). These and other theaters, along with the new skyscrapers, were part of the reconstruction project in the aftermath of the Japanese bombing.[71] Before the city was shell-shocked again in 1937, Shanghai emerged as the most dazzling metropolis in the East. The streamline aesthetic, accentuated with vertical lines and neon lights echoed and amplified the international aesthetic of the machine age. Films made in the period, whether soft or hard, scrambled to capture the urban landscape's glittering allure. Many films' title sequence simply became a condensed city symphony flaunting the seductive skyline and the hieroglyphic neon writings.

How did Liu and his cohorts reconcile the seeming contradiction between the soft look they advocated (and made) and the hard gears of film technology and social engineering it represented? To be sure, the soft aesthetics' apparent hard dimensions should not be confused with the overt political content the hard films depicted. Instead of a hairsplitting

7.9 A cinema built in the 1930s: the international style of the Metropol (*The Builder* 1, no. 3 [1933]; architect: Zhao Shenchen).

analysis of both sides' often self-contradictory rhetoric, the magazine's overall graphic design offers unexpected insights.

An abundance of illustrations embellish *Modern Screen.* At the outset, the images betray a passion for a soft look embodied by the numerous carefully crafted nude or seminude pictures of Chinese or Western movie stars and models. These images manifest the prevalent fascination with the so-called fleshy feeling (*rougan*) of the modern girl—with her mixture of sensuality and energy, primitive aura and modern flavor, erotic appeal and athletic power. The cult of flesh apotheosized here sometimes borders on soft porn, as shown in the drawings illustrating Huang Jiamo's article, "'Soft' Film versus 'Hard' Film." The article title is "presented" by a maiden with flowing hair, her hands holding a bundle of fabric over her private parts. At the end of the article, a woman's plump arm and a leg are crossed together with celluloid lace accentuating the sensuality of her curving limbs. These close-ups of female body parts (lips, eyes, or legs) framing the text share a seductive vernacular with the ads for nail polishes, stockings, and other adornments of the modern female body. The soft aesthetic thus appears feminine, or hyperfeminine, yet with a twist as the body parts with their streamlines also invoke parts in a machine. The frequently featured nude or seminude portraits were taken by editorial members. They prided themselves as skilled photographers or filmmakers and presented these images as "art."

Both anonymous and noted film actresses were subjects of the elaborate nude photography. Veteran director Dan Duyu, who began his career in the early 1920s and shot the sexy swashbuckling beauties in *Cave of the Spider Spirit,* contributed several nude photographs. With elegantly posed women against pastoral backgrounds, the pictures are meant to be studies of "light and shadow." Another eye-catching studio nude study features actress Hu Shan (cousin of the Queen of Cinema Hu Die). With her bare back facing the camera, Hu Shan's face turns to the viewer with an obvious pride in her own body. This is a modern girl self-assured about her photogenic, streamline curves (fig. 7.10).

The nude as a legitimate artistic subject had only been established in China after Liu Haisu, the French-educated modern painter and principal of the Shanghai Fine Arts Academy (the first Western style art school in China), won the legal battles to use nude models in the 1920s.[72] As an arbiter of Western inspired modern art, Liu may have succeeded in making a distinction between nudity and pornography, respectable art and the sex industry. The triumph did not, however, belong to Liu alone. The entry of the well-proportioned female body into public view inadvertently signaled not only the birth of a new profession for women, but more importantly, affirmed the centrality of female body in modern imagination and social change. The incident coincided not only with the increasing public presence of Chinese women as full-fledged social subjects (though still employed as "objects"), but also with their growing consciousness and control over their body. This was best exemplified in the life and work of Pan Yuliang, a former prostitute-turned-art student of Liu and, after a few years studying in Europe, a professor at the Shanghai Fine Art School and the Nanjing Central University. Pan's nude stud-

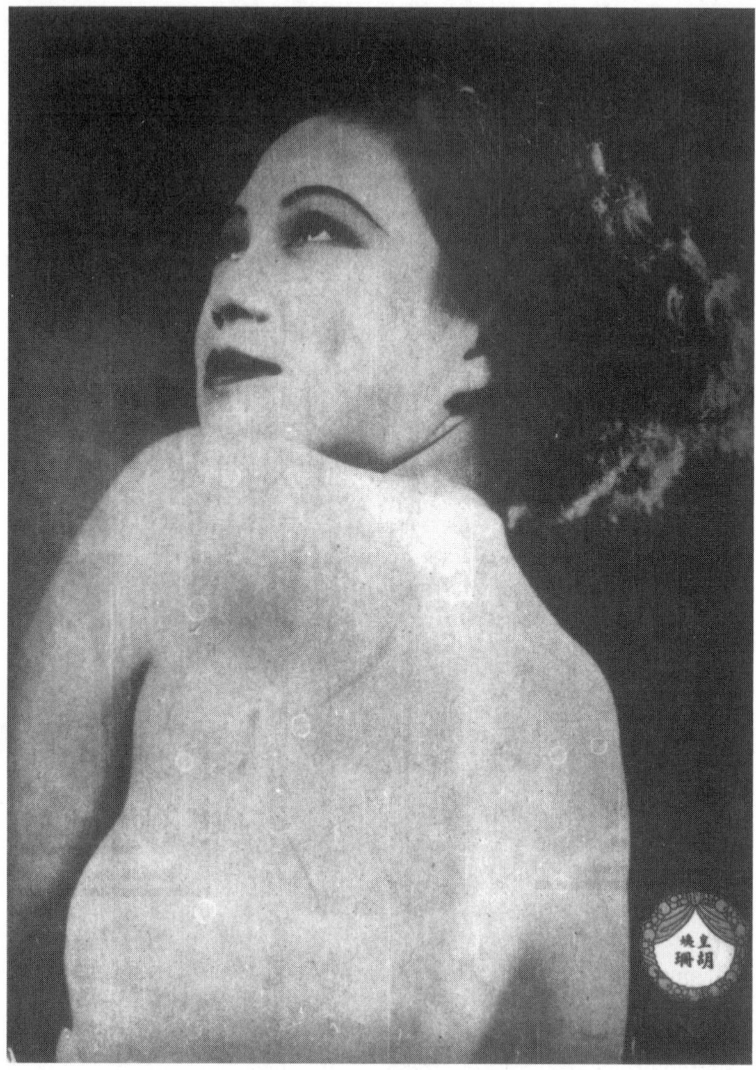

7.10 "The speed of flesh": Hu Shan. (*Modern Screen*)

ies (of herself and other women) appeared in the first National Art Exhibition in Nanjing in 1929.[73] Journalists who were trying to damage her public image dug up Pan's past as a prostitute and a concubine of the man who redeemed her from brothel. Clearly, the moralists resented her subject matter as much as her radical transformation from a lowly prostitute to a prominent modern artist and public figure.[74] Pan's fate was remarkably similar to actress Xuan Jingling's, as detailed in the opening of this book.

The controversy over nudity was also part and parcel of a larger debate over "beauty"—or what constituted a beautiful life—in the late 1920s. The advocates and practitioners of the "beautiful life," influenced by a mixture of romanticism and neoclassicism, held the view that nudity was a crucial agent and symbol of a modern, sensuous, and fulfilled life. In his book *The Beautiful View of Life,* Zhang Jingsheng, the sensationalized champion and theoretician of this lifestyle, recommends nudity as a way of attaining a healthy, aesthetic body. Zhang's views are unabashedly antitraditional, at times verging on eugenics. He argues against having shame in one's own body and suggests that bad clothes not only harm body but also inhibit natural socialization between the sexes. Body beautification begins by practicing nudity, which allows the body to reembrace nature and strips away civilization's confines. However, this is not easily done in a country like China where males and females were traditionally not supposed to court or touch publicly. He prescribes discretion yet perseverance:

> In a society like ours it is certainly difficult to practice nudity publicly. Only in moonlit night one could take a walk in the open, unpopulated space alone or together with one's family or close friends. When inside one's own room, one should form the habit of practicing nudity. If there is bed suitable for sleeping nude, one should do so. It will make one's body feel happy, and also save money spent on clothes.[75]

If Zhang's nude aesthetic stems from a romantic return to natural state of being, the nudes in *Modern Screen* celebrate urban civilization, incorporating the romantic ethos into the machine age. Dan Duyu's pastoral nudes and other carefully crafted seminude studies in theatrical or "ethnic" costume reveal a curious blending of primitivism and modernism, the soft flesh and the hardware of photography. Beside static studio works, which might have been provided by the photo shops advertised in the magazine, there are far more snapshots of scantily clad movie stars engaged in sports, dance, or other physical activities in *Modern Screen.* The editors seemed particularly fond of stars in swimsuits, both male and female, on the beach or not. The aesthetes of the soft film found their quintessential form in the "athletic and beautiful" body, which combined the erotic appeal of both organic nature and material civilization.

The cult of the nude signaled the entrance of a new constellation of screen actors who, despite their on-screen images as oppressed peasants or workers, were marketed for their Hollywood-style physiques and athleticism. They were not just movie stars, but *modeng* creatures embodying lifestyles associated with "self-winding" watches, Buick cars, and motorbikes. One contributor to *Modern Screen* simply equates *modeng* with stars in terms of their unique physique: "He (or she) is no fragile 'sick-man of the Orient,' nor is he (or she) a fat person with a heavy head and swollen body. He (or she) is tall, with firm muscles, bright and clear eyes and eyebrows, and strong limbs. He (or she) possesses a realistic, strong beauty of a human body [*rentimei*], can perform graceful and tender movements, but can also perform virile and forceful actions."[76] The soft film aesthetic was obviously derived from the contemporary international discourse and praxis of nude painting, photography, and nudism, which centered on the transformed epistemological and aesthetic status of the body and modern technology in the 1920s and 1930s. In more synthetic and tangible forms it registered how the body—especially the female body—was at once liberated from reproductive functions but trapped in the second nature of machines, including the camera. The soft aesthetic gave expression to a new physiognomy and sexual appeal characterized by hyperfemininity, androgyny, and machine aesthetics in Chinese metropolitan centers.

The quintessence of the machine aesthetic, of course, was speed. But its soft or erotic countenance required bodily energy and form. In "On Film Rhythm," Liu Na'ou again emphasizes that it is the "form of art, not just content, that reflects the epoch." This form is defined in terms of temporality and kinesthetic movement. Speed, the annihilation of space by time, was a chief hallmark of modernity. According to Liu, it is not speed per se but the "sense of speed" (*kuaigan*), or the sensation it induces, that defines the appeal of cinema. This sense of speed, which in turn generates rhythm, may be obtained by driving a Roadster, dancing to jazz music, or watching a movie. Liu prefers the terms *movie* and *motion pictures* to *film* or *cinema* for the connotation of movement.[77]

The analogy between dance and movies makes particular sense; the cult of social dance in the industrial era, as Deleuze noted, partly derived from the cult of the machine, wherein the human body was incorporated into the metallic and mechanical rhythm of the modern era.[78] Cinematic form, generating the twin-pleasure of the "sense of flesh" and the "sense of speed," thus corresponds to the very physiognomy of a mass-mediated urban life, characterized by the intensification of desire, commodification of social relations, and consumption of (leisure) time. Social dance became so popular that it became a kinetic icon; in China's jazz age it was conceivably a gigantic sensory machine of the crowd. As an antidote to alienation, boredom, and isolation, ballroom dancing and cinema became the quintessential forms of mass enjoyment, accentuated by the spread of the gramophone. At the same time, the systematic commodification of this commingled form of metropolitan pleasure, embodied in the dancing hostess, turned it into a covert sex-industry and an emblem of urban modernity. Many of the diligent cinephiles were also dance maniacs. Cheng Bugao, director of *Wild Torrent* and *Spring Silkworms*, was famous for his dance passion. Treating dancing almost as a form of fieldwork, Cheng found that "there is so much to savor when one holds a dancing hostess, listening to her telling life stories full of sad or happy encounters, reunions and separations."[79]

Prior to Liu's direct involvement in cinema, the intertwining of flesh and speed, of embodiment and technology was already well articulated in his fiction writing in the New Sensationalist mode. The Sensationalists (including Xu Xiacun, author of "Modern Girl" and Shi Zhecun, author of "At Paris Theater," and Mu Shiying) were Shanghai literary dandies influenced by their Japanese contemporaries, especially the so-called *xinkankakuha* writers Yokomitsu Riichi, Tanizaki Jun'ichiro, Yasunari Kawabata, and Kataoka Teppei, in addition to the French writer Paul Morand. They sought to create a new, sensuous prose form portraying Shanghai urban life, using a host of modernist and cinematic techniques. Liu was the group's fountainhead. Reportedly half-Japanese and half-Taiwanese, Liu received his formative education in Japan and was fluent in Japanese and had a good knowledge of French and English. Arriving in Shanghai in 1924 to attend a French Jesuit University, Liu was a typical Shanghai cosmopolitan emigré. He quickly improved his Chinese, translated several Japanese writers, and became an ardent practitioner and publisher of the New Sensationalist writing.[80]

His collection of short stories, *Scène* (*Dushi fengjingxian*, 1930),[81] canvasses the urban landscape of Shanghai and a motion-charged lifestyle of modern girls and dandies who frequent urban venues such as cafés, dance halls, and movie theaters. An advertisement for his book of stories in *La nouvelle littérature* (*Xin wenyi*), a journal edited by Liu himself, offers a succinct description of the work and Liu as the literary dandy and aficionado of modern life: "Mr. Na'ou is a sensitive man. With his special talent, he wields a sharp scalpel to dissect airplanes, movies, jazz, skyscrapers, eroticism, the high speed of long-bodied cars, and the mass production of modern life."[82]

True to this advertisement, the book is like a collection of musings on these modern venues, vehicles, and actions. Almost unfailingly, each story features the encounter between a modern girl and a dandy, both often with ambiguous national or racial identities.[83] The pace at which the relationships develop and dissolve is as fast as the sports cars they drive or the jazz tunes they dance to, and as ephemeral as the fashion they wear. The dandies are fascinated with the modern girl's exotic looks and with the tempo of urban fads they embody. But ultimately, the dandies find themselves outwitted or overpowered by the girls, whose "sense of flesh" prove too *matérielle* and whose cultural complexity prove too hard to penetrate.[84]

"The Two Who Suffer from the Lost Sense of Time" in *Scène* captures the pregnant mixture of speed and flesh.[85] The story opens at the horse-racing track in downtown Shanghai, where a dandy called H catches a glimpse or, rather, a whiff of a perfumed girl in the midst of an intense race. He turns around and sees a "sporty modern woman whose elastic muscles softly vibrate under French silk as though she was doing light exercises." Both have bet on the same horse and win. They quickly find themselves walking out of the racing court and stroll down the street as lovers. "Taking walks is an inseparable element in modern courtship, because it's the only way to demonstrate the existence of ephemeral love," intones the narrator. They stop at a café, then pass the three "monster-like" department stores on Damalu (Nanjing Road). On the way, H is enthralled by the sight of a Frontenac 1929, but he reminds himself that he has a "fair sex" to attend to at the moment. They soon land at a dance hall, in time for the tea dance. Rivaling another dandy called T, H seizes the chance to waltz with the girl. While swirling to the music, H tries to persuade her to leave the dance hall with him to get rid of the meddling T. Her reply startles him: "Ah, you're a real kid. Why have you been so clumsy—eating ice cream, taking a walk, all those nuisances. Don't you know that lovemaking should be done in a car and in the wind? . . . I have never spent more than three hours with a gentleman. This is already an exception."[86] This modern girl is obviously living and moving at a much faster pace than both dandies, who have lost the "sense of time." She has welded her sexuality into a sports car, her body into the machine, which inspires in the dandy both desire and anxiety. With her fashionable "opera-bag" in hand, the girl swiftly leaves the two men for another appointment. As in other stories in *Scène,* the despondent dandies are left feeling not so much embarrassed as alienated by their inability to catch up with the "feel of speed." For them, the city and the modern girl are often interchangeable, at once alluring and menacing. Yet the dandy who indulges in urban material culture and libidinal economy is, for Liu, also a potential revolutionary, like Baudelaire's flâneur.

Liu's enthusiasm for the cameraman's centrality in modernist film aesthetics evokes Dziga Vertov's theorization of the "kino eye." Vertov's revolutionary flâneur incorporates the technology of movie camera to give direct representation to urban life (in Moscow) as lived, nonalienated modern experience. The "perfectible eye" of the camera, more "truthful" than the human eye, can capture the "feel of the world" and potentially change the world through critical production.[87] Vertov's name often graces *Modern Screen.* Stills of his documentary *Enthusiasm* display a curious collage of "mechanical civilization" (*jixie wenming*), sports culture, and primitive tribal dance. Other Russian film theorists and directors are also frequently cited. In an article on the "material" (or subjects) of film, Liu cites Pudovkin to support his argument that "film as a new art ought to possess its own unique newness. . . . As a new expressive form, cinema has its own particular grounding, its own language."[88] Similarly, the production of a modern "sense" mediated by mechanically induced movement also evokes Eisenstein's fascination with biomechanics and his experiment with "expressive movement" as an acting style inspired by machines.

Liu's emphasis on cinema's ontological (or photographic) uniqueness resonates with the international avant-garde's intervention in the medium's formal possibilities as an instrument for artistic revolution, giving life back to art. On the other hand, the Chinese modernists' love for Hollywood, their seemingly aberrant taste in "low genres" (such as physical comedy and the musical), and "classicist" nude pictures reflect the ambiguous genesis of Soviet cinema, which actively appropriated American cinema. As Yuri Tsivian's study suggests, works by Kuleshov, Gardin, and others at the turn of the 1920s demonstrated a visible "Americanization" in the speed of editing, closeness of framing, and above all the adoption of "American montage."[89] At the same time, the intellectuals' fascination with "cinematic pulp fiction"—for example, Eisenstein's interest in serial queen dramas—exemplifies the interconnection and persistence of two Americanisms in the transition from an old to a new political and cinematic regime.

The dialectical relation between classical cinema and modernism, and between the Hollywood vernacular and avant-garde in the Russian-Soviet film is germane to the contention and interrelation among the competing Shanghai moderns. Shanghai filmmakers too tried to create a "contemporary" Chinese cinema befitting its era and in dialogue with international modernism. The ideological divide between them was made clear, however, after the Japanese invasion of Manchuria. The left-wing embraced nationalism and an anti-Kuomintang approach, whereas the modernists tried to escape it by clinging to aesthetics. The former increasingly associated Hollywood—and indeed most foreign cultural or political powers—with the enemy. The modernists, some with strong (in the case of Liu even with umbilical) ties to Japan, were more attracted to cosmopolitan flânerie than patriotic rhetoric. They choose aesthetics over politics, the dance-machine over war machine, celluloid dreams over urgent reports from the frontline in Manchuria or the slums in the city. In that regard, their consuming passion for the soft aesthetic, in some measure, turned into a form of escapism. It came dangerously close to anaestheticizing social and political consciousness at a time when the democratic promise held by mass culture and cinema was seriously challenged by the rise of fascism and the exigencies of the war across the international horizon.

GIRL IN DISGUISE, IMAGE IN DISPUTE

While the left-wing screenwriters embraced a form of revolutionary masculinity hardened by nationalism, the modernists were preoccupied with apotheosizing the modern girl as the hybrid emblem of the machine age and cosmopolitan consumption. Like their counterparts, the modernists also put their theory to practice. Among the handful of films on which *Modern Screen* editors moonlighted as screenwriters or directors, *Girl in Disguise* (*Huashen guniang,* Yihua, 1936) exemplified the soft film for both sides of the debate.

Girl in Disguise is a crowd-pleaser with mixed elements from Zheng Zhengqiu's ethical melodramas (minus the tragedy) and Hollywood's romantic comedies. But its popularity had much to do with its "queer" plot, in which Liying (played by Yuan Meiyun), a girl from Singapore, poses as a boy named Shouben (which means "guarding the origin") when she visits her lineage-obsessed grandfather in Shanghai. The masquerade and mistaken gender identity create comic, embarrassing situations. Along the way, a young woman falls in love with the "girl in disguise," while the "boy" becomes infatuated with a Shanghai dandy (fig. 7.11). Playing with the flexibility or artificiality of gender identity, *Girl in Disguise* capitalizes on the appeal of Shanghai's androgynous fashions in the 1930s. It became an instant hit when it was released in the summer of 1936, serving as a palatable "ice cream for the eyes" to thousands of moviegoers who sought refuge from heat—and from national or personal troubles—in the air-conditioned theaters.

Unlike other films mentioned in this chapter, the film was a talkie; the implementation of sound was near completion. Its sound track gives this soft film an added appeal aimed at pleasing the petty urbanites' senses. Secondly, several years after the 1932 bombing of Shanghai, the city's economic and cultural life had not only rebounded but also seemed to reach a new high point. New skyscrapers and cinemas rose, nightlife flourished, and more people and commodities flowed in and out of the city. By then, *Modern Screen* had ceased publication, and the left-wing film

7.11 *Girl in Disguise:* the pleasure of cross-dressing. (Courtesy of the China Film Archive)

criticism had also lost much of its foothold in the press. At the same time, the debate over soft film was giving way to discourse on creating a "national defense" cinema in the face of the imminent all-out Japanese invasion. *Girl in Disguise* cinematically materializes the modernists' persistent fascination with the chameleon-like modern girl while the business of national salvation was left to the patriots.

The central concept, according to its creators, is the persistent problem of gender bias or discrimination in Chinese society, even in a high-modern Shanghai. Liying assumed double gender identities the moment she was born because her parents were obliged to produce a boy to cure the patriarch's illness caused by anxiety over genealogical discontinuity. At home in tropical Singapore, however, she is the beloved daughter of her parents and the envy of her friends as she grows into a beauty. When she becomes eighteen, the patriarch orders her parents to send the "grandson" to Shanghai to prepare for his career as the future heir. A commotion of activities ensues. In order to transform Liying into Shouben, a tailor makes suits for her and a barber chops off her long hair. Liying boards the steamship for Shanghai with a wig packed in her luggage.

If her girlhood seemed easy and carefree in Singapore, Shanghai proves to be a metropolis of confusing desire and, paradoxically, a stronghold of traditional patriarchal forces as well. Liying's double life gets her entangled in unexpected familial and social situations. The grandfather loves his only grandson so much that he wants him to sleep in the same bed—as he and Liying's father once did. She is also taken to the Yong'an Department Store to shop for shaving blades, although she has no need for any male toiletries. A matchmaker brings would-be brides' pictures for Shouben to make his picks. While Liying enjoys her androgynous look and to some extent the "same-sex" flirtations with girls and boys, she eventually finds all the procedures to remold her into a male heir unbearable to say the least. She uses every possible moment to reclaim her femininity, particularly by "impersonating" a female role during a Peking opera performance on the patriarch's birthday.

The film's critics engaged neither the provocative representations of a Singaporean Chinese girl's gender trouble nor her troubled relationship to her "native" city of Shanghai. Inevitably, Liying's identity is revealed. In a soft shot framed diagonally to stress the shocking revelation and its dizzying effect, the grandfather glimpses her breasts protruding under her pajamas when he wakes to Liying's scream in a nightmare. After the initial shock, the grandfather quickly comes back to his senses and accepts Liying the granddaughter, who promptly changes into a *qipao* dress. Meanwhile, a telegram from Singapore announces the arrival of a real son. Thus all ends well: the gender confusion is resolved and the patriarch gets an heir (fig. 7.12).

Girl in Disguise's detractors found it a typical "low-taste" crowd-pleaser with nothing but a few "meaningless games" and "comic gags." The gender-bending elements were dismissed as part and parcel of "ice-cream for the eyes" formulated to "anaesthetize" the audience in a time when the fate of the nation was at stake.[90] Another critic simply discredited the relevance of gender bias critique, arguing that the "recent total collapse of the rural economy has forced traditionally 'heavily' valued men also to the point of mere survival." "Their status is as pitiable as that of women's. Thus the custom of 'valuing boys over girls' has been alleviated. . . . Therefore, [this old saying] does not mean so much anymore, because women are no longer looked down upon."[91]

While the film's ending clearly caters to the entrenched patriarchal values that persist even among residents of a metropolis, the proposition that gender bias in Chinese society was no longer a relevant problem is not only disconcerting but historically inaccurate. The implicit argument in such an observation is that class was a more urgent and "contemporary" issue, whereas the gender question was by that time passé and had been resolved by modernization. Moreover, this critic saw the new urban proletariat or underclass as a primarily male social body, oblivious to the fact that modernity had created new gender hierarchies while reinforc-

7.12 *Girl in Disguise:* the pressure of family values. (Courtesy of the China Film Archive)

ing old ones. Certainly, the rapid urbanization and industrialization gave women unprecedented opportunities to enter the workforce and various public arenas, but the gender bias fostered and institutionalized by time-honored cultural norms has retained a firm place in the Chinese consciousness until this day.

Girl in Disguise symptomatically exposes gender trouble in a modern city despite the seeming liberation of modern girls (and boys). The modern girl portrayed by the New Sensationalist fiction tends to be a hyperbolic imaginary creature, or, rather, the modernist dandy's projection of his contradictory cosmopolitan fantasies involving a playful self-emasculation. The cultural and cinematic vernacular employed by *Girl in Disguise* spoke to an audience consisting mostly of petty urbanites rather than highbrow fiction readers and connoisseurs of avant-garde aesthetics. The medium's commercial requirements evidently pushed soft film advocates to tilt to the prosaic entertainment end of the spectrum of their aesthetic, showcasing its fleshy content more than speedy mechanic form. The cinematic modernism was less about Liu's formal concerns than about the *appearances* or vernacular registers of modern life, such as fashion, makeup, urban milieu, and transportation.[92] Yet, through its preoccupation with gender and sexuality in a world city, the film highlights one of the chief concerns of the New Sensationalist writing. If the modern girl in their textual inscription and abstraction seems rootless, floating, and unbounded by marriage and family, the more mundane and concrete troubles Liying/Shouben encounters create comic and ironic effects appealing to audiences of popular cinema.

"Disguise" becomes the inevitable tactic with which the modern woman negotiates these conflicting demands on her gender role. The constant shifting in and out of male or female accouterments does not simply constitute frivolous comic relief but in fact reveals the real predicament of the modern girl. She feels straightjacketed by prescribed old gender norms on one hand, and the impossibility to freely experiment with androgyny and female intimacy on the other. A couple of cartoons published in a trade journal at the time capture both the fascination and apprehension about the "girl in disguise." One of them depicts a woman embracing a "man." The caption: "Just one step further, that Miss will surely be disappointed. For the handsome Mister will turn out to be a girl in 'disguise'!" Another one by the same cartoonist portrays a group of bare-chest men staring at a fully dressed young "man," sweating profusely under the scorching sun. The caption: "'Girl in disguise' can only fan herself strenuously in summer, because she cannot bare her chest as others. If she did that, she would reveal her true form!"[93]

Female androgyny, cross-dressing and same-sex intimacy are attributes of the modern girl that captivated intellectuals and petty urbanites in 1930s urban China.[94] Young women flaunted their androgynous fashion, often copied from their screen idols, on the street and in photo studios. The cross-dressing woman was at once seen as a spectacle of freakish curiosity and a sign of cosmopolitanism; she was censored or "corrected" when perceived to threaten patrilineage. The real problem with *Girl in Disguise* was not, as one critic claimed, that "it had nothing to do with contemporary life." Rather, it had everything to do with the gender question and urban modernity in that period. But the film's provocative premise was ultimately undone by its narrative framing. The edgy sexual politics embedded in the film gets compromised at the end, when a son is promptly delivered to fill in the position of a male heir, disqualifying Liying. The modern girl with dubious gender and social identity has been reformed into a good girl, while same-sex affection has been replaced by heterosexual courting rituals, complete with a matchmaker.

SUN YU'S "CHOP-SUEY" STYLE

No discussion of the 1930s contentious film culture would be complete without assessing Sun Yu's contributions; he was actively involved in—and denounced by—both modernist and left circles. In many respects, Sun's work exemplified and redefined vernacular modernism by negotiating and venturing beyond competing modernist claims and expressions. A full assessment of his output before the outbreak of the war in 1937, when Sun left Shanghai for his hometown Chongqing, is not possible here.[95] Rather, I try to place this auteur's work in relation to the questions raised above. I focus on his writings in *Modern Screen* and some features of his films that formed a consistent lyrical visual style, investigated the transition to the metropolis (and beyond), and romanticized revolutionary cosmopolitanism.

Enamoured with both literature and film, Sun had something in common with Tian Han and Liu Na'ou, respective figureheads of the hard and soft film camps. Yet he was not entangled by the love-hate sentiments that most Japan-educated intellectuals felt toward their host-country-turned-enemy. Sun had a solid Sino-American education that allowed him to delve into both classical Chinese poetry and American-style filmmaking. His studies in Jazz Age America imparted a combination of youthful energy, poetic romanticism, social concern, and an unstinting optimism to his films. He grasped the essence of the medium and the demands of his epoch, resulting in a succession of works that helped create the Lianhua "visual style" and a progressive cosmopolitan strand of Shanghai cinema.[96]

The inaugural issue of *Modern Screen* also launched Sun's column, "The Cinematic Chop-Suey House" (*Dianying zasuiguan*).[97] In a series of essays, the "poet of the silver screen" articulated his alternately passionate and abrasive views on cinema, society, and politics. These writings covered a wide range of topics and shed important light on his "writings" on the screen. In "Auspicious Opening," Sun spells out the sources for the metaphor "chop-suey house" and its hybrid content: a northern style sidewalk vendor-made stew made of chopped lamb and oxen entrails and strong spices. Transplanting it from northern China to the streets of Shanghai, Sun believed this quotidian dish was exactly what people without fur coats needed on a cold winter day—cheap but heartwarming, nourishing and energizing. This hearty domestic dish would appeal to Chinese filmmakers and moviegoers because their hearts had turned "cold" by the sluggish development of Chinese cinema. He candidly acknowledges the vernacular origins of his recipe:

> The kind of things sold at the Cinematic Chop-Suey House will of course be disorganized, unstructured: there are intestines, stomachs as well as theories about techniques, sketches of life; there are goat heads, perhaps also dog meat; there is something sweet, something sour, perhaps also something hot. For those who come to eat the chop-suey at my little shop, don't hope to find sea cucumbers or swallow nests because my shop does not have these. But if your

heart has turned cold, please do come into my little place to get warmed up.[98]

This "chop-suey" caters to customers of modest means. The mixing of northern food and southern service indicates a certain kind of popular yet spicy cinematic aspiration for the country as a whole. But creating such a quotidian feast to help revitalize Chinese cinema and restore warmth in the Chinese audiences seems a tall order. Sun makes clear his reluctance to subject this home-style enterprise to any lofty ideology. In "My Mission," his second essay, he does not compare his profession as a director (and a writer) with a priest, a great statesman, or a master educator who professes to save the nation. Instead he identifies himself with a little chop-suey shop vendor, who does not have a trendy "ism" to spice up his chop-suey stew.

His six extant films—*Wild Rose* (*Ye meigui*), *The Blood of Passion on the Volcano* (*Huoshan qingxue*), *Little Toys* (*Xiaowanyi*), *Daybreak* (*Tianming*), *Big Road* (*Da lu*), and *Queen of Sports* (*Tiyu huanghou*)—were made within four years in the aftermath of the 1932 bombing. At that time, the film industry was changing drastically. The intensified political climate and modernization process in Shanghai left indelible marks on this group of thematically and stylistically consistent works.

Taken together, these works may be seen as parts of a larger work unified by female protagonists usually played by either Li Lili or Wang Renmei, two rising stars with athletic sexiness and youthful energy. This consistency may also be attributed to the fact that Sun himself wrote most of the scripts, which did not subscribe to any single ideology. Similar to many films of the time, these films almost unfailingly follow the trajectory of youths migrating to Shanghai from pastoral villages. They are motivated by the oppression of feudalism and imperialism, and lured by urban modernity. The country, at least in its predestruction state, was usually the fountainhead of poetry for both the protagonist and the filmmaker, whereas the city was the bastion of sin, the laboratory of modern subjectivity and revolutionary ideals. Nearly all of the films (with the exception of *Queen of Sports*) focus on the "working people on the bottom of the society."[99] We witness how the country girls and boys transform into sophisticated urban subjects. They become workers, students, prostitutes, social flowers, athletes, artisans, bohemian artists or revolutionaries. They were the true faces of Shanghai: migrants from the Jiangnan region famous for its lush fields, waterways, silk, and rice.

Wild Rose, his earliest extant film, contains many of these features that extended into subsequent films. Written in the wake of September 8, 1931, which marked the Japanese occupation of Manchuria, it portrays a "healthily beautiful and patriotic girl in a fishing village" near the mouth of Wusong River (today's Huangpu River).[100] Xiaofeng (played by Wang Renmei) is the "commander" of a contingent of children playing soldiers around the village. Jiang Bo (Jin Yan), a student of the Shanghai Fine Arts Academy from a rich urban family "discovers" the new image of China's daughter and, of course, his own Cinderella in the barefoot, healthy, and naturally beautiful Xiaofeng.[101] (The two actors tied the knot within two years.) He paints a portrait of her and eventually takes her to the city after a fire kills her father and destroys their home—an obvious allegorical reference to Japanese aggression.

Xiaofeng's entry to the city on Jiang Bo's automobile is a significant, albeit clichéd, element in the city film idioms. The modern vehicle carries the country girl into the urban wonderland and she is led to shop for clothes and get a perm. The sequence is reminiscent of similar sequences in Murnau's *Sunrise* (1927) and Vidor's *The Crowd* (1928). Adorned with an artificial rose Jiang gave her, Xiaofeng has magically turned into a modern girl. However, upon her arrival at Jiang's palatial modern home, her fradulant urban identity is exposed when she throws away her high heels and goes barefoot. Her silk stockings slide down her strong legs in front of the outraged patriarch.

The couple is promptly driven out of the house and forced to support themselves, living on the bottom rung of the society. They move into a *longtang* where several families share a simple row house. (Sun was the first to use a manually operated crane-up device to shoot the cramped housing condition vertically.)[102] The couple's nuptial home is a makeshift structure on the rooftop but yields a generous view of the city's skyline that reminds Jiang of his sojourn as an art student in Paris.[103] Jiang joins his friend Xiao Li (played by Zheng Junli) to paint billboards on the street while Xiaofeng serves as the team's cook. The gendered division of labor here remains traditionally coded, but the four of them form a communal family, a kinship that recurs in *Big Road* (and several Chinese films later on, such as *Street Angel* [1937] and *Crows and Sparrows* [1949]).

Of course, such a fairy tale home proves fragile and is soon torn apart by poverty and misfortune. Jiang cannot sell his "Wild Rose" portrait. Xiaofeng picks up a wallet on the street, which accidentally sends Jiang and his comrades to jail. In order to have Jiang freed, Xiaofeng asks Jiang's father for help. He agrees, but on the condition that she leave her love. Xiaofeng subsequently "disappears" to become a textile worker, only reappear again at the film's "bright tail," when the four friends are united on the street, marching to join "volunteers" for the war against (Japanese) invaders. Jiang Bo jumps out of a dancehall window to join the patriotic parade, indeed prefiguring the trope of passing from "night[life]" to "morning" or from the dream factory to the social reality of the street. The country's nostalgic poetry is thus rewritten, superimposed by cadences composed in tune with the city's rhythm and the time's spirit. The last poetic intertitle indicates: "Like four children, they march forward, arm in arm, on the life's path with smiles and courage."[104]

More interested in lyrical distention than narrative cohesion, revolutionary romanticism than ideological dogmatism, Sun created his films as though he was connecting self-sustaining poetic stanzas into a loose verse. Each of these parts, often set in disparate geographical locations (country and city, China and elsewhere), carries different genre markers and politically "incoherent" messages due to shifting formal structures and often dramatic changes in characters' action (with little if any psychological motivation). It is as though the films were intended for varied audiences, and as such they convey and process competing aesthetic and ideological orientations. Such a chop-suey style is most evident in *Blood of Passion,* also made in 1932, which received mixed reviews. Perhaps Sun Yu's most fantastic film, its plot seems like a poetic concoction rather than a realist tale of a young peasant's international journey toward self-reinvention.

The plot can be divided into to two symmetrical parts according to its geographical distribution and drastic narrative rupture. The first, smaller part is set in the typical Jiangnan country, whereas the second, more fanciful part takes the characters to an exotic volcanic island in Nanyang. Like *Wild Rose,* the film begins in an idyllic setting, Village of Willow Flowers. A series of shots in soft daylight depict the timeless serenity and beauty of the countryside: rippling lake, swimming ducks, plowing water buffalos, herds of sheep, and farmers pumping the waterwheels for irrigation. Song Ke (played by Zheng Junli) is a young farmer who helps his father farm and plays with his beloved sister Lihua (fig. 7.13). But this lyrical landscape is soon ravaged by an evil landlord who orders the abduction of the sister and the killing of the father. Song must flee the village but vows to eradicate all "monsters among humanity."

Years later—as the film enters the second part and a different mode—Song appears in an entirely foreign tropical setting: a cabaret bar. The island, with a bustling port and the bar full of drunken American soldiers and local hooligans, strikes the viewer as a miniature Shanghai. Yet the exotic location, especially the volcano looming large behind the town, gives the film a touch of the fantastic and allegorical. The location's sensual appeal, while allowing Sun Yu to employ "soft" elements to titillate Shanghai moviegoers, suggests his (and Lianhua's) desire to continue courting the Nanyang audience. Rather than simply turning into a prole-

7.13 *The Blood of Passion on the Volcano* (1933): idyllic countryside. (Courtesy of the China Film Archive)

tarian in the city, Song Ke is refashioned as a cosmopolitan subject with a political passion that outstrips both patriotism and parochialism. Described as the "man who never laughs," he attends more to his old localized identity than to an abstract national allegiance. While both parts of the film contain progressive elements that fuel revolutionary passion, they are also suffused with the poetry of nature and love, though with different nuances and intensities. The innocence Song lost he redeems through revenge and eroticism.[105]

The second half's revenge and romantic narrative create an impression that the characters have been reincarnated from the first half of the film. The latter presents an afterlife, an alternate world—one that is not necessarily better but offers possibilities for retribution and redemption. Not only does Song reinvent himself as a cosmopolitan anarchist, but for some unexplained reason the villainous landlord finds his way to the island as well. The symmetrical structure is further reinforced by the appearance of Liuhua (who bears the namesake of Song's village and is played by Li Lili, Sun's leading lady for many subsequent films). Liuhua's name, background, and her naughty way of wrinkling her nose remind him of his dead sister. Yet she is obviously a modern girl by virtue of her profession as a cabaret performer (dancing in Hawaiian-style straw skirt, and again, barefoot) (fig. 7.14). In terms of iconography and screen persona, Li Lili's character (as with her next role in *Daybreak*) is almost a

7.14 *The Blood of Passion on the Volcano:* the lovers reunite on the beach under the moon. (Courtesy of the China Film Archive)

replica of Marlene Dietrich in Josef von Sternberg's *The Blue Angel* (1930) and *Dishonored* (1931). She uses makeup and plays a gramophone; in a soft scene she plays the record with her toes. Liuhua falls for the "man who never laughs" and tries to win his heart with wine and sensual dancing under moonlight on the beach. But Song holds back his desire: "The revenge is not done yet, and so I cannot accept your feelings." True to the film's title, he eventually carries out his revenge on top of an active volcano. After a strenuous struggle amid rolling rocks and flowing lava, Song manages to push the "monster" into the burning crater (fig. 7.15). While the eruption abates, the lovers reunite on the beach. Song holds Liuhua in his arms, walking toward the ocean under tropical moonlight. He is finally ready to consummate their passion; the "man who never laughs" is also finally able to smile again.

The hyperbolic plot, radical incongruity between diverse narrative components, and erratic character transformation (rather than development) in both *Wild Rose* and *Blood of Passion* demonstrate Sun's distinctive brand of vernacular modernism à la cinematic "chop-suey." While his creative energy and progressive outlook were welcomed by the left critics, the romantic sensibility and poetic elements in the films were deemed "unrealistic" or plainly foreign, the latter singled out as the common "malaise" of Lianhua productions.[106] A review in *Chenbao* accused *Wild Rose* of being "poisonous" because of its "worship of individualism,

7.15 *The Blood of Passion on the Volcano:* revenge on the volcano. (Courtesy of the China Film Archive)

advocacy of aestheticism, and sentimental humanism." A flower like "wild rose," the critics contended, would "intoxicate the audience so much that they would turn numb." With regard to *Blood of Passion,* they criticized the "foreign style" fencing in the duel scene and Li Lili's erotic dancing in the straw skirt.[107] Su Feng's review in the same paper simply disparaged the use of the volcano as a "novel and curious" but "unreal," "unnecessary" setting. Song Ke's name was considered too literary, not fit for a farmer. (Simple but also stereotypical peasant names Song Ah-da or Song Dabao were suggested as alternatives, revealing the critic's own patronizing view of laborers.) The critic expressed his annoyance at the hints of fashion, such as Zheng Junli's *modeng* perm and Li Lili's makeup, as unbefitting progressive characters. Above all Su Feng was critical of Sun's lack of class consciousness, despite the latter's professed concern to "depict the suffering of the lower classes." He saw Song Ke's revenge as a merely incidental case and thus hardly representative of class struggle.

In his memoir written decades later, Sun again defended *Blood of Passion*'s ending:

> [T]he young peasant Song Ke I created may look like a "superman" who engages in a personal protest and strife. What I had in mind was, if a farmer from a poor remote village was portrayed as a mature, political leader armed with progressive thinking and the consciousness of relying on the great power of organized masses to

> topple the ruling class, then Song Ke would no longer be just an ordinary young farmer with a rebellious spirit.[108]

This kind of less-than-ideal representation of the proletarian hero or heroine may not have conformed to the ideological agenda of the dogmatic left critics. But through the combination of their ordinary or imperfect action and romantic yearnings, Song Ke's and Liuhua's images, at once idealist and worldly, transcended the divides between the real and fantastic, the rural and urban, the local and global. As such they catered to a particular transnational spectatorship that craved recognizable cultural references (the village) and cosmopolitan imaginaries (the volcanic island). Such a cinematic "chop-suey" is made of a recipe that would stimulate both the mind and the body, releasing daily anxiety as well as galvanizing hope for a better tomorrow.

Sun Yu created his corpus and style against a spectacular but also spectacularly uneven urban modernity. In the first half of the 1930s Shanghai was a city full of promised fortunes and fame, as well as abject poverty and brutal violence. Sun aimed to expose these drastic contrasts and to instigate possible transformations in everyday life and social structure through a particular film language. This cinematic vernacular is composed with rapid shifts in locations, tones of narration, and character transformation. His films incorporated American genre modes, such as urban melodramas of King Vidor and Frank Borzage and sports/campus films that flaunted "YMCA-type" youthful body and energy.[109] On the other hand, Soviet montage theory and techniques further enabled him to articulate social contradictions and utopian aspirations.

While other filmmakers had to wake up from their "pink dream" or "silver dream," Sun embarked on making progressive yet romantic celluloid dreams for the masses—including workers as well as other petty urbanites. As Ding Yaping points out, Sun's commitment to both social progress and cinematic innovation led him to create a particular film language that may be called "unofficial/popular discourse," which for my purpose, may be reformulated as a "vernacular discourse."[110] The popular cinema of the 1920s, in particular the phenomenon of the martial arts film, had opened up a discursive space that was not explicitly politically charged (though never apolitical). The cinema of the 1930s, inflamed by pervasive patriotic fervor and marked by the "left turn," saw radical changes in film culture. Sun was quick to perceive and articulate this change by updating both the form and content of cinematic vernacular modernism.

In conclusion, the animosity between the left critics and the modernists appears to be founded upon diverging views of cinema's political instrumentality versus its entertainment function. This chapter has shown that the seeming polarity in fact masks complex exchanges and interaction between the two camps that cannot be reduced to diametrically opposed views on questions of content versus form, politics versus aesthetics, or art versus market. The left critics and filmmakers were also interested in formal elements (montage, in particular), while the modernists were hardly oblivious to the dominance of capitalism and colonial presence in China. They shared an ambivalence toward Hollywood cinema and a fascination with the Japanese and European avant-garde, though to varying degrees and for different reasons. These conflicting yet overlapping forces spurred rivalries among different cultural communities, as well as creativity and competition that shaped the "golden age" as an assemblage of competing temporalities.

Ultimately, the polemic skirmishes and film practices address the critical question of spectatorship and the identity of Shanghai cinema in a politically volatile time. The modernists celebrated cosmopolitan, promiscuous (sexually, culturally, and politically speaking) character of Shanghai cinema, whereas the left critics (more than the left-wing filmmakers) tried to streamline it into a national cinema and a political weapon. The competing formulas they offered through criticism, translation, scripts, and actual films offered antidotes to the alienation and fragmentation of everyday life in a Shanghai engulfed by modern splendor and misery: champagnes and perfumes alongside blood, sweat, and garbage. The medium of cinema, which until the turn of the decade had been primarily used for entertainment and enlightenment outside the intellectual mainstream, was now charged with the burden of radical social change to save the nation. More crucially, and disquietingly, the war between hard and soft films yielded a cacophony of explanations of the sensory and political economy of the time embodied in the fate of the modern girl and her sexuality; she had to be objectified or domesticated, one way or another. Sun Yu's works, while also products of this contentious time and milieu, went further in exploring the progressive potential of vernacular modernism while refusing to surrender to dogmatism.

CHAPTER EIGHT

SONG AT MIDNIGHT

ACOUSTIC HORROR AND THE GROTESQUE FACE OF HISTORY

AS XINHUA COMPANY'S[1] first conscious attempt at a horror film (*kongbu pian*), *Song at Midnight* (*Yeban gesheng,* 1937) generated massive interest and trepidation. The film is obviously modeled on Rupert Julian's *The Phantom of the Opera,* the sensational horror film released by Universal Pictures in 1925, which features Lon Chaney (dubbed as *Lang-que-nei* in Chinese) in his most famous role.[2] It departs significantly from the silent American antecedent, however. Ma-Xu Weibang's (1905–61)[3] version transforms both a nineteenth-century Parisian Gaston Leroux novel and a Hollywood horror flick into a modern Chinese gothic tale with an ambiguous political and aesthetic message (fig. 8.1).

Song at Midnight retains several key elements of the original: the formula of romance plus horror, the disfigured face, the sexual obsession, the allusion to a revolutionary past, the use of the architectural space of a theater, and finally, the shadowplay effect. In the Chinese version, not only do all the characters take on Chinese names and historically specific identities, the sound track foregrounds and materializes the singing that the silent predecessor lacked. The American version, despite its flirtation with shadowplay and other elements found in Weimar cinema, is largely filmed in the Hollywood paradigm. Although heavily indebted to the American film for thematic structure, stylistically *Song at Midnight* shows more affinity with German expressionist drama and cinema. In a curious way, *Song at Midnight* stands as an instance where both European and

8.1 Ad for *Song at Midnight* (1937). (Courtesy of the China Film Archive)

American influence on Chinese cinema converged and diverged. Adaptation as mimetic act occasions a process of deformation and reformation, which constitutes, in essence, a particular "horrific" form. The film's horror and violence, amplified by its haunting soundtrack and eponymous theme song, echoed contemporary feelings of uncertainty and fear on the eve of the Sino-Japanese war.

Song at Midnight dramatizes an itinerant troupe's strange experiences in an abandoned theater (fig. 8.2). Interestingly, the film's horror effect and its commercial success were enhanced by the use of the Lyrical Theater for its premiere.[4] Its February 1937 release created a sensation in Shanghai, as the popular silent film actor Gong Jianong recalled:

> Before *Midnight* officially premiered at the Lyric Theater, Zhang Shankun [the producer], who knew the importance of publicity, had a huge portrait of the disfigured character hung up in front of the theater gate. Green bulbs were used for the eyeballs in the demonic face, further increasing its hideousness and the sense of horror. The following day, a newspaper reported that a child had been scared to death [by the portrait], and this immediately received lots of attention. Zhang Shankun seized the opportunity and spread the news further, stirring up the whole of Shanghai. The premier of *Midnight* was timely. Newspaper advertisements for it carried the phrase "Please don't take your children with you," which stimulated the curiosity of the audience all the more, and they rushed to see the film. The film was sold out for more than thirty days at the theater, and held the box-office record for domestic-made films in 1936. Jin Shan and Hu Ping became popular stars instantly, and the director Ma-Xu Weibang solidified his peculiar status as the authority on the horror film. The foundation of the Xinhua Company was thus solidified by *Midnight*.[5]

The sensational effect produced by the superimposition of the phantom singer's grotesque face on the facade of the Lyric Theater proved to be an effective strategy for galvanizing the audience's appetite for reverse mimesis and sensory stimulation. The "projection" of the singer's body on the architectural structure (particularly a cinema) also underscored the tension-ridden relationship between body and space, the abject and the representational, in the film and in the horror genre in general.

Given the film's mass appeal and its influence on later film history, both the film and its context tell us much about the interaction between film culture and national culture in that immediate prewar period. The dynamic yet often conflicting relationship between the film's visual style and its acoustic qualities reveal the unresolved tensions between silent

8.2 The abandoned theater. (Courtesy of the China Film Archive)

and sound film, as well as between the various ideologies and aesthetics competing at this crucial moment in Chinese culture. Produced at the demise of the silent period, *Song at Midnight* not only provides a dark and grotesque view of its epoch but also urgently provides an alternative to mainstream "national defense" films. It attempts to reconcile silent and sound film and to legitimize a popular art cinema in the midst of a national crisis. The phantom lover's scarred face and the disembodied voice are the uncanny sites at which unconsummated desire and incomplete history resurface and erupt.

The main plot unfolds in the same theater in two time periods: the early Republican period of the 1910s and a decade later with the return of the repressed love and traumatic memory. Thus the film presents itself as a historiographic project in which repressed history and memory are embodied in the hero's disfigured face and the heroine's mental derangement. This cinematic historiography is emphatically somatic and visceral, writing this strong tale of modern China in "the most physiological of genres," one that thrives on "preliterate, somatic modes of knowing."[6] The repetition, or rather revision, of history and its troubled redemption (through the "awakening" heroine) points to the vulnerability of this bodily inscribed history. Moreover, the film's constant allusion to the historical kinship between theater and cinema—especially the reference to the early New Drama, a catalyst for the emergence of Chinese cinema—also makes this film a meditation on film history.

The richness of *Song at Midnight* springs as much from its implosive textuality as the multiple historical dimensions wrought on the skin of the film. *Laborer's Love* (1922) provided the possibility for probing the "beginning" of early Chinese cinema in the teahouse milieu and an emerging film world within the broader vernacular culture. As a romance that ends in horror and destruction rather than a matrimonial happy ending, *Song at Midnight* registers the impeding end of an era, which, however, refuses any simple closure.

THE THEATER OF SOUND AND FURY

The aftershocks of the arrival of sound at the end of the 1920s lasted well beyond the mid-1930s.[7] Sound functioned as a critical catalyst in the golden age of Chinese silent film. The advent of sound highlighted and complicated the linguistic application of the vernacular in cinema. It triggered a new tide of public discourse on cinema's ontology and ideological function, as well as a series of sound experiments that reshaped the sensorial experience in and outside movie theaters.

The desire to naturalize the mechanical correspondence between the articulation of sound and its source generated both excitement and anxiety about the aesthetic efficacy and social meaning of this new acoustic "dominant," to borrow a term conceived by the Russian linguists, to integrate sound and meaning into an "inseparable whole" in the study of poetry. Roman Jakobson, the leading voice of the prague school of linguistics and semiotics, defined it as "the focusing component of a work of art: it rules, determines, and transforms the remaining components. . . . It is the dominant which guarantees the integrity of the structure."[8] In other words, the acoustic dominant does not exist in isolation; it is part of a dynamic system when it interacts with other elements and brings about structural change. Moreover, the notion may be applied to the "art of a given epoch," beyond the poetic work for which the term was first conceived. In this spirit, I apply the concept to the advent of sound in Shanghai cinema and its impact on the transforming film world. While it ended a long silent era, the new acoustic dominant also signaled a new beginning in Chinese film history with mixed repercussions.

The ascendance of the acoustic dominant in Chinese film history between 1930 and 1936 was characterized by a heterogeneous body of practice. Not only did silent films continue to be made and perfected, early sound film was also divided by a number of technologies—ranging from the use of phonographs, separate wax disks, and finally movie-tone film stock. This was in part carried over from the sound practices of silent film. American observers in the mid-1920s reported, for instance, that during the showing of a domestic film in a Shanghai theater, a Russian orchestra played foreign music, "being in toto a peculiar conglomeration, including music from *Madam Butterfly*, and from other musical plays." (The presence of a Russian orchestra is hardly surprising as many Russians fled the 1917 revolution and came to live in Shanghai.) In some theaters in Tianjin, however, "music . . . is sometimes offered through the medium of a phonograph, upon which Chinese or foreign pieces may be played." Because foreign music was still rather alien to the Chinese audience at large, in strictly Chinese theaters only Chinese records were selected.[9]

Indeed, in the films of this period, the line between silent and sound is hard to draw. Although many perceived the arrival of sound as an assault on the "great deaf"—as silent film was fondly called at the time—this reaction was complicated by a mixture of wonder and awe. The onset of sound, along with the coming of age of the music-recording industry, radically redefined the meaning of the body in cinema and resulted in a reordering of the sensory hierarchy in the larger arena of vernacular culture. Many silent and early sound films used sound to embellish visual attraction and dramaturgy rather than to conceal the process of narration. The "song and dance" film (*gewu pian*), a genre foregrounding the body in motion, for instance, had much music and was the most apt vehicle for early sound experiments.

The ascendance of the acoustic dominant, extending more than a half decade, coincided with the onslaught of Hollywood sound films in the Chinese market on one hand and Japanese military invasion on the other. The implementation of sound proved an intense cultural drama at times bordering on horror and violence. Sound thus became an important component in the formation of a certain "aesthetic of emergency" that accompanied the emergence of the left-wing cinema and then the "national defense" cinema. A strand of these cinemas (such as Sun Yu's and Cai Chusheng's films) was popularized through the use of sound and, in particular, the invention of the theme song. Some theme songs became hits, generating sensations beyond movie theaters. Moreover, they also served the purpose of mobilizing the masses' political consciousness and commitment to the patriotic cause. The most celebrated examples include "Song of the Big Road" (*Dalu ge*) in *Big Road*, "The Song of the Graduates" (*Biye ge*) in *Plunder of Peach and Plum* (1934), and the "The Marching of the Volunteers" (*Yiyongjun jinxingqu*) in *Children of Troubled Times* (1935). The last was adopted by the People's Republic of China as the national anthem.

The transition to sound necessarily brought the issue of speech into the forefront. Early sound experiments hardly attended to dialogue, but rather focused on inserting musical numbers into narrative space or simply used them to display the aural spectacle. Some later attempts at producing films with "total dialogue" (*quanbu yousheng duibai*) tried obsessively to reproduce dramatic speech (as many sound film actors came from spoken drama backgrounds) at the expense of diegetic absorption. The same happened with the use of sound effects. Many early sound films neglected sound effects altogether, producing a ghostly quiet diegetic space in which characters deliver disembodied lines, whereas other films, devoid of pronounced dialogue, used sound effects for comic relief or to create a particular ambiance. These divergent attempts at incorporating or excluding speech, sometimes simply for technical or financial reasons, speak to a polyphonic conception of sound cinema.

The end of the silent period is commonly designated as 1936, after major Chinese studios succeeded in making synchronized "total" sound films (which include musical score, speech and sound effects), and after most urban theaters had completely installed sound equipment. However, silent films continued to be made sporadically until 1938 and were shown in small theaters or rural areas for many years afterward. Silent film's memory and aesthetic sensibility were carried over into the sound era, despite the increasingly marginal status of that form.

Notably, the companies heralding sound experimentation had also been the chief players in the martial arts film craze. Hu Die, Xu Qingfan, and Wu Suxin, among other actresses made famous by their roles as martial heroines reinvented themselves to fit into their new sound film roles.[10] Their early sound productions manifest a passionate initiative similar to the initiatives channeled into creating martial arts special effects, such as the spectacle of flying. The first Chinese "sound" film using a wax disk, *The Singing Girl Red Peony* (Mingxing, 1930), starring Hu Die, is a story about a Peking opera actress whose quest for personal happiness ends in tragedy. The film boasted Peking opera tunes sung by the protagonist. The second experiment, *The Singing Beauty* (*Yu meiren*, Youlian, 1931), also contained musical numbers, which were advertised as the film's chief attraction. Both companies used different names for their sound productions. Mingxing used "Minzhong" while Youlian used "Yimin." Though their quality was far from ideal, the early sound films turned out to be hot commodities. The exhibition rights of *Red Peony* were bought by Nanyang distributors for more than ten times the price of a silent film. *Singing Beauty*, though not the "first" and lacking a complete sound track, still made a profit five to six times more than its silent production.[11]

The results of these experiments were uneven. Various efforts were made to improve the quality of acoustics and synchronization. Hu Die recalls that *Red Peony* was made in cooperation with the Pathé recording company in Shanghai. The recording proved to be a difficult job; it took five or six attempts before a line was properly recorded at the same pace as the image track. The projection situation was often comedic when the disk and the film played out of sync.[12] While *Red Peony* used postrecording on wax disks, *Singing Beauty* tried the reverse, producing the sound disk first and then playing it during the shooting. However, because of the differences in the speed of the phonograph, the camera and the projector, the "synchronization" of sound and image track turned out to be an ordeal.[13] Moreover, strictly speaking, both were only partial-sound films. *Red Peony* lacked sound effects, whereas *Singing Beauty,* due to financial constraints, left much dialogue and music unrecorded. Technology was the main attraction for these films, very much in the "display" spirit characteristic of early exhibition practice. In a sense, early sound cinema can be seen as the next cinema of attractions (and distractions) wave, following the martial-arts film.

Dissatisfied with the wax disk's nonsynchronous effects, other companies tried the sound-on-film technology with the help of foreign expertise. The first synchronized film (Kinotone), *Peace after Storm* (*Yuguo tianqing,* Da Zhongguo and Jinan, 1931), was the result of a joint venture by two small companies that sent a production team to Japan to use the equipment there (fig. 8.3). The event produced a big sensation in the media. A Chinese student wrote from Japan about his encounter with the team, praising their effort to make a "complete sound film with singing, dialogue, martial arts, and romance." With five musicians and two phoneticians working hard, the film will have "melodious music and soft-spoken dialogue, as well as all the sounds of the universe." Compared to the "sandy" effect of the wax disk used in *Red Peony,* the quality of *Peace after Storm* would be on a par with foreign talkies.[14] *Movie Magazine* carried a picture of sample strips of the film to demonstrate the wonder of acoustic celluloid; another picture showed the in-studio shooting with a big boomer extended over the orchestra.[15] One advertisement for the film in *Movie Weekly* dramatized the event thus: "The film has twelve reels, and is 14,134 inches long. It has 977 lines of dialogue, consisting of 6935 sentences. There are four original composed songs and other contemporary Peking opera tunes. The score contains twenty-six melodies that are played according to the plot."[16] It seems the adoption of the synchronized film stock also made possible the use of extensive dialogue, as exemplified by the making and promotion of *Peace after Storm.* The obsession with the quantity of lines and musical embellishment suggest a conception of sound film that still regarded sound as the attraction rather as tool of narration. Because of its Japanese connection, however, the

8.3 Ad for *Peace after Storm,* one of the early sound experiments. (Courtesy of the China Film Archive)

public resisted the film after its release, and the Chinese film world refused to credit it as the first domestically made synchronized film.[17]

Tianyi proved its business acumen in the transition from wax recording to synchronization. Shortly after its first sound film made on wax disk (*The Tolling Bell* [*Zhongsheng*]) was destroyed in a studio fire, it quickly built a new glass studio and secured a loan for a sound camera from an American company to make *Spring Arrives in the Singing World* (*Gechang chunse,* 1931). Tianyi planned to produce the first film with the latest technology—Movietone—and thereby establish its leading position in sound film. Abandoning its initial plan to travel to Japan, the company hired two American cameramen at astronomical salaries and imported the most up-to-date equipment from the United States.[18] The film was based on a successful New Drama piece called *The Beautiful Dancing Girl* (*Wunü meiguniang*) that was playing at the Xiaowutai Theater, a venue the Shao family established in 1922. The film received mixed reviews. The viewers had become more critical after the initial enchantment with sound experiments wore off. While one critic questioned the authenticity of the nativeness of the production; another viewer from Canton expressed his disappointment with its incomplete song recordings.[19] A more demanding critic pointed to its "squared" framing, overuse of close-ups, and unrealistic or missing narrative elements. In the end, "it did not leave any deep impression on the audience except for the lingering singing."[20] Tianyi's costly experiment in synchronized filmmaking, however, did not end the practice of partial sound film—either on wax disk or sound stock, usually without a full score or sound effects. The terrain of film production and exhibition remained largely nonsynchronous until 1936, allowing for the competition, coexistence, and combination of a variety of technologies and aesthetics.

Technical ordeals aside, early sound films commonly privileged singing girls and self-reflexive references to the theater world. The musical numbers were not usually integrated into the narratives but were sung by characters playing characters and dubbed by famous vocalists, hence the term *xi zhong xi* (play within a play). Indeed, the possibility of conflating the singing voice of an opera star (such as Mei Lanfang in the case of *Red Peony*) and the face of a film star like Hu Die was one of the attractions of the sound film. As Hu Die later recalled, after the release of the film, her fans came to regard her as the original singer and invented stories to explain how she learned Peking opera. As she noted: "I am not Mei Lan*fang* [square], but Mei Lan*yuan* [round]. It was the round gramophone record [*yuanpan*] that was singing for me!"[21]

The anecdote underscores the permeability of the theater and film, which became more pronounced with the advent of reproducible sound.

It also foregrounded the fundamentally *asynchronistic* relationships of body, face, and voice in the cinematic space, despite the frenzy for synchronization. The proliferation of the Chinese character for song (*ge*) in early sound-film titles is indicative of a film culture captivated by the sonic spell, and influenced by Hollywood musicals as well as traditional Chinese opera. The split body of the screen actor and the singer in the recording studio underscores the disunity inherent in what Mary Ann Doane aptly calls the "fantasmatic body" reconstituted by technology.[22]

Chinese cinema's romance with Peking opera has a long history. In 1905, the Fentai Photo Studio in Beijing filmed the Peking opera actor Tan Xinpei, inaugurating what Mary Farquhar and Chris Berry call the "shadow opera" tradition in Chinese film.[23] In 1920 and 1924, Mei Lanfang performed in several short films made by the Commercial Press and the Minxin Company, respectively. The films consisted mostly of episodes accentuating choreographed movement.[24] The early sound film once more turned to Peking opera, only this time emphatically focusing on the aural aspect. This cross-fertilization lent popularity to both art forms and their stars.[25] Most of the early sound films embellished with operatic tunes were modern tales about the melodramatic fate of the singer. The play within a play formula allowed parallel unfolding of different kinds of theater practice (e.g., opera versus spoken drama), as well as the interface of the theater world and the cinema world.

Two Stars (1931), an extant film with a partial sound track recorded on wax disk, is a typical example of this doubling formula and uses a "star is born" tale (fig. 8.4).[26] The "two stars" reflect the constellation of the theater and film galaxies, also suggested by the comic moniker for the studio, Yinghang, literally the Milky Way. In the narrative, a film production team on location in scenic Hangzhou overhears a girl singing who turns out to be Li Yueying, the daughter of a recently retired Nanyang musician. The crew is so captivated that they summon another director from Shanghai to see (and hear) if she is right for the starring role in his film.

The film within the film is structured around the process of shooting a Peking opera about the Tang emperor Xuanzong's love for his concubine. In the course of filming, the on-stage theatrical love story gets intertwined with the backstage romance between the actors (famous opera actress Zi Luolan opposite Lianhua's poster-boy Jin Yan). The constant shift between classical costumes and modern fashion, the archaic Peking opera sets and place of contemporary urban leisure (such as a miniature golf course and dance hall) echoed the shift between silence and sound, as well as the cinematic and dramatic. The long takes of the scene of Zi Luolan singing in her operatic role are contained in rather static framing redolent of a stage tableau as though the audience is suddenly transported to an opera theater.

8.4 *Two Stars* (1931). (Courtesy of the China Film Archive)

This scene of *live* singing is contrasted with a later scene when singing becomes disembodied. At a company party celebrating the film's success, a tango dance is interrupted when a giant radio at the center of the dance floor is turned on. The radio is broadcasting the film live from the theater at the moment when the concubine starts to sing the opera tune. While everyone listens raptly, the actress is saddened by the song because it evokes her unrequited love for the actor. The radio reproduces the film event as a sound event; at the same time, the recorded voice being played at the theater uncannily returns, with a new layer of mediation, to the source of its bodily origin. The singer listens to her own voice, now loaded with her ambivalence.

The spectacle of singing in these early sound films proves to be rather discontinuous and volatile. The fate of the singer in *Two Stars,* as in *Red Peony,* is a tragic one. The female protagonist eventually renounces the freedom and romantic love associated with the public articulation of her voice. Red Peony loses her voice onstage after suffering from her good-for-nothing husband's physical and psychological abuse. As a consequence, she is demoted from being a top star to playing minor roles. In *Two Stars,* the rising talent Li Yueying eventually leaves the urban "Milky Way" riddled with both glamour and pain after a thwarted love affair with the male star. Similarly, *Singing Beauty* and *Spring Arrives to the Singing World* portray the unhappy endings of singing girls' backstage lives. In all these instances, the voice of the singing girl is the source of both attraction and eventual (self-)destruction.

The dramatic conflict is often predicated on the conflict between the public and the private, usually in the form of a woman's career and her personal life, and between free love and moral strictures imposed by social norms, that is, arranged marriage or the sanctity of family. The voice of the singer thus becomes the site of both dramatic and social tension associated with new technology. Just as the female knights-errant in martial arts films embodied an anarchic tendency, charging the silent screen with an exploding energy, the singing girl's aural excess both stimulated and unsettled the still predominantly silent film scene.

As the advent of sound challenged the practice of screenwriting, the tension between the verbal and visual presentation in silent film was now complicated by the relationship between image and sound. Significantly, the voice of the singing girl in early sound films is often pitched against musical writing. At the end of *Red Peony,* her tragedy is explained away thus: "Hers is a hopeless case. It's all because she is uneducated and has sung too many old opera tunes."[27] Illiteracy was a traditional stigma associated with majority of actors, who typically entered a theatrical troupe instead of school as children due to poverty. Her singing is singled out as the source of calamity, and she alone has to bear the consequences of her gift, or rather, the public consumption of it. In a sense, singing is equated with orality, and thus is more in tune with popular culture than with literary culture.

Singing Beauty is another case in point. The film deserves a closer look because it foreshadows many elements found in *Song at Midnight.* The heroine again sings in a song and dance troupe; she is the object of desire for several men around her, including the troupe's playwright. He is so infatuated with her beauty and talent that he decides to write a play especially for her. This play within the play is based on a classical Peking opera (the legend of Xiangyu and his concubine Yu Ji) and offers a mirror image of the romance between the actress and the playwright. Upon learning that the singing girl has become engaged to the son of the troupe's leader, the playwright leaves the troupe after a failed attempt to disfigure his own face with nitric acid—a motif central to *Song at Midnight.* Using acid to "liquidate" his handsome face is an act of "concretizing or eternalizing love" (*gu'ai*), so his undying love would be permanently etched in scars. However, his servant stops this act of self-destruction. Instead, he goes into a voluntary exile only to become seriously injured in a car accident, leaving him with a scarred face and a crippled leg. Years later, when he meets the singing girl who is just about to get married, his old scar bursts open and he quickly dies of both physical and emotional pain (fig. 8.5).

The film ends in the death of the playwright who, before leaving the

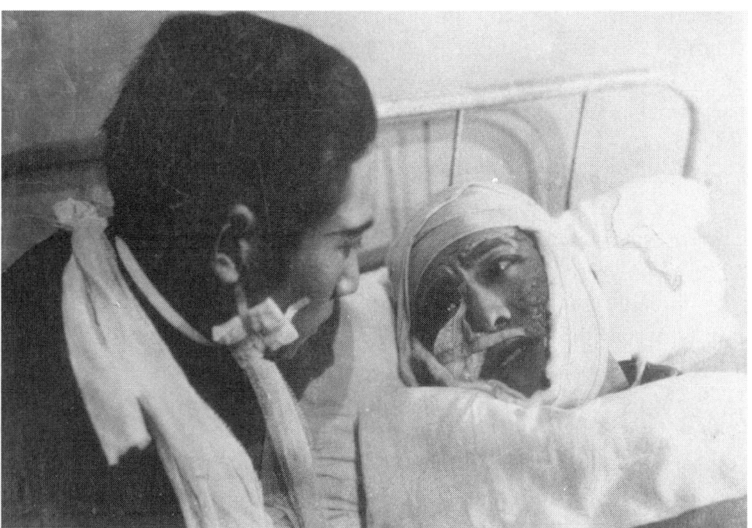

8.5 The disfigured face in *The Singing Beauty* (1931). (Courtesy of the China Film Archive)

"sordid" world for good, asks the actress to sing the songs he wrote for her. Overwhelmed by grief and guilt, she dies at his bedside, thus bringing a romantic tragedy to a "perfect" conclusion. The playwright's unfulfilled desire is redeemed by the girl's remorse and a private performance—returning the songs to him as a ritual sacrifice. The song that brought her fame is now turned into a swan song for an unrequited love. The songwriter's death makes it imperative for her to die as well, for without the authorization of his compositions, she remains voiceless.

The advent of sound provided the opportunity for cinema to actively draw on various old and new forms: the "song and dance" theater, the "beauty meets scholar" story of Butterfly fiction, and the Hollywood formula of backstage drama.[28] In a transformation of an old motif the beauty becomes the singing girl and the scholar the musician or songwriter. This transfiguration was certainly mediated by sound, yet the persistent melodramatic impulse (note that the Greek *melos* means "song") demonstrates the roots of early sound film in the narrative conventions of the vernacular culture at large. Technically, it also allowed the cinematic mise-en-scène of different bodies inhabiting the "same" sound and narrative space.

The plight of the playwright cum songwriter demonstrated the dilemma the screenwriter faced in a new way of "composing" for the screen. Significantly, in the years following the first experiments, a group of young composers and songwriters appeared on the film scene. Xian Xinghai (1905–45), Nie Er (1912–35), Ren Guan (1900–41), and An E became important forces in creating Chinese film music. Among them, Xian Xinghai composed the score and songs for *Song at Midnight.* As opposed to the scholar or literary writer that had dominated the silent screen, the composer or opera playwright signaled the birth of a new male subject. The female singer's success, once taking on a life of its own, often proves to be too excessive to be contained by the original, and self-centered, intention of the composer. The films' tragic endings thus raise a fundamental question concerning the relationship between the singer and the writer, connected or divided by technology.

THEME SONG AS THE LOCUS OF THE NEW DOMINANT

The early sound films that situate the singer at the dramatic center in effect constitute an ambivalent discourse on the ontological meaning and cultural implication of sound cinema. Yet, the singer's rise and fall cannot be dissociated from the songs she transmits and popularizes. These early sound films relied heavily on theme songs that was emblematic of the sonic age, as a nodal point in a larger acoustic space where a set of leisure practices converged. Some theme songs even become vital forces in mobilizing the masses for national salvation. The theme songs circulated, in a variety of forms, generating multifaceted mass phenomena that redefined the meaning of movie-going and the theater as public space. The eponymous theme song of *Song at Midnight,* like many others, not only helped to draw audiences to the theater but eventually acquired a life of its own, assuming the role of an aural memento by which the film would be remembered decades later.

The symbiosis between the singing girl and the male composer, a reflection of the troubled marriage between sound and cinema, is perhaps best exemplified in Sun Yu's *Wild Flowers* (*Yecao xianhua;* Minxin/Lianhua, 1930), the first film to use a theme song for quasi-diegetic purposes.[29] In the film a young musician (Jin Yan) discovers that the flower-vending girl he rescued from a car accident (Ruan Lingyu) has a beautiful "oriole-like" voice. He invites her to play the leading singer in the opera he is writing. Her debut turns out to be an astounding success and she becomes a star overnight. The musician proposes marriage, but the girl, pressured by his rich father and fearful of ruining his future, feigns disinterest. Toward the end of the film, weakened by her longing, she faints and spits blood on the stage. Subsequently, she loses her voice. The musician returns and comforts her by saying, "Don't worry. From now on, let me be your voice."[30]

The film has been regarded as an example of the ambiguous image of the modern woman in Shanghai.[31] What I find most revealing about this film is its unique place in the implementation of sound. Not only is its subject matter preoccupied with the production of sound and its reception, the film literally inserts a sound product—namely, the theme song—in the diegetic space. Sun is best known for his films *Daybreak, Queen of Sports, Big Road,* and other canonical films of the golden age. Little attention has been paid to Sun Yu's sporadic yet pioneering experiment with sound in that period. Prior to his work with Lianhua, he had experimented with the use of recorded music for his films. During the exhibition of *Tears of Xiaoxiang* (1928), a martial arts–magic spirit film, he arranged to play recorded Chinese pipe music when a poem written in archaic style appeared in an intertitle card. The poetic lines were thus animated by the music and appeared to address the audience without the visible presence of the speaking body. Years later Sun called the event "perhaps the first film song in a Chinese silent film."[32] Of course, the use of music in the movie theater was nothing new. Where there were no musicians, recorded music was habitually used.[33] Sun's ingenious innovation, however, was the first attempt to "synchronize" silent speech with an external sound source, thereby carving out a momentary virtual sound space in the diegetic space, while also carrying over the tradition of accompaniment.

Sun's play with both silent and sound techniques indicates an ambiguous moment in Chinese film history when disparate aesthetic practices converged in the movie theater. He was completing his film education in the United States at a crucial time for sound experimentation. The introduction of Vitaphone in 1926, the release of *Don Juan* the same year, and *The Jazz Singer* a year later are together commonly recognized as the moments inaugurating sound's full admission to cinema, despite the fact that these early sound films are far from complete talkies. Returning to China where the film industry was entering the heyday of silent film, Sun nevertheless brought his exposure to sound film into his work. As in the case of other national cinemas, China's protracted transition was partly determined by economic and technological disadvantage but also conditioned by a certain political and aesthetic resistance toward American talkies. American sound films had been shown at numerous first-run theaters in major cities since 1929, but they were not welcome because of the unintelligibility of the language and lack of adequate resources for simultaneous translation. For example, one critic points to the unintelligibility of not just English but also various accents and dialects in imported talkies, so they were even more difficult to watch than foreign silent films. He compared the frustration to watching a fine opera performance by Mei

Lanfang without knowing anything about Peking opera.[34] My interviews with several old Shanghai moviegoers also confirm this. It was more of a trend and as a way of showing one's social status that a certain audience went to see the foreign talkies. (Later on, earphones were provided to solve the translation problem.) The Chinese audience at large quickly returned to the more comfortable environment of homemade silent films and partial-sound films.

Sun's experiment in *Tears of Xiaoxiang* led him to create a full-fledged theme song for *Wild Flowers.* Sun's penchant for enhancing the role of songs in his films may have as well sprung from his lyrical impulse. The possibility of literally and musically articulating poems with the aid of sound technology, however rudimentary at the time, seemed alluring not only for expanding the sensory pleasure of cinema. It would also be instrumental for reviving the oral and tonal quality of classical Chinese poetry, which was supposed to be sung or chanted. When Sun wrote the theme song "Looking for My Brother" (*Xunxiong ci*) for *Wild Flowers,*[35] he employed a professional composer (his brother Sun Chengbi) to write the score. The recording was contracted to the Great China Recording Company with the two stars Jin Yan and Ruan Lingyu, and accompanied by the Carlton Theater Orchestra, using a combination of Chinese and Western instruments. When the film was publicly shown, Sun spent three days in the theater taking charge of the phonograph himself to ensure the "lip-sync" effect of the singing, before he could entrust the task to the assistants he had trained.[36]

The theme song's contribution to the film's success went beyond the confines of the auditorium. In fact, the theme song proved to be a complex cultural event in itself. The film functioned at best as its surrogate parent. Recorded in advance, the album *Looking for My Brother* was released simultaneously with the film. It was repeatedly advertised in, for instance, *Yingxi zazhi,* a monthly put out by Lianhua's publishing division.[37] Issue number 10 from 1930 alone carried three advertisements for the film—two of them about the song's appeal. Located in the inside cover, promotional text for the film outlines several special features of the film above the illustration of the embracing couple against Shanghai's silhouetted modern skyline. In addition to the theme (*juzhi*), sets (*beijing*), and comic relief (or interludes, *chuancha*), the theme song (*tige*) is a main attraction. The advertising verse about the song reads

A play within a play
Looking for my brother over thousands of miles
Sung together by Jin and Ruan
It's both sad and empowering.

The reader is also promised that the power of the song is so strong that the song will "wind around the roof beam of your house for three days" after seeing the film. This description, somewhat hyperbolic due to the use of a classical idiom, signaled the emergence of a mass phenomenon that not only crossed the division between the public and private spheres, but also significantly broadened the experiential horizon of the film.

The other large advertisement in the same issue of *Film Magazine* relates the theme song to a different sensorial regime (fig. 8.6). The left half of the page shows an illustration of the two stars singing, in costume. The text indicates that the song sheet for the theme song, in both Chinese and English, can be purchased at major bookstores and movie theaters for twenty cents. The right half of the page, however, promotes the Xinyue (New Moon) recording company, which produced the album. It lists more than two dozen albums of original sound (*yuanyin*) recordings, and includes "Looking for My Brother." The illustration immediately above the list depicts, if in an overstated way, the emergence of a particular audience. A young man dressed in a Chinese robe and vest sits in a rattan chair with his head resting on a pillow listening intently to a huge record. The "title" of the record is actually the trademark of the recording company, the New Moon. The central idea of the advertisement is spelled out in the text below, under the rubric "A Shortcut for Learning a Song." Lamenting the difficulty of learning songs, the caption goes on to say that "only the records of the New Moon company contain clear and accurately pronounced sentences, and those wishing to learn new songs will thus most likely succeed [by listening to them]."

Clearly, as illustrated by these advertisements, an emerging listening subject, partially overlapping with the film spectator, began to occupy a substantial place with considerable autonomy in the everyday world of leisure consumption around 1930. The record's mass appeal lies in its democratic potential—that everyone could learn to *sing* like film stars, if not act like them. The theme song could be acquired separately from the film and be played over and over again in one's living room thus triggering a gradual yet profound transformation in the structure of the cinematic experience as a whole. The theme song as a new attraction was incorporated into the space of the film narrative and the theater, yet circulated as a commodity in bookstores, music shops, and private living rooms. It constituted the nexus of the "system" of "films, radio, and magazines" in a restructured "culture industry."[38] As a cultural object that is inherently mobile and malleable, the theme song functioned as a catalyst in linking previously disparate urban spaces within a shared cultural geography of leisure consumption.

Because of its cohesive as well as destabilizing role in the transition to

8.6 *Wild Flowers* (1930): ad for the album with the theme song "Looking for Brother," and other Xinyue albums (from *Yingxi zazhi,* vol. 1, no. 10, 1930).

sound, the theme song crystallizes the new dominant in the Shanghai film culture in the first half of the 1930s. Insofar as this epoch is highly uneven culturally and technologically, it is also a "shifting dominant" because it emerges from the horizon of a cluster of "transitional regions"[39] —the silent film, multiple sound technologies, theater, the phonograph, radio, magazines, and last but not least, the street. Theme songs were played through loudspeakers in front of the theater as a strategy to entice the audience. Gong Jianong recalled how, in promoting the film *Twin Sisters* (*Zimei hua,* Mingxing, 1933), Mingxing studio had the theater playing the theme song "Lullaby" (*Cuimianqü*) in front of the Central Theater where the film premiered. The passersby were told that one could learn the song quickly by watching the movie. A song sheet was also included in its premiere catalogue. The film was a huge success. Another sensationally popular film, *Fisherman's Ballad* (*Yu guang qu,* Lianhua, 1932), premiered at the Lyrical Theater and sold records of the eponymous theme song before the film's release in order to rival *Twin Sisters Flowers.* "So when the film was first shown, everywhere people were already singing 'Clouds float in the sky above the sea . . .'" Both films ran continuously for almost three months.[40]

The ascendance of the new dominant had implications for the configuration of space and time in cinematic perception as a whole. According to Roman Jakobson, visual signs are organized for the most part in a "spatial dimension," whereas auditory signs (such as speech) are primarily ordered temporally.[41] The theme song, stemming from the marriage between the visual art of the cinema and the auditory (as well as performative) art of the theater, became a "transitional region" in which such a spatial and temporal division collapsed. As an audiovisual experience that exceeded the confines of the movie theater, it was mapped onto the multiple temporalities manifested in its various incarnations or extensions. As such, it intimated the emergence of an acousticized spectatorship that brought together nonsynchronous aesthetic tastes and social experiences.

As a linchpin between the visual and the auditory regimes of perception and diverse narrative elements, the theme song became the site where a particular libidinal economy was produced. The contemporary slogan of the "union of sight and sound" (*shengse lianyin*), used liberally in advertisements as well as popular discourse, is redolent with erotic connotations. The indulgence in *shengse*—the enjoyment of music, songs, dance, wine, and visual delight—has always been linked to sensual and sexual pleasures in its idiomatic usage. *Lianyin,* on the other hand, literally means "tie the knot," or "marriage." The amorous relationship between the singing girl and the composer-writer so prevalent in early sound films may be viewed in light of this marriage between the senses and the technologies that convey them. However, that romance, as we have seen, is fraught with tension and subject to tribulations caused by existing social and material conditions.

If the reproducibility of the visual image was at the heart of the "optical unconscious" in the search for a film language in the early-mid 1920s, then the reproduction of sound—and hence theme songs—posed a similar, though qualitatively different, shift in the 1930s. Both processes witnessed a transformation from self-reflexive experimentation to integration. In time, the status of mass produced copies became less a challenge to authenticity than a widely accepted new order of things.

The implementation of sound generated multiple versions of duplication, as the movie theater became a dynamic and at times chaotic laboratory. Much of the discussion provoked by the frantic yet innovative attempts to "tie the knot" between the theater and the cinema on the one hand, and sight and sound on the other, centered on the question of fidelity or authenticity in various forms of synchronization. However, the actual screening of a film often led to unexpected results that disrupted a uniform experience because of differences in the theaters and in the skills of projectionists and phonograph operators. Despite the rhetoric about the appeal of a reproduction of the original sound of a song, the listeners' lived experiences of the song in different media and contexts render the notion of origin evasive; the contexts of the performance were constantly fractured and multiplied. In fact, Jin Shan, who played the phantom singer in *Song at Midnight,* lip-synched the songs to the famous singer-composer Shen Jialun's recorded voice. Both Mei Lanfang and Shen Jialun are thus the phantom origins of the singing roles on the screen at the beginning and the end of the transition to sound, respectively. In Shen's case, because the plot explicitly revolves around the reproduction of voice and identity in a haunted theater, the ambiguity in the relationship between the original and the copied voice is doubly played out on and off the screen.

The ambivalence toward the legitimacy of the singer as an authority of knowledge makes the film an exemplary case for reflecting on the complexity of film history at the closing of the silent period and the golden age. The eponymous theme song of the film, with lyrics by the left-wing playwright and poet Tian Han and music by Xian Xinghai stems from the complex genealogy of the production and consumption of early sound film generally and the theme song specifically outlined so far. In the early partial-sound films, the presence of the singer as the embodiment of the new dominant was always foregrounded, both technically and diegetically; it was even more so when mismatching resulted in an unintended separation of the body from its sound space. The figure of the singer and the importance of the theme song in *Song at Midnight*, however, assert their force through a deliberate mechanism of invisibility and the elusive movement of the grotesque ventriloquist. The theme song seems more internalized by the diegesis or serves as an active narrative vehicle, while the singing subject becomes radically disembodied—by the disfigurement and his ghostly presence in the theater's attic. However, this narrative internalization of the singing coinciding with the phantom's self-imposed internment in an abandoned theater is by no means seamless. The interplay between the shadow and the body, between the onstage and backstage singing, between the image track and the sound track, and between the past and the present yields a surplus of meaning that demands careful disentanglement.

ACOUSTIC HORROR IN *SONG AT MIDNIGHT*

Song at Midnight is a film about the life of a theater—how it was resurrected only to become the stage of turmoil and violence once again. The screenwriter cum director Ma-Xu Weibang, songwriter Tian Han, and the main actors all came from theater backgrounds. The plot was also in itself a self-referential tale about a troupe encountering the haunting spirit of an early theater practice in the aftermath of the Republican revolution in the 1910s. The theater as a dramatic form here is neither traditional Chinese opera nor the spoken drama, but a sinicized version of the Western opera. The choice of this theatrical form is significant. The spoken drama, a favored art form among the students and the urban petty bourgeoisie at large, would have been a natural model for the sound film. Instead it was based on a combination of the traditional opera and the modern "song and dance" revue theater (*gewu ju*) that supplied readymade resources for the early sound experiments.[42] Musical numbers augmented cinema's appeal without having to be rigorously incorporated into the diegesis of a film. The sonic boom, at least at the initial stage, provided the occasion for the amplification and reordering of sensory stimulation rather than narrative enhancement.

The shifts between the tableau presentation of theatrical singing and the cinematic mode of backstage romance requiring more sophisticated camera work and editing also created a new space for gender performance. This space, as configured through the various early attempts to insert traditional or modern opera singing into the narrative space of the silent film is inherently heterotopic and shifting. In this cinematically constructed "singing field," the boundary between various kinds of dramatic theater and the movie theater gets blurred. It was a space of confusion as well as innovation. Although the advent of sound was initially regarded by some filmmakers and critics as a regressive turn back to when the cinema and drama cross-fertilized, the return to theater proved to be a dynamic event.

In this sense, the trope of the face so crucial to the horror effect of the film may be viewed in tandem with the use and abuse of face and surface in the fictional and real drama alike. The interplay between the onstage performance and the backstage drama is paralleled by the interplay between the outside (the theater front) and the inside (the auditorium). The tension between the theatrical convention and filmic impulse, between the "cinema of attractions" and "cinema of narrative integration" is replayed here in a sound film made at the end of the silent period. In *Song at Midnight* the insertion of sound, the singing voice in particular, demanded a new way of organizing narrative space. The troubled sound space in the film, evolving around the voice of the phantom singer, is thus also the space in which the dramatic tension between face and voice, surface and depth gets articulated. Because the grotesque face and the disembodied voice form a symbiotic existence, and constitute the main attraction and narrative nexus of the film, it is imperative to consider the meaning of defacing in relation to the problem of voicing. The grotesque face, which mirrors the gothic architecture of the theater, serves both a living synecdoche of the physical setting and a key element of the mise-en-scène in the film.

Song at Midnight consistently invokes the aesthetic of shadowplay characteristic of both early Chinese silent film and German expressionist cinema. Indeed, the entire film, shrouded in the nocturnal *Stimmung* (mood) created by shadows and veiled lighting,[43] pays stylistic tribute to silent cinema. *Song at Midnight* begins with a few beams of light bursting through leaden clouds while the camera draws us closer to a desolate theater. Accompanied by eerie music, the camera focuses on an announcement in front of the theater, inviting developers to demolish the theater and build modern housing on the site (fig. 8.7). The announcement is dated August 1926. In the ensuing silence, the camera pans slowly around the ruined walls as if caressing a disfigured face and gradually penetrates the building and the basement. An old hand with long nails suddenly appears in the frame, holding an oil lamp. A huge shadow is cast on the wall (fig. 8.8). In low-key lighting, the hunchbacked janitor with long, disheveled hair is finally discerned in close-up. He opens a letter and reads it slowly. The letter brings the news that the Angel troupe is coming to stage a last performance in the theater. A gust of wind interrupts him; withered leaves flutter on the ground. The camera then cuts back to the facade of the theater looming in darkness, followed by a shot of the interior of the tower covered with spider webs. A giant shadow of a human figure in a long cape is projected on the wall.

The songs in the film ("Hot Blood" [*Rexue*] and "The Love of the Yel-

8.7 The theater is to be demolished . . . (Courtesy of the China Film Archive)

8.8 The shadow of the phantom singer. (Courtesy of the China Film Archive)

low River" [*Huanghe zhi lian*]) are themes of both the film and the plays within the film—occupy much of the diegetic space. Their presence, however, is predicated on the interplay, or shadow-play, between the disembodiment and embodiment of the phantom who inhabits the theater. The onstage singing is constantly disrupted or interjected by a voice arising from behind the stage. The sound track at times takes on a life of its own and produces the effect of musical accompaniment. The disjunction between the voice and its bodily origin, between the shadow and its substantive source is at the center of the unsettling relation between the theatrical and the cinematic, the silent and sound components in the film.

The director Ma-Xu Weibang started his career in the Shanghai film industry during the heyday of the silent period and over time became known for his indulgence in the strange and the esoteric (fig. 8.9). Trained as a painter, he taught at the Shanghai Fine Arts Academy. He joined Mingxing in 1924 as an actor and art designer. Besides designing title cards and sets, he played several secondary roles and quickly rose to the rank of assistant director, working side by side with Zheng Zhengqiu. After leaving Mingxing, he became involved in small companies that allowed him more directorial control.

The figure of the stranger and motifs of a deserted place and the nocturnal recur in his work. With *The Stranger on the Love Scene* (*Qingchang guairen,* Langhua, 1926), Ma-Xu made his debut as a screenwriter and director. Although the film is not extant, a Langhua *tekan* (special issue) on

8.9 *Song at Midnight*'s director Maxu Weibang. (Special issue on *Qingchang guairen*)

8.10 *The Stranger on the Love Scene* (1926). (Special issue on *Qingchang guairen*)

the film, which contains dozens of still photos, a synopsis, and a script for the intertitles, provides a comprehensive view of it.[44] The most striking feature, relevant to my analysis of *Song at Midnight,* is the figure of the stranger (*guairen*) and his narrative function (fig. 8.10). Iconographically, the strangeness of the man is marked by his physiognomic and sartorial oddity, constituted through makeup or masquerade. An old man with a long white beard, he wears an eye patch. He wears a top hat and carries a stick, and his menacing figure is wrapped in a long, black cape—a costume associated with strange or uncanny characters in Weimar cinema (e.g., *Student of Prague, The Cabinet of Dr. Caligari, Nosferatu*) and the American horror film, in particular, *The Phantom of the Opera.* In the film, the stranger turns out to be a servant who tries to help his master and other young people in obtaining their love. Interestingly, Ma-Xu chose to play the stranger himself. Among other knightly deeds, the disguised matchmaker ghostwrites love letters and comes to the lovers' rescue in moments of danger. He usually contrives a pretext to leave his master's house in the evening to carry out his missions under the cover of darkness. In the end, after many twists and turns, the lovers are reunited and the stranger's identity is revealed.

The strange and its enabling of romance proved to be Ma-Xu's enduring passion. In the heyday of martial arts–magic spirit craze, he directed and starred in *The Stranger of Dark Night* (*Heiye guairen,* 1928) and *The*

Strange Knight-Errant in the Deserted Pagoda (*Huangta qixia,* 1929), both for the Jinlong Company. In *The Cry of the Apes in a Deserted Valley* (*Konggu yuansheng,* 1930), a bizarre film about the abductions of young virgins by men dressed in ape skins, Ma-Xu continued his exploration of the strange in the liminal overlap between mystery and horror. His fascination with the deceptiveness of surface was further played out in the contrast between the ape-skin costume and Western suits worn by the men. The violence toward women by modern scientific men and the shock effect it produced constitute the basic theme of this incipient horror film. The moment of truth arrives when the men are stripped of their hairy ape-skin body suits. Again, Ma-Xu himself played the role of the "mysterious guest"—the modern knight-errant in a dark hooded cape who comes and goes without leaving a trace. Very similar to the stranger in *The Stranger on the Love Scene,* he looms surreptitiously on the edge of the main action yet functions as an active agent propelling narrative progression.

The figure of the strange is inseparable from his ambiguous identity and shifting movement in space. His double role as both an insider and outsider endows him with the mysterious power to intervene at crucial moments. However, this power is predicated on masquerade and invisibility, the stylistic articulation of which often takes on the form of shadowplay. In *The Cry of the Apes,* the audience is alerted to the presence of the "mysterious guest" by the unwitting projection of his shadow on a windowpane. The movement of the shadow not only announces his elusive existence, but also comments on the instability of the narrative space, as the truth keeps receding from the spectator's view: seeing is *not* believing.

Shadowplay and its power to induce terror and suspense became more complicated in *Song at Midnight* because of the incorporation of sound. Significantly, on the three occasions in the film when the theme song is heard, the phantom singer Song Danping never *physically* appears. In fact, in his first appearance the phantom singer is a combination of his shadow on the wall and his disembodied singing voice. The song is heard amid a group of shots of the deserted theater and the sound of rain, wind, and the bamboo clock used by the night watchman.[45] The voice, emanating from the giant shadow on the wall, generates deep echoes in the theater. As the singing flows, the scene cuts to an equally desolate house across the street and then to its balcony where a white-clad woman emerges and listens intently (fig. 8.11). We realize that the song is addressed to her (because of the direct address "O, my girl" in the lyrics). Her vacuous eyes and long, disheveled hair, clue us into her madness. The gothic ambiance is accentuated by the presence of her companion, a

8.11 Li Xiaoxia with the wet nurse. (Courtesy of the China Film Archive)

hunchbacked old woman servant (her wet nurse) holding a flickering candle.[46] As the story unfolds, we learn that the deranged woman is Li Xiaoxia, Song Danping's beloved from a decade ago.

It was in this very theater they fell in love—he was the actor on the stage and she was the spectator in the balcony reserved for local notables. The face-to-face encounter and eye contact in the space of the live theater proved too dangerous in a society that still classed actors with prostitutes. A liaison between a landlord's daughter and an actor could not be tolerated, let alone consummated. Her rich father denied them permission to marry, and a local tyrant who desired Li Xiaoxia had Song beaten and disfigured with nitric acid (fig. 8.12). The attack ended Song's acting career as well as the romance, for he would not let Li see his scarred face. This dramatic turn of events caused Li to have a nervous breakdown. Instead of abandoning Li altogether, Song takes up residence in the attic of the deserted theater; from there he glimpses Li in her house across the street. Every night he sings "Song at Midnight" to console her. His disappearance is thus compensated by his voice, which fills the theater every night. Even as his body is reduced to a shadow, his voice is given spatial depth and volume.

The past persists through Song's nightly singing, which is charged with repressed desire. Although Li Xiaoxia is the intended listener, she cannot determine the real source of the voice and the true identity of the singer because of her insanity. The singing thus hovers in the border

8.12 Song Danping in the torture chamber. (Courtesy of the China Film Archive)

space between the diegetic and nondiegetic, as exemplified in the three instances when the theme song is heard in the film. Sung in its entirety at the beginning of the film, the lyrics of the song encapsulates the nocturnal *Stimmung* of the mise-en-scène while offering a poetic summary of the plot:

> Fireflies fly in the sky,
> Foxes and rats walk on the high platform;
> A human figure accompanies a lonesome lamp,
> There is the third sounding from the night-watch man.
> The wind blows sadly, the rain pours,
> Flower petals drop randomly, leaves are fallen;
> In this pervasive dark night,
> Who is awaiting the daybreak with me?[47]

The singer describes his "form" as being as "hideous as a ghost" but vows to fight against the "feudal devil" to his "last breadth." The singer's existence is signaled by the shadow on the wall. The image track shows close-ups of Li's expressionless face and her hunchback wet nurse, juxtaposed with montage shots of lyrical imagery of the images mentioned in the lyrics.[48]

The second time, only the middle stanza is sung by Sun Xiao'ou, a handsome young actor of the Angel troupe. After Sun traces the singing

8.13 Following the singing, Sun Xiaoou finds the phantom singer in the attic. (Courtesy of the China Film Archive)

voice to the attic, Song tells him the tragic story and asks Sun to disguise himself as the youthful Song (fig. 8.13). Song directs Sun's view to the balcony across the street and says, "Look! She is still there waiting for me." Next, we see Li in a long shot walking in the woods toward the source of the singing, which turns out to be Sun rather than Song. In the woods shrouded in milky misty lighting, Li and Sun "reenact" the scene in which Li and Song had their first tryst ten years earlier. The pattern of repetition is unmistakable. Sun becomes Song's double or the embodiment of the shadow. When day is about to break, Sun vanishes from the scene just as a ghost or a vampire who cannot be exposed to daylight.

The song's last occurrence comes at the end of the film, after Song has revealed his identity and his grotesque face to the man who destroyed his love. At this point in the story, the tyrant is now about to violate Sun's girlfriend Lüdie while Sun performs onstage. After the tyrant falls out of a window and dies on the street in front of the theater, Song, like a *deus ex machina,* descends to the stage on a rope suspended from the ceiling. Song's unexpected reappearance creates a great commotion in the theater. The audience, which turns into a frenzied mob, chases him to a desolate tower in the woods and sets fire to it, as in a ghost exorcism. In the end, Song's burning body falls into the river, vanishing from the human world altogether. His fall is illustrated by loud sound effects; the vibrating sound waves echo the wild torrents. As Song's body is swallowed by the waves, his last stanza of the theme song is drowned out—staged against a sublime landscape filled with romantic pathos of *Sturm and Drung* (a raging river, a heavy, leaden sky, and the dark earth). The rapid zoom-out image track shows Sun and Li in a reincarnation of an earlier romantic passion, standing on a cliff before a stagy backdrop of a dawn sky.

In outlining the disembodied occurrences of the theme song in *Song at Midnight,* my intention is to show that it serves as a metadiegetic vehicle that at once functions as the dominant and eludes the confines of the narrative space superimposed on the haunted theater. The etymology of *diegesis* (narration) in Greek, as Michel de Certeau has shown, is rooted in "itinerary," that which "guides" and "transgresses." It is made of movements, "concerning the deformation of figures." Its operation transforms static places (such as a tomb) into dynamic space with "transportable limits."[49] Unlike the film's other two songs embedded within plays, "Song at Midnight" is a metatheme of the film as a play and the play as a film. It animates a gravelike place and transforms it into a lived space for personal and collective drama. Hovering always at a remove from the image track yet framing the film as a whole, the song exceeds the diegetic absorption of a single plot and becomes the nodal point of multiple narratives (both theatrical and filmic) and temporalities. The shadow as the voice's carrier shifts constantly in and out of the body, as well as on- and off-stage. In other words, the voice *is* the timeless "spirit," indeed a revenant, who inhabits and enlivens the deserted theater, linking the past and the present. The sublime power of the voice is predicated on the body's invisibility; when the grotesque body actually emerges onto the stage and exposes the disfigured face as a material evidence of a historical trauma, it quickly meets its ultimate destruction.

PERMUTATIONS OF THE GROTESQUE FACE

Among all the thematic and stylistic similarities, the grotesque face in both the American *The Phantom of the Opera* and the Chinese *Song at Midnight* films serves as the material token of trauma and a metaphor (in its etymological sense of "vehicle") for horror. The grotesque face of Lon Chaney's phantom made *The Phantom of the Opera* so hair-raising and sensational. Holding a skull in his hand, a stagehand describes the phantom's face as a "leperous parchment" without a nose but with truncated eye sockets ("holes") filled with dull-colored beads. The havoc that the phantom wreaks upon the opera house makes headlines in the Parisian newspapers. Similarly, Song Danping's disfigured face in *Song at Midnight* is the pivotal point of a multilayered social drama.

The revelation of the grotesque face in both films announces not only the surfacing of truth but also a crucial narrative transition, when the onstage drama and backstage romance intertwine. The phantom steps out of the shadows and thereby realigns the voice and its bodily source—with dire consequences. Early in *The Phantom of the Opera,* Erik announces to Christine that he is the one who "imparted the full measure" of opera to her through his coaching behind the wall. "Soon this voice will take form" to "command" her love. After he exposes his face, which causes her to faint, Christine also physically disappears from the stage. The film increasingly gravitates toward the backstage; depth and interiority begin to replace, or overshadow, surface and frontality.

A similar pattern occurs in *Song at Midnight.* Song Danping's grotesque face appears for the first time when Sun traces the voice. Instead of revealing his face, which is veiled under a black cloth, Song shows the young man two photographs of his youthful face from ten years ago. The ensuing flashback (absent in the Hollywood version) quite literally unravels the events leading to the disfigurement. In a long take, the gauze that wrapped Song's injured head is unwound layer after layer, "an act resembling the shedding of a cocoon, stressing his metamorphosis."[50] The still-blood stained face with swollen cicatrices frightens the people in the room as well as Song himself. He walks to the mirror, shouting "No! No!" By revealing his face and the historical truth beneath it to Sun, Song's voice reunites with his body. This reunion is in part vicariously carried out by the young singer, whose visage and voice resemble Song's. Through this doppelganger, Song meets his deranged lover "in person" for the first time in a decade.

Wolfgang Kayser's definition of the grotesque is relevant here: the grotesque signifies the "fusion of realms which we know to be separated, the abolition of the law of statics, the loss of identity, the distortion of 'natural' size and shape, the suspension of the categories of objects, the destruction of personality, and the fragmentation of the historical order."[51] The prominence of the grotesque face highlights the role that makeup, and its ability to distort "'natural' size and shape" play in horror. It is perhaps not surprising that Ma-Xu Weibang was often compared to Lon Chaney. His passion for grotesque makeup and roles (as in *The Stranger on the Love Scene*) won him the title of the "oriental Lon Chaney." Chaney was known to the Chinese audience as the "man with a thousand faces" (*qianmianlang*).[52] The ability to transform one face into a "thousand" other faces is not simply a marker of an actor's flexibility; it underscores a conception of the face as a locus for multilayered and fluctuating meaning beyond "face" value. As a surface given to endless deformation and transformation, the grotesque face is also isomorphic to the chameleon-like film screen, which is open to all possible experience, including the most inchoate and unspeakable.

The mirror, an important tool for make-up, finds its proper place in a film about a phantom singer and his grotesquely made-up face, and his double. The mirror was deployed as one of the key mise-en-scène elements in Weimar cinema, beginning with *Student of Prague,* in which the mirror ceases to yield the student's reflection after he has sold his soul to the devil. The mirror serves not only as the means through which the grotesque face is revealed, but also the space where the ambiguous relationship between surface and depth, the original and the copy, manifests itself. Christine has to pass a mirror-door to enter the subterranean world of the phantom, whereas Song encounters his own deformed face in the mirror after the gauze is stripped away. The moment Song breaks the mirror is the moment when he declares his "death" and never appears on the stage again.

Rather than fashioning a mirror image of the Hollywood model, *Song at Midnight* disfigures the original in many respects. This disfigurement lies in a different articulation of the theater space and gender relations. In terms of the spatial mise-en-scène, *Song at Midnight* turns *The Phantom of the Opera,* quite literally, upside down. Instead of taking up residence in the mystic subterranean chamber, separated by the mirror door and labyrinthine passages that form the nether world of horror, Song lives on top of the theater—like the Hunchback of Notre Dame, which allows him to linger in the human world and even to command an advantageous point-of-view. He can see his beloved nightly through the window and communicates with her by singing. The theater space in *Song at Midnight* is significantly simplified yet highly stylized. Moreover, the number of characters and the size of the "audience" are also smaller, further accentuating the stagy, expressionist look of the film.

Ma-Xu's aesthetic investment in the grotesque face was by no means peculiar to him, although he was the one who perfected the horror genre in China's prewar film industry. The fascination with the grotesque face and the technique of facial makeup in the silent period peaked in the martial arts–magic spirit film. This was in part because the genre's fantastic tales demanded a more sophisticated use of makeup to present the ghosts, spirits, and demons that populate these films. Film magazines at the time carried numerous articles conceptualizing their importance or introducing practical techniques of screen makeup. Hu Zhongbiao's "A Study on the Makeup of Demons and Devils," for instance, offers a lengthy deliberation on the aesthetic significance of "demons and devils" in providing "spice" to stimulate the audience's "appetite." The author also comments on differences in iconographical features of the otherworldly creatures between the East and the West due to disparate religious backgrounds. The Western devil often has horns or a tail, whereas the Chinese counterpart tends to have a protruding growth on top of the head or long hair-tufts on the sides of the face. Hu offers detailed description of specific techniques of makeup, emphasizing the materiality of the process, which involves the use of "makeup items" (*jiazhuangpin*) or masks. Hu boldly predicts that a particular genre of "demon and devil" film will become a lasting "spice" in the world of cinema.[53] Foregrounding the grotesque (male) face as a marker of artistry presented an important challenge to a star culture in the early 1930s, when male dandies' smooth pale faces dominated the film screens.

Against the background of the national crisis, the grotesque faces in some films appear visibly invested with political meaning. In *Hearts United in Life and Death* (*Shengsi tongxin*, Mingxing, 1936), a left-wing sound film scripted by Yang Hansheng and directed by Ying Yunwei (1904–67),[54] the grotesque face plays a pivotal role. Despite its overt political message and realist mode of narration, the film contains many stock images of horror. Elements that later appeared in *Song at Midnight* include rats and snakes in a nightmarish scene, mirrors and photographic effects to introduce the grotesque character,[55] and, of course, visual play with shadows. The film, like *Song at Midnight*, is set in the period of the Northern Expedition (*Beifa*, 1925–27). A captured revolutionary (Yuan Muzhi) escapes from prison, and a young man (also played by Yuan) returning from Nanyang is arrested because he looks identical to the revolutionary. The revolutionary, whose face is scarred in a fire during escape, returns to the city and meets the innocent young man's fiancée. Out of guilt and sympathy, the revolutionary secretly leaves a sack of rice in front of her door, recalling the figure of the knightly stranger in the late silent film. Over time, the fiancée's political consciousness awakens under the revolutionary's influence. At the end of the film, the revolutionary dies in a battle to free the prisoners. In his footsteps, the couple joins the Northern Expedition army, marching to the front. In a striking ending, the dead revolutionary seems resurrected; his larger-than-life ghostly image is superimposed over the marching army. This image is matched by the collective singing of the theme song, "The March of the New China," on the sound track.

The permutations of the grotesque face and the figure of the double in these films, Chinese or Western, weave together an intertextual matrix from which *Song at Midnight* is derived and which it updates. This chain of influence or confluence attests to the horror genre's international appeal, which, as Carol Clover argues, is germane to the uniqueness of the cinema in the production of sensation, or a certain "cinefantastic." Focusing on its structural proximity to folklore or oral narrative, Clover explicates why "cinematic conventions of horror are so easily and so often parodied":

> The free exchange of themes and motifs, the archetypal characters and situations, the accumulation of sequels, remakes, imitations. This is a field in which there is in some sense no original, no real or right text, but only variants; a world in which, therefore, the meaning of the individual example lies outside itself. The "art" of the horror film, like the "art" of pornography, is to a very large extent the art of rendition, and it is understood as such by [a] competent audience. A particular example may have original features, but its quality as a horror film lies in the way it delivers the cliché.[56]

The incipient Chinese horror film, which Ma-Xu helped to consolidate, constitutes one of the cinematic folktale genres that thrive on seriality, variation, and transnational appeal, in a way similar to the martial arts–magic spirit film. *Song at Midnight* was addressed to a knowing audience with prior exposure to the genre in its various incarnations, which was nonetheless inclined to be shocked by the unique, locally colored ways in which the "cliché" was delivered.

One key aspect through which *Song at Midnight* alters the archetypal tale and the grotesque face of *The Phantom of the Opera* and other Chinese predecessors is the change in gender. The singer, both onstage and backstage, becomes exclusively male, while the singing girl is split in two: the female spectator Li Xiaoxia and the young male actor Sun Xiao'ou. This change is thought-provoking, not the least because the deprivation of the female voice acquires a new expression. Song Danping is not just a singer; he is the *author* of the songs and the plays staged within the film. The voice of the singing girl in early sound films served as a symbol for sound technology, and it was through her voice that she was presented as object of desire. By the time of *Song at Midnight,* the sound film had passed that early stage romancing with the new medium. It was as if once experimentation lost its novelty, the female voice lost its function as a vehicle, bringing the actual behind-the-scenes songwriter to the fore to sing his own music.

What remains troubling, however, is how the male singer represses or defers his sexual desire and political commitment, which are perceived as threatening to the social order. The hero's disfigurement is the price for crossing several boundaries, between classes, writing and voice, art and politics. Unlike the rich, handsome urbane writers who court poor singing girls in a number of early sound films, the male singer here comes from a lower class. He is labeled a "plaything" (*xizi*), a derogatory term traditionally reserved for actors, who sold their art if not their bodies. Disfigurement did more than deprive Song Danping of his living as an actor; it also effectively dehumanized him. The nitric acid literally "branded" him as a "wild animal" (*yeshou*). After meeting his grotesque face in the mirror, he asks the servant to tell Li that he is from now on "dead"—"a ghost, a wild animal."

This deformation of a handsome face to a grotesque one is central to the production of terror as "the ruling principle of the sublime." Edmund Burke in his post-Enlightenment aesthetic theory opposed the beautiful to the sublime. As James Donald observes, Burke's theory of the sublime is at the outset akin to Freud's notion of the "uncanny" and Todorov's poetics of the "fantastic." Burke locates, however, the source of terror in the readily visible physiological form and immensity of nature rather than in the illusive or abstract boundaries between the real and unreal, subject and object, time and space: "He [Burke] invokes stormy oceans, wild cataracts, dark towers and demons to convey the forces that overwhelm human reason and imagination and produce a response of awe and terror: his sublime involves powerful emotions ultimately reducible to visceral processes of pleasure and pain."[57] In light of this physiological and somatic reading of the sublime, it is possible to see the grotesque face as a "visceral" form of horror resulting from the collapsed boundary between culture and nature in modern consciousness. And this collapse is borne out in the transformation of a physical theater, which, throughout the film, undergoes animistic metamorphoses from a desolate castle to an urban gathering place, and then to a house of violence once again in the end. The theater as the "home" of the uncanny (*unheimlich*) is extended to an awe-inspiring landscape montage (both visual and auditory) of the jungle, torrential river, thunder and wind. For Burke, the sublime as an emergent aesthetic category stood for a certain masculine sensibility in a post-Enlightenment Europe. The transfiguration of the "beautiful" into the grotesque face in *Song at Midnight,* set in the disenchanted post-May Fourth period, may be seen as the moment instantiating the disfigured male singer as a new aesthetic and political subject. Song Danping's "beautiful" voice is superimposed on, or indeed "sublimated" in, the mise-en-scène of horror. His identity as a talented actor and romantic revolutionary is fractured by the disfigurement and his subsequent "burial" inside the theater living among snakes and spiders, whereas the theater appears as a castle situated in an awe-inspiring landscape.

The sublimation of masculine desire and gender reconfiguration in the film, however, demands further explanation in another direction, which concerns the question of spectatorship. The change of the social roles between the romantic couple directs our attention to the image of the female spectator. Before her nervous breakdown, Li Xiaoxia used to occupy the balcony with her family. As a daughter in a gentry family who enjoys going to the theater, hers is a typical image of the female spectator who patronized teahouses or theater houses, and the movie theaters. Romance between male actors and female spectators was a recurring phenomenon that frequently scandalized the public. Before the tragedy, we see her watching Song's performance through her binoculars. Her amorous gaze is met by Song's eyes. The mise-en-scène and framing emphasize the act of looking and the erotic nature of the theater as a public space where different sexes and classes intermingle. The love between Li and Song ends in personal catastrophe for both and results in the desolation of the theater for a decade. Significantly, Li's active spectatorship is replaced by her dedicated listening after Song's disfigurement. But isolated and deranged, she listens from a distance to a disembodied voice.

This transformation encapsulates the industry's *painstaking* transition to synchronized total sound cinema. Spatially, this transposition is articulated through the move from the balcony in the theater to the balcony of Li's house; the pleasure of looking does not so much give way as to enhance the thrill of listening. As the theater becomes a grave for the defaced hero, Li's palatial home is turned into a madhouse. At the end of the film, she is released from her disoriented state, when she suddenly awakens to the sound of the theme song. But this can only happen after the audience turns into a mob, whose torching of the deserted tower in the woods forces Song to jump into the river. The last sounds in *Song at Midnight* no longer issue from Song's shadow or that of his double Sun Xiao'ou but from an unidentifiable off-screen source. The aural sublimation is now complete.

THE PHANTOM SINGER AS THE "RECORDER OF HISTORY"

The interplay between shadow and body, voice and face, in *Song at Midnight* is staged on the ruins of history as well as a theater. The phantom figure's historical dimensions are strikingly concrete: as a reminder of the Republican revolution in the early 1910s and as an icon for the Northern Expedition that ended the warlord period. The film itself was made another decade later, in the midst of the movement for "national salvation." There is an invisible sliding in periodization here. It was fairly common for 1930s films to use the warlord period as a historical space characterized by a perpetual sense of crisis, allegorically projected onto the contemporary national emergency. This temporal indeterminacy, I believe, is deliberate, since it allows the convergence and collision of distinctive historical experience.

The film may thus be viewed in a larger historical frame. The first appearance of the theme song foreshadows the persistence of history and its haunting spirit. The second stanza of the theme song contains these ambiguous lines:

> . . . I want to be forever the one buried in the grave
> Buried together with my original name in the world
> I want to be the recorder of history who survived the punishment
> [*xingyu shichen*]
> Who wrote exhaustively about injustice in the human world.

The allusion to the "recorder of history" is crucial for understanding the song as a hermeneutic key to the film as a whole. The historical figure invoked here is no doubt Sima Qian of the Western Han dynasty, the first historiographer in Chinese (written) history. His status as a tragic icon of historical truth is commonly linked to castration, the punishment he received from the Emperor Wu, who resented his defense of a Han general's surrender to the Xiongnu "barbarians." After his release from prison, Sima Qian devoted himself to completing his historiographic project.[58] The archaic Chinese term for castration is "punishing by corrosion" (*fuxing*), which echoes the corrosive disfigurement by nitric acid that befalls Song Danping.[59] In drawing a parallel between the castration of the "recorder of history" and his own mutilation, which in effect impaired his masculinity, the phantom singer equates their deformities. Sima Qian's imprisonment is thus projected onto Song's voluntary exile in the deserted theater, the torture chamber of his soul.

Even more intriguing is the elusive allusion to his "original" name, that is, his former self. When the young singer Sun Xiao'ou traces the phantom voice to the attic Song reveals himself to be the famous revolutionary actor Jin Zhijian. The literal meaning of the name, "as hard (or enduring) as gold," obviously stands for both his revolutionary zeal and his romantic devotion. The semantic richness of gold is given a specific historicity when Song Danping tells the younger actor that his original self, in the photograph taken in 1913, used to be a leader of the student movement when he was at his "golden age" (*huangjin shidai*). But the revolution was soon aborted, and he had to go underground by joining the Qiuliu troupe under the pseudonym Song Danping, the stage name under which he became famous. In the second photograph he presents, he no longer appears as the student leader in his school uniform but as an actor in a hooded cape.

The phantom singer's self-portrayal as a modern "recorder of history" is enhanced by further evidence of historical sedimentation. If his evocation of the ancient historiographer seems a bit far-fetched, the allusion to the catalytic change in politics and culture in the 1910s endows the film with historical immediacy. The troupe that Jin Zhijian (the youthful Song) joined and used as a refuge is named Qiuliu (autumn willow). The abortion of the Republican revolution in the early 1910s saw the dissolution of many New Drama troupes that had played a key role in disseminating ideas about democracy, republicanism, and modernity. One of the most important troupes of that period was Chunliu (spring willow). The troupe had been founded by a group of Chinese students in Japan in 1907.[60] On the eve of the revolution, several important Chunliu members returned to China, using drama as a means of political mobilization as well as popular entertainment.[61] After Yuan Shikai (1859–1916) betrayed the Republic and enthroned himself as the emperor, his regime suppressed the New Drama movement, which at that time had become synonymous with revolution. Song Danping's exile in the gravelike theater is thus metaphoric of the New Drama movement that died out or went underground.

The connection between Chunliu and Qiuliu is made more explicit when Song Danping presents Sun Xiao'ou with the play *Hot Blood* (*Rexue*), which he had written a decade earlier and revised during his exile in the theater (fig. 8.14). One of the plays that the Chunliu troupe staged in Japan was also called *Hot Blood* (a.k.a. *Hot Tears*). At this second moment of revelation, Song identifies himself as a writer and aligns himself more closely with the ancient historian. The play performed by Chunliu and "authored" by Song Danping was an adaptation of a French play inspired by the French Revolution.[62] By handing down a script of Chinese and Western theatrical and revolutionary heritage, Song Danping's gesture also suggests the complex nature of the transmission of culture and history. This gesture extends a metacommentary on the production of *Song at Midnight,* derived from international sources. The play has to be revised and restaged at different points of history because the personal and collective experiences that underscore its popularity have been restructured. The revised play is presented to the Angel troupe as a gift; its contemporary relevance will attract an audience back to the deserted theater before its demolition.

The motif of generational shift and heritage can be probed further in relation both to film history and to another strand of the New Drama and its representative figure, Zheng Zhengqiu. In the history of modern Chinese drama, Chunliu represents the "foreign" side of the New Drama by virtue of its origin outside China and its adherence to formal unity and the use of standard Mandarin; it is the progenitor of the Western style *huaju,* or spoken drama. Zheng Zhenqiu is, on the other hand, often associated with the "native" strand of the New Drama that stemmed from

8.14 Song Danping acting in the play *Hot Blood.* (Courtesy of the China Film Archive)

student theater activities in missionary schools in urban China and evolved into a more hybrid form. This native form of the New Drama liberally combines elements from Western spoken drama, the Japanese new-style drama, and traditional Chinese theater. It is, on the whole, more improvisational and entertaining. Comic interludes and impromptu speeches are common, and there is little inhibition against using local dialects during performance. Works in this style came to be called civilized plays for their advocacy of modern values and lifestyle while paying due respect to everyday reality.

Zheng Zhengqiu came to the fore of the theater world first through his review column in the progressive newspaper *Min li bao,* and subsequently through his acting, script writing, and directing. Although most prerevolutionary theater groups disbanded under either political or financial pressures, Zheng's Xinmin troupe, which was associated with the Asia Company and instrumental in making *A Difficult Couple,* thrived because its popular plays featured earthy messages rather than outdated revolutionary rhetoric. Zheng's innovative scripts and directing style, plus his sensitivity to the audience and especially women's taste and expectations, were largely responsible for the revival of the civilized play. This was later dubbed the "Jiayin Restoration" (*Jiayin zhongxin;* the year 1914 was a Jiayin year in the Chinese lunar calendar).[63] The revived civilized play supplied both plot material and human resources to the nascent Chinese filmmaking enterprise. With the founding of Mingxing in

1922, the union between cinema and drama was complete, although tensions persisted.

Zheng's chief contribution to the New Drama during and after the Jiayin boom can be attributed to his ability to take the audience seriously in his reform of drama's style and content. This resonates with Song Danping's timely help to the Angel troupe as he presents them with an updated version of an old play that might reverse declining audience numbers and a difficult financial crisis. (The box-office revenues will sustain the troupe for only five more days.) Zheng's phantom presence in *Song at Midnight* is perhaps made more relevant by the fact that he had died shortly before the production of the film, on July 16, 1935, at the age of forty-six. The passing of one of the most important figures in early Chinese cinema resulted in a collective mourning throughout the film world in Shanghai. His death, together with the suicide of female star Ruan Lingyu and the drowning of the film composer Nie Er in Japan during the same year, marked a symbolic ending to the silent period.[64]

As a sound film that meditates on its symbiotic relation to silent film and the New Drama, *Song at Midnight* presents the phantom singer as the mediator between these different historical periods and aesthetic realms. The phantom singer's multiple identities represent the formative decades in the history of modern Chinese drama and cinema. At once dead and living, he is a witness as well as an agent of a history repressed and repeated.

EMERGENCY EXPRESSIONS

The contemporary urgency created by the crisis in the North, where the Japanese army was making a rapid advance toward the interior, is couched in *The Romance of the Yellow River,* another play staged within a film. Tellingly, the advertisement posted in front of the theater calls it a "new style historical operetta" (*xinxing lishi geju*). The story, though set in the Song dynasty under the threat of the Mongols from the North, is an allegory for the contemporary national crisis. A boy from the south side of the river is in love with a girl on the north side. The boy crosses the river to meet his girl. While paddling in the river, he sings:

> I'd rather be a fish in the Yellow River
> Than a slave without a country
> A *wangguonu* cannot act freely
> A fish can still stir the waves
> It can topple the Barbarian's ship,
> It can stop them crossing the river . . .

The phrase *wangguonu* (a slave without a country) was gaining high currency in the rhetoric of national salvation during this period. The love story, presented in the broad mythic strokes of a folktale yet clothed as a Western-style operetta, is an onstage version of the offstage romance between the phantom singer and his deranged lover, separated by a river as well as social boundaries. The ancient patriotic fervor is mobilized to give a historical depth to the anti-Qing Republican revolution and the anti-Japanese war.

The incorporation of the play further underscores the historiographic nature of *Song at Midnight,* which is permeated with a sense of repetition and emergency. Not only does the film end with the eruption of the crowd, which echoes similar endings in many "national defense" films (e.g., *Big Road, Children of Troubled Times, Hearts United in Life and Death*), the film as a whole is structured around a series of crises. Tian Han "edited" Ma-Xu's script and wrote the lyrics, certainly giving the film a more progressive discourse. However, the crisis expressed in the film is more culturally embedded than simply politically informed. It works through a range of anxieties regarding technology, film history, and multinational aesthetics. Beyond the multiple layers of history that give the film its semantic richness visceral impact, its formal expression in an aesthetic of emergency deserves further examination.

Two seemingly unrelated aspects in the film provide some entry points to this question: the expressionist visual style and Angel troupe's financial crisis. While the former speaks to an aspiration for making art cinema, the latter suggests its difficulty in a time of political and economic turmoil. *Song at Midnight* is, in fact, about the life of a theater. After the ominous opening, the camera work, lighting, and sets are dominated by an expressionist visual style. The distinctive feature of Weimar expressionist cinema, generally regarded as the origin of the horror film, is its antinaturalist narrative pattern and visual style. If dream, fantasy, and delirium make up the basic narrative language of Weimar cinema, the exaggerated sets irreverent of perspective and balance constitute the skewed structure of expressionist mise-en-scène. "By comparison to the then-established conventions of film imagery," such a space has been viewed as "a world internally [gone] awry."[65]

The space in *Song at Midnight* may also be described in such terms. The mise-en-scène's instability embodied by the Gothic theater is caused by physical and social forces. The camera work helps to construct a nonnaturalist space resisting contiguity and symmetry, and the hyperbolic plot is thus "justified" by an improbable space—the imaginary "theater" that links the tower where Song sings to the balcony where Li listens. Besides such spatial distortion, the image track is also replete with shots in slanted framing or filtered through a blurred lens. They are often accompanied by dramatic sound imagery, which intensifies the sense of disorientation and crisis. After Song reveals his true identity to the young singer, tilted shots begin to crowd the film space. Some examples:

- After the failure of the revolution, Song, escaping from persecution, rides on horseback in the jungle through pouring rain. The speed of the shot seems to force the frame to tilt. (Sound track: horse hooves and thunder storm.)
- Li Xiaoxia has a nervous breakdown after learning of Song's "death." (Sound track: drums)
- The villain threatens to shoot the young singer. Song comes to his rescue. After revealing his grotesque face, he executes his own revenge. (Sound track: orchestra in fast tempo, the noise of the crowd.)
- Li hears the truth and sees a spinning blurred world. (Sound track: shouting of the crowd.)

These fast and jerky shots generate both dread and excitement (fig. 8.15).[66] The subjective slanted frame and blurred vision are especially pertinent for expressing Li's deranged state of mind—the liminal space in which the division between past and present is suspended. The viewer is repeatedly pulled into a world of madness and disorder. The frequency of these scenes provides the film with a basic mood of distress and horror effected by the stimulation of optical nerves rather than psychologized characterization.

Such expressive visual coding is largely absent in most national defense films, which resorted to a realist or even propagandist mode of narration. It is perhaps not so surprising that mainstream Chinese film historiographies excluded Ma-Xu's works in the canon of the left-wing cinema; instead, he is often labeled a filmmaker who indulged in petit-bourgeois taste:

> *Song at Midnight* exposes, to a certain extent, the tyranny of the feudal ruling class and depicts Song Danping's struggle against the feudal forces. However, Song Danping's individual-centered heroism, strife, petit-bourgeois fervor, and his "entangled" romance with Li Xiaoxia, all of which the filmmaker endorses and eulogizes, are incompatible with the guiding ideology of the national defense film movement. On the level of artistic expression, the director also copies wholesale the style of Hollywood horror film such as *Phantom of the Opera*. And this undermines what small valuable content there is in the film.[67]

8.15 Emergency expression: tilted framing. (Courtesy of the China Film Archive)

Such criticism, informed by an ideology that favors socialist realism, simplistically opposes form to content. Any formal experiment that attempts to seek alternative paths in negotiating the aesthetic and the political was deemed dubious if not dismissed outright. The visual style and the acoustic composition of *Song at Midnight* are far from a simple mimicry of Hollywood. The explicit borrowing of German expressionism and the sedimentation of specific historical experiences give the film poignant expressions of perhaps a combined optical and political "unconscious,"[68] rather than a mere reflection of a preconceived agenda.

The relationship between form and content in the film is, to be sure, a troubled one. A sense of competition pervades the film—between the foreign versions and the Chinese adaptation, between German expressionism and Hollywood illusionism, between the theater's tableau quality and slowness and the cinema's montage density and speed, between silence and sound, between sensuous music and the mechanical speech of standard vernacular Chinese, and between obsessive visual stylization and hyperbolic political rhetoric.[69] A heterogeneous, uneasy mix of aesthetic choices and ideological avenues were available to the makers of this and other films made at this time. This generation of filmmakers was poised on the threshold linking the silent and sound film and had been nourished by a modernist culture in the first half of the 1930s. *Song at Midnight* presents an experiment that is innovative, thrilling, and politically stimulating while also commercially viable.

The second aspect concerns the financial crisis of the Angel troupe. Significantly, the box-office crisis is bound to the social and physical instability of the theater space and the whims of the audience. The stylistic expressions of the aesthetic, technological, and ideological dissonance in the film evolves toward the production of the last show, or swan song, as it were, in the moribund theater. There is no narrative motivation for the Angel troupe to arrive there on a stormy night. Besides sustaining themselves financially, the troupe tries to revive the theater and its surrounding community, so selecting an appropriate script is essential. The first play, *The Romance of the Yellow River,* an allegory for the contemporary national crisis, fails to attract a large audience; this may well have been a commentary on the failure of some of the propagandist "hard" films. The box-office returns barely support the troupe for a few days, and the local people circulate rumors about the troupe's imminent bankruptcy. Hearing that, the troupe director complains, "It's just too hard to know the psychology of the audience here." The financial crisis thus reflects a crisis of spectatorship. The phantom singer's script rescues the troupe and resuscitates a large throng of spectators. The play, set during the French Revolution, advocates the ideal of democracy and a more utopian world community than *Romance of the Yellow River.* If the more nationalist inflected *Romance of the Yellow River,* set in a mythological time and space, stands for the national defense film, *Hot Blood,* with its translated cosmopolitan message and modern style, seems to offer an alternative response to the question of emergency and its aesthetic solution.

In the film, *Hot Blood* momentarily revives the theater the day it opens—with the theater bathed in sunshine and crowded with an enthusiastic audience—it also brings about its doomsday. As soon as the curtain opens, the onstage story and backstage drama begin to intersect in a way that strangely repeats the past. The rapid crosscutting and chase scenes propel the film's sense of emergency. When the villain falls to his death in front of the theater, where he had disfigured Song Danping ten years ago, history comes full circle. And when Song Danping descends to the stage, exposing his grotesque face, the line between past and present, between representation and reality, collapses beyond repair.

The true horror of the film takes place when the audience becomes transformed into a carnivalesque crowd. What do they want from the theater? What do they want of the man with the grotesque face? As the crowd rushes onto the stage interrupting and becoming part of the show, the boundary between the proscenium and the auditorium devolves in this eruption of an anarchic social body. The drama quickly extends into the realm of nature as the crowd chases the phantom singer into the woods. The sound track is filled with shouting and drumming, while

Song climbs to the top of the tower only to fall like a dark angel of history in a Benjaminian sense: "His face is turned toward the past. . . . He sees only one single catastrophe which keeps piling wreckage upon wreckage and hurls it in front of his feet."[70]

Although we do not witness the demolition of the theater, the burning of the tower serves as a metonym for its destruction and the revolt of the masses. While the images of fire and an agitated crowd chasing an enemy were common endings for national defense films, the moral ambiguity of the relationship between the crowd and the phantom singer makes it impossible to read the sequence as a replay of the theme of national salvation. In fact, it bears more than a passing resemblance to the ending of James Whale's *Frankenstein* (1931), in which the monster, chased by a mob, climbs to the top of the mill and then falls into the water. To take Song Danping, a former revolutionary and actor, for a national enemy would be misreading. Similarly, the crowd, with its unmotivated violence, refuses to be viewed as a mobilized mass marching to the war front or join the revolution. Rather, this crowd, at once chaotic and energetic, evokes the grotesque body in the medieval carnival described by Mikhail Bakhtin.[71] The grotesque body is a folk body that temporarily defiles order and decorum. As a ritual body it also serves as the site for transformation and history-making. The collapse of the boundary between the proscenium and the auditorium signaled the fusion of the two halves of the grotesque body: the phantom and the audience. The juxtaposition of revolution and revulsion through the hero's disfigurement, as Yomi Braester suggests, "fleshes out the inner contradictions of revolutionary utopia and underscores contemporary doubts about appealing to the masses."[72] Thus revolution is transmogrified into ritual violence, as in the aftermath of the French, Chinese Republican, and later, the Communist revolutions. Horror, showing the unspeakable visually, acoustically, and viscerally, is the aesthetic embodiment of history at such moments of danger. It expresses an emergency operation—the search for a cinematic language and an audience at a crucial juncture in film and national culture.

Although Song Danping dies at the end of *Song at Midnight,* the grotesque face endured. The disfigured face marked Ma-Xu's artistry and was a deviant strand of the aesthetic orientation of the period. After the war broke out, Ma-Xu stayed in Shanghai and made several more horror films, such as *The Haunted House* (*Guwu xingshi ji,* 1938), *The Poetic Soul and the Cold Moon* (*Lengyue shihun,* 1938), and *The Leper Girl* (*Mafeng nü,* 1939). (The latter centers around disfigurement caused by a sexually transmitted disease and its spread.[73]) In 1941, *Song at Midnight II* (*Xu Yeban gesheng*), in which Song Danping makes a "homecoming," was released.

This time, the good-hearted phantom (looking more like Nosferatu than Erik in *The Phantom of the Opera*) takes on a more sinister form and executes more hair-raising deeds. *The Autumn Crabapple* (*Qiu Haitang*) made in 1943 is again about a disfigured singing actor and his disenchanted love. In 1947, Ma-Xu moved to Hong Kong, taking his mastery of horror with him. Ever since, Hong Kong cinema has provided an immense body of horror and phantom films, and Hong Kong has replaced Shanghai as the chief dream factory in the Chinese-speaking world.[74]

ENVOI

Thus founded on the rupture between a past that is its object, and a present that is the place of its practice, history endlessly finds the present in its object and the past in its practice. Inhabited by the uncanniness that it seeks, history imposes its law upon the faraway places that it conquers when it fosters the illusion that it is bringing them back to life.

—MICHEL DE CERTEAU

SO MUCH HAS changed since the first foreign "electric shadowplay" arrived in a Shanghai teahouse in the summer of 1896, and since some of the first films were shot in a photo shop's courtyard in Beijing in the autumn of 1905. Most people who once contributed to the building of a film world and thus to the remaking of a new China in the early decades of the twentieth century have passed away; some died only recently. Most films from that era have been lost to fires, wars, or the sheer force of time. Yet something has remained in the form of memories, reincarnated in different registers and locations. Watching the vivid images of select preserved examples of early Chinese films on the large screen in Teatro Verdi in Pordenone, Italy, in the company of an international assembly of silent film fans and scholars, or on the video screen in a cold room by myself in the archive in Beijing, and now on the computer or DVD screens in the comfortable setting of the living room, is to witness the persistent apparitions of an early history. It is about seeing resemblance in difference, the past in the present, and vice versa.

The initial work for this book started in the mid-1990s, on the eve of the centenary of cinema and amidst the onset of a whirlwind of economic and cultural transformations in China. I remember shuttling between three continents, from Pordenone Silent Film Festival in Italy, to the dusty, "premodern" archives and libraries in Beijing and Shanghai, and back to the University of Chicago where this project formed part of a vibrant wave of discussions on early cinema and modernity. Finishing the book around the Chinese cinema's centenary, I felt that I had traveled great distances, both real and imaginary, to get in touch with a historical experience that keeps receding from our grasp as we traverse a minefield of ever greater collective amnesia. The long process of completing the book, however, inadvertently allowed my arguments to be measured against the epochal change on the heel of a new century in China.

This change once again has remapped the city of Shanghai—the display window of Chinese modernity and its gateway to the world—and also the material and spiritual topography of China as a whole. It was indeed uncanny to journey across building-zones in the city to get to libraries and archives. I witnessed, on the one hand, the tearing down of old movie theaters and neighborhoods once inhabited by the people who once saw the events mentioned in this book, and on the other, the erection of new skyscrapers and entertainment complexes (including several multiplexes built by Hollywood companies). The Yangjingbang canal and the entertainment district built on or around it almost a century ago is now an expressway somersaulting over the city center, shooting, via tunnels under the Huangpu River, right into the Pudong area, Shanghai's own, brand new "Manhattan." The Great World entertainment center, now closed for renovation and an uncertain destiny, looks dwarfed, besieged by a web of elevated expressways and giant, cold commercial buildings in the vicinity. How ironic that the Paris Theater on Huaihai Road featured in Shi Zhecun's story (see chapter 2) is now the site of a chic commercial building called Times Square. It's not clear whether it is intended as a memorial of the bygone years or a hymn to the breathlessly hectic present in the former French concession. The "New Heaven and Earth" (Xin Tiandi), a popular shopping and leisure plaza and a product of postmodern architectural facelift of the old vernacular housing, is only a stone's throw away. And the dusty, dilapidated Xujiahui reading room for classical documents and the Republican period materials is now housed in the new, air-conditioned Shanghai Municipal Library on Western Huaihai Road. The white towering building now is but one of many solid markers designed to separate the past from the present.

Over the past decade, this revamped metropolitan space has once again become a hotbed of mass culture. Teahouse culture seems to have returned, accompanied by new variants such as KTV or movie bars showing VCD or DVD movies and Internet cafés. While many unprofitable cinemas have been turned into teahouses, coffeehouses, or nightclubs, some have rebaptized themselves with the famous names used in old Shanghai and remodeled their theaters into entertainment centers. Several renovated luxurious viewing rooms (or *mini ting*) are complete with coffee tables, cocktails, and discreet lovers' seats (*yuanyang zuo*, "mandarin duck seats") or family "balconies." Cheaper all-night shows also attract restless youth and homeless migrant souls. TV dramas and films based on the life of old Shanghai were among the latest fads in visual production and consumption.

Nostalgia in the form of selective, reproducible old Shanghai images—from fashion models to film stars, from art deco architecture to calendar posters—fills the urban landscape, as well as overwhelming the urban imagination. At the same time, history seems to have been held hostage by an invisible hand, barring it from showing its scarred face. The prevailing ideology today invites us to marvel at the spectacle of a postmodern Shanghai and a postsocialist China with remarkable GNP growth, and to attribute them to the grand design of a new market economy policy and to a partnership with the forces of globalization. We are asked to celebrate a pure present, a clean slate, accentuated by the floods of light on the Bund at night and by the fireworks on national holidays.

However, history tells us that modernization comes with a price. That is partly why I choose to end the main body of the book with *Song at Midnight*, and its lessons for history and historiography. The disfigured phantom singer haunts us to this day because he is the undead who refuses to allow us to forget the past, and a poignant reminder of the "spectral" nature of the present. This figure of the revenant marks the site of "difference" of the jarring and coevality of global modernity. It arrives, constantly, in the form of the "ghosts of what had been past and the premodern culture of reference that had not yet died, returning from a place out of time to haunt and disturb the historical present."[1] Dipesh Chakrabarty, in a similar spirit, lucidly characterizes this "historical difference" as wedged in the inchoate space between the godless, disenchanted Enlightenment narrative of modernity on the one hand, and the persistence of a life-world still populated by gods, spirits, and magic powers on the other; between an empty, homogenous time and a time full of ruptures, fragments, and heterogeneity; between a universalist totalizing analytic impulse set out to "demystify" ideology and a hermeneutic approach invested in details and affect, locality and diversity.[2] And this space is not so much the irreconcilable physical or discursive gap between the West and the rest, as a shared world of thought and experiences irrevocably connected by the Enlightenment legacy.

I see Shanghai and its cinematic legacy as an instance of this "difference"; it is a haunted site of modernity. Shanghai was and seems to continue as an uncanny "scandal" in the translation (and not transition, as Chakrabarty stresses) of modernity between Europe and China, between a lingering past filled with vernacular "superstitions" and rituals and a secular national culture represented by a May Fourth ideology. It is not a matter of judging who is the villain and who is the victim, as both were deeply implicated and intertwined in the same drama, however much later historiography was tinted with the interests of the victors. Nowhere was the convoluted translation more evident than in the makeup of the metropolitan culture of Shanghai and its cinema—from the anachronistic architectural collections to the worldly tastes of the petty urbanites to the Yangjingbang legacy, both as regards language and culture. Shanghai cinema as the embodiment of a mass-mediated vernacular modernism was neither completely bad nor completely good, neither purely Chinese nor a Hollywood copycat. The same may be said of that Chinese brand of Enlightenment fastidiously translated and transmitted by elitist intellectuals, operating through their ostensibly instrumentalist vernacular movement.

If these two tendencies diverged in terms of approaches and effects, they were united in a common pursuit of a form of modernity aimed at democracy and renewed global visibility for an old country burdened with distinctively ambivalent traditions. The May Fourth project, following a time-honored pedagogical tradition, assigned the primacy to the written word, which in actuality still eluded the masses. The builders and inhabitants of a film world in Shanghai and beyond, however, seized upon modern visual (and auditory) technologies as new mimetic machines that lent expression to the very process of modernization, and its translation.

Like Yangjingbang pidgin speech, first produced in the rough translation and instant transaction between foreigners and locals at the moment of Shanghai's emergence, vernacular modernism is hardly an oxymoron. It is the very symptom and form of the effects of Enlightenment and modern cosmopolitanism resulting from colonial expansions and the spread of industrial capitalism, which upset and even inverted the relationship between the metropole and the periphery. Vernacular modernism perceives cinema as a discursive and sensory apparatus enabling the audiences to overcome the shock of the new and formulate their own terms of mediation of modern everyday life. If Shanghai cinema had as its unannounced agenda to "provincialize" Hollywood, it did so through both the acknowledgement of the latter's indispensability as an inventor of a new "universal language" and its inherent inadequacy when "spoken" in other places.

Ideologically as well as pragmatically, Shanghai cinema had to devise a vernacular that could negotiate both the lofty ideas of the nationalist May Fourth New Culture movement (which sought to translate and transfer European Enlightenment and scientism), as well as the Hollywood cinematic idioms marketed as a global vernacular for the masses regardless of class, gender, and race. It embraced many late Qing reformist and May Fourth ideas such as women's liberation, public education, and the "strengthening of the nation," while also, as an industry and a business, catering to and cashing on popular beliefs in Confucianism, Buddhism, and Daoism. It vehemently fought the incursions of Hollywood cinema while also relishing in borrowing and transmuting its star systems, genre formulas, and special effects. Thus, it is hardly surprising that the forms and genres that best exemplify vernacular modernism are those "translatable" genres or "body genres" that made sense to the mass audience, translated from both Chinese and non-Chinese repertoires, such as the melodrama, the martial arts film, and horror. With its multifarious offerings—realist, fantastical, or otherwise—Shanghai cinema provided easy-to-digest primers for modern life and its many competing explanations, and new challenges. More importantly, emerging at a time when all sensory and intellectual resources were undergoing radical transformation, stimulated by modern technologies and ideas, the cinema effectively became a "vernacular scene" for assembling and rehearsing various gender roles and fashioning new sociopolitical subjectivities.

Vernacular modernism is an assemblage of multiple temporalities and sensibilities, as well as of content and form. It could be cultivated by individual filmmakers, as in the case of Zheng Zhengqiu, Cai Chusheng, and Sun Yu who articulated their personal visions for a collective experience, each in their own way. Unlike political modernism and literary modernism that often fed into elitist and nativist agendas, vernacular modernism is at once a representational and performative form aimed at the masses. It accounts for their participation as both actors and spectators in the construction of a technologically mediated modern world and of their local, national, and global citizenship.

I have kept using the term *Shanghai cinema* rather than *Chinese cinema* because just like the city that fostered it and the Hong Kong cinema that followed in its footsteps, Shanghai cinema was neither completely national nor completely international. Shanghai cinema helped to amplify and define a form of cosmopolitanism as a popular translation enterprise mobilizing all sensory and semiotic resources, which, as seen in the Yangjingbang speech and its spatial practice (discussed in chapter 2), foregrounded the incommensurability, and the injustices, inherent in the transition of capitalism to the non-Western world. Yet the "open-air" translators and bricoleurs of the film world in Shanghai found ingenious solutions creating their own grammars and glossaries that not simply matched the imported categories, but also invented vocabularies and new tools suited for asserting their own voices and interests.

The writing of this history of early Shanghai cinema is in large measure inspired by such a translation. Not only did I translate piles of materials from Chinese into English, I also had to translate what for the most part are vernacular materials into a scholarly language, or at least the language of a self-appointed historian. It has been a daunting but also rewarding experience. It forced me to juggle different approaches and to search for the optimal pace and presentational style for this balancing act. More crucially, it has compelled me to reconsider the relationship between the vernacular movement proper as part of the Chinese Enlightenment and the more diffusive, and sometimes subversive, vernacular modernism created and transmitted through the cinema and the related mass media, in addition to considering the relationship between Shanghai cinema and world cinema. I have also had to think long and hard about why the unique physical and social infrastructure of Shanghai's metropolitan culture matters so much in understanding these relationships. Therefore, this "local" history is not merely a special guidebook to my beloved native city and to a wonderful film tradition. Its aim is also to open a new form of conversation with certain towering themes in the existing historiography of modern China and, indeed, that of global modernity as a whole. I believe the phenomenological politics and poetics of the body, of affect, and of memory, which is at the center of this book, has something to offer for the reconsideration of the foundations of that project.

For the French historian Paul Veyne, the assertion "history does not exist," is not so much a nihilist form of relativism as an admission that history is not and cannot be a bounded, coherent, and closed entity to be "objectified" from a safe, "scientific" distance.[3] Rather, borrowing Genette's dictum, he reiterates that "it's *diegesis* and not *mimesis*."[4] While I am passionate about getting closer to certain matters of fact, and about tracing their genealogies and competing claims surrounding them, I am not driven by any compulsive search for illusory scientific exactness. I do not believe that anyone can ipso facto reconstruct history as it once was. To do so would mean the past is dead and has no relation to the present whatsoever. The very fragmentary nature of archival remains and the scarred, multilayered urban landscape that houses the memories of the past already pronounce that any history is necessarily mutilated knowledge. I did not discover the history of Shanghai cinema in some sealed tomb of the past, but encountered its vestiges and manifestations in the troubled present. By virtue of being lodged in the now and here it irresistibly shapes and constitutes our present and future.

ABBREVIATIONS

FZS	Cheng Jihua, Li Shaobai and Xing Zuwen. *Zhongguo dianying fazhanshi* 中國電影發展史 [History of the Development of Chinese Cinema]. 2 vols. Beijing: Zhongguo dianying, 1981.
GJN	Gong Jianong. *Gong Jianong congying huiyilu* 龔家農從影回憶綠 [Robert Kung's Memoires of his Silver Screen Life]. 3 vols. Taipei: Wenxing shudian, 1966–67.
LLWX	Luo Yijun et al., eds. *Zhongguo dianying lilun wenxuan* 中國電影理論文選 1920–1989 [Anthology of Chinese Film Theory and Criticism]. 2 vols. Beijing: Wenhua yishu, 1992.
SSND	Chen Bo and Yi Ming, eds. *Sanshi niandai Zhongguo dianying pinglun xuan* 三十年代中國電影評論選 [An Anthology of Chinese Film criticism of the 1930s]. Beijing: Zhongguo dianying, 1993.
WSDY	Zhongguo dianying ziliaoguan [China Film Archive], ed. *Zhongguo wusheng dianying* 中國無聲電影 [Chinese Silent Film]. Beijing: Zhongguo dianying, 1996.
WSDYJB	Zhongguo dianying ziliaoguan [China Film Archive], ed. *Zhongguo wusheng dianying juben* 中國無聲電影劇本 [Chinese Silent Film Scripts], 3 vols. Beijing: Zhongguo dianying, 1996.
WSDYS	Li Suyuan and Hu Jubin. *Zhongguo wusheng dianyingshi* 中國無聲電影史 [History of Chinese Silent Film]. Beijing: Zhongguo dianying, 1997.
YXSH	*Yingxi shenghuo* 影戲生活 [Movie Weekly]

NOTES

INTRODUCTION

1. Walter Benjamin, "Theses on the Philosophy of History," in *Illuminations*, ed. Hannah Arendt (New York: Harcourt, Brace and World, 1968), pp. 262, 264.
2. Referred to hereafter as *Amorous History*.
3. Li Suyuan and Hu Jubin, *Zhongguo wusheng dianyingshi* (History of Chinese Silent Film) *WSDYS*, 2 vols. (Beijing: Zhongguo dianying, 1996). In the past researchers had very limited access to extant material due both to inadequate management of the archive and tight government control of material from the Republican period. Foreign scholars have not been allowed to consult such material until recently. I chanced upon the film while researching at the China Film Archive in Beijing in the summer of 1995.
4. Some representative works in this trend are Roger Holman, ed., *Cinema 1900–1906: An Analytical Study* (Brussels: Fédération Internationale des Archives du Film, 1982); John Fell, ed., *Film Before Griffith* (Berkeley: University of California Press, 1983); Jay Leyda and Charles Musser, eds., *Before Hollywood* (New York: American Federation of the Arts, 1987); Noël Burch, *Life to Those Shadows*, trans. and ed. Ben Brewster (Berkeley: University of California Press, 1990). The most representative work that maps out the patriarchal structure of looking through the psychoanalytic method is Laura Mulvey's seminal essay, "Visual Pleasure and Classical Narrative," *Screen* 16, no. 3 (1975): 6–18.
5. For a concise sketch of the rise of early cinema as a critical concept, see Thomas Elsaesser's, "General Introduction—Early Cinema: From Linear History to Mass Media Archaeology," ed., Thomas Elsaesser, *Early Cinema: Space, Frame, Narrative* (London: BFI, 1990). The volume contains some pioneering studies on early cinema from multiple perspectives. However, it does not concern early non-Western cinemas at all.
6. See, for example, Patrice Petro, *Joyless Streets: Women and Melodramatic Representation in Weimar Germany* (Princeton, N.J.: Princeton University Press, 1989); Miriam Hansen, *Babel and Babylon: Spectatorship in American Silent Film* (Cambridge, Mass.: Harvard University Press, 1991); Giuliana Bruno, *Streetwalking on a Ruined Map: Cultural Theory and the City Film of Elvira Notari* (Princeton, N.J.: Princeton University Press, 1993); Ann Friedberg, *Window Shopping: Cinema and the Postmodern* (Berkeley: University of California Press, 1993); Shelly Stamp, *Movie-Struck Girls: Women and Motion Picture Culture after the Nickelodeon* (Princeton, N.J.: Princeton University Press, 2000); and Jennifer Bean and Diane Negra, eds., *A Feminist Reader in Early Cinema* (Durham, N.C.: Duke University Press, 2002); Antonia Lant and Ingrid

Periz, eds., *The Red Velvet Seat: Women's Writings on the Cinema, the First Fifty Years* (London and New York: Verso, forthcoming).

7. For a brief assessment of this emergent scholarship in China, see my article, "Teahouse, Shadowplay, Bricolage: *Laborer's Love* and the Question of Early Chinese Cinema," in *Cinema and Urban Culture in Shanghai, 1922–1943*, ed. Yingjin Zhang (Palo Alto: Stanford University Press, 1999).
8. Since the 1980s, some European and Japanese scholars (e.g., Marie-Claire Quiquemelle, Regis Bergeron, Marco Müller, Tadao Sato, Fumitoshi Karima) have also produced some interesting work, mostly as catalogue essays for retrospectives of Chinese film held in the early 1980s. See for example, Centre de documentation sur le cinéma chinois, *Ombres électriques: Panorama du cinéma chinois 1925–1982* (Paris, 1982); Marie-Claire Quiquemelle and Jean Loup Passek, eds., *Le cinéma chinois* (Centre Georges Pompidou: Paris, 1985); the National Film Center at the Tokyo Kokuritsu Kindai Bijutsukan (The National Museum of Modern Art, Tokyo), *Chugoku eiga no kaiko (1922–1952)* (A Retrospective of Chinese Cinema, 1922–1952) (Tokyo, 1984); *Chugoku eiga no kaiko (1932–1964)* (A Retrospective of Chinese Cinema, 1932–1964) (Tokyo, 1988); and *Sun Yu kandoku to Shanghai eiga no nakamatachi—Chugoku eiga no kaiko* (Sun Yu and His Shanghai Colleagues: Retrospective of Chinese films) (Tokyo, 1992).
9. Li Suyuan and Hu Jubin, *Zhongguo wusheng dianyingshi* (History of Chinese Silent Film) (Beijing: Zhongguo dianying, 1996).

10. Hu Jubin, *Projecting a Nation: Chinese Cinema Before 1949* (Hong Kong University Press, 2003); Laikwan Pang, *Building a New China in Cinema: The Cinematic Left-wing Cinema Movement 1932–1937* (London: Rowman and Littefield, 2002).
11. For an early attempt to theorize nonsynchronicity, see Ernst Bloch, "Nonsynchronism and the Obligation to Its Dialectics," trans. Mark Ritter, *New German Critique* 11 (Spring 1977): 22–38.
12. Printed in the programs of the Afanggong Theater for *Amorous History*, parts 1 and 2, August 1931.
13. The reference to Lillian Gish is an allusion to Xuan Jinglin's real life story. Her original name was Tian Jinlin. While in the brothel she used the nickname Xiao Jinmudan (Little Golden Peony). The veteran director Zheng Zhengqiu helped her to adopt the stage name Xuan Jinglin, obliquely alluding to Lillian Gish (Ganlixu, in Chinese transliteration). Tan Chunfa, *Kai yidai xianhe—Zhongguo dianying zhifu Zheng Zhengqiu* (The Pioneer—Zheng Zhengqiu, the Father of Chinese Cinema) (Beijing: Guoji wenhua chuban gongsi, 1992), p. 308.
14. These three films were actual Mingxing productions that year.
15. Zhong Dafeng and Shu Xiaomin, *Zhongguo dianyingshi* (History of Chinese Film) (Beijing: Zhongguo guangbo dianshi, 1995), p. 14.
16. Xuan Jingling, "Wode yingmu shenghuo" (My Life on the Silver Screen), *Zhongguo dianying* (Chinese Cinema), no. 3 (Dec. 1956): 72–74. See also Zhang Shichuan, "Zi wo daoyan yilai" (Since I Started Directing), *Mingxing banyuekan* (Mingxing bimonthly) 1, no. 5 (1935). Zhang recalls first seeing

Xuan as a little girl with pigtails riding donkeys in the New World amusement center, where he worked as a manager. Years later, while he was casting for the film *Last Conscience* (Zuihou de liangxin, 1925), he managed to find Xuan, who had become a prostitute out of poverty, and asked her to play a minor role. After the successful release of the film, the company paid two thousand Chinese dollars to redeem her from the brothel.

17. The social status of the company in particular and the film world in general was significantly enhanced when Hong Shen (1894–1955), a Harvard-trained professor of English and drama at Fudan University, joined Mingxing as a screenwriter. Hong Shen's decision to enter the nascent, yet lowly film industry in the company of ex-prostitute Xuan aroused shock among intellectuals, including his family and friends. Film at the time was still regarded as a low entertainment form rather than art. His action was labeled by a Fudan colleague as "prostitution of art." Hong Shen was nevertheless resolute. See Hong Shen, "Wo de dagu shiqi yijing guo le ma?" (Has the time of my drumming passed already?), *Hong Shen quanji* (Collected Works of Hong Shen) (Beijing: Zhongguo xiju, 1957), 4:517. Xuan starred in *The Mistress's Fan* (Shao nainai de shanzi, 1926), scripted and directed by Hong Shen.

18. For a groundbreaking study on the "exhibitionist" mode of presentation of early cinema, which challenges the prevalent "voyeurist" paradigm used in studies of classical Hollywood cinema, see Tom Gunning, "Cinema of Attractions: Early Film, Its Spectator and the Avant-Garde," *Wide Angle* 8, no. 3 and 4 (1986): 63–70. Miriam Hansen has described such a presentational practice in terms of "excess of appeal," "diversity and display," and "public performance." See her *Babel and Babylon*, chapter 1, "A Cinema in Search of a Spectator: Film-Viewer Relations before Hollywood."

19. Andreas Huyssen, *The Great Divide: Modernism, Mass Culture, Postmodernism* (Bloomington: Indiana University Press, 1986), chapter 4, "The Vamp and the Machine."

20. Walter Benjamin, "One Way Street," *Walter Benjamin: Selected Writings Volume 1. 1913–1926*, eds., Marcus Bullock and Michael W. Jennings (Harvard University Press, 1996), p. 476.

21. Due to the immense success, Xuan's salary was doubled for the first time. The film was among the eight Chinese films brought to the Moscow International Film Festival in 1935, which were then toured around major European cities. See Hu Die, *Yinghou shenya* (The Career of the Queen of Cinema) (Hangzhou: Zhejiang renmin, 1986), pp. 163–67.

22. She actually made her second comeback to the screen in 1956, playing a role in *The Family* (*Jia*) based on Ba Jin's famous novel.

23. Tom Gunning, "An Aesthetic of Astonishment: Early Film and the (In)credulous Spectator," *Art and Text* 34 (Spring 1989): 31–45.

24. Zhong Yuan, "Guan 'Yingmu yanshi' hou" (After watching *An Amorous History of the Silver Screen*), *Yingxi shenghuo* (hereafter *YXSH*) (1931), 1, no. 34: 15–17.

25. Tom Gunning, "An Aesthetic of Astonishment," p. 43.

26. Hans Ulrich Gumbrecht, "A Farewell to Interpretation," in *Materialities of Communication,* ed. Hans Ulrich Gumbrecht and K. Ludwig Pfeiffer (Palo Alto: Stanford University Press, 1994), pp. 398–99.

CHAPTER ONE

1. Foucault defines episteme as an "epistemological field," in which "conditions of possibility" of a prevalent form of historical experience and knowledge may be identified. Michel Foucault, *The Order of Things: An Archaeology of the Human Sciences* (New York, Pantheon Books, 1971), xxii.
2. Vachel Lindsay, *The Art of the Moving Picture* (Liveright Publishing Company, 1970; originally published by The Macmillan Company in 1915). Miriam Hansen finds the locus of this "universal language" or "visual Esperanto" in the institutionalization of narrative cinema as a representational system and the emergence, or construction, of a mass spectatorship. See her comments on Lindsay's and others' views in *Babel and Babylon: Spectatorship in American Silent Film* (Cambridge, Mass.: Harvard University Press, 1991), pp. 76–89; and chapter 7, "Film History, Archaeology, Universal Language," about Griffith's implementation of the utopian vision.
3. Miriam Hansen, "The Mass Production of the Senses: Classical Cinema as Vernacular Modernism," *Modernism / Modernity* 6, no. 2 (1999): 68.
4. Jonathan Friedman, *Cultural Identity and Global Process* (London: Sage, 1994), p. 230.
5. Linda Williams, "Film Bodies: Gender, Genre, and Excess" in *Film Genre Reader II,* ed. Barry Keith Grant (Austin: University of Texas Press, 1995), pp. 140–58.
6. Rey Chow, *Woman and Chinese Modernity: The Politics of Reading between East and West* (Minneapolis: University of Minnesota Press, 1991). For a detailed study of this literature's late Qing precursors and their relations to modernity, see David Der-wei Wang. *Fin-de-siècle Splendor: Repressed Modernities of Late Qing Fiction, 1849–1911* (Palo Alto: Stanford University Press, 1997).
7. Leo Charney and Vanessa R. Schwartz, eds., introduction to *Cinema and the Invention of Modern Life* (Berkeley: University of California Press, 1995), p. 1
8. Ibid., p. 8.
9. Ibid., p. 10.
10. Wolfgang Schivelbusch, *Railway Journey: The Industrialization of Time and Space in the Nineteenth Century* (Berkeley: University of California Press, 1986 [1977]).
11. Lynn Kirby, *Parallel Tracks: The Railroad and Silent Cinema* (Durham, N.C.: Duke University Press, 1997), p. 7.
12. Anne Friedberg, *Window Shopping: Cinema and the Postmodern* (Berkeley: University of California Press, 1993), pp. 2–3.
13. Walter Benjamin, *The Arcades Project,* trans. Howard Eiland and Kevin McLaughlin (Cambridge, Mass.: Harvard University Press, 1999), pp. 416–55.
14. Lauren Rabinovitz, *For the Love of Pleasure: Women, Movies and Culture in Turn-of-the-Century Chicago* (New Brunswick, N.J.: Rutgers University Press, 1998).

15. Susan Buck-Morss, "The Flâneur, the Sandwichman, and the Whore: The Politics of Loitering," *New German Critique* 39 (1986): 99–140.
16. Rabinovitz, *For the Love of Pleasure*, pp. 180–81.
17. Ibid., p. 184.
18. David Bordwell, *On the History of Film Style* (Cambridge, Mass: Harvard University Press, 1997), pp. 141–46.
19. Ben Singer, *Melodrama and Modernity: Early Sensational Cinema and Its Contexts* (New York: Columbia University Press, 2001).
20. Ibid, p. 65. According to Singer, the term was originally coined by Michael Davis, a New York social reformer, in his book, *The Exploitation of Pleasure* (New York: Russell Sage Foundation, 1911).
21. Ibid., pp. 90–97.
22. Ibid., pp. 294–95.
23. Miriam Hansen, "Benjamin and Cinema: Not a One-Way Street," *Critical Inquiry* 25, no. 2 (Winter 1999): 313.
24. Ibid., p. 321.
25. Wolfgang Schivelbusch, *The Railroad Journey*, pp. 52–69.
26. Tom Gunning, "The Whole Town Is Gawking: Early Cinema and the Visual Experience of Modernity," *Yale Journal of Criticism* 7, no. 2 (1994): 191.
27. Walter Benjamin, "The Work of Art in the Age of Mechanical Reproduction," in *Illuminations*, ed. Hannah Arendt (New York: Harcourt, Brace and World, 1968), pp. 220–22.
28. Miriam Hansen, "Benjamin and Cinema," p. 312.
29. Ibid., p. 321.
30. Ibid., p. 329.
31. André Bazin, "Charlie Chaplin," in *What Is Cinema?* vol. 1, trans. Hugh Gray (Berkeley: University of California Press, 1967), p. 152.
32. See He Xiujun, "Zhang Shichuan he Mingxing yingpian gongsi" (Zhang Shichuan and Mingxing Company), in *WSDY*, p. 1520.
33. Gunning, "An Aesthetic of Astonishment," p. 129.
34. Walter Benjamin, "A Short History of Photography," *Screen* 13 (Spring 1972 [1931]): 7.
35. Hansen, "Benjamin and Cinema," p. 340.
36. Benjamin, *Illuminations*, pp. 36–37.
37. See Benjamin, "Flâneur," in *Selected Writings*, vol. 1; Georg Simmel, "Mental Life of the Metropolis," in *On Individuality and Social Forms*, ed. Donald Levine (Chicago: University of Chicago Press, 1971).
38. Gunning, "The Whole Town Is Gawking."
39. Miriam Hansen, "America, Paris, and the Alps: Kracauer (and Benjamin) on Cinema and Modernity," in *Cinema and the Invention of Modern Life*, ed. Leo Charney et al., pp. 362–402.
40. Miram Hansen, "The Mass Production of the Senses: Classical Cinema as Vernacular Modernism," *Modernism / Modernity* 6, no. 2 (1999): p. 60.
41. Ibid., 61–62. See also Yuri Tsivian, "Between the Old and the New: Soviet Film Culture in 1918–1924," *Griffithiana* 55/56 (1996): 15–63.

42. Miriam Hansen, "Fallen Women, Rising Stars, New Horizons: Shanghai Silent Film As Vernacular Modernism," *Film Quarterly* 54, no. 1 (2000): 10–22.
43. Ibid., p. 14.
44. See for example, John Brinckerhoff Jackson, *Discovering the Vernacular Landscape* (New Haven, Conn.: Yale University Press, 1984), p. 85.
45. See the essays in Mete Turan, ed., *Vernacular Architecture: Paradigms of Environmental Response* (Aldershot, England: Avebury, 1990).
46. Amos Rapoport, "Defining Vernacular Design," in *Vernacular Architecture*, ed. Turan, pp. 76–77. Note that figure 4:2 in his article indicates that the "vernacular" and the "popular" occupying the broad middle in the continuum.
47. Johanna Drucker, *The Visible Word: Experimental Typography and Modern Art, 1909–1923* (University of Chicago Press, 1994), p. 141.
48. Ibid., pp. 142–43.
49. Bozkurt Güvenç, "Vernacular Architecture as a Paradigm: Case Argument," in Turan, ed., *Vernacular Architecture*, pp. 286–88.
50. Sheldon Pollock, "Cosmopolitan and Vernacular in History," *Public Culture* 12, no. 3 (Fall 2000): 624. For a recent collective effort to redefine cosmopolitanism, focusing particularly on its affective, nonelite, and non-Western centered articulations, see Bruce Robbins, ed., *Cosmopolitics: Thinking and Feeling Beyond the Nation* (Minneapolis: University of Minnesota Press, 1998).

51. Xiong Yuezhi and Xu Min, *Wanqing wenhua* (Culture of the Late Qing Period), vol. 6 in *Shanghai tongshi* (A Survey History of Shanghai) (Shanghai: Shanghai renmin, 1999), p. 496. For a list of select vernacular newspapers published in Shanghai see pp. 501–2. See also Ma Guangren, ed., *Shanghai xinwen shi 1850–1949* (History of Journalism in Shanghai, 1850–1949) (Shanghai: Fudan daxue, 1996), pp. 282–87.
52. Zhou Wu and Wu Guilong, *Wanqing shehui* (Late Qing Society), vol. 5 in *Shanghai tongshi* (A Survey History of Shanghai), ed. Xiong Yuezhi (Shanghai: Shanghai renmin, 1999), p. 391.
53. Ma Guangren, ed., *Shanghai xinwen shi*, pp. 286–87.
54. The most established text that holds this orthodox view is Cheng Jihua, et al., *Zhongguo dianying fazhan shi* (History of the Development of Chinese Cinema, 2 vols.) (Beijing: Zhongguo dianying, 1981), hereafter as *FZS*. The earliest serious treatment on early film history by Zheng Junli, an important left-wing actor and director in the 1930s, is in retrospect a more nuanced and sophisticated account from a Marxist perspective. Yet in Zheng's equally evolutionist chronology, popular genres such as the martial arts film are dismissed and the left-wing political cinema is privileged. See his *Xiandai Zhongguo dianying shilüe* (A Concise History of Modern Chinese film), in *Zhongguo yishu fazhan shi* (A History of the Development of Art in Modern China) (Shanghai: Liangyou, 1936). For a critical assessment of various approaches in Chinese film historiography, see Yingjin Zhang, introduction to *Cinema and Urban Culture in Shanghai*, pp. 5–12.
55. Ke Ling, "Shi wei 'Wusi' yu dianying hua yi lunkuo" (An Attempt at Draw-

ing a Contour for the May Fourth Movement and the Cinema) [1983], in *Ke Ling dianying wencun* (Selected Extant Writings of Ke Ling), ed. Chen Wei (Beijing: Zhongguo dianying, 1992), pp. 286–302. Ke Ling entered the Shanghai film world as a left-wing writer in the early 1930s.

56. See Vera Schwarcz, *The Chinese Enlightenment: Intellectuals and the Legacy of the May Fourth Movement of 1919* (Berkeley: University of California Press, 1986).
57. Chow Tse-Tsung, *The May Fourth Movement: Intellectual Revolution in Modern China* (Cambridge, Mass.: Harvard University Press, 1960), p. 59. The journal had only shifted to the use of the vernacular the year before, in 1918.
58. Walter Ong, *Orality and Literary: The Technologizing of the Word* (Methum and Co. Ltd., 1982; reprinted by Routledge, 1988). Ong's study has admittedly a transhistorical scope rather than a focus on the impact of industrial capitalism and modern print technology on the orality-writing dynamic and cultural identity. For a seminal study on the latter, see Benedict Anderson, *Imagined Communites: Reflections on the Origin and Spread of Nationalism* (New York: Verso, 1983).
59. See Nie Gannu, *Cong baihuawen dao xin wenzi* (From Vernacular Language to New Writing) (Shanghai: Dazhong wenhua, 1936), pp. 48–53.
60. See Raymond Williams, *Keywords: A Vocabulary of Culture and Society* (New York: Oxford University Press, 1983), pp. 126–28.
61. In his book, *The City in Modern Chinese Literature and Film: Configuration of Space, Time, and Gender,* Yingjin Zhang also attempted to apply Benjamin's concept to the Chinese context (pp. 128–33).
62. Walter Benjamin, *Charles Baudelaire: A Lyric Poet in the Era of High-Capitalism* (New York and London: Verso, 1983), pp. 109–45.
63. Ibid., "The Flâneur," passim. "Botanizing on the asphalt" is congruous with "seasickness on dry land." The latter appears in "Franz Kafka: On the Tenth Anniversary of His Death," in *Illuminations,* p. 130. Both descriptions are suggestive of Benjamin's conception of the cosmopolitan life as a manifestation of a modern cosmology that violently juxtaposes the present and the archaic, culture and nature. For an unconventional application of Benjamin's idea to anthropological inquiries, see Michael Taussig, *Mimesis and Alterity: A Particular History of the Senses* (New York: Routledge, 1993), especially chapter 2, "Physiognomic Aspects of Visual Worlds," pp. 19–32.
64. Lydia Liu gives two examples from two classical texts, Tao Qian's *Soushen houji* (Sequel to Catching Spirits) and Cao Xueqin's *Honglou meng* (Dream of the Red Chamber). In the first case, experience has to do with Chinese medical knowledge related to divination. The latter example has, however, direct reference to sensory knowing connected to tasting, seeing and hearing. See *Translingual Practice: Literature, National Culture and Translated Modernity. China, 1900–1937* (Palo Alto, Calif.: Stanford University Press, 1995), p. 316. For a study on the uses or adaptations of the term in the modern discourse and practice of Chinese medicine, see Xianglin Lei, "How Did Chinese Medicine Become Experiential? The Political Epistemology of *Jingyan,*" *Positions* 10, no. 2 (Fall 2002): 333–64.

65. For an informative study on Hu Shi's intellectual career, see Min-chih Chou, *Hu Shih and Intellectual Choice in Modern China* (Ann Arbor: University of Michigan Press, 1984).
66. Hu Shi, "Wenxue gailiang chuyi" (Some modest proposals for the reform of literature), *Xin qingnian* 2, no. 5 (January 1917); translation from Kirk Denton, ed., *Modern Chinese Literary Thought: Writings on Literature, 1893–1945* (Palo Alto, Calif.: Stanford University Press, 1996), pp. 123–39. *New Youth* published the first piece of fiction written in the vernacular by Lu Xun in January 1918. Hu Shi first experimented with vernacular writing and publishing when he studied in new-style schools in Shanghai as a teenager, 1904–10, before he left for America. See Hu Shi, "Sishi zishu" (An Autobiography Written at the Age of Forty), in *Hu Shi zizhuan* (Autobiography of Hu Shi), ed. Cao Boyuan (Hefei: Huangshan shushe, 1986 [1935]), pp. 54–62.
67. Translation from Kirk Denton, *Modern Chinese Literary Thought,* p. 124.
68. Ibid., passim.
69. In an effort to rescue vernacular literature from the past and "restore" its canonical status or historical significance, Hu Shi wrote *Baihua wenxue shi* (History of Vernacular Literature) (Changsha: Yuelu shushe, 1986 [1928]).
70. Translation from Kirk Denton, *Modern Chinese Literary Thought,* p. 137.
71. Hu Shi, *Changshiji* (Experiments) (Shanghai: Yadong tushuguan, 1922 [1920]), pp. 91–93. The poem was written on October 10, 1920.

72. According to this preface, the first three editions sold about ten thousand copies within two years, a phenomenal number for a poetry collection (p. 1).
73. Ibid., pp. 2–3; emphasis added.
74. See Rey Chow, *Woman and Chinese Modernity: The Politics of Reading between West and East,* chapter 4, "Loving Women: Masochism, Fantasy, and the Idealization of the Mother." Bound feet did, however, play a concrete role in Hu Shi's personal experience. Before he went to America, he was engaged to a woman with bound feet whom his mother chose for him in his native Anhui province. When he was studying at Columbia, he fell in love with an American woman. Unable to absolve his feeling of moral obligation, he married the Chinese woman upon returning to China.
75. The representative work of this approach is Christian Metz, *Film Language* (New York: Oxford University Press, 1974).
76. Paul Stoller, *Sensuous Scholarship* (Philadelphia: University of Pennsylvania Press, 1997).
77. The term is coined by Michael Jackson, *Path Toward a Clearing: Radical Empiricism and Ethnographic Inquiry* (Bloomington: Indiana University Press, 1989), as quoted in Thomas J. Csordas, "Introduction: The Body as Representation and Being-in-the-World," in *Embodiment and Experience: The Existential Ground of Culture and Self* (New York: Cambridge University Press, 1994), p. 10.
78. Thomas Csordas, introduction to *Embodiment and Experience,* p. 12.
79. Vivian Sobchack, "Phenomenology and the Film Experience," in *Viewing*

Positions: Ways of Seeing Film, ed. Linda Williams (New Brunswick, N.J.: Rutgers University Press, 1997), pp. 36–58. The article is taken from Sobchack's book, *The Address of the Eye: A Phenomenology of the Film Experience* (Princeton: Princeton University Press, 1992).

80. Siegfried Kracauer, "Photography" (1927), trans. Thomas Levin, *Critical Inquiry* 19 (Spring 1993), p. 433.
81. Siegfried Kracauer, *Theory of Film: The Redemption of Physical Reality* (Princeton: Princeton University Press, 1997), pp. 71–72.
82. Steven Shaviro argues, "The cinematic apparatus is a new mode of embodiment; it is a technology for containing and controlling bodies, but also for affirming, perpetuating, and multiplying them, by grasping them in the terrible, uncanny immediacy of their images. . . . The body is a necessary condition and support of the cinematic process: it makes that process possible, but also continually interrupts it, unlacing its sutures and swallowing up its meanings." *The Cinematic Body* (Minneapolis: Minnesota University Press, 1993), pp. 256–57.
83. See Susan Buck-Morss, "The Cinema Screen as Prosthesis of Perception: A Historical Account," in C. Nadia Seremetakis, ed., *The Senses Still: Perception and Memory as Material Culture* (Boulder, Colo.: Westview Press, 1994), pp. 45–63.
84. Michael Taussig, *Mimesis and Alterity,* p. 24.
85. See Miriam Hansen's remarks on the textual history of the book in her introduction to Kracauer's *Theory of Film,* vii–xlv.
86. Kracauer, "Photography," pp. 422–23; emphasis added.
87. Ibid., pp. 426–29.
88. See Thomas Levin's footnote, ibid., p. 423. Those theatrical productions were said to be the forerunners of the "musicals." See also Karsten Witte, "Introduction to Siegfried Kracauer's 'The Mass Ornament,'" *New German Critique* 5 (1975): 63.
89. Siegfried Kracauer, *The Mass Ornament,* trans. Thomas Levin (Cambridge, Mass.: Harvard University Press, 1995), p. 77. This idea foreshadows the observation he made in the essay on photography, that "[f]or the first time in history, photography brings to the fore the entire natural shell" (Kracauer, "Photography," p. 422).
90. "Assemblage" and "body without organs" are two key concepts in Gilles Deleuze and Félix Guattari's collaborative works, developed fully in *A Thousand Plateaus: Capitalism and Schizophrenia* (Minneapolis: University of Minnesota Press, 1987). For Deleuze and Guattari, "assemblage" constitutes the dynamic integration of the body and the machine in capitalist production, which I find germane to Kracauer's conception of the "mass ornament."
91. Emphasis on "aesthetic pleasure" was original. As Karsten Witte rightly points out, this legitimation is conditional. "It is valid only if the aesthetic expression of the masses is not separated from the acknowledgment of their political authority." The "mass ornament" as later deployed by the Nazi regime certainly bespeaks its negative or reactionary orientation. "Introduction to Siegfried Kracauer's *The Mass Ornament,*" p. 64.

92. Siegfried Kracauer, *The Mass Ornament,* op. cit.
93. Kracauer, "Photography," pp. 435–36; emphasis added.
94. This view resonates with Benjamin's conviction of the cinema as being the exemplary means for "the everyday reschooling for the mimetic faculty" in modernity. Michael Taussig, *Mimesis and Alterity,* p. 29.
95. Karsten Witte, "Introduction to Siegfried Kracauer's 'The Mass Ornament,'" p. 64.
96. Gongsun Lu, *Zhongguo dianying shihua* (Historical Accounts of Chinese Cinema), Hong Kong: Guangjiaojing, 1976, pp. 50–52.
97. Wang Hanlun, "Yingchang huiyilu" (Memoires of the Film Studio), *Liangyou,* no. 64 (December 1931): 32.
98. The director Ren Jinping who introduced Wang to Mingxing Company, describes her as someone who "enjoys [using] English . . . [and] has extensive social contacts." She also worked as a private teacher for a family in Hong Kong after leaving the typist position. Ren Jinping, "Wang Hanlun nüshi" (Miss Wang Hanlun), *Dianying zazhi* (Movies Monthly) 1, no. 1 (May 1924).
99. Wang Hanlun, "Wo ru yingxi jie shimo" (How I Entered the Film World), *Dianying zazhi* 2, no. 1 (1925).
100. Wang Hanlun, "Wode congying jingguo" (My Experience with the Cinema), in *WSDY,* pp. 1471–75 [originally published in *Zhongguo dianying* no. 2, 1956].
101. Zhang Shichuan, "Zi wo daoyan yilai," *Mingxing banyuekan* 1, no. 4 (1935): 16.

102. At the turn of the twentieth century, this practice was carried over to the modern spoken drama and subsequently cinema for some time.
103. The term "taste for reality" is adapted from Vanessa R. Schwartz, "Cinema Spectatorship before the Apparatus: The Public Taste for Reality in Fin-de-Siècle Paris," in Linda Williams, ed., *Viewing Positions: Ways of Seeing Film* (New Brunswick, N.J.: Rutgers University Press, 1997), pp. 87–113.
104. For a comprehensive account of early Chinese film actresses including some mentioned here, see Michael Chang, "The Good, the Bad, and the Beautiful: Movie Actresses and Public Discourse in Shanghai, 1920s–1930s," in *Cinema and Urban Culture,* ed. Yingjin Zhang, pp. 128–59.
105. Gongsun Lu, *Zhongguo dianying shihua* (Historical Accounts of Chinese Cinema), (Hong Kong: Guangjiaojing, 1976), pp. 39–41, 53–54.
106. There were two other famous modern girls known also by their "foreign" names—Miss A. A. (Ace Ace) and Miss S. S. (Shanghai Style). Miss. A. A.'s real name is Fu Wenhao, and she also appeared in films. She was allegedly the first Chinese woman to obtain a driver's license in the International Settlements of Shanghai. Cheng Bugao, *Yingtan yijiu* (Reminiscences of the Film World) (Beijing: Zhongguo dianying, 1983), p. 57.
107. Gong Jianong congying huiyilu (Gong Kung's Memoirs of His Silver Screen Life; hereafter abbreviated as *GJN*), vol. 1, Taipei: Wenxing shudian, 1966–67, p. 123.
108. Wang Hanlun, "Wode congying jingguo," pp. 1476–77. The original English title for the film is *Blind Love.* For a synopsis of the film, see Zhongguo dianying ziliaoguan (China Film Archive), ed., *Zhongguo wusheng dianying*

juben (Chinese silent film scripts), 3 vols. Beijing: Zhongguo dianying, 1996 (hereafter *WSDYJB*), pp. 1849–50.

109. See He Naihan's detailed reportage on Wang's trip to Ha'erbin, "Nüxing Wang Hanlun lai Ha xianji ji" (A report on the female star Wang Hanlun's trip to offer her art in Ha'erbin), *Xin yinxing yu tiyu shijie* (Silverland / Sports World), vol. 3, no. 21 (May 1930):19, 21.

110. Paul Zumthor, 'Body and Performance." In Gumbrecht et al., eds., *Materialities of Communication.* (Palo Alto, Calif.: Stanford University Press, 1994), p. 224.

CHAPTER TWO

1. That is, after New York, London, Berlin, Chicago, and Paris.
2. *All About Shanghai: A Standard Guidebook,* with an introduction by H. J. Lethbridge, (Hong Kong: Oxford University Press, 1983; originally published by the University Press, Shanghai, 1934–35), p. 1.
3. The following are some notable titles in Shanghai studies from these perspectives: Harriet Sergeant, *Shanghai: A Collision Point of Cultures* (London: John Murray, 1998 [1991]); Betty Peh-T'i Wei, *Shanghai: The Crucible of Modern China* (Hong Kong and New York: Oxford University Press, 1987); Christopher Howe, ed., *Shanghai: Revolution and Development in an Asian Metropolis* (New York: Cambridge University Press, 1981); Elizabeth Perry, *Shanghai on Strike: The Politics of Chinese Labor* (Palo Alto, Calif.: Stanford University Press, 1993); Jeffrey Wasserstrom, *Student Protests in Twentieth-Century China: The View from Shanghai* (Palo Alto, Calif.: Stanford University Press, 1991); Emily Honig, *Sisters and Strangers: Women in the Shanghai Cotton Mills* (Stanford University Press, 1986); Frederik Wakeman Jr., *Policing Shanghai 1927–1937* (Berkeley: University of California Press, 1995); Bryna Goodman, *Native Place, City, and Nation: Regional Networks and Identities in Shanghai, 1853–1937* (Berkeley: University of California Press, 1995); and Christian Henriot, *Shanghai 1927–1937: Municipal Power, Locality, and Modernization* (Berkeley: University of California Press, 1993).
4. Leo Ou-fan Lee, *Shanghai Modern: The Flowering of a New Urban Culture in China, 1930–1945* (Cambridge, Mass: Harvard University Press, 1999).
5. Other notable efforts include Zhang Yingjin's *The City in Modern Chinese Literature and Film:* Configuration of Space, Tim, and Gender (Palo Alto, Calif.: Stanford University Press, 1996) and Shih Shu-Mei's *The Lure of the Modern: Writing Modernism in Semicolonial Shanghai* (Berkeley: University of California Press, 2001).
6. It became a county seat more than seven hundred years ago and set up a customs house three hundred years ago. Its ties with the surrounding Jiangnan region, the source of raw material and goods as well as prospective citizens, were very important for its southern regional identity.
7. *Haipai* originally refers to a particular style and commercial practice of painting originated in the Shanghai region in the late Qing period but its usage was gradually extended to opera, literature, and lifestyle as a whole. See Xiong Yuezhi and Zhang Min, *Wanqing wenhua,* p. 33.

8. Jonathan Hay, "Painting and the Built Environment in Late-Nineteenth-Century Shanghai," *Chinese Art: Modern Expressions,* ed. Maxwell K. Hearn and Judith G. Smith (New York: The Metropolitan Museum of Art, 2001), p. 87.
9. The figures are from Zhen Zu'an, *Bainian Shanghai cheng* (A Century of the City of Shanghai) (Shanghai: Xuelin, 1999), p. 230.
10. For a detailed analysis of the changing cartography of the city in late 19th century, see Ye Kaidi, "Nali shi Shanghai?" (Where was Shanghai?), *Ershiyi shiji,* no. 48 (June 1998): 72–88.
11. For a discussion of Shanghai's *shi* character (as opposed to *cheng*), see Xu Daoming, *Haipai wenxue lun* (On Shanghai Style Literature) (Shanghai: Fudan daxue, 1999), pp. 31–58. *Shi* is an integral aspect of *xiaoshimin,* or the petty urbanites. *Shi* is also linked to "urban" or "urbane" in a modern sense whereas *cheng* is not.
12. The first tram was put in use in 1908, followed by trackless streetcars in the International Settlement in 1914.
13. See Xiong Yuezhi, "Shanghai zujie yu Shanghai shehui sixiang bianqian" (Shanghai Concessions and the Changes in Social Thought), *Shanghai yanjiu luncong* no.2 (1989). *Chang* was also translated as "ground" in the Shanghai cartography of the late nineteenth century. See Ye Kaidi (Kathrine Yeh), "Nali shi Shanghai?" p. 74.
14. On *haipai,* see also Li Tiangang, *Wenhua Shanghai* (Cultural Shanghai) (Shanghai jiaoyu, 1998), pp. 3–34. Li defines *haipai* as essentially a modern urban mass culture with Chinese characteristics, or "simply, the culture of city dwellers" (p. 29).

15. Both *hai* and *yang* connote vastness, the far away, and open-mindedness. The city has (or had) a number of other "aquatic" names—such as *Hu* derived from fishing and *Shen* after the nearby river—all related to Shanghai's relation to the ocean and surrounding bodies of water.
16. As quoted in Zhen Zu'an, *Bainian Shanghai cheng,* p. 358.
17. Ma Xuexin et al, eds., *Shanghai wenhua yuanliu cidian* (A Lexicon on the Origins of Shanghai Culture) (Shanghai shehui kexue, 1992), p. 525.
18. Other treaty ports, especially Canton under the strong influence of the British colonial culture of Hong Kong also saw the flourishing of a locally inflected pidgin English. For a study of the history of the sociolinguistic phenomenon, see Zou Zhenhuan, "Shijiu shiji xiabanqi Shanghaide 'Yingyu re' yu zaoqi Yingyu duben jiqi yingxiang" (Shanghai's "English fever" in the Latter Half of the Nineteenth Century and the Early English Readers and Their Effect"), in Ma Changlin ed., *Zujie li de Shanghai* (Shanghai's Foreign Concessions) (Shanghai shehui kexueyuan, 2003), pp. 93–106.
19. See Cao Juren, *Shanghai chunqiu* (Shanghai Chronicles) (Shanghai renmin, 1996), p. 177. Cao also cites one example of Yangjingbang use of Chinese syntax to speak English: "A boat has two eye. / No eye, how can see. / No can see, how can go."
20. Yao Gonghe, *Shanghai xianhua* (Idle Talk of Shanghai) (Shanghai: Shangwu yinshuguan, 1926 [1917]), pp. 30–31. In the opening of the book, Yao

states that "from a political point of view, Shanghai may be the entry point for foreign invasion. But from a material point of view, Shanghai is really the cradle of [modern] civilization for the whole country."

21. A reverse kind of pidgin in Shanghai dialect could be found in many foreign language newspapers. See Xiong Yuezhi and Xu Min, *Wanqing wenhua,* p. 49.
22. Cai Fengming, *Shanghai dushi minsu* (Shanghai Urban Folklore) (Shanghai: Xuelin, 2001), pp. 173, 201.
23. For a study on the late Qing publishing fever see Leo Ou-fan Lee and Andrew J. Nathan, "The Beginning of Mass Culture: Journalism and Fiction in the Late Ch'ing and Beyond," in David Johnson, Andrew J. Nathan, Evelyn S. Rawski, eds., *Popular Culture in Late Imperial China.* Berkeley: University of California Press, 1985, pp. 360–95. See also, Xiong Yuezhi and Xu Min, *Wanqing wenhua,* chapter 2.
24. Marcia Yonemoto, "The Spatial Vernacular in Tokugawa Maps," *Journal of Asian Studies,* 59, no. 3 (2000): 647–66.
25. See Tess Johnson and Deke Erh, *A Last Look: Western Architecture in Old Shanghai* (Hong Kong: Old China Hand Press, 1993).
26. Leo Ou-fan Lee, *Shanghai Modern,* p. 12.
27. See Li Jiang, "Lilong jutaku" (Rowhouses), *Sinica* 11, no. 7 (2000): 40–42. *Lilong* is another name for *longtang.* Li argues the sound of *long* (in the Shanghai dialect) is derived from "row"—this would be a typical example of Yangjingbang pidgin.

28. Ackbar Abbas, "Cosmopolitan De-scriptions: Shanghai and Hong Kong," *Public Culture* 12, no. 3 (Fall 2000): 774.
29. On such "high-minded" forms of cosmopolitanism, see Joseph Levenson's seminal study, *Revolution and Cosmopolitanism: The Western Stage and Chinese Stages* (Berkeley: University of California, 1971).
30. The term "unintended city" is coined by the Indian architect and social activist Jai Sen to designate the "space where the disenfranchised and the marginal sections of society live in contradiction [though never separate] to elite urban utopias. It is the "often unintended result of planning and social programs and policies, as opposed to direct exploitation." "The Unintended City," *Seminar,* no. 200 (April 1976). (As quoted in Ranjani Mazumdar, "Urban Allegories: The City in Bombay Cinema, 1970–2000," Ph.D. diss. NYU, 2000, pp. 50–51.)
31. Shanghai tongshe, ed., *Shanghai yanjiu ziliao* (Research Materials on Shanghai) (1936), p. 324.
32. Xiong Yuezhi and Xu Min, *Wanqing wenhua,* p. 480.
33. *Dianshizhai huabao,* vol. 1, no. 1, 1884.
34. Xiong Yuezhi and Xu Min, *Wanqing wenhua,* p. 482.
35. This sketch of the atmosphere of the Shanghai teahouse culture is based on a reading of *Tuhua ribao* (The Illustrated Daily), July 1908–February 1909.
36. Tom Gunning, "The Cinema of Attractions: Early Film, Its Spectator and the Avant-Garde." *Wide Angle* 8, nos. 3, 4 (Fall 1986): 63–70.
37. Gunning, "The Cinema of Attractions," p. 57.

38. *Tuhua ribao,* vol. 1, no. 1, 1908.
39. Shen Lixing, "Jiu Shanghaide shijie 're'" (The World Fever in Old Shanghai), in *Shanghai shehui daguan* (An Overview of Shanghai Society), ed. Shi Fukang, (Shanghai shudian, 2000), p. 277.
40. Zhou Shixun ed., *Shanghai daguan* (A Panorama of Shanghai) (Shanghai: Wenhua meishu tushu gongsi, 1933), section on "Shanghai zhi sige shijie" (Four Worlds in Shanghai).
41. Tu Shiping, ed., *Shanghaishi daguan* (Shanghai Panorama) (Zhongguo zazhitushu gongsi, 1948), part 2, chapter 27, section 5. This kind of "tower" replaces the function of pagodas for obtaining the pleasure of a commanding view of the landscape from a vantage point, only now the landscape viewed is the city. Zheng Yimei et al., *Shanghai jiuhua* (Old Shanghai Tales) (Shanghai wenhua, 1986), p. 105.
42. *Xin Shanghai* (New Shanghai) (Shanghai yinshuguan, 1930), pp. 127–28.
43. Walter Benjamin, "Grandville, or the World Exhibition," in *The Arcades Project,* translated by Howard Eiland and Kevin McLaughlin; ed. Rolf Tiedmann (Cambridge, Mass.: Harvard University Press, 1999), p. 7.
44. Jonathan Hay, "Painting and the Built Environment in Late-Nineteenth-Century Shanghai," p. 75. Hay distinguishes "the architecture of spectacle" from "architecture of permanence," referring to monumental civic buildings, and "architecture of displacement," which consisted of buildings built by and for migrants and sojourners from other parts of China.

45. The term is borrowed from Wen-hsin Yeh, "Shanghai Modernity: Commerce and Culture in a Republican City," *China Quarterly* (1997), p. 392.
46. It was observed that the French concession where the New World stood was more liberal than the British controlled international concession. Zheng Yimei et al, *Shanghai jiuhua,* p. 114.
47. See Bao Tianxiao, *Chuanyinglou huiyilu xubian* (Sequel to the Reminisces of the Bracelet Shadow Chamber) (Hong Kong: Dahua, 1973), pp. 93–94.
48. Zhang Shichuan, "Zi wo daoyan yilai" (Since I Started Directing), *Mingxing banyuekan* vol, 1, no. 5 (1935). Zhang was the nephew of Wang Guozhen, the proprietress of the establishment.
49. See Yao Gonghe, *Shanghai xianhua,* p. 48. The term, derived from the words *kitten* (*mao'er*) and *hats* (*mào'er*) refers to women impersonating men with hair covered up, and suggests fashion (as in *shimao*).
50. Zhou Shixun, ed., *Shanghaishi daguan,* section on "Shanghai zhi baihuo gongsi" (Department Stores in Shanghai) (Shanghai: Wenhua meishu tushu gongsi, 1933). The author defines the department store (*baihuo gongsi,* literally a company with hundreds of goods) as "a big market that both collects goods from all over the world and also deals in national products."
51. Sincere Co. Ltd., *The 25th Anniversary Celebration Album,* 1924. The album also boasts the writings and calligraphy of major literary figures, including Kang Youwei, Zhou Shoujuan, (Shen) Zhengya, and Xu Zhuodai. Zhou contributed a particularly interesting "futuristic" entry on what Sincere would look like on its fiftieth anniversary.

52. Ann Friedberg, *Window Shopping: Cinema and the Postmodern* (Berkeley: University of California Press, 1993), pp. 29–32.
53. Ellen Thorbecke, *Shanghai* (Shanghai: North-China Daily News and Herald Ltd., 1941), p. 49.
54. An important precursor of the amusement halls and rooftop gardens in late nineteenth century is the large private garden-turned public leisure establishment, such as Zhang Yuan, Dangui Yuan, and Xu Yuan. Xu Yuan was allegedly the first venue that exhibited an "Occidental shadowplay" in Shanghai, in 1896.
55. Zhang Shichuan, who was the nephew of Jing Runsan, the founder and owner of the New World, allegedly came up with the passage idea. See Cheng Bugao, *Yingtan yijiu* (Reminiscences of the Film World) (Beijing: Zhongguo dianying, 1983), p. 64. The tunnel collapsed in 1930, which caused the subsequent shutdown of the north building.
56. For a study that brought the term "petty urbanites" to critical focus in Western scholarship on Shanghai modern history, see Wen-hsin Yeh, "Progressive Journalism and Shanghai's petty urbanites: Zou Taofen and the *Shenghuo* Enterprise," in *Shanghai Sojourners,* ed. Frederic Wakeman and Wen-hsin Yeh (Berkeley: Center for Chinese Studies Monograph Series, 1992), pp. 186–238.
57. I concur with Haochan Lu that the difficulty with defining the petty urbanites sociologically is due to the fact that they are not a fixed social category. See his *Beyond the Neon Lights: Everyday Shanghai in the Early Twentieth Century* (Berkeley: University of California Press, 1999), p. 167. Its chief characteristics are diversity, fluidity, and mobility, and as such it demands a cultural analysis that takes into account, among other things, the Yangjingbang character of the metropolis.
58. Shen Yanbing (Mao Dun), "Fengjiande xiaoshimin wenyi" (The Feudal Art of the Petty Urban Dwellers), *Dongfang zazhi* 30, no. 3 (Jan. 1, 1933), in *Yuanyang hudie pai yanjiu ziliao,* ed. Wei Shaochang, pp. 47–52.
59. As quoted in Chang-tai Hung, *Going to the People: Chinese Intellectuals and Folk Literature, 1918–1937* (Cambridge, Mass.: Harvard University Press, 1985), p. 14.
60. Lu Hongshi and Shu Xiaoming, *Zhongguo dianyingshi* (A History of Chinese Cinema), (Beijing: Wenhua yishu, 1998), p. 6.
61. Synopsia in Zhu Tianwei and Wang Zhenzhen, eds., *Zhongguo yingpian dadian 1905–1930* (Encyclopedia of Chinese Films) (Beijing: Zhongguo dianying, 1996), pp. 5–6.
62. These experiments are comparable to films such as *Rube and Mandy at the Coney Island* (1903), *Uncle Josh at the Picture Show* (1902), and many of Griffith's Biograph shorts.
63. For more on the content and making of these shorts, see Qian Huafo, "Yaxiya yingxi gongside chengli shimo" (The Origins of the Founding of the Asia Company), *WSDY,* 1455–58. Qian, an actor of both civilized play and Peking Opera, was one of the actors in this and several other films.

64. Shanghai tongshe, *Shanghai yanjiu ziliao xuji,* pp. 541–42. While these early venues have Chinese names transliterating foreign terms, many later ones carried meaningful Chinese names. This "bilingual" character of the theaters' names and its transformation over time is again a testimony to Yangjingbang as a "spatial vernacular."
65. Both were built or converted in 1912 in the aftermath of the Republican revolution when many teahouses, which had functioned as theaters, changed the names to theater houses or stages. Xinxin Wutai originally opened as Dangui Chayuan by Xia brothers who contributed to many early films. It was converted from part of the Louwailou Amusement Hall. In 1916, the new management leased the location from its owner, the Wing'an Department Store and changed the name to Tianzhan Wutai. Ma Xuexin et al., *Shanghai wenhua yuanliu cidian,* p. 670.
66. The actors of the Xinmin troupe actually participated in the war as well as in the film. This might be an early example of docudrama in China, although the absence of an extant print makes it hard to determine the degree of its docudramatic quality. See the advertisement in *Shenbao* for "Shanghai War" used by Jay Leyda in *Dianying: An Account of Films and the Film Audience in China* (Cambridge, Mass.: MIT Press, 1972), p. 12. Leyda's caption erroneously called the film "War in Wu Han."
67. Guan Haifeng and Zhang Shichuan founded the Huanxian Company in Xujiahui, one of the ephemeral enterprises.

68. Yuan Jin, *Yuanyang hudie pai* (The Mandarin Ducks and Butterflies School) (Shanghai: Shanghai shudian, 1994), p. 5. For a different account of the origin of the term see Ping Jinya, "'Yuanyang hudie pai' mingming de gushi" (The Story behind the Naming of the 'Mandarin Ducks and Butterflies'), in Wei Shaochang, *Yuanyang hudie pai yanju ziliao,* vol. 1, pp. 179–81. According to Ping, also a Butterfly author, the term came up at a dinner party when Liu Bannong, a May Fourth writer, called the novel *Jade Pear Spirit* a Butterfly novel. Liu also observed that many popular writers adopted pen names that contained Chinese characters for butterfly or other birds or insects.
69. Perry Link, *Mandarin Ducks and Butterflies: Popular Fiction in Early Twentieth-Century Chinese Cities* (Berkeley: University of California Press, 1981), p. 10. For a discussion on the public reception of traditional vernacular storytelling, see Patrick Hanna, *The Chinese Vernacular Story* (Cambridge, Mass.: Harvard University Press, 1981).
70. Perry Link, *Mandarin Ducks and Butterflies,* p. 6. According to the sources cited by Link, there was a six-fold expansion of printing industry in Shanghai from the early twentieth century to the early 1930s. New-style schools increased from 4,000 in 1905 to more than 120,000 by the late 1910s in China (p. 10).
71. Ibid., pp. 11–12.
72. For a sample of early "film stories" written in the semivernacular style, which was commonly used by Butterfly writers, see Tao Hancui, *(Huitu) Yingxi daguan* (An Illustrated Anthology of Shadowplays) (Shanghai shijie

shuju, 1924). Most stories were derived from European and American films and meant to provide models for Chinese cinema. See also Die Lu, ed., *Yingxi xiaoshuo sanshizhong* (Thirty Film Stories) (Shanghai: Jinzhi tushuguan, 1925). The latter includes a dozen of Chinese film stories, such as *Yan Ruisheng,* a big hit released in 1920.

73. Cheng Shuren, ed., *Zhonghua yingye nianjian* (Yearbook of Chinese Film) (Shanghai, 1927), section on "Yingye chubanwu" (film publications).
74. Xu Chiheng ed., *Zhongguo yingxi daguan* (Filmdom in China) (Shanghai: Hezuo, 1927), section on "Guanyu yingxi chubanwu zhi diaocha" (research on film publications).
75. It is possible that the precedence of film magazine publication in China can be found in the various *youxi* (literally, play or entertainment) or New Drama magazines, and to some extent, the popular Butterfly literary magazines. The latter were run by almost the same group of people who enthusiastically crossed from one entertainment form to another in that rapidly changing time.
76. Some of the translations of the magazines' titles are mine. The rather literal renditions are meant to show the prevalent use of the term *shadowplay* in the film discourse in that period.
77. Li Suyuan and Hu Jubin, *WSDYS,* p. 179. For a comprehensive and annotated account of film publications 1921–49, see Zhang Wei, Yinxian and Chen Jin, "Zhongguo xiandai dianying chubanwu zongmu tiyao" (A Concise Annotated Bibliography of Film Publications in Modern China) *Shanghai dianying shiliao* (1994), vol. 2, pp. 212–88; vol. 3, pp. 289–344.
78. *Dianying zhoubao,* 1925, no. 1 (April): 1.
79. Ibid., 11.
80. In fact, it was a period when a new generation of Chinese film stars with athletic bodies (such as the legendary couple Jin Yan and Wang Renmei) began to take over the center stage. It was certainly connected to the Nationalists' modernizing drive, in particular the New Life movement.
81. On the intersection between cinema, social dance, and political culture in Republican China, see Andrew Field, "Selling Souls in Sin City: Shanghai Singing and Dancing Hostesses in Print, Film, and Politics, 1920–40," in Yingjin Zhang, ed., *Cinema and Urban Culture in Shanghai,* pp. 99–127.
82. Gong Jianong, *GJN,* pp. 154–55, 31–32.
83. The idea of the Queen of Sports was obviously inspired by the title the "Queen of the Cinema" bestowed on Hu Die in 1933.
84. See Qing Ren, "Quanguo yundonghui li guanyu dianying fangmian de zhongzhong" (Diverse Things Surrounding Film During the National Sports Games), *Mingxing banyuekan,* no. 27 (1933): 7–8. The reporter also mentioned that Li Lili, the star who played the Queen of Sports, even hired a personal coach to improve her athletic skills in Nanjing. Many other stars who took an active interest in sports also arrived at the stadium to view the event, creating sensation as well as commotion.
85. Interview with Ms. Cheng Ying, Shanghai, October 1997.
86. At a few theaters earphones were installed for simultaneous interpretation.

The literal translation by a disembodied and technologically mediated voice was, however, not quite the same as the gesticulating and atmosphere-generating "interpreter" inside the auditorium. Interviews with Mr. Shu Yan in Beijing and Ms. Cheng Ying in Shanghai in the fall of 1997.

87. The genealogy goes back even further to the Symbolist poets active in the 1920s. See Harry A. Kaplan, "The Symbolist Movement in Modern Chinese Poetry," diss., Harvard University, 1989; Heinrich Fruehauf, "Urban Exoticism in Modern Chinese Literature, 1910–1933," diss., University of Chicago, 1990. For other treatments of the modernist movements in early twentieth-century China, see Randolph Trumbull, diss., "The Shanghai Modernists" (Stanford University, 1989); Yingjin Zhang, *The City in Modern Chinese Literature and Film* (Palo Alto: Stanford University Press, 1966), chapter 6, "The Circulation of Temporality and Eroticism in Shanghai." Leo Ou-fan Lee's *Shanghai Modern* and Shih Shu-mei's *The Lure of the Modern* are two recent studies that covered the subject substantially. I will have more to say on the controversy surrounding "soft cinema" in chapter 7.

88. This "translation" practice is further complicated by the fact that the Japanese writers were initially influenced by the French writer Paul Morand. Morand visited Shanghai in 1928. See Yan Jiayan's, introduction, *Xin ganjue pai xiaoshuo xuan* (An Anthology of the New Sensationalist Fiction) (Beijing: Renmin wenxue, 1985), pp. 1–6. For a more recent and perceptive study on the New Sensationalist literature in China, see also Wu Zhongjie and Wu Lichang, eds., *Zhongguo xiandaizhuyi xunzong 1900–1949* (Tracing Chinese Modernism, 1900–1949) (Shanghai: Xuelin, 1995), pp. 381–416.

89. These English and French translations of book or journal titles are original.

90. Yan Jiayan, ed., *Xin ganjue pai xiaoshuo xuan;* Liu Na'ou, *Dushi fengjingxian* (Shanghai: Shuimo shudian, 1930); Shi Zhecun, *One Rainy Evening* (Beijing: Panda / Chinese Literature Press, 1994).

91. Wang Ruiyong, "Shanghai yingyuan bianqian lu" (A Record of the Changes in Shanghai Cinema Theatres), in *Shanghai dianying shiliao* (Historical Material on Shanghai Cinema) 5 (1994), p. 86.

92. It is only fleetingly suggested that the film was an UFA production rather than a Hollywood film. The fact that the story was set in a "Parisian" theater in the French concession and a European film was shown there indicates that there was a certain measure of resistance to the Hollywood cinema among the intellectuals. In the story, the male character tries to explain to the girl what UFA was: "UFA is a leading German film maker. They turn out some excellent films. They're my favorites. I think they're better than anything that comes out of Hollywood" (p. 28).

93. Morodin could be a misspelling for Ivan Mozhukhin.

94. Zhecun Shi, "At the Paris Theatre," in *One Rainy Evening* (Beijing: Panda/ Chinese Literature Press, 1994), p. 38.

95. Shu-Mei Shi, *The Lure of the Modern,* pp. 342–54.

96. Cheng Shuren, *Zhonghua yingye nianjian,* "Zhonghua yingyeshi," p. 17.

97. See my article, "The Shanghai Factor in Hong Kong Cinema: Historical Perspectives," *Asian Cinema* 10, no.1 (Fall 1998): 146–59.

98. Jay Leyda, *Dianying,* pp, 24–27.
99. Thomas Bender, "The Culture of the Metropolis" (review essay), *Journal of Urban History* 14 (1988): 492–93.
100. Kevin Hetherington, *The Badlands of Modernity: Heterotopia and Social Ordering* (London and New York: Routledge, 1997), pp. 6–9.
101. Laikwan Pang, *Building a New China in Cinema: The Cinematic Left-wing Cinema Movement, 1932–1937* (Lanham, Md. and London: Rowman & Littlefield, 2002), p. 166. See Chapter 7 "A Shanghai Cinema or a Chinese Cinema?" for an insightful discussion on the relationship between this cinema movement and national identity.
102. Li Suyuan and Hu Jubin, *WSDYS,* pp. 95–96.

CHAPTER THREE

1. Lu Xun, "Shanghai wenyi zhi yipie" (A Glance at the Shanghai Arts), in *Lu Xun quanji,* vol. 4, p. 293; "Chengzha de fanqi" (The Surfacing of Dregs), *Lu Xun quanji,* vol. 4, p. 323.
2. Edward Gunn, *Rewriting Chinese: Style and Innovation in Twentieth-Century Chinese Prose* (Palo Alto, Calif.: Stanford University Press, 1991). Gunn's purpose is to uncover how "a Chinese educated elite [followed] what they perceived as the example of foreign nations in creating a national language, and [to] further [debate] the nature and role of that language in writing as part of a nation-building enterprise." See especially chapter 5, "Creative Stylists in Literature: 1918–42," pp. 95–133.
3. These terms were still relatively new to Chinese filmmakers as they had only been translated recently. According to Cheng Bugao's account, Zhang and Zheng's early filming experience was largely improvisational and collaborative. A detailed shooting script was an unknown concept until much later. Zheng's scripts, based on the models of Peking opera and modern spoken drama, consisted of rough outlines of scenarios (*mubiao*), allowing much room for actors' improvisation. See Cheng Bugao, *Yingtan yijiu* (Reminiscences of the Old Film World) (Beijing: Zhongguo dianying, 1983), pp. 108–10. See also Kou Tianwu, "Zhongguo dianyingshi shangde 'diyi'" (The "firsts" in Chinese film history), *Yingshi wenhua,* no. 2, 1989, p. 267. Cheng and Kou give different dates for the "first" full-fledged film script. Cheng recalls Xia Yan's *Torrent* (*Kuangliu*) of 1932 as the first instance of a real film script, whereas Kou attributes the "first" to Hong Shen's *Shen tu shi* published in 1925. It should be noted, however, that a "film script" as such was also quite a recent development in American film production, and Zhang was made aware of this through his conversations with a film professor from Columbia University who visited Zhang's company in the early 1920s. See Wang Suping, "Zhongguo dianying tuohuangzhede zuji—zaoqi dianying daoyan tanyilu" (Footprints of the pioneers of Chinese cinema—Early film directors on their art), *Yingshi wenhua* no. 2 (1989): 308. I will discuss in more detail the issue of screenwriting in chapter 5.
4. Gongsun Lu, *Zhongguo dianying shihua,* vol. 1: 46–48.
5. See *FZS,* vol. 1, p. 59. To date this work is the most comprehensive survey

of Chinese cinema up until 1949 but with obvious ideological biases. Tan Chunfa's book on Zheng Zhengqiu, however, revises this picture. According to his findings, *Laborer's Love* and *The King of Comedy* were shown at the Embassy Theater to a full house. Late arrivals had only standing room. Tan Chunfa, *Kai yidai xianhe,* p. 248.

6. See, for instance, the Hong Kong Arts Center and the Hong Kong Chinese Film Association's Programme for Hong Kong Arts Festival, 1984: *Tansuode niandai—Zaoqi Zhongguo dianying zhan* (Early Chinese Cinema: The Era of Exploration).
7. "Chronotope" is a key concept of Bakhtin's historical poetics. Literally meaning "time space," it refers to the "intrinsic connectedness of temporal and spatial relationships that are artistically expressed in literature." See Mikhail Bakhtin, *The Dialogical Imagination,* ed., Michael Holquist; trans. Caryl Emerson and Michael Holquist (Austin: University of Texas Press, 1981), p. 84. Although Bakhtin's original idea primarily concerns the novel, the concept has been widely adopted in critical interpretations of other cultural texts and their relationships to dynamic cultural systems.
8. This "laborer," as I will show later, is not an idealized proletarian as would have been pictured by the May Fourth discourse. Rather, as a carpenter turned fruit vendor, his image comes closer to a typical petty urbanite. Because he is a returnee from the overseas, this petty urbanite possesses a cosmopolitan aura as well.

9. Back cover of Noël Burch's *To the Distant Observer* (Berkeley: University of California Press, 1979).
10. Ibid., p. 27.
11. Cheng Shuren, *Zhonghua yingye nianjian,* p. 179.
12. *FZS,* vol. 1, pp. 53–54.
13. Tom Gunning, "Film History and Film Analysis: The Individual Film in the Course of Time," *Wide Angle* 12, no. 3 (July 1990): 5.
14. Ibid., p. 6.
15. Ibid., pp. 13–14.
16. *FZS,* vol. 1, pp. 8–9.
17. Translation adapted from Jay Leyda, *Electric Shadows,* p. 2. The original essay in Chinese also contains a description of a film about a train arriving at a station which "shook the entire room." *Youxibao,* no. 74 (September 5, 1897).
18. See Yong Li, "Woguo diyizuo yingyuan jin hezai?" (Where is China's First Movie Theater Today?), *Shanghai dianying shiliao* (Historical Materials on Shanghai Cinema) (Shanghai dianyingju shizhi bangongshi, n.d.), no. 5, pp. 99–100. Years later, Ramos rebuilt it into a concrete structure, expanding the space to hold 710 seats.
19. Liao Ben, *Zhongguo gudai juchang shi* (History of China's Ancient Theaters) (Zhengzhou: Zhongguo guji, 1997), pp. 92–98.
20. Ibid., p. 160.
21. Ibid., p. 162. For the social and political impact the ascendance of modern playhouse in urban China had on the formation of modern subjectivity, see

Joshua Goldstein, "From Teahouse to Playhouse: Theaters As Social Text in Early Twentieth-Century China," *Journal of Asian Studies* 62, no. 3 (August 2003): 753–80.

22. Cheng Bugao, *Yingtan yijiu*, pp. 84–87.
23. "Chaguan yu yinyue chalou" (Teahouse and music tearoom), in *Shanghai chunqiu* (Vicissitudes of Shanghai), ed. Tu Shiping (Hong Kong: Zhongguo tushu jicheng gongsi, 1968). The book appears to be a reprint of *Shanghai daguan* (An Overview of Shanghai) published in Shanghai in the 1940s. For a brief discussion on the "Hale's Tour Car," see Douglas Gomery, *Shared Pleasures: A History of Movie Presentation in the United States* (Madison: University of Wisconsin Press, 1992), p. 10.
24. Qian Huafuo, *Sanshi nian lai zhi Shanghai*, pp. 12–13.
25. See his *Xiandai Zhongguo dianying shi lüe*, p. 11.
26. For a fairly comprehensive genealogy and stylistic analysis of shadowplay in China and its export to foreign countries, see Dong Jingxin, "Zhongguo yingxi kao" (An Examination of Chinese Shadowplay), *Juxue yuekan* 3, no. 11 (1934): 1–19.
27. Cheng Shuren, "Zhonghua yingye shi" (pp. 1–15), in *Zhonghua yingye nianjian*, ed Cheng Shuren. The original account of the story, "Li furen" (Lady Li), can be found in *Hanshu*.
28. For visual illustrations of "leather shadow puppets," see A Wei, ed., *Piyingxi* (Shadowplay) (Beijing: Zhaohua meishu, 1955). Zhang Yimou's film, *To Live* (1994), contains vivid scenes of shadowplay and its milieu.
29. Dong Jingxin, "Zhongguo yingxi kao," pp. 5–8. Dong's article also included a list of some major titles of shadowplay programs, p. 18.
30. "Cong yingxi dao dianying" (From Shadowplay to Cinema), in *Shanghai fengwu zhi* (Gazetteer of Shanghai Lore), ed. Wu Qiufang (Shanghai: Shanghai wenhua, 1982), p. 256.
31. For a concise history of *wenmingxi*, see Ouyang Yuqian's memoir "Tan wenmingxi" (On the Civilized Play), in *Zhongguo huaju yundong wushinian shiliaoji* (Collection of Historical Materials on Fifty Years of Chinese Spoken Drama Movement) (Beijing: Zhongguo xiju, 1958), vol. 1, 48–108.
32. See also Wang Zilong, *Zhongguo yingjushi* (A History of Chinese Cinema and Drama) (Taipei: Jianguo, 1950), pp. 1–5.
33. Zhong Dafeng, "Lun yingxi" (On "shadowplay"), *Beijing dianying xueyuan xuebao*, no. 2 (1985): 54–92, and "Zhongguo dianyingde lishi jiqi gengyuan: zailun 'yingxi'" (The History of Chinese Cinema and Its Sources: Once More on "Shadowplay"), *Dianying yishu*, no. 1 (1994): 29–35; no. 2 (1994): 9–14.
34. Lin Niantong, "Zhongguo dianyingde kongjian yishi" (The Sense of Space in Chinese Cinema), *Zhongguo dianying yanjiu* (Dianying: An Interdisciplinary Journal of Chinese Film Studies) (Hong Kong: Hong Kong Chinese Film Association, 1984), vol. 1, pp. 58–78.
35. Zheng Yimei and Xu Zhuodai, *Shanghai jiuhua* (Old Shanghai Tales) (Shanghai: Shanghai wenhua, 1986), p. 112.
36. *Yingshi wenhua*, no. 2 (1989): 302.

37. Gongsun Lu, *Zhongguo dianying shihua,* vol. 1, p. 13.
38. I put quotation marks around *narrative* because it does not carry the same meaning as "narrative cinema" as an established institution. In fact, this short feature, despite its vague line of causality, was filmed mainly as a "documentary" presentation. The camera setup is a static long shot. The whole reel constituted a single long take. "If the reel is finished while the action or expression [of the actor] has not, the next reel will continue with the same action." Zhang Shichuan, "Zi wo daoyan yilai."
39. Zhong Dafeng, "Lun 'yingxi,'" p. 63.
40. Gunning, "The Cinema of Attractions," p. 64.
41. The popular play was derived from Wu Yanren's eponymous story published in a literary journal in 1907. Wu deployed first-person narration, combining Western-style fiction and traditional Chinese storytelling to create a "true record" incorporating real locations and personalities, a style popular in late Qing narrative fiction. See Zhang Wei, 'Pilu yijian yanmo le qishi wuniande shishi" (Unveil Historical Evidence Lost for 75 Years), in *Zhongguo jindai wenxue zhengming* (Debates on Modern Chinese Literature) (Shanghai shudian, 1987), vol. 1, pp. 159–61.
42. Synopsis in Zhu Tianwei and Wang Zhenzhen, eds., *Zhongguo yingpian dadian,* p. 7.
43. The film (nonextant) premiered at the Embassy Theater and made a huge profit. Xu Chiheng, "Zhongguo yingxi zhi shuyuan" (Tracing the Origin of Chinese Shadowplay), in *Zhongguo yingxi daguan,* p. 3.

44. A synopsized script was published in the November issue of *Yingxi zazhi* in 1921, which is considered the first text that approximates a script. A detail-rich story version can be found in Die Lu, *Yingxi xiaoshuo sansh izhong* (Thirty Film Stories) (Shanghai: Jinzhi tushuguang, 1925), pp. 117–19. The film was reported a hit in Beijing as well. An advertisement from Zhongtian Cinema calls the movie a "picture that sends a warning to the world." It also stresses the attraction of "real locations" and that the film sets an example of how Chinese cinema has advanced in recent years. The film was reportedly shown continuously (with no intermissions) for five days. As late as 1940, the linked play-film was performed at the Xinguang Grand Theater in Shanghai. The advertisement indicates that Shanghai dialect was used. Both items are found in the "Yan Ruisheng" folder (no. 121–42) at the China Film Archive.
45. *Shenbao,* July 19, 1921. The film was premiered on July 1 and was shown for a week at the Olympic Theater. Judging from the date of this advertisement, the film seemed to be on view in Shanghai beyond July 7. "Baihuali" and "Fuyuli" mentioned in the list of locations are *longtang* names.
46. Xu Chiheng, *Zhongguo yingxi daguan,* p. 3.
47. Note, too, that photography in China at the time was called, via Japanese, *xiezhen* (true depiction).
48. André Bazin, "The Ontology of the Photographic Image," in his *What Is Cinema?* vol. 1, p. 15.
49. Ibid., p. 14.

50. He Xiujun thought her husband "went too far" with playing *xutou* (selling points) in this film. Due to its gory details, the film was banned by the municipal government. See He Xiujun, "Zhang Shichuan he Mingxing yingpian gongsi," in *WSDY,* p. 1520.
51. *FZS,* vol. 1, p. 59.
52. The early 1920s in Chinese history is marked by several important events: the birth of the Chinese Communist party, and, under the mediation of Comintern, the first collaboration between Sun Yat-sen's Nationalist party and the Communist party in order to reclaim power from warlords in a post-imperial, war-torn China.
53. Thomas Elsaesser, introduction to *Early Cinema: Space, Frame, Narrative,* pp. 167–68.
54. *Laohuzao* (literally, tiger stove) is a rudimentary teahouse with an open storefront, hereafter referred to as teashop. For more on this particular Shanghai urban spatial feature and public space in general, see Lu Hanchao, "Away from Nanking Road: Small Stores and Neighborhood Life in Modern Shanghai," *Journal of Asian Studies* 54, no. 1 (1995): 93–123. For a more detailed description of the teashop in the Republican period, see Bao Jing, ed., *Lao Shanghai jianwen* (Impressions of Old Shanghai) (Shanghai: Shanghai guoguang shudian, 1947), vol. 2, 52–53. Bao depicts the teashop as a public space patronized mainly by people from the lower social strata. It functioned as a bathroom in summer and cheap hotel for the homeless in winter. Hooligans and thieves also constituted a major clientele.

55. A typical example of this genre is *Ruby and Mandy at Coney Island* (1903).
56. Hong Shi et al., "Zhongguo zaoqi gushipian chuangzuo tansuo" (Explorations on the Creation of Early Chinese Narrative Cinema), *Dianying yishu,* no. 1 (1990): 39.
57. For lack of a more pertinent term, *leisure class* used here refers to a particular urban social group emerging in the Chinese cities around the turn of last century. They include gangsters, dandies, gamblers, high-class prostitutes, and those who ran the mass entertainment establishments. Shanghai dialect has a particular word for this group: *baixiangren* (people who play).
58. For the original use of the concept *bricoleur* in anthropological theory, see Claude Lévi-Strauss, *The Savage Mind* (Chicago: University of Chicago Press, 1966), pp. 16–33. The term is first used in film history by Alan Williams to describe the heterogeneity of the origins of cinema as a cultural and technological medium. See his *Republic of Images: A History of French Filmmaking* (Cambridge, Mass.: Harvard University Press, 1992), pp. 8–9.
59. Thomas Elsaesser, "Film History and Visual Pleasure: Weimar Cinema" in *Cinema Histories / Cinema Practices,* ed. Patricia Mellencamp (Los Angeles: AFI, 1984), pp. 76–78.
60. In addition, Zheng Zhenqiu's role as the doctor is also suggestive of his family background in the pharmaceutical (and sometimes opium) business; his other given name is Yaofeng, which has a reference to medicine (*yao*). Such self-referential practice (characters assuming the same last names of the actors) continued well into the 1930s, as in *Big Road* (1934), for example.

61. For a historical investigation of the Chinese communities in that region, see Maurice Freedman, "The Chinese in Southeast Asia: A Longer View," in *The Study of Chinese Society: Essays by Maurice Freedman* (Palo Alto, Calif.: Stanford University Press, 1979). For a rich cultural history of the Chinese diaspora as a whole, see Lynn Pan, *Sons of the Yellow Emperor: The Story of the Overseas Chinese* (London: Secker and Warburg, 1990).
62. Film magazines often carried news and serious articles on the subject. See, for example, Huo Wenzhi, "Yingpian gongxiao tan" (On Film's Function), *Dianying zazhi,* no. 6, 1924, in which he relates the impact of a documentary film on Shanghai Jingwu Martial Arts Society on the Chinese audience in Singapore. Gu Jiancheng, "Guozhi yingpian yu Nanyang huaqiao" (Domestic Films and Overseas Chinese in Nanyang), *Mingxing tekan no. 16: Tade tongku* (Mingxing special issue, no. 16, *Her Sorrows*), 1926 And Wu Xiwen, "Guochan yingpian yu Nanyang wenhua" (Chinese Film and Nanyang culture), *Zhongnan qingbao* 2, no. 2 (Mar. 1935): 20–22.
63. Ma Junxiang, "Zhongguo dianying qingxiede qipao xian" (The Slanting Starting Line of Chinese Cinema), *Dianying yishu,* no. 1 (1990): 9.
64. Miriam Hansen, "Adventures of Goldilocks: Spectatorship, Consumerism and Public Life," *Camera Obscura* 22, no. 2 (January 1990): 57.

CHAPTER FOUR

1. C. J. North, "The Chinese Motion Picture Market," *Trade Information Bulletin,* no. 467 (United States Department of Commerce, Bureau of Foreign and Domestic Commerce, May 4, 1927). Using a tanner's yard as a theater, and with the projector perched on a pile of books atop a shaky table, the exhibition situation was certainly more congenial to the teahouse mode than that of the movie-only theater with its dark and luxury interior. Such discrepancy shows the unevenness of the moviegoing experience in China at the time. Despite the penetration of cinema into the rural area, full-fledged movie theaters were concentrated in major urban centers.
2. Ibid., foreword.
3. Ibid., p. 2.
4. Michael Walsh, "No Place for a White Man: United Artists' Far East Department: 1922–1929," *Asian Cinema* 7, no. 2 (Winter 1995): 20, 30.
5. North's report cites an embarrassing episode illustrating this problem. At a theater "catering to the poorer, uneducated Chinese, [t]he picture was a foreign comedy with the captions, shop-front lettering, etc., all reading backward, the film evidently having been incorrectly inserted in the projector. However, no one seemed to notice the difference and the film was not changed throughout the performance." "The Chinese Motion Picture Market," pp. 15–16.
6. Michael Walsh, "No Place for a White Man," p. 31.
7. Ibid.
8. *Yingxi chunqiu,* no. 5 (1925): 6, 9, 14.
9. Ibid., p. 2.
10. Ibid., p. 5.

11. The Ramos Amusement Co., being an agent for Famous Players-Lasky, was also the chief broker of cheap American films and contributed directly to the rampant presence of American films in China. Ramos paid only a flat rate of 150 silver dollars per print for films that were at least two years old. "Famous Players were getting something for nothing—picking up cash for old prints in a territory that thus far they had no interest in exploiting themselves." See Walsh, "No Place for a White Man," p. 21. One might infer that his retirement also meant a diminished market for the American products.
12. Bu Jiangjun, "Zhongyang daxiyuan kaimu zhishen." *Dianying zhoubao,* no. 1 (1925): 13. The theater had been an important forum for the civilized play and modern Peking opera performances.
13. "Shanghai dianying faxing fangyinye yaoshi lu" (A Record of the Important Events in Film Distribution and Exhibition in Shanghai), *Shanghai dianying shiliao* 5 (1994), pp. 113, 115.
14. Wu Guifang ed., *Shanghai fengwuzhi,* pp. 258–59.
15. *GJN,* p. 18.
16. For a sampling of these reports, see Cheng Shuren, *Zhonghua yingye nianjian,* section on "Guochan yingpian xiaolu zhi baogao" (Reports of Chinese Pictures from Foreign Markets).
17. Wang Ruiyong, "Shanghai yingyuan bianqian lu" (A Record of the Changes in Shanghai Cinema Theaters) *Shanghai dianying shiliao* 5 (1994): 82–98. Specific addresses of the venues are also given though many of them are no longer standing. Odeon was among a sizable number of theaters destroyed by Japanese bombing in 1932.
18. C. J. North, "The Chinese Motion Picture Market," p. 15.
19. Siegfried Kracauer, "Cult of Distraction: On Berlin's Picture Palaces," *The Mass Ornament,* pp. 323–24.
20. Xu Chiheng, *Zhongguo yingxi daguan* (ads unpaginated).
21. Kracauer, "Cult of Distraction," p. 325.
22. Xu Chiheng, *Zhongguo yingxi daguan,* section on "Theater Companies—Chinese Management," p. 1. Entering the theater was, as described by a journalist of the time, like entering a "palace." Its facade was built with "manmade stones" (*renzao shi*), "strong and elegant"; the interior was decorated with numerous plaster statues (*Shenbao,* August 8, 1926).
23. The term is borrowed from Jonathan Crary, "Unbinding Vision: Manet and the Attentive Observer in the Late Nineteenth Century," in *Cinema and the Invention of Modern Life,* ed. Leo Charney et al., pp. 46–71. Crary is concerned with a perceptual tension imbued in the discourse on visual attention against the backdrop of modernity in late nineteenth century Paris. I find his take on the problem germane to the issue here, namely, the ambiguous relation between indulgence of visual pleasure and the need to discipline or "direct" that pleasure. The effect is an attention that constantly vacillates between ephemeral immobilization and persistent distraction.
24. Jianyun, "Dao yan" (introduction), *Chengxing Gu'er jiuzuji tekan* (*Morning Star's* Special issue on *Orphan Rescues Grandfather* (Chengshe, 1923), p.3.

25. The film is not extant. See original synopsis and dialogues in the "special issue" mentioned above. The series was edited by Ren Jinping, chair of the society and director of publicity for Mingxing. A modified script appears in Ah Ying, ed., *Zhongguo xinwenxue daxi* (A Comprehensive Collection of Chinese New Literature) (1927–37), vol. 13 (Shanghai: Shanghai wenyi, 1987).
26. Gu Jianchen, "Zhongguo dianying fada shi" (A History of the Development of Chinese Film), in Cheng Shuren, ed. *Zhonghua yingye nianjian* (Yearbook of Chinese Film), Shanghai, 1934.
27. Xu Chiheng, *Zhongguo yingxi daguan,* pp. 6–9.
28. The film was reportedly shown in Shanghai, Nantong, and Nanjing and was brought to New York as well (*FZS,* pp. 41–24). See also Ouyang Yuqian, "Dianying banlu chujia ji" (Entering cinema halfway), *Dianying yishu,* no. 3 (1959): 70–74, 80.
29. Ouyang Yuqian, *Zi wo yanxi yilai* (Since I Started Acting) (Beijing: Zhongguo xiju, 1959), pp. 91–94.
30. Hu Die, *Yinghou shengya,* pp. 16–21. In the same year, a young American woman, a certain Miss Bailey, briefly ran a film school in Shanghai. Her major Chinese collaborator was Zhang Shewo, a prominent Butterfly writer who was also an aficionado of Western drama; see Xu Chiheng, *Zhongguo yingxi daguan,* p. 8. Some of the students were later employed to play roles in some films made by the British-American Tobacco Co. (*FZS,* p. 124).

31. *Yingxi chunqiu,* no. 4 (1925): 15.
32. *Yingxi chunqiu,* no. 5 (1925): 17. In the same "Replies" column in that issue there is another letter from Chinese students in Berlin who praised the editors' effort to promote new Chinese culture and arts and offered to help to make Chinese film known to the Europeans. The editors wrote back with gratitude and a request for reciprocal information about foreign film culture (18–19).
33. Recruitment advertisement in *Dianying zazhi,* no. 6 (1924).
34. Zhou Jianyun and Wang Xuchang, "Yingxi gailun" (An Introduction to Shadowplay), *LLWX,* vol. 1, p. 11.
35. The school address (Gengqin alley on Xinzha Road) appears to have been the same as the film company, which later moved to a larger location. It is possible the school was part of the fund-raising campaign to set up the new company. See Cheng Shuren, "Specialists Trained Abroad" (p. 1), in his *Zhonghua yingye nianjian.* For more on Shengzhou, see the section on "Hushang ge zhipian gongsi zhi chuangli shi ji jinguo" (The History of the Founding of Film Companies in Shanghai), in Xu Chiheng, *Zhongguo yingxi daguan,* pp. 10–11.
36. Zhou and Wang, "Yingxi gailun," p. 13. Li Suyuan points out that the confusion of naming at that period should alert us to the fact that "it is not the naming per se, but rather people's perception of the cinema at that time, that is the point of departure of our research on Chinese early cinema." Li Suyuan, "Guanyu Zhongguo zaoqui Li Lun" (On Early Chinese Film Theory), *Dangdai dianying,* no. 4 (1994): 23.

37. This probably explains why the so-called expressive drama (*biaoqing ju,* which literally means "facial expression drama") is listed in the chart below as an immediate antecedent, after vernacular modern drama, to the shadowplay.
38. Zhou and Wang, "Yingxi gailun," p. 14.
39. Gu Kengfu, "*Yingxi zazhi* fakanci." The quotations here are from the full text collected in *LLWX,* pp. 3–10.
40. The primary place given to acting is pertinent to the early experiments that relied heavily on actors' improvising and formulaic performance at once. Gu himself was also a teacher at the Mingxing Film School. He joined the Da Zhonghua Company as director in 1924 and began to edit *Dianying zazhi.*
41. There is no better example than the docudramatic film *Yan Ruisheng* (1921) which Gu participated in making.
42. Gu Kengfu, "*Yingxi zazhi* fakanci," p. 9.
43. The attention paid to psychology and neurology is hardly surprising given the fact that Freudian psychoanalytical theory and other schools of psychology had been widely translated into Chinese in this period. For a study on the introduction of psychoanalysis in China and its influence on literary discourse, see Jingyuan Zhang, *Psychoanalysis in China: Literary Transformations 1919–1949* (Ithaca: Cornell University East Asia Program, 1992). Bertrand Russell's visit to China and his lectures on "The Analysis of Mind" delivered in Beijing in 1920 triggered widespread interest in psychology and behaviorism (pp. 10–13).
44. Georg Simmel, "The Metropolis and Mental Life," pp. 325–26.
45. Zhou and Wang, "Yingxi gailun," p. 17; emphasis added.
46. Michael Taussig, *Mimesis and Alterity,* pp. 20–23.
47. Chen Shouying, "'Kan jingtou' yu 'dui jingtou' zuoxi" (Looking at the Camera or Acting to the Camera), *Dianying zazhi,* no. 13 (1925).
48. Zhou and Wang, "Yingxi gailun," p. 18.
49. Ibid., pp.18–19.
50. Hu Die recalls that in order to learn how to drive a car, she and another actress-to-be Xu Qinfang, who later became a popular martial-arts film star, had the ingenious idea of renting a taxi, then asking the cab driver to take them to the suburbs. There they let the driver "rest" in the back seat while they practiced driving. Afterwards they paid the driver double the fare. Hu Die, *Yinghou shengya,* p. 21.
51. Zhou and Wang, "Yingxi gailun," p. 19.
52. In his introduction to the special issue for *Orphan Rescues Grandfather,* Zhou Jianyun offers a few concrete examples of "national" approaches, more in terms of screen realism than political doctrine. He contends that, because not all Chinese wear Western suits, it is not necessary to have actors wear them regardless of situations. Similarly, Chinese gardens deserve to be used as locations and filmed for their elegant beauty. *Gu'er jiuzu ji tekan* (Special Issue on Orphan Rescue, Grandfather) (Mingxing Company, 1923), p. 4.
53. Zhou and Wang, "Yingxi gailun," pp. 21–22.
54. Ibid., p. 23.

55. Ibid.

56. See Gregory L. Ulmer, *Applied Grammatology: Post(e)-Pedagogy from Jacques Derrida to Joseph Beuys* (Baltimore: The Johns Hopkins University Press, 1985), pp. 173, 179. The last chapter, "Film: Sergei Eisenstein," deals more directly with the implication of film and other visual or electronic media for "applied grammatology" as a popular pedagogy (pp. 265–315).

57. Tan Xinpai's art, as mentioned earlier, was made into the first Chinese-produced film at the Fengtai Photo Studio in Beijing in 1905. In 1920, another famous Peking opera actor Mei Lanfang came to Shanghai to perform and happily accepted the invitation from the Commercial Press Film Department to film some episodes of the plays he was performing. See Mei Lanfang, *Wode dianying shenghuo* (My Film Life) (Beijing: Zhongguo dianying, 1962), pp. 3–10. In 1923 and 1924, Mei was involved in a number of more "sophisticated" filming projects of his art. In his memoir he recalls the problems he had with the filming crew as he could not accept at first their method of "chopping up" his continuous movement and singing. When a dance episode from *Farewell My Concubine* was filmed in a theater in Beijing, he told the cameraman that they should "try to make the film look connected even though it is actually shot in fragments." "Just like a puzzle can be put together from disparate pieces and look complete" (p. 14).

58. *Furen ruzi* refers to uneducated people as a whole. It is characteristic of the Confucian doctrine to equate the "uncultivated" men with women and children who are almost by definition ignorant because of illiteracy and low social status within the patrilineal system.

59. This echoes the educational aim of the early production policy of the Commercial Press Film Department. In 1926, during the heyday of commercial cinema, the film department was disassociated from the press and became the Guoguang Company, which made five narrative films before closing down in 1927 (*FZS,* pp. 39–40).

60. Xu Chiheng, *Zhongguo yingxi daguan,* pp. 10–11.

61. See, for example, Sun Shiyi, "Yingju zhi yishu jiazhi yu shehui jiazhi" (The Artistic Value Versus the Social Value of Cinema), "Wang xiacheng de yingju" (The Cinema that Caters to the Lower Strata), and Jin Cao, "Zhongguo dianying yu yishu" (Chinese Cinema and Art), all collected in *LLWX,* pp. 69–71, 76–80, 90–96. I have encountered countless articles in the early film magazines that actively participated in this public discourse for establishing cinema's social and cultural legitimacy.

62. *Gu'er jiuzu ji tekan* (Mingxing Company, 1923), pp. 6–8. Notably, Zhou Jianyun, one of the authors of *Introduction,* co-wrote the intertitles with Zheng Zhengqiu.

63. Zheng Zhengqiu, "Fenmochang zhongde zahuodian" (The Grocery Store in the World of Theater), cited in *GJN,* p. 74.

64. *LLWX,* pp. 66–68. The article was originally published in *Shanghai yi furen tekan* (Special Catalogue for *A Woman of Shanghai*) by the Mingxing Company in July 1925.

65. Several Chinese workers were locked out by a Japanese-owned textile mill

during a strike. One worker was killed in the protest, which quickly ignited a mass rally on the Nanjing Road. The demonstration was met with violent suppression by the British controlled police force. For an account of the incident, see Jonathan Spence, *The Search for Modern China,* p. 340.

CHAPTER FIVE

1. Jian Sheyu, "Guan Mingxing shezhi zhi *Guer jiuzu ji*" (Watching *Orphan Rescues Grandfather* by the Star Company), *Ziyoutan fukan* (The Free Conversations Supplement) *Shenbao,* December 26, 1923.
2. A practice that bears some resemblance to the "commedia dell'arte" in Italy of the Renaissance period. For a definition of "commedia dell'arte," see Karl Beckson and Arthur Ganz, *A Reader's Guide to Literary Terms* (New York: The Noonday Press, 1960), pp. 30–31.
3. Some chief polemics against the Butterfly fiction by Lu Xun, Qu Qiubai, Mao Dun and others, as well as the defenses made by the popular writers are collected in Wei Shaochang, ed., *Yuanyang hudie pai yanjiu ziliao,* vol. 1.
4. Bao Tianxiao, "Wo yu dianying" (The Cinema and I), *Chuanyinglou huiyi lu* (Hong Kong: Dahua, 1971), pp. 95–96.
5. A Hollywood film would have indicated one as the story creator and the other as the screenwriter. In the Chinese case, there was actually a third writer credited—the calligrapher who rendered the intertitles.
6. Zhou Jianyun and Cheng Bugao, *Bianjuxue* (The Science of Screenwriting), in *LLWX,* pp. 35–46. Zhou also coauthored the *Introduction* to the course literature discussed in chapter 4. Cheng was one of Mingxing's leading directors and cinematographers.
7. Ibid., 38; emphasis added. See also Wang Fangzheng, "Zhuanshu zimude yidian xiao jingyan" (Some Experiences on Composing Intertitles), *Dianying zhoubao,* 3 (1925): 9. Wang proposes that the writing style of intertitles for each film should be consistent, and attentive to the educational level and regional specificity of the audiences. On the whole, however, Wang is inclined toward simpler language, especially for the sake of "women and children" who detest (or ignore) long and difficult intertitles.
8. This is also true of the moviegoing experience of the period. Mr. Shu Yan, a former critic, told me that while the literate and literary people could get a concise synopsis (or *shuomingshu,* pamphlet of explication) written in an ornate mixed classical and vernacular (*buwen bubai*) Butterfly style language in the theater lobby, most women and illiterate spectators enjoyed the loud, colorful, and exaggerated commentary of the "explicator." In other words, the combination of different forms of verbal production paralleled the heterogeneity of the audiences with different degrees of access to language and representation.
9. Hu Ying, *Tales of Translation: Composing the New Woman in China, 1899–1918* (Palo Alto: Stanford University Press, 2000), p. 5.
10. Ibid., p. 12. The term *contact zone* is developed by Mary Louise Pratt in her book, *Imperial Eyes: Travel Writing and Transculturation* (New York: Routledge, 1992).

11. Lydia Liu, *Translingual Practice: Literature, National Culture, and Translated Modernity, China, 1900–1937* (Palo Alto: Stanford University Press, 1995).
12. Xu's stage name is Xu Banmei. He went to Japan to study physical education and founded China's first institute of physical education after returning to China. After several years in the theater, he and Wang Youyou founded the Kaixin [Fun] Film Company in 1925, which specialized in physical comedies. For more on his background in the theater see his *Huaju shichuangqi huiyilu* (Memoir of the Beginning of Chinese Spoken Drama) (Beijing: Zhongguo xiju, 1957).
13. The book, like most theoretical texts on film at the time, was based on translations and compilations of Western and Japanese sources, but was also heavily inflected by the author's own opinions. Xu Zhuodai, *Yingxi xue* (Shanghai: Huaxian shangyeshe tushubu, 1924). Hou Yao, *Yingxi juben zuofa* (Shanghai: Taidong tushuju, 1925).
14. *Sannian yihou, Minxin tekan* (Minxin special issue on *Three Years Later*), no. 4, December 1926.
15. For a definition of the soul and its two components *hun* (the sentient animal soul) and *po* (the after-birth personality), see Wolfram Eberhard, *A Dictionary of Chinese Symbols* (London: Routledge, 1983), pp. 270–71. For a nuanced anthropological study of this subject, especially regarding the "number" of souls and its relationship to personality, see Stevan Harrell, "The Concept of Soul in Chinese Folk Religion," *Journal of Asian Studies* 38, no. 3 (May 1979): 519–28. The play that best exemplifies the importance of the soul in traditional Chinese drama is Tang Xianzu's *Peony Pavilion* of the late Ming period.
16. See Anders Hansson, *Chinese Outcasts: Discrimination and Emancipation in Late Imperial China* (Leiden: E. J. Brill, 1996), especially Chapter 3, "Musicians' Households."
17. Lu Xun, "Shexi," in *Lu Xun quanji* (Beijing: Renmin wenxue, 1981), vol. 1, pp. 559–70. Interestingly, Lu Xun preferred the open-air rural theater to the cramped theater house in the city. In his description of the theater, he mentioned seeing ghost characters from a famous Buddhist tale. See also David Johnson's discussion on the pedagogical function of the theater in David Johnson et al., eds., *Popular Culture in Late Imperial China* (Berkeley: University of California Press, 1985).
18. Ouyang Yuqian, *Zi wo yanxi yilai,* p. 59. In this memoir, he also recalls how his childhood penchant for acting was influenced by the leather-puppet shadowplay (p. 4).
19. Lu Xun, "Lun Zhaoxiang zhilei" (On Photography, etc.), in *Lu Xun quanji,* vol. 1, pp. 181–90.
20. The association of new electronic media with paranormal and spiritual phenomena is not unique to China. For a brilliant study on the subject in the American context, see Jeffrey Sconce, *Haunted Media: Electronic Presence from Telegraphy to Television* (Durham: Duke University Press, 2000). The Chinese responses indicated, however, a certain anxiety about Western incursions on both Chinese territories and traditions.

21. *FZS,* p. 10. However, Cixi was a big fan of photography. As the most powerful imperial sitter who loved *huazhuang xiang* (makeup portraits, meaning the sitter poses as a dramatic character), her photos circulated widely among the general populace. See Ma Yunzeng et al., *Zhongguo sheyingshi: 1840–1937* (A History of Photography in China) (Beijing: Zhongguo sheying, 1987), pp. 63–64. A contemporary poem also recorded Cixi's photo sessions in the court, in which she appeared as Guanyin (a female Buddha). See Liu Lu ed., *Qinggong cixuan* (Selected Ci Poetry from the Qing Court) (Beijing: Zijincheng, 1985), pp. 101–2
22. Hou Yao, *Yingxi juben zuofa,* p. 1.
23. The script of *The Abandoned Wife* includes 136 scenes that are not divided down to shots. They are organized according to interior scenes and on location exterior scenes.
24. Xu's view is strikingly similar to that of Paul Wegener, also screenwriter and star of *Student of Prague.* For a persuasive account of Wegener's view on the uniqueness of the cinema and the importance of its cinematographic properties, as opposed to drama and literature, see Kristin Thompson, "*Im Anfang War* . . . Some Links between German Fantasy Films of the Teens and the Twenties," in *Before Caligari: German Cinema, 1895–1920,* ed. Paolo Cherchi Usai (Pordenone, Italy: Le Giornate del Cinema Muto and Edizioni Biblioteca dell'Immagine, 1990), pp. 138–61.
25. This resolution has affinity to Chinese Buddhist notions of the soul, which, in one interpretation, passes through several purgatories and then reaches a dark room where it has to look for a skin so that it can be reborn (Eberhard, p. 271). In other words, the skin may be seen as a kind of "shadow" in which the soul seeks appearance and life, illusive as it may again be.
26. Kracauer, "Photography," p. 430.
27. Annette Michelson, "The Art of Moving Shadows," in *The Art of Moving Shadows,* catalogue of the exhibition "On the Art of Fixing a Shadow, 7 May–30 July 1989," ed. Annette Michelson (Washington D.C.: National Gallery of Art, 1989), p. 16.
28. Xu Zhuodai, *The Science of Shadowplay,* p. 68.
29. Ibid., pp. 9, 75. In one instance, almost the entire cast and the production personnel have *ying* (shadow) in their first name, as would siblings in a large Chinese family. In fact, *yingren* (the people of shadows) has always been a common appellation for people involved in the film world.
30. Lu Xun, "Lun zhaoxiang zhilei," in *Lu Xun quanji,* vol. 1, pp. 183–85. Lu Xun further remarked that when the "self-begging picture" disappeared and the photograph only showed the awe-inspiring face, he could not help but think that this was only the half of the self-begging-the-self picture, as the other self was rendered invisible.
31. Homi Bhabha, "Signs Taken for Wonders: Questions of Ambivalence and Authority Under a Tree Outside Delhi, May 1817," in *"Race," Writing, and Difference,* ed. Henry Louis Gates, Jr. and Kwame Anthony Appiah (Chicago: University of Chicago Press, 1986), p. 175.
32. Tom Gunning, "Phantom Images and Modern Manifestations: Spirit Pho-

tography, Magic Theater, Trick Films, and Photography's Uncanny," in *Fugitive Images: From Photography to Video,* ed. Patrice Petro (Bloomington: Indiana University Press, 1995), p. 67.

33. On the kinship between photography and cinema, and the play or tension between stillness and movement, beginning with Lumière's first screening in 1895, see Patrick Loughney, "Still Images in Motion: The Influence of Photography in the Early Silent Period," and Annette Michelson, "The Art of Moving Shadows," both in *The Art of Moving Shadows,* ed. Michelson.
34. Eduardo Cadava, "Words of Light: Theses on the Photography of History," in *Fugitive Images,* ed. Patrice Petro, p. 226.
35. *FZS,* p. 91.
36. Guy de Maupassant, "The Diamond Necklace," in *Selected Tales of Guy De Maupassant,* ed. Saxe Commins (Random House, 1950), pp. 137–44.
37. The French catalogue for the 1982 retrospective show of Chinese cinema, *Ombres électriques,* has this film at the very beginning, calling it "le plus ancien film chinois qui ait été conservé, et par chance il est absolument impeccable." The observation of *A String of Pearls* as an "impeccable" work of art, however, is suggestive of its narrative artfulness and skillful cinematic techniques. The catalogue also describes the "modern style" of the intertitles in the cards with text in English, which "ne manquent pas de charme" (p. 7).
38. Karl Marx, *Capital* (New York: International, 1977), vol. 1, pp. 74–75.

39. W. J. T. Mitchell, *Iconology: Image, Text, Ideology* (Chicago: University of Chicago Press, 1986), p. 193.
40. As quoted in Miriam Hansen, *Babel and Babylon,* p. 188.
41. Miriam Hansen, "Mass Culture as Hieroglyphic Writing: Adorno, Derrida, Kracauer," *New German Critique* 56 (Spring/Summer 1992): 48–9. Hansen's reading of the "scriptural" patterning in Griffith's *Intolerance* provides a good example here. She argues that the disguising of the script (writing) as a pure image in the film is connected to the "forgetting" of the historical transition from image to writing. It is symptomatic of the "reification of mimetic capacities under the universal law of commodity culture." Paradoxically, it also constitutes the "very condition" of decipherment. *Babel and Babylon,* p. 192.
42. Annette Michelson, "The Art of Moving Shadows," p. 16.
43. Rachel O. Moore, *Savage Theory: Cinema as Modern Magic* (Durham: Duke University Press, 2000), p. 10.
44. Hou Yao, *Yingxi juben zuofa,* p. 54.
45. Thorstein Veblen, *The Theory of the Leisure Class* (New American Library, 1953 [1899]), p. 126.
46. Hou Yao, "*Yichuan zhenzhu* de sixiang" (The Ideas in *A String of Pearls*), *Yichuan zhenzhu,* a special issue of the Great Wall Motion Picture Company productions, Shanghai, 1926; reprinted in *WSDY,* pp. 299–300.
47. Li Suyuan, "Zhongguo zaoqi dianyingde xushi moshi" (The Narrative Paradigm of Early Chinese Cinema), *Dangdai dianying,* no. 3 (1993): 32–3.
48. For an insightful analysis of European avant-garde and modernist film the-

ory's relation to primitivism, see Rachel Moore, *Savage Theory,* chapter 1, "The Moderns."

49. Yang Liansheng, "The Concept of 'Pao' as a Basis for Social Relations in China," in *Chinese Thought and Institutions,* ed. John K. Fairbank (Chicago: University of Chicago Press, 1957), pp. 5–8; 49. See also Paul Varo Martinson, "Pao Order and Redemption: Perspectives on Chinese Society and Relation Based on a Study of the Chin P'ing Mei," Ph.D. diss., University of Chicago, 1973.
50. Yang Liansheng, "The Concept of 'Pao,'" p. 6.
51. Several scholars have pointed to the great impact Buddhist narrative and arts had on Chinese literature and other arts. See, for example, Victor H. Mair, *Tang Transformation Texts: A Study of the Buddhist Contribution to the Rise of Vernacular Fiction and Drama in China* (Cambridge, Mass.: Council on East Asian Studies, Harvard University Press, 1989).
52. See Perry Link, *Mandarin Ducks and Butterflies,* pp. 196–235.
53. Chow goes on to say, "A mode of narration that invites disbelief by inflating a society's addictive ideologies (such as fatalism) to such melodramatic proportions is fundamentally dangerous for the society." Rey Chow, *Woman and Chinese Modernity,* p. 65.
54. A prominent example is Wu Yanren's story *Heiji yuanhun* (1907), which was adapted to theater and film as discussed in chapter 3. Despite the "real record" (*shilu*) style of the main story, its prelude uses a popular contemporary legend of retribution concerning the angry soul of a Buddha, who allowed his and other statues in a Tibetan temple to be melted for minting money by the Qing army in dire need. Transmigrating back to India and waiting in vain for the Chinese to replace the statues, the Buddha reincarnated as poppies and then opium to inundate China as a way of retrieving the overdue debt. See Zhang Wei, "Pilu yijian yanmo le qishi wuniande shishi."
55. The film had another title, *Way Down West,* which was meant to be a counterpart to Griffith's *Way Down East.* For a list of Griffith's films shown in China in the mid-1920s, see Zheng Junli, *Xiandai zhongguo dianying shilüe,* pp. 38–9.
56. The prominent Zhang family of Cantonese origin comprised of eleven brothers with the same father but different mothers. It is thus not mere coincidence that the film is about "brothers" feuding over treasure. The fifth brother in the family, Zhang Huichong, had his own company and is known as the first martial-arts film star. The seventh, Zhang Daming, was the notorious ex-husband of the legendary actress Ruan Linyu who committed suicide in 1935, largely due to the scandalous unresolved legal battle between her and Zhang.
57. Yu is played by Wu Suxin, Zhang's girlfriend in real life. She played almost all the female leading roles in Huaju productions from 1927 to 1931. The title card introduces her role as "the cohabitant 'wife' of Xin and the two did not have an official wedding." *Tongju* (cohabitation) was a vogue among young people who considered themselves to be moderns. They chose "ro-

mantic and free love" as a protest against the feudal practice of arranged marriage. See Roxane Witke, "Transformation of Attitudes Towards Women During the May Fourth Era of Modern China," PhD. diss., University of California–Berkeley, 1970, especially chapter 5, "Free Love and Marriage."

58. The mise-en-scène here is very similar to the "theft" scene in *A String of Pearls,* except here the sleeping figures are not of a couple, but two young women. Thus the loss of the pearls is not associated with a family problem that would need to be solved as in the other film.
59. Ben Singer, "Female Power in the Serial-Queen Melodrama: The Etiology of an Anomaly," in *Silent Film,* ed. Richard Abel (New Brunswick, N.J.: Rutgers University Press, 1996), p. 166. For a more extensive study on the subject, see his book, *Melodrama and Modernity.*
60. Ben Singer, "Female Power in the Serial-Queen Melodrama," pp. 169–170.
61. Tom Gunning, "'Now You See It, Now You Don't': The Temporality of the Cinema of Attractions," in *Silent Film,* ed Richard Abel, p. 75.
62. V. Propp, *Morphology of the Folktale,* trans. Laurence Scott (Austin: University of Texas Press, 1968), especially chapter 3, "The Function of Dramatis Personae," pp. 25–65.
63. See Alan Dundes's introduction to *Morphology of the Folktale,* Ibid., xii–xiv.
64. Unlike *Lustrous Pearls,* this film about treasure hunting begins with a single hero who bids farewell to his "sister" (girlfriend) and leaves for a mine far away. The "national treasure," which remained a phantom object in the film, is only nominally present in a treasure chart, stolen and found after many tribulations. Before he founded his own company, Zhang Huichong was a sailor on a freight ship and then a major actor in the film department at the Commercial Press from 1922 to 1924, where he received his training as an actor and a film entrepreneur. In his memoir Gong Jianong describes Zhang Huichong as the first versatile modern film actor who could ride a horse, drive a car, and swim, in addition to having a magician's hand. After gambling all his fortune away he led a small circus and performed in the Nanyang region. According to Gong, Zhang founded his company with his share of his father's inheritance (*GJN,* pp. 83–84).
65. Tianyi's productions as a whole (especially the "classical costume drama" and the "martial arts" genre) enjoyed most popularity among the Nanyang diaspora communities in the 1920s. In 1936, its headquarters moved to Hong Kong before the Japanese invasion. In 1937, its name was aptly changed to the Nanyang Film Company. In 1950, it was renamed Shao Father and Sons. In 1957, the two younger brothers, Shao Yifu and Shao Renmei, who had been running a distribution company in Singapore and Malaysia, returned to Hong Kong to found the Shao Brothers (Hong Kong) and instituted the Cantonese language production group. Shao Father and Sons limited its business to theater management and distribution from that point on. See Du Yunzhi, *Shaoshi dianying wangguo mixin* (The Secrets of the Shaos' Film Kingdom) (Taipei: Ni wo ta dianshi zazhishe, 1979). Du's oral history reveals many details of the competition and in-fights between the

brothers and their sons over the decades, which were exacerbated by the destruction of film vaults by fire.

66. For a synopsis of the film, see *WSDYJB*, pp. 1603–4. It was a common practice for competing companies to make films with same (or similar) titles, based on the same (or similar) stories. Many commercial wars were waged over the so-called twin cases (*shuangbao an*). In 1932, under the influence of the left-wing cinema, Tianyi also adapted Maupassant's "Necklace" into *One Night Glamour* (*Yiye haohua*).
67. Marshall Berman, *All That Is Solid Melts Into Air: The Experience of Modernity* (New York: Penguin Books, 1982). The original phrase is from Karl Marx's *Communist Manifesto.*
68. This pedagogical moment also suggests the persistent influence of some early cinematic genres such as educational documentaries about plants, minerals, and bacteria that were also modern attractions.
69. Walter Benjamin, "The Storyteller," in *Illuminations*, p. 87.
70. Tian Han, "Yige weiwanchengde yingsede meng—*Dao minjian qu*" (An Unfinished Silver Dream: *Going to the People*) in his *Wangshi zhuihuailu* (Beijing: Zhongguo dianying, 1981), pp. 2–7. The films discussed here are not extant. My discussion is based on the written sources.
71. *WSDYJB*, pp. 934–30 (originally published in *Shenbao, Bengfu zengkan* (local supplement), May 14, 1926.
72. As we shall see in chapter 7, Tian Han becomes a driving force in the left-wing cinema of the 1930s, which was overwhelmingly devoted to the cause of mobilizing the people for patriotic causes.
73. Its antecedent may be found in Zhang Huichong's *Seizing a National Treasure* mentioned above. In it the girl surprises the spectator by turning herself into a supple and smart heroine who rescues the hero trapped under a huge bronze clock.
74. The idea of "types" as opposed to characters is in part inspired by Tom Gunning's paper, "Pathé and Cinematic Conte-Tale: Storytelling in Early Cinema," presented at the fourth DOMITOR Conference, Paris, Dec. 1996.

CHAPTER SIX

1. *Shenguai* has also been translated literally as "gods and monsters." I choose "magic spirit" for the visual spectacle it created and the important associations it had with contemporary discourses on magic.
2. *WSDYS*, p. 239.
3. In the genre's early stage, Tianyi, enticed by business opportunities in the diaspora, merged with a Nanyang distribution company (headed by Cheng Bilin) to form Tianyi-Qingnian. They produced a great number of "classical costume" films that were both shown domestically and exported to Nanyang. The collaboration ended in 1928 when Tianyi began to have direct control in the region. Tianyi's expansion into Nanyang was largely triggered by the competition between Tianyi and the Liuhe consortium. The latter, under the shrewd management of Zhou Jianyun, recruited the

influential Nanyang distributor Wang Yuting and formed a virtual sanction against Tianyi. See Du Yunzhi, *Shaoshi dianying wangguo mixin*, pp. 26–17; 30–33. See also Tong Gong, "Wuhu huoshao" (Alas, Fire), *YXSH* 1, no. 18 (1931): 2. Tong Gong is critical of the way Nanyang distributors manipulated the price of martial arts films, reinforcing competition and the genre's mass production.

4. See for instances, Tong Gong, "Wuhu huoshao," and Li Changjian, "Shengguaipian zhen hairen" (The Magic-Spirit Film Is Really Harmful), *YXSH* 1, no. 7 (1931): 10. The Emei Mountain in Sichuan province is a famous pilgrimage site and one of the favorite destinations for these escapades.
5. For instance, some viewers would start burning incense and bowing to the image of Ne Zha (a mythic child hero in *Fengsheng bang*) appearing on the silver screen. Huang Yicuo, "Guochan yingpiande fuxin wenti" (The Problem of Reviving the Domestic Cinema), *Yingxi zazhi*, 1:7/8 (June 1930): 24. The specific film referred to here is *The Birth of Ne Zha* (*Ne Zha chushi*, Changcheng, 1928).
6. Walter Benjamin, "Theses on the Philosophy of History," in *Illuminations*, pp. 261–62.
7. One fan described Xia Peizhen, who starred in *Burning*, as a typical modern woman with a masculine aura. See, Jiang Zhenxin, "Xiandai nü dianxing—Xia Peizhen" (A Typical Modern Woman—Xia Peizhen) *YXSH* 1, no. 16 (1931): 10. Another fan was particularly impressed by Wu Lizhu, the "oriental Fairbanks," and considered her martial skills "authentic." Han Chao, "Tan guochan wuxiapian" (On the Domestically Made Martial Arts Film), *YXSH* 1, no. 29 (1931): 2–3.
8. Rick Altman, "An Introduction to the Theory of Genre Analysis," *American Film Musical* (Bloomington: Indiana University Press, 1987), pp. 9; 1–2.
9. Stuart Kaminsky and Jeffrey Mahan, *American Television Genres* (Chicago: Nelson-Hall, 1986), p. 17.
10. Ying Dou, "Shenguai ju zhi wo jian" (My Opinion on the Magic-Spirit Film) [1927], in *WSDY*, pp. 662–63.
11. See Jin Taipu, "Shenguaipian chajin hou—jinhou de dianyingjie xiang nali zou?" (After the Censoring of the Magic-Spirit Film—Where is the Film World Heading?), *YXSH* 1, no. 32 (1931): 1–4. The critic traces the film genre to the storytelling practice in the teahouse. However, stories told in that fashion remained idealist (*weixinde*), or invisible. Although the reformed theater with "magic devices" could present some of the fantastic features in the vernacular tales, ordinary people usually could not afford this type of live show. Most small cinemas in the Shanghai area were near factories and farms and thus were ideal for attracting this type of audience to see the wonders of the magic-spirit film.
12. Ma Junxiang, "Zhongguo dianying qingxiede qipao xian," p. 11.
13. The lead actor Wang Yuanlong (who also directed one episode) of *Four Heroes of the Wang Family* (*Wangshi sixia;* Dazhonghua beihe, 1927) wrote in his memoir how he himself was impressed by the grandiose set of the film. All four films in the series were big hits in Shanghai in 1927–29. "Zi wo ru

yingjie yilai" (Since I Entered the Film World), *Linxing* 3 (1933): 10. Dissatisfied with the exterior footage of landscape, they made a set so big that it "occupied the entire glass studio."

14. James Liu, *The Chinese Knight-Errant* (Chicago: University of Chicago Press, 1967), pp. 4–6.
15. Sima Qian, *Shiji,* vol. 86, pp. 2515–2538; vol. 124, pp. 3181–3190.
16. See Chen Mo, *Daoguang xiaying mengtaiqi—Zhongguo wuxia dianying lun* (A Sword-and-Shadows Light Montage for the Knight-Errant: On Chinese Martial Arts Film) (Beijing: Zhongguo dianying, 1996), pp. 15–22.
17. Mingxing reportedly had plans to adapt the novel onto the screen. See Qing Ping, "Cong wuxia dianying shuodao Huoshao Hongliansi he Shuihu" (From Martial Arts Film to *Burning* and *On the Water Margins*), *YXSH,* 1, no. 3 (1931): 7–8. The author predicts that if the film were well made, "not only would the majority of lower class people hurry to see it but the educated would also be attracted to it."
18. The term *wuxia* designated the new style martial arts fiction was coined by Japanese novelists in the nineteenth century and was subsequently borrowed by Chinese writers living in Japan. Ye Hongsheng, *The Art of Wuxia Fiction* (Taipei: Lianjing publishing, 1994), p. 11, as quoted in Sam Ho, "From Page to Screen: A Brief History of *Wuxia* Fiction," in *Heroic Grace; The Chinese Martial Arts Film,* ed. David Chute and Cheng-Sim Lim (Los Angeles: UCLA Film and Television Archive, 2003), p. 14.
19. Che Mo, *Daoguang xiaying mengtaiqi,* p. 32–35.

20. Jia Lielei, "Zhongguo wuxia dianying yuanliu lun" (On the Origin of the Chinese Martial Arts Film), *Yingshi wenhua,* 5 (1992): 213. Xiang Kairan was inspired by folk tales in the Hunan region where the novel was set. See Zhang Gansheng, *Minguo tongsu xiaoshuo lungao* (Chongqing: Chongqing, 1991), pp. 111–24. Before becoming a popular writer, Xiang had been involved in the anti-Yuan Shikai revolution and subsequently studied in Japan. He was said to be the only martial arts fiction writer who mastered the arts he wrote about. In 1927, after Xiang returned to his native Hunan, another writer by the name Zhao Shaokuang continued to write the remaining episodes.
21. The director Zhang Shichuan was allegedly attracted to the novel when he tried to find out what had distracted his son from his homework (*GJN,* p. 157).
22. Arthur Asa Berger, "Preface," *Popular Culture Genres: Theories and Texts* (Newbury Park, Calif.: SAGE, 1992), xiii.
23. Jia Leilei, "Zhongguo wuxia dianying yuanliu lun," p. 216. Ren Pengnian, also the director of *Yan Ruisheng,* founded his own company, Yueming, in 1927; it was one of the major producers of the martial arts film. His wife was Wu Lizhu, the "Oriental Female Fairbank."
24. *For the Sake of Justice* (*Dayi mieqin* [a.k.a. *Xiayi yuan*], 1922) and *The Patriotic Umbrella* (*Aiguo san,* 1923).
25. See Guan Haifeng, "Wo paishe *Hongfeng kulou* zhi jingguo" (How I Made *Red Skeleton*), in *Zhongguo dianying,* 5 (1957), pp. 60–61.

26. Xinya's advertisement, as quoted in Li Suyuan and Hu Jubin, *WSDYS,* p. 77. The director Guan Haifeng later also made two proto-"martial arts" films, *The Chivalric Boy* (*Xiayi shaonian;* 1924) and *Revenge of the Filial Daughter* (*Xiaonü fuchou ji,* 1925), the latter starring Wu Suxin, who played the heroine in *Lustrous Pearls.*
27. *GJN,* 1: 83–84.
28. Both are famous Ming novels of the "magic-spirit" genre. In 1927 alone, Da Zhonghua released three ten-reel films adapted from *Investiture of Gods.* There were about eight films adapted from *Journey to the West* by various studios.
29. *Xiyouji Pansi dong tekan* (Special Catalogue on *Journey to the West, The Cave of the Spider Spirit*) (Shanghai yingxi, 1927), quoted in *WSDYS,* p. 216.
30. Cheng Xiaoqing, "Lishi yingpian de liyong ji nandian" (The Uses of the Historical Film and its Difficulties) [1927], *WSDY,* p. 633. The critic observed that historical subjects were more likely to attract overseas Chinese and Western audiences.
31. I consider *Romance of the West Chamber* (mentioned in chapter 5) an exemplary text for the clash between *wen* and *wu*. The dream sequence in which Zhang Sheng rides the "enlarged" phallic brush pen in the sky is a metonymic display of the scholar's anxiety as a sexually and politically impotent subject in a time of social disarray. In *Red Heroine,* to be discussed later in this chapter, the last name of the scholar figure, a cousin of the heroine, is incidentally Wen, played by the director Wen Yimin.
32. Yao Gengchen, "Tan wuxia pian" (On the Martial Arts Film) [1927], *WSDY,* p. 670.
33. As the film is not extant, the discussion is based on the synopsis and still photos published in *Dianying yuebao* 7 (Oct. 1928). Despite sharing the same family name and middle name the two were not relatives. Zhang Huimin is said to have had a strong interest in aviation as well. The first Chinese encounter with the flying machine took place in 1911, when the French pilot René Vallon came to Shanghai and entertained the urban crowd with his flight skills. He was, however, killed in a flying accident the same year. Betty Peh-T'i Wei, *Crucible of Modern China* (Hong Kong: Oxford University Press, 1987), p. 195.
34. Flying as a motif of the modern fairy tale had appeared in *The Flying Shoes* (*Feixing xie;* Minxin, 1928) one year earlier. The film was allegedly based on a German folktale. Another contemporary film, *The Great Flying Bandit* (*Feixing dadao,* a.k.a. *Little Sister, I Love You,* 1929), made by Dan Duyu, also rests its attraction on flight. This action film involves five brothers trying to court a modern girl. The mise-en-scène includes the bandit's flying house (which has two hidden wings, a police helicopter, a flying vehicle on which a musical show is advertised, a motorcycle, and a car. At the end, after a suspenseful fight in the flying house, the girl descends into the ocean with a parachute. Her lover from the city reappears and carries her away in the car without leaving a trace. Synopsis in *WSDYJB* 2:1729–731.

35. Roy Bhaskar, *Reclaiming Reality: A Critical Introduction to Contemporary Philosophy* (London: Verso, 1989), p. 42.
36. Juanhong, "Hangkong daxia" (The Great Knight-Errant of Aviation), *Dianying yuebao,* no. 7 (October 1928).
37. Sun Shiyi, "Dianyingjie de guju fengkuangzheng" (The Craze for the Old Drama in the Film World) [1926], *WSDY,* pp. 643–45.
38. E. Chang, "Guzhuangpian zhong zhi ying zhuyi zhe" (Things to Consider in the Classical Costume Drama) [1927], *WSDY,* p. 654.
39. It is unclear which film the critic was referring to. In 1927, one of the numerous classical costume films based on *Journey to the West* is called *Zhu Bajie the Pig Tours Shanghai* (*Zhu Bajie you Shanghai*). The three-reel short comedy is clearly in the tradition of early Mingxing comedies such as *The King of Comedy* and *Laborer's Love.* Such modern remaking of the classical novel culminated in Mingxing's *New Journey to the West* (*Xin Xiyouji*) of 1929, sporting a female lead with the name of Miss K. and urban venues such as the dance hall.
40. Friedrich G. Jünger, as quoted in Hermann Bausinger, *Folk Culture in a World of Technology,* trans. Elke Dettmer (Bloomington: Indiana University Press, 1990), p. 10.
41. Ibid., pp. 16–17.
42. Translation by J. D. Schmidt, in his book, *Within the Human Realm: The Poetry of Huang Zunxian, 1848–1905* (Cambridge: Cambridge University Press, 1994), pp. 270–71. See also the section on "Huang Zunxian and Modern Science," pp. 181–94. Huang played with and "updated" traditional poetic allusions in poems by, for instance, Meng Jiao (751–814), the mid-Tang poet, to describe modern objects and the sensibilities they evoked. Huang opened the first poem in the set thus: "My thoughts whirl like a wheel, when it's time to part, / Turning at the rate of 10,000 RPM [literally, 'ten thousand times every fifteen minutes (*ke*)]." Schmidt points out this is a "clever transformation of Meng Jiao's lines", "My Thoughts whirl like a wheel when it's time to part / Ten thousand times each single day"; but Huang accelerates the speed of the whirling thoughts to correspond with the increased tempo of modern life" (p. 190).
43. On the "science fantasy" genre in late Qing fiction, see David Der-wei Wang, *Fin-de-siècle Splendor,* chapter 5, "Confused Horizons: Science Fantasy" (Palo Alto, Calif.: Stanford University Press, 1991) pp. 252–312; see also Masaya Takeda, *Tobe! Dai-Sei teikoku* (Fly! Great Qing Empire) (Tokyo: Riburupoto, 1988).
44. Huang Zunxian, "On Climbing the Eiffel Tower," in Schmidt, *Within the Human Realm,* p. 275.
45. *Dianshizhai huabao* 1:4 (1898). For a translation of the caption in English, see David Arkush and Leo O. Lee eds., *Land without Ghosts: Chinese Impressions of America from the Mid-Nineteenth Century to the Present* (Berkeley: University of California Press, 1989), pp. 120–21. The book also contains, however, two political poems written by Huang while serving as the Chinese

consul-general in San Francisco from 1882–85, expressing his disillusionment with social injustice in America, especially racial discrimination against Chinese immigrants (pp. 61–70).

46. See Liang Qichao, *Yingbing shihua* (Discourse on Poetry in the Ice Room) (Beijing: Renmin wenxue, 1959), pp. 2, 24, 51. See also his remarks (with entire quotes of the original) on Jiang Wanli's poems on the submarine and the airplane (pp. 136–37), which Liang found to be similar examples of the "poetic revolution."

47. Frank Dikötter, *Sex, Culture and Modernity in China: Medical Science and the Construction of Sexual Identities in the Early Republican Period* (Honolulu: University of Hawaii Press, 1995), p. 21.

48. Gan Yonglong, "Jixie ren" (The machine-man), *Dongfang zazhi* 8, no. 8 (August 1911): 22. The magazine switched to the vernacular in 1920 under the impact of the New Culture movement. See Chow Tse-Tsung, *The May Fourth Movement,* p. 181.

49. The chief theoretician for this discourse is Yan Fu, also a major translator of Western texts (in particular those of British liberalism). On Yan Fu and his important role in the late Qing reform, see Benjamin Schwartz, *In Search of Wealth and Power* (Cambridge, Mass.: Harvard University Press, 1964). Yan Fu was also instrumental in introducing the concept of science into modern Chinese thought. For an excellent discussion on Yan Fu and the question of science, see Wang Hui, "The Fate of 'Mr. Science' in China: The Concept of Science and Its Application in Modern Chinese Thought," *Positions* 3, no. 1 (Spring 1995): 1–68.

50. See Chang-tai Hung, *Going to the People: Chinese Intellectuals and Folk Literature, 1918–1937* (Cambridge, Mass.: Harvard University Press, 1985), especially chapter 1, "The Discovery of Folk Literature" and chapter 7, "Intellectuals and the Folk."

51. As quoted in Chow Tse-Tsung, *The May Fourth Movement,* p. 328.

52. The term is a direct translation of Eucken's concept *Lebensanschauung.* Zhang was a student of Bergson and Eucken while studying in Europe. With the latter he coauthored *Das Lebensproblem in China und in Europa* (Leipzig, 1922). See Chow Tse-Tsung, *The May Fourth Movement,* p. 333 (including the footnote on the same page).

53. Ibid., pp. 333–35. For a concise review and analysis of Zhang's ideas and the debate as a whole, see also Fan Dainian, "Dui 'Wusi' Xinwenhua yundongde zhexue fansi—ji ershi niandai chu de kexue yu renshenguan da lunzhan" (A Philosophical Reflection on the May Fourth New Culture Movement—On the Great Debate on Science and View of Life in the Early Twentieth Century), in *Kexue shi lunji* (An Anthology of Essays on the History of Science), ed. Fang Lizhi (Hefei: Zhongguo kexue jishu daxue, 1987), pp. 255–76. Rather than ruling out the importance of science altogether, as Fan points out, Zhang was proposing a nonpositivist approach, which emphasized methodology rather than object of study, contingency rather than causality or quantification (p. 263).

54. The term "metaphysics" in Chinese translation is *xuanxue,* which also re-

ferred to philosophy in general as opposed to science. *Xuanxue* also carries the connotation of spiritualism and esoterism. *Xuan* in particular refers to strange or paranormal phenomena that are beyond ordinary or rational comprehension. *Xuanji,* or strange coincidence/device, is a commonly deployed narrative and mise-en-scène strategy in martial arts–magic spirit film. In the latter usage, *xuan* becomes a materialized and embodied entity with the aid of cinematic technology.

55. Ding Wenjiang, "Xuanxue yu kexue," *Nuli zhoubao,* April 12, 1923: 48–49. Collected in Yadong tushuguan, ed., *Kexue yu renshengguan* (Science and the View of Life) (Shanghai, 1923), pp. 1–30.
56. Chow Tse-Tsung, *The May Fourth Movement,* p. 334.
57. Such a contradiction attests to Horkheimer and Adorno's thesis that enlightenment internalizes myth and thereby creates a new form of mythology and totalitarianism. Conversely, archaic myths are placed on a secularizing trail. See Max Horkheimer and Theodor Adorno, *Dialectic of Enlightenment* (1944), trans. John Cumming (New York: Herder and Herder, 1972), pp. 6–9.
58. These include Luo Zhixi, *Kexue yu xuanxue* (Shanghai: Commercial Press, 1927; 1930); Peng Kang, "kexue yu renshenguan—jin ji nian lai Zhongguo sixiangjie de zong jiesuan," *Wenhua pipan,* no. 3 (1928); Wang Gangshen, *Kexue lun ABC* (Shanghai shuju, 1928). Sources from Fan Dainian, "Dui 'Wusi' Xinwenhua yundongde zhexue fansi," endnotes, pp. 275–276.
59. The technique is called *jieding,* "connecting the roofs." Dong entered Mingxing as an apprentice. After assisting the shooting of *Orphan Rescues Grandfather,* he began to operate a camera independently in 1924 and is credited as the first cinematographer who used double exposure in *The Good Brother* (*Hao xiongdi*), in which one actor played two brothers. He is also the first cameraman who collaborated with a sound technician in producing China's first sound film (on wax disk), *The Singing Girl Red Peony* (Mingxing, 1931). In his later years, he served as the technical consultant for the Shaw Brothers Co. in Hong Kong.

60. He Xiujun, "Zhang Shichuan he Mingxing yingpian gongsi" (Zhang Shichuan and the Mingxing Film Company), in *WSDY,* p. 1528. The author is Zhang's widow who wrote the memoir in 1965. According to He, the article in the American magazine contained no more than a few foreign terms, so Dong had to resort to his homespun methods to achieve the intended special effect.
61. In Chinese folklore and as a literary trope, female warriors were often called *jingguo yinxiong* (heroes with headdress). Invariably, the female knights-errant in the "martial arts" film appear in a headdress covering her long hair, the marker of her original femininity. Fan Xuepeng, who starred in *Red Heroine,* recalls that she had the idea of dying her character with "red ink" to make her authentically "red." Because of that, the film was more popular with the Nanyang audience and as a result, the company earned a large profit. She claims Mingxing partly borrowed this idea in portraying Honggu (Red Maiden) in *Burning.* Fan Xuepeng, "Wo de yinmu shenghuo

de huiyi" (Remembering My Life on the Silver Screen)[1956], in *WSDY*, p. 1480.

62. *Dingying yuebao* and *Yingxi shenguo* (*YXSH*), two leading film magazines during the height of the genre craze between 1928 and 1932, carried numerous articles on makeup, tricks, and sets. The critic Jin Taipu sees the "magic-spirit" film itself is about making secrets "public," which explains its attraction because it satisfies the audience's curiosity for revealing what lay behind the mysterious. Jin Taipu, "Shenguaipian chajin hou," p. 2.
63. The term is derived from Matei Calinescu, *Five Faces of Modernity: Modernism, Avant-Garde, Decadence, Kitsch, Postmodernism* (Durham: Duke University Press, 1987). Calinescu identifies these "faces" as distinctive aesthetic categories of modernity. The martial arts–magic spirit film apparently blends some of these categories in a way that dissolves the boundary between high and low.
64. Marcel Mauss, "Techniques of the Body," *Economy and Society* 2, no. 1 (February 1973): 73, 75.
65. Sam Ho, "From Page to Screen," p. 14.
66. Robert Stam, "Specificities: From Hybridity to the Aesthetics of Garbage," *Social Identities* 3, no. 2 (1997): 279. Stam's argument is derived from his analysis of Afro-diasporic and Brazilian cinemas and popular culture. In light of Bakhtin's conception of "chronotopic multiplicity," Stam argues for an alternative aesthetic that is not built on binarism and linear temporality but on a productive "redemption of detritus." What I find particularly suggestive is his substitution of the term "premodern" ("that embeds modernity as telos") with "paramodern," a term that allows the nonlinear collage of the most archaic and the postmodern resources for cultural production.
67. The female knight-errant figure goes back to the Tang period—such as the legendary Hua Mulan, made internationally famous by Maxine Hong Kingston's fiction and the Disney animated film *Mulan*—and was often associated with its subordination to filial piety and masquerading as male. For an account of the *nüxia* image in traditional folklore and history, see Wang Li, *Zhongguo gudai haoxia yishi* (Ancient Chinese Gallant Knights-Errant and Chivalrous Subjects) (Hefei: Anhui renmin, 1996), chapter 5, "Nüxia ji xia zhi funü guan" (Female Knights-Errant, Knight-Errantry and Views on Women), pp. 134–60.
68. The late Qing novel *Ernü yingxiong zhuan* (A Tale of Heroes and Lovers) was an important precedent for this genre. See David Wang's perceptive analysis of the novel and its influence on subsequent literary production in *Fin-de-siècle Splendor*, pp. 156–74.
69. More famous productions (such as *Burning*) are not included as they do not concentrate on the image of the heroine alone. *WSDYJB* contains extant plot summaries (and sometimes complete scripts of intertitles from theater pamphlets or film magazines) of these films.
70. Youlian was founded in 1925 by Chen Kengran, Xu Bibo, and others. One of its first productions was a documentary shot on the spot about the May 30 incident on Nanjing Road that year. Its leading actresses Xu Qing-

fang hid the camera in her wide trousers to avoid police confiscation. Xu Bibo, "Jilupian 'Wusan huchao' paishe jingguo" (How the Documentary *The May Thirtieth Shanghai Surge* Was Made), *Zhongguo Dianying* 5 (1957): 62.

71. The motifs of the martial heroine's apprenticeship with the ape-man and her unrequited love can be traced to one of the earliest literary works of the genre about Yuenü and her sword fighting skill from the first century. It has been passed down and rewritten countless times, including the version by Jin Yong. See Chen Mo, *Daoguang xiaying mengtaiqi,* p. 28.

72. Xu joined Youlian in 1925 when it was newly established. Besides her screen image as a heroine, she was also the screenwriter and star of *The Knight-Errant with a Double Swords* (*Shuangjian xia,* 1928). She joined Mingxing in 1933 after Youlian ceased operation due to the Japanese bombing of Shanghai in January 1932.

73. In her name, the character for *Yun* has the "grass" radical on top of "cloud." But both characters (with or without the radical) are pronounced the same.

74. Wu's English name is White Rose Woo, so the name of the heroine is actually that of the actress. Notably, Wu also served as the assistant director of the film.

75. This scene of her gender transformation was done through a set of shots using a curtain, a screen, and a mirror. Bai's costume and makeup were allegedly influenced by *Three Musketeers,* which was widely popular in China. *Zhongguo dianying* (Chinese Cinema: A Documentary Film), part 4 (coproduced by Center for Research on Chinese Film and Chinese Film Archive, 1996).

76. It was, for instance, used as an incipient narrative device as seen in *Laborer's Love.* The rope also plays an important role in *Red Heroine* in escape and rescue scenes. Of course, the rope is an essential prop in the Westerns widely seen in China at the time. Also as in *Laborer's Love* the staircase in the middle of the set is turned into a slide, like when the carpenter-vendor "produces" injured bodies for his future father-in-law.

77. This scene, except for the beginning, is missing from the extant print I saw. It is possible that it was censored. The description is from the synopsis reprinted in *WSDYJB,* pp. 1826–828.

78. Donna Haraway, *Simians, Cyborgs, and Women: The Reinvention of Nature* (London: Free Associations Books, 1991), p. 150.

79. Wang Chaoguang, "Sanshi niandai chuqi de Guomingdang dianying jiancha zhidu" (The Film Censorship System of the Nationalist Party in the Early 1930s), *Dianying yishu* 3 (1997): 63.

80. See Prasenjit Duara, "Knowledge and Power in the Discourse of Modernity: The Campaign against Popular Religion in Early Twentieth-Century China," *Journal of Asian Studies* 50, no. 1 (February 1991): 67–83.

81. Zhongguo jiaoyu dianying xiehui, ed., *Zhongguo dianying nianjian* (The Cinematographic Yearbook of China) of 1934, compiled by the official China Educational Film Association and prefaced by the minister of propaganda Chen Lifu, is a publication that demonstrates the Nationalists' systematic effort to control the film industry for the purpose of nation building. The cen-

tral theme of the book is education through cinema. A whole section is devoted to introducing foreign practices of film censorship, which is followed by a section on "Chinese film administration" offering detailed description of the NFCC's establishment and a list of censored domestic and imported films.

82. See Song Jie's article, "Dianying yu shehui lifa wenti" (Cinema and the Problem of Social Law-making), *Dongfang zazhi* (Feb. 1925): 79–94. After introducing (or translating) a large amount of material on film censorship in the West, Song proposes the necessity of establishing film censorship in China but stresses that it should be in the form of "people's film censorship" rather than officially controlled.
83. For a comprehensive study on the subject, see Xiao Zhiwei's dissertation, "Film Censorship in China, 1927–1937," chapter 2, "Film Censorship in China 1911–1938." As Xiao points out, the earlier attempts at censorship before the Nationalists came to power in 1927, hence the beginning of the so-called Nanjing decade, were sporadic and hardly institutionalized. The appendix in Xiao's dissertation includes translations of some of them.
84. Among the foreign films banned because of their representation of religious and occult material were *Ben Hur, The Ten Commandments, Alice in Wonderland,* and *Dr. Frankenstein* (ibid., p. 231).
85. Wang Chaoguang, "Sanshi niandai chuqi de Guomingdang dianying jiancha zhidu," p. 63. The original source of this information is NFCC, "Dianying jiancha gongzuo zong baogao" (A General Report on the Work on Film Censorship), and Luo Gang, "Zhongyang dianjianhui gongzuo gaikuang" (An Overview of the Work of the NFCC), both in *Zhongguo dianying nianjian* (1934).
86. Lu Xun, "Youwu xiangtong" (Each Supplies What the Other Needs), *Xin qingnian* 6, no. 6 (Nov. 1919), collected in *Lu Xun quanji,* vol. 1, pp. 364–65. In the essay, Lu Xun attributes the "knightly" or martial style to Northern writers and the sentimental style to the Southern writers.
87. Qu Qiubai, "Guimenguan yiwai de zhanzhen" (The War Outside of the Gate of Hell), in Wei Shaochang, *Yuanyang hudie pai yanjiu ziliao,* p. 22.
88. Qu Qiubai, "Puluo dazhong wenyi de xianshi wenti" (The Actual Problem of Proletarian Popular Literature and Art), in Wei Shaochang, *Yuanyang hudie pai yanjiu ziliao,* p. 28. The original article was written on Oct. 25, 1931 and published in *Wenxue* (Literature), a League of Left Writers publication, in March 1932.
89. Shen Yanbing, "Fengjiande xiaoshimin wenyi," pp. 48–49.
90. Benjamin, "On the Mimetic Faculty," in *Reflections,* p. 333.
91. Jennifer Bean, "Technologies of Early Stardom and the Extraordinary Body," *Camera Obscura* 48 (vol. 16, no. 3, 2001): 46–7.
92. See Richard Dyer, "Entertainment and Utopia," in *The Cultural Studies Reader,* ed. Simon During (London & New York: Routledge, 1993), pp. 371–81.
93. Ibid., p. 49.
94. Ibid., p. 48.
95. Shen Yanbing, "Fengjiande xiaoshimin wenyi," p. 48. Shen used this as an

example to prove the point that the genre was not capable of carrying modern and serious messages and could only remain a vehicle for feudal ideas.

96. Wu Xiwen, "Guochan yingpian yu Nanyang wenhua," p. 21.
97. Prasenjit Duara, "Knowledge and Power in the Discourse of Modernity," p. 75.
98. See Rey Chow, *Primitive Passions,* pp. 4–11.
99. Ibid., p. 18.
100. Paul G. Pickowicz, "Melodramatic Representation and the 'May Fourth' Tradition of Chinese Cinema," p. 296.
101. Despite Lu Xun's overall negative view of the popular cinema, he nevertheless enjoyed moviegoing. He reportedly relished Mickey Mouse cartoons with his son. Gu Yuanqing and Gao Jinxian, "Lu Xun yu dianying" (Lu Xun and the cinema), *Dianying yishu* 4 (1979), pp. 41–48.
102. *Romance of the West Chamber* is a good example of the temple's function as such a liminal space. In order to concentrate on study, young scholars often take residence there to prepare for the imperial exams, as Zhang Sheng did in the film.
103. Wang Chaoguang, "Sanshi niandai chuqi de Guomingdang dianying jiancha zhidu," p.64.
104. Ibid., p. 65.

CHAPTER SEVEN

1. For a book-length study devoted to the left-wing cinema, see Laikwan Pang's *Building a New China in Cinema* (Landham, Md.: Rowman and Littlefield, 2002).
2. The second half of the 1940s, after the Japanese lost the war and the Shanghai film industry regained independence and flourished again, has been commonly designated the second golden age.
3. Sun Yu calls 1932 the year when Chinese cinema made a "left turn." See his article, "Huiyi Wusi yundong yingxiangxiade sanshi niandai dianying" (Remembering the '30s Cinema Under the Influence of the May Fourth Movement). *Dianying yishu,* no. 3 (1979): 8.
4. Chris Berry, "Chinese Left Cinema in the 1930s: Poisonous Weeds or National Treasures?" *Jump Cut* 34 (1989): 87–94.
5. A 141 film showcase, including 27 films from 1922 to 1937, screened in Beijing and Shanghai in 1982, and in Milan and Paris in 1984. The program toured a number of European cities in various formats. The Film Center at the National Museum of Modern Art in Tokyo also held similar exhibitions in 1984, 1988, and 1991.
6. For a report on the conference, see Jian Yong and Tian Jin, "Tantao Zhongguo dianying lishi jingyande yici shenghui" (A Grand Conference for Exploring the Historical Experience of Chinese Film History), *Dianying yishu,* no. 11 (1983): 10–11.
7. An example of such publications is Lu Si's *Yingping yijiu* (Reminiscences of Film Criticism) (Beijing: Zhongguo dianying, 1984).
8. The document was published in *Wenxue daobao,* no. 6–7, October 1931. See

Li Shaobai, "Jianlun Zhongguo sanshi niandai 'dianying wenhua yundong' de xingqi" (A Concise Treatise on the Rise of the "Film Culture Movement" in China in the '30s), *Dangdai dianying,* no. 3 (1994): 79–80. In my interview with the important 1930s film critic Shu Yan, he also stressed that the term "left-wing" was hardly used at the time. He said that the term "New Film Culture movement" laid emphasis on film as "culture" as opposed to commodity (November 16, 1996).

9. In 1932, several American business interests attempted to form U.S.-registered, Shanghai-based studios to make films for the Chinese market. As with similar situations in the mid-1920s, they were met with strong opposition. For a sample of the polemics against the American movies at the time, see Yi Lang's (Lin He) article, "Mei ziben jingong Zhongguo dianyingjie hou zengyang tupo muqian de weiji" (How to overcome the current crisis caused by the American capital's invasion of the Chinese film industry), *Dianying yishu,* 1, no. 3 (1932). See also Wang Suping, "Liangge yingpian gongsi de 'liuchan' shimo" (On the "Abortion" of Two Film Companies), *Yingshi wenhua,* no. 1 (September 1988): 282–87.
10. Yi Lang (Lin He), "Mei ziben jingong Zhongguo dianyingjie hou zengyang tupo muqian de weiji," p. 82.
11. Yang Hansheng, "Zuoyi yundongde ruogan lishi jingyan" (Some Historical Lessons From the Left-Wing Cinema Movement), *Dianying yishu,* 11 (1983): 2.
12. Mingxing spent most of its resources on the implementation of sound at that time, whereas Lianhua seized the opportunity to make films for a market not yet entirely ready for the talkies.
13. See Lu Si, "Zhongguo zuoyi dianying huigu" (Remembering the Chinese Left Cinema Movement), in *Yingping yijiu,* p. 85.
14. The English term appears in the original. "*Chuncan* zuotanhui" (Workshop on *Spring Silkworms*), in Chen Bo and Yi Ming, eds., *Sanshi niandai Zhongguo dianying pinglun wenxuan* (An Anthology of '30's Chinese Film Criticism), (Beijing: Zhongguo dianying, 1993), hereafter *SSND,* pp. 250–51. The article was originally published in the Daily Supplement on film, *Chengbao,* Oct. 8, 1933. Interestingly, Cheng also acknowledged the addition of materials such as statistical tables that enhanced the "documentary" look of the film. The same issue also carried other news on recent developments in Russian film and drama.
15. Lu Xun, for instance, translated and introduced Iwasaki Hisashi's work. See "Xiandai dianying yu youchan jieji" (Modern Cinema and the Bourgeoisie), *Lu Xun quanji,* vol. 4, pp. 389–413.
16. "Su'e laihua yingpiande yige xiaotongji" (A Brief Account of Films Imported from Soviet Union), *Yingmi zhoubao* (Movie Fans Weekly) 1, no. 5 (Oct. 24, 1934): 86.
17. Yang Hansheng, "Zuoyi yundongde ruogan lishi jingyan," p. 3.
18. Ibid.
19. Lu Si, *Yingping yijiu,* pp. 4–10.

20. Ibid., pp. 14–5. In general, however, one or more critics were assigned to a certain theater and reviewed all the programs there (p. 10).
21. Lin He, "Zuoyi juliande yingping xiaozu ji qita" (Left-wing Dramatists Group etc.), *Dianying yishu,* no. 9 (1980): 59–60.
22. For a vivid and detailed report on a series of these "tea party" seminars in 1934, see Qi Xin, "Ji disici dianchahui" (A Record of the Fourth Film Tea Party) and other articles in *Yingmi zhoubao* vol. 1, no. 4 (Oct. 17, 1934): 70–74.
23. At the time the average salary for a journalist was 50 yuan, and a junior college professor earned about 60 yuan a month. Interview with Shu Yan (November 16, 1996).
24. See the section on a dance hall incident involving some fashionable critics and a college-educated hostess in Qi Xin's article, "Liandaren chi jiangcha," *Yingmi zhoubao* vol. 1, no. 4: 74.
25. The only active woman critic was Hu Ping, also an actress.
26. Zheng Zhengqiu, "Ruhe zoushang qianjin zhi lu" in *SSND,* pp. 614–17, *Mingxing yuebao,* vol. 1, no. 1 (May 1933).
27. Gu Menghe, "Yi Tian Han tongzhi zai Nanguoshe de dianying chuangzuo" (Remembering Comrade Tian Han's Film Work at the "Southern-Country Society"), *Dianying yishu,* no. 4 (1980): 56.
28. Tian Han, "Wode ziwo pipan," (My Self-Critique) (1930), quoted in Chen Daicheng, "Wei zaochengde meng" (The Unrealized Dream), *Dianying yishu,* no. 11 (1980): 49.
29. Tian Han, "Yinse de meng," *Yingxing,* no. 5 (1927).
30. On the "pure film movement" and Tanizaki's role in it, see Joana Bernardi, *Writing in Light: The Silent Scenario and the Japanese Pure Film Movement* (Detroit: Wayne State University, 2001), especially chapters 4–6.
31. Tian Han, "Yinse de meng," Tian Han's (translated) film theory was quickly accepted and spread by other writers. See, for instance, Wei Nan's elaboration of the "day dream" thesis in his article, "Dianyingde wenyihua" (Transforming Cinema into Art), in Lu Mengshu, ed. *Dianying yu wenyi* (Cinema and the Arts—A Special Supplement of Yinxing), (Shanghai: Liangyou tushu, 1928), pp. 1–15. The author argues for the elevation of the status of the screenwriter, in "transforming" shadowplay into an art form.
32. In Japanese film historiography, Tanizaki's view of cinema was influenced by German expressionist theater and cinema. Tian Han saw *The Cabinet of Dr. Caligari* in Japan in 1921 and was shocked by its "sharp and strange beauty." See his *Yinse de meng* (Silver Dream) (Zhonghua shuju, 1928), p. 52.
33. Gu Menghe, "Yi Tian Han tongzhi zai Nanguoshe de dianying chuangzuo," p. 57.
34. This can be glimpsed even in a fictional text. In Junijiro Tanizaki's novel, *Some Prefer Nettles,* translated from the Japanese by Edward G. Seidensticker (New York: Knopf, 1955 [1928]), the male protagonist, a fashionable Tokyo dandy of refined tastes, relates how he acquired a copy of an exquisite edi-

tion of *Arabian Nights* from Shanghai. Tanizaki may have been referring to his own frequent trips to the Asian metropolis of the time.

35. I have found several production stills and Tian Han's handwriting in a special file at the China Film Archive. Samples of Tian Han's handwriting contain the word "masochism" in English. The stills show, among other scenes, the encounter on the train, Li's whipping of Sun (with Li dressed in male attire), and the lakeside shooting.
36. In his memoir, Gong Jianong's description of the film does not mention the sadomasochist sex scene or the shooting. Instead, he remembered the film primarily as a "scenic publicity" film, in which the phantom gives the young man from Shanghai a tour around the lake. See *GJN*, pp. 115–18. Tian Han's modern tale bears affinity to classical tales about the legendary lake and the beauties bred by it, in particular late Ming writer Zhang Dai's *Xihu mengxun* (In Search of Dreams at the West Lake).
37. Qian Bai, "Guan Mingxingde 'Hubian chunmeng' hou" (After Viewing Mingxing's *Spring Dream at the Lakeside*) *Mingxing tekan*, no. 27 (1927), collected in *WSDY*, 1168.
38. Xu Xiacun, "Modern Girl," in Yan Jiayan, *Xinganjuepai xiaoshuo xuan* (An Anthology of New Sensationalist Fiction) (Beijing: Renmin wenxue chubanshe, 1985), pp. 30–35 [Originally published in *Xin wenyi*, 1, no. 3 (1929)]. For a detailed historical study on the cafe waitress and her "labors and desires" in Japan in the 1920s and 1930s, see Miriam Silverberg, "The Cafe Waitress Serving Modern Japan," in Stephen Vlastos, ed., *Mirror of Modernity: Invented Traditions of Modern Japan* (Berkeley: University of California Press, 1998), pp. 208–28.
39. Besides this film, Cai Chusheng also wrote two other scripts in the same vein in this period, *Spring in the South* (*Nanguo zhichun*, Linhua, 1932), which he directed, and *Spring Tides* (*Chunchao;* Hemintong, 1933) directed by Zheng Yinshi.
40. Paul Pickowicz, "The Theme of Spiritual Pollution in Chinese Films of the 1930s," *Modern China* 17 (1991): 47.
41. A female writer assuming a male name to publish her autobiographical novel is a motif picked up again in Cai's *New Woman* two years later. See the synopsis by Cai in *WSDYJB*, pp. 2242–44.
42. See Li Lili, "Huiyi he Cai Chusheng tongzhi zai yiqi gongzuo de nianyue" (Recollections of the Years Working Together with Comrade Cai Chusheng), *Dianying yishu*, no. 6 (1979): 31.
43. Xi Naifang, "Ping "Fenghongse de meng"—Meiguopian de yingxiang" (On *Pink Dream*—The Influence of American Film), *SSND*, pp. 325–27 (originally published in *Chengbao*'s daily film supplement, Sept. 6, 1933).
44. Su Feng, "Zhishi yige meng" (Only a Dream), *Chengbao*'s daily film supplement, September 6, 1932.
45. Lu Si, *Yingpin yijiu.*
46. Tian Han, "Cong yingse zhi meng li xingzhuanlai" (Awaking from the Silver Dream), in *WSDY*, pp. 472–75 [*Dianying*, no. 1, 1930].

47. Another example was the famous *Welcome Danger* incident that took Shanghai by storm in 1930. Hong Shen, a drama professor at Fudan University and a well-known screenwriter, stood up in the middle of the screening at the Grand Theater and called for a collective protest to the humiliating depiction of Chinese in Harold Lloyd's slapstick comedy. In the article Tian Han refers specifically to the scene in which Lloyd passes a stick to two Chinese men who beat each other with it (ibid., p. 474).
48. The film is not extant. A complete script can be found in *WSDYJB*, pp. 2250–81. Prior to this film, Bu had also been chastised by the left critics for his compounded "humanist," "feudal," and "petty-bourgeois" sentiments and aesthetics in his earlier films including *Hubian chunmeng, Taohua qixue ji,* (1931), *Lian'ai yu yiwu* (1930), *Rendao* (1932) and *Xu gudu chunmeng* (1932).
49. For an insightful analysis of the multiple types of women, see Yingjin Zhang, "Engendering Chinese Filmic Discourse of the 1930s: Configurations of Modern Women in Shanghai in Three Silent Films," *Positions* 2, no. 3 (1994): 603–28, especially, 612–16.
50. Such screenplays may be seen as a new variant of the "revolution plus love" literature prevalent in early twentieth century. See Liu Jianmei's detailed study of this literary phenomenon, *Revolution Plus Love: Literary History, Women's Bodies, and Thematic Repetition in Twentieth-Century Chinese Fiction* (Honolulu: University of Hawaii Press, 2003), especially chapters 2–4.
51. Tian Han's political turn and new conviction in the ideological function of cinema is obviously a result of Soviet influence. See Lu Wei, *Tian Han juzuolun* (On Tian Han's Playwriting) (Nanjing daxue, 1995), p. 120.
52. These three were among the five scripts written for Yihua, which produced some of the most radical films in 1933–35. Due to the precarious political situation, Tian Han's name did not appear in some of the films' credits.
53. Su Feng and Lu Si, "Women de pipan" (Our Criticism), *SSND,* pp. 113–16 (*Chengbao*'s film supplement, Dec. 31, 1932).
54. Cai's other preconversion film *Spring in the South* revolves around a modern man's entanglement with three (types of) women, and also was denounced by the left critics.
55. Chen Wu, "Guanyu *Xinnüxing* de yingpian, piping ji qita" (Criticism of *New Woman,* and more), *SSND,* pp. 345 (*Zhonghua ribao,* March 2, 1935).
56. See, for instance, Kristine Harris, "The New Woman Incident: Cinema, Scandal, Spectacle in 1935 Shanghai," in *Transnational Chinese Cinemas: Identity, Nationhood, Gender,* ed. Sheldon H. Lu (Honolulu: University of Hawaii Press, 1997), pp. 277–302.
57. Ai Xia also wrote a few scripts, including *A Modern Girl* (*Xiandai yi nüxing,* 1933), starring herself. The story is about Putao, a modern girl who has a relationship with a married journalist and goes to any length to maintain this love. In the end she was put into the prison where she meets her old friend, a revolutionary woman. Upon release, Putao decides to embark on a "progressive road." Although there is at this point not much more mate-

rial available for analysis, it is interesting to observe that Ai Xia's script gives her a bright open possibility. For a synopsis, see *WSDYJB,* pp. 2449–51 (*Mingxing yuebao* 1, no. 2, 1935).

58. See Cai Hongsheng, *Cai Chusheng de chuangzuo daolu* (Cai Chusheng's Creative Path) (Beijing: Wenhua yishu, 1982), p. 13.
59. Ibid., p. 21.
60. *Film Art* was, however, forced to cease publication by the Nationalist censors after only four issues.
61. The aforementioned *Movie Weekly* cost 50 cents per copy, so 20 cents was a real bargain for such a "quality" magazine. "Bianzheshi" (Editorial Room), *Xiandai dianying,* no. 2 (April 1, 1933): 31.
62. For examples, Ai Xia, "Ai de zimei" (Love's Sister), in *Xiandai dianying,* no. 1, p. 12; Li Lili's poem, "Zai Xihu she 'Tianming' waijing guituzhong" (On the Way Back from Filming *Daybreak*), in *Xiandai dianying,* no. 2, p. 1.
63. Huang Jiamo, "'Yiandai dianying' and Zhongguo dianyingjie" ('Modern film' and the Chinese Film Industry) *Xiandai dianying,* no. 1 (1933): 1.
64. See Lu Jiefu, "Cong dazhonghua shuoqi" (Beginning with the Issue of Popularization), *Xiandai dianying,* no. 2 (1933): p. 12; and Tian Wa, "Dazhonghua zhuanmaidian" (The Specialty Store on Popularization), *Xiandai dianying* no. 3 (1933): 27.
65. Jiamo, "Xiandai de guanzhong ganjue" (The Feeling of Modern Audiences), *Xiandai dianying,* no. 3 (1933): 9.
66. Xia Yan, "Baineizhang de 'shengyiyan'—shui shahai le Zhongguo xinsheng dianying" ("The Commercial Eye" of Glaucoma-infected Vision"—Who Killed the Newborn Chinese Cinema), *Chengbao*'s film supplement, July 3, 1934.
67. In that sense, the "soft film" was hardly a new category but rather took on a more salient modernist form. See Kwok & M. C. Quiquemelle, "Chinese Cinema and Realism" in *Film and Politics in the Third World,* ed. John D. H. Downing (New York: Praeger, 1987), p. 182.
68. *Xiandai dianying,* no. 6 (1933): 3.
69. Liu Na'ou, "Zhongguo dianying de shendu wenti" (The Problem of Depth Description in Chinese Film), *Xiandai dianying,* no. 3 (1933).
70. Lu Si, "Lun dianying piping de jizhun wenti" (On the Question of Basic Criteria of Film Criticism), *SSND,* pp. 791–819 [serialized in *Minbao*'s film supplement *Yingtan,* March 1–9, 1935].
71. The Metropol, for example, had a striking presence with its blue, lustrous facade accentuated by red neon lights. It is only a stone's throw away from Grand and Calton. There was a female nude statue in the foyer, and the auditorium had deep green upholstered seats, red silk ribbon on the ceiling, and four pretty female ushers. See Yi Feng, "Shehui bujingqi zhong Da Shangahai yingxi kaimu" (The Metropol Opens Despite the Recession) *Mingxing,* no. 28 (1933): 50.
72. Michael Sullivan, *Art and Artists in Twentieth Century China* (Berkeley: University of California Press, 1996), pp. 44–46.
73. Ibid., pp. 58–59.

74. Under pressures from both society and her family (she was the second wife of the man who redeemed her from the brothel), Pan eventually returned to Paris in 1935 and continued her art career there until her death in 1983. Pan Yuliang's life is the subject of Huang Shuqin's film *Soul of Painting* (*Hua hun,* 1996), adapted from Ye Nan's eponymous biography and starring Gong Li.
75. Zhang Jinsheng, *Meide renshengguan* (The Beautiful View of life) (Shanghai: Beixin shuju, 1925), p. 62. Several pictures featuring nude practitioners in Europe were used to illustrate his argument in the book.
76. Xu Meiyun, "Yige modeng yanyuan" (A Modern Actor), *Xiandai dianying,* no. 5 (1933): 12.
77. *Xiandai dianying,* no. 6 (1933).
78. Gilles Deleuze, *Cinema I: The Movement Image,* trans. Hugh Tomlinson and Barbara Habberjam (London: Athlone Press, 1986), p. 40.
79. As quoted in "Tiaowu de zimei" (The Dance Sisters), *Diansheng* 3, no. 6 (1934): 117.
80. Liu was killed by an unidentified assassin in Shanghai in 1939. For more on Liu's life and career, see Shih Shu-mei, "Gender, Race, and Semicolonialism: Liu Na'ou's Urban Shanghai Landscape," *Journal of Asian Studies* 55, no. 4 (Nov. 1996): 934–56.
81. Liu Na'ou, *Dushi fengjing xian* (The Horizon of the Metropolitan Landscape) (Shanghai: Shuimo shudian, 1930). *Scène* is the original French title. The book is written in Chinese.
82. Translation adopted from Shih Shu-mei, "Gender, Race, and Semicolonialism," p. 934.
83. For instance, the modern girl in Xu Xiacun's story "Modern Girl" is Japanese. The dandy in Liu Na'ou's "Bones of Passion" is a French man.
84. Liu Na'Ou's story "Reqing zhigu" (Bones of Passion) is a good example (*Scène,* pp. 67–87). The French term appears at the end of the story, in a letter supposedly "written" in French by the modern girl who turns out to be a married woman. She has sought money from the French man to save her husband's small flower-vending business.
85. Liu Na'ou, "Liangge shijiande buganzheng zhe," in *Scéne,* pp. 89–106
86. Ibid., p. 104.
87. Annette Michelson, introduction, to *Kino-Eye: The Writings of Dziga Vertov,* ed. Michelson, trans., Kevin O'Brien. (Berkeley: University of California Press, 1984), xix, xxv.
88. Liu Na'ou, "Lun Qucai" (On [Film's] Subject Matter), *Xiandi dianying,* no. 4 (1933): 2.
89. Yuri Tsivian, "Between the Old and the New."
90. Mu Weifang, "'Huashen guniang'" (Girl in Disguise), *SSND,* pp. 832–33 (*Minbao*'s supplement, *Yingtan,* 7 June 1936).
91. Gao Feng, "'Huashen guniang' ji qita" (Girl in Disguise etc.), *SSND,* pp. 834–36 (*Dawangbao,* June 20, 1936).
92. Bai Zi, "*Huasheng guniang* gongzuo riji" (Work log of *Girl in Disguise*); *Huasheng guniang tekan* (1936), microfilm, China Film Archive. Apparently,

Yuan Meiyun was very keen on her male garbs. She took walks "incognito" in her male suits. She also went to the Datong Photo Studio to have pictures taken in her suits.

93. Ibid. The cartoonist's name is Jiang Dongliang.
94. For a discussion on the proliferation of, and debates over, translated Western discourses on homoeroticism in Republican China, see Tze-lan Deborah Sang's article, "Translating Homosexuality: The Discourse of *Tongxing'ai* in Republican China (1912–1949)," in *Tokens of Exchange: The Problem of Translation in Global Circulations,* ed. Lydia H. Liu (Durham: Duke University Press, 1999), pp. 276–304. Sang observes that the profusion of public discussions on female same-sex love went hand in hand with an increased male scrutiny of a female experience previously largely confined to the private sphere. This was accompanied by a concerted action to stigmatize and prohibit female same-sex love in the name of science.
95. Sun Yu's film career began in 1927 when he joined the Great Wall Company as an assistant director. In 1928–29 he wrote and directed his first two films, *Xiaoxiang Tears* (Xiaoxiang lei) and *Playboy Swordsman* (Fengliu jianke), both martial arts subjects though with a poetic touch. He then joined Lianhua while making *Spring Dream in the Old Capital* (*Gudu chunmeng;* Minxin, 1930).
96. Peter Rist, "Visual Style in the Shanghai Films Made by the Lianhua Film Company (United Photoplay Service): 1931–37," *The Moving Image: The Journal of the Association of Moving Image Archivists* (2001), pp. 210–16.

97. *Zasui* is a cheap northern dish made of chopped and stewed entrails of lamb and oxen. The English pidgin term "chop-suey," which I choose as a translation, both refers to stir-fry dishes with similar or other cheap ingredients common in American Chinatowns.
98. Sun Yu, "Dianying zaisuiguan: Kaizhang daji" (Cinematic Chop-Suey House: An Auspicious Opening), *Xiandai dianying,* no. 1 (1933): 22–23.
99. Sun Yu, *Dalu zhi ge,* p. 119.
100. Ibid., p. 123.
101. As with *Roadside Flower,* this film was also apparently inspired by and reworked the story of *La dame aux camellia,* which enjoyed enormous popularity in China. Dong Xinyu offers a perceptive analysis of the imprint of this "Camellia" prototype on Chinese film melodrama about aborted free love in her *Kan yu beikan zhijian* (Between Seeing and Being Seen) (Beijing shifan daxue, 2000), pp. 86–90.
102. Wang Renmei, *Wode chengming yu buxing* (Shanghai wenyi, 1985), p. 108.
103. A similar setting is found in the first half of *Daybreak* made a year later. Indeed, while other films of the period often feature middle-class homes with city views as a given, Sun Yu insistently give the working class also a share of that view and thus a sense of city ownership.
104. According to Wang Renmei's recollections, Sun Yu deleted another sentence ("The life's path is uneven with obstacles, but they ignore them") and instead had the camera tracking the four pairs of youthful, strong legs

marching in synchrony, stepping over boulders. Wang, *Wode chengming yu buxing,* pp. 107–8.

105. The script was originally titled *Revenge on the Volcano* (*Huoshan fuchouji*). "Blood of Passion" (*qingxue*) has an obvious erotic meaning, although Sun Yu insisted that the change of title was motivated by the desire to get away from a mere "personal revenge" theme. Sun Yu, "Daoyan 'Huoshan qingxue ji'" (Notes on Directing *Blood of Passion on the Volcano*), *SSND,* p. 132 [*Shibao,* September 15, 1932].
106. Xi Naifang and Huang Zibu, "*Huoshan qingxue,*" *SSND,* p. 135 [*Chengbao's* daily film supplement, September 16, 1932].
107. Ibid., 133–35.
108. Sun Yu, *Dalu zhi ge,* p. 123.
109. Paul Pickowicz, "The Themes of Spiritual Pollution in Chinese Films of the 1930s," p. 51.
110. Ding Yaping, "Lishi de jiulu—Zhongguo dianying and Sun Yu" (The Old Path of History—Chinese Cinema and Sun Yu), *Beijing dianying xuebao,* no. 4 (November 2000): 3–4.

CHAPTER EIGHT

1. Xinhua had come into existence in the mid-1930s sound boom. Its founder Zhang Shankun was a key figure in the film scene in the mid- to late 1930s and in Occupied Shanghai after the war broke out. As had Zhang Shichun before him, Zhang Shankun came from the teahouse background. After a brief career in a tobacco company, and through his involvement in a powerful triad (The Green Gang), he climbed to a managerial position in the Great World, the famous amusement center, and the adjacent Gongwutai Theater.
2. The Chinese rendering of the title, "The Ghostly Shadow in the Field of Singing" (*Gechang meiying*), aptly translates a Western "phantom" into a Chinese idiom for the supernatural figure.
3. His original surname was Xu. Because he is married into his wife's family, presumably as an adopted male heir, he took on his wife's last name as well, hence the rather unusual double surname.
4. Lyrical Theater (Jincheng) was located at the intersection of today's Beijing Road and Guizhou Road. The theater was built in 1934, the same year Xinhua was founded.
5. *GJN,* p. 407.
6. Linda Badley, *Film, Horror, and the Body Fantastic* (Westport, Conn.: Greenwood Press, 1995), pp. 8, 11. On horror as a "body genre," see Carol J. Clover, "Her Body, Himself: Gender in the Slasher Film," in *Fantasy and the Cinema,* ed. James Donald (London: British Film Institute, 1989), pp. 91–133. See also Linda Williams, "Film Bodies: Gender, Genre, and Excess," in *Film Genre Reader II,* ed. Barry Keith Grant (Austin: University of Texas Press, 1995), pp. 140–58.
7. According to a U.S. Department of Commerce Report from 1930: "The ex-

hibition of the first sound and talking pictures in the Shanghai theaters in February 1929 took the motion-picture public of Shanghai by storm. Since then no less than 12 theaters in Shanghai have installed or are about to install sound equipment, and most first-class theaters show nothing but sound pictures. Outside of Shanghai, sound equipment has been installed in Hong Kong, Canton, Tientsin, Hankow, Peiping and Nanking" (E. L. Way, ed., "Motion Pictures in China," *Trade Information Bulletin,* no. 722 [U.S. Department of Commerce, Bureau of Foreign and Domestic Commerce, 1930]: 5).

8. Roman Jakobson, "The Dominant," in *Language in Literature,* eds. Krystyna Pomorska and Stephen Rudy (Cambridge, Mass.: Belknap Press, 1987), p. 41.
9. C. J. North, "The Chinese Motion Picture Market," pp. 8, 16–17.
10. Lianhua, the left-leaning company established in 1930, was slow in embracing sound. This procrastination was due to a number of reasons; one central concern was that the crude quality of early sound film was not appropriate for its campaign of "reviving the national film." Making silent films, with sound only as occasional embellishment, quickly became Lianhua's production philosophy. See "Lianhua jinhou zhipian jihua" (The Future Plan for Film Production at Lianhua), *Yingxi zazhi* 2, no. 2 (Oct. 31, 1931): 22–23.
11. Xu Bibo, "Zhongguo yousheng dianying de kaiduan" (The Beginnings of Chinese Sound Cinema), *Zhongguo Dianying,* no. 4 (1957): 58–62. Xu wrote the script for the film. To promote the film, *YXSH* (1, no. 9 [March 1931]) devoted a special issue to it, with a synopsis, song lyrics, and other items of interest.
12. Hu Die, *Yinghou shengya,* pp. 91–94. It happened frequently that one heard a male voice while there was a woman speaking on the screen. See also *GJN,* pp. 209–10.
13. *Singing Beauty* was sold to a distributor in Canton. After overcoming some technical problems, such as the matching of "sound" and "mouth," the film premiered there on September 19, 1931. The theater was located in the heart of the city near the bus terminal, which greatly boosted box-office returns. Ji Cheng, "*Yu Meiren* zai Guangzhou" (*Singing Beauty* in Canton), *YXSH* 1, no. 38 (Oct. 3, 1931).
14. Yun Qin, "Cong *Genü Hongmudan* shuodao *Yuguo tianqing*" (From *The Singing Girl Red Peony* to *Peace after Storm*), *YXSH,* 1, no. 21 (June 6, 1931): 8–9.
15. The caption reads: "Dear readers, you often go enjoy sound films, and perhaps you are aware that some of them have sound. But because of your [ignorant] situation, you may not know how it was done. We hereby show you two strips of film from *Peace after Storm.* Please pay attention to the side bar with uneven coloring—that is precisely the source of sound waves," *Yingxi zazhi,* no. 9 (April 1931): 3.
16. *YXSH,* 1, no. 24 (June 27, 1931). In the same issue, a picture of the "Movietone" strip was shown, along with a picture of the star Huang Naishuang dancing.

17. See for instance, Tanjingdeng (Carbon Light), "Zhen mei lianchi ya!" (How Shameless!), *YXSH* 1, no. 26 (July 11, 1931): 3.
18. Kamola (Camera), "Tianyi gongsi shezhi shengpian zhi jinguo" (How Tianyi Came to Make Sound Film), *YXSH* 1, no. 20 (June 6, 1931): 4–7.
19. Xiaoyuan, "Qingwen Tianyi gongsi" (Some Questions for the Tianyi company), *YXSH* 1.35 (12 Sept. 1931): 27–28; and Chen Guoxin, "Guan guochan shengpian *Gechang chunse hou*" (After Seeing the Domestically Made Sound Film *Spring Arrives in the Singing World*), *YXSH* 1, no. 47 (1931): 2–3.
20. Sha, "Guan *Gechang chunse hou*" (After Seeing *Spring Arrives to the Singing World*), *YXSH* 1, no. 50 (Dec. 26, 1931): 15–17.
21. Hence the wordplay on *fang* (square), a homophone of the *fang* in Mei Lanfang, and *yuan* (round), which refers to the shape of a record album. Hu Die, *Yinghou shengya*, p. 96.
22. Mary Ann Doane, "The Voice in the Cinema: Articulation of Body and Space," in Elisabeth Weis and John Belton, eds., *Film Sound* (New York: Columbia University Press), 1985, pp. 163–64.
23. Mary Farquhar and Chris Berry, "Shadow Opera: Toward a New Archaeology of the Chinese Cinema," *Post Script* 20, no. 2–3 (Winter/Spring & Summer 2001): 25–42.
24. The shorts were shown with other films in a variety of manners. The song lyrics appeared as intertitles. Those made by Minxin were later incorporated into Lianhua's (into which Minxin merged) first feature *Spring Dream in the Old Capital* (1930), accompanied by a phonograph. Mei Lanfang, *Wode dianying shenghuo*, pp. 3–10, 13–20.

25. For an informative and insightful essay on the "modernization" of the Peking opera star (including Mei Lanfang), see Isabelle Duchesne, "The Chinese Opera Star: Roles and Identity," in *Boundaries in China*, ed. John Hay (London: Reaktion Books, 1994), pp. 217–330.
26. The sound track is not extant. The film also contains dancing episodes performed by (but shot separately) the Mingyue singing and dancing troupe. Wang Renmei, *Wo de chengming yu buxing*, pp. 112–23. According to Wang, these episodes were among several experimental "singing and dancing" sound films using wax disk technology. They were supposed to be shown before a feature. But in this case, they were incorporated into the film despite lack of narrative connection.
27. *FZS*, p, 163.
28. This may have been partly influenced by Hollywood musicals that were shown at first-run sound theaters in Shanghai. The June 1930 issue of the magazine, *Xin yinxing yu tiyu*, for instance, carries a big advertisement for Warner Brother's release *Show of Shows*. Its Chinese title is "Xi zhong xi" (Play within a play) (p. 14).
29. Wang Wenhe, *Zhongguo dianying yinyue xunzong* (Beijing: Zhongguo guangbo dianying, 1995), p. 9.
30. The film is not extant. For a complete original script, see *Sun Yu dianying juben xuanji* (Selected Film Scripts by Sun Yu) (Beijing: Zhongguo dianying, 1981). Sun Yu reportedly admitted the influence of Frank Borzage's *Seventh*

Heaven (1927)—one of Fox's first Movietone films—on this film. See Yi Zhong, "Cong *Gudu chunmeng* shuodao *Yecao xianhua* ji *Lian'ai yu yiwu*" (From *Spring Dream in the Old Capital* to *Wild Flowers* and *Love and Duty*), *Yingxi zazhi* 2, no. 2. (Oct. 1, 1931): 30.

31. See Yingjin Zhang, "Engendering Chinese Filmic Discourse of the 1930s."
32. Quoted in Wang Wenhe, *Zhongguo dianying yingyue xunzong,* p. 8.
33. Ibid., pp. 6–7.
34. Huo Shan (Volcano), "Duiyu yousheng dianyingde quexian" (The Shortcomings of Sound Film), *YXSH,* vol. 1, no. 51 (2 Jan. 1932): 4–5. The report from the American consulates in Shanghai obviously overestimated the size of the English-speaking population there at the time (E. L. Way, ed., "Motion Pictures in China," p. 5).
35. On the whole Sun Yu's language is very modern and shows the influence of the May Fourth vernacular literature. His song lyrics retain traces of classical poetry and folk song, however. "Looking for My Brother," for instance, has an eight-line stanza that alternates between lines with three and five characters. In all there are four verses, with the "brother" and "sister" singing two verses each. Both in form and content, it resembles a folksong.
36. Wang Wenhe, *Zhongguo dianying yinyue xunzong,* p. 90. Besides the theme song, another important diegetic piece of music, the humoresque by the Czech composer Antonin Dvorák, played by the male protagonist in the film when expressing his love, was also "synchronized" by a record.
37. Lianhua had offices in Hong Kong, Shanghai, and Tianjin. In fact, *Wild Flowers* was produced by Minxin, but "published" or distributed by the newly founded Lianhua.
38. Max Horkheimer and Theodor W. Adorno, *Dialectic of Enlightenment,* p. 120.
39. Ibid., pp. 44–45.
40. *GJN,* pp. 295–96.
41. Roman Jakobson, "On the Relation between Visual and Auditory Signs," in *Language in Literature,* p. 469.
42. The most famous "song and dance" troupe at the time, the "Mingyue gewutuan," headed by Li Jinghui and featuring would-be movie stars Li Lili and Wang Renmei, was an important supplier of musical material and talent to the emerging sound film industry. Li Minghui promoted the numbered musical notation, standard Chinese, and children's literature and education. All the troupe members learned *guoyu,* partly for singing the songs he wrote. The troupe was officially incorporated into Lianhua in 1931, and participated in the production of several films. See Wang Renmei, *Wo de chengming yu buxin,* chapters 2 and 3. Nie Er, the young musician who composed the theme song in *Children of Troubled Times* (the future national anthem of the PRC) for the film, was also a Mingyue member.
43. For a discussion on the significance of *Stimmung* in the Weimar cinema, see Lotte H. Eisner, *The Haunted Screen: Expressionism in the German Cinema and the Influence of Max Reinhardt,* trans. Roger Greaves (Berkeley: University of California Press, 1973), pp. 199–206. According to Eisner's definition, *Stimmung,* an effect of lighting, suggests the "vibrations of the soul," which

"hovers around objects as well as people." She continues, "This *Stimmung* is most often diffused by a 'veiled,' melancholy landscape, or by an interior in which the etiolated glow of a hanging lamp, an oil lamp, a chandelier, or even a sunbeam shining through a window, creates penumbra." Although Eisner's view is at times impaired by her obsessive critique of the German "psyche," her highlighting of the key stylistic elements in the Weimar cinema is helpful. This description applies to *Song at Midnight* to some extent as well.

44. *Qingchang guairen* (Shanghai: Langhua yingpian gongsi), April 1924.
45. The "bamboo clock," consisting of a hallowed bamboo stem and a stick, is a device traditionally used to indicate the time at night according to the position of the moon.
46. Another hunchback in the film is the night watchman in the theater. Interestingly, the two old characters serve the dual function of both the servants and the parents to the male and female protagonists. Together they seem to form a deformed family, marked by physical or mental handicap and divided by historical trauma. The hunchback is one of the typical characters in horror films. See Drake Douglas, *Horrors!* (New York: Overlook Press, 1989), the section on "The Hunchback," pp. 299–332. The other types Douglas examines include the Vampire, the Werewolf, the Monster, the Mummy, the Walking Dead, the Schizophrenic, and the Phantom. The main character in *Song at Midnight* clearly belongs in the international family of phantoms.

47. The lyrical mood here is also evocative of the figure of the esoteric, strange and dissent in classical Chinese literary tradition, for examples, Qu Yuan's *Chu Ci,* and Pu Songling's *Liaozhai zhiyi.* For a perceptive study of the latter, see Judith Zeitlin, *Historian of the Strange* (Palo Alto, Calif.: Stanford University Press, 1993). The association with Qu Yuan is not entirely arbitrary, since Tian Han was heavily influenced by a combination of Chinese esoteric poetry, Japanese modernism, and Western romantic poets such as Goethe and Whitman.
48. A ghost, according to the traditional belief, does not possess a shadow, and that is how one can tell a ghost from a living person. In the case of Song Danping, because he is not really dead, the shadow-body may stand as a liminal form between a ghost and a living person.
49. Michel de Certeau, *The Practice of Everyday Life,* trans., Steven Rendall (Berkeley: University of California Press, 1984), p. 129.
50. Yomi Braester, *Witness Against History: Literature, Film, and Public Discourse in Twentieth-Century China* (Palo Alto, Calif.: Stanford University Press, 2003), p. 99.
51. Wolfgang Kayser, *The Grotesque in Art and Literature,* translated by Ulrich Weisstein (Bloomington: Indiana University Press, 1983), p. 185.
52. *YXSH,* vol. 1, no. 4 (1931): 2.
53. Hu Zhongbiao, "Shenguai muogui huazhuang zhi yanjiu" (Studies on the Makeup of Demons and Spirits), *Dianying yuebao,* no. 7 (Oct. 10, 1928).
54. Ying also directed *Plunder of Peach and Plum* (1934), the first "total" sound

film made with sound equipment devised by Chinese technicians. Prior to his entry into the film world, like other prominent directors of the period, Yin had been active in the spoken drama scene.

55. In one interesting instance of the uncanny use of sound in relation to the face, a portrait of her fiancé on the wall suddenly "talks" to the woman, encouraging her to work harder for the revolutionary cause.

56. Carol Clover, "Her Body, Himself: Gender in the Slasher Film," in *Fantasy and the Cinema,* ed. James Donald (London: British Film Institute, 1989), p. 94.

57. James Donald, "The Fantastic, the Sublime and the Popular: Or, What's At Stake in Vampire Films?" in *Fantasy and the Cinema,* p. 240.

58. The corpus of this project as a whole is known as *Shiji,* or *Records of the Historian.* It was written ca. 104–91 and consists of 130 books. It covers the period from the mythical Yellow Emperor to the contemporary events during the reign of Emperor Wu of the Han Dynasty; the contents range from biographies of famous figures to peasant uprisings, from portrayals of ethnic minorities to descriptions of commercial life. The genres and methods used by Sima Qian were adopted by later historians and historiographers. The work as a whole has also been considered an exemplary literary landmark. Sima Qian is credited as the first historian who adopted the genre of biography in the writing of history.

59. The reference to nitric acid has, however, a more direct connection to modern science and military technology. My thanks to James St. André who alerted me to the prevalent motif of vitriol-throwing in late Victorian English detective fiction, which was translated into Chinese. The practice of using nitric acid in incidents involving thwarted love has been a persistent part of urban lore in Shanghai.

60. Incidentally, the name of one of the Chunliu playwrights was Song Chiping; only the middle character differs from Song Danping. Whereas *chi* means obsession, *dan* has connotations of loyalty and devotion. Ouyang Yuqian describes playwrights like Song and others as being primarily influenced by their literati background, and hence reluctant to embrace more radical ideas and values. Their protagonists tend to be romantic and gallant yet tragic, and they often renounce the world through suicide or escape in the end; see his "Tan wenmingxi," pp. 206–7.

61. For a first-hand account of the Chunliu troupe, see Ouyang Yuqian, "Huiyi Chunliu" (Remembering Chunliu), collected in his *Zi wo yanxi yilai* (Since I Started Acting) (Beijing: Zhongguo xiju, 1959), pp.155–89.

62. A full-length version of the play in Chinese, translated and modified by Xu Banmei, is included in *Zhongguo zaoqi huaju xuan* (Selected Early Chinese Spoken Drama Plays), ed. Wang Weimin (Beijing: Zhongguo xiju, 1989), pp. 307–44.

63. See Zhong Dafeng et al., "From Wenmingxi (Civilized Play) to Yingxi (Shadowplay)," p. 49.

64. Nie Er died just one day after Zheng, on July 17, 1935.

65. Andrew Tudor, *Monsters and Mad Scientists,* as quoted in Mark Jancovich, *Horror,* p. 53.
66. Notably, Universal Pictures' *The Phantom of the Opera* has none of these features.
67. *FZS,* pp. 490–91.
68. Here it is possible to connect Benjamin's conception of photography's capacity to reveal the "optical unconscious" and Frederic Jameson's proposition that narrative interpretation has to be informed by an underlining "political unconscious." For both, the "unconscious" stands for a particular historically *formed* experience that cannot be simply reduced to the level of content alone. Benjamin is more attentive to the technological singularity and representational challenge posed by the photographic medium, whereas Jameson is primarily concerned with the form of the novel. See Walter Benjamin, "A Short History of Photography" and Fredric Jameson, *The Political Unconscious: Narrative as a Socially Symbolic Act* (Ithaca: Cornell University Press, 1981).
69. A contemporary critic, writing shortly after the premiere of the film, commented on the problem of sound recording in the film, that the volume of the sound effects tended to drown out the dialogue. What he found most attractive about the film was these poetic staging of the nocturnal scene, with a cold moon and the misty lighting. He also argues that the form of horror is very appropriate for the subject matter, which presents the ghost as a human being and an embodiment of the "conflict between emotion and reason." Ye Di, "Yeban gesheng" (Song at Midnight), in *SSND,* pp. 471–73 [*Da wanbao,* Feb. 22, 1937].
70. Benjamin, "Theses on the Philosophy of History," in *Illuminations,* p. 257.
71. Mikhail Bakhtin, *Rabelais and His World,* trans. Hélène Islowsky (Bloomington: Indiana University Press, 1986), pp. 304–67.
72. Yomi Braester, *Witness Against History,* p. 81.
73. The Hong Kong catalogue for the retrospective of *Early Chinese Cinema: The Era of Exploration* (Hong Kong Arts Center and Hong Kong Chinese Film Association, 1984) describes this film as "reminiscent of *Song at Midnight* in its treatment of images and heralds the style of 'Film Noir' in the forties."
74. The persistent return of the grotesque face and the proliferation of the horror and other "body genres" in Hong Kong in ensuing decades further underscores the significance of *Song at Midnight* in Chinese film and cultural history. The film's latest incarnation was *The Phantom Lover* (with same Chinese title, *Yeban gesheng*) made in 1995, on the eve of the "turn-over" of Hong Kong to China, and featured the mega–pop star Leslie Cheung (Zhang Guorong), who composed and sang film's songs. The film was again a huge hit. The nocturnal singing of this early sound film echoes until this day, not least because Leslie Cheung killed himself by jumping off a high-rise hotel in central Hong Kong on April 1, 2003. His death prompted a mass mourning both in the city and around the world, on the street, and in cyberspace.

ENVOI

1. Harry Harootunian, *History's Disquiet: Modernity, Cultural Practice, and the Question of Everyday Life* (New York: Columbia University Press, 2000), p. 17.
2. Dipesh Chakrabarty, *Provincializing Europe: Postcolonial Thought and Historical Difference* (Princeton: Princeton University Press, 2000), pp. 17–8.
3. Paul Veyne, *Writing History,* trans. Mina Moore-Rinvolucri (Middletown, Conn.: Wesleyan University Press, 1984 (1971), pp. 15–30.
4. Ibid., p. 5.

GLOSSARY

aimeiju	愛美劇
Aipulu (Apollo)	愛普盧
Aodi'an (Odéon)	奥迪安
babu zhuyi	八不主義
baguwen	八股文
baihua	白話
baihua yundong	白話運動
baixiangren	白相人
Baiyuan laoren	白猿老人
Bali daxiyuan	巴黎大戲院
bao	報
Bao Tianxiao	包天笑
baolupian	暴露片
baoying	報應
beifa	北伐
bianhuan	變幻
bianju	編劇
biaoyan	表演
bishi pian	裨史片
bizhen	逼眞
bolaiping	舶來品
buwen bubai	不文不白
Cai Chusheng	蔡楚生
Changcheng	長城
Changjiang	長江
Changming hanshou yingxi xuexiao jiangyi	昌明函授影戲學校講義
changpian zhengju	長片正劇
changshi	嘗試
chayuan	茶園
Chen Duxiu	陳獨秀
Chen Kaige	陳凱歌
Cheng Bugao	程步高
chi	池
chifei	赤匪
chuan	串
chuancha	穿插
chuanqi	傳奇

chuchu wei xingqu shishang,yiji boren yican 處處惟興趣是尚,以冀博人一粲
chujian chubao, jiuliang jipin 除奸除暴救良濟貧
Da Shanghai jihua 大上海計划
Dashijie 大世界
datuanyuan 大團圓
dazhong 大眾
delüfeng 得律風
Demokelaxi xiansheng 德莫克拉西先生
dianchahui 電茶會
dianying 電影
dianying mingxing 電影明星
dianying shi yanjing de bingqilin, xinling de shafayi 電影是眼睛的冰淇琳,心靈的沙發椅
dianying xiaoshuo 電影小說
dianying zasuiguan 電影雜碎館
diaobangzi 吊膀子
dingmin lun 定命論
Dong Keyi 董克毅
dongya bingfu 東亞病夫
dongzuo 動作
dushi guanzhong 都市觀眾

dushi sanwen 都市散文
er wo tu 二我圖
erchong zhi yi 二重之役
fan ouxiang zhuyi 反偶像主義
Fan Xuepeng 范雪朋
fangjiao 放脚
fayang guoguang 發揚國光
feilü feima 非驢非馬
feixia 飛俠
fen shen xiang 分身像
fen shuoming 分說明
fenchang fenmu 分場分幕
fengsuhua 風俗畫
fengxing quanqiu 風行全球
fugu 復古
fuguo qiangbin 富國強兵
fuxing 腐刑
fuxing guopian 復興國片
gailiang jingxi 改良京戲
ge 歌
geju 歌劇
gewu ju 歌舞劇
gewu pian 歌舞片

gewu zhizhi	格物至致
Gong Jianong	龔家農
Gu Kenfu	顧肯夫
gu'ai	固愛
guairen	怪人
Guaixia	怪俠
Guan Haifeng	管海峰
guanzhong xinli	觀眾心理
Gu'er jiuzu ji	孤兒救祖記
guju xinbian	古劇新編
guochan	國產
guofang dianying	國防電影
guopian zhi gong	國片之宮
guoyu	國語
gushipian	故事片
guzhuangju	古裝劇
haipai	海派
haishang	海上
Han Wudi	漢武帝
heiqi bandeng	黑漆板凳
Hong Shen	洪深
Hongkou da xiyuan	虹口大戲院
Hou Yao	侯曜
Hu	滬
Hu Die	胡蝶
Hu Shi	胡適
huabao	畫報
huahua shijie	花花世界
huaji xiju	滑稽喜劇
Huaju	華劇
huaju	話劇
Huang Zunxian	黃遵憲
huangjin shidai	黃金時代
Huanxian	幻仙
huayang zaju	華洋雜居
huazhuang xiang	化妝像
huodong xiezhen	活動寫眞
huo wenxue	活文學
huohai	禍害
huoshao	火燒
jianghu	江湖
jianguang doufa	劍光斗法
jiaohua	教化
jiaojihua	交際花
jiating gongsi	家庭公司

jiating wenti ju 家庭問題劇
jiayin zhongxing 甲寅中興
jiazhuangpin 假裝品
jieshuo 解說
jiguan 機關
jiguan bujing 機關布景
jingji 經濟
jingkuangshi 鏡框式
jingli 經歷
jingpai 京派
jingyan 經驗
jingyanzhuyi 經驗主義
jixie ren 機械人
jixie wenming 機械文明
juben huang 劇本荒
jun'eiga 純映畫
juzhi 劇旨
kai yanjie 開眼界
kaibu 開埠
kan xiyangjing 看西洋鏡
kangbadu 康白度
kanke 看客

Ke Ling 柯靈
kexue shen 科學神
kexue yu renshengguan zhizheng 科學與人生觀之爭
kexue yu xuanxue 科學與玄學
kongbu pian 恐怖片
kuaigan 快感
kunqu 昆曲
Lang Que-nai 郎卻乃
laohuzao 老虎灶
laogong 勞工
leidesi 累得死
Li Lili 黎麗麗
Li Zeyuan 李澤源
Liang Qichao 梁啓超
Lianhe 聯合
Lianhua 聯華
Lianhuan tuhua 連環圖畫
lianhuanxi 連環戲
liantai benxi 連台本戲
lilong 里弄
linghun 靈魂
lingong xuexiao 傭工學校

lishi xiangzhao	力士香皂
Liu Na'ou	劉吶鷗
liyuan	梨園
longtang	弄堂
Lu Xun	魯迅
Luo Mingyou	羅明佑
lutian tongshi	露天通事
Mao Dun (Shen Yanbing)	茅盾(沈雁冰)
mao'er xi	髦兒戲
Ma-Xu Weibang	馬徐維邦
Mei Lanfang	梅蘭芳
mini ting	迷你廳
mingshi fengliu	名士風流
Mingxing	明星
Mingxing yingpian gufen youxian gongsi	明星影片股份有限公司
Minxin	民新
minzhonghua	民眾化
modeng	摩登
modeng nülang	摩登女郎
mubiao	幕表
muwei	幕味
namowen	拿摩溫
Nanyang	南洋
neixin biaoyan	內心表演
Nie Er	聶耳
niucha	牛茶
niupeng	牛棚
nüxia	女俠
Ouhua	歐化
Ouyang Yuqian	歐陽予倩
piaoyouhui	票友會
pingmin jiaoyu	平民教育
piyingxi	皮影戲
puluo	普羅
qianmianlang	千面郎
qianyi mohua	潛移默化
qimeng	啓蒙
Qinglian ge	青蓮閣
qipao	旗袍
qiu ji tu	求己圖
Qu Qiubai	瞿秋白
quanbu yousheng duibai	全部有聲對白
quanguo yundonghui	全國運動會
Quanye julebu	全夜俱樂部

raoliang sanri	繞梁三日
Ren Pengnian	任彭年
rentimei	人體美
renxia haoyi	任俠好義
Renxin zai jishi, miaoshou ke huichun	仁心在濟世, 妙手可回春
rongzhu xin lixiang yi ru jiu fengge	熔鑄新理想於舊風格
rougan	肉感
Ruan Lingyu	阮玲玉
ruanpian	軟片
ruanxing dianying	軟性電影
Saiyinsi xiansheng	賽因斯先生
shan you shan bao, e you e bao	善有善報, 惡有惡報
Shanghai	上海
Shanghai da xiyuan	上海大戲院
Shanghai meishu zhuanke xuexiao	上海美術專科學校
Shanghai qi	上海氣
shangwu jingshen	尚武精神
shangwu yinshuguan	商務印書館
Shao shi xiongdi	邵氏兄弟
Shao Yifu	邵逸夫
Shao Zuiweng	邵醉翁
shehui lunli pian	社會倫理片
shehui pian	社會片
shehui xinwen	社會新聞
Shen	申
shengjiangji	升降機
shengse lianyin	聲色聯姻
Shenjiang yi da wutai	申江亦大舞臺
shenlin qi jing	身臨其境
shenmi ke	神密客
shenqi/shenguai	神奇/神怪
Shenzhou pai	神州派
shexi	社戲
shi de jingyanzhuyi	詩的經驗主義
Shibao	時報
shidai	時代
shijie	世界
shijie datong	世界大同
shijie geming	詩界革命
shijiere	世界熱
shili yangchang	十里洋場
Shi Zhecun	施蟄存

shimpai geki 新派劇
shishen 失身
shisu 世俗
shizhuang yanqingpian 時裝言情片
shouying 手影
shuangbao an 雙胞案
shuoming 説明
shuomingshu 説明書
Sima Qian 司馬遷
simiao 寺廟
su 俗
Sulian jingtou 蘇聯鏡頭
Sun Yat-sen (Sun Zhongshan) 孫中山
Sun Yu 孫瑜
Tan Xinpei 譚鑫培
tanci 彈詞
Tang San Zang 唐三藏
tekan 特刊
Tian Han 田漢
tianqiao 天橋
tianren heyi 天人合一
Tianyi 天一
ticai ge (tige) 題材歌（題歌）
tichang guohuo 提倡國貨
tishen 替身
tixian 體現
tiyan 體驗
tongju 同居
Tongqing 同慶
tongshi 通事
tongsu 通俗
tu'an shi 圖案式
Tuhua lan 圖畫欄
tuolike 托里克
Wanguo bolanhui 萬國博覽會
wangguonu 亡國奴
Wang Hanlun 王漢倫
Wang Xuchang 汪煦昌
Wang Zilong 王子龍
Wang Yuanlong 王元龍
wei rensheng de yishu 爲人生的藝術
wen 文
Wen Yimin 文逸民
Wenming yaji 文明雅集
wenming jiehun 文明結婚

wenmingjiao	文明腳
wenmingxi	文明戲
wenxue geming	文學革命
wenxue yanjiuhui	文學研究會
wenyan	文言
wenyanwen	文言文
woyou	臥遊
Wu Lizhu	鄔麗珠
Wu Suxin	吳素馨
wusi yundong	五四運動
wutaiju	舞台劇
wuxia	武俠
wuxia kuang	武俠狂
wuxia shenguai pian	武俠神怪片
wuzhi wenming	物質文明
xi	戲
Xi yuan	西園
xi zhong xi	戲中戲
Xia Peizhen	夏佩珍
Xia Yan	夏衍
Xiahun	俠魂
xiake	俠客
Xian Xinhai	冼星海
xiangzuozhuan	向左轉
xiao shimin	小市民
xiao zichan jieji	小資產階級
Xie Jin	謝晉
xiesheng shi	寫生式
xin	新
xin ganjue pai	新感覺派
Xin Qingnian	新青年
xinchao	新潮
xingfengji	興奮劑
xingyu shichen	刑餘史臣
xinju	新劇
Xinmin	新民
xinqi	新奇
xinshi xuetang	新式學堂
Xinshijie	新世界
xinxing lishi geju	新型歷史歌劇
xiren dianying	戲人電影
xiushen	修身
xiyang yingxi	西洋影戲
xiyuan	戲園
xizi	戲子

Xu Banmei	徐半梅
Xu Qinfang	徐琴芳
Xu Yuan	徐園
Xu Zhuodai	徐卓呆
Xuan Jinglin	宣景琳
xuanji	玄机
xuanxue gui	玄學鬼
xueben	血本
xunxiongci	尋兄詞
Yang Naimei	楊耐梅
Yang Xiaozhong	楊小仲
yangchang	洋場
yangpai	洋派
yanjiang	演講
Yanqing pian	言情片
yanshi	艷史
Yaxiya	亞細亞
ye huayuan	夜花園
yeshou	野獸
yi wu chuanqing	以物傳情
yiban furen ruzi	一般婦人孺子
yichang	夷場
Yin Mingzhu	殷明珠
ying	影
yingjie	影界
yingpianju	影片劇
yingpingren	影評人
yingxi	影戲
yingxi xiaoshuo	影戲小說
yingxing dianying	硬性電影
yingye jia liangxin	營業加良心
yinse shijie	銀色世界
yipian gongsi	一片公司
yiren	异人
yishi	意識
youlechang	遊樂場
Youlian	友聯
youxi	遊戲
Yuan Muzhi	袁牧之
yuanding	園丁
yuanquan shi	圓圈式
yuanxiao	元宵
yuanxing	原型
yuanyang hudie	鴛鴦蝴蝶
yuanyang zuo	鴛鴦座

yuanyin 原音
yuanzhi 原質
Yueming 月明
yugong 寓公
yule pian 娛樂片
yumang 愚盲
Yun Gu 芸姑
zaofei 造匪
zaomeng 造夢
zaoqi dianying 早期電影
Zhang Huichong 張惠沖
Zhang Huimin 張惠民
Zhang Shankun 張善琨
Zhang Shichuan 張石川
zhanghui 章回
zhen 珍
Zheng Yimei 鄭逸梅
Zheng Zhenqiu 鄭正秋
zhengdang 正當
zhengli guogu 整理國故
zhenshixing 眞實性
zhenzhu 珍珠

Zhongguo yingpian zhizao youxian gongsi 中國影片製造有限公司
Zhongguo yingxi yanjiushe 中國影戲研究社
Zhonghua yingye xuexiao 中華影業學校
zhongxue weiyong, xixue weiti 中學爲用, 西學爲體
Zhongyang daxiyuan 中央大戲院
Zhongyang yingxi gongsi 中央影戲公司
Zhou Jianyun 周劍雲
zhuangyuan 狀元
ziqiang 自強
zong shuoming 總説明
zoumadeng 走馬燈
zujie 租界
zuoyi dianying 左翼電影
zuoyou 坐遊

FILMOGRAPHY

Note: Many translations are original, some are my own.

BAIYAN NÜXIA *(The Female Knight-Errant White Swallow)* 白燕女俠
Fudan, 1928
Scr/Dir: Yu Boyan
Cast: Zhang Lingqun, Qian Siying, Zhao Yongni, Yu Hanmin, Hua Wanfang

CHEZHONG DAO *(Robbery on a Train)* 車中盜
Commercial Press Motion Picture Section, 1920, 6000 feet
Scr: Chen Chunsheng (adapted from a translated novel)
Dir: Ren Pengnian
Ph: Liao Enshou
Cast: Ding Yuanyi, Bao Guirong, Zhang Shengwu

CHUANJIABAO *(A Family Treasure)* 傳家寶
Shanghai yingxi, 1926. 9 r
Dir: Dan Duyu
Ph: Dan Ganting
Cast: Yin Minzhu, He Rongzhu, Chen Baoqi, Gu Yunjie, Zhou Hongquan, Wang Qiefu

CHUNCAN *(Spring Silkworms)* 春蠶
Mingxing, 1933, 10 r
Scr: Xia Yan
Dir: Chen Bugao
Ph: Wang Shizhen
Cast: Xiao Ying, Yan Xuexian, Gong Jianong, Ai Xia, Gao Jingping, Zheng Xiaoqiu

DA LU *(Big Road)* 大路
Lianhua (second studio), 1935, sound effects and music, 10 r
Scr/Dir: Sun Yu
Ph: Hong Weilie
Music: Nie Er
Cast: Jin Yan, Chen Yanyan, Li Lili, Zhang Yi, Zheng Junli, Luo Peng, Han Langen, Zhang Zhizhe, Shang Guanwu, Liu Qian, Liu Jiqun, Hong Jingling

DA NAO GUAI JUCHANG *(Strange Happenings at the Theater)* 大鬧怪劇場
Mingxing, 1922, 3 r

Scr: Zheng Zhengqiu
Dir: Zhang Shichuan
Ph: Carl Gregory
Cast: Yan Zhongying, Zheng Zhegu

DAO MINJIAN QU *(Going to the People)* 到民間去
Nanguo dianying she, 1926, unfinished
Scr/Dir: Tian Han
Cast: Tang Huaiqiu, Tang Lin, Yi Su, Ye Dingluo, Jiang Guangchi, Li Jinfa, Zhong Zitong, Boris, Piniek, Mme Weifudingsawa (?)

DINGJUNSHAN *(Mount Dingjun)* 定軍山
Fengtai Photographic Studio, extracts, 1905, 3 r, opera film.
Ph: Liu Zhonglun
Cast: Tan Xinpei

DUANDI YUYIN *(Lingering Sound of a Broken Flute)* 斷笛餘音
a.k.a. FENTOU ZHI WU *(Dance in Front of the Tomb)* 墳頭之舞
Shanghai College of Arts, 1927, unfinished
Scr/Dir: Tian Han
Ph: Ou Xiafeng, Zhang Huiling

DUHUI DE ZAOCHEN *(Morning in a Metropolis)* 都會的早晨
Lianhua, 1933, 12 r
Scr: Cai Chusheng
Dir: Cai Chusheng
Ph: Zhou Ke
Cast: Wang Renmei, Gao Zhanfei, Yuan Congmei, Wang Guilin, Tang Huaiqiu

DUO GUOBAO *(Seizing a National Treasure)* 奪國寶
Lianhe, 1926, 9 r
Dir: Zhang Huichong
Cast: Zhang Huichong, Xu Su'e, Fei Baiqing

DUSHI FENGGUANG *(Metropolitan Scenes)* 都市風光
Diantong, 1935, 10 r, sound
Scr/Dir: Yuan Muzhi
Ph: Wu Xinxian
Cast: Zhang Xinzhu, Tang Na, Zhou Boxun, Bai Lu, Wu Yin, Cai Ruohong

ERBAIWU BAIXIANG CHENGHUANGMIAO *(The Silly in Town God's Temple)* 二百五白相城皇廟
Asia, 1913
Dir: Zhang Shichuan

Ph: Essler
Cast: Ding Chuhe

FEIXING DADAO *(The Great Flying Bandit)* 飛行大盜
a.k.a. *Little Sister, I Love You*
Shanghai Film Company, 1929
Dir/Ph: Dan Duyu
Cast: Yin Mingzhu, Dan Erchun, Han Langen

FENGYUN ERNÜ *(Children of Troubled Times)* 風雲兒女
Diantong, 1935, sound
Scr: Tian Han.
Scenario: Xia Yan
Dir: Xu Xingzhi
Ph: Wu Xinxian
Cast: Yuan Muzhi, Wang Renmei, Tan Ying, Gu Menghe, Lu Luming, Wang Guilin

FENHONGSE DE MENG *(Pink Dream)* 粉紅色的夢
Lianhua, 1932, 10 r
Scr/Dir: Cai Chusheng
Cast: Gao Zhanfei, Xue Linxian, Liu Jiqun, Han Langeng, Tan Yin, Zheng Junli

FEIJIAN NUXIA *(Heroine with a Flying Sword)* 飛劍女俠
Xinren, 1928
Dir: Cheng Bugao
Cast: Li Manli, Ren Chaojun

GECHANG CHUNSE *(Spring Arrives at the Singing World)* 歌場春色
Tianyi, 1931, 8 r, sound
Scr: Yao Sufeng.
Adaptation: Qiu Qixiang.
Dialogue: Chen Dabei.
Dir: Li Pingqian
Ph: Bert Cann, Yan Bingheng, Zhou Shilu
Cast: Xuan Jinglin, Zhang Yonggui, Chen Yitang, Wu Suxin, Xu Qinfang, Yang Naimei, Zi Luolan, Pu Jinghong

GENÜ HONG MUDAN *(The Singing Girl Red Peony)* 歌女紅牡丹
Mingxing, 1930, 9 r, film with sound on wax disks
Scr/Titles: Hong Shen
Dir: Zhang Shichuan
Ph: Dong Keyi

Cast: Hu Die, Wang Xianzhai, Xia Peizhen, Gong Jianong, Wang Jiting, Tang Jie, Tan Zhiyuan, Zhu Xiuying, Xiao Ying

GONGFU GUONAN *(Share the Burden of the National Crisis)* 共赴國難
Lianhua, 1932, 7 r
Scr: Cai Chusheng, with Sun Yu, Wang Cilong, Shidong Shan
Dir: Cai Chusheng, with Sun Yu, Wang Cilong, Shidong Shan
Ph: Zhou Ke
Cast: Wang Cilong, Gao Zhanfei, Zong Weigeng, Zheng Junli, Jiang Junchao, Chen Yanyan

GUDU CHUNMENG *(Spring Dream in the Old Capital)* 故都春夢
Lianhua, 1930, 10 r
Scr: Zhu Shilin, Luo Mingyou
Dir: Sun Yu
Ph: Huang Shaofen
Cast: Wang Ruilin, Lin Chuchu, Ruan Lingyu, Liu Jiqun, Luo Huizhu

GU'ER JIU ZU JI *(Orphan Rescues Grandfather)* 孤兒救祖記
Mingxing, 1923, 10 r
Scr: Zheng Zhengqiu
Dir: Zheng Zhengqiu
Ph: Zhang Weitao
Cast: Wang Hanlun, Zheng Xiaoqiu, Zheng Zhegu, Wang Xianzhai, Zhou Wenzhu, Ren Chaojun, Shao Zhuanglin

HAISHI *(Sea Oath)* 海誓
Shanghai yingxi gongsi, 1921, 6 r
Dir/Ph: Dan Duyu
Cast: Yin Mingzhu, Zhou Guoji, Dan Erchun, Chen Baoqi, He Rongzhu

HANGKONG DAXIA *(The Great Knight-Errant of Aviation)* 航空大俠
Huaju, 1928
Dir: Chen Tian
Ph: Tang Jianting
Cast: Zhang Huimin, Wu Suxin, Chen Fei, Liang Saizhen

HEIJI YUANHUN *(Victims of Opium)* 黑籍冤魂
Huanxian Film Company, 1916, 4 r
Dir: Guan Haifeng
Ph: A. Lauro
Cast: Zha Tianying, Xu Banmei, Zhang Shichuan, Huang Xiaoya, Huang Youya, Hong Jingling

HEIYE GUAIREN *(The Stranger of Dark Night)* 黑夜怪人
Jinlong, 1928
Dir: Hong Ji, Ma-Xu Weibang,

HONGFEN KULOU *(Red Beauty and Skeleton)* 紅粉骷髏
a.k.a. SHI ZIMEI *(Ten Sisters)* 十姊妹
New Asia Film Company, 1921, 14 r
Scr: Guan Haifeng
Dir: Guan Haifeng
Ph: Liao Enshou
Cast: Yin Xianfu, Shen Fengying, Chai Shaoyong, Lu Manshu, Hong Jingling, Wang Guilin

HONG LEI YING *(Shadow of Red Tears)* 紅淚影
Mingxing, 1931, 20 r
Scr/Dir/Titles: Zheng Zhengqiu
Asst. Dir: Cai Chusheng
Ph: Dong Keyi
Cast: Hu Die, Zheng Xiaoqiu, Xia Peizhen, Gong Jianong, Gao Qianpin

HONG XIA *(The Red Heroine)* 紅俠
Youlian, 1929, 10 r
Dir: Lincoln Yao (Yao Shiquan) (on print), Wen Yimin (in official sources)
Ph: Yao Shiquan
Cast: Fan Xuepeng (Van Shi Bong), Zhu Shaoquan, Wen Yimin, Shang Guanwu, Xu Guohui

HONG YANG HAOXIA ZHUAN *(The Legend of the Great Knight-Errant Hong Yang)* 洪羊豪俠傳
Xinhua, 1935, sound
Scr: Wang Zhongxian (adpated from the eponymous Peking opera)
Dir: Yang Xiaozhong
Ph: Shen Yongshi
Cast: Wang Huchen, Xu Qinfang, Tong Yuejuan, Tian Fang

HONGLOU MENG *(Dream of the Red Chamber)* 紅樓夢
Fudan, 1927, 20 r
Dir: Ren Pengshou, Yu Boyan
Ph: Wang Shizhen
Cast: Lu Jianfen, Wen Yimin, Zhou Kongkong, Fan Xuepeng, Wang Xieyan, Huang Yueru, Xing Banmei, Wang Yiming, Wang Yiman

HUAJI DAWANG YOU HUA JI *(The King of Comedy's Journey to China)* 滑稽大王游華記

Mingxing, 1922, 3 r
Scr: Zheng Zhengqiu
Dir: Zhang Shichuan
Ph: Goodyear (?) (British resident)
Cast: Ricard Bell (British resident), Zheng Zhengqiu, Wang Xianzhai

HUA MULAN CONGJUN *(Hua Mulan Joins the Army)* 花木蘭從軍

Tianyi, 1927, 10 r
Scr: Liu Huogong
Dir: Li Pingqian
Ph: Wu Weiyun
Cast: Hu Shan, Zhu Gang, Zhang Zhenduo, Zhang Zhizhi

HUANGJIANG NUXIA *(Swordswoman from the Huangjiang River)* 荒江女俠
Episode 6 (of 13), DANAO LUJIAOGOU *(Big Trouble at Deer Horn Gulch)* 大鬧鹿角溝

Youlian, 1930, 10 r
Scr: Gu Mingdao (adapted from his serialized novel)
Dir: Chen Kengran, Zheng Yisheng, Shang Guanwu
Ph: Yao Shiquan
Cast: Xu Qinfang, He Zhizhang, Zheng Yisheng, Shang Guanwu

HUANGTA QIXIA *(The Strange Knight-Errant in the Deserted Pagoda)* 荒塔奇俠

Jinlong, 1929
Scr: Ni Gulian
Dir: Hong Ji
Ph: Zhou Tingxi
Cast: Hua Wanfang, Ma-Xu Weibang, Chen Kai, Xiao Sheng

HUASHEN GUNIANG *(Girl in Disguise)* 化身姑娘

Yihua, 1936, 10 r, sound
Scr: Huang Jiamo
Dir: Fang Peiling
Ph: Yao Shiquan
Cast: Yuan Meiyun, Wang Yin, Han Langen, Zhou Xuan, Wang Guilin, Jiang Xiu

HUBAIN CHUNMENG *(Spring Dream on the Lakeside)* 湖邊春夢

Mingxing, 1927, 9 r
Scr: Tian Han
Dir: Bu Wancang
Ph: Dong Keyi, Shi Shipan

Cast: Gong Jianong, Yang Naimei, Xiao Ying, Tang Jie, Mao Jianpei, Lin Zhusan.

HUO WUCHANG *(A Living Wuchang)* 活五常
a.k.a. XINNIANG HUAJIA YU BAI WUCHANG *(The Bridal Sedan Meets Pale Wuchang)* 新娘花嫁與白五常
Asia, 1913, 2 r
Dir: Zhang Shichuan
Ph: Essler
Cast: Qian Huofo, Ma Qingfeng, Guo Yongfu, Wang Xihua

HUODONG YINGXIANG *(The Mobile Safe)* 活動銀箱
Kaixin, 1925, 3 r
Scr: Xu Zhuodai
Dir: Wang Youyou, Xu Zhuodai
Ph: Kawatani Shodaira
Cast: Xu Zhuodai, Wang Youyou, Zhou Fengwen, Zhou Kongkong

HUOSHAN QINGXUE *(The Blood of Passion on the Volcano)* 火山情血
Lianhua, 1932, 10 r
Scr: Sun Yu
Dir: Sun Yu
Ph: Zhou Ke
Cast: Li Lili, Zheng Junli, Tan Ying, Liu Jiqun.

HUOSHAO HONGLIAN SI *(The Burning of the Red Lotus Temple)* 火燒紅蓮寺
(14 episodes, 1928–31)
Mingxing, part 1, 1928, 11 r
Scr: Zheng Zhengqiu
Dir: Zhang Shichuan
Ph: Dong Keyi
Cast: Zheng Xiaoqiu, Xia Peizhen, Tan Zhiyuan, Xiao Ying, Zheng Shaofan, Zhao Jingxia, Gao Lihen

KONGGU LAN *(Orchid in the Empty Valley)* 空穀蘭
Mingxing, 1925, 11 r
Scr: Bao Tianxiao (adapted from the eponymous novel)
Titles: Zheng Zhengqiu
Dir: Zhang Shichuan
Ph: Dong Keyi
Cast: Zhang Zhiyun, Yang Naimei, Zhu Fei, Zheng Xiaoqiu, Song Chanhong, Zhao Zhen, Wang Jiting, Ma-Xu Weibang, Ren Chaojun, Wang Xianzhai

KONGGU YUANSHENG *(The Cry of Apes in a Deserted Valley)* 空穀猿聲
Tianma, 1930
Dir: Ma-Xu Weibang
Cast: Wang Mengfei, You Guangzhao, Tan Yuesun, Fu Meina, Yuan Yijun, Jing Fansan, Zhao Songjiao

KUANG LIU *(Wild Torrent)* 狂流
Mingxing, 1933, 8 r
Scr/Titles: Xia Yan
Dir: Cheng Bugao
Ph: Dong Keyi
Cast: Hu Die, Gong Jianong, Xia Peizhen, Tan Zhiyuan, Zhu Guyan

LAOGONG ZHI AIQING *(Laborer's Love)* 勞工之愛情
a.k.a. ZHIGUOYUAN
Mingxing, 1922, 3 r
Scr/Dir: Zhang Shichuan, Zheng Zhengqiu
Cast: Zheng Zhegu, Yu Yin, Zheng Zhengqiu

LIANHUA JIAOXIANGQU *(Lianhua Symphony)* 聯華交響曲
(an omnibus film of eight shorts)
Lianhua, 1937
Scr: Cai Chusheng, Fei Mu, Tan Youliu, He Mengfu, Zhu Shilin, Shen Fu, Sun Yu
Dir: Situ Huimin, Fei Mu, Tan Youliu, He Mengfu, Zhu Shilin, Shen Fu, Sun Yu, Cai Chusheng
Cast: Lan Ping, Mei Xi, Shen Fu, Li Zhuozhuo, Chen Yanyan, Zheng Junli, Ba Lu, Liu Qiong, Li Qing, Zong You, Luo Peng, Heng Li, Shang Kouwu, Ge Zuozhi, Wang Cilong, Yin Xiucen

MALU TIANSHI *(Street Angel)* 馬路天使
Lianhua, 1937, 10 r, sound
Scr/Dir: Yuan Muzhi
Ph: Wu Xinxian
Cast: Zhao Dan, Zhou Xuan, Wei Heling, Zhao Huichen, Wang Jiting, Qian Qianli, Yuan Shaomei, Lin Jinyu

MITU DE GAOYANG *(Lost Lambs)* 迷途的羔羊
Lianhua, 1936, 5 r (?)
Scr/Dir: Cai Chusheng
Ph: Zhou Daming
Cast: ge Zuozhi, Chen Juanjuan, Li Zhuozhuo, Zheng Junli

MUXING ZHI GUANG *(Maternal Light)* 母性之光
Lianhua, 1933, 10 r
Scr: Tian Han
Dir: Bu Wangcang
Ph: Huang Shaofen
Cast: Jin Yan, Chen Yanyan, Li Zhuozhuo

NANFU NANQI *(The Difficult Couple)* 難夫難妻
a.k.a. DONGFANG HUAZHU *(Wedding Festivities)* 洞房花燭
Asia Film and Theater Company, 1913, 2 r
Scr: Zheng Zhengqiu
Dir: Zhang Shichuan
Ph: Essler

NEZHA CHUSHI *(Nezha is Born)* 那吒出世
Changcheng, 1927, 10 r
Scr: Sun Shiyi
Dir: Li Zeyuan
Ph: Li Wenguang
Cast: Lei Xiadian, Zhang Zhede, Liu Jiqun, Liu Hanjun

NULING FUCHOU JI *(Revenge of an Actress)* 女伶復仇記
a.k.a. MANGMUDE AIQING *(Blind Love)* 盲目的愛情
Hanlun, 1929
Scr: Bao Tianxiao
Dir: Bu Wangcang
Ph: Liang Lingguang
Cast: Wang Hanlun, Gao Zhanfei, Fei Baiqing, Cai Chusheng

NÜXIA BAIMEIGUI *(The Valiant Girl White Rose)* 女俠白玫瑰
Huaju, 1929
Scr: Gu Jianchen
Dir: Zhang Huimin
Ph: Tang Jianting
Cast: Wu Suxin, Ruan Shengduo, Sheng Xiaotian

NÜXIA HEI MUDAN *(The Female Knight-Errant Black Peony)* 女俠黑牡丹
Yueming, 1931
Scr: Wen Bojiu
Dir: Ren Pengnian
Ph: Ren Pengshou
Cast: Wu Lizhu, Cha Ruilong, Wang Hancheng

NÜXIA LI FEIFEI *(The Female Knight-Errant Li Feifei)* 女侠李飛飛
Tianyi, 1925, 10 r
Scr: Shao Cunren, Gao Lihen
Titles: Zhao Tieqiao
Dir: Shao Zuiweng
Ph: Xu Shaoyu
Cast: Feng Jühua, Wei Pengfei, Zhang Yi'er, Zhou Tianbei, Feng Kecheng

PANSI DONG *(The Cave of the Spider Spirit)* 盤絲洞
Shanghai Film Company, 1927, 10 r
Scr: Guan Ji'an
Dir: Dan Duyu
Ph: Dan Ganting
Cast: Yin Mingzhu, Wu Wenchao, Jiang Meikang, Zhou Hongquan, Wang Qiefu

QI NUZI YU MEIYAN *(The Amazing Woman Yu Meiyan)* 奇女子餘美艷
Naimei, 1928, 9 r
Scr: Zheng Yingshi
Dir: Shi Dongshan. Asst. Dir: Cai Chusheng
Ph: Shi Shipan
Cast: Yang Naimei, Zhu Fei, Gao Zhanfei, Zhou Kongkong, Gao Qianpin, Yan Gongshang, Yuan Yijun

QIFU *(The Abandoned Wife)* 棄婦
Changcheng, 1924, 11 r
Scr: Hou Yao
Dir: Li Zeyuan, Hou Yao
Ph: Cheng Peishuang
Cast: Wang Hanlun, Gan Yushi, Pu Jun, Hu Caixia, Chen Yimeng

QINGCHANG GUAIREN *(The Stranger on the Love Scene)* 情場怪人
Langhua, 1926
Scr/Dir: Ma-Xu Weibang
Titles: He Xiaochen
Ph: Luo Hongyi
Cast: Yu Shuxiong, Shen Qiuying, Wu Xiaying, He Xiaochen, Zhang Wuzhi, Wei Bang, You Guangzhao

SANGE MODENG NUXING *(Three Modern Women)* 三個摩登女性
Lianhua, 1933
Scr: Tian Han
Dir: Bu Wancang
Ph: Huang Shaofen
Cast: Ruan Lingyu, Jin Yan, Li Zhuozhuo, Chen Yanyan

SHENGSI TONGXIN *(Hearts United in Life and Death)* 生死同心
Mingxing, 1936, 9 r, sound
Scr: Yang Hansheng
Dir: Yin Yunwei
Ph: Wu Xinxian
Cast: Yuan Muzhi, Chen Bo'er, Li Qing, Liu Liying, Ying Yin

SHENNU *(Goddess)* 神女
Lianhua, 1934, 10 r
Scr/Dir: Wu Yonggang.
Ph: Hong Weilie
Cast: Ruan Lingyu, Li Qian, Zhang Zhizhe, Li Junpan

SHENXIAN BANG *(The Magic Club)* 神仙棒
Kaixin, 1926, 8 r
Dir: Wang Youyou
Ph: Kawatani Shodaira
Cast: Wang Youyou, Ouyang Yuqian, Fang Hongye, Xia Yuerun, Zhou Fengwen, Zhang Zhi'er, Qin Haha

SI JIE CUN *(Four Heroes Village)* 四傑村
Zhongguo yingpian zhizao youxian gongsi, 1919, opera film, shot in Nantong.
Dir. Lu Shoulian
Ph. Galkin(?) (American resident)

SI ZIMEI *(Four Sisters)* 四姊妹
Lianhua, 1935
Scr/Dir: Yang Xiaozhong
Ph: Zhuang Guojun
Cast: Liang Saizhen, Liang Saizhu, Liang Saishan, Liang Saihu, Jiang Junchao, Liu Jiqun

TAO LI JIE *(Plunder of Peach and Plum)* 桃李劫
Diantong, 1934, sound
Scr: Yuan Muzhi
Dir: Ying Yunwei
Ph: Wu Weiyun
Cast: Yuan Muzhi, Chen Bo'er, Tang Huaiqiu, Zhou Boxun

TIANMING *(Daybreak)* 天明
Lianhua, 1933, 11 r
Scr/Dir: Sun Yu
Ph: Zhou Ke
Cast: Gao Zhanfei, Li Lili, Ye Juanjuan, Yuan Congmei

TIEBAN HONGLEILU 鐵板紅淚彔
Mingxing 1933, 10 r
Scr: Yang Hansheng
Dir: Hong Shen
Ph: Dong Keyi
Cast: Wang Ying, Chen Ningqiu, Wang Zhengxin

TIXIAO YINYUAN *(Fate in Tears and Laughter)* 啼笑姻緣
Mingxing, 1932, 6 episodes, part sound
Scr: Yan Duhe (adapted from the eponymous novel by Zhang Henshui)
Dir: Zheng Zhengqiu
Ph: Dong Keyi, Wang Shizhen, James Williamson
Cast: Hu Die, Zheng Xiaoqiu, Xiao Ying, Wang Xianzhai, Yan Xuexian, Gong Jianong

TIYU HAUNGHOU *(Sports Queen)* 體育皇后
Lianhua, 1934. 10 r
Scr/Dir: Sun Yu
Ph: Qiu Yizhang
Cast: Li Lili, Zhang Yi, Yin Xu, Bai Lu, Wang Moqiu, Gao Weilian, He Feiguang, Shang Guanwu, Li Junpan, Han Langen, Liu Jiqun, Yin Xiulin

WANGSHI SIXIA *(Four Heroes of the Wang Family)* 王氏四俠
Dazhonghua beihe, 1927, 10 r
Scr/Dir: Shi Dongshan
Ph: Zhou Shimu
Cast: Wang Yuanlong, Wang Xuechang, Wang Yingzhi, Wang Zhengxin, Wang Naidong, Zhou Wenzhu, Xie Yunqing

WU FU LIN MEN *(Mascot Is Coming Here)* 五福臨門
a.k.a. FENGLIU HESHANG *(The Playboy Monk)* 風流和尚
Asia, 1913, 3 r
Dir: Zhang Shichuan
Ph: Essler
Cast: Qian Huofo, Ding Chuhe, Ma Qingfeng, Wang Bingseng, Liu Ziqing, Zhang Cuicui

XI XIANG JI *(Romance of the Western Chamber)* 西廂記
Minxin, 1927, 4035 feet
Scr: Hou Yao
Titles: Pu Shunqing
Dir: Hou Yao, Li Minwei
Ph: Liang Linguang
Cast: Li Dandan, Lin Chuchu, Ge Cijiang, Li Minwei

XIAO WANYI *(Little Toy)* 小玩意
Lianhua, 1933, 11 r
Scr: Sun Yu
Dir: Sun Yu
Ph: Zhou Ke
Cast: Ruan Lingyu, Li Lili

XIN NÜXING *(New Woman)* 新女性
Lianhua (second studio), 1934, part sound
Scr: Sun Shiyi
Dir: Cai Chusheng
Ph: Zhou Daming
Music: Nie Er
Cast: Ruan Lingyu, Wang Moqiu, Zheng Junli, Yin Xu

XIN TAOHUA SHAN *(The New Peach Blossom Fan)* 新桃花扇
Xinhua, 1935, sound
Scr/Dir: Ouyang Yuqian
Ph: Yu Shengsan
Cast: Jin Yan, Hu Ping, Tong Yuejuan, Zhang Shiyun, Wang Cilong, Gu Menghe, Dai Yanfang

XIN XI YOU JI *(New Journey to the West)* 新西游記
Mingxing, part 2, 1929, 10 r (in all 3 episodes 1929–30)
Titles: Zheng Zhengqiu
Dir: Zhang Shichuan
Ph: Dong Keyi
Cast: Zheng Xiaoqiu, Xia Peizhen, Wang Jiting, Huang Junfu, Tan Zhiyuan

YAN RUISHENG 閻瑞生
Zhingguo yingxi, China Film Research Society, 1921, 14 r
Scr: Chen Chunsheng
Dir: Ren Pengnian
Ph: Liao Enshou
Cast: Chen Shouzhi, Shao Peng, Wang Caiyun

YE MEIGUI *(Wild Rose)* 野玫瑰
Lianhua, 1931, 9 r
Scr/Dir: Sun Yu
Ph: Yu Xingsan
Cast: Wang Renmei, Jin Yan, Ye Juanjuan, Zheng Junli, Han Lan'gen.

YE MINGZHU *(Lustrous Pearls)* 夜明珠
Huaju, 1927, 9 r
Scr: Zhang Huimin
Dir: Chen Tian
Ph: Tang Jianting
Cast: Zhang Huimin, Wu Suxin, Liang Saizhen, Ruan Shengduo, Wu Susu, Zhang Yuepeng, Tang Jianting

YEBAN GESHENG *(Song at Midnight)* 夜半歌聲
Xinhua, 1937, sound
Scr/Dir: Ma-Xu Weibang
Ph: Yu Xingshan, Xue Boqing
Music: Xian Xinhai
Cast: Hu Ping, Jin Shan, Zhou Wenzhu, Shi Chao, Xu Manli, Gu Menghe, Wang Weiyi

YECAO XIANHUA *(Wild Flowers)* 野草閒花
Minxin/Lianhua, 1930, 11 r, part sound (songs)
Scr/Dir: Sun Yu
Ph: Huang Shaofen
Cast: Ruan Lingyu, Jin Yan, Liu Jiqun

YICHUAN ZHENZHU *(A String of Pearls)* 一串珍珠
Changcheng, 1925, 10 r
Scr: Hou Yao
Dir: Li Zeyuan
Ph: Cheng Peishuang
Cast: Lei Xiadian, Liu Hanjun, Liu Jiqun, Zhai Qiqi, Huang Zhihuai, Xing Shaomei

YINGSHEN YI *(The Invisible Coat)* 隱身衣
Kaixin, 1925, 3 r
Scr: Xu Zhuodai
Dir: Xu Zhuodai, Wang Youyou
Ph: Kawatani Shodaira
Cast: Wang Youyou, Xu Zhuodai

YINHAN SHUANGXING *(Two Stars)* 銀漢雙星
Lianhua, 1931, 12 r, part sound
Original story: Zhang Henshui
Scr: Zhu Shilin
Dir: Tomsie Sze (Shi Dongshan)
Ph: Zhou Ke
Cast: Raymond King (Jin Yan), Violet Wong (Zi Luolan), Wang Cilong, Gao Chien Fei (Gao Zhanfei)

YINMU YANSHI *(An Amorous History of the Silver Screen)* 銀幕艷史
Mingxing, 2 parts, 1931, 18 r
Dir: Cheng Bugao
Titles: Zheng Zhengqiu
Ph: Dong Keyi
Cast: Xuan Jinglin, Tan Zhiyuan, Wang Zhengxin, Xiao Ying, Gao Qianpin, Liang Saizhen

YIYE HAOHUA *(One Night of Glamour)* 一夜豪華
Tianyi, 1932, 9 r, sound
Scr: Su Yi
Dir: Shao Zuiweng
Ph: Wu Weiyun, Zhou Shilu
Cast: Xhen Yumei, Hu Shan, Sun Min

YU GUANG QU *(The Fishermen's Ballad)* 漁光曲
Lianhua, 1932, part sound
Scr/Dir: Cai Chusheng
Ph: Zhou Ke
Cast: Wang Renmei, Luo Peng, Yuan Congmei, Han Langen, Tang Tianxiu, Shang Guanwu, Qiu Yiwei

YU LI HUN *(Jade Pear Spirit)* 玉梨魂
Mingxing, 1924, 10 r
Scr: Zheng Zhengqiu (adapted from the eponymous novel by Xu Zhenya)
Dir: Zhang Shichuan, Xu Hu
Ph: Wang Xuchang
Cast: Wang Hanlun, Wang Xianzhai, Yang Naimei, Zheng Zhegu, Huang Jungu, Ren Chaojun

YU MEIREN *(The Singing Beauty)* 虞美人
Youlian, 1931 (film with sound on wax disks, produced under the name of the Yiming Film Company)
Scr: Xu Bibo
Dir: Chen Kengran
Ph: Liu Liangchan, He Zhigang
Cast: Xu Qinfang, Zhu Fei, Shang Guanwu

YUGUO TIANQING *(Peace After Storm)* 雨過天青
Huaguang, 1931, 12 r, sound
Scr: Xie Shihuang
Dir: Xia Chifeng
Ph: K. Henry
Cast: Chen Qiufeng, Huang Naishuang, Lin Ruxin, Zhang Zhizhi, Liu Yixin

ZHIFEN SHICHANG *(Rouge Market)* 脂粉市場
Mingxing, 1933, 6r
Scr: Xia Yan
Dir: Zhang Shichuan
Ph: Dong Keyi
Cast: Hu Die, Gong Jianong

ZIMEI HUA *(Twin Sisters)* 姊妹花
Mingxing, 1933, 11r
Dir: Zheng Zhengqiu
Ph: Dong Keyi
Cast: Hu Die, Zheng Xiaoqiu, Xuan Jinglin, Tan Zhiyuan, Gu Meijun

BIBLIOGRAPHY

CHINESE AND JAPANESE SOURCES

Books and Articles

A Wei, ed. *Piyingxi* [*Shadowplay*]. Beijing: Zhaohua meishu, 1955.

Ah Ying, ed. *Zhongguo xinwenxue daxi* [A Comprehensive Collection of Chinese New Literature] (1927–37). Vol. 13. Shanghai: Shanghai wenyi, 1987.

Bai Zi. "*Huashen guniang* gongzuo riji" [Work log of *Girl in Disguise*]. *Huasheng guniang tekan* (1936). Microfilm. China Film Archive.

Bao Jing, ed. *Lao Shanghai jianwen* [Impressions of Old Shanghai]. Shanghai: Shanghai guoguang shudian, 1947.

Bao Tianxiao. *Chuanyinglou huiyilu xubian* [Sequel to the Reminiscences of the Bracelet Shadow Chamber]. Hong Kong: Dahua, 1973.

———. *Chuanyinglou huiyi lu* [Reminiscences of the Bracelet Shadow Chamber]. Hong Kong: Dahua, 1971.

Cai Chusheng. *Cai Chusheng xuanji* [Selected Writings of Cai Chusheng]. Edited by Mu Yi and Fang Sheng. Beijing: Zhongguo dianying, 1988.

Cai Fengming. *Shanghai dushi minsu* [Shanghai Urban Folklore]. Shanghai: Xuelin, 2001.

Cai Hongsheng. *Cai Chusheng de chuangzuo daolu* [Cai Chusheng's Creative Path]. Beijing: Wenhua yishu, 1982.

Cao Boyuan, ed. *Hu Shi zizhuan* [Autobiography of Hu Shi]. Hefei: Huangshan shushe, 1986.

Cao Juren. *Shanghai chunqiu* [Shanghai Chronicles]. Shanghai renmin, 1996.

Chen Bo and Yi Ming, eds. *Sanshi niandai Zhongguo dianying pinglun xuan* [An Anthology of Chinese Film Criticism of the 1930s]. Beijing: Zhongguo dianying, 1993.

Chen Bohai and Jin Yuan, eds. *Shanghai jindai wenxue shi* [History of Modern Chinese Literary History]. Shanghai: Shanghai renmin, 1993.

Chen Congzhou and Zhang Ming, eds. *Shanghai jindai jianzhu shigao* [History of Modern Shanghai Architecture]. Shanghai: Sanlian shudian, 1988.

Chen Daicheng. "Wei zaochengde meng" [The Unrealized Dream]. *Dianying yishu*, no. 11 (1980): 49.

Chen Dieyi et al., eds. *Dianying huanghou jinian ce—Hu Die nüshi zhuanji* [Commemorative Album of the Queen of Cinema—A Biography of Miss Hu Die]. Shanghai: Mingxing ribaoshe, August 1933.

Chen Gaoyong. "Zenyang shi Zhongguo xiandaihua" [How to Modernize China]. *Shenbao yuekan* [Shen Pao monthly supplement] 2, no. 7 (1933): 47–52.

Chen Mo. *Daoguang xiaying mengtaiqi—Zhongguo wuxia dianying lun* [A Sword-and-Shadows Light Montage for the Knight-Errant: On the Chinese Martial Arts Film]. Beijing: Zhongguo dianying, 1996.

Chen Shouying. "'Kan jingtou' yu 'dui jingtou' zuoxi" [Looking at the Camera or Acting to the Camera]. *Dianying zazhi,* no. 13, 1925.

Chen Yanqiao. *Shanghai meishu yundong* [The Shanghai Art Movement]. Shanghai: Dadong shuju, 1951.

Chen Zizhang. *Zhongguo jindai wenxue zhi bianqian* [The Transformation of Modern Chinese Literature]. Shanghai: Zhonghua shuju, 1930.

Cheng Bugao. *Yingtan yijiu* [Reminiscences of the Film World]. Beijing: Zhongguo dianying, 1983.

Cheng Jihua, Li Shaobai and Xing Zuwen. *Zhongguo dianying fazhan shi* [History of the Development of Chinese Cinema]. 2 vols. Beijing: Zhongguo dianying, 1981.

Cheng Shuren, ed. *Zhonghua yingye nianjian* [Yearbook of Chinese Film]. Shanghai, 1927.

Chugoku eiga no kaiko (1922–1952) [A Retrospective of Chinese Cinema, 1922–1952]. Tokyo: Tokyo Kokuritsu Kindai Bijutsukan, 1985.

Chugoku eiga no kaiko (1932–1964) [A Retrospective of Chinese cinema, 1932–1964]. Tokyo: Tokyo Kokuritsu Kindai Bijutsukan, 1988.

Die Lu, ed. *Yingxi xiaoshuo sanshi zhong* [Thirty Film Stories]. Shanghai: Jingzhi tushuguan, 1925.

Ding Yaping. "Lishi de jiulu–Zhongguo dianying and Sun Yu" [The Old Path of History—Chinese Cinema and Sun Yu]. *Beijing dianying xuebao,* Nov. 4, 2000.

Dong Guangbi. *Zhongguo jinxiandai kexue jishu shi lungang* [Outline of the History of Modern Chinese Science and Technology]. Changsha: Hunan jiaoyu, 1992.

Dong Jingxin. "Zhongguo yingxi kao" [An Examination of Chinese Shadowplay]. *Juxue yuekan* 3, no. 11 (Nov. 1934): 1–19.

Dong Xinyu. *Kan yu beikan zhijian* [Between Seeing and Being Seen]. Beijing: Beijing shifan daxue, 2000.

Du Yunzhi. *Shaoshi dianying wangguo mixin* [The Secrets of the Shao's Film Kingdom]. Taibei: Ni wo ta dianshi zazhishe, 1979.

———. *Zhongguo dianying shi* [History of Chinese Film]. 2 vols. Taibei: Taiwan shangwu yinshuguan, 1972.

———. *Zhongguode dianying* [Chinese Cinema]. Taibei: Huangguan, 1978.

Fan Dainian, "Dui 'Wusi' Xinwenhua yundongde zhexue fansi—ji ershi niandai chu de kexue yu renshenguan da lunzhan" [A Philosophical Reflection on the May Fourth New Culture Movement—On the Great Debate on Science and View of Life in the Early Twentieth Century]. In *Kexue shi lunji* [An Anthology of Essays on the History of Science], edited by Fang Lizhi, pp. 255–76. Hefei: Zhongguo kexue jishu daxue, 1987.

Fang Lizhi, ed. *Kexue shi lunji* [An Anthology of Essays on the History of Science]. Hefei: Zhongguo kexue jishu daxue, 1987.

Ge Gongzhen. *Zhongguo baoxue shi* [History of Chinese Newspapers]. Beijing: Zhongguo xinwen, 1985 (1927).

Ge Yihong et al. *Zhongguo huaju tongshi* [History of Chinese Spoken Drama]. Beijing: Wenhua yishu, 1990.

Gong Jianong. *Gong Jianong congying huiyilu* [Robert Kung's Memoires of His Silver Screen Life]. 3 vols. Taipei: Wenxing shudian, 1966–67.

Gongsun Lu. *Zhongguo dianying shihua* [Historical Accounts of Chinese Cinema]. 2 vols. Hong Kong: Nantian shuye gongsi, n.d.; repr. Hong Kong: Guangjiaojing, 1976.

Gu Jiancheng, "Guozhi yingpian yu Nanyang huaqiao" [Domestic Films and Overseas Chinese in Nanyang]. *Mingxing tekan no. 16: Tade tongku* [Mingxing special issue, no. 16, *Her Sorrows*], 1926.

Gu Menghe. "Yi Tian Han tongshi zai Nanguoshe de dianying chuangzuo" [Remembering Comrade Tian Han's Film Work at the "Southern-Country Society"]. *Dianying yishu,* no. 4 (1980): 56.

Gu Yuanqing and Gao Jinxian. "Lu Xun yu dianying" [Lu Xun and the Cinema]. *Dianying yishu* 1979, no. 4, 41–8.

Gu'er jiuzu ji tekan [Special Issue on *Orphan Rescues Grandfather*]. Chenxing Society, 1923.

Guan Wenqing. *Zhongguo yingtan waishi* [An Unofficial History of the Chinese Film World]. Hong Kong: Guangjiaojing, 1976.

Guangbo dianying dianshi bu dianying ju dangshi ziliao zhengji gongzuo xiaozu, Zhongguo dianying yishu yanjiu zhongxin, ed. *Zhongguo zuoyi dianying yundong* [The Chinese Left-Wing Cinema Movement]. Beijing: Zhongguo dianying, 1993.

Guo Yanli. *Zhongguo jindai wenxue fazhan shi* [History of the Development of Modern Chinese Literature]. Vol. 2. Jinan: Shandong jiaoyu, 1991.

Hong Shen. *Hong Shen wenji* [Collected Works of Hong Shen]. Vols. 1 and 4. Beijing: Zhongguo xiju, 1957.

Hong Shi. "Wusheng de cunzai" [Silent Existence]. Preface to *Zhongguo wusheng dianying* [Chinese Silent Film]. Beijing: Zhongguo dianying, 1996.

Hong Shi et al. "Zhongguo zaoqi gushipian chuangzuo tansuo" [Explorations of the Creation of Early Chinese Narrative Cinema). *Dianying yishu* 1990, no. 1: 22–47.

Hong Kong Arts Center and the Hong Kong Chinese Film Association. *Tansuode niandai—Zaoqi Zhongguo dianying zhan* [Early Chinese Cinema: The Era of Exploration]. Program for Hong Kong Arts Festival. Hong Kong, 1984.

Hou Yao. *Yingxi juben zuofa* [The Techniques of Writing Shadowplay Scripts]. Shanghai: Taidong tushuju, 1925.

Hu Die. *Yinghou shengya: Hu Die huiyi lu* [The Career of the Queen of Cinema: Hu Die's Memoire]. Hangzhou: Zhejiang renmin, 1986.

Hu Shi. *Baihua wenxueshi* [History of Vernacular Literature]. Changsha: Yuelu shushe, 1986 [1928].

———. *Changshiji* [Experiments]. Shanghai: Shanghai shudian, 1982 [1920].

Hu Zhichuan and Chen Shen, eds. *Zhongguo zaoqi sheying zuopin xuan (1840–1919)* [A collection of pictures of early-period Chinese photography, 1840–1919]. Beijing: Zhongguo sheying, 1987.

Huang Zunxian. *Renjing lu shicao jianzhu* [An Annotated Collection of *Poetry from the Human Realm*]. 2 vols. Shanghai: Guji, 1981.

Jia Leilei. "Zhongguo wuxia dianying yuanliu lun" [On the Origin of the Chinese Martial Arts Film]. *Yingshi wenhua,* no. 5 (1992): 204–24.

Jian Yong and Tian Jin. "Tantao Zhongguo dianying lishi jingyande yici shenghui" [A Grand Conference for Exploring the Historical Experience of Chinese Film History]. *Dianying yishu,* no. 11, 1983.

Jiang Yinghao. *Chuantong yu xiandai zhijian—Zhongguo jindai wenxue lun* [Between Tradition and Modernity: On Modern Chinese Literature]. Hong Kong: Wende wenhua shiye youxian gongsi, 1991.

Jianyun. "Dao yan" (introduction). *Chengxing Gu'er jiuzuji tekan* (*Morning Star's* Special issue on *Orphan Rescues Grandfather*). Chengshe, 1923.

Ke Ling. *Ke Lin dianying wencun* [Selected Extant Writings of Ke Ling]. Edited by Chen Wei. Beijing: Zhongguo dianying, 1992.

———. "Shi wei 'Wu Si' yu dianying hua yi lunkuo" [An Attempt at Drawing a Contour for the May Fourth Movement and the Cinema]. In *Zhongguo dianying yanjiu.* Hong Kong: Chinese Film Association, 1983.

Kou Tianwu, "Zhongguo dianyingshi shangde 'diyi'" [The "firsts" in Chinese film history]. *Yingshi wenhua,* no. 2 (1989): 267.

Li Jiang. "Lilong jutaku" [Rowhouses]. *Sinica* (in Japanese), 11, no. 7 (2000): 40–42.

Li Lili. "Huiyi he Cai Chusheng tongzhi zai yiqi gongzuo de nianyue" [Recollections of the Years Working Together with Comrade Cai Chusheng]. *Dianying yishu,* no. 6 (1979): 31.

Li Shaobai. *Dianying lishi ji lilun* [Film History and Theory]. Beijing: Wenhua yishu, 1991.

———. "Jianlun Zhongguo sanshi niandai 'dianying wenhua yundong' de xingqi" [A Concise Treatise on the Rise of the "Film Culture Movement" in China in the '30s]. *Dangdai dianying,* 1994, no. 3.

Li Suyuan. "Guanyu Zhongguo zaoqi dianying lilun" [On Early Chinese Film Theory]. *Dangdai dianying,* 1994, no. 4.

———. "Zhongguo zaoqi dianyingde xushi moshi" [The Narrative Paradigm of Early Chinese Cinema]. *Dangdai dianying* 1993, no.6: 28–34.

Li Suyuan and Hu Jubin. *Zhongguo wusheng dianyingshi* [*WSDYS,* History of Chinese Silent Film]. Beijing: Zhongguo dianying, 1997.

Li Tiangang. *Wenhua Shanghai* [Cultural Shanghai]. Shanghai jiaoyu, 1998.

Lian Yantang. "Liang Qichao de 'shijie geming' lun he shige chuangzuo" [Liang Qichao's View on the "Poetic Revolution" and the Creation of Poetry]. In *Zhongguo jindai wenxue yanjiu ji* [Anthology of Studies on Modern Chinese Literature], edited by Shekeyuan wenyansuo jindai wenxue yanjiuzu. Beijing: Zhongguo wenlian, 1986.

Liang Qichao. *Yingbingshi shihua* [Discourse on Poetry in the Ice Room]. Beijing: Renmin wenxue, 1959.

Liao Ben, *Zhongguo gudai juchang shi* [History of China's Ancient Theaters]. Zhengzhou: Zhongguo guji, 1997.

Lin He. "Zuoyi juliande yingping xiaozu ji qita" [Left-Wing Dramatists Group, etc.]. *Dianying yishu* 1980, no. 9.

Lin Niantong. "Zhongguo dianyingde kongjian yishi" [The Sense of Space in Chinese Cinema]. In *Zhongguo dianying yanjiu* [Dianying: An Interdisciplinary Journal of Chinese Film Studies], no. 1: 58–78. Hong Kong: Hong Kong Chinese Film Association, 1984.

Liu Lu, ed. *Qinggong cixuan* [Selected *Ci* Poetry from the Qing Court]. Beijing: Zijincheng, 1985.

Liu Na'ou. *Dushi fengjing xian* [Scène]. Shanghai: Shuimo shudian, 1930.

Liu Peiqian, ed. *Da Shanghai zhinan* [A Guide for Greater Shanghai]. Shanghai: Guoguang shudian, 1936.

Lu Hongshi and Shu Xiaoming, *Zhongguo dianyingshi* [A History of Chinese Cinema]. Beijing: Wenhua yishu, 1998.

Lu Mengshu, ed. *Dianying yu wenyi* (*Yinxing* haowai) [Cinema and the Arts—A Special Supplement of *Yinxing*]. Shanghai: Liangyou tushu yinshua youxian gongsi, 1928.

Lu Si. *Yingping yijiu* [Reminiscences of Film Criticism]. Beijing: Zhongguo dianying, 1984.

Lu Wei. *Tian Han juzuolun* [On Tian Han's Playwriting]. Nanjing daxue, 1995.

Lu Xun. Lu Xun quanji [Collected Works by Lu Xun]. Beijing: Renmin wenxue, 1982 (1931).

Luo Yijun. "Wenhua chuantong yu zhongguo dianying lilun" [Cultural Tradition and Chinese Film Theory]. *Dianying yishu* 1992, no.4: 20–30.

Luo Yijun et al., eds. *Zhongguo dianying lilun wenxuan 1920–1989* [Anthology of Chinese Film Theory and Criticism]. 2 vols. Beijing: Wenhua yishu, 1992.

Luo Zhixi. *Kexue yu xuanxue* [Science versus Metaphysics]. Shanghai: Commercial Press, 1927.

Ma Guangren, ed. *Shanghai xinwen shi 1850–1949* [History of Journalism in Shanghai, 1850–1949]. Shanghai: Fudan daxue, 1996.

Ma Junxiang. "Zhongguo dianying qingxiede qipao xian" [The Slanting Starting Line of Early Chinese Cinema]. *Dianying yishu* 1990, no.1: 6–21.

Ma Xuexin et al., eds. *Shanghai wenhua yuanliu cidian* [A Lexicon of the Origins of Shanghai Culture]. Shanghai shehui kexue, 1992.

Ma Yunzeng et al. *Zhongguo sheyingshi: 1840–1937* [A History of Photography in China]. Beijing: Zhongguo sheying, 1987.

Mei Lanfang. *Wode dianying shenghuo* [My Film Life]. Beijing: Zhongguo dianying, 1962.

Nie Gannu. *Cong baihuawen dao xin wenzi* [From Vernacular Language to New Writing]. Shanghai: Dazhong wenhua, 1936.

Ouyang Yuqian. "Tan wenmingxi" [On the "Civilized Play"]. In *Zhongguo huaju wushinian shiliao xuan* [Collection of Historical Materials on Fifty Years of Chinese Spoken Drama Movement]. Vol. 1: 48–108. Beijing: Zhongguo xiju, 1958.

———. *Zi wo yanxi yilai* [Since I Started Acting]. Beijing: Zhongguo xiju, 1959.

Peng Kang. "Kexue yu renshenguan—jin ji nian lai Zhongguo sixiangjie de zong jiesuan." *Wenhua pipan*, 1928, no. 3.

Ping Jinya. "'Yuanyang hudie pai' mingming de gushi" [The Story behind the Naming of the "Mandarin Ducks and Butterflies"]. In *Yuanyang hudie pai yanjiu ziliao,* edited by Wei Shaochang, pp. 179–81. Shanghai: Wenyi, 1984, vol. 1.

Qian Huafo. "Yaxiya yingxi gongside chengli shimo." In *WSDY,* edited by Zhongguo dianying ziliaoguan, 1455–58.

Qian Huafuo and Zheng Yimei. *Sanshi nian lai zhi Shanghai* [Thirty Years of Shanghai]. Shanghai: Shanghai shudian, 1984 (1947).

Qu Qiubai. "Dazhong wenyi de wenti" [Questions Concerning Mass Culture]. In *Qu Qiubai xuanji* [Selected Writings of Qu Qiubai]. Beijing: Renmin, 1985.

Rong Tianyu. *Zhongguo xiandai qunzhong wenhua shi* [History of Modern Chinese Mass Culture]. Beijing: Wenhua yishu, 1986.

Sannian yihou. *Minxin tekan* [Minxin Special Issue on *Three Years Later*], no. 4 (December 1926).

Shanghai diansheng zhoubao, ed. *Dianying nianjian* [Cinema Yearbook]. Shanghai: Yuanxia gongsi, 1936.

"Shanghai dianying faxing fangyingye yaoshi lu" [A Record of the Important Events in Film Distribution and Exhibition in Shanghai]. *Shanghai dianying shiliao* 5 (1994).

Shanghai shi tongji [Statistics of Shanghai]. Shanghai: Shanghai shi difang xiehui [Shanghai Civic Association]. 1933.

Shanghai tongshe, ed. *Shanghai yanjiu ziliao* [Research Materials on Shanghai]. Shanghai: Shanghai shudian, 1984 (1936).

———. *Shanghai yanjiu ziliao xuji* [Sequel to Research Materials on Shanghai]. Shanghai: Zhonghua shuju, 1939.

Shanghai yanjiu zhongxin, Shanghai renmin, eds. *Shanghai qibainian* [Seven Hundred Years of Shanghai]. Shanghai: Shanghai renmin, 1991.

Shen Lixing. "Jiu Shanghaide shijie 're'" [The World Fever in Old Shanghai]. In *Shanghai shehui daguan* [An Overview of Shanghai Society], edited by Shi Fukang. Shanghai shudian, 2000.

Shen Yanbing (Mao Dun). "Fengjiande xiaoshimin wenyi" [The Feudal Arts of the Petty Urban Dwellers]. In *Yuanyang hudie pai yanjiu ziliao,* edited by Wei Shaochang, pp. 47–52. Vol. 1. Originally published in *Dongfang zazhi* 30, no. 3 (Jan. 1, 1933).

Sima Feng. *Zhongguo dianying wushinian* [Fifty Years of Chinese Cinema]. Taibei: Huanding wenhua, 1983.

Sima Qian. *Shiji* [Records of the Historian]. Beijing: Zhonghua shuju, 1959.

Song Jie. "Dianying yu shehui lifa wenti" [Cinema and the Problem of Social Law-making]. *Dongfang zazhi* (Feb. 1925): 79–94.

Sun Shiyi. "Yingju zhi yishu jiazhi yu shehui jiazhi" [The Artistic Value versus the Social Value of the Cinema]. In *LLWX,* edited by Luo Yijun et al. 1: 69–71.

Sun Yu. *Dalu zhi ge* [Song of the Big Road]. Edited by Shu Qi and Li Zhuotao. Taipei: Yuanliu, 1990.

———. "Huiyi Wusi yundong yingxiangxiade sanshi niandai dianying" [Remembering the '30s Cinema under the Influence of the May Fourth Movement]. *Dianying yishu,* 1979, no. 3.

———. *Sun Yu dianying juben xuanji* [Selected Film Scripts by Sun Yu]. Beijing: Zhongguo dianying, 1981.

Sun Yu kandoku to Shanghai eiga no nakamatachi—Chugoku eiga no kaiko [Sun Yu and His Shanghai Colleagues: A Retrospective of Chinese Films]. Tokyo: Tokyo kokuritsu kindai bijutsukan, 1992.

Tade tongku Mingxing tekan, no. 16 [Mingxing Special Issue, *Her Sorrows*]. 1926.

Takeda, Masaya. *Tobe! Dai-Sei teikoku. Kindai Chugoku no genso kagaku* [Fly! Great Qing Empire. The Imaginary Science of Modern China]. Tokyo: Riburupoto, 1988.

———. *Shincho eshi Go Yujo no jikenjo* [The Current-Events Pictures of the Qing Dynasty Painter Wu Youru]. Tokyo: Seihinsha, 1998.

Tan Chunfa. *Kai yidai xianhe—Zhongguo dianying zhi fu Zheng Zhengqiu* [The Pioneer—Zheng Zhengqiu, the Father of Chinese Cinema]. Beijing: Guoji wenhua chuban gongsi, 1992.

Tao Hancui, trans. and ed. *(Huitu) yingxi daguan* [An Illustrated Anthology of Shadowplays]. Shanghai: Shijie shuju, 1924.

Tian Bengxiang. *Zhongguo xiandai bijiao xiju shi* [A Comparative History of Modern Chinese Drama]. Beijing: Wenhua yishu, 1993.

Tian Han. "Nanguo she shilüe" [A Brief History of the Nanguo Society]. In *Zhongguo huaju wushinian shiliao xuan,* 1: 113–38. Beijing: Zhongguo xiju, 1958.

———. *Yingshi zhuihuai lu* [Memories about the Events in Cinema]. Beijing: Zhongguo dianying, 1981.

———. *Yinse de meng* [Silver Dream]. Zhonghua shuju, 1928.

Tian Qing. *Zhongguo xiju yongdong* [The Movement of Chinese Drama]. Shanghai: Shangwu yinshuguan, 1944.

Tu Shiping, ed. *Shanghai chunqiu* [Vicissitudes of Shanghai]. Hong Kong: Zhongguo tushu jicheng gongsi, 1968.

———. *Shanghaishi daguan* [Shanghai Panorama]. Zhongguo zazhitushu gongsi, 1948.

Wang Chaoguang. "Sanshi niandai chuqi de Guomingdang dianying jiancha zhidu" [The Film Censorship System of the Nationalist Party in the Early 1930s]. *Dianying yishu* 1997, no. 3: 63.

———."Minguo nianjian Meiguo dianying zai hua shichang yanjiu" [American Cinema in the Chinese Market during the Republican Period]. *Dianying yishu* 1998, no. 1: 57–64.

Wang Gangshen. *Kexue lun ABC* [The ABC of the Study of Science]. Shanghai: Shanghai shuju, 1928.

Wang Guowei. *Renjian cihua xinzhu* [New Annotated Discourse on Poetry of the Human Realm]. Jinan: Qilu shushe, 1981.

Wang Hanlun. "Wode congying jingguo" [My Experience with the Cinema]. In Zhongguo dianying ziliaoguan, pp. 1471–75. *WSDY.* Originally in *Zhongguo dianying* 1956, no. 2.

Wang Li. *Zhongguo gudai haoxia yishi* [Ancient Chinese Gallant Knights—Errant and Chivalrous Subjects]. Hefei: Anhui renmin, 1996.

Wang Renmei. *Wo de chengming yu buxing—Wang Renmei huiyilu* [My Success and Tragedy—a Memoir by Wang Renmei]. Shanghai: Shanghai wenyi, 1985.

Wang Ruiyong. "Shanghai yingyuan bianqian lu" [A Record of the Changes in Shanghai Cinema Theatres]. In *Shanghai dianying shiliao* [Historical Material on Shanghai Cinema], no. 5 (1994).

Wang Suping. "Liangge yingpian gongsi de 'liuchan' shimo" [On the "Abortion" of Two Film Companies]. *Yingshi wenhua,* 1988, no. 1.

———. "Zhongguo dianying tuohuangzhede zuji—zaoqi dianying daoyan tanyilu" [Footprints of the pioneers of Chinese cinema—Early film directors on their art]. *Yingshi wenhua,* 1989, no. 2 : 308.

Wang Weimin, ed. *Zhongguo zaoqi huaju xuan* [Selected Early Chinese Spoken Drama Plays], pp. 307–44. Beijing: Zhongguo xiju, 1989.

Wang Wenhe. *Zhongguo dianying yinyue xunzong* [Tracing Chinese Film Music]. Beijing: Zhongguo guangbo dianying, 1995.

Wang Zilong. *Zhongguo yingjushi* [A History of Chinese Cinema and Drama]. Taipei: Jianguo, 1950.

Wei Shaochang, ed. *Yuanyang hudie yanjiu ziliao* [Research Material on the Mandarin Ducks and Butterflies Literature]. 2 vols. Shanghai: Wenyi, 1984.

Wu Guifang, ed. *Shanghai fengwu zhi* [Gazetteer of Shanghai Lore]. Shanghai: Shanghai wenhua, 1982.

Wu Hao et al., eds. *Duhui modeng: yuefengpai 1910s–1930s* [Calendar Posters of the Modern Chinese Women]. Hong Kong: Sanlian shudian, 1994.

Wusi yilai dianying juben xuanji. Vol. 1. Beijing: Zhongguo dianying, 1962.

Wu Xiwen. "Guochan yingpian yu Nanyang wenhua" [Domestic Film and Nanyang Culture]. *Zhongnan qingbao* 2, no. 2 (Mar. 1935): 20–22.

Wu Yigong et al. *Shanghai dianying zhi* [Gazetteers of Shanghai Cinema]. Shanghai shehui kexueyuan, 1999.

Wu Zhongjie and Wu Lichang, eds. *Zhongguo xiandaizhuyi xunzong 1900–1949* [Tracing Chinese Modernism]. Shanghai: Xuelin, 1995.

Xia Yan. *Xian Yan dianying juzuo ji* [Xia Yan's Film Scripts]. Beijing: Zhongguo dianying, 1985.

Xiong Yuezhi and Xu Min. *Wanqing wenhua* [Culture of the Late Qing Period]. Vol. 6 in *Shanghai tongshi* [A Survey History of Shanghai], edited by Xiong Yuezhi. Shanghai: Shanghai renmin, 1999.

Xu Banmei. *Huaju shichuangqi huiyilu* [A Memoir of the Beginning of Chinese Spoken Drama]. Beijing: Zhongguo xiju, 1957.

Xu Bibo. "Jilupian 'Wusan huchao' paishe jingguo" [How the Documentary *The May Thirtieth Shanghai Surge* Was Made]. *Zhongguo dianying,* 1957, no. 5: 62.

———. "Zhongguo yousheng dianying de kaiduan" [The Beginning of Chinese Sound Cinema]. *Zhongguo dianying* 1957, no. 4: 58–62.

Xu Chiheng, ed. *Zhongguo yingxi daguan* [Filmdom in China]. Shanghai: Hezuo, 1927.

Xu Daoming. *Haipai wenxue lun* [On Shanghai Style Literature]. Shanghai: Fudan daxue, 1999.

Xu Gongmei. *Dianying fada shi* [History of the Development of the Cinema]. Shanghai: Shangwu yinshuguan, 1938.

Xu Zhuodai. *Huaju shichuangqi huiyilu* [A Memoir from the Formative Era of the Spoken Drama]. Beijing: Zhongguo xiju chubanshe, 1957.

———. *Yingxi xue* [The Science of Shadowplay]. Shanghai: Huaxian shangyeshe tushubu, 1924.

Xuan Jingling. "Wode yingmu shenghuo." *Zhongguo dianying* 1956, no. 3: 72–75.

Yadong tushuguan, ed. *Kexue yu renshengguan* [Science and the View of Life]. Shanghai: Yadong tushuguan, 1923.

Yan Jiayan, ed. *Xin ganjue pai xiaoshuo xuan* [An Anthology of the New Sensationist Fiction]. Beijing: Renmin wenxue, 1985.

Yang Cun. *Zhongguo dianying sanshinian* [Thirty Years of Chinese Film]. Hong Kong: Shijie, 1954.

Yao Gonghe. *Shanghai xianhua* [Idle Talk of Shanghai]. Shanghai: Shangwu yinshuguan, 1926 (1917).

Ye Kaidi, "Nali shi Shanghai?" [Where was Shanghai?]. *Ershiyi shiji,* no. 48 (June 1998): 72–88.

Yi Bing et al., eds. *Lao Shanghai guanggao* [Advertisements from old Shanghai]. Shanghai: Shanghai huabao, 1995.

Yichuan zhenzhu tekan [Special Issue of *A String of Pearls*]. Changcheng huapian gongsi (Great Wall Film Company), 1926.

Yong Li. "Woguo diyizuo yingyuan jin hezai?" [Where Is China's First Movie Theater Today?]. In *Shanghai dianying shiliao* [Historical Materials on Shanghai Cinema], 5. Shanghaishi dianyingju shizhi bangongshi, 1994.

Yuan Jin. *Yuanyang hudie pai* [The Mandarin Ducks and Butterflies School]. Shanghai: Shanghai shudian, 1994.

Yuan Rongchun and Guanghua Hu. *Zhonghua minguo meishu shi 1911–1949* [History of Art in Republican China]. Chengdu: Sichuan meishu, 1991.

Yuguo tianqing tekan [Special issue of *Peace after Storm*]. Huguang pianshang yousheng dianying gongsi [Huaguang movietone Film Lit. Co.], 1931.

Zhang Gansheng. *Minguo tongsu xiaoshuo lungao* [Studies on Popular Fiction of the Republican Period]. Chongqing: Chongqing, 1991.

Zhang Hengshui. *Xiezuo shengya huiyi* [Remembrances of My Career as a Writer]. Beijing: Renmin wenxue, 1982.

Zhang Jingsheng. *Meide renshengguan* [The Beautiful View of Life]. Shanghai: Beixin shuju, 1925.

Zhang Junxiang et al. *Zhongguo dianying da cidian* [China Cinema Encyclopedia]. Shanghai cishu, 1995.

Zhang Ruoyin, ed. *Zhongguo xin wenxue yundong shi ziliao* [Materials on the History of the New Chinese Literature]. Shanghai: Shanghai shudian, 1982 [1934].

Zhang Wei. "Pilu yijian yanmo le qishi wuniande shishi" [Unveil Historical Evidence Lost for Seventy-five Years]. In *Zhongguo jindai wenxue zhengming* [Debates on Modern Chinese Literature]. 1: 159–61. Shanghai shudian, 1987.

Zhang Wei et al. *Lao Shanghai ditu* [Maps of Old Shanghai]. Shanghai huabao, 2001.

———, Yinxian and Chen Jin. "Zhongguo xiandai dianying chubanwu zongmu tiyao" [A Concise Annotated Bibliography of Film Publications in Modern China]. *Shanghai dianying shiliao.* 1994.

Zhang Zhenhua. "'Shanghai' dianyingde dansheng jiqi meixue tezheng" [The Birth of Shanghai Cinema and Its Aesthetic Characteristics]. *Dianying yishu,* 1992, no. 3: 62–65.

Zhao Shikai and Xu Zhihao, eds. *Zhongguo yingxi daguan* [An Overview of Chinese Shadowplay]. Xian: Shaanxi renmin, 1989.

Zhe Fu. *Jiu Shanghai mingxinpian* [Postcards of Old Shanghai]. Shanghai: Xuelin, 1999.

Zhen Zu'an. *Bainian Shanghai cheng* [A Century of the City of Shanghai]. Shanghai: Xuelin, 1999.

Zheng Junli. *Xiandai Zhongguo dianying shilüe* [A Concise History of Modern Chinese Film]. In Li Puyuan et al, *Zhongguo jindai yishu fazhan shi* [A History of the Development of Art in Modern China]. Shanghai: Liangyou, 1936.

Zheng Yimei. *Huaju chuangshiqi huiyilu* [A Memoire from the Formative Era of Spoken Drama]. Beijing: Zhongguo xiju, 1957.

———. *Yingtan jiuwen—Dan Duyu yu Yin Mingzhu* [Tales from the Old Film World—Dan Duyu and Yin Mingzhu]. Shanghai: Shanghai wenyi, 1982.

Zheng Yimei and Xu Zhuodai, *Shanghai jiuhua* [Old Shanghai Tales]. Shanghai wenhua, 1986.

Zhong Dafeng. "Lun yingxi" [On "Shadowplay"]. *Beijing dianying xueyuan xuebao* no. 2 (1985): 54–90.

———. "Zhongguo dianyingde lishi jiqi gengyuan: zailun 'yingxi'" [The History of Chinese Cinema and Its Sources: Once More on "Shadowplay"]. *Dianying yishu,* 1994, no. 1: 29–35; no. 2: 9–14.

Zhong Dafeng and Shu Xiaomin. *Zhongguo dianyingshi* [History of Chinese Film]. Beijing: Zhongguo guangbo dianshi, 1995.

Zhong Lei. *Wushinian lai de Zhongguo dianying* [Fifty Years of Chinese Film]. Taibei: Zhengzhong shuju, 1965.

Zhongguo dianying [Chinese Cinema: A Documentary Film]. Coproduced by Center for Research on Chinese Film and Chinese Film Archive, 1996.

Zhongguo dianying ziliaoguan (China Film Archive), ed. *Zhongguo wusheng dianying* [Chinese Silent Film]. *WSDY.* Beijing: Zhongguo dianying, 1996.

———. *Zhongguo wusheng dianying juben* [Chinese Silent Film Scripts]. 3 vols. *WSDYJB.* Beijing: Zhongguo dianying, 1996.

Zhongguo jiaoyu dianying xiehui, ed. *Zhongguo dianying nianjian* [The Cinematographic Yearbook of China]. Shanghai, 1934.

Zhou Jianyun and Cheng Bugao. *Bianjuxue* [The Science of Screenwriting]. In *LLWX,* vol. 1, edited by Luo Yijun et al. Beijing: Wenhua yishu, 1992.

Zhou Jianyun and Wang Xuchang. "Yingxi gailun" [An Introduction to Shadowplay]. Edited by Luo Yijun et al. *LLWX.* Vol. 1. Beijing: Wenhua yishu, 1992.

Zhou Shixun, ed. *Shanghai daguan* [A Panorama of Shanghai]. Shanghai, Wenhua meishu tushu gongsi, 1933.

Zhou Wu and Wu Guilong. *Wan Qing shehui* [Late Qing Society]. Vol. 5 of *Shanghai tongshi* [A Survey History of Shanghai]. Edited by Xiong Yuezhi. Shanghai: Shanghai renmin, 1999.

Zhu Tianwei and Wang Zhenzhen, eds. *Zhongguo yingpian dadian 1905–1930* [Encyclopedia of Chinese Films]. Beijing: Zhongguo dianying, 1996.

Zou Zhenhuan, "Shijiu shiji xiabanqi Shanghaide 'Yingyu re' yu zaoqi Yingyu duben jiqi yingxiang" [Shanghai's "English fever" in the Latter Half of the Nineteenth Century and the Early English Readers and Their Effect"]. In *Zujie li de Shanghai* [Shanghai's Foreign Concessions], pp. 93–106. Edited by Ma Changlin. Shanghai shehui kexueyuan, 2003.

Newspapers and Journals before 1949

(Note: some translations are original while others are mine.)

Baihuabao [Vernacular Newspaper] 白話報
Chenbao [Morning Daily] 晨報
Chenxing [Morning Star] 晨星
Diansheng [Cinema Voice] 電聲
Dianshizhai huabao [Dianshizhai Illustrated] 點石齋畫報
Diantong banyuekan [Denton Gazette] 電通半月刊
Dianying huabao [Movie Pictorial] 電影畫報
Dianying manhua [Cinema Cartoons] 電影漫畫
Dianying wenhua [Film Culture] 電影文化
Dianying xiju [Film and Drama] 電影戲劇
Dianying xinwen [Movie News] 電影新聞
Dianying yishu [Movie Art] 電影藝術
Dianying yuebao [Cinema Monthly] 電影月報
Dianying zazhi [Movie Monthly] 電影雜誌
Dianying zhoubao [Saturday Screen News] 電影周報
Dianying zhoubao/Tiaowu shijie [Movie Weekly/The Dancing World] 電影周報/跳舞世界
Dongfang zazhi [Eastern Miscellany] 東方雜誌
Huabao [Pictorial Weekly] 畫報
Juxue yuekan [Monthly Journal of Theater Studies] 劇學月刊
Liangyou huabao [The Young Companion] 良友畫報
Lianhua huabao [Lianhua Pictorial] 聯華畫報
Lianhua zhoubao [Lianhua Weekly] 聯華周報
Lingxing [Theater-Screen Stars] 伶星
Minbao [People's Daily] 民報
Mingxing banyuekan [Mingxing Bimonthly] 明星半月刊
Mingxing yuebao [Mingxing Monthly] 明星月報
Qingqing dianying [Qingqing Film] 青青電影
Shenbao [Shanghai Daily] 申報
Shibao [Times] 時報
Shidai dianying [Cinema of the Epoch] 時代電影
Tuhua ribao [Illustrated Daily] 圖畫日報
Xiandai dianying [Modern Screen] 現代電影
Xiju yu dianying [Theater and Cinema] 戲劇與電影
Xin Shanghai [New Shanghai] 新上海

Xin yinxing [New Silver Star] 新銀星
Xin yinxing yu tiyu shijie [Silverland/Sports World] 新銀星與體育世界
Yingmi zhoubao [Movie Fan's Weekly] 影迷周報
Yingmu zhoubao [Screen Weekly] 銀幕周報
Yingwu xinwen [Movie-dance News] 影舞新聞
Yingxi chunqiu [Movie Weekly] 影戲春秋
Yingxi shenghuo [Movie Life] 影戲生活
Yingxi shijie [Motion Picture World] 影戲世界
Yingxi zazhi [Film Magazine] 影戲雜誌
Yingxing [Silver Star] 銀星
Yisheng (dianying yu yinyue) [Art Sound (film and music)] 藝聲（電影與音樂）
Youxibao [Leisure and Entertainment] 遊戲報
Youxi zazhi [Leisure and Entertainment Magazine] 遊戲雜誌

WESTERN LANGUAGE SOURCES

Abel, Richard, ed. *Silent Film.* New Brunswick, N.J.: Rutgers University Press, 1996.

Abbas, Ackbar. "Cosmopolitan De-scriptions: Shanghai and Hong Kong." *Public Culture* 12, no. 3 (Fall 2000), 769–86.

Adorno, Theodor W. "For the Record: Adorno on Music Reproducibility." Translated by Thomas Levin. *October* 55 (Winter 1990): 23–47.

All About Shanghai: A Standard Guidebook. With an introduction by H. J. Lethbridge. Hong Kong: Oxford University Press, 1983. Originally published by the University Press, Shanghai, 1934–1935.

Allen, Robert and Douglas Gomery. *Film History: Theory and Practice.* New York: Knopf, 1985.

Altman, Rick. *American Film Musical.* Bloomington: Indiana University Press, 1987.

———. "An Introduction to the Theory of Genre Analysis." *American Film Musical.* Bloomington: Indiana University Press, 1987.

———. "Sound Space." In *Sound Theory, Sound Practice,* edited by Rick Altman, pp. 46–64. New York: Routledge, 1992.

Anderson, Benedict. *Imagined Communites: Reflections on the Origin and Spread of Nationalism.* New York: Verso, 1983.

Anderson, Marston. *The Limits of Realism: Chinese Fiction in the Revolutionary Period.* Berkeley: University of California Press, 1990.

Appadurai, Arjun. *Modernity at Large: Cultural Dimensions of Globalizations.* Minneapolis, Minn.: University of Minnesota Press, 1996.

Arkush, David and Leo O. Lee, eds. *Land without Ghosts: Chinese Impressions of America from the Mid-Nineteenth Century to the Present.* Berkeley: University of California Press, 1989.

Badley, Linda. *Film, Horror, and the Body Fantastic.* Westport, Conn.: Greenwood Press, 1995.

Bakhtin, Mikhail. *The Dialogical Imagination: Four Essays.* Translated by Caryl Emerson and Michael Holquist. Austin: University of Texas Press, 1981.

———. *Rabelais and His World.* Translated by Hélène Iswolsky. Bloomington: Indiana University Press, 1986.

Bausinger, Herman. *Folk Culture in a World of Technology.* Translated by Elke Dettmer. Bloomington: Indiana University Press, 1990.

Bazin, André. *What Is Cinema?* Vol. 1. Translated by Hugh Gray. Berkeley: University of California Press, 1967.

Bean, Jennifer. "Technologies of Early Stardom and the Extraordinary Body." *Camera Obscura* 48, vol. 16, no. 3 (2001): 9–56.

Bean, Jennifer and Diane Negra, eds. *A Feminist Reader in Early Cinema.* Durham, N.C.: Duke University Press, 2002.

Beckson, Karl and Arthur Ganz. *A Reader's Guide to Literary Terms.* New York: The Noonday Press, 1960.

Bender, Thomas. "The Culture of the Metropolis" (review essay). *Journal of Urban History* 14 (1988): 492–502.

Benjamin, Walter. *The Arcades Project.* Translated by Howard Eiland and Kevin McLaughlin. Edited by Rolf Tiedmann. Cambridge, Mass: Harvard University Press, 1999.

———. *Charles Baudelaire: A Lyric Poet in the Era of High-Capitalism.* New York and London: Verso, 1983.

———. *Illuminations: Essays and Reflections.* Edited by Hannah Arendt. New York: Harcourt, Brace and World, 1968.

———. *Reflections: Essays, Aphorisms, Autobiographical Writings.* Translated by Edmund Jephcott. Edited by Peter Demetz. 1st ed. New York: Harcourt Brace Jovanovich, 1978.

———. *Selected Writings. Volume 1. 1913–1926.* Edited by Marcus Bullock and Michael W. Jennings. Harvard University Press, 1996.

———. "A Short History of Photography." *Screen* 13 (Spring1972): 5–26 (1931).

Berger, Arthur Asa. Preface to *Popular Culture Genres: Theories and Texts.* Newbury Park, Calif.: SAGE, 1992.

Bergeron, Régis. *Le cinéma chinois 1984–1997.* Aix-en-Provence, France: Institut de l'Image, 1997.

Berman, Marshall. *All That Is Solid Melts into Air: The Experience of Modernity.* New York: Penguin Books, 1988.

Bernardi, Joana. *Writing in Light: The Silent Scenario and the Japanese Pure Film Movement.* Detroit: Wayne State University, 2001.

Berry, Chris. "Chinese Left Cinema in the 1930s: Poisonous Weeds or National Treasures?" *Jump Cut* 34 (1989): 87–94.

———, ed. *Perspectives on Chinese Cinema.* London: British Film Institute, 1991.

Bhaskar, Roy. *Reclaiming Reality: A Critical Introduction to Contemporary Philosophy.* London: Verso, 1989.

———. "The Sublimative Text: Sex and Revolution in *Big Road.*" *East-West Film Journal* 2, no. 2 (June 1988): 68–86.

Bhabha, Homi. "Signs Taken for Wonders: Questions of Ambivalence and Authority Under a Tree Outside Delhi, May 1817." In *"Race," Writing, and Differ-*

ence, edited by Henry Louis Gates, Jr. and Kwame Anthony Appiah, pp. 163–84. Chicago: University of Chicago Press, 1986.

Bloch, Ernst. "Nonsynchronism and the Obligation of Its Dialectics." Translated by Mark Ritter. *New German Critique* 11 (Spring 1977): 22–38.

Bordwell, David. *On the History of Film Style.* Cambridge, Mass: Harvard University Press, 1997.

Bordwell, David and Kristin Thompson. *Film Art: An Introduction.* New York: McGraw-Hill, 1990.

Braester, Yomi. *Witness Against History: Literature, Film, and Public Discourse in Twentieth-Century China.* Palo Alto, Calif.: Stanford University Press, 2003.

Brown, Bill. *The Material Unconscious: American Amusement, Stephen Crane, and the Economy of Play.* Cambridge, Mass.: Harvard University Press, 1996.

Brownell, Susan. *Training the Body for China: Sports and Moral Order in the People's Republic.* Chicago and London: University of Chicago Press, 1995.

Bruno, Giuliana. *Streetwalking on a Ruined Map: Cultural Theory and the City Film of Elvira Notari.* Princeton, N.J.: Princeton University Press, 1993.

Buck-Morss, Susan. "The Cinema Screen as Prosthesis of Perception: A Historical Account." In *The Senses Still: Perception and Memory as Material Culture,* edited by C. Nadia Seremetakis, pp. 45–63. Boulder, Colo.: Westview Press, 1994.

———. "The Flâneur, the Sandwichman, and the Whore: The Politics of Loitering." *New German Critique* 39 (1986), pp. 99–140.

Burch, Noël. *To the Distant Observer.* Berkeley: University of California Press, 1979.

———. *Life to Those Shadows.* Translated and edited by Ben Brewster. Berkeley: University of California Press, 1990.

Burke, Edmund. *A Philosophical Enquiry into the Origin of our Idea of the Sublime and Beautiful.* Edited by James T. Boulton. London: Routlege and Kegan Paul, 1958 (1757).

Cadava, Eduardo. "Words of Light: Theses on the Photography of History." In *Fugitive Images: From Photography to Video.* Edited by Patrice Petro, pp. 220–44. Bloomington: Indiana University Press, 1995.

Calineascu, Matei. *Five Faces of Modernity: Modernism, Avant-Garde, Decadence, Kitsch, Postmodernism.* Durham: Duke University Press, 1987.

Cambon, Marie. "The Dream Palaces of Shanghai: American Films in China's Largest Metropolis Prior to 1949." *Asian Cinema* 7, no. 2 (Winter 1995): 34–45.

Cavell, Stanley. *The World Viewed: Reflections on the Ontology of Film.* Cambridge, Mass.: Harvard University Press, 1979.

Centre de documentation sur le cinema chinois. *Ombres électriques: Panorama du cinéma chinois 1925–1982.* Paris, 1982.

Chakrabarty, Dipesh. *Provincializing Europe: Postcolonial Thought and Historical Difference.* Princeton: Princeton University Press, 2000.

Chang, Michael G. "The Good, the Bad, and the Beautiful: Movie Actresses and Public Discourse in Shanghai, 1920s–1930s." In *Cinema and Urban Culture in Shanghai, 1922–43,* edited by Yingjin Zhang. pp. 128–59. Palo Alto, Calif.: Stanford University Press, 1999.

Charney, Leo and Vanessa R. Schwartz, eds. *Cinema and the Invention of Modern Life.* Berkeley: University of California Press, 1995.

Chou, Min-chih. *Hu Shih and Intellectual Choice in Modern China.* Ann Arbor: University of Michigan Press, 1984.

Chow, Rey. *Primitive Passions: Visuality, Sexuality, Ethnography, and Contemporary Chinese Cinema.* New York: Columbia University Press, 1995.

———. *Woman and Chinese Modernity: The Politics of Reading between West and East.* Minneapolis: University of Minnesota Press, 1991.

Chow, Tse-Tsung. *The May Fourth Movement: Intellectual Revolution in Modern China.* Cambridge: Harvard University Press, 1960.

Clover, Carol J. "Her Body, Himself: Gender in the Slasher Film." In *Fantasy and the Cinema,* edited by James Donald, pp. 91–133. London: British Film Institute, 1989.

Crary, Jonathan. *Techniques of the Observer: On Vision and Modernity in the Nineteenth Century.* Cambridge, Mass.: MIT Press, 1990.

Csordas, Thomas J. "Introduction: The Body as Representation and Being-in-the-World." In *Embodiment and Experience: The Existential Ground of Culture and Self,* edited by Csordas. New York: Cambridge University Press, 1994.

Debord, Guy. *Society of the Spectacle.* Detroit: Black and Red, 1983.

De Certeau, Michel. *The Practice of Everyday Life.* Translated by Steven Rendall. Berkeley: University of California Press, 1984.

———. *The Writing of History.* Translated by Tom Conely. New York: Columbia University Press, 1988.

Deleuze, Gilles. *Cinema I: The Movement Image.* Translated by Hugh Tomlinson and Barbara Habberjam. London: Athlone Press, 1986.

Deleuze, Gilles and Félix Guattari. *A Thousand Plateaus: Capitalism and Schizophrenia.* Minneapolis: University of Minnesota Press, 1987.

Denton, Kirk, ed. *Modern Chinese Literary Thought: Writings on Literature, 1893–1945.* Stanford University Press, 1996.

Dikötter, Frank. *Sex, Culture and Modernity in China: Medical Science and the Construction of Sexual Identities in the Early Republican Period.* Honolulu: University of Hawaii Press, 1995.

Doane, Mary Ann. "The Voice in the Cinema: Articulation of Body and Space." In *Film Sound,* edited by Elisabeth Weis and John Belton, pp. 163–76. New York: Columbia University Press, 1985.

Donald, James, ed. *Fantasy and the Cinema.* London: BFI, 1989.

Douglas, Drake. *Horrors!* New York: The Overlook Press, 1989.

Drucker, Johanna. *The Visible Word: Experimental Typography and Modern Art, 1909–1923.* Chicago: University of Chicago Press, 1994.

Duara, Prasenjit. "Knowledge and Power in the Discourse of Modernity: The Campaign against Popular Religion in Early Twentieth-Century China." *Journal of Asian Studies* 50, no. 1 (February 1991): 67–83.

Duchesne, Isabelle. "The Chinese Opera Star: Roles and Identity." In *Boundaries in China,* edited by John Hay, pp. 217–330. London: Reaktion Books, 1994.

Dyer, Richard. "Entertainment and Utopia." In *The Cultural Studies Reader,* edited by Simon During, pp. 371–81. London and New York: Routledge, 1993.

———. *Stars.* London: BFI, 1979.

Eberhard, Wolfram. *A Dictionary of Chinese Symbols.* London: Routledge, 1983.

Eisner, Lotte H. *The Haunted Screen: Expressionism in the German Cinema and the Influence of Max Reinhardt.* Translated by Roger Greaves. Berkeley: University of California Press, 1973.

Elley, Derek, ed. "Peach Blossom Dreams: Silent Chinese Cinema Remembered." *Griffithiana* 60/61 (October 1997): 127–79.

Elsaesser, Thomas. "Film History and Visual Pleasure: Weimar Cinema." In *Cinema Histories/Cinema Practices,* edited by Patricia Mellencamp, pp. 47–84. Los Angeles: AFI, 1984.

———, ed. *Early Cinema: Space, Frame, Narrative.* London: BFI, 1990.

Esherick, Joseph W., ed. *Remaking the Chinese City: Modernity and National Identity, 1900–1950.* Honolulu: University of Hawaii Press, 1999.

Fairbank, John K. ed. *Chinese Thought and Institutions.* Chicago: University of Chicago Press, 1957.

Farquhar, Mary, and Chris Berry. "Shadow Opera: Toward a New Archaeology of the Chinese Cinema." *Post Script* 20, no. 2–3 (Winter/Spring and Summer 2001): 25–42.

Fell, John, ed. *Film Before Griffith.* Berkeley: University of California Press, 1983.

Field, Andrew. "Selling Souls in Sin City: Shanghai Singing and Dancing Hostesses in Print, Film, and Politics, 1920–40." In *Cinema and Urban Culture in Shanghai,* edited by Yingjin Zhang, pp. 99–127.

Foucault, Michel. *The Order of Things: An Archaeology of the Human Sciences.* New York, Pantheon Books, 1971.

Freedman, Maurice. *The Study of Chinese Society: Essays by Maurice Freedman.* Palo Alto, Calif.: Stanford University Press, 1979.

Friedberg, Anne. *Window Shopping: Cinema and the Postmodern.* Berkeley: University of California Press, 1993.

Friedman, Jonathan. *Cultural Identity and Global Process.* London, Sage, 1994.

Fruehauf, Heinrich. *Urban Exoticism in Modern Chinese Literature, 1910–1933.* Ph.D. dissertation. University of Chicago, 1990.

Garsault, Alain, Jean-Paul Tchang and Paul-Louis Thirard. "Le 'groupe de Shanghai.'" *Positif,* no. 242 (May 1981): 49–54.

Giddens, Anthony. *The Consequences of Modernity.* Palo Alto, Calif.: Stanford University Press, 1990.

Gledhill, Christine, ed. *Home Is Where the Heart Is: Studies in Melodrama and the Woman's Film.* London: BFI, 1987.

Goldman, Merle, ed. *Modern Chinese Literature in the May Fourth Era.* Cambridge, Mass.: Harvard University Press, 1977.

Goldstein, Joshua. "From Teahouse to Playhouse: Theaters as Social Text in Early Twentieth-Century China." *Journal of Asian Studies* 62, no. 3 (August 2003): 753–80.

Gomery, Douglas. *Shared Pleasures: A History of Movie Presentation in the United States.* University of Wisconsin Press, 1992.

Goodman, Bryna. *Native Place, City, Nation: Regional Networks and Identities in Shanghai, 1853–1937.* Berkeley: University of California Press, 1995.

Goody, Jack and Ian Watt. "The Consequence of Literacy." *Comparative Studies in Society and History* 5 (1962–63): 304–45.

Gumbrecht, Hans Ulrich. "A Farewell to Interpretation." In *Materialities of Communication,* edited by Hans Ulrich Gumbrecht and K. Ludwig Pfeiffer, pp. 398–99. Palo Alto, Calif.: Stanford University Press, 1994.

———. *In 1926: Living at the Edge of Time.* Cambridge, Mass.: Harvard University Press, 1997.

Gunn, Edward. *Rewriting Chinese: Style and Innovation in Twentieth-Century Chinese Prose.* Palo Alto, Calif.: Stanford University Press, 1991.

Gunning, Tom. "An Aesthetic of Astonishment: Early Cinema and the (In)credulous Spectator." *Art and Text* 34 (Spring 1989): 31–45.

———. "The Cinema of Attractions: Early Film, Its Spectator and the Avant-Garde." *Wide Angle* 8, nos. 3, 4 (1986): 63–70.

———. "Film History and Film Analysis: The Individual Film in the Course of Time." *Wide Angle* 12, no. 3 (July 1990): 4–19.

———. "'Now You See It, Now You Don't': The Temporality of the Cinema of Attractions." In *Silent Film,* edited by Richard Abel, pp. 71–84. Rutgers University Press, 1996 (1993).

———. "Pathé and Cinematic Conte-Tale: Storytelling in Early Cinema." Paper presented at the fourth DOMITOR Conference, Paris, December 1996.

———. "Phantom Images and Modern Manifestations: Spirit Photography, Magic Theater, Trick Films, and Photography's Uncanny." In *Fugitive Images: From Photography to Video,* edited by Patrice Petro, pp. 42–71. Bloomington: Indiana University Press, 1995.

———. "The Whole Town Is Gawking: Early Cinema and the Visual Experience of Modernity." *Yale Journal of Criticism* 7, no. 2 (1994): 189–201.

Güvenç, Bozkurt. "Vernacular Architecture as a Paradigm—Case Argument." In., *Vernacular Architecture: Paradigms of Environmental Response,* edited by M. Turan, pp. 286–88. Aldershot; England: Avebury, 1990.

Hanna, Patrick. *The Chinese Vernacular Story.* Cambridge, Mass.: Harvard University Press, 1981.

Hansen, Miriam. "Adventures of Goldilocks: Spectatorship, Consumerism and Public Life." *Camera Obscura* 22, no. 2 (Jan. 1990): 50–71.

———. *Babel and Babylon: Spectatorship in American Silent Filem.* Cambridge, Mass.: Harvard University Press, 1991.

———. "Benjamin and Cinema: Not a One-Way Street." *Critical Inquiry* 25, no. 2 (Winter 1999): 307–43.

———. "Fallen Women, Rising Stars, New Horizons: Shanghai Silent Film As Vernacular Modernism." *Film Quarterly* 54, no. 1 (2000): 10–22.

———. "Mass Culture as Hieroglyphic Writing: Adorno, Derrida, Kracauer." *New German Critique* 56 (Spring/Summer 1992): 32–73.

———. "The Mass Production of the Senses: Classical Cinema as Vernacular Modernism." *Modernism/Modernity* 6, no. 2 (1999): 59–77.

Hansson, Anders. *Chinese Outcasts: Discrimination and Emancipation in Late Imperial China.* Leiden: E. J. Brill, 1996.

Harraway, Donna. "The Actors Are Cyborg, Nature Is Coyote, and the Geography

Is Elsewhere: Postscript to 'Cybors at Large." In *Technoculture,* edited by Constance Penley and Andrew Ross. University of Minnesota Press, 1991.

———. *Simians, Cyborgs, and Women: The Reinvention of Nature.* London: Free Association Books, 1991.

Harrell, Stevan. "The Concept of Soul in Chinese Folk Religion." *Journal of Asian Studies* 38, no. 3 (May 1979): 519–28.

Harootunian, Harry. "The Benjamin Effect: Modernism, Repetition, and the Path to Different Cultural Imaginaries." In *Walter Benjamin and the Demands of History,* edited by Michael P. Steinberg, pp. 62–87. Ithaca: Cornell University Press, 1996.

———. *History's Disquiet: Modernity, Cultural Practice, and the Question of Everyday Life.* New York: Columbia University Press, 2000.

Harris, Kristine. "The New Woman Incident: Cinema, Scandal, and Spectacle in 1935 Shanghai." In *Transnational Chinese Cinemas: Identity, Nationhood, Gender,* Sheldon Hsiao-peng Lu, pp. 277–302. Honolulu: University of Hawaii Press, 1997.

Hay, Jonathan. "Painting and the Built Environment in Late-Nineteenth-Century Shanghai." In *Chinese Art: Modern Expressions,* edited by Maxwell K. Hearn and Judith G. Smith, pp. 61–101. New York: The Metropolitan Museum of Art, 2001.

He, Xiujun. "Histoire de la compagnie shanghaienne Mingxing et de son fondateur Zhang Shichuan." Translated by Jean-Paul Tchang. In *Le cinema chinois,* edited by Marie-Claire Quiquemelle and Jean Loup Passek. Paris: Centre George Pompidou, 1985.

Henriot, Christian., *Shanghai 1927–1937; Municipal Power, Locality, and Modernization* Berkeley: University of California Press, 1993.

Hetherington, Kevin. *The Badlands of Modernity: Heterotopia and Social Ordering.* London and New York: Routledge, 1997.

Ho, Sam. "From Page to Screen: A Brief History of *Wuxia* Fiction." In *Heroic Grace; The Chinese Martial Arts Film,* edited by David Chute and Cheng-Sim Lim. Los Angeles: UCLA Film and Television Archive, 2003.

Holman, Roger, ed. *Cinema 1900–1906: An Analytical Study.* Brussels: Fédération Internationale des Archives du Film, 1982.

Hong Kong Urban Council and The Hong Kong International Film Festival. *The China Factor in Hong Kong Cinema.* Hong Kong Urban Council, 1990.

Honig, Emily. *Sisters and Strangers: Women in the Shanghai Cotton Mills.* Palo Alto, Calif.: Stanford University Press, 1986.

Horkheimer, Max and Theodor W. Adorno. *Dialectic of Enlightenment.* Translated by John Comming. New York: Continuum, 1994.

Howe, Christopher, ed. *Shanghai: Revolution and Development in an Asian Metropolis.* New York: Cambridge University Press, 1981.

Hu Jubin. *Projecting a Nation: Chinese Cinema before 1949.* Hong Kong University Press, 2003.

Hu Ying. *Tales of Translation: Composing the New Woman in China, 1899–1918.* Palo Alto, Calif.: Stanford University Press, 2000.

Hung, Chang-tai. *Going to the People: Chinese Intellectuals and Folk Literature, 1918–*

1937. Cambridge, Mass.: Council on East Asian Studies, Harvard University, 1985.

Huyssen, Andreas. *After the Great Divide: Modernism, Mass Culture, Postmodernism.* Bloomington: Indiana University Press, 1986.

Jackson, John Brinckerhoff. *Discovering the Vernacular Landscape.* New Haven: Yale University Press, 1984.

Jakobson, Roman. *Language in Literature.* Edited by Krystyna Pomorska and Stephen Rudy. Cambridge: Belknap Press, 1987.

Jameson, Fredric. *The Political Unconscious: Narrative as a Socially Symbolic Act.* Ithaca: Cornell University Press, 1981.

Jancovich, Mark. *Horror.* London: Batsford, 1992.

Johnson, David, Andrew J. Nathan, and Evelyn S. Rawski, eds. *Popular Culture in Late Imperial China.* Berkeley: University of California Press, 1985.

Johnson, Tess, and Deke Erh. *A Last Look: Western Architecture in Old Shanghai.* Hong Kong: Old China Hand Press, 1993.

Kaminsky, Stuart and Jeffrey Mahan. *American Television Genres.* Chicago: Nelson-Hall, 1986.

Kaplan, Harry Allan. "The Symbolist Movement in Modern Chinese Poetry." Ph.D. dissertation. Harvard University, 1983.

Karatani, Kojin. *Origins of Modern Japanese Literature.* Edited by Brett de Bary. Durham: Duke University Press, 1993.

Kayser, Wolfgang. *The Grotesque in Art and Literature.* Translated byUlrich Weisstein. Bloomington: Indiana University Press, 1983.

Kern, Stephen. *The Culture of Time and Space: 1880–1918.* Cambridge, Mass.: Harvard University Press, 1983.

Kirby, Lynn. *Parallel Tracks: The Railroad and Silent Cinema.* Durham, N.C.: Duke University Press, 1997.

Kluge, Alexander and Oskar Negt. *The Public Sphere and Experience.* Peter Libanyi et al., trans., with a foreword by Miriam Hansen. Minneapolis: University of Minnesota Press, 1993.

Kracauer, Siegfried. *The Mass Ornament.* Translated by Thomas Levin. Cambridge, Mass.: Harvard University Press, 1995 [1965].

———. "Photography." Translated by Thomas Levin. *Critical Inquiry* 19 (Spring 1993): 421–36 (1927).

———. *Theory of Film: The Redemption of Physical Reality.* Princeton: Princeton University Press, 1997 (1960).

Kwok and M. C. Quiquemelle, "Chinese Cinema and Realism." In *Film and Politics in the Third* World, edited by John D. H. Downing, pp. 181–98. New York: Praeger, 1987.

Lant, Antonia and Ingrid Periz, eds. *The Red Velvet Seat: Women's Writings on the Cinema, the First Fifty Years.* London: Verso, forthcoming.

Latour, Bruno. *We Have Never Been Modern.* Translated by Catherine Porter. Cambridge, Mass.: Harvard University Press, 1993.

Lee, Leo Ou-fan. *Shanghai Modern: The Flowering of a New Urban Culture in China, 1930–1945.* Cambridge, Mass: Harvard University Press, 1999.

———. "The Tradition of Modern Chinese Cinema: Some Preliminary Explorations and Hypotheses." In *Perspectives on Chinese Cinema,* edited by Chris Berry. London: BFI, 1991.

Lee, Leo Ou-fan and Andrew J. Nathan. "The Beginning of Mass Culture: Journalism and Fiction in the Late Ch'ing and Beyond." In *Popular Culture in Late Imperial China,* edited by David Johnson, Andrew J. Nathan, Evelyn S. Rawski, pp.360–395. Berkeley: University of California Press, 1985.

Lefevbre, Henry. *Critique of Everyday Life.* Translated by John Moore. London: Verso, 1991.

Lei, Xianglin. "How Did Chinese Medicine Become Experiential? The Political Epistemology of *Jingyan.*" *Positions* 10, no. 2 (Fall 2002): 333–64.

Lent, John, ed. *The Asian Film Industry.* London: Christopher Helm, 1990.

Lévi-Strauss, Claude. *The Savage Mind.* Chicago: University of Chicago Press, 1966.

Leyda, Jay. *Dianying: An Account of Films and the Film Audience in China.* Cambridge, MA: MIT Press, 1972.

Leyda, Jay and Charles Musser, eds. *Before Hollywood: Turn of the Century Films from American Archives.* New York: American Federation of Arts, 1987.

Levenson, Joseph. *Revolution and Cosmopolitanism: The Western Stage and the Chinese Stages.* Berkeley: University of California Press, 1971.

Li Cheuk-to. "A Gentle Discourse on a Genius: Sun Yu. Eight Films of Sun Yu." *Cinemaya* 11 (1991): 53–63.

Lin Yü-sheng. *The Crisis of Chinese Consciousness: Radical Antitraditionalism in the May Fourth Era.* Madison: University of Wisconsin Press, 1979.

Lindsay, Vachel. *The Art of the Moving Picture.* Liverright Publishing Company, 1970. Originally published by The MacMillan Company, 1915.

Link, Perry E. *Mandarin Ducks and Butterflies: Popular Fiction in Early Twentieth-Century Chinese Cities.* Berkeley: University of California Press, 1981.

Liu, James. *The Chinese Knight-Errant.* Chicago: University of Chicago Press, 1967.

Liu, Jianmei. *Revolution Plus Love: Literary History, Women's Bodies, and Thematic Repetition in Twentieth-Century Chinese Fiction.* Honolulu: University of Hawaii Press, 2003.

Liu, Lydia. *Translingual Practice: Literature, National Culture, and Translated Modernity. China, 1900–1937.* Palo Alto, Calif.: Stanford University Press, 1995.

Lu Hanchao. "Away from Nanking Road: Small Stores and Neighborhood Life in Modern Shanghai." *Journal of Asian Studies* 54, no. 1 (1995): 93–123.

———. *Beyond the Neon Lights: Everyday Shanghai in the Early Twentieth Century.* Berkeley: University of California Press, 1999.

Ma Ning. "The Textual and Critical Difference of Being Radical: Reconstructing Chinese Leftist Films of the 1930s." *Wide Angle* 11, no. 2 (1989): 22–31.

Mair, Victor H. *Tang Transformation Texts: A Study of the Buddhist Contribution to the Rise of Vernacular Fiction and Drama in China.* Cambridge, Mass.: Council on East Asian Studies, Harvard University Press, 1989.

Marks, Laura U. *The Skin of the Film: Intercultural Cinema, Embodiment, and the Senses.* Durham, N.C.: Duke University Press, 2000.

Martinson, Paul Varo. "Pao Order and Redemption: Perspectives on Chinese Society and Relation Based on a Study of the Chin P'ing Mei." Ph.D. dissertation. University of Chicago, 1973.

Marx, Karl. *Capital.* Vol. 1. New York: International, 1977.

Maupassant, Guy de. "The Diamond Necklace." In *Selected Tales of Guy De Maupassant,* edited by Saxe Commins, pp. 137–44. New York: Random House, 1950.

Mauss, Marcel. "Techniques of the Body." *Economy and Society* 2, no. 1 (February, 1973): 70–88 (1935).

Mazumdar, Ranjani. "Urban Allegories: The City in Bombay Cinema, 1970–2000." Ph.D. dissertation. New York University, 2000.

Metz, Christian. *Film Language.* New York: University of Oxford Press, 1974.

Michelson, Annette, ed. *The Art of Moving Shadows.* Catalogue of the exhibition "On the Art of Fixing a Shadow." May 7–July 30, 1989. Washington D.C.: National Gallery of Art, 1989.

———, ed. *Kino-Eye: The Writings of Dziga Vertov.* Translated by Kevin O'Brien. Berkeley: University of California Press, 1984.

Mitchell, W. J. T. *Iconology: Image, Text, Ideology.* Chicago: University of Chicago Press, 1986.

Moore, Rachel O. *Savage Theory: Cinema as Modern Magic.* Durham: Duke University Press, 2000.

Mulvey, Laura. *Visual and Other Pleasures.* Bloomington: Indiana University Press, 1989.

———. "Visual Pleasure and Narrative Cinema." *Screen* 16, no. 3 (1975): 6–18.

North, C. J., ed. "The Chinese Motion Picture Market." *Trade Information Bulletin,* no. 467, pp. 1–42. United States Department of Commerce, Bureau of Foreign and Domestic Commerce, May 4, 1927.

Ong, Walter. *Interfaces of the Word: Studies in the Evolution of Consciousness and Culture.* Ithaca: Cornell University Press, 1977.

———. *Orality and Literary: The Technologizing of the Word.* Methum and Co. Ltd., 1982; reprinted by Routledge, 1988.

Pan, Lynn. *In Search of Old Shanghai.* Hong Kong: Joint Publishing Company, 1983.

———. *Sons of the Yellow Emperor: The Story of the Overseas Chinese.* London: Secker and Warburg, 1990.

Pang, Laikwan. *Building a New China in Cinema: The Cinematic Left-wing Cinema Movement 1932–1937.* Lanham, Md.: Rowman and Littefield, 2002.

Perry, Elizabeth. *Shanghai on Strike: The Politics of Chinese Labor.* Stanford University Press, 1993.

Petro, Patrice. *Joyless Streets: Women and Melodramatic Representation in Weimar Germany.* Princeton, N.J.: Princeton University Press, 1989.

Pickowicz, Paul. "The Theme of Spiritual Pollution in Chinese Films of the 1930s." *Modern China* 17, no. 1 (1991): 38–75.

———. "Melodramatic Representation and the 'May Fourth' Tradition of Chinese Cinema." In *From May Fourth to June Fourth: Fiction and Film in Twentieth-Century China,* edited by Ellen Widmer and David Der-wei Wang. Cambridge, Mass.: Harvard University Press, 1993.

Pollock, Sheldon. "Cosmopolitan and Vernacular in History." *Public Culture* 12, no. 3 (Fall 2000): 591–625.

Pratt, Mary Louise. *Imperial Eyes: Travel Writing and Transculturation.* London; New York: Routledge, 1992.

Propp, Vladimir. *Morphology of the Folktale.* Translated by Laurence Scott. Austin, TX: University of Texas Press, 1968.

Quiquemelle, Marie-Claire and Jean Loup Passek, eds. *Le Cinema Chinois.* Paris: Centre Georges Pompidou, 1993.

Rabinovitz, Lauren. *For the Love of Pleasure: Women, Movies and Culture in Turn-of-the-Century Chicago.* New Brunswick, N.J.: Rutgers University Press, 1998.

Rapoport, Amos. "Defining Vernacular Design." In *Vernacular Architecture: Paradigms of Environmental Response,* edited by M. Turan. Aldershot; England: Avebury, 1990.

Rist, Peter. "Visual Style in the Shanghai Films Made by the Lianhua Film Company (United Photoplay Service): 1931–37." *The Moving Image: Journal of the Association of Moving Image Archivists* 1, no. 1 (spring 2001).

Robbins, Bruce, ed. *Cosmopolitics: Thinking and Feeling beyond the Nation.* Minneapolis: University of Minnesota Press, 1998.

Sang, Tze-lan Deborah. "Translating Homosexuality: The Discourse of *Tongxing'ai* in Republican China (1912–1949)." In *Tokens of Exchange: The Problem of Translation in Global Circulations,* edited by Lydia H. Liu, pp. 276–304. Durham: Duke University Press, 1999.

Sergeant, Harriet. *Shanghai: A Collision Point of Cultures.* London: John Murray, 1998 (1991).

Schivelbusch, Wolfgang. *Railway Journey: The Industrialization of Time and Space in the Nineteenth Century.* Berkeley: University of California Press, 1986 (1977).

Schmidt, J. D. *Within the Human Realm: The Poetry of Huang Zunxian, 1848–1905.* Cambridge, UK: Cambridge University Press, 1994.

Sconce, Jeffrey. *Haunted Media: Electronic Presence from Telegraphy to Television.* Durham: Duke University Press, 2000.

Simmel, Georg. *On Individuality and Social Forms.* Edited by Donald N. Levine. Chicago: University of Chicago Press, 1971.

Schwartz, Benjamin. *In Search of Wealth and Power.* Cambridge, Mass.: Belknap Press, 1964.

Schwartz, Vanessa R. "Cinema Spectatorship before the Apparatus: The Public Taste for Reality in Fin-de-Siècle Paris." In *Viewing Positions: Ways of Seeing Film,* edited by Linda Williams, pp. 87–113. New Brunswick, N.J.: Rutgers University Press, 1997.

Schwarcz, Vera. *The Chinese Enlightenment: Intellectuals and the Legacy of the May Fourth Movement of 1919.* Berkeley: University of California Press, 1986.

Shaviro, Steven. *The Cinematic Body.* Minneapolis: Minnesota University Press, 1993.

Shi, Zhecun. *One Rainy Evening.* Beijing: Panda / Chinese Literature Press, 1994.

Shih, Shu-mei. "Gender, Race, and Semicolonialism: Liu Na'ou's Urban Shanghai Landscape." *The Journal of Asian Studies* 55, no. 4 (Nov. 1996): 934–56.

———. *The Lure of the Modern: Writing Modernism in Semicolonial Shanghai.* Berkeley: University of California Press, 2001.

Silverberg, Miriam. "The Cafe Waitress Serving Modern Japan." In *Mirror of Modernity: Invented Traditions of Modern Japan,* edited by Stephen Vlastos, pp. 208–28. Berkeley: University of California Press, 1998.

Singer, Ben. "Female Power in the Serial-Queen Melodrama: The Etiology of an Anomaly." In *Silent Film,* edited by Richard Abel, pp. 263–297. New Brunswick, N.J.: Rutgers University Press, 1996.

———. *Melodrama and Modernity: Early Sensational Cinema and Its Contexts.* New York: Columbia University Press, 2001.

Sklar, Robert. *Movie-Made America: A Cultural History of American Movies.* New York: Vintage Books, 1975.

Sobchack, Vivian. *The Address of the Eye: A Phenomenology of the Film Experience.* Princeton: Princeton University Press, 1992.

Spence, Jonathan. *The Search for Modern China.* New York: W. W. Norton, 1990.

Stam, Robert. "Specificities: From Hybridity to the Aesthetics of Garbage." *Social Entities* 3, no. 2 (1997): 275–290.

Stamp, Shelly. *Movie-Struck Girls: Women and Motion Picture Culture after the Nickelodeon.* Princeton, N.J.: Princeton University Press, 2000.

Stoller, Paul. *Sensuous Scholarship.* Philadelphia: University of Pennsylvania Press, 1997.

Sullivan, Michael. *Art and Artists in Twentieth Century China.* Berkeley: University of California Press, 1996.

Taussig, Michael. *Mimesis and Alterity: A Particular History of the Senses.* New York: Routledge, 1993.

Thompson, Kristin. "*Im Anfang War* . . . : Some Links between German Fantasy Films of the Teens and the Twenties." In *Before Caligari: German Cinema, 1895–1920,* edited by Paolo Cherchi Usai, pp. 138–161. Pordenone, Italy: Le Giornate del Cinema Muto and Edizioni Biblioteca dell'Immagine, 1990.

Thorbecke, Ellen. *Shanghai.* Shanghai: North-China Daily News and Herald Ltd., 1941.

Trumbull, Randolph. "The Shanghai Modernists." Ph.D. dissertation. Stanford University, 1989.

Tsivian, Yuri. "Between the Old and the New: Soviet Film Culture in 1918–1924." *Griffithiana* 55/56 (1996): 15–63.

Turan, Mete, ed. *Vernacular Architecture: Paradigms of Environmental Response.* Aldershot, England: Avebury, 1990.

Ulmer, Gregory L. *Applied Grammatology: Post(e)-Pedagogy from Jacques Derrida to Joseph Beuys.* Baltimore: Johns Hopkins University Press, 1985.

Veblen, Thorstein. *The Theory of the Leisure Class.* The New American Library, 1953 (1899).

Veyne, Paul. *Writing History.* Translated by Mina Moore-Rinvolucri (Middletown, Conn.: Wesleyan University Press, 1984 (1971).

Wakeman, Frederik Jr. *Policing Shanghai, 1927–1937.* Berkeley: University of California Press, 1995.

Walsh, Michael. "No Place for a White Man: United Artists' Far East Department: 1922–1929." *Asian Cinema* 7, no. 2 (Winter 1995): 18–33.

Wang, David Der-wei. *Fin-de-siècle Splendor: Repressed Modernities of Late Qing Fiction, 1849–1911*. Palo Alto, Calif.: Stanford University Press, 1997.

Wang, Hui. "The Fate of 'Mr. Science' in China: The Concept of Science and Its Application in Modern Chinese Thought." *Positions* 3, no. 1 (Spring 1995): 1–68.

Warner, Mariana et al. *Cinema and the Realm of Enchantment: Lectures. Seminars and Essays by Marina Warner and Others*. London: BFI, 1993.

Wasserstrom, Jeffrey. *Student Protests in Twentieth Century China: The View from Shanghai*. Palo Alto, Calif.: Stanford University Press, 1991.

Way, E. L., ed. "Motion Pictures in China." *Trade Information Bulletin,* no. 722, pp. 1–16. United States Department of Commerce, Bureau of Foreign and Domestic Commerce, 1930.

Wei, Betty Peh-T'i. *Shanghai: The Crucible of Modern China*. Hong Kong and New York: Oxford University Press, 1987.

Williams, Alan. *Republic of Images: A History of French Filmmaking*. Cambridge, Mass.: Harvard University Press, 1992.

Williams, Linda. "Film Bodies: Gender, Genre, and Excess [1991]." In *Film Genre Reader II,* edited by Barry Keith Grant, pp. 140–58. Austin: University of Texas Press, 1995.

Williams, Raymond. *Keywords: A Vocabulary of Culture and Society*. New York: Oxford University Press, 1983 (1976).

Witke, Roxane. "Transformation of Attitudes towards Women during the May Fourth Era of Modern China." Ph.D. dissertation. University of California, Berkeley, 1970.

Witte, Karsten. "Introduction to Siegfried Kracauer's 'The Mass Ornament.'" *New German Critique* 5 (1975): 59–66.

Wu, Hung. "The Early Pictorial Representations of Ape Tales: An Interdisciplinary Study of Early Chinese Narrative Art and Literature." *T'oung Pao* 73 (1987): 86–112.

Xiao, Zhiwei. "Film Censorship in China, 1927–1935." Ph.D. dissertation. University of California, San Diego, 1994.

Yang, Liansheng. "The Concept of 'Pao' as a Basis for Social Relations in China." In *Chinese Thought and Institutions,* edited by John K. Fairbank. Chicago: University of Chicago Press, 1957.

Yeh, Wen-hsin. "Progressive Journalism and Shanghai's Petty Urbanites: Zou Taofen and the *Shenghuo* Enterprise." In *Shanghai Sojourners,* edited by Frederic Wakeman and Wen-hsin Yeh, pp. 186–238. Berkeley: Center for Chinese Studies Monograph Series, 1992.

———. "Shanghai Modernity: Commerce and Culture in a Republican City." *China Quarterly* (1997): 375–94.

Yonemoto, Marcia. "The Spatial Vernacular in Tokugawa Maps." *Journal of Asian Studies* 59, no. 3 (2000): 647–66.

Zeitlin, Judith. *Historian of the Strange: Pu Songling and the Chinese Classical Tale*. Palo Alto, Calif.: Stanford University Press, 1993.

Zhang, Jingyuan. *Psychoanalysis in China: Literary Transformations 1919–1949.* Ithaca, N.Y.: Cornell East Asia Program, 1992.

Zhang, Yingjin. *The City in Modern Chinese Literature and Film: Configuration of Space, Time, and Gender.* Palo. Alto, Calif.: Stanford University Press, 1996.

———."Engendering Chinese Filmic Discourse of the 1930s: Configurations of Modern Women in Shanghai in Three Silent Films." *Positions* 2, no. 3 (Winter 1994): 603–28.

———, ed. *Cinema and Urban Culture in Shanghai, 1922–1943.* Palo Alto, Calif.: Stanford University Press, 1999.

Zhang, Zhen. "Cosmopolitan Projections: World Literature on Chinese Screens." In Robert Stam and Alessandra Raengo, eds. *A Companion to Literature and Film.* London: Blackwell, 2004.

———. "Teahouse, Shadowplay, Bricolage, *Laborer's Love* and the Question of Early Chinese Cinema." In *Cinema and Urban Culture in Shanghai, 1922–1943,* edited by Yingjin Zhang. Palo Alto, Calif.: Stanford University Press, 1999.

———. "The Shanghai Factor in Hong Kong Cinema: Historical Perspectives." *Asian Cinema* 10, no. 1 (Fall 1998): 146–59.

Zhong Dafeng, Zhang Zhen and Zhang Yingjin. "From 'Civilized Play' (*Wenmingxi*) to 'Shadow Play' (*Yingxi*): The Foundation of Shanghai Film Industry in the 1920s." *Asian Cinema* 9, no. 1 (Fall 1997): 46–64.

Zumthor, Paul. "Body and Performance." In *Materialities of Communication,* edited by Hans Ulrich Gumbrecht and K. Ludwig Pfeiffer and translated by William Whobrey, pp. 217–26. Palo Alto, Calif.: Stanford University Press, 1994.

INDEX